This Day in Network Radio

Also by Jim Cox
and from McFarland

The Great Radio Audience Participation Shows: Seventeen Programs from the 1940s and 1950s (2001; paperback 2008)

The Great Radio Soap Operas (1999; paperback 2008)

Sold on Radio: Advertisers in the Golden Age of Broadcasting (2008)

Radio Speakers: Narrators, News Junkies, Sports Jockeys, Tattletales, Tipsters, Toastmasters and Coffee Klatch Couples Who Verbalized the Jargon of the Aural Ether from the 1920s to the 1980s— A Biographical Dictionary (2007)

The Great Radio Sitcoms (2007)

The Daytime Serials of Television, 1946–1960 (2006)

Music Radio: The Great Performers and Programs of the 1920s through Early 1960s (2005)

Mr. Keen, Tracer of Lost Persons: A Complete History and Episode Log of Radio's Most Durable Detective (2004)

Frank and Anne Hummert's Radio Factory: The Programs and Personalities of Broadcasting's Most Prolific Producers (2003)

Radio Crime Fighters: Over 300 Programs from the Golden Age (2002)

Say Goodnight, Gracie: The Last Years of Network Radio (2002)

This Day in Network Radio

A Daily Calendar of Births, Deaths, Debuts, Cancellations and Other Events in Broadcasting History

Jim Cox

McFarland & Company, Inc., Publishers
Jefferson, North Carolina, and London

LIBRARY OF CONGRESS CATALOGUING-IN-PUBLICATION DATA

Cox, Jim, 1939–
This day in network radio: a daily calendar of
births, deaths, debuts, cancellations and other events
in broadcasting history / Jim Cox
p. cm.
Includes bibliographical references and index.

ISBN 978-0-7864-3848-8
softcover : 50# alkaline paper ♾

1. Radio broadcasting — United States — History — Chronology.
I. Title.
PN1991.3.U6C693 2008 384.510973 — dc22 2008036008

British Library cataloguing data are available

Manufactured in the United States of America

McFarland & Company, Inc., Publishers
Box 611, Jefferson, North Carolina 28640
www.mcfarlandpub.com

For Oscar Hoffmeyer,
colleague for decades,
Comrade for Life

Acknowledgments

My heart overflows with profound appreciation for Irene Heinstein who painstakingly supplied hundreds and very likely thousands of hours of research in seeking the most elusive details in the lives of some of the personalities in this volume. I've noted before that she possesses an extraordinary ability for finding stuff that escapes the notice of some of her contemporaries. Once again I've confirmed her knack for ferreting out the obscure as she turned her full focus to this project. I can't recall a single instance that a birth date or place, death date or place — which so many times would seem out of the reach of some other historiographers — has thwarted Irene. This is, in fact, the kind of challenge she thrives on. On so many occasions she totally overwhelmed me with her intuitive initiative to look more deeply than typical researchers might to pursue a tiny ambiguous fact, to check little-known newspapers in wayside places, to track down ship passenger manifests of a century or more ago to learn who arrived in America under what name and at what age, and to search databases that most of us never knew existed. As a paid subscriber to many of these sources, she possesses contacts that aren't accessible to most of us. She looks until she can corroborate beyond any reasonable doubt what simply would be a lost opportunity for many. All of us who can be classified as passionate vintage radio buffs can be infinitely grateful that Irene is on the job. So many times, she is able to locate and correct erroneous data that, regrettably, has been repeated over and over. Thank you for all of us, Irene. Your input is wide-ranging and I speak for many in acknowledging your incredible drive.

There are others who have made worthy contributions to this volume: Jim Carstensen, Chris Chandler, Claire Connelly, Christopher Conrad, Steve Darnall, Doug Douglass, Jack French, Jay Hickerson, Joy Jackson, Stuart Lubin, John Rayburn, Ron Sayles, Chuck Schaden, David Schwartz, Derek Tague, Janet Waldo, and Jim Widner. I am blessed by the friendship of most and honored to be part of their team.

There is a cluster within the hobby that perpetuates all we do as radio researchers, and they wholeheartedly support my small efforts in preserving old time radio. Their names are familiar to many for the many wonderful and enduring efforts they make in diverse areas: Jim Adams, Frank Bresee, Bob Burchett, Steve Darnall, Jack French, Tom Heathwood, Jay Hickerson, Walden Hughes, Ken Krug, Patrick Lucanio, and Chuck Schaden. I'm grateful to each one for the assistance they render to us all.

And of course Sharon Cox, my paramount champ, is always by my side, allowing me to relive my dreams of yesteryear. To her I am forever in debt and express my deepest gratitude.

Finally, thank you, dear reader, for the encouragement you bring to vintage radio. May our collective pursuits continue to prosper in order that folks like you can learn from them and be entertained by them for a very long while.

Contents

Preface

A second-grade youngster was asked which he preferred — plays aired on the radio or plays carried on television.

"Oh, on the radio!" he replied without a moment's hesitation.

"And why is that?" his inquisitor probed.

The child meditated briefly. Suddenly, an inspiration turned his expression into wild-eyed excitement. "Because," said he, "I can see the pictures better!"

I'm hoping that you'll see them better too, as you read the words and hear the sounds and see the pictures this book brings to mind — sounds and word pictures that have emanated across the ether for as long as eight or nine decades.

The premise is simple.

For many years I have wondered what matters of consequence took place in radio on a given date. From time to time, while stumbling across a number of intriguing facts in the course of performing an array of media research quests — encountering specific dates that a show began or ended, or a luminary was born or died, or discovering a watershed event that had a powerful impact on the industry — I occasionally ruminated over what else might have occurred on that exact date. Of course, I was particularly curious about dates that were memorable or important to me for explicitly personal reasons, just as I think anyone might be about red-letter days with special import for his or her own life. Nevertheless, my curiosity got the better of me at last — this tome is an attempt to scratch a nagging itch that was previously unscratchable.

At the outset I should establish that my intent never was to rewrite history; it wasn't to fine-tune every entry that some of my esteemed, scholarly colleagues have furnished in well-known and frequently-used books that inhabit our bookshelves. Most passionate radiophiles are familiar with a handful of works by several contemporary authors that fairly well cover the territory. They've enumerated the names of shows and personalities which especially amused or enlightened audiences during the Golden Age of radio. (For our purposes in this text, the Golden Age will be considered as the third of a century spanning the latter 1920s to the early 1960s.) Here I am attempting to add to the data others have provided, interpret it in my exacting style, and exhibit it in a format that is patterned after the Gregorian calendar — which I believe to be an innovation.

In the Golden Age, radio was surely one of our national American treasures — a trusted, reliably dependable source of entertainment, information and inspiration. And lest the reader mistakenly assume that this volume runs the gamut of what has transpired in radio history, he should be forewarned by an upfront admission: instead of being intentionally *comprehensive*, the work is more precisely an account that provides data specifically selected due to their probable appeal to a widespread reading audience. I focus on (1) occasions, practices and decisions that left indelible marks on broadcasting (they appear in the text under the heading "Sound Bite"); (2) the programming that filled the airwaves (programs are clearly identified as "Debuting" and "Canceled") and (3) the personalities most identified with those series (noted under the headings "Births" and "Deaths").

It should be noted that for the third group I have diligently sought to present the headliners as well as individuals fairly obscure to most ears in a wide range of genres. This group encompasses network, station and ad agency executives, producers, directors, writers, announcers, actors, comedians, singers, impresarios, instrumentalists, emcees, quizmasters, newscasters, commentators, consultants, gossipmongers, sportscasters, tipsters, experts and authorities, disc jockeys, talk show hosts, sound technicians, engineers, commercial hawkers, pollsters, evangelists, animal and baby imitators, impersonators, panelists and the like. You'll probably find — intentionally so — as disparate a group of individuals as you will encounter anywhere in radio history documentaries, again *representative* of the personalities that populated the airwaves in the epoch particularly under concentration.

While I have attempted to be faithful by including events, shows and people that (a) significantly influenced the medium in the United States since the national networks were formed in the mid 1920s, and (b) will appeal to those today who are disciples of some era of the phenomenon (whether by avocation, livelihood, or historical pursuits or otherwise), I admit a fallibility in not being able to select every drama or comedian that a reader might have retained on a personal list of favorites. Without including the universe of candidates available among all shows and stars, there is simply no way to reasonably cover that vast sphere. Despite the handicap, I approached this opportunity pensively, seeking to answer the simple question: What would my readers actually *expect* to find included here? I asked that of myself again and again, and attempted to be as impartial in responding to that inquiry as I possibly could be.

In pursuing this project, my overriding aim from the outset was to *get it right*— nothing more; nothing less. The researchers assisting me have been steadfastly focused on providing accurate documentation. I have been aware of their laboring studiously over a single detail about an individual's life literally for hours before illumination arrived and satisfaction was achieved. On the other hand, in a few cases noted in the text, every search to ferret out an elusive fact ended fruitlessly. I believe most of those experiences concluded with the dual emotions of failure and resolve: an inability to fill in the blank segued into knowing the pursuit had been given our best shot, netting redoubled efforts to get the next one.

In this unwavering quest I have had to right some wrongs from my past: while verifying dates a program aired or a person lived, I made some painful discoveries that sometimes convinced me my own data currently in print is incorrect. To make it accurate, I have relied upon federal and state government records as well as the archives of *The New York Times* and *Time* magazine. At the same time, I have compared published radio logs in a collection of major newspaper markets aired on identical dates, and checked a multiplicity of similar verifiable sources to determine authentic citations. All of this, of course, has been tested against information supplied by databases, websites, books, magazines, newspapers, newsletters and other publications and resources currently available. As a result, I believe some erroneous information presently in circulation can be held to a fresh and dependably reliable standard. Accomplishing that has been a rewarding byproduct in the challenges pursued.

At the same time, I would be woefully negligent if I failed to admit that I'm absolutely positive this book is not without error. Mistakes creep in through careless transmission, transpositions and, of course, including imperfect data. The work has been proofed by manifold trained professionals who give careful attention to every detail, yet we are all guilty of unintentional, embarrassing oversights. For that reason, your indulgence is deeply implored. As author, I take full responsibility for whatever mistakes and inconsistencies you may find, despite our dogged efforts. I am convinced, nevertheless, that I have sincerely tried to give you the most accurate source of documentation currently available on the material presented.

The text of the entries has been arranged in the following order for each day of the 366-day Gregorian calendar;

Sound Bite — An important moment in broadcasting
Debuting — Programs making their first network appearance on a given day (with brief summary of premise, principals, and so on)
Canceled — Programs making their network swansong on a given day
Birth — Personalities who were born on a given day (with brief overview of career highlights in mixed genres)
Death — Personalities who died on a given day

Not every one of these sectors is present for every day. Indeed, all could not possibly apply universally.

Furthermore, you will note that the entries are offered in a very distinctive style: while they are as concise as I can make them, there is a sensation of immediacy about them by their limited use of prepositions, conjunctions and punctuation marks, in particular, creating an opening for saying more in less space. Until you arrive at the conclusion of an entry, you'll find semicolons and dashes separating clauses instead of periods, supplying greater connectivity between passages than you might otherwise experience with sentences. After you have read a few of the entries, you'll likely pick up the flow and rhythm of the prevailing pattern throughout the calendar.

Canceled items usually inform you of the network carrying a series when it left the air, which may or may not have been the network acknowledged in *Debuting*. Many programs were aired on different networks at different times.

Death items tell you where an individual died (if known), data not included in the biographical vignettes under *Birth*.

A few statistics may interest, amuse or enlighten you about the content. There are 83 sound bites included in the text, 363 debuting shows highlighted, 345 canceled features identified, 968 personalities introduced, and 868 deaths for a total of 2,627 entries. Three dates — February 8 and 14, and June 10 — are the most popular birthdays, producing eight airtime luminaries each among those in this register. Numerous dates afford seven birthdays. Conversely, there are eight deaths on three different dates — January 3 and 29, and July 4 — representing the most on single days. October saw more debuting series than any other (49) while August saw the least (9). Not surprisingly, more series were canceled in June than at any other time of year (60), while August saw the fewest shows go away (15). June also witnessed more birthdays (102) while September experienced the fewest (72). More of these personalities died in January than any other month (94) while the fewest passed in April (60).

There were a handful of major national networks during radio's Golden Age and they are labeled in the text like this:

NBC — National Broadcasting Company, which operated two networks until the mid 1940s; the programming in this volume refers to that of the NBC Red network, a chain that went on the air on November 15, 1926, and persisted as NBC after the Blue chain was sold

NBC Blue — National Broadcasting Company Blue network, sold in July 1943, temporarily designated the Blue network, and renamed ABC in 1945

ABC — American Broadcasting Company, the new moniker of the NBC Blue web after it was sold

CBS — Columbia Broadcasting System, or the Columbia Phonograph Broadcasting System at its inception on September 27, 1927, then Columbia before the triple call letters came into common usage

MBS — Mutual Broadcasting System, formed September 29, 1934 after four influential stations comprising the Quality Network altered the earlier appellation

While *This Day in Network Radio* likely won't be a volume that you'll sit down and devour from cover to cover, perhaps it's one that will be a constant reminder — as you delve into it again and again on a specific date, or search its contents for an intriguing fact or figure — how fortunate we all are that Heinrich Hertz, Guglielmo Marconi, Nathan Stubblefield, Reginald Fessenden, Lee de Forest, Edwin Armstrong, Frank Conrad, David Sarnoff, William Paley and legions of auxiliary visionaries among the early practitioners did their thing by pursuing unappeasable dreams. The venue that resulted from their collective efforts has satisfied some of us with millions of hours of entertainment value over these decades.

It's my hope that this text helps you reprise a great deal of what you have loved most — and found most compelling — about network radio. It's a sound that, for some who have liberally invested part of their lives in it, won't ever go away.

Can you see the pictures?

The Calendar

The broadcast series and personalities selected are representative *of network-syndicated radio since the 1920s but* not all-inclusive*; most shows selected aired for one season or beyond or they or their stars made a substantial impact on the medium; "bka" means "best known as."*

January 1

Sound Bites

NBC takes over operations of RCA's New York WJZ outlet Jan. 1, 1927, effectively establishing foundation for second nationwide chain, incorporating former Radio Group network (handful of stations connected by sub-grade Western Union circuitry as opposed to AT&T lines used by NBC)—second web announced in December 1926; on Jan. 1, Radio Group joins New York WEAF-based web broadcasting Graham McNamee play-by-play coverage of Rose Bowl gridiron match featuring Alabama, Stanford (7–7 tie); WJZ net contributes six affiliates; WEAF cluster designated "Red" network, WJZ band identified as "Blue," believed based on circuits on map colored by AT&T engineers separating dual chains.

On Jan. 1, 1928, NBC is comprised of 48 stations, a 153 percent increase since chain was formed 13-and-a-half months earlier with 19 affiliates, radically escalating its coverage reach, impact.

Federal Communications Commission—acting in 1940 after review of handful of experimental non-commercial FM (frequency modulation) stations—approves commercial FM radio effective Jan. 1, 1941, on 40 channnels boasting wide band of 42–50 MHz; lowest five channels reserved for educational outlets.

For 45 minutes on Jan. 1, 1950, CBS airs *Years of Crisis*, first of 12 annual entries in which handful of noteworthies engage in freewheeling erudite exchange on precarious state of global affairs at present; with eminent CBS news guru Ed Murrow moderating forum of award-winning CBS reporter-analysts, questions fielded by panel of correspondents; CBS mogul William S. Paley later observes it "sounded like pieces which might be written 50 years from now by top historians, certainly not by guys who have lived through most of the period"; summarizing *Years of Crisis* broadcasts, media pundits Stanley Cloud, Lynne Olson typify affair as "a significant national event ... conversation was absolutely brilliant"; sets precendent for TV's countless year-end reviews since.

ABC splits its radio chain into quartet of subchains Jan. 1, 1968: Contemporary Network—brief news reports, content tempting to young people, Entertainment Network—news, features, personalities-oriented for middle-of-road stations, FM Network—four minutes of news-on-hour, Information Network—five-minute news reports hourly, extended newscasts, commentary, sports; ABC affiliates proliferate as result, some markets supporting multiple ABC outlets; when its transmission link switches to satellite in 1982, allowing concurrent transmission on manifold transponders, ABC creates still more webs.

Debuting

Hopalong Cassidy, Jan. 1, 1950, MBS; western adventure drama aimed at juveniles, probably dads, too; cattle rancher Cassidy (William Boyd) bore image of hero-detective to his plains neighbors as he chased lawbreakers, brought them to justice escorted by clumsy sidekick Jack (California) Carlson (Andy Clyde, Joe Duval); with novel antecedents, Hoppy movies emerged 1930s starring Boyd in 66 Saturday matinees 1935–48 resulting in merchandising mania turning him into multimillionaire by endorsements on comic books, lunch pails, candy bars, clothing, bicycles, roller skates, furniture — more than 2,000 items; on NBC-TV 1949–51, another 52 episodes syndicated; final new radiocast March 15, 1952 with repeats airing on CBS Mountain States regional web April 26-Dec. 27, 1952.

On Stage (*Cathy and Elliott Lewis On Stage*), Jan. 1, 1953, CBS; anthology drama; "by some accounts the best radio anthology ever heard" affirmed a wag; Lewises among busiest talents on air as they put together mix of classic, original narratives with adventure, satire, comedy, melodrama, mystery tinges; West Coast thespians turned up — Harry Bartell, William Conrad, Mary Jane Croft, John Dehner, Paul Frees, Joseph Kearns, Jack Kruschen, Peter Leeds, Sheldon Leonard, John McIntire, Howard McNear, Tyler McVey, Frank Nelson, Jeanette Nolan, Peggy Webber, Paula Winslowe, more; final broadcast Sept. 30, 1954.

The Story of Mary Marlin (premiered on Chicago WMAQ Oct. 3, 1934-Dec. 31, 1934), Jan. 1, 1935, NBC; daytime serial; U. S. Sen. Joe Marlin (Robert Griffin) of Iowa vanished for long time in Asian wilds, declared dead, spouse Mary (Joan Blaine, Anne Seymour, Betty Lou Gerson, Muriel Kirkland, Eloise Kummer, Linda Carlton) appointed to fill his office; surprisingly, Joe reappeared now and then but with amnesia; when he was home vixen Bunny Mitchell (Fran Carlon) tried to get her hooks into him while David Post (Carlton Brickert) loved Mary, wished they were wed, creating awkward moments for her as she tried to hold emotions in check; despite her problems, it must have seemed glamorous existence to housewives at home without modern conveniences to assist as they performed drudgery jobs; serial silent 1945–51; final broadcast April 11, 1952.

Canceled

The NBC Radio Theater, Jan. 1, 1960, NBC; debut April 27, 1959.

Births

Ted Cott, Jan. 1, 1917, Poughkeepsie, N.Y.; announcer, director, emcee; first radio gig at 16 announcing for a Brooklyn station, progressively moving to nearby WNYC at $150 monthly, WNEW at $600 monthly, CBS introducing *Major Bowes' Original Amateur Hour* at $1,500 monthly; *Society Girl* director 1939–40, *So You Think You Know Music?* master of ceremonies 1939–41, *The Pause That Refreshes on the Air* interlocutor 1947–49; elevated to NBC vice presidency 1950, general manager of its NY radio-TV outlets; same duties with Dumont TV net/local station before operation folded mid 1950s; International Academy of Television Arts and Sciences presents Ted Cott Award annually to a board member contributing appreciably; d. June 12, 1973.

Xavier Cugat, Jan. 1, 1900, Tirona, Spain; impresario bka "King of the Rumba," fronted outfit with Waldorf Astoria Hotel venue; radio gigs under sundry monikers 1933–48; copied by Desi Arnaz, Perez Prado; attracted girl singers Rita Hayworth, Abbe Lane, Charro (last two among four wives); d. Oct. 27, 1990.

Norma Jean Nilsson, Jan. 1, 1938, Hollywood, Calif.; actress (film, radio), bka *Father Knows Best* sitcom younger daughter Kathy Anderson 1949–54.

Deaths

Jack Fraser, Jan. 1, 2000, Winter Park, Fla.; b. Feb. 4, 1908. Larry Klee, Jan. 1, 1957, Westport, Conn.; b. July 24, 1914. Jack Latham, Jan. 1, 1987, Palm Springs, Calif.; b. Dec. 27, 1914. Jane Morgan, Jan. 1, 1972, Burbank, Calif.; b. Dec. 6, 1880.

January 2

Sound Bites

While many ministers viewed radio warily in its formative years, Dr. E. J. Van Etten, pastor of Pittsburgh's Calvary Episcopal Church, saw enormous outreach potential; on Jan. 2, 1921 KDKA aired first church service to go across ether from his parish; in time, some religious as well as web officials broke with those classifying radio "tool of the devil" to foster *Back to the Bible, The Baptist Hour, The Catholic Hour, Church of the Air, The Eternal Light, The Hour of Decision, Hymns of All Churches, The Lutheran Hour, Music and the Spoken Word from the Crossroads of the West, The National Radio Pulpit, National Vespers, The Old-Fashioned Revival Hour, The Voice of Prophecy*, more.

Most visible outcome of CBS mogul William S. Paley's infamous 1940s "talent raids" at rival webs evidenced by comic Jack Benny switching sides (most coveted "prize" in those pursuits said pundits); Benny was NBC mainstay 16 years, mostly Sunday at 7 P.M.; on Sunday, Jan. 2, 1949 at 7 P.M. *The Jack Benny Program* premiered on CBS, stayed put to 1958 end of radio run (including repeats), continued on CBS-TV to 1964, final year on NBC-TV 1964–65; his shift to CBS signified how deeply acquisitions cut into other chains' artist arsenals.

Debuting

The George Jessel Show (*George Jessel Variety Hour, Thirty Minutes in Hollywood, For Men Only, George Jessel Jamboree, George Jessel's Celebrity Program, This Is Show Business, George Jessel Salutes*), Jan. 2, 1934, CBS; comedy variety; critic's assessment of ex-vaudevillian Jessel's radio ventures depicted lackluster shows mustering modest excitement, ratings — sans encore seasons; Jessel's series off ether 1940–53; final broadcast Jan. 28, 1954.

Johnny Presents, Jan. 2, 1934, NBC; music, variety, drama; umbrella appellation embracing programming with Philip Morris Co. mascot ex-bellhop Johnny Roventini shilling under diverse themes: orchestras of Leo Reisman, Russ Morgan, Johnny Green, Ray Bloch — sometimes with narratives, *Johnny Presents Dramatized Short Stories, Johnny Presents Philip Morris Playhouse, Johnny Presents Ginny Simms*, added formats, headliners; *Playhouse* most memorable — *Johnny Presents* brand aired 1939–44, without it 1948–49, 1951–53, drifted to CBS-TV 1953–54; final radiocast with that banner Jan. 15, 1946.

Canceled

Backstage Wife, Jan. 2, 1959, CBS; debut Aug. 5, 1935. *The Kate Smith Show*, Jan. 2, 1959, MBS; debut March 17, 1931. *Our Gal Sunday*, Jan. 2, 1959, CBS; debut March 29, 1937. *The Road of Life*, Jan. 2, 1959, CBS; debut Sept. 13, 1937. *This Is Nora Drake*, Jan. 2, 1959, CBS; debut Oct. 27, 1947.

Births

Julius LaRosa, Jan. 2, 1930, Brooklyn, N.Y.; actor (stage, TV), disc jockey, personal appearance /recording artist, vocalist bka "singer fired on air by Arthur Godfrey" for perceived "lack of humility" *Arthur Godfrey Time* musical variety feature CBS Oct. 19, 1953, date Godfrey's public prestige suffered huge setback as legions of doting fans departed, never recouping past level; LaRosa also appeared on *Arthur Godfrey and His Friends* revue CBS-TV concurrently; "discovered" by Godfrey while singing with U. S. Navy Band, job awaited him on Navy release — joined Godfrey troupe Nov. 19, 1951, instant audience favorite; years later LaRosa dubbed ex-mentor "not a very nice man"; recorded hits on Cadence, RCA Victor labels; *The Julius LaRosa Show* headliner backed by Russ Case Orchestra CBS Radio 1953–54; career moved from radio-TV to gigs at cabarets like Rainbow and Stars, jazz rooms like Michael's Pub, Carnegie Hall, Philadelphia Academy of Music, summer fairs, school auditoriums, ballparks, nightclubs; DJ at New York WNEW early 1970s; theater roles in *Come Blow Your Horn, Guys and Dolls, Kiss Me Kate, West Side Story*; acted in *Another World* daytime serial NBC-TV 1980.

James Melton, Jan. 2, 1904, Moultrie, Ga.; vocalist (tenor) — concert tours, film, radio, recordings, TV bka recurring artist e.g., *The Jack Benny Program* 1933–34, *The Palmolive Beauty Box Theater* 1934–37, *The Bell Telephone Hour* and *Voice of Firestone* 1940s-50s; d. April 21, 1961.

Death

Jack Carson, Jan. 2, 1963, Encino, Calif.; b. Oct. 27, 1910.

January 3

Sound Bite

On Jan. 3, 1930 at age 39 David Sarnoff—his employer's general manager since May 1921—is installed as president of Radio Corporation of America, parent of National Broadcasting Co., over which he will have sweeping say; star reaches celestial heights, perch from which he oversees dual radio networks plus development of TV this visionary has already labeled "the future of broadcasting."

Debuting

The A&P Gypsies, Jan. 3, 1927, NBC; impresario Harry Horlick conducted orchestra in musical feature named for sponsor (The Great Atlantic & Pacific Tea Co.), common in era; show originated March 17, 1924 on New York WEAF (future NBC flagship); persisted on NBC to June 6, 1927, resumed Sept. 12, 1927-Sept. 7, 1936, concurrent run on NBC Blue Sept. 3, 1931-June 16, 1932.

Terry Regan, Attorney at Law, Jan. 3, 1938, NBC Blue; daytime-primetime serial; forerunner of string of aural courtroom counselors (Nancy James, Perry Mason, Portia Manning, et al.); title role in sunshine played by Jim Ameche, after dark by Arthur Jacobson; Regan's secretary Sally Dunlap played by Fran Carlon, Betty Winkler respectively; final broadcast Aug. 30, 1938.

True or False, Jan. 3, 1938, MBS; quiz; with quizmasters Dr. Harry Hagen. Eddie Dunn, feature tossed seven true-false questions to contestants, each theoretically increasingly tougher, winners vying for jackpot question, larger prize at end; format shift in 1948 saw rivals try to guess true-false answers to four of five proffered questions, jackpot at end worth $2,500, big money in those days; silent 1943–48, 1951–53, plus shorter spells; final broadcast Feb. 4, 1956.

Woman in White, Jan. 3, 1938, NBC; daytime serial; nursing grad Karen Adams, 30 (Luise Barclay, Betty Ruth Smith, Betty Lou Gerson, Peggy Knudsen) dedicated self to benefit others, "a modern day Florence Nightingale" uttering familiar aphorism daily: "If there is any kindness I can show, or any good that I can do to any fellow being, let me do it now, for I shall not pass this way again"; orphaned, as eldest she guided siblings Betty, John, all residing in home of Uncle Bill, Aunt Helen; her true love died so she wed another who had affair with John's wife (of such was matinee misery); after serial's absence 1942–44, resumed sans beleaguered Karen, now with nurse Eileen Holmes (Sarajane Wells) as heroine sweet on Dr. Paul Burton (Ken Griffin); final broadcast May 28, 1948.

Canceled

The Quiz Kids, Jan. 3, 1954, CBS; debut June 28, 1940. *The Robert Q. Lewis Show*, Jan. 3, 1959, CBS; debut April 7, 1945. *Wendy Warren and the News*, Jan. 3, 1958, CBS; debut June 23, 1947.

Birth

Maxene Andrews, Jan. 3, 1916, Mound, Minn.; vocalist (second soprano)—film, public appearances, radio, recordings, stage bka one of venerated Andrews Sisters trio; recorded 1,800 songs, sold 90 million platters; *The Andrews Sisters Eight-to-the-Bar Ranch* ABC 1944–46, *Club Fifteen* CBS 1947–53 notable audio gigs; d. Oct. 21, 1995.

Deaths

Edwin D. Canham, Jan. 3, 1982, Guam; b. Feb. 13, 1904. Milton Cross, Jan. 3, 1975, New York City, N.Y.; b. April 16, 1897. Irving Kaufman, Jan. 3, 1976, Indio, Calif.; b. Feb. 8, 1890. Floyd Mack, Jan. 3, 1983, Newark, Ohio; b. Oct. 23, 1912. Pat McGeehan, Jan. 3, 1988, Burbank, Calif.; b. March 4, 1907. Howard McNear, Jan. 3, 1969, San Fernando Valley, Calif.; b. Jan. 27, 1905. Peter Van Steeden, Jr., Jan. 3, 1990, New Canaan, Conn.; b. April 3, 1904. Murray Wagner, Jan. 3, 1994, Westlake Village, Calif. (California Death Index states he died Dec. 15, 1993 while SSDI displays date shown here); b. Dec. 17, 1914.

January 4

Sound Bites

New York WEAF owned by AT&T — on cutting edge of early radio development — bands with Boston WNAC owned by John Shepard III Jan. 4, 1923 to concurrently air single program: five-minute saxophone solo originating at WEAF, sent to Boston via telephone line circuitry; labeled inaugural "network" broadcast, it wouldn't be repeated until June 7, 1923 when four outlets fused.

ESPN Radio Network with sports talk and call-in programming becomes functional Jan. 4, 1992; dual features — *Fabulous Sports Babe*, *Sportsbeat* — are regular offerings in web's early life; collegiate as well as professional sports news, commentary, game-day reporting of athletic events, interviews with sports figures (franchise owners, players, analysts, etc.), interaction with listeners.

Debuting

The Fred Waring Show (profuse sobriquets), Jan. 4, 1931, NBC; maestro perfectionist Waring produced symphony of sound every outing with esteemed, trained, stable orchestra (The Pennsylvanians), chorus, vocalists, specialty acts; "beautiful music" creations on par with *The Bell Telephone Hour*, *Voice of Firestone*; identified by unique glee club blend instantly distinguishing it from rivals; final web broadcast Oct. 4, 1957, syndicated 1957–60 (156 half-hours).

The Intimate Revue, Jan. 4, 1935, NBC Blue; comedy; although series was history in three months, it gave national venue to one stellar comedian of 20th century from which Bob Hope rose to fame as broadcast, movie, recording, personal appearance, advertising legend; successively followed by *Atlantic Family* 1935–36, *Rippling Rhythm Revue* 1937, mere preludes to NBC series star headlined Sept. 27, 1938-April 21, 1955, repeats Sept. 28, 1956-March 21, 1958, on NBC-TV 1953–67, many occasional video specials in subsequent decades.

Canceled

The Adventures of Bill Lance, Jan. 4, 1948, ABC; debut April 23, 1944. *Major Bowes' Original Amateur Hour*, Jan. 4, 1945, NBC; debut March 24, 1935.

Deaths

Les Brown, Jan. 4, 2001, Los Angeles, Calif.; b. March 14, 1912. Bob Montana, Jan. 4, 1975, Meredith, N.H.; b. Oct. 23, 1920.

January 5

Canceled

David Harum, Jan. 5, 1951, CBS; debut Jan. 27, 1936. *Romance*, Jan. 5, 1957, CBS; debut April 19, 1943.

Deaths

Hans Conried, Jan. 5, 1982, Burbank, Calif.; b. April 15, 1917. Ross Graham, Jan. 5, 1986, Fort Worth, Texas; b. Aug. 8, 1905. Stuart Metz, Jan. 5, 1994, Pine Island, Minn.; b. March 20, 1908.

January 6

Debuting

The CBS Radio Mystery Theater, Jan. 6, 1974, CBS; anthology crime drama; ambitious comeback for audio's dead dramatic programming (abandoned after CBS's final remnants left ether Sept. 30, 1962); fostered by producer-director Himan Brown who lobbied for return to those days of yesteryear, convincing web brass to try it; E. G. Marshall (later Tammy Grimes) beckoned listeners to "come in," a squeaking door still needed oil (holdover prop from Brown's *Inner Sanctum Mysteries*); 195 original dramas plus repeats aired with Brown proving Americans would tune in again; narratives were often of ordinary people whose greed led them to commit crime; among players were East Coast thespians Mason Adams, Joan Banks, Jackson Beck, Ralph Bell, Roger DeKoven, Robert Dryden, Elspeth Eric, Mary Jane Higby, Leon Janney, Joseph Julian, Teri Keane, Mandel Kramer, Berry Kroeger, Joan Lorring, Ian Martin, Grace Matthews, Paul McGrath, Bret Morrison, Arnold

Moss, Santos Ortega, Bryna Raeburn, William Redfield, more; final broadcast Dec. 31, 1982.

The Halls of Ivy, Jan. 6, 1950, NBC; lighthearted narrative of fictitious liberal arts college with president William Todhunter Hall (Ronald Colman), spouse Victoria Cromwell (Vicky) Hall (Benita Hume Colman); creator Don Quinn penned scripts for Jim and Marian Jordan (*Fibber McGee & Molly*) before inspiring campus plots; final radiocast June 25, 1952, CBS-TV exposure Oct. 19, 1954-Oct. 13, 1955.

The Saint, Jan. 6, 1945, NBC; private eye detective mystery; markedly well-heeled Saint — Simon Templar (Edgar Barrier, Brian Aherne, Vincent Price, Tom Conway) — passed time dining at posh bistros, indulging in arts, solving crimes at times to consternation of N Y. P. D., sometimes bending law doing so; love interest Patricia Holmes (Louise Arthur) was in some of run while houseboy Happy (Ken Christy), cabbie Louie (Larry Dobkin), police inspector Fernak (John Brown, Theodore von Eltz) often around; born in novelist Leslie Charteris' fiction, 10 theatrical films, one made-for-TV flick, syndicated TV series produced in England 1963–66, intermittent NBC-TV incarnation 1967–69, spotty new CBS-TV episodes 1978–80; final radiocast Oct. 21, 1951.

Canceled

Dr. Christian, Jan. 6, 1954, CBS; debut Nov. 7, 1937. *Lora Lawton*, Jan. 6, 1950, NBC; debut May 31, 1943.

Birth

Dan S. Cubberly, Jan. 6, 1917, Colorado; announcer, newscaster bka *Yours Truly — Johnny Dollar* interlocutor 1951–54; introduced plethora of crimefighting fare in 1950s: *Fort Laramie*, *Frontier Gentleman*, *The Judge*, *The Lineup*, *Night Watch*, plus *Romance*, *Whispering Streets*; premiered as newsman at Olympia, Wash. KGY 1938, Phoenix KOY 1940; d. Oct. 6, 1991.

Deaths

Alice Frost, Jan. 6, 1998, Naples, Fla.; b. Aug. 1, 1905. Johnny Johnston, Jan. 6, 1996, Cape Coral, Fla.; b. Dec. 1, 1915. Bob Lemond, Jan. 6, 2008, Bonsall, Calif.; b. April 11, 1913. John W. Vandercook, Jan. 6, 1963, Delhi, N.Y.; b. April 22, 1902.

January 7

Debuting

The Crime Files of Flamond, Jan. 7, 1953, MBS; crime drama; psychologist Flamond (Arthur Wyatt, Myron "Mike" Wallace, Everett Clarke), born into Radioland sans given moniker, approached crimesolving by concentrating on *why* felonies committed, at drama's end revealing guilty parties; assisting in his pursuits, secretary Sandra Lake (Patricia Dunlap, Muriel Bremner) whom he platonically addressed as "Miss Lake"; series dispatched by transcription from Chicago WGN 1946–48; final net broadcast Feb. 27, 1957.

Gene Autry's Melody Ranch, Jan. 7, 1940, CBS; soul-filled Western ballads ("Back in the Saddle Again," "Cool Water," "Don't Fence Me In," "Tumbling Tumbleweeds"), humor, pithy adventure narratives — combination drawing listeners from multi-ages; host dubbed "America's Favorite Cowboy" performed in broadcasting, film, on records, at personal appearances onstage, rodeos; final broadcast (after extended interval off air Aug. 1, 1943-Sept. 23, 1945) May 13, 1956, *The Gene Autry Show* CBS-TV July 23, 1950-Aug. 7, 1956.

Inner Sanctum Mysteries, Jan. 7, 1941, NBC Blue; horror anthology drama; grinning disposition of chilling-voiced "Raymond" (Raymond Edward Johnson, Paul McGrath, House Jameson) beckoned "friends of the Inner Sanctum" to grisly tales of macabre, mayhem, murder; *The CBS Radio Mystery Theater* three decades hence borrowed squeaking door, "Come in!" salutation, "pleasant dreeeammmsss" farewell delivered by host E. G. Marshall (creator-producer-director Himan Brown tied to both dramas); syndicated TV series 1954 hosted by McGrath; final radiocast Oct. 5, 1952.

Meet Corliss Archer, Jan. 7, 1943, CBS; teen sitcom with Priscilla Lyon, Janet Waldo, Lugene Sanders as namesake; web's response to NBC's *A Date with Judy* 1941–50; 17 timeslots, three chains put show at disadvantage to like fare, dulled ratings; protagonist flanked by parents, boyfriend (Dexter Franklin with five actors in role), comrades; final broadcast Sept. 30, 1956.

The Red Skelton Show (*Avalon Time*, *The Raleigh Cigarette Program*), Jan. 7, 1939, NBC; comedy variety; clown who made reading (misreading) lines art form got bigger laughs by purposely lousing up dialogue ("I don't write 'em, I just read 'em" he often said); visual artist capitalized on ways unseeing home audience knew what he was doing, turning every situation into laughter; as pantomimist, superb, but his familiar characterizations endeared him to fans who reveled — lame-brained Clem Kadiddlehopper, Junior "the mean widdle kid," Freddie the Freeloader, San Fernando Red, Bolivar Shagnasty, henpecked George Appleby, Willie Lump-Lump, et al.; lots of guest stars dropped by plus cadre of talents who sang or played regularly in sketches like Janette Davis, Verna Felton, Red Foley, Marlin Hurt, Curt Massey, Ozzie and Harriet Nelson; on TV he was a natural, shifting easily to home screens — show never missed a season in two decades NBC/CBS 1951–71; final radiocast May 26, 1953.

The Second Mrs. Burton, Jan. 7, 1946, CBS; daytime serial; Terry Burton (Sharon Douglas, Claire Niesen, Patsy Campbell, Teri Keane) of namesake fame not only was second bride of Stan Burton (Dwight Weist), she played second fiddle to Mother Burton (Charme Allen, Evelyn Varden, Ethel Owen), snobby socialite mom-in-law though — to her credit — cheery, patient Terry weathered those intrusions better than Stan; in fairly genteel storyline, realism surfaced more often than most; series earned dubious distinction of last network soap opera leaving air on infamous "day radio drama died" Nov. 25, 1960.

Births

Art Baker (Arthur Shank), Jan. 7, 1898, New York City, N.Y.; actor (film), announcer, blue-collar businessman, emcee, quizmaster, toastmaster-lecturer, vocalist bka *People Are Funny* original host 1942, dispatched by producer John Guedel late 1943 despite NBC protests — Baker suing Guedel, losing — replaced by Art Linkletter; Baker found new career in 51 celluloid productions 1946–66 e.g., *Abie's Irish Rose* 1946, *The Farmer's Daughter* 1947, *Walk a Crooked Mile* 1948, *Any Number Can Play* 1949, *Voyage to the Bottom of the Sea* 1961, *Young Dillinger* 1965; d. Aug. 26, 1966.

Hilmar Robert Baukhage, Jan. 7, 1889, LaSalle, Ill.; commentator, emcee, journalist (Associated Press, magazines, Army newspaper), news anchor (TV) bka *The National Farm and Home Hour* 1932–37 and *Baukhage Talking* hosts 1937–53; one critic labeled him "the consummate professional journalist," said he "never used his first name, either on the air or in his personal life" yet he "tried to present an accurate, evenhanded view of current events," was "widely respected for his objectivity"; another acknowledged him as "originator of the casual, down-to-earth news-reporting style that ... is still being used by many newscasters"; co-anchor with Jim Gibbons of *News and Views*, ABC-TV daily newscasts baptism 1948; magazine columnist, Armed Forces broadcaster afterward; d. Jan. 31, 1976.

Deaths

Donald I. Ball, Jan. 7, 1974; b. Feb. 8, 1904. Irene Beasley, Jan. 7, 1980, Ardsley, N.Y.; b. Jan. 28, 1904. Richard Kollmar, Jan. 7, 1971, New York City, N.Y.; b. Dec. 31, 1910.

January 8

Debuting

A Man Named Jordan (Rocky Jordan), Jan. 8, 1945, CBS West Coast; international intrigue drama; hero (Jack Moyles, George Raft) operated Café Tambourine — in Istanbul in forerunner series, Cairo in latter — site of dangerous pursuits, profit-driven, focused on crime, mystery, gorgeous female with wily charms or blend of those; quest for "dames in trouble to lost souls seeking help" gave culinary artist incentive to get up every day; show off air, changing titles, locales April 20, 1947-Oct. 31, 1948; final broadcast Aug. 22, 1951.

The Screen Guild Theater (*The Gulf Screen Guild Show*, *The Gulf Screen Guild Theater*, *The Lady Esther Screen Guild Theater*, *The Camel Screen Guild Players*, *Stars in the Air*, *Hollywood Soundstage*), Jan. 8, 1939, CBS; anthology drama variety; George Murphy, Roger Pryor were early hosts; renowned legends of silver screen in humorous sketches, stunts, film adaptations (initial season) with films only thereafter, big-budget "salaries" awarded Motion Picture Relief Fund; players: Gracie Allen, Edward Arnold, Jack Benny, Humphrey Bogart, Barbara Britton, George Burns, James Cagney, Ronald Colman, Gary Cooper, Larry "Buster" Crabbe, Joan Crawford, Bing Crosby, Marlene Dietrich, Brian Donlevy, Nelson Eddy, Clark Gable, Judy Garland, Betty Grable, Cary Grant, Phil Harris, Rita Hayworth, John Hodiak, Bob Hope, Van Johnson, Art Linkletter, Fred MacMurray, Gregory Peck, Walter Pidgeon, Vincent Price, Edward G. Robinson, Mickey Rooney, Dinah Shore, Ann Sothern, Shirley Temple, Audrey Totter, more; pundit vowed show paled beside *Screen Directors' Playhouse*— with same talent, writing/staging superior here, said he; final broadcast June 29, 1952.

Births

Roger Bower, Jan. 8, 1903, New York City, N.Y.; actor, announcer, director, emcee, producer, sound effects technician bka *Can You Top This?* moderator MBS 1940–45; premiered on ether over New York WMCA 1927, shifted to WOR 1928 producing-directing *The Witch's Tale* 24 years; first eyewitness reporter for Macy's Thanksgiving Day parade; other series produced and/or directed: *The Crime Club, The Adventures of Leonidas Witherall, The Paul Winchell-Jerry Mahoney Show, The Rookies, The Grummits, Leave It to Mike, Secret Missions, Take a Note, Famous Jury Trials, It Pays to Be Ignorant*; *Stop Me if You've Heard This One* emcee, radio-TV versions; d. May 17, 1979.

Sam Cowling (Samuel Taggert Cowling II), Jan. 8, 1914, Indiana; comedian, vocalist bka *The Breakfast Club* humorist 1937–68 ("Fiction and Fact from Sam's Almanac"); initially appeared at venue with The Romeos quartet but his one-liner gags proved asset as foil to toastmaster Don McNeill; also heard regularly on *Club Matinee* NBC Blue 1937–43; d. Feb. 14, 1983.

Charles Osgood (Charles Osgood Wood III), Jan. 8, 1933, New York City, N.Y.; author, banjoist, commentator, correspondent, emcee, organist, pianist, writer bka *The Osgood File* observations commentary sometimes expressed in rhyming couplets CBS 1971-present ("See you on the radio"), *Sunday Morning* newsmag host CBS-TV 1994-present; still active on New York flagship station WCBS; *ABC News* reporter 1963–67, *Newsmark* public affairs discussion host CBS 1980s, anchored TV fare like *CBS Sunday Night News* early-mid 1970s, *CBS Early Morning News* 1987–92; penned five tomes 1980s-90s including *See You on the Radio*; dozen honorary degrees (10 doctorates), three George Foster Peabody Awards, instrumentalist with Boston Pops, New York Pops, Mormon Tabernacle Choir, organist for a Philadelphia drama on radio debut.

Sander Vanocur, Jan. 8, 1928, Cleveland, Ohio; actor, correspondent, educator, entrepreneur-media mogul, print journalist (*The Manchester Guardian, The New York Times, The Washington Post*), wire journalist (United Press, BBC North American Service) bka reporter for dual chains—*CBS World News Roundup* 1954, *NBC News on the Hour* 1957–71; NBC-TV *Today* show White House/national political/ Washington correspondent, *Huntley-Brinkley Report* nightly newscast contributing editor, *First Tuesday* monthly magazine host 1969–70; lectured at Duke University early 1970s; *The Washington Post* TV critic 1975–77; ABC News 1977–92 as chief diplomatic correspondent; appeared in half-dozen theatrical films 1971–97; anchored two History Channel features 1995–2002; headed Santa Barbara, Calif. media consulting enterprise since.

Deaths

Walter Kiernan, Jan. 8, 1978, Daytona Beach, Fla.; b. Jan. 24, 1902. Olin Tice, Jan. 8, 1998, Blythewood, S.C.; b. Aug. 23, 1919.

January 9

Sound Bite

Antitrust suits against National Broadcasting Co. and investigation by Federal Communications Commission into its dual networks results in NBC separating its broadcast operations, creating on Jan. 9, 1942 the Blue Network Co., Inc.; Red Network is known from that time forward as NBC; NBC finds buyer for Blue in 1943 after FCC orders divestiture of one of net's chains.

Debuting

Roadshow, Jan. 9, 1954, NBC; magazine feature; at start Bill Cullen presided over three-hour Saturday matinee marathon later expanded into five-and-a-half hours that provided impetus, incentive for NBC's programming innovation *Monitor* (airing 40 hours per weekend at start, lasting 20 years); games, prizes, safety tips, music, news, travel features blazed trail for service that defied most well-worn schedule limitations; final broadcast June 11, 1955.

Screen Director's Playhouse (*NBC Theater*, *Screen Director's Guild*), Jan. 9, 1949, NBC; anthology drama; major Hollywood icons in celebrated celluloid narratives; distinguished by superior writing, directors' narration, interaction with stars, similar to concluding moments of *Lux Radio Theater* sans commercial endorsements; headliners appearing included Lucille Ball, Tallulah Bankhead, Jeff Chandler, Joseph Cotten, Kirk Douglas, Dorothy McGuire, Dick Powell, Edward G. Robinson, Barbara Stanwyck, Jimmy Stewart, Claire Trevor, Margaret Truman, John Wayne, Jane Wyatt, more; final broadcast Sept. 28, 1951.

Canceled

The Howard Miller Show, Jan. 9, 1959, CBS; debut July 18, 1955. *X-Minus One*, Jan. 9, 1958, NBC; debut April 24, 1955.

Birth

Murat Bernard (Chic) Young, Jan. 9, 1901, Chicago, Ill.; illustrator bka *Blondie* creator, newspaper comic strip appearing since Sept. 8, 1930, radio manifestation 1939–50, proliferating merchandise, branding extensions; d. March 14, 1973.

Deaths

Arthur Lake, Jan. 9, 1987, Indian Wells, Calif.; b. April 17, 1905. Bernie Smith, Jan. 9, 1990; director (*You Bet Your Life*), b. ca. 1914 (infinite sources exhausted for exact date, locations without firm authentication).

January 10

Births

Donald Gardiner, Jan. 10, 1916, New York City, N.Y.; announcer, newscaster bka longtime ABC employee 1943 (when still Blue network) to death 34 years hence; after being NBC page, joined Winston-Salem WAIR, Washington WRC covering President Franklin D. Roosevelt's third inaugural at latter gig 1941; introduced *David Harding—Counterspy*, *Dick Tracy*, *Gangbusters*, *When a Girl Marries* while dispatching *Monday Morning Headlines* 1944–58, *Tomorrow's Headlines* 1948–49; d. March 27, 1977.

Donald Herbert Lowe, Jan. 10, 1911, Hartford, Conn.; actor (radio, stage), announcer, assistant station manager, emcee, publicist, vocalist, writer; onstage with Westbury, Conn. stock company year before joining Boston WBZ as actor, relief announcer followed by gigs at other New England stations, myriad duties, eventually at small New York City outlet, hired by NBC 1933, soon dispatched to its Washington, D.C. WRC, returned to New York 1934 for series beamed to nation: *David Harding—Counterspy*, *Dunninger—the Mentalist*, *Ethel and Albert*, *The Fat Man*, *Lorenzo Jones*, *The Metropolitan Opera Auditions of the Air*, *Mr. President*, *The Moylan Sisters*, more; d. June 1, 1991.

Deaths

Al Goodman, Jan. 10, 1972, New York City, N.Y.; b. Aug. 5, 1890. Frank Parker, Jan. 10, 1999, Titusville, Fla.; b. April 29, 1903. Donald Voorhees, Jan. 10, 1989, Cape May Court House, N.J.; b. July 26, 1903.

January 11

Births

Eugene Lock Baker, Jan. 11, 1910, Portland, Ore.; announcer, disc jockey, vocalist; aspiring singer whose idol was John Charles Thomas, performed with Columbia Symphony Orchestra, *Songs of a Dreamer* vocalist 1942–44; not wanting to gamble future, pursued debating, dramatics, music in school; stints at Portland, Chicago, Los Angeles stations; introduced net audiences to passel of largely Chicago-based shows late 1930s, 1940s—*Family Theater*, *The First Nighter*, *Golden Days of Radio*, *Houseboat Hannah*, *Knickerbocker Playhouse*, *Lum and Abner*, *Midstream*, *Queen for a Day*, *The Quiz Kids*; d. Aug. 14, 1981.

Carl Caruso, Jan. 11, 1917, Boston, Mass.; announcer, director, emcee; interlocutor 1940s, 1950s series *The Adventures of Leonidas Witherall*, *Bandwagon Mysteries*, *Bobby Benson's Adventures*, *High Adventure*, *My Friend Irma*, *The Mysterious Traveler*, *Rogue's Gallery*, *The Shadow*; *Spin the Picture* game show host Dumont TV 1949; ABC employee 1963–83.

Leonard G. (Len) Sterling, Jan. 11, 1924, Arizona; actor, announcer, vocalist; presented 1940s *Boake Carter*, *The FBI in Peace & War*, *Joyce Jordan—Girl Interne*, *Pot o' Gold*, *We Are Always Young*, more acting in *Cavalcade of America* (where he also sang), *The Eternal Light*, *The Search That Never Ends*, sponsor's rep on *The Brighter Day*, *Life Can Be Beautiful*; d. Sept. 3, 1995.

Deaths

Frank D. Barton, Jan. 11, 1995, Tucson, Ariz.; b. July 21, 1909. Isabel Randolph, Jan. 11, 1973, Los Angeles, Calif.; b. Dec. 4, 1889.

January 12

Debuting

Sam 'n' Henry, Jan. 12, 1926, Chicago WGN; forerunner venerated sitcom *Amos 'n' Andy* aired locally, nationally under sundry appellations March 19, 1928-Nov. 25, 1960; final broadcast of predecessor series Dec. 18, 1927.

Birth

Martin Agronsky, Jan. 12, 1915, Philadelphia, Pa.; commentator, newscaster, print journalist bka *The ABC Morning News* commentator 1944-ca. 1956; concurrent newsman for Washington, D.C. WMAL, New York WABC; wore "extremely liberal" label; staffer, correspondent or contributor to *The Palestine Post*, *The Christian Science Monitor*, *Newsweek*, *Foreign Affairs*, *The Chicago Tribune*, *The London News-Chronicle*, International News Service; transitional journalist shifted to TV as one of video's foremost opinion interviewers ABC, NBC, CBS, PBS 1950s-70s; acclaimed syndicated-TV *Agronsky & Company* 1976–88 re-titled *Inside Edition* when he left—critics credited him for launch of "granddaddy of all the modern talking-heads pundit shows"; d. July 25, 1999.

Deaths

H. Jon (Tex) Antoine, Jan. 12, 1983, New York City, N.Y.; b. April 21, 1923. Helen Claire, Jan. 12, 1974, Birmingham, Ala.; b. Oct. 18, 1911. Betty Lou Gerson, Jan. 12, 1999, Los Angeles, Calif.; b. April 19, 1914.

January 13

Debuting

Al Pearce and His Gang, Jan. 13, 1934, NBC Blue; comedy; frequently as self-conscious door-to-door salesman Elmer Blurt, Pearce gathered about him a bunch of zany comics whose nonsensical abilities tickled the nation's funnybone when it was most needed; show skipped back-and-forth between three chains to Oct. 25, 1947, persisting only with brief daytime, primetime CBS-TV runs in 1952.

Birth

Elmer Holmes Davis, Jan. 13, 1890, Aurora, Ind.; author, commentator, correspondent, editor, newscaster, print journalist bka nightly/weekly/weekend news analyst appearing under own moniker 1939–55; *Radio Guide* claimed he had "an Oxford brain, an Indiana twang that reeked of neutrality"; *The New York Times* reporter 1910–24; short story author for *Harper's*, *The New Yorker*, *The Saturday Review of Literature*; U. S. Office of War Information director 1942–45; d. May 18, 1958.

Deaths

Charlotte Holland, Jan. 13, 1997, London,

England; b. Feb. 9, 1915. Frank Waldecker, Jan. 13, 1995, Needham, Mass.; b. Nov. 20, 1909.

January 14

Debuting

The Affairs of Dr. Gentry, Jan. 14, 1957, NBC; daytime serial; with this NBC inaugurated its final serialized yarn; key figures with infinitely more fascinating lives than those of patients were Dr. Anne Gentry (Madeleine Carroll), Dr. Philip Hamilton (Paul McGrath); epigraph which she read at start of every episode promised: "In everyone's life there are moments of great happiness ... moments of deep sorrow ... there is doubt and deceit ... but there is also hope, faith, and the courage to go on ... I am Anne Gentry ... mine is such a story"; one of NBC's attempts to fill multihour matinee holes in wake of collapse of *Weekday* 1955–56 which swept away most of web's longrunning serial goods, interrupting listening habits that persisted for 25 years; final broadcast April 24, 1959.

Births

George Ansbro, Jan. 14, 1915, Brooklyn, N.Y.; announcer, author, commercial spokesman, newscaster, vocalist bka *Young Widder Brown* daytime serial narrator 1938–56 surpassing peers (he termed it "18 years of the most excruciating radio torture ever devised by Frank and Anne Hummert"); recurring interlocutor of big band remotes fronted by Charlie Barnet, Xavier Cugat, Jimmy Dorsey, Tommy Dorsey, Eddie Duchin, Benny Goodman, Gene Krupa, Guy Lombardo, Glenn Miller, Chick Webb, more; familiar voice all over dial, often linked 1930s-50s to Hummert productions (*The American Album of Familiar Music, Chaplain Jim U.S.A., Manhattan Merry-Go-Round, Mr. Keen—Tracer of Lost Persons, Mrs. Wiggs of the Cabbage Patch, Waltz Time*); scads more series e.g. *Coast-to-Coast on a Bus, Lowell Thomas and the News, Manhattan Maharajah, Pick a Date with Buddy Rogers, Sammy Kaye's Sunday Serenade, What Makes You Tick?, When a Girl Marries*; ABC-TV daily newscast host with John Charles Daly late 1940s; *Dr. I. Q., the Mental Banker* roving announcer ABC-TV 1953–54 ("I have a lady in the balcony, doctor" infamous aphorism); 1990 retirement ended 59-year career, final staffer to serve ABC-NBC dually.

William Bendix, Jan. 14, 1906, Manhattan, New York City, N.Y.; actor (stage, film, radio, TV), grocer bka *The Life of Riley* patriarch, blue-collar guy with trouble getting things right, on radio 1944–51, TV 1953–58; support player, infrequent star 64 theatrical films 1940s-50s e.g. *Wake Island, A Bell for Adano, Sentimental Journey, The Blue Dahlia, The Time of Your Life, The Babe Ruth Story, A Connecticut Yankee in King Arthur's Court, The Life of Riley, Kill the Umpire, Detective Story*; concurrently in surfeit of 1940s-50s aural anthologies—*Cavalcade of America, The Columbia Workshop, Hollywood Star Playhouse, The Hour of Mystery, The Lady Esther Screen Guild Theater, Lux Radio Theater, This Is Hollywood*, more, plus early TV narratives—*Fireside Theater, Lux Video Theater, Philco Television Playhouse, Robert Montgomery Presents, Wagon Train, Playhouse 90, Schlitz Playhouse of Stars, The Untouchables, General Electric Theater*, et al.; d. Dec. 14, 1964.

Mark Goodson, Jan. 14, 1915, Sacramento, Calif.; announcer, director, disc jockey, program inventor, TV game show guru, co-owner Goodson and [Bill] Todman Productions; baptism as San Francisco DJ 1938, regional *Quiz of Two Cities* host, created *Pop the Question*; New York 1941 directing web-based *Appointment with Life, Portia Faces Life, The Kate Smith Show* drama vignettes; established permanent career by designing *Winner Take All* radio run 1946–52 TV 1948–52; repertoire sampling 30+ mostly TV contrivances: *Beat the Clock, Card Sharks, Family Feud, Hit the Jackpot, I've Got a Secret, Judge for Yourself, Match Game, Missing Links, The Name's the Same, Password, Play Your Hunch, The Price Is Right, Rate Your Mate, Snap Judgment, Spin to Win, Tattletales, To Tell the Truth, What's My Line?*; d. Dec. 18, 1992.

David Gothard, Jan. 14, 1911, Beardstown, Ill.; actor (stage, radio) bka *The Romance of Helen Trent* daytime serial longsuffering suitor Gil Whitney CBS 1936–37, 1944–60; performed with local theater groups in Los Angeles before hitching ride to Chicago to try radio—offered announcing job in 1932 that led to dramatic roles on *The Adventures of the Thin Man* (as lead), *Bachelor's Children, Big Sister, Hilltop House, The O'Neills, The Right to Happiness, Woman in White*; d. Aug. 2, 1977.

George Herman, Jan. 14, 1920, New York City, N.Y.; correspondent, newscaster, writer bka CBS newsman 1950s-80s (*CBS World News Roundup*, more); launched CBS career 1944 as newswriter, White House correspondent 1950s-60s, covered Supreme Court 1960s-70s, *Face the Nation* moderator CBS-TV 1969–83; retired from CBS 1987 after 43 years; d. Feb. 8, 2005.

George Arthur Putnam (at times identified as George Arthur to dodge mix-up with separate announcing-newscasting George Putnam), Jan. 21, 1914, Middletown, N.Y.; announcer, newscaster bka interlocutor on enduring NBC washboard weepers *Lorenzo Jones, Portia Faces Life* while credited by a source with 55 aural series; among 1940s-50s introductions: *Joe and Mabel, Justice Triumphs, Lucky U Ranch, Short Short Story* as *George Putnam and the News* aired 1943–44; two 10-minute newscasts daily on New York WEAF, NBC flagship outlet while on web programs; premiered on air at San Diego KGB mid 1930s, shifted to New York CBS 1938, moved to NBC shortly thereafter; following radio halcyon days, announced at Los Angeles TV station KNXT; d. April 8, 1975.

Deaths

Don Carney, Jan. 14, 1954, Miami, Fla.; b. Aug. 19, 1886.

January 15

Debuting

House Party, Jan. 15, 1945, CBS; daytime audience participation series hosted by Art Linkletter; final radiocast Oct. 13, 1967, simulcast CBS-TV Sept. 1, 1952 to aural run's end, *The Art Linkletter Show* video extension to Sept. 5, 1969.

Canceled

Double or Nothing, Jan. 15, 1954, ABC; debut Sept. 29, 1940. *Johnny Presents*, Jan. 15, 1946, NBC; debut Jan. 2, 1934.

Births

Alvin Robinson, Jan. 15, 1913, Apache, Okla.; announcer, magazine sales, theater manager; joined Tulsa KVOO, moved to Gotham, NBC page, six weeks hence auditioned/won spot as NBC staff announcer without specific shows.

Deaths

William C. Bivens, Jan. 15, 1984, Charlotte, N.C.; b. March 24, 1915. Bob Sabin, Jan. 15, 1959, Los Angeles, Calif.; b. Jan. 18, 1912. Ruth Warrick, Jan. 15, 2005, Manhattan, New York City, N.Y.; b. June 29, 1916.

January 16

Debuting

I Love a Mystery, Jan. 16, 1939, NBC West Coast web, transferred to full NBC net Oct. 2, 1939; mystery adventure serial; narrative from prolific, esteemed pen of Carleton E. Morse focused on triple figures of Hollywood A-1 Detective Agency, often carried them to exotic locales, provided merry chases, fantastic exploits for fans; Doc Long (Jim Boles, Barton Yarborough), Jack Packard (Robert Dryden, John McIntire, Jay Novello, Michael Raffetto, Russell Thorson), Reggie Yorke (Tom Collins, Walter Paterson, Tony Randall) seamlessly combined suspense, private eye breed into unique feature; trilogy full-length films released 1945, TV reprise flick 1970s not credible, 1980s comic strip met limited interest, Morse wrote *Stuff the Lady's Hatbox* novel based on show just before 1993 demise; final radiocast Dec. 26, 1952.

Canceled

Band of America, Jan. 16, 1956, NBC; debut Feb. 18, 1927 (*Cities Service Concert*). *Club Fifteen*, Jan. 16, 1953, CBS; debut June 30, 1947. *Your Hit Parade*, Jan. 16, 1953, NBC, video extension on NBC, CBS to April 24, 1959; debut April 20, 1935.

Births

Goodman Ace (Goodman Aiskowitz), Jan. 16, 1899, Kansas City, Mo.; actor, columnist, gagwriter, journalist, scriptwriter bka *Easy Aces*,

Mr. Ace and Jane scribe-thespian playing self in both homespun comedies with spouse Jane Sherwood Ace; *The Kansas City Post-Journal* drama critic also reviewed films for KMBC 1927–32; when talent didn't arrive once, Ace told "keep talking"—enlisted wife who was at studio—their gab loved by listeners, netted twice-weekly feature 1930–32, projected duo to Chicago chains 1932–45, 1948, syndication 1945–46; he penned gags for Tallulah Bankhead, Milton Berle, Perry Como, Danny Kaye, Bob Newhart; wrote *Saturday Review* column for years; d. March 25, 1982.

Jay Hanna (Dizzy) Dean, Jan. 16, 1910, Lucas, Ark.; baseball pitcher (St. Louis Cardinals, Chicago Cubs, St. Louis Browns), sportscaster bka *Game of the Day* play-by-play announcer 1951–53 (*Game of the Week* ABC-TV, CBS-TV 1953–65), *Dizzy Dean* radio host 1948, 1951; entered broadcasting full time 1941 but back to field briefly 1947; colorfully massacred English language to fans' delight; elected to Baseball Hall of Fame 1953; d. July 17, 1974.

John (Bud) Hiestand, Jan. 16, 1907, Madison, Wis.; actor (radio, film, TV), announcer; beckoned 1940s-50s listeners to *The Edgar Bergen Hour, The George Burns and Gracie Allen Show, The Great Gildersleeve, Kay Kyser's Kollege of Musical Knowledge, Let George Do It, Meet Corliss Archer*, more; played on *The Cinnamon Bear, Young Love*; 10 B-movies 1943–71; introduced *Ford Theater* 1949–57 to viewers of three chains, sitcoms *The Adventures of Hiram Holiday* NBC 1956–57, *My Living Doll* CBS 1964–65, *Green Acres* CBS 1965–71, *Hogan's Heroes* CBS 1965–71, *The Second Hundred Years* ABC 1967–68; d. Feb. 5, 1987.

John B. Kennedy, Jan. 16, 1895, Quebec, Canada; announcer, analyst, emcee, newscaster, print journalist (multiple newspapers, edited Knights of Columbus' *Columbia, Collier's* as associate, managing editor); while at latter joined New York WJZ 1926 part time as announcer, newscaster, overseeing *The Collier Hour* NBC 1927–32, elevated to full time NBC 1933; web newscasts under his moniker, intermittent breaks 1933–51 (last two years ABC), local nightly newscasts New York WNEW 1941–44, WOR mid 1940s, Philadelphia WFIL 1948; hosted *Radio City Party* 1934–35, presented *General Motors Concert, The Packard Hour*, moderated *The People's Rally* 1930s; d. July 22, 1961.

Dwight Weist, Jan. 16, 1910, Palo Alto, Calif.; actor (film, radio, stage), announcer, educator, emcee, entrepreneur, voiceover artist, writer bka "man of 1,000 voices" with versatile dialectical range, *Search for Tomorrow* daytime serial interlocutor CBS-TV 1951–82; announced, wrote for Columbus, Ohio WAIU in ethereal debut; played with Ohio stock companies; late 1930s-1960s installments *Andy Hardy, Buck Rogers in the 25th Century, The March of Time, The Second Mrs. Burton, The Shadow, Texaco Star Theater, Treasury Star Parade, Valiant Lady*, more; presented *The Aldrich Family, Big Town, Grand Slam, Inner Sanctum Mysteries, Official Detective*, more; co-founded Weist-Barron School of TV-Commercial Acting, teaching 35 years; *We the People* host CBS-TV 1948–50 (radio carryover); voiced radio-TV commercials, narrated TV travelogues, Pathé newsreels, acted in five cinematic films, narrated 27 more; d. July 16, 1991.

Deaths

Ray Barrett, Jan. 16, 1973, Fort Lauderdale, Fla.; b. Sept. 1, 1907. Carl Eastman, Jan. 16, 1970, New York City, N.Y.; b. June 13, 1908. Arturo Toscanini, Jan. 16, 1957, Riverdale, N.Y.; b. March 25, 1867.

January 17

Debuting

Ben Bernie, the Old Maestro, Jan. 17, 1930, NBC Blue; musical variety; neither musician (while he *could* fiddle), super impresario, arranger, comic or talent scout but—alleged a pundit—a "personality" who held audiences at rapt attention with unique speech style (expressions, clipped *g*'s, etc.), attracting huge following by 1933; final broadcast March 5, 1943 (ill—he left show Jan. 15, 1943).

Births

Hugh E. Brundage, Jan. 17, 1915, Montana; actor (*Mr. Smith Goes to Washington* film 1939), announcer, news anchor-director (local TV); introduced listeners to *The Old Fashioned Revival Hour* ca. 1940s, *Aunt Mary* 1942–51, *Heart's Desire* 1946–48, *Junior Miss* 1948–50 among duties; staffer with six Los Angeles radio-TV outlets; d. March 31, 1972.

Warren Hull, Jan. 17, 1903, Gasport, N.Y.; actor (film, radio, stage), announcer, emcee, producer, vocalist, writer bka *Strike It Rich* master of ceremonies ca. 1949–1957; elected officer first year of American Federation of Radio Artists 1937; introduced aural features *The Jack Haley Show, The Maxwell House Show Boat, Your Hit Parade*, acted in *The Gibson Family, Log Cabin Jamboree*, hosted *Vox Pop, Mother Knows Best, Radio City Matinee* (latter daytime variety show on New York WNBT television 1946); d. Sept. 14, 1974.

Charles Knox Manning, Jan. 17, 1904, Worcester, Mass.; actor (film, radio), announcer, emcee; hired to act by Boston station 1930, soon announcing, multi on-air tasks, working series aired by Yankee, Don Lee networks (latter after shifting to West Coast); joined Los Angeles KNX; American Federation of Radio Artists (AFRA) elected him president 1952 as group expanded to TV (AFTRA); narrated 52 movies, appeared in 20 more 1939–53; welcomed radio listeners to *The Adventures of Sherlock Holmes, Stars Over Hollywood*, more than dozen others, some he hosted; d. Aug. 26, 1980.

Dallas S. Townsend, Jr., Jan. 17, 1919, New York City, N.Y.; newscaster bka CBS news vet 1941–85; briefly news editor at New York WQXR before joining CBS as news editor, correspondent, anchoring one of net's dual major daily news features — *CBS World News Round-up* — mornings mid 1950s-early 1980s (minus 1961–63 when he anchored other signature show — *The World Tonight*); also dispatched *CBS News on the Hour* at intervals 1955–85; d. June 1, 1995.

Deaths

Richard Crenna, Jan. 17, 2003, Los Angeles, Calif.; b. Nov. 30, 1927.

January 18

Debuting

Aunt Jenny's Real Life Stories (premiered as Aunt *Jenny's True Life Stories*), Jan. 18, 1937, CBS; anthological daytime serial; only recurring voices were Jenny (Edith Spencer, Agnes Young) — narrating five-installment-per-tale chapters of mythical Littleton's denizens, announcer Dan Seymour — sampling cakes, pies, fries, turnovers, fritters, dumplings, etc. Jenny made with sponsor's shortening ("For all you bake or fry, rely on Spry!"), birdman Henry Boyd, whose fowl language imitated whistling canary in Jenny's sunlit kitchen; daily she left fans with an inspirational bromide, her "golden thought for today"; drama one of minuscule handful with closed-end (ultimate conclusion) storylines, lasting nearly two decades; final broadcast Nov. 16, 1956.

Canceled

Blind Date, Jan. 18, 1946, NBC; debut July 8, 1943.

Births

Roderick G. (Rod) O'Connor, Jan. 18, 1914, Houston, Texas; actor (film, radio, TV), announcer, emcee; pilgrimage to big time included 1930s-mid 1940s: Minneapolis WTCN, San Luis Obispo, Calif. WVEC, Idaho Falls, Idaho KID, Ogden, Utah KLO, Salt Lake City, KUTA, KSL, Minneapolis WCCO, Chicago WGN, Los Angeles KHJ; mid 1940s-50s introductions of *Command Performance, The Count of Monte Cristo, Duffy's Tavern, Family Theater, Glamour Manor, Guest Star, Murder Is My Hobby, People Are Funny*, more, plus acting in *Crime Is My Pastime*, hosting *Cascade of Stars*; uncredited roles in 1948 theatrical releases *The Fuller Brush Man, A Southern Yankee*; bit part in *Fury* episode NBC-TV 1955; d. June 5, 1964.

Robert Cook Sabin, Jan. 18, 1912, Illinois; announcer, newscaster, sportscaster bka *Modern Romances* narrator 1936–37 (only validated web series); moved to Gary, Ind. WIND as newscaster 1942, Monterey, Calif. KDON 1946 as sportscaster; d. Jan. 15, 1959.

Lucille Wall, Jan. 18, 1899, Chicago, Ill.; actress (radio, TV) bka *Portia Faces Life* daytime serial namesake attorney Portia Blake Manning for full CBS/NBC run 1940–51, *Lorenzo Jones* daytime serial feminine lead Belle Jones NBC

1940–55; broke into radio at Newark WJZ 1927, appeared on *The Collier Hour*, *The First Nighter*, *Sherlock Holmes*, *True Confessions*, more; appeared in *General Hospital* soap as Nurse March ABC-TV 1963–76, 1982; d. July 11, 1986.

Deaths

Art Balinger, Jan. 18, 1980, Alhambra, Calif.; b. Feb. 4, 1898. Joan Banks, Jan. 18, 1998, Los Angeles, Calif.; b. Oct. 30, 1918. Harry Fleetwood, Jan. 18, 2004, New York City, N.Y.; Sept. 15, 1917. Ray Morgan, Jan. 18, 1975, Los Angeles, Calif.; b. Dec. 15, 1917.

January 19

Debuting

Official Detective, Jan. 19, 1947, MBS; police investigative drama inspired by tales in magazine of same name; among "the men who guard your safety and protect your home" hard-boiled detective Lt. Dan Britt (Joe McCormack, Ed Begley, Craig McDonnell), Sgt. Al Bowen (Tom Evans, Louis Nye) pulled few punches delivering behind-scenes look at metro police operation, adapting real cases against murderers, arsonists, thieves, counterfeiters, gangsters as own; critic maintained "the same thing was done better on *The Lineup* and much better on *Dragnet*"; Everett Sloane hosted fleeting anthology on syndicated TV 1957; final radiocast March 7, 1957.

Births

Norman Barry, Jan. 19, 1909, St. Louis, Mo.; accountant, announcer, newscaster, sportscaster; Chicago broadcasting career launched WIBO 1930 included trial TV efforts, eventually encompassed WENR, WMAQ, NBC starting 1934; chain claims Barry featured "on many network programs" although only one certified, *Dan Harding's Wife*, late 1930s; d. Dec. 25, 1997.

Dirk Fredericks (Frederick W. Duerk), Jan. 19, 1919, New York City, N.Y.; announcer, emcee; hosted only web series *Music Tent* 1955; joined ABC 1950, remained 26 years to death; one of four roving inquisitors finding studio contestants for *Dr. I. Q.—the Mental Banker* ABC-TV 1953–54, 1958–59; d. Dec. 31, 1976.

Anne (Shumacher Ashenhurst) Hummert, Jan. 19, 1905, Baltimore, Md.; advertising agency executive, journalist, producer bka collaborator with spouse Frank bringing 125+ recurring series to radio, half open-ended soap operas with ongoing story lines, rest split in juvenile adventure serials, musicales, mysteries 1931–60; never surpassed duo branded "most prolific producers in broadcasting" (more detail under Frank's entry June 2); d. July 5, 1996, New York City, N.Y.

Lanny Ross, Jan. 19, 1906, Seattle, Wash.; disc jockey, recording artist, vocalist (lyric tenor) bka singer for score of national series 1929–57, eight dubbed *The Lanny Ross Show*, another *Lanny Ross and His State Fair Concert*, plus *The Lanny Ross Show* NBC-TV 1948–49; forsook law ambitions, promising athletics path to pursue entertainment; as network exposure subsided, became New York disc jockey WCBS late 1950s-1960s; d. April 25, 1988.

Alexander Woollcott (Woolcott also), Jan. 19, 1887, Phalanx, N.J.; actor (stage), announcer, author, commentator, emcee, journalist, lecturer bka *The Town Crier* host-commentator 1930, 1933–35, 1937–38, *A Christmas Carol* host-narrator annually 1934–42; drama critic of dailies trio—*The New York Times*, *The New York World*, *The New York Herald* intermittently 1914–32, but banned by Schuberts (and thereby his paper, *Times*) from their multiple theaters 1916; nonconformist, egotistical, abrasive style often branded him "misfit"—loved ridiculing people, put screws to some he interviewed on air, not widely accepted then; influence extensive, powerful—he could "make or break a play, film or celebrity" noted critic; frequent guest on radio's *Information Please*, *People's Platform*, *Stage Door Canteen*; d. Jan. 23, 1943.

January 20

Births

George Burns (Nathan Birnbaum), Jan. 20, 1896, New York City, N.Y.; actor (stage, film, radio, TV), author, producer (McCadden Productions) bka *The George Burns and Gracie Allen Show* family sitcom patriarch as himself 1932–50, CBS-TV extension 1950–58; consummate straight man fed lines to Gracie whose wacky character carried show; played title role star of trilogy of acclaimed theatrical releases: *Oh, God!* 1977, *Oh, God! Book II* 1980, *Oh, God! You Devil* 1984; confident he'd live to 100, did; d. March 9, 1996.

Deaths

Alan Freed, Jan. 20, 1965, Palm Springs, Calif.; b. Dec. 15, 1922. Don Stanley, Jan. 20, 2003, Los Angeles, Calif.; b. Aug, 5, 1917.

January 21

Debuting

The Fat Man, Jan. 21, 1946, ABC; detective drama with private eye Brad Runyon (J. Scott Smart) tipping scales at 237 pounds, whose rare brushes with jocularity were never a lapse to resolute commitment in nailing criminals; another sleuth (*Sam Spade*, *The Thin Man*) from Dashiell Hammett fiction, this time swapping chatter with secretary Lila North (Mary Patton), girlfriend Cathy Evans (Amzie Strickland), police Sgt. O'Hara (Ed Begley); Smart reprised lead in 1951 theatrical film; final broadcast Sept. 26, 1951.

Births

Eugenia Lincoln (Jinx) Falkenburg, Jan. 21, 1919, Barcelona, Spain; actress (film, stage), commentator, dancer, sportscaster, vocalist bka *Meet Tex and Jinx* 1947, 1948, *Leave It to the Girls* panelist 1945–49; dubbed "Mr. Brains and Mrs. Beauty," Tex McCrary and wife Jinx joined Ed, Pegeen Fitzgerald, Dorothy Kilgallen, hubby Richard Kollmar in perpetuating early morning spousal breakfast chats on New York radio (theirs ran 1946–60); she was swimming champ in Chile, tennis champ in Brazil, statuesque form projected her into 23 mostly B movies, Broadway; huge GOP fund-raiser; d. Aug. 27, 2003.

J. Carrol Naish (Joseph Patrick Carrol Naish), Jan. 21, 1897, New York City, N.Y.; actor (stage, film, radio, TV) bka dialect thespian, fluent in many languages in sundry mediums; *Life with Luigi* protagonist Luigi Basco, Italian immigrant running Chicago antique emporium with unbridled quest to be best U. S. citizen possible despite obstacles created by language, mistaken meanings 1948–54; d. Jan. 24, 1973.

Deaths

Bob Dwan, Jan. 21, 2005, Santa Monica, Calif.; b. April 1, 1915. Peggy Lee, Jan. 21, 2002, Bel Air, Calif.; b. May 26, 1920.

January 22

Debuting

The Adventures of Christopher London, Jan. 22, 1950, NBC; intercontinental crime drama; hero (Hollywood movie legend Glenn Ford) was globetrotting troubleshooter pursuing quests in far away places with strange-sounding names; inspired by *Perry Mason* creator Erle Stanley Gardner, though its five-month run hints inspiration not enough; final broadcast June 5, 1950.

Births

Anne Elstner, Jan. 22, 1899, Lake Charles, La.; actress (radio, stage), entrepreneur bka *Stella Dallas* daytime serial heroine NBC 1938–55; already acting on Broadway, this queen of matinee misery played in *Moonshine and Honeysuckle* NBC 1930–33 en-route to crowning achievement with roles in *Brenda Curtis*, *The Fat Man*, *The Gibson Family*, *Great Plays*, *Heartthrobs of the Hills*, *The Heinz Magazine of the Air*, *Just Plain Bill*, *Maverick Jim*, *The March of Time*, *Mr. Keen—Tracer of Lost Persons*, *Pages of Romance*, *Tish*, *Wilderness Road*; as radio faded, with spouse she operated Stella Dallas' Rivers Edge Restaurant at Lambertville, N.J.; d. Jan. 29, 1981.

Frank Ernest Hemingway, Jan. 22, 1903, Brookings, S.D.; actor (radio, stage), announcer, dialectician (French, German, Japanese, Scotch, others), newscaster; onstage before radio at Bend, Ore. KNBD 1937 colorizing newscasts with dialects; Portland, Ore. KOIN 1939, then KGW, KEX, Los Angeles KMPC 1945, KHJ, Don Lee Network, ABC West Coast radio-TV; mid 1940s-early 1950s beckoned fans to *Breakfast at Sardi's* (*Breakfast in Hollywood*), *Deadline Mystery*, *Voice of the Nation*, et al., *Roy Rogers Show* actor; d. June 25, 1989.

Guy Savage, Jan. 22, 1906, Tulsa, Okla.; announcer, newscaster, sportscaster, vocalist bka *Play Broadcast* interlocutor 1940–41 (only confirmed net series); journey carried him from singing on Houston KTRH where he debuted 1930 to San Antonio KABC 1937 as sportscaster, Chicago WGN 1938–41 initially as newscaster before transferring to sportscasting, sports reports at two more Houston outlets — KLEE 1948, KXYZ 1950–60; d. Aug. 31, 1981.

Charles Robert Warren, Jan. 22, 1917, Plainview, Neb.; actor, announcer, composer, newscaster bka *The Lawrence Welk Show* interlocutor 27 years, ABC-TV 1955–71, syndicated 1971–82; opened *This Is Your Life* NBC-TV 1952, *The Girl in My Life* ABC-TV 1973–74; acted in radio's *Death Valley Sheriff* late 1940s-early 1950s, presenting *Archie Andrews, Cloak and Dagger, Confidentially Yours, The Jane Pickens Show, Radio City Playhouse, X-Minus One*, more; *Eve Knew Her Apples* 1945 flick composer; Philadelphia KYW newsman 1946; d. Dec. 28, 1984.

Richard G. (Dick) Willard, Jan. 22, 1914, Binghamton (unverified), N.Y.; announcer, disc jockey, emcee, producer; on national radio scene late 1930s-mid 1950s (hired by WOR he stayed 44 years), DJ for *Easy Does It, Mutual Matinee*, host of *Take It Easy Time*, opened *Mary Margaret McBride* (*Martha Deane*), *The Shadow, The Strange Dr. Weird*; d. Sept. 6, 2000.

Deaths

Parker Fennelly, Jan. 22, 1988, Peekskill, N.Y.; b. Oct. 22, 1891. Billy May, Jan. 22, 2004, San Juan Capistrano, Calif.; b. Nov. 10, 1916. Arch Presby, Jan. 22, 2007, Escondido, Calif.; b. Aug. 27, 1907.

January 23

Births

Florence Halop, Jan. 23, 1923, Jamaica Estates, Queens, N.Y.; actress (film, radio, TV) bka recurring voice in sitcom-comedy-dramatic roles: *Duffy's Tavern, The Falcon, The Jimmy Durante Show, Meet Millie, The Jack Paar Show*; bit parts in movie trio —*Nancy Drew, Reporter* 1939, *Junior G-Men* 1940, *The Glass Bottom Boat* 1966; TV regular for *Don Ameche's Musical Playhouse* 1950–51, *St. Elsewhere* pesky patient Mrs. Hufnagel 1984–85, *Night Court* feisty bailiff Florence Kleiner 1985–86; d. July 15, 1986.

Deaths

Harry Kramer, Jan. 23, 1996, Sarasota, Fla.; b. Feb. 9, 1911. Alexander Woollcott, Jan. 23, 1943, New York City, N.Y.; b. Jan. 19, 1887.

January 24

Births

Alwyn E. Bach, Jan. 24, 1898, Springfield, Mass.; announcer bka interlocutor in network radio's first decade for musical fare like *Heel Hugger Harmonies, Enna Jettick Melodies, The Lehn and Fink Serenade, Luden's Novelty Orchestra, Real Folks, Stars of Melody*; joined Springfield WBZ mid 1920s, on hand as it affiliated with NBC 1926 (call letters moved to Boston 1931, Springfield outlet re-lettered WBZA); Bach named "senior announcer" at WBZ late 1920s; recipient Good Diction Award 1930 from American Academy of Arts and Sciences; d. May 14, 1993.

Earl Godwin, Jan. 24, 1881, Washington, D.C.; commentator, newscaster, print journalist (*The Baltimore Sun, The Washington Star, The Montreal Star, The New York World, The New York Times, The Washington Times-Herald*) bka newscaster on multiple series: *Earl Godwin and the News* 1935–41, 1944–49, *Watch the World Go By* 1942–44; Franklin D. Roosevelt christened him "the Earl of Godwin" appointing chair for him near presidential desk at White House press conferences — Godwin covered all national political campaigns Wilson to FDR; d. Sept. 23, 1956.

Marvin Kaplan, Jan. 24, 1924, Brooklyn, N.Y.; actor (stage, film, radio, TV), voiceover artist bka *Meet Millie* sitcom poet wannabe Alfred E. Printzmetal 1951–54, on CBS-TV 1952–56 wherein stocky-bodied, round-faced, bespectacled comic thespian with distinctive Brooklynese inflection was ideal for eccentric figure he played; same with *Alice* restaurant patron-telephone lineman Henry Beesmyer CBS-TV 1978–85; silver screen escapades

1950–76 included *Francis the Talking Mule, I Can Get It for You Wholesale, The Fat Man, Angels in the Outfield, Wake Me When It's Over, The Nutty Professor, It's a Mad Mad Mad Mad World, The Great Race, Freaky Friday*; spoke lines for scads of TV cartoons 1960s-1990s e.g. *The C. B. Bears, The Smurfs, Saturday Supercade.*

Walter Kiernan, Jan. 24, 1902, New Haven, Conn.; commentator, emcee, syndicated columnist (*One Man's Opinion*), wire service journalist (Associated Press, International News Service) bka *Monitor* co-communicator 1955–60, *Weekday* 1955–56, *Weekend* host 1953–55; interview series *Kiernan's Corner* 1945–48, *Mystery File* master of ceremonies 1950–51, commentator on *One Man's Opinion* 1949–51, *Cliché Club moderator* 1950, several more entries in similar vein; joined New York WJZ 1943 with news feature, signifying transition print to electronic media; on New York WOR Radio, TV 1958–69 under *One Man's Opinion* moniker; many TV exploits 1948–55 e.g. moderating *Who Said That?* NBC 1951–54, *I've Got a Secret* panelist CBS 1952; d. Jan. 8, 1978.

Deaths

Gordon MacRae, Jan. 24, 1986, Lincoln, Neb.; b. March 12, 1921. J. Carrol Naish, Jan. 24, 1973, La Jolla, Calif.; b. Jan. 21, 1897. Tom Shirley, Jan. 24, 1962, New York City, N.Y.; b. Dec. 1, 1899.

January 25

Debuting

The Guiding Light, Jan. 25, 1937, NBC; daytime serial; most enduring drama in broadcast history launched with minister as central figure, Dr. John Ruthledge (Arthur Peterson), preaching to choir, everybody else in nonsectarian rural congregation at Five Points; tale evolved from his homilies to foibles of Bauer clan at mid-century including Papa (Theodore Goetz), Meta (Jone Allison), Trudy (Laurette Fillbrandt), Bill (Lyle Sudrow), Bill's wife Bertha (Charita Bauer) who became family's matriarch; in 1980s they passed, others arrived as modern interpretation played out on CBS-TV dating to June 30, 1952, still airing in 2008; final radiocast June 29, 1956.

My Son Jeep, Jan. 25, 1953, NBC; domestic sitcom; frothy tale of widowed physician Robert Allison (Donald Cook, Paul McGrath) of Grove Falls raising two kids, Jeep (Martin Huston, Bobby Alford), Peggy (Joan Lazer); title hinted he doted on one; others in cast: housekeeper Mrs. Bixby (Leona Powers), Allison's receptionist/heartthrob Barbara Miller (Lynn Allen, Joyce Gordon); silent for 28 months, restored in 1955, filling weeknight hole; final broadcast Nov. 9, 1956.

Canceled

The National Farm and Home Hour, Jan. 25, 1958, NBC; debut Sept. 30, 1929. *We, the People*, Jan. 25, 1951, NBC; debut Oct. 4, 1936.

Birth

Roy A. Rowan, Jan. 25, 1920, Encino, Calif.; actor, announcer, entrepreneur bka Lucille Ball CBS-TV domestic sitcom announcer for *I Love Lucy* 1951–57, *The Lucy-Desi Comedy Hour* 1957–60, *The Lucy Show* 1962–68, *Here's Lucy* 1968–74; broadcast quests began at Kalamazoo, Mich. WKZO 1939, Schenectady WGY, Buffalo WGR-WKBW, Chicago WGN 1943, Hollywood KNX 1944; opened radio's *The Adventures of Philip Marlowe, The Amazing Mr. Tutt, Columbia Presents Corwin, Crime Classics, Escape, Gunsmoke, Meet Corliss Archer, My Little Margie, Our Miss Brooks, Rogers of the Gazette, Romance, Yours Truly—Johnny Dollar*, more; in 1950s-70s TV announced *Earn Your Vacation, Those Whiting Girls, It's Always Jan, How's Your Mother-in-law?, The Joker's Wild*, others; acted in made-for-TV flick *Incident in San Francisco* 1971; part owner three radio stations—San Jose/Stockton, Calif., Las Vegas, Nev.; managed Beverly Hills branch media brokerage house 1968–90 before operating Rowan Media Brokers, Encino, Calif. 1990–97; d. May 10, 1998.

Deaths

Ted Mallie, Jan. 25, 1999, Jamaica, N.Y.; b. June 3, 1924. Robert Rockwell, Jan. 25, 2003, Malibu, Calif.; b. Oct. 15, 1920.

January 26

Canceled

Monitor, Jan. 26, 1975, NBC; debut June 12, 1955.

Births

Arthur Kohl, Jan. 26, 1908, Chicago, Ill.; actor (radio, TV) bka *Archie Andrews* teen sitcom patriarch Fred Andrews 1947–53; inexhaustible Chicago soap opera thespian (*Bachelor's Children, Betty and Bob, The Right to Happiness, The Road of Life, The Story of Mary Marlin*, more) 1930s-early 1940s; *Famous Jury Trials* solo recorded TV exhibition Dumont 1950; d. Dec. 17, 1972.

William (Billy) Redfield, Jan. 26, 1927, Manhattan, New York City, N.Y.; actor (stage, radio, film, TV), author, raconteur, writer; aural support roles on *The Brighter Day, David Harum, Have Gun—Will Travel, Mr. Keen—Tracer of Lost Persons, Young Doctor Malone, Yours Truly—Johnny Dollar*, eventually *The CBS Radio Mystery Theater*; Broadway stage debut at nine in *Swing Your Lady* 1936 followed by *Our Town* 1938, *Junior Miss* 1941, *A Man for All Seasons* 1961, *You Know I Can't Hear You When the Water's Running* 1968, more; ongoing roles in four early TV series: *Jimmy Hughes—Rookie Cop* 1953, *The Marriage* 1954, *Kitty Foyle* 1958, *As the World Turns* 1958; 20 theatrical motion pictures 1939–78 including *One Flew Over the Cukoo's Nest* 1975, parts in 69 solo episodes of TV dramatic fare 1949–76, five made-for-TV flicks 1961–75; co-created *Mr. Peepers* TV sitcom, penned *A View with Alarm* stage play, published memoir *Letters from an Actor*, on talk show circuit sharing experiences; d. Aug. 17, 1976.

Deaths

Victor Lindlahr, Jan. 26, 1969, Miami Beach, Fla.; b. Feb. 14, 1897. Gertrude Warner, Jan. 26, 1986, New York City, N.Y.; b. April 2, 1917.

January 27

Sound Bite

Opposition arrives to NBC's dual-chain dominance of nationwide ether on Jan. 27, 1927 as United Independent Broadcasters, Inc. established by New York talent agent Arthur Judson; needing investors, Columbia Phonograph Co. (Columbia Records) pays debts during April 1927; net starts airing Sept. 18, 1927, renamed Columbia Phonograph Broadcasting System; "Columbia bought the operating rights of United Independent," says *Fortune*, "which wasn't even operating"; unable to sell sufficient air time to advertisers, Columbia sells to new bloc Sept. 25, 1927; after several years, that faction will turn it to profit.

Debuting

Clara, Lu 'n' Em, Jan. 27, 1931, NBC Blue (premiered over Chicago WGN June 16, 1930); comedic serial; debuted as weeknight feature but quickly moved to weekdays Feb. 15, 1927, becoming first soap opera aired by chain in sunshine hours, setting pattern for much more to follow; focused on trio of gossipy neighbors finding mirth in life's experiences; originating parts of chatty housewives were Louise Starkey, Isabel Carothers, Helen King, replaced by Fran Harris, Dorothy Day, Harriet Allyn; off air 1936–42; final broadcast Dec. 4, 1942.

David Harum, Jan. 27, 1936, NBC; daytime serial with dark nuances; New England banker Harum (Craig McDonnell, Cameron Prud'homme, Wilmer Walter) mired in "helping those who need help" while "outwitting those who are too clever and scheming in helping themselves," chasing kidnappers, exposing diabolical plots, nailing rapscallions of sundry intents, true "helping hand" figure of soap opera (e.g. *Big Sister, Just Plain Bill, Ma Perkins*); aided in some pursuits by Susan Price Wells (Peggy Allenby, Joan Tompkins, Gertrude Warner); Harum stemmed from 1898 novel, 1934 film starring Will Rogers; acclaimed after New York WOR premiered it in 1935; profitable vehicle for B. T. Babbitt Co. pushing Bab-O cleanser via incessant premiums; final broadcast Jan. 5, 1951.

Births

Nancy Dickerson (Whitehead) (Nancy Conners Hanschman), Jan. 27, 1927, Wauwatosa, Wis.; author, educator, producer, reporter, socialite; perhaps unaware of Mary Marvin Breckinridge, hired by Ed Murrow summer 1939 as sole feminine member of famed "Murrow Boys" covering European theater in World War II for CBS as she — Dickerson — wrote in *Among Those Present* 1976 "she" was "first woman reporter at CBS"; despite error, Dickerson wasn't inconsequential — opened doors for lady journalists that hadn't been nearly as wide; joined CBS 1954, *Face the Nation* associate producer, on air as correspondent 1960–63, NBC News Washington bureau 1963–70; produced syndicated TV programs next, won Peabody for "784 Days That Changed America — Watergate to Resignation"; Fox News commentator 1986–91; interviewed multi heads of state for PBS; frequently held lavish parties for D.C. bureaucrats at two area estates; d. Oct. 18, 1997.

Howard McNear, Jan. 27, 1905, Los Angeles, Calif.; actor (radio, film, TV), voiceover artist bka *Gunsmoke* western narrative Doc Charles Adams CBS 1952–61, *The Andy Griffith Show* sitcom barber Floyd Lawson CBS-TV 1961–67; discerning as ace operator Clint Barlow in syndicated *Speed Gibson of the International Secret Police* 1937–38, paved way for support roles in aural fare: *The Adventures of Nero Wolfe, The Adventures of Philip Marlowe, The Affairs of Ann Scotland, The Casebook of Gregory Hood, Fibber McGee & Molly, The Lineup, Maisie, One Man's Family, The Six Shooter, Tales of the Texas Rangers, Yours Truly—Johnny Dollar*, more; 28 theatrical movies 1954–66, recorded voiceovers for two TV animated cartoons, in one made-for-TV flick, 81 episodes of scattered video features — dramas, sitcoms, variety shows; d. Jan. 3, 1969.

Merrill Mueller, Jan. 27, 1916, New York City, N.Y.; commentator, correspondent, newscaster bka key overseas reporter in World War II for NBC from European, Pacific theaters, providing pool coverage feeds to all radio chains several months; *Merrill Mueller News Commentary* 1945–46; NBC workhorse throughout 1940s-60s, frequently on *Monitor* 1955–70 as newscaster, host of half-hour news specials; contributed to NBC-TV coverage afternoon of President John F. Kennedy's assassination (Nov. 22, 1963), with Jay Barbree co-anchored multiple space launches NBC Radio; joined ABC Radio 1970 anchoring most of Apollo 13 crisis coverage, ABC newscaster 1970–80; d. Nov. 30, 1980.

Deaths

Louis (Lou) Crosby, Jan. 27, 1984, Australia; b. 1911 (rigorous efforts to confirm exact date unproductive), Lawton, Okla.; actor, announcer, producer — *Gene Autry's Melody Ranch, The Roy Rogers Show*. Ed Ford, Jan. 27, 1970, Greenport, N.Y.; b. June 13, 1887. Bill Kennedy, Jan. 27, 1997, Palm Beach, Fla.; b. June 27, 1912. Edward P. Morgan, Jan. 27, 1993, McLean, Va.; b. June 23, 1910. Jack Paar, Jan. 27, 2004, Greenwich, Conn.; b. May 1, 1918. Bill Rogers, Jan. 27, 1996 (last residence New Milford, N.J.); b. Nov. 17, 1916. Dick Wesson, Jan. 27, 1979, Costa Mesa, Calif.; b. Feb. 20, 1919.

January 28

Canceled

George Jessel Salutes (last in series), Jan. 28, 1954, ABC; debut Jan. 2, 1934.

Births

(Elizabeth) Irene Beasley, Jan. 28, 1904, Whitehaven, Tenn.; composer, educator, emcee, entrepreneur, pianist, producer, vocalist, writer bka *Grand Slam* musical quiz mistress of ceremonies-producer-writer CBS 1943–53; on radio at Memphis 1928 followed by year in Chicago theaters, studios, clubs, on to New York 1929 joining CBS, continuing in nightclubs, vaudeville houses across U. S.; pioneered singing commercials; radio career embraced *The Fitch Bandwagon, Good Neighbors, Old Dutch Girl, RFD #1, Raising a Husband*; during radio heyday she owned Mississippi corn, cotton plantation; retired from radio mid 1950s, turning to real estate for livelihood; d. Jan. 7, 1980.

Briggs, Donald P. (Lester B. Sprawls), Jan. 28, 1911, Chicago, Ill.; actor (stage, film, radio, TV), announcer (*The First Nighter*), brokerage salesman, producer bka recurring thespian in string of 1930s-40s soap operas: *Betty and Bob, David Harum, Girl Alone, Hilltop House, Life Begins, Perry Mason, Portia Faces Life, The Story of Bess Johnson*; versatile utility player in solo roles on *Columbia Workshop*, *The FBI in Peace & War*, *Grand Hotel*, *Mr. Keen—Tracer of Lost Persons*, *The Sheriff*, more; co-produced *The Army Hour* 1942–45; typecast as suave, sinister villain 37 mostly B-movies 1936–76; left Hollywood for Broadway, summer stock, tours; career climaxed with TV parts in *Cameo Theater*, *Pulitzer Prize Playhouse*, *Robert Montgomery Presents*, *Studio One*, *Suspense*, *Tales of Tomorrow*, *The Web*, like fare; d. Feb. 3, 1986.

Arthur James Gary, Jan. 28, 1914, New York City, N.Y.; announcer, newscaster bka interlocutor for *The Colgate Sports Newsreel/Bill Stern Sports* and other appellations ca. 1937-ca. 1956; broadcasting career extending 1936–84 welcoming radio listeners to *The Amazing Mr. Malone*, *The Eternal Light*, *For the Record*, *Living*, *News of the World*; d. Oct. 31, 2005.

Arnold Moss, Jan. 28, 1910, Brooklyn, N.Y.; actor (stage, film, radio, TV), announcer, author, educator (Brooklyn College), voiceover artist, writer; debuted onstage in *Peter Pan* at Eva La Gallienne's Civic Repertory Theater in New York 1929; on Broadway while teaching drama, speech; more than 30 stage roles by 1981, often regional productions; made-for-TV flicks, some voiceover work, 18 Hollywood films, dozens of TV episodes; wrote *The Cross and the Arrow*, penned more than 60 installments *The CBS Radio Mystery Theater*, other shows; American Foundation for the Blind talking books narrator, created crossword puzzles for *The New York Times*; acted in/introduced legions of 1930s-80s radio series e.g. *Big Sister*, *The CBS Radio Mystery Theater*, *The Columbia Workshop*, *Grand Central Station*, *The Guiding Light*, *Inner Sanctum Mysteries*, *The March of Time*, *Mollé Mystery Theater*, *The New York Philharmonic Symphony Orchestra*, *Stella Dallas*, *Valiant Lady*; d. Dec. 15, 1989.

William S. Paley, Jan. 28, 1901, Chicago, Ill.; Columbia (Phonograph) Broadcasting System CEO-chairman-majority stockholder-president 1928–90 bka flamboyant playboy, iron-willed, competitive broadcasting czar; set industry practices, trends while turning CBS into major communications powerhouse, force to be reckoned with on multiple levels; nurtured personal radio loyalty long past that of chief rival peer; d. Oct. 26, 1990.

Deaths

Ward Byron, Jan. 28, 1996, Roslyn, Long Island, N.Y.; b. June 2, 1906. Roger DeKoven, Jan. 28, 1988, New York City, N.Y.; b. Oct. 22, 1906. Murray Forbes, Jan. 28, 1987, Los Angeles, Calif.; b. July 20, 1906. John MacVane, Jan. 28, 1984, Brunswick, Maine; b. April 29, 1912. Ed Reimers, Jan. 28, 1986, Nevada City, Calif.; b. Oct. 26, 1912.

January 29

Canceled

The CBS Radio Adventure Theater, Jan. 29, 1978, CBS; debut Feb. 5, 1977.

Birth

Don Morrow, Jan. 29, 1927, Stanford, Conn.; announcer arriving in Radioland almost too late, presenting *The Dizzy Dean Show*, *The Adventures of Rin Tin Tin* early to mid 1950s; greater presence in TV mid 1950s-late 1980s presiding over game shows *Camouflage*, *Science All-Stars*, *Let's Play Post Office*, *Sale of the Century*, introducing *Arthur Murray Party*, *The Edge of Night*, *General Electric Theater*, *The Loretta Young Show*, *Martin Kane—Private Eye*, *Rin Tin Tin*, *This Is Your Life*, *Wide Wide World*, more.

Deaths

Frank Black, Jan. 29, 1968, Atlanta, Ga.; b. Nov. 28, 1894. Jimmy Durante, Jan. 29, 1980, Santa Monica, Calif.; b. Feb. 10, 1893. Anne Elstner, Jan. 29, 1981, Doylestown, Pa.; b. Jan. 22, 1899. Leif Erickson, Jan. 29, 1986, Pensacola, Fla.; b. Oct. 27, 1911. Mandel Kramer, Jan. 29, 1989, Westchester, N.Y.; b. March 12, 1916. John Larkin, Jan. 29, 1965, Hollywood, Calif.; b. April 11, 1912. Bill Shadel, Jan. 29, 2005, Renton, Wash.; b. July 31, 1908. Joan Tompkins, Jan. 29, 2005, Orange County, Calif.; b. July 9, 1915.

January 30

Debuting

Mark Trail, Jan. 30, 1950, MBS; juvenile

adventure derived from Ed Dodd comic strip; decades before it became "in thing" woodsman-forest ranger Trail (Matt Crowley, John Larkin, Staats Cotsworth), devoted to conservation, sought to preserve nature from whatever might spoil it, relying on a couple of helpers in saving the planet, albeit without surnames: Scotty (Ben Cooper, Ronald Liss), Cherry (Joyce Gordon, Amy Sidell); final broadcast June 27, 1952.

Canceled

This Is Your FBI, Jan. 30, 1953, ABC; debut April 6, 1945.

Births

Conrad Ambress Binyon, Jan. 30, 1931, Los Angeles County, Calif.; actor (stage, film, radio) bka *One Man's Family* drama grandson Hank Herbert (son of "bewildering offspring" Hazel) NBC 1939–50; running parts on 1940s *The Life of Riley, Major Hoople, Mayor of the Town, The Nebbs*, sporadic roles on *Smilin' Ed and His Buster Brown Gang*; in films at six months of age, turned into *Our Gang* movie regular, *The Boy from Stalingrad* key juvenile role 1943, in 27 theatrical releases 1940–50, 23 of them uncredited; called for Air National Guard duty in Korean War, ditching acting to devote 20 years to military service.

Tammy Grimes, Jan. 30, 1934, Lynn, Mass.; actress (film, stage, TV), emcee bka *The CBS Radio Mystery Theater* hostess 1982, superseding enduring host E. G. Marshall in capacity; frequently on Broadway, star of four-week-long ABC-TV sitcom *The Tammy Grimes Show* 1966, more than 40 guest appearances on TV series, in 27 films made-for-TV or shown in cinema houses.

Deaths

Pegeen Fitzgerald, Jan. 30, 1989, New York City, N.Y.; b. Nov. 24, 1904. Ed Herlihy, Jan. 30, 1999, Manhattan, New York City, N.Y.; b. Aug. 14, 1909. John McIntire, Jan. 30, 1991, Pasadena, Calif.; b. June 27, 1907. Jacques Renard, Jan. 30, 1973, Miami, Fla.; b. May 15, 1897. Dorothy Thompson, Jan. 30, 1961, Lisbon, Portugal; b. July 9, 1894.

January 31

Sound Bite

The Lone Ranger (premier), Jan. 31, 1933; definitive western thriller; initially beamed from WXYZ Detroit to handful Michigan outlets; powerful radio production empire resulted; flagship series carried by MBS chain 1934; mythical hero featured with exploits appealing to legions, transcended generations; epic masked rider of the plains, peacemaking "champion of justice" impersonated by George Seaton 1933, Earl Graser 1933–41, Brace Beemer 1941–56; sidekick Tonto (John Todd) in full run, producer George W. Trendle, wordsmith Fran Striker; final broadcast May 25, 1956, NBC, new episodes ended Sept. 3, 1954; ABC-TV embodiment Sept. 15, 1949-Sept. 12, 1957, CBS-TV animated extension Sept. 10, 1966-Sept. 6, 1969.

Births

Tallulah Bankhead, Jan. 31, 1902, Huntsville, Ala.; actress (stage, film, radio, TV), hostess bka *The Big Show* mistress of ceremonies 1950–52, a series NBC publicists touted as the medium's last gasp as TV unremittingly siphoned away advertisers, audiences; dubbed herself "Queen of the Kilocycles," Bankhead suggesting she accepted radio offers "only when poverty stricken"; previously triumphant onstage in New York, London productions (*The Little Foxes, The Skin of Our Teeth, Private Lives*) but by then on the downside of a heralded career to be followed by guest star roles on the likes of *Lucy* TV shows; d. Dec. 12, 1968.

Edward (Eddie) Cantor (Isadore Itzkowitz), Jan. 31, 1892, New York City, N.Y.; comedian, emcee, quizmaster, recording artist, stage performer, vocalist bka *The Eddie Cantor Show* master of ceremonies 1931–49 under multiple monikers at intervals; vaudeville-burlesque comic singer tabbed "Banjo Eyes"; acclaimed singing-dancing-clowning act on *Ziegfeld Follies* bills with W. C. Fields, Will Rogers 1917–19; appeared in *The Eddie Cantor Story* 1953, 22 more motion pictures; early proponent of including live studio audience at broadcasts, convincing NBC to add spectators for impulsive applause; d. Oct. 10, 1964.

Garry Moore (Thomas Garrison Morfit), Jan. 31, 1915, Baltimore, Md.; announcer, comedian, emcee bka *The Garry Moore Show* host 1949–51 radio, 1950–58 daytime TV, primetime TV 1950–51, 1958–67, *I've Got a Secret* panel moderator 1952–67; versatility, gregarious personality, able associates let him excel wherever he performed, said pundits; d. Nov. 28, 1993.

Deaths

Howard Barlow, Jan. 31, 1972, Bethel, Conn.; b. May 1, 1892. Hilmar Robert Baukhage, Jan. 31, 1976, Washington, D.C.; b. Jan. 7, 1889.

February 1

Debuting

Big Jon and Sparkie, Feb. 1, 1950, ABC; juvenile variety feature; one of two (other *No School Today*) for tykes hosted by Jon Arthur in which star impersonated hundreds of character voices, often relying on turntable for help; singing, storytelling, serialized narratives, appeals for better hygiene, exchanges with pals of Sparkie, "the little elf from the land of make-believe, who wants more than anything else ... to be a real boy"; originated weekdays over Cincinnati WSAI 1948, beamed to America from there; final broadcast ABC 1958.

Canceled

My True Story, Feb. 1, 1962, MBS; debut Feb. 15, 1943. *The Sears Radio Theater*, Feb. 1, 1980, CBS; debut Feb. 5, 1979 (repeated episodes under banner *The Mutual Radio Theater* aired March 3, 1980-Dec. 19, 1980 on MBS). *Winner Take All*, Feb. 1, 1952, CBS; debut June 3, 1946.

Deaths

Jack Bailey, Feb. 1, 1980, Santa Monica, Calif.; b. Sept. 15, 1907. Milton Biow, Feb. 1, 1976, New York City, N.Y.; b. July 24, 1892. Anne Burr, Feb. 1, 2003, Old Lyme, Conn.; b. June 10, 1920. Mary Jane Higby, Feb. 1, 1986, New York City, N.Y.; b. June 29, 1909. Hedda Hopper, Feb. 1, 1966, Hollywood, Calif.; b. June 2, 1890. L.A. (Speed) Riggs, Feb. 1, 1987, Goldsboro, N.C.; b. Feb. 18, 1907.

February 2

Debuting

Twenty Questions, Feb. 2, 1946, MBS; quiz; answers to queries revealed to studio audience via cards unseen by onstage panel, radio fans clued via filtered offstage "mystery voice" whisperer; panel defined animal/vegetable/mineral item with yes-no questions; mostly of one clan, panel consisted of Fred Van Deventer, Florence Rinard (Fred's spouse), Bobby McGuire (Fred/Florence's son), fourth chair mixed—Nancy Van Deventer (daughter), producer Herb Polesie, guests; moderator MBS sportsman Bill Slater; Fred, Florence, Herb survived to play game on TV: NBC/ABC/Dumont 1949–55; final radiocast March 27, 1954.

Births

Charles James Correll, Feb. 2, 1890, Peoria, Ill.; actor (film, radio, stage), director, pianist, producer, tradesman, vocalist bka *Amos 'n' Andy* characters Andrew H. Brown, Henry Van Porter, dozens of added figures; partnership with Freeman Gosden (Amos) formed shortly after meeting in 1919, extending rest of their lives, briefly commanding largest number of Americans concurrently focused on single amusement; infamous characters launched as *Sam 'n' Henry* over Chicago WGN Jan. 12, 1926, continuing network airtime persisted to *The Amos 'n' Andy Music Hall* final broadcast Nov. 25, 1960, unprecedented for aural comic characters; d. Sept. 26, 1972.

Jascha Heifetz, Feb. 2, 1901, Vilnius, Russia; concert artist, violinist bka *The Bell Telephone Hour* initial (April 27, 1942), dominant "guest artist" (with 54 appearances) 1942–58; idolized by comedian Jack Benny, tongue-in-cheek, propitiously comparing self with legendary virtuoso; at first Heifetz disdained radio, concentrated on audiences in concert halls until persuaded he'd captivate millions simultaneously with his music; d. Dec. 10, 1987.

Haleloke Kahauolopue, Feb. 2, 1923, Hilo, Hawaii; hula dancer, personal appearance/recording artist, vocalist bka *Arthur Godfrey Time* variety revue Hawaiian singer CBS Radio-TV 1950–55, *Arthur Godfrey and His Friends* CBS-TV 1950–55; one of many artists Godfrey fired in exhibit of iron will; performed on

Hawaii Calls originating in Hawaii CBS 1945, promoted to solo vocalist 1946; met Godfrey there 1950—invited to join New York cast; popularity led to production of Haleloke doll sold in 1950s; after dismissal April 15, 1955, settled in Union City, Ind. with friends met at Godfrey shows—was traveling companion to Stella Keck after Keck's spouse died 1962; d. Dec. 16, 2004.

Frank Munn, Feb. 2, 1894, Bronx, N.Y.; recording artist, vocalist (tenor), bka singing star of musicales produced by Frank, Anne Hummert, billed by publicists "the golden voice of radio" and "dean of the ballad singers"; lead artist on five 1930s-40s Hummert-backed series: *The American Album of Familiar Music, American Melody Hour, Lavender and Old Lace, Sweetest Love Songs Ever Sung, Waltz Time*, a trio of those airing concurrently for years on varied weeknights; retired at 51 (1945), preferring leisure over work; d. Oct. 1, 1953.

Cal (Calvin) Tinney, Feb. 2, 1908, Pontotoc County, Okla.; actor (film, radio, TV), columnist, disc jockey, emcee, entrepreneur, newscaster bka "a sort of latter-day Will Rogers" dispensing barnyard humor to amuse; went on Tulsa KVOO as advertiser 1932, in New York same year acting on *The March of Time*; other gigs into 1950s—*The Cal Tinney Show* (DJ), *If I Had a Chance* (master of ceremonies), *Youth vs. Age* (quizmaster), *Stop Me If You've Heard This One* (panelist), *Sizing Up the News* (commentator), *Vanity Fair* (comic), *Robinson Crusoe Jr., Show Boat* (acting on both); played in film, TV; d. Dec. 2, 1993.

Deaths

Dick Dudley, Feb. 2, 2000, Lancaster, Pa.; b. April 22, 1915. Bert Parks, Feb. 2, 1992, La Jolla, Calif.; b. Dec. 30, 1914. Willard Waterman, Feb. 2, 1995, Burlingame, Calif.; b. Aug. 29, 1914.

February 3

Debuting

Red Ryder, Feb. 3, 1942, NBC Blue West Coast; juvenile western adventure; "America's famous fighting cowboy," Colorado cattle-rancher Ryder (Reed Hadley, Carlton KaDell, Brooke Temple), was—like some of his Radioland neighbors—an unofficial lawman by nature, tracking cattle rustlers, bank robbers, claim-jumpers who threatened peaceful frontier coexistence; companions were sidekick Buckskin Blodgett (Horace Murphy), Navajo ward Little Beaver (Tommy Cook, Frank Bresee, Henry Blair, Johnny McGovern, Sammy Ogg) founding one of radio's first mixed clans; Ryder born in Fred Harman short stories followed by 1938 comic strip, 1940 12-part movie serial; final broadcast date unclear—initial run ended MBS Sept. 9, 1942, resumed on unidentified dates MBS 1948–49 with hint it may have persisted into 1951 though it hasn't been substantiated.

Births

Martin Block, Feb. 3, 1903, Los Angeles, Calif.; announcer, disc jockey bka DJ revolutionizing industry, personalizing profession at New York WNEW *Make Believe Ballroom* 1935–54; first of breed starring in own right, copied by legions emulating his success formula; touted by ABC publicists as "that old Block magic" on 1954–61 turntable feature; d. Sept. 19, 1967.

Nelson Case, Feb. 3, 1910, Long Beach, Calif.; announcer, emcee, impresario, newscaster, panel moderator, pianist, vocalist, voiceover artist (TV commercials) bka introducing Johnny ("Call for Philip Morris") Roventini 1930s-40s ("And here comes Johnny now, stepping out of thousands of store windows to greet you!"); soft-spoken salesman for Procter & Gamble's flagship Ivory soap ("Ninety-nine and forty-four one hundredths percent pure—it floats!") on plethora of daytime serials (*Big Sister, The Right to Happiness, The Road of Life*, more) 1940s-50s; d. March 24, 1976.

Deaths

Donald P. Briggs, Feb. 3, 1986, Los Angeles, Calif.; b. Jan. 28, 1911. Jody Gilbert, Feb. 3, 1979, Los Angeles, Calif.; b. March 18, 1916. Al Lewis, Feb. 3, 2002, Huntington Beach, Calif.; b. Oct. 25, 1912. Joe Ripley, Feb. 3, 1993, Massapequa, N.Y.; b. July 18, 1913.

February 4

Sound Bite

General Mills, Inc. reveals in a *Broadcast-*

ing piece published Feb. 4, 1946 that it has earmarked $5 million—*half* its annual advertising appropriations for 1946—to radio; indicates depth of commitment to aural broadcasting by one of nation's prime food manufacturers during medium's heyday.

Debuting

The American School of the Air, Feb. 4, 1930, CBS; instructional feature; cited as "perhaps the most outstanding show in educational radio," offered as a teaching supplement twice-a-week entry at start, moving in 1939 to weekdays, beamed in 1941 to 15 nations; final broadcast April 30, 1948.

Dick Tracy/The Adventures of Dick Tracy, Feb. 4, 1935, CBS; juvenile police serial; based on Chester Gould comic strip initiated 1931, its gritty realism evolving into tryout on New England NBC outlets 1934; police detective Richard (Dick) Tracy (Matt Crowley, Barry Thomson, Ned Wever) of unnamed crime-ridden city flanked by spouse Tess Trueheart (Helen Lewis), son Dick Jr. (Andy Donnelly, Jackie Kelk), assistant Patrick (Pat) Patton (Walter Kinsella); what is hokey today glued small fry to radios then; movie serials, full-length films, ABC-TV series 1950–51, animated TV cartoons, documentaries, comics, published works, endless merchandise perpetuated myth; final radiocast July 16, 1948.

Canceled

True or False, Feb. 4, 1956, MBS; debut Jan. 3, 1938.

Births

Arthur (Art) Leroy Balinger (in some references, Ballinger), Feb. 4, 1898, Troy, Ohio; actor, announcer, commercial spokesman bka late 1940s-50s voice introducing *Here's Morgan*, *Mr. and Mrs. North*, *The Philip Morris Playhouse*, *The Roy Rogers Show*, *This Is Your Life*; plugged Studebaker automobiles on Buster Keaton TV series 1949; *Dragnet* thespian stock company member for NBC-TV episodes 1955–59, 1967–70; occasional TV roles on *Adam-12*, *Code Red*, *Ellery Queen*, *77 Sunset Strip*; d. Jan. 18, 1980.

John Gordon (Jack) Fraser, Feb. 4, 1908, Lawrence, Mass.; announcer, editor, newscaster, producer, vocalist, writer bka presiding at TV exhibition at 1939 New York World's Fair with President Franklin D. Roosevelt speaking; left Providence, R.I. station for New York WMCA, then WOR followed by NBC 1936, acquiring 1940s shows in dual genres (*John Gordon Fraser and the News*, *Your Gospel Singer*); dispatched news at WJZ between web-based gigs; at launch of *Monitor* weekend magazine marathon 1955, remaining 19 years editing, writing, producing; retired to Florida 1974, hired by Rollins College radio station 1978–90; d. Jan. 1, 2000.

Janet Waldo (Lee), Feb. 4, 1919, Grandview, Wash.; actress (stage, film, radio, TV), voiceover artist bka *Meet Corliss Archer* teen sitcom protagonist CBS/NBC/ABC 1943–43, 1944–45, 1946–48, 1949–53; performed in church plays as youth, college plays, signed for bit parts in movies followed by eternal teen Corliss Archer on radio, *The Adventures of Ozzie and Harriet* (radio/TV), *The Gallant Heart*, *One Man's Family*, *People Are Funny*, *The Red Skelton Show*, *Star Playhouse*; voice of Judy Jetson in animated *The Jetsons* ABC-/CBS-/NBC-/syndicated TV 1962–67, 1969–76, 1979–81, 1982–83, 1985, 1987; her comments added to *The Jetsons—The Complete First Season* DVD released 2004.

Deaths

Jim Ameche, Feb. 4, 1983, Tucson, Ariz.; b. Aug. 6, 1915. John Dehner, Feb. 4, 1992, Santa Barbara, Calif.; b. Nov. 23, 1915. Jerome Hines, Feb. 4, 2003, New York City, N.Y.; b. Nov. 8, 1921. Philip Tonken, Feb. 4, 2000, Washington, D.C.; b. April 13, 1919.

February 5

Debuting

Amanda of Honeymoon Hill, Feb. 5, 1940, NBC Blue; daytime serial; Hummert property where simple lass from sticks Amanda Dyke (Joy Hathaway) wed Edward Leighton (Boyd Crawford, George Lambert, Staats Cotsworth) who hailed from well-heeled aristocratic Dixie clan—and what became of pair, ties to inlaws regularly in jeopardy; announcer Frank Gallop's sober manner challenged daily as he presented "Amanda of Honeymoon Hill, the story of a young girl laid against a tapestry of the deep South"; final broadcast April 26, 1946.

General Mills Radio Adventure Theater (*The CBS Radio Adventure Theater*), Feb. 5, 1977, CBS; anthology drama; hosted by Tom Bosley, built upon acclaimed late entry *The CBS Radio Mystery Theater* 1974–82 returning drama to aural ether for enjoyment of new, earlier generations; twice-weekly trial didn't replicate *Mystery Theater's* success; final broadcast Jan. 29, 1978.

The Sears Radio Theater (*The Mutual Radio Theater*), Feb. 5, 1979, CBS; anthology drama; in revival of old time radio drama on heels of *The CBS Radio Mystery Theater*, *General Mills Radio Adventure Theater* earlier in 1970s, with original production team of Elliott Lewis, Fletcher Markle, five familiar names hosted original plays weeknights: Monday (westerns)—Lorne Greene, Tuesday (comedy)–Andy Griffith, Wednesday (mystery)—Vincent Price, Thursday (drama)—Cicely Tyson, Friday (adventure)—Leonard Nimoy, Richard Widmark; actors: Elvia Allman, Eve Arden, Parley Baer, Hans Conried, Mary Jane Croft, Howard Culver, John Dehner, Howard Duff, Sam Edwards, Virginia Gregg, Jim Jordan, John McIntire, Tyler McVey, Marvin Miller, Shirley Mitchell, Frank Nelson, Jeanette Nolan, Vic Perrin, Elliott Reid, Lurene Tuttle, Janet Waldo, Peggy Webber, more; heavy investments by sponsor/chain/producers, although listeners tuned out, previously scheduled repeats filling contracted time; final broadcast Feb. 1, 1980; reprised sans underwriter as *The Mutual Radio Theater* March 3, 1980-Dec. 19, 1980.

Deaths

Court Benson, Feb. 5, 1995, Mount Kisco, N.Y.; b. Nov. 4, 1914. Carroll Carroll, Feb. 5, 1991, West Hollywood, Calif.; b. April 11, 1902. Bud Hiestand, Feb. 5, 1987, Newport Beach, Calif.; b. Jan. 16, 1907. Larry Lesueur, Feb. 5, 2003, Washington, D.C.; b. June 10, 1909.

February 6

Debuting

Night Beat, Feb. 6, 1940, NBC; crime drama; *Chicago Star* reporter Randy Stone (Frank Lovejoy) worked after sunset pursuing stories of human interest, depravity, narrating his tales in first person; final broadcast Sept. 25, 1952.

Canceled

Hop Harrigan, Feb. 6, 1948, MBS; debut Aug. 31, 1942.

Births

Bennett Kilpack, Feb. 6, 1883, Long Melford, West Suffolk, England; actor (stage, radio) bka *Mr. Keen, Tracer of Lost Persons* crime-detective mystery as "the kindly old tracer" seeking clues to disappearances, murders of endless victims NBC Blue/CBS/NBC 1937–50; moved to U. S. 1908, launched career 1910 with *Othello* touring stage outfit, successively gaining more Shakespearean roles on Broadway; following disconnect including World War I, other pursuits, returned to stage, by 1927 finding radio ripe for thespians; aural credits for score of features e.g. *Alias Jimmy Valentine*, *Believe It or Not*, *David Harum*, *Doc Barclay's Daughters* (lead), *Grand Central Station*, *Great Plays*, *Hilltop House*, *Seth Parker*, *The Shadow*, *Young Widder Brown*, more; departed *Mr. Keen* Oct. 26, 1950 due to cancer, expecting to return but unable to; d. Aug. 18, 1962.

John Lund, Feb. 6, 1911, Rochester, N.Y.; actor (film, radio), announcer, businessman bka Hollywood silver screen legend turning up in 29 movies 1946–78 including *The Night Has a Thousand Eyes*, *My Friend Irma*, *My Friend Irma Goes West*, *The Mating Season*, *The Battle at Apache Pass*, *High Society*, *Battle Stations*, *The Wackiest Ship in the Army*, *If a Man Answers*; except uncredited role in 1978, left films early 1960s to focus on business interests; on radio acted in 1940s-50s *Academy Award Theater*, *Chaplain Jim U.S.A.*, *NBC Star Playhouse*, *Screen Director's Playhouse*, *Suspense*, *Yours Truly—Johnny Dollar*, introduced *The Bob Crosby Show*; d. May 10, 1992.

Deaths

Frankie Laine, Feb. 6, 2007, San Diego, Calif.; b. March 30, 1913.

Robert St. John, Feb. 6, 2003, Waldorf, Md.; b. March 9, 1902.

February 7

Births

William (Bill) S. Johnstone, Feb. 7, 1908,

Brooklyn, N.Y.; actor (stage, radio, film, TV) bka *As the World Turns* daytime serial figure Judge James 'Father' Lowell CBS-TV 1956–78; audio portfolio embraced *The Adventures of Ozzie and Harriet, The Lineup* (in which he played lead Lt. Ben Guthrie), *Mark Sabre* (namesake), *Maudie's Diary, My Favorite Husband, Nick Carter—Master Detective, Portia Faces Life, Pursuit, The Shadow, The Whistler* (lead); onstage 1926, acted in multi plays thereafter; 1950 TV series *Tom Corbett—Space Cadet,* six solo TV drama episodes 1953–55, made-for-TV flick 1986, TV miniseries 1986, often uncredited in 13 theatrical movies 1948–64; d. Nov. 1, 1996.

Robert Robinson Stephenson, Feb. 7, 1901, England; announcer, director, producer; focused on few 1940s web entries, producing-directing *The Bob Hope Show,* welcoming listeners to *Jeff Regan—Investigator, Romance, Yours Truly—Johnny Dollar*; d. Sept. 5, 1970.

February 8

Births

Donald I. Ball, Feb. 8, 1904, Block Island, R.I.; CBS staff announcer while with New York WABC (chain's 1930s flagship outlet), hotelier; moved to radio at Columbus, Ohio WCAH after managing local lodging property; d. Jan. 7, 1974.

Truman Bradley, Feb. 8, 1905, Sheldon, Mo.; actor (film, radio, stage), announcer (radio, TV), broadcast executive, entrepreneur, newscaster, producer, salesman, writer bka *The Ford Sunday Evening Hour* interlocutor 1932–38, racking up 39,000 miles commute by air from Chicago ethereal duties for weekly Detroit-based show; welcomed listeners to aural venues headlined by Dinah Shore, Don Ameche, George Burns and Gracie Allen, Frank Sinatra, Red Skelton, Shirley Temple, Rudy Vallee in 1930s-40s; narrated *Jack Armstrong—the All-American Boy, The Lady Esther Screen Guild Theater, The Prudential Family Hour, The Story of Mary Marlin, Suspense*; bit parts in 37 largely B-flicks 1938–52 with a few standouts: *Northwest Passage, The Horn Blows at Midnight, I Wonder Who's Kissing Her Now, Call Northside 777, Fighter Squadron*; introduced syndicated TV anthology *Science Fiction Theater* 1955–57; d. July 28, 1974.

Robert Dryden, Feb. 8, 1917, New York, N.Y.; actor (stage, radio, TV, film) bka *The CBS Radio Mystery Theater* crime anthology star 243 times CBS 1974–82; typecast by protruding portfolio of 1940s-50s crime series: *The Adventures of Superman, The Adventures of the Falcon, Bandwagon Mysteries, The Big Story, Big Town, Call the Police, Calling All Cars, Casey—Crime Photographer, The Fat Man, The FBI in Peace & War, Gangbusters, I Love a Mystery, Mystery Theater, Renfrew of the Mounted, Robert Kilgore—Public Defender, Scotland Yard, Space Patrol, True Detective Mysteries, Yours Truly—Johnny Dollar,* handful beyond crimefighting (*Ford Theater, The Right to Happiness, Studio One,* et al.); initiated career in summer stock at Virginia's Barter Theater; in TV series *Tom Corbett—Sace Cadet* 1950, *The Edge of Night* 1966; 25 solo episodes of TV dramas 1955–77, five B-motion pictures 1957–75; d. Dec. 16, 2003.

Edward Fitzgerald, Feb. 8, 1893, Troy, N.Y.; commentator bka *The Fitzgeralds* wedded couple breakfast chat 1945–47, show airing locally New York WOR 1940–82; fostered programming breed copied by other New York married entertainers and more than 75 scattered across U. S.; d. March 22, 1982.

Taylor Grant (Grant T. Cushmore), Feb. 8, 1913, Philadelphia, Pa.; newscaster, sportscaster bka *Headline Edition* speaker 1945–55; news-sports reporter at Philadelphia WCAU 1938–45 before ABC weeknight quarter-hour also carried Sunday nights 1952–54; ABC-TV quarter-hour newscast with anchor John Charles Daly weeknights except Tuesday 1953–54, that night anchored by Grant; cited as "a champion of civil rights and a die-hard liberal"; d. Feb. 24, 1998.

Irving Kaufman, Feb. 8, 1890, Syracuse, N.Y.; emcee, vocalist; not-well-recalled host of less-than-memorable late 1920s-early 1940s series *The Palmolive Community Sing, Happy Jim Parsons, The Happy Rambler, The Piano Troubadours, Lazy Dan the Minstrel Man, Radio Revels*; d. Jan. 3, 1976.

Walter Myron McCormick, Feb. 8, 1907, Albany, Ind.; actor (stage, radio, film, TV) bka *South Pacific* figure Luther Billis, only original cast member for full Broadway run of 1,925 performances 1949–53; toured with medicine show at 11, played theater stages at 25, a founder of Cape Cod summer stock with budding artists Jimmy Stewart, Henry Fonda, Margaret Sullivan; never overcame acute stage fright; screen debut in *Winterset* 1936, more celluloid including *No Time for Sergeants* 1958, *The Hustler* 1961; leading man/villain in radio's *Central City, Ford Theater, Gangbusters, Helpmate, Joyce Jordan—Girl Interne, Listening Post, The Man Behind the Gun, The March of Time, Mr. District Attorney, Passport for Adams, Portia Faces Life, Studio One*; TV roles: *Alfred Hitchcock Presents, Naked City, Pursuit, The Untouchables*; d. July 30, 1962.

Peter Roberts, Feb. 8, 1918, unconfirmed location; announcer, newscaster; initial break occurred at Philadelphia KYW 1940s, then WPTZ-TV in same market; by 1948 introduced *Who Said That?* to national audience, followed in 1950s by *The Adventures of the Falcon, The Big Guy, The Forty Million, The Maginficent Montague, Meet the Press* (aural version), *Monitor*; beyond network duties, newscaster at multi New York stations (WOR, WINS, WPAT), worked with DJ John A. Gambling, comics Bob [Elliott] & Ray [Goulding] early morning shifts through 1980s; celebrated 90th birthday in Ottawa, Canada Feb. 8, 2008.

Deaths

George Herman, Feb. 8, 2005, Washington, D.C.; b. Jan. 14, 1920. Johnny Jacobs, Feb. 8, 1982, Los Angeles, Calif.; b. June 22, 1916. Marvin Miller, Feb. 8, 1985, Santa Monica, Calif.; b. July 18, 1913.

February 9

Sound Bite

NBC inaugurates "The Source," youth-oriented radio hookup on Feb. 9, 1979 with one-hour transcribed Willie Nelson concert following earlier acclaim achieved by ABC with live-on-tape music specials for young people in mid 1970s; "The Source" expands May 28, 1979 to include more musical concerts plus two minutes of youth-oriented reports hourly within daily six-hour timeframe; youth news feeds stretched to run 24 hours daily starting Sept. 1, 1979.

Births

(Waldo) Brian Donlevy, Feb. 9, 1901, Cleveland, Ohio; actor (stage, film, radio, TV), producer; relinquished prospective military career for stage which projected him to Hollywood films—played in 95 theatrical movies 1923–69 with 41 appearances in TV sundry roles, guest shots 1949–67; radio activity included *The Court of Human Relations, Crime Doctor, Dangerous Assignment, The Eno Crime Club, Hillbilly Heartthrobs, The Screen Guild Theater, Silver Theater, Suspense*; d. April 5, 1972.

Bob Hite, Feb. 9, 1914, Decatur, Ind.; announcer, newscaster bka voice in early color era on CBS-TV stating "CBS presents this program in color"; from late 1930s-late 1950s offered surplus of aural shows: *Casey—Crime Photographer, The CBS Radio Workshop, The Challenge of the Yukon, Cimarron Tavern, The Green Hornet, The Kathy Godfrey Show, The Lone Ranger, Ned Jordan—Secret Agent*, more; retired CBS 1979, moved to Florida; d. Feb. 18, 2000.

Charlotte Holland (Wanamaker), Feb. 9, 1915, Chicago, Ill.; actress (radio, film) bka *This Is Nora Drake* daytime serial heroine NBC 1947–49; while playing in anthology dramatic fare like *The Mysterious Traveler*, favored soap operas e.g. *Against the Storm, Big Sister, Lone Journey, The Open Door, Joyce Jordan—M.D.*; when spouse, actor-director Sam Wanamaker (of emporium fame) was blacklisted by Sen. Joseph McCarthy witchhunts at mid 20th century, she was giving birth to future actress Zoë Wanamaker (May 13, 1949); resigned career to raise family in exile in London where Sam continued working but Charlotte was in bit part in 1965 theatrical film *Promise Her Anything*; d. Jan. 13, 1997.

Harry Kramer, Feb. 9, 1911, Philadelphia, Pa.; announcer, emcee, news analyst bka *The CBS Evening News* voice beckoning behind camera 1962–71 "Direct from our CBS newsroom in New York ... this is ... *The CBS Evening News* ... with Walter Cronkite ... and ..." (naming reporters, their locations for telecast); identifiably foreboding voice two hours before on CBS-TV daytime "dark" serial *The Edge of Night* 1958–72 ("Theeeeee Edggggeeee of Niiihhhttt!"); *Dance Barn* host on New York WNEW 1930s-40s, analyst for WNEW *New York Lighting Electric Stores News*; late 1930s-mid 1950s narrated *The Alfredo Antonini Orchestra, Hits and Misses, Mike and Buff's Mail Bag, Mr. Keen—Tracer of Lost Persons, Our Gal Sunday*; introduced *Winner Take All, The Mel Torme Show, The Red Buttons Show* CBS-TV early 1950s; retired CBS 1972; d. Jan. 23, 1996.

Wilmer Leslie Walter, Feb. 9, 1881, Philadelphia, Pa.; actor bka *David Harum* daytime serial namesake helping-hand New England banker who crusaded "for love ... for happiness ... and the good way of life" NBC Blue/NBC 1936–41; in same period played masculine lead Andy Gump on *The Gumps* CBS 1934–37 with tale's roots in Sidney Smith comic strip 1917–59; d. Aug. 23, 1941.

Deaths

Eddy Duchin, Feb. 9, 1951, New York City, N.Y.; b. April 1, 1909. Percy Faith, Feb. 9, 1976, Van Nuys, Calif.; b. April 8, 1908.

February 10

Birth

Jimmy Durante (James Francis Durante), Feb. 10, 1893, New York City, N.Y.; actor (stage, film, radio, TV), comedian, pianist, vocalist bka *The Jimmy Durante Show* comedy variety series headliner (under multiple monikers) NBC/CBS 1933, 1934, 1943–50, NBC-TV 1954–56; raspy-voiced comic-singer is recalled for catchphrases "Everybody wants to git into de act!," "I've got a million of 'em!," "Goodnight, Mrs. Calabash, wherever you are!," signature solo "Inka Dinka Doo"; one pundit assessed "he turned his fractured English with mispronunciations and malapropisms and honky-tonk piano into a winning routine that never failed to charm an audience"; carried act from speakeasy to vaudeville, Broadway, films, radio, television; guest on every other comic's radio/TV series; d. Jan. 29, 1980.

Deaths

Virginia Payne, Feb. 10, 1977, Cincinnati, Ohio; b. June 19, 1910. Carl Warren, Feb. 10, 1968, Norwalk, Conn.; b. Oct. 30, 1905.

February 11

Debuting

The Chamber Music Society of Lower Basin Street, Feb. 11, 1940, NBC Blue; parody of Metropolitan Opera, classical music via hot swing tunes while rhetoric poked fun at liberated listeners' preferences proving radio loved a good spoof; legendary announcer Milton J. Cross, Met interlocutor, added impetus to model in heyday; after assorted intervals final broadcast Aug. 2, 1952.

Yours Truly, Johnny Dollar, Feb. 11, 1949, CBS; mystery crime drama; in unusual twist Dollar (Charles Russell, Edmond O'Brien, John Lund, Gerald Mohr, Bob Bailey, Bob Readick, Mandel Kramer) was insurance investigator whose cases inevitably led to murder, crime he was better at solving than local law enforcement; with "action-packed expense account" tabulated at end of tales, he was characterized as thinly veiled playboy, authoritative, dynamic, charming; modern day icon to hero-worshipers of golden age radio; series sustained as CBS axed most of its standing schedule in late 1960, persisted to Sept. 30, 1962.

Death

William Conrad, Feb. 11, 1994, North Hollywood, Calif.; b. Sept. 27, 1920.

February 12

Debuting

The Adventures of Superman, Feb. 12, 1940, MBS; juvenile adventure serial initially heard in limited test markets 1938–40; "the man of steel" exhibited superhuman powers thwarted only by kryptonite from his birth planet, yet hid his identity as newspaper reporter Clark Kent (Clayton "Bud" Collyer, Michael Fitzmaurice); flanked by cohorts Lois Lane (Joan Alexander), Jimmy Olsen (Mitch Evans, Jackie Kelk), Perry White (Julian Noa) who were struck dumb when it came to figuring out who he actually was; derived from comic book hero, Superman spawned merchandising industry that included film, radio, TV, commodities by zillions; final radiocast March 1, 1951.

Canceled

Wild Bill Hickok, Feb. 12, 1956, MBS; debut May 27, 1951.

Births

Joseph Henry Garagiola, Feb. 12, 1926, St. Louis, Mo.; author, major league baseball player (St. Louis Cardinals, Pittsburgh Pirates, Chicago Cubs, New York Giants 1946–54), sportscaster bka *Baseball Game of the Week* host NBC-TV 1961–64, 1975–88; *Monitor* interviewer-commentator-segment host early 1960s-1975; *Today* sports commentator 1967–75, 1991–92; *To Tell the Truth* syndicated version moderator 1977–78; penned *Baseball Is a Funny Game* 1960, *It's Anybody's Ballgame* 1988; local TV commentator for New York Yankees, California Angels; Ford Frick Award recipient 1991 for superior broadcasting achievements from Baseball Hall of Fame.

Lorne Greene, Feb. 12, 1915, Ottawa, Ontario, Canada; actor (stage, film, radio, TV), entrepreneur (launched Toronto's Academy of Radio Arts, marketed reverse stopwatch), narrator, newscaster bka *Bonanza* frontier figure "Hoss" Cartwright NBC-TV 1959–73; five dozen more TV performances, 87 theatrical, made-for-TV films; *The Sears Radio Theater* (*The Mutual Radio Theater*) anthology drama host Monday nights CBS/MBS 1979–81; designated "The Voice of Canada" for nightly newscasts on Canadian Broadcasting Corp. 1939-ca. 1942; d. Sept. 11, 1987.

Joseph Kearns, Feb. 12, 1907, Salt Lake City, Utah; actor (stage, radio, film, TV), educator, organist bka *Our Miss Brooks* sitcom school superintendent Edgar T. Stone CBS 1948–57, CBS-TV 1953–55, *The Jack Benny Program* sitcom character Ed, security guard at underground vault CBS ca. 1940s-50s, CBS-TV 1953–61; *Dennis the Menace* sitcom neighbor George Wilson CBS-TV 1959–62; financed eduction teaching theatrical makeup; theater, radio pipe organist (years later included Wurlitzer in Hollywood home); acted on aural ether 1930s-50s in more than two dozen crime, sitcom features e.g. *The Adventures of Sam Spade, The Amos 'n' Andy Show, Crime Classics, A Date with Judy, Gunsmoke, Have Gun—Will Travel, I Deal in Crime, The Joan Davis Show, The Lineup, The Mel Blanc Show, My Favorite Husband, Pursuit, Suspense, The Whistler, Yours Truly—Johnny Dollar*; parts in 37 added solo video jaunts 1951–61—dramas, sitcoms, variety shows, played in 1949 made-for-TV flick, nine theatrical motion pictures 1947–59 including *Anatomy of a Murder*; d. Feb. 17, 1962.

Kenneth Roberts, Feb. 12, 1910, Bronx, N.Y.; actor (film, stage, TV), ad salesman, announcer, artist, composer, disc jockey, pianist, quizmaster, scriptwriter bka *Love of Life* daytime serial interlocutor CBS-TV 1951–80; after amateur theatricals hired to announce, play piano, sell advertising by Brooklyn WLTH 1930 followed by WPCH, WMCA, CBS announcing staff, WMGM 1952 DJ; while penning scripts for *The Campbell Playhouse* ca. 1938–41, emceeing *Quick as a Flash* 1944–47, presented radio fans with 45 ongoing series e.g. *Brenda Curtis, Casey—Crime Photographer, Crime Doctor, Grand Central Station, Hour of Charm, Johnny Presents, Joyce Jordan—Girl Interne, The Life of Mary Sothern, The Shadow, This Is Nora Drake, You Are There*; multi fleeting early TV entries, played support parts 21 times in TV dramas 1961–2004, 14 made-for-TV flicks, four TV mini series, 25 theatrical movies including *Radio Days*; composed score for 1985 filmography *Junior*, storyboard for 1997 movie *The Night Flier*.

Death

Edwin C. Hill, Feb. 12, 1957, St. Petersburg, Fla.; b. April 23, 1884.

February 13

Debuting

Pat Novak for Hire, Feb. 13, 1949, ABC; crime detective drama; aired unspecified dates on ABC West Coast hookup 1946–47; series thrust Jack Webb to national acclaim (left title role to Ben Morris spring 1947)—first of five times Webb went sleuthing followed by Johnny Madero, Jeff Regan, Joe Friday, Pete Kelly; campy, predictable plots often led to knockout blonde/brunette/redhead, thereafter to Novak getting rap on head, waking up to explain presence alongside dead body to curious cops; Novak relied on Frisco seaside chum Jocko Madigan (Jack Lewis, Tudor Owen) for tidbits of helpful info—problems arose as Madigan wasn't sober much; Inspector Hellman (John Galbraith, Raymond Burr) never liked Novak very much, offering little help either; final broadcast June 25, 1949.

Canceled

The Hormel All-Girl Band and Chorus, Feb. 13, 1954, CBS; debut Nov. 27, 1949.

Births

Edwin D. Canham, Feb. 13, 1904, Auburn,

Maine; commentator, newscaster, journal editor, religious official bka *The Christian Science Monitor* editor 1960s; *Christian Science Views* (aka *Monitor Views*) host-commentator 1945-ca. 1959; *Headlines and Bylines* radio correspondent 1937–38, other pithy series followed; Christian Science Church president 1966–75; d. Jan. 3, 1982.

Eileen Farrell, Feb. 13, 1920, Willimantic, Conn.; concert artist, educator, vocalist (soprano) bka *The Bell Telephone Hour* guest artist (22 appearances) 1942–58, habitual gigs with *Voice of Firestone* 1940s-50s, *The NBC Symphony Orchestra* 1937–63; Metropolitan Opera Co. member 1960–64; performed with operatic units in Tampa, Chicago, San Francisco; voice instructor for trio of institutions of higher learning; d. March 23, 2002.

Pauline Frederick, Feb. 13, 1908, Gallitzin, Pa.; author, commentator, copywriter, newscaster, print/wire service journalist bka "first full-fledged woman correspondent and opened doors for women's acceptance in television and radio journalism" affirmed NBC News producer Beryl Pfizer; *The Washington Star*, North American Newspaper Alliance, *U. S. News and World Report* contributor; part time copywriter for ABC Radio newsman H. R. Baukhage; ABC hired her full time 1946 where she soon aired six morning radio, three telecasts weekly: *Pauline Frederick and the News* 1946–75; covered U. N. 28 years for ABC/NBC; first of her gender to win George Foster Peabody Award for distinguished reporting 1954; first of gender to moderate presidential debate 1976; first feminine president U. N. Correspondents Association; 23 honorary degrees; d. May 9, 1990.

Deaths

Daniel Golenpaul, Feb. 13, 1974, New York City, N.Y.; b. June 3, 1900. Lily Pons, Feb. 13, 1976, Dallas, Texas; b. April 12, 1898.

February 14

Canceled

The Cisco Kid, Feb. 14, 1945, MBS (syndicated 1947–56); debut Oct. 2, 1942.

Births

Mel Allen (Melvin Allen Israel), Feb. 14, 1913, Birmingham, Ala.; announcer, sportscaster bka "Voice of the Yankees" 1939–64; trademark yell "How about that!"; introduced diverse 1940s non–sport features: *The Army Hour*, *The Chesterfield Supper Club*, *Kitty Foyle*, *Truth or Consequences*; hosted *Monitor* NBC weekend info/entertainment marathon 1961–63; presided over half-hour syndicated TV series *This Week in Baseball* 1977–96; revealed he preferred audio to video —"on radio you could choose your direction, but on TV you always had ... the director telling you they were going to cut away to some cheesecake in upper right field"; d. June 16, 1996.

Peggy Allenby (McGovern), Feb. 14, 1901, New York City, N.Y.; actress (film, radio, TV) bka *The Edge of Night* daytime serial character Mattie Lane Grimsley CBS-TV 1956–66; appeared in 1922 silent film *The Man Who Came Back*; prolific 1930s-50s washboard weeper thespian in *Aunt Jenny's Real Life Stories*, *David Harum*, *Easy Aces*, *Life Can Be Beautiful*, *The Light of the World*, *Rich Man's Darling*, *The Road of Life* while earning nighttime credits for *Archie Andrews*, *It's Higgins — Sir*, *Les Miserables*, *Mr. Keen —Tracer of Lost Persons*, *The Orange Lantern*, *The Palmolive Beauty Box Theater*, *Your Unseen Friend*; TV series (beyond *Edge*): *The Herb Shriner Show* CBS 1949, *First Love* NBC 1954; played in handful of dramatic video roles elsewhere 1951–64; d. March 23, 1966.

Jack Benny (Benjamin Kubelsky), Feb. 14, 1894, Chicago, Ill.; comedian (radio, stage, TV), violinist bka *The Jack Benny Program* star (as himself); consummate, unparalleled entertainer with penchant for recurring gags (miserliness, violin ineptitude); marked by identifying mannerisms; master of timing; interacted with cadre of recurring funny figures, guests; possibly most universally beloved showman of era; radio 1932–58, TV 1950–65; d. Dec. 26, 1974.

Hugh Malcolm Downs, Feb. 14, 1921, Akron, Ohio; announcer, emcee bka *Today* newsmagazine host NBC-TV 1962–71, *20/20* newsmagazine host/cohost ABC-TV 1978–99; introduced *The Dave Garroway Show* to radio fans 1947, 1949–50, *Monitor* co–communicator NBC Radio 1955–59; all over early TV in ties to *Kukla, Fran and Ollie* 1949-early 1950s, *Hawkins Falls* 1951–54, *Home* 1954–57, *The Tonight Show* 1957–62, *Concentration* 1958–69; *Guinness Book of Records* claimed he presided over more TV hours than anyone else by 1985.

Jessica Dragonette, Feb. 14, 1900, Calcutta, India; author, entertainer (concerts, radio, stage, TV), recording artist, vocalist (soprano) bka *Cities Service Concert* featured artist 1930–37; a pundit allowed *Cities Service* entry "came of age ... with the arrival of Jessica Dragonette"; glowing reviews lauded her as "the Jenny Lind of the air," "girl with the smile in her voice," "Queen of Radio," "Princess of Song," "Greta Garbo of the airwaves"; in time disenchanted by *Cities Service* format, she asked that operettas be included to add speaking roles, yet it didn't happen; Dragonette left in a huff for *The Palmolive Beauty Box Theater* as some adoring fans turned against her for her handling of it; *Beauty Box* lasted a season and Dragonette never reclaimed earlier iconic status at *Cities Service* even with comeback try on *Saturday Night Serenade* 1941–45; d. March 18, 1980.

Victor Hugo Lindlahr, Feb. 14, 1897, Montana; author, commentator, entrepreneur bka nutrition series host under own moniker 1938–53 preceded by *Journal of Living* 1937–38; penned *You Are What You Eat* 1942, more tomes perpetuating entrepreneurial enterprise; one of earliest ethereal advocates of health, diet issues; linked commercially on radio, TV with health supplement Serutan ("Serutan is Natures spelled backwards"); d. Jan. 26, 1969.

Tyler McVey, Feb. 14, 1912, Bay City, Mich.; actor (film, stage, radio, TV), announcer, director, producer bka American Federation of Television and Radio Artists (AFTRA) national president, earlier president of Los Angeles American Federation of Radio Artists (AFRA) unit 1938–43; career began in amateur plays in hometown, joined New York-New England drama entourage at 21, then into West Coast radio acting late 1930s-early 1980s in score of features: *Dr. Christian, Dragnet, Fibber McGee & Molly, Gene Autry's Melody Ranch, The George Burns and Gracie Allen Show, Glamour Manor, The Great Gildersleeve, The Jack Benny Program, Lux Radio Theater, One Man's Family, The Red Skelton Show, The Sears/Mutual Radio Theater, Today's Children, Wild Bill Hickok*; 42 theatrical films 1951–75 including *The Day the Earth Stood Still, From Here to Eternity, The Caine Mutiny, Seven Days in May, Hello, Dolly!*; in TV dramas like *Bonanza, Climax!, Lassie, My Friend Irma*, more; d. July 4, 2003.

Grace Valentine (Grace Sharrenberger Snow), Feb. 14, 1884, Springfield, Ohio; actress (film, radio, TV) bka *Stella Dallas* daytime serial colorful rooming house landlady-confidante Minnie Grady NBC 1938–55; bearing distinctive gravel voice, maintained sustaining role in *Lone Journey*, sporadic parts in *Mr. Keen—Tracer of Lost Persons*; performed in 14 theatrical motion pictures 1915–33, mostly silent films, plus two solo TV episodes 1949; d. Nov. 12, 1964.

Deaths

Bob Brown, Feb. 14, 1988, Lexington, Ky.; b. Dec. 7, 1905. Sam Cowling, Feb. 14, 1983, Fresno, Calif.; b. Jan. 8, 1914. Cy Harrice, Feb. 14, 2007, Kelly, Wyo.; b. March 1, 1915.

February 15

Debuting

My True Story, Feb. 15, 1943; romance anthology drama; "confession magazine of the air" with narratives drawn from pages of *True Story* magazine; closed-ended melodrama, each episode complete; final broadcast Feb. 1, 1962 beyond conventional "day drama died" at rival CBS, always airing elsewhere.

Canceled

Juvenile Jury, Feb. 15, 1953, NBC; debut June 15, 1946.

Stop the Music!, Feb. 15, 1955, CBS; debut March 21, 1948.

Births

Patricia Marie (Patty) Andrews, Feb. 16, 1918, Mound, Minn.; vocalist (lead soprano)—film, public appearances, radio, recordings, stage bka one of the infamous Andrews Sisters trio; recorded 1,800 songs, sold 90 million platters; *The Andrews Sisters Eight-to-the-Bar Ranch* ABC 1944–46, *Club Fifteen* CBS 1947–53 notable audio gigs; only sibling still alive (late 2007), resided Northridge, Calif.

Frank Behrens, Feb. 15, 1919, Sheboygan, Wis.; actor (radio, TV, film), gagwriter bka prolific daytime serial thespian: *Arnold Grimm's Daughter, Caroline's Golden Store, The Guiding Light, Joyce Jordan—Girl Interne, Lorenzo Jones, The Right to Happiness, The Road of Life, Woman in White* plus juvenile adventure *Jack Armstrong—the All-American Boy*; slid easily into TV drama 1955–64 in almost two dozen solo episodes of *The Honeymooners*, *Peter Gunn*, *The Ann Sothern Show*, *The Twilight Zone*, *The Untouchables*, et al. while also playing in two theatrical films—*Wake Me When It's Over*, *Shock Treatment*; penned one-liners for comics Don Knotts, Tony Randall; d. Dec. 15, 1986.

Mary Jane Croft (Lewis), Feb. 15, 1916, Muncie, Ind.; actress (radio, film, TV), voiceover artist; started at Cincinnati WLW; all over dial 1940s-50s: *The Abbott and Costello Show*, *The Mel Blanc Show*, *Beulah*, *Blondie*, *Crime Classics*, *Dr. Christian*, *Fibber McGee & Molly*, *The Frank Fontaine Show*, *Honest Harold*, *Lady of the Press*, *Mayor of the Town*, *Meet Corliss Archer*, *One Man's Family*, *Onstage with Cathy and Elliott Lewis*, *Our Miss Brooks*, *The Screen Guild Theater*, *Suspense*, *Too Many Cooks*, *The Whistler*, more; *The Adventures of Ozzie and Harriet* sitcom as Clara Randolph 21 episodes ABC-TV 1956–66; *The Lucy Show* 1962–68, *Here's Lucy* 1970–74 sitcoms as Mary Jane Lewis total 28 times CBS-TV; 13 scattered TV roles, two added series—*I Married Joan* 1952, *The People's Choice* 1955, two made-for-TV flicks, two cinema films; d. Aug. 24, 1999.

Harfield Weedin, Feb. 15, 1916, Tennessee; director, producer, station executive, writer; launched radio career at Austin, Tex. during college years, later managing KTBC there owned by Lyndon, Lady Bird Johnson; following World War II Navy stint with AFRS, joined Hollywood ABC scripting *The Abbott and Costello Show*, *Meet Corliss Archer*, directing *Marvin Miller Storyteller*, producing *Dr. I. Q.*, *You Bet Your Life* (some shows in dual mediums); coproduced Ralph Edwards' *End of the Rainbow* NBC-TV 1958; hired at Los Angeles KNX Radio 1961, eventually rising to CBS Radio West Coast program director to retirement 1982; elected Pacific Pioneer Broadcasters president; d. June 8, 1993.

Deaths

Charles Irving, Feb. 15, 1981, Minneapolis, Minn.; b. July 30, 1912. Jan Miner, Feb. 15, 2004, Bethel, Conn.; b. Oct. 15, 1917. John Richbourg, Feb. 15, 1986, Nashville, Tenn.; b. Aug. 20, 1910. Louis Roen, Feb. 15, 1993, San Diego, Calif.; b. March 13, 1905. Howard K. Smith, Feb. 15, 2002, Bethesda, Md.; b. May 12, 1914. Harold True, Feb. 15, 1973, Fort Lauderdale, Fla.; b. April 1, 1891.

February 16

Births

Edgar Bergen, Feb. 16, 1903, Chicago, Ill.; comedian, ventriloquist bka *The Edgar Bergen-Charlie McCarthy Show* straight man put words in mouths of marionettes Charlie McCarthy, Mortimer Snerd, Effie Klinker, Podine Puffington, Lars Lindquist NBC/CBS 1937–56; though act was visual, worked well on radio—yet when applied on *Do You Trust Your Wife?* quiz CBS-TV 1956–57 it bombed; it had huge draw in vaudeville, road shows, nightclubs, theaters; d. Sept. 30, 1978.

Robert Maurice Campbell, Feb. 16, 1922, Detroit, Mich.; actor, announcer, director, producer; introducing *Out of the Deep* persisting six weeks at NBC 1945–46 only confirmed chain radio credit; produced, directed Broadway plays, ABC-TV's *All-Star News* 1952–53; d. May 1981 (multiple sources ineffective in validating date, place).

Wayne (Clay) Howell (Wayne H. Chappelle), Feb. 16, 1921, Lexington, Ky.; actor (stage), announcer, disc jockey, emcee, newscaster, sportscaster bka *Miss America Beauty Pageant* interlocutor NBC-TV 1966–85, filled same slot on *Broadway Open House* 1950–51, *The Jonathan Winters Show* 1957, *Concentration* 1958–61; Charleston, S.C. WTMA sports reporter 1940; opened 1940s-60s *Honeymoon in New York*, *The Jane Pickens Show*, *The Martin and Lewis Show*, *Monitor*, *Name That Tune*, *The NBC Radio Theater*, *The $64,000 Question*, hosted DJ entry *The Wayne Howell Show* 1950, *Wayne Howell and the News* 1949–50/1951; retired from NBC after 39 years 1985; performed regularly with Pompano Beach (Fla.) Players in retirement; d. July 8, 1993.

Delbert Eugene (Del) Sharbutt, Feb. 16, 1912, Fort Worth, Texas; announcer, emcee, vocalist bka Campbell Soup Co. spokesman for soup, juice, pasta, sauce ("Uuummmm ... uuummmm ... ggoood!") on plethora of 1930s-50s aural series: *Amos 'n' Andy*, *The Campbell Playhouse*, *Club 15*, *The Jack Carson Show*, *The Lanny Ross Show*, *Life Begins*, *The Man I Married*, *Meet*

Corliss Archer, *Request Performance*, *You're the Expert*; launched career singing on Fort Worth WBAP 1928, moved to New York CBS 1934 to announce—acquired three dozen gigs as interlocutor—*The Ask-It Basket*, *Lavender and Old Lace*, *Meet Mr. McNutley*, *Singin' Sam*, et al.; joined NBC, on final season *Your Hit Parade* NBC-TV 1957–58, retiring from that web 1980s; d. April 26, 2006.

Deaths

William Gargan, Feb. 16, 1979, on plane enroute from New York-San Diego; b. July 17, 1905. Richard C. Harkness, Feb. 16, 1977, Washington, D.C.; b. Sept. 29, 1907. Kenneth Williams, Feb. 16, 1984, Los Angeles, Calif.; b. April 12, 1914.

February 17

Births

Walter Lanier (Red) Barber, Feb. 17, 1908, Columbus, Miss.; announcer, sportscaster bka Brooklyn Dodgers commentator 1939–53, subsequently Pathé News film commentator; identifying aphorism "Oh-ho, doctor!"; *The Red Barber Show* host-interviewer CBS 1946–50; *Monitor* sports figure interviews, comments NBC 1955–66; as colleague Mel Allen narrated soap operas, Barber did unusual stuff, too, like ebullient commercial spokesman for Procter & Gamble's Fluffo shortening on NBC 1950s episodes *Pepper Young's Family*; sports comments Fridays NPR *Morning Edition* late in career; d. Oct. 22, 1992.

Staats Cotsworth, Feb. 17, 1908, Oak Park, Ill.; actor (stage, film, radio, TV), painter, photographer bka *Front Page Farrell* soap opera namesake newsman David Farrell early 1950s; quiver filled with roles on similar fare—*Amanda of Honeymoon Hill*, *Big Sister*, *Lone Journey*, *Lorenzo Jones*, *Marriage for Two*, *The Right to Happiness*, *The Second Mrs. Burton*, *Stella Dallas*, *When a Girl Marries*; regular on *Casey—Crime Photographer* (lead), *Cavalcade of America*, *The Man from G-2*, *The March of Time*, *Mark Trail*, *Mr. and Mrs. North* (as Lt. Bill Weigand), *Rogue's Gallery*, more in golden era, *The CBS Radio Mystery Theater* 1970s; three theatrical films, countless TV roles including continuing parts in *As the World Turns*, *The Edge of Night*; d. April 9, 1979.

Mark Hiram Hawley, Feb. 17, 1910, New York City, N.Y.; announcer, consultant, director, newscaster, producer bka "The Voice of Pathé News" narrating newsreels screened in cinema houses 1930s-40s; hired from Buffalo WMAK by CBS 1929, announcing Guy Lombardo's first New Year's Eve aircast from Roosevelt Hotel; in 1930s on *Death Valley Days*, *The Fred Allen Show*, *Mr. District Attorney*; New York WOR newscaster 1935–41, same at CBS 1941–43; established Honolulu Fleet Motion Picture Office with U. S. Navy in World War II, producing-directing training films; NBC-TV employee 1947–50; managed Reno KOLO Radio 1955; later industrial management consultant; d. Sept. 5, 1986.

Deaths

Jerry Felding, Feb. 17, 1980, Toronto, Canada; b. June 17, 1922. Joseph Kearns, Feb. 17, 1962, Los Angeles, Calif.; b. Feb. 12, 1907.

February 18

Debuting

Cities Service Concert (*Highways in Melody*, *Cities Service Band of America*, *Band of America*), Feb. 18, 1927, NBC; sterling music feature offered booming bass band at inception, then classical-semiclassical-operatic-pop orchestra, pop-only entourage, returning to brass with heavy march accent; four impresarios—Edwin Franko Goldman, Rosario Bourdon, Frank Black, (and most memorably) Paul Lavalle 1944–56, clarinetist in Goldman reign 1927; soloists, ensembles included Jessica Dragonette, Lucille Manners, James Melton, Frank Parker, Robert Simmons, The Cavaliers, Ken Christy Chorus; final broadcast Jan. 16, 1956.

No School Today, Feb. 18, 1950, ABC; juvenile variety feature; one of two (other *Big Jon and Sparkie*) for tykes hosted by Jon Arthur who impersonated hundreds of character voices, often relying on turntable for help; singing, storytelling, serialized narratives, appeals for better hygiene, exchanges with pals of Sparkie, "the little elf from the land of make-believe, who wants more than anything else ... to be a real boy";

originated Saturdays in Cincinnati — with weekday hour, Arthur had unprecedented seven hours of network performance time weekly to entertain small fry; final broadcast May 22, 1954.

Births

William Lawrence (Bill) Cullen, Feb. 18, 1920, Pittsburgh, Pa.; announcer, emcee, host, quizmaster, TV panelist bka TV game show guru extraordinaire, *I've Got a Secret* panelist 1952–67; *This Is Nora Drake* narrator 1947–51; guessing game host 1940s-50s radio giveaways *Catch Me If You Can, Fun For All, Hit the Jackpot, Quick as a Flash, Stop the Music!, Walk a Mile, Winner Take All*; presided on *Roadshow* NBC 1954, progenitor of *Monitor* that Cullen hosted 1971–73; conducted wake-up show New York WNBC mid 1950s; place in ethereal history set running legions of TV games 1952–86, perhaps more than anyone else: *Give and Take, Winner Take All, Who's There, Why?, Quick as a Flash, Name That Tune, Bank on the Stars, Place the Face, Down You Go, The Price Is Right, Eye Guess, Three on a Match, Winning Streak, Blankety Blanks, Pass the Buck, The Love Experts, Chain Reaction, Blockbusters, Child's Play, Hot Potato, The Joker's Wild*; d. July 7, 1990.

Wayne King, Feb. 18, 1901, Savannah, Ill.; saxophonist fronting big band (branded "The Waltz King"); did remotes plus played 15 network, syndicated radio series 1930–47, nine named *Wayne King Orchestra*; established unknown Lady Esther cosmetic line almost solo after creators put his entourage on national airwaves — so successful was he on six *Lady Esther Serenade* features, salary escalated from $500 weekly to $15,000; d. July 16, 1985.

Lee Aubrey (Speed) Riggs, Feb. 18, 1907, Silverdale, N.C.; announcer, auctioneer, commercial spokesman bka tobacco auctioneer on Lucky Strike cigarette commercials pervading *Information Please* ca. 1940–44, *The Jack Benny Program* 1944–55, *Your All-Time Hit Parade* 1943–44, *Your Hit Parade* ca. late 1930s-1953, other shows; picked by American Tobacco president George Washington Hill to give memorable twist to cigarette advertising (spiel ended "Sol-l-l-d to A-merican!"); transferred to video commercials when they appeared 1950s (*The Jack Benny Program, Your Hit Parade* prevailing); d. Feb. 1, 1987.

John Howard (Jack) Slattery, Feb. 18, 1917, Kansas City, Mo.; announcer bka *Art Linkletter's House Party* audience participation interlocutor 1945–67 on radio, 1959–70 on TV ("Come on in ... it's Art Linkletter's House Party!"); soft-spoken fellow opening show over din of studio chatter welcomed precocious juveniles, held mini model home as host conducted game "What's in the House?," revealed prizes; *You Bet Your Life* comedy-quiz announcer 1947; d. Oct. 29, 1979.

Deaths

Bob Hite, Feb. 18, 2000, West Palm Beach, Fla.; b. Feb. 9, 1914. Nat Shilkret, Feb. 18, 1982, Long Island, N.Y.; b. Dec. 25, 1889.

February 19

Debuting

Renfro Valley Folks (*Renfro Valley Barn Dance, Renfro Valley Sunday Mornin' Gatherin,' Renfro Valley Country Store*), Feb. 19, 1938, MBS; country music jamboree; impetus of John Lair, who created-hosted all Renfro Valley series; Appalachian nod to picking, singing pop country ballads, hoedown tunes, sacred songs performed by mountain acts, guest stars, live audience singing; for years Saturday night shindigs followed by Sunday morning hymn fests; final net broadcast Dec. 28, 1951 although syndicated barn dance still distributed.

Births

Sanford (Sandy) George Becker, Feb. 19, 1922, New York City, N.Y.; actor, announcer, emcee, voiceover artist bka *Young Doctor Malone* soap opera lead (Jerry Malone) 1947–60; thespian or narrator, 1940s-50s aural series: *Backstage Wife, The Columbia Workshop, Hilltop House, Life Can Be Beautiful, Now Hear This, The Shadow, Stepping Out, Take It or Leave It, Treasury Agent*; hosted local daily TV shows for tots on New York WABD, WNEW mid 1950s-late 1960s; voiceover roles of TV cartoon trio: *King Leonardo and His Short Subjects* 1960–63, *The Underdog Show* 1966–68, *Go Go Gophers* 1968–69; d. April 9, 1996.

Lyle Sudrow (Lisle K. V. Sudrow), Feb. 19, 1921, Los Angeles, Calif.; actor (radio, TV, film) bka *The Guiding Light* daytime serial weakened male Bert Bauer perpetuating/returning overbearing mate Bertha's nagging with betrayals, alcoholism CBS 1947–56, CBS-TV 1952–59; aural credits for *The Big Guy, House in the Country, The Mysterious Traveler, Portia Faces Life, The Road of Life, Special Agent, When a Girl Marries*; from 1963–65 in half-dozen solo roles of TV dramas (*Dr. Kildare, Ben Casey*, etc.); uncredited parts in trio of theatrical films 1963–66; d. May 6, 2006.

Deaths

Quincy Howe, Feb. 19, 1977, New York City, N.Y.; b. Aug. 17, 1900. Fort Pearson, Feb. 19, 1989, Alameda County, Calif.; b. May 3, 1909. Don Rickles, Feb. 19, 1985, Los Angeles, Calif.; b. Oct. 7, 1927.

February 20

Canceled

The Jack Kirkwood Show, Feb. 20, 1953, MBS-Don Lee; debut May 17, 1943.

The Lineup, Feb. 20, 1953, CBS; debut July 6, 1950.

Births

Nadine Connor (Evelyn Nadine Henderson), Feb. 20, 1907, Los Angeles, Calif.; vocalist (lyric soprano) bka *The Railroad Hour* fourth most enduring costar, appearing with Gordon MacRae 27 times 1948–54; Metropolitan Opera Co. member 1931–51; intermittent guest *Voice of Firestone* simulcasts 1950s plus few ordinary radio gigs; d. March 1, 2003.

John Charles Daly, Jr., Feb. 20, 1914, Johannesburg, South Africa; emcee, executive, newscaster bka *What's My Line?* panel moderator CBS-TV 1950–67, CBS Radio 1952–53 ("Come in and sign in, please!"); ABC-TV evening news anchorman 1953–57, 1958–60 while vice president-news, special events, public affairs, religious/sports programming; *The World Today, You Are There, Report to the Nation* correspondent CBS Radio 1940s; *Voice of America* director 1967–68; d. Feb. 25, 1991.

Gale Gordon (Charles T. Aldrich, Jr.), Feb. 20, 1906, New York City, N.Y.; actor (stage, film, radio, TV) bka radio veteran with running, sporadic roles in three dozen audio series, frequently know-it-all, unbending stuffed shirts like *The George Burns and Gracie Allen Show* (neighbor Harry Morton), *Junior Miss* (patriarch Harry Graves), *Fibber McGee & Molly* (Mayor Homer La Trivia, weatherman "Foggy" Williams), *The Great Gildersleeve* (neighbor Rumson Bullard), *Our Miss Brooks* (principal Osgood Conklin), *My Favorite Husband* (banker Rudolph Atterbury); nemesis to scatterbrained figures portrayed by Lucille Ball in TV sitcoms *I Love Lucy, The Lucy-Desi Comedy Hour, The Lucy Show, Here's Lucy, Life with Lucy* 1951–86; d. June 30, 1995.

Richard Lewis (Dick) Wesson, Feb. 20, 1919, Shoshone, Idaho; announcer, disc jockey, sportscaster opening late 1940s-early 1950s *Hollywood Open House, Invisible Walls, Space Patrol, ABC Radio Workshop*; DJ at Portland, Ore. KALE 1947, sports reporter at rival KPOJ 1950; *The Walt Disney Show* ABC-/NBC-TV interlocutor 1954–79; d. Jan. 27, 1979.

Deaths

Rosemary DeCamp, Feb. 20, 2001, Torrance, Calif.; b. Nov. 14, 1910. Edgar Fairchild, Feb. 20, 1975, Woodland Hills, Calif.; b. June 1, 1898. Walter Winchell, Feb. 20, 1972, Los Angeles, Calif.; b. April 7, 1897.

February 21

Deaths

Don Dowd, Feb. 21, 1977, Punta Gorda, Fla.; b. March 22, 1905. Morton Gould, Feb. 21, 1996, Orlando, Fla.; b. Dec. 10, 1913. Jane Pickens, Feb. 21, 1992, Newport, R.I.; b. Aug. 10, 1908. Hal Stone, Feb. 21, 2007, Phoenix, Ariz.; b. June 10, 1931.

February 22

Debuting

The George Burns and Gracie Allen Show (debuting segment of *The Robert Burns Panatella Program*), Feb. 22, 1932, CBS; principals as selves in family sitcom accentuating Gracie's zany, illogical conclusions, George and recurring cast's reactions; after ratings slipped in 1941, focus turned from playing unwed singles to married broadcasting couple similar to Jack Bennys proving right move; final half-hour broadcast May 17, 1950, sporadic five-minute features Nov. 18-Dec. 29, 1959, CBS-TV extension Oct. 12, 1950-Sept. 22, 1958.

Scattergood Baines, Feb. 22, 1937, CBS West Coast; comedy serial; in dual incarnations in mythical village of Coldriver, separate figures encircled hardware store proprietor Baines (Jess Pugh, Wendell Holmes) first time around labeled "benevolent force, wise and friendly, ... used psychology and the powers of persuasion to get people to do what was best for them"; in reprise branded "the best-loved, most cussed-at, and by all odds the fattest man" in town; flanked by Hippocrates Brown (John Hearne), others in first incarnation, Hannibal Gibbey (Parker Fennelly), more townsfolk in second; final broadcast of first June 12, 1942; returned to air Feb. 10, 1949 with final broadcast Oct. 26, 1949.

Births

Bess Kathryn Johnson, Feb. 22, 1901, Elkins, W. Va.; actress (radio, TV), ad spokeswoman bka *Hilltop House* daytime serial social caseworker Bess Johnson MBS/CBS 1937–41, *The Story of Bess Johnson* boarding school headmistress Bess Johnson CBS/NBC 1941–42; played in *Today's Children*; one of first ladies to deliver commercial plugs — on multi shows for Lady Esther cosmetics (appeared as "Lady Esther"), Palmolive soap (gave sponsor's pitches on *Hilltop House* beyond starring in soapy saga); played in an episode of *Armstrong Circle Theater* NBC-TV 1951 before joining *Search for Tomorrow* daytime serial as heroine's meddling mom-in-law Irene Barron CBS-TV 1951–54, 1960–61; d. January 1975 (exact date elusive), New York City, N.Y.

Don Pardo (Dominick George Pardo), Feb. 22, 1918, Westfield, Mass.; announcer, newscaster bka *Saturday Night Live* interlocutor NBC-TV 1975–81, 1982–2008 (and counting), one of two people (other Bob Hope) given NBC lifetime contracts; ethereal career began opening 1940s-50s *Barry Craig — Confidential Investigator, Dimension X, Just Plain Bill, Let's Go Nightclubbing, The Magnificent Montague, The Mindy Carson Show, X-Minus One*, orchestras, other features, dispatching headlines on sundry NBC news venues, interviewing guests on 1950s-60s *Monitor* segments; welcomed viewers to video's *The Jonathan Winters Show* 1956–57, TV game shows *Droodles* 1954, *The Price Is Right* 1956–63, *Jeopardy* 1964–75, 1978–79.

Robert George Young, Feb. 22, 1907, Chicago, Ill.; actor (film, radio, TV), emcee, entrepreneur-businessman, producer bka *Father Knows Best* family sitcom patriarch Jim Anderson 1949–54 radio, TV 1954–60, TV reruns 1960–80; *Marcus Welby, M.D.* namesake star ABC-TV 1969–76; half-owner Rodney-Young Productions airing *Father Knows Best*; durable silver screen career starting 1928 with first of 98 primarily B-flicks; of his celluloid activities he allowed: "I was an introvert in an extrovert profession — all those years at MGM I hid a black terror behind a cheerful face"; appeared in dozen made-for-TV movies, two more video series — *A Window on Main Street* 1961–62, *Little Women* 1972; battled alcohol addiction, making unsuccessful attempt on own life 1991; d. July 21, 1998.

February 23

Sound Bite

Radio Act of 1927 passed by Congress Feb. 18 enacted Feb. 23, 1927 as President Calvin Coolidge signs into law; sets Federal Radio Commission five-member panel drawn from five geographical regions of nation, appointed to overlapping six-year terms; one of FRC's biggest tasks is licensing stations, with profound implication fo chains; precursor of Federal Communications Commission.

Births

William L. Shirer, Feb. 23, 1904, Chicago, Ill.; author, columnist, commentator, correspondent, newscaster, print journalist (*The Paris Tribune, The Chicago Tribune, The Paris Herald*), wire journalist (International News Service) bka first "Murrow Boy" hired by CBS chief foreign correspondent Edward R. Murrow 1937, covered war run-up in Europe to 1940 when he went to New York; 1939–47 gigs *CBS World News Roundup, Columbia Presents Corwin, William L. Shirer News and Commentary, World News Roundup/World News Tonight*; penned nine volumes of wartime experiences, traveled lecture circuits, recalled history via newspaper column; despite good fortune, abrasive aristocratic arrogance rubbed colleagues wrong way including peers, Murrow, CBS chairman William S. Paley, who fired him in 1947 — Shirer continued tirades at MBS to 1949 before leaving radio to focus on writing; d. Dec. 28, 1993.

Thomas Llyfwny Thomas, Feb. 23, 1912, Maesteg, South Wales; machinist, concert and recording artist, vocalist (baritone), voice instructor bka *Voice of Firestone* guest artist (43 times) late 1940s-mid 1950s; *National Radio Auditions* winner 1932 followed by *Palmolive Beauty Box Theater* singing roles with Jessica Dragonette; *The Metropolitan Opera Auditions of the Air* winner 1937; billed as "beloved singer of stage and radio" on dual Frank and Anne Hummert-produced aural features —*Manhattan Merry-Go-Round* 1943–49, *Your Song and Mine* 1948 — while appearing on NBC *Highways in Melody* concerts 1948; final career years coached voice among Southwestern students; d. April 17, 1983.

Death

Tiny Ruffner, Feb. 23, 1983, Mt. Clemens, Mich.; b. Nov. 8, 1899.

February 24

Births

Joe Laurie, Jr. (Leiser Lurie), Feb. 24, 1891, Moscow, Russia; actor (radio, stage), emcee, humorist, writer bka *Can You Top This?* panelist 1940–54; *The Fleischmann Hour* guest in myriad appearances with showman Rudy Vallee 1937; *We Are Always Young* daytime serial running role 1941; *Variety* columnist, with Abel Green co–wrote 600-page essay *Show Biz: From Vaude to Video* released 1952; d. April 29, 1954.

Ted Mack (Edward Maguiness), Feb. 24, 1904, Greeley, Colo.; clarinetist, emcee, impresario, saxophonist, talent scout bka successor to Major Edward Bowes, re–launching Bowes' pioneer talent auditions — *Ted Mack's Original Amateur Hour*, radio Sept. 29, 1948-Sept. 18, 1952, TV Jan. 18, 1948-Sept. 27, 1970, ultimately embracing all four video chains; d. July 12, 1976.

Deaths

(Big) Jon Arthur, Feb. 24, 1982 (final residence Fremont, Calif.); b. June 14, 1918. Forrest E. Boone, Feb. 24, 1982, Rancho Park, Calif.; b. Oct. 11, 1893. Taylor Grant, Feb. 24, 1998, Glenside, Pa.; b. Feb. 8, 1913. Conrad Nagel, Feb. 24, 1970, New York City, N.Y.; b. March 16, 1897. Dinah Shore, Feb. 24, 1994, Beverly Hills, Calif.; b. March 1, 1917. Henry J. Taylor, Feb. 24, 1984, New York City, N.Y.; b. Sept. 2, 1902.

February 25

Canceled

Modern Romances, Feb. 25, 1955, NBC; debut Oct. 7, 1936.

Births

James Gilmore (Jim) Backus, Feb. 25, 1913, Cleveland, Ohio; actor (stage, radio, film, TV), author, director, emcee, panelist, voiceover artist, writer bka booming-voiced beetle-browed actor giving life to nearsighted cartoon figure Mr. Magoo in theaters/syndicated TV 1960–62/NBC-TV 1964/CBS-TV 1977/reruns ad infinitum, also prosperous self–indulgent ascot-attired Thurston Howell III of *Gilligan's Island*/*Gilligan's Planet* sitcoms CBS-TV 1964–67/1982–83; legions of film portrayals, most prestigious as James Dean's ineffectual dad Frank Stark in *Rebel Without a Cause* 1955; hosted radio's *Jim Backus Variety* CBS 1942, *The Jim Backus Show* MBS 1947–48, ABC 1957–58; thespian in 1940s-50s audio shows headlined by Alan Young, Bob Burns, Danny Kaye, Edgar Bergen, George Burns and Gracie Allen, Judy Canova, Kate Smith, Mel Blanc, Penny Singleton, plus *The Big Talent Hunt*, *The Columbia Workshop*, *Fibber McGee & Molly*, *Gaslight Gayeties*, *The Great Gildersleeve*, *Lum and Abner*, *Matinee at Meadowbrook*, *The Sad Sack*, *Stella Dallas*; countless TV parts; d. July 3, 1989.

David Kelley Roberts, Jr., Feb. 25, 1912, Jacksonville, Fla.; NBC staff announcer from 1936, apprenticing in guest relations, enlisting in web's announcing institute prior to full time service; d. Dec. 24, 1996.

Death

Vincent Pelletier, Feb. 25, 1994, Los Angeles, Calif.; b. March 21, 1908.

February 26

Canceled

Dragnet, Feb. 26, 1957, NBC; debut June 3, 1949. *Ed Wynn*, Feb. 26, 1945, NBC Blue; debut April 26, 1932. *The Prudential Family Hour of Stars*, Feb. 26, 1950, CBS; debut Aug. 31, 1941.

Births

Mason Adams, Feb. 26, 1919, Brooklyn, N.Y.; actor (radio, stage, TV), voiceover artist (commercials) bka *Pepper Young's Family* daytime serial namesake hero 1945–59, managing editor Charlie Hume of *Lou Grant* newspaper drama starring Ed Asner CBS-TV 1977–82, enduring ad spokesman for J. M. Smucker jams, jellies, preserves ("With a name like Smucker's, it *has* to be good!"); more radio credits for *The Adventures of Superman, Big Sister, Big Town, Gasoline Alley, Hearthstone of the Death Squad, The Road of Life*; community theater, college, stock productions before World War II — he admitted loving stage most, playing there throughout career; in many TV dramas, often shows underwritten by American Tobacco, Ford, U. S. Steel; d. April 26, 2005.

Donald Baker, Feb. 26, 1903, Ontario, Canada; announcer, composer, organist, pianist; introduced *The Columbia Workshop, Information Please, Pursuit, Strike It Rich* and organist for *My Best Girls, Sing for Your Dough, This Day Is Ours*; staff musician at New York WOR 1934–35 after launching career as band pianist and playing organ at Gotham's Rialto and Rivoli theaters and London's Sidney Bernstein Theater; similar capacity for New York's Paramount Theater 1935–48; joined CBS 1943, transferred to Hollywood 1949 to serve chain's O-and-O outlet KNX rest of life; d. Nov. 12, 1968.

Dick Dunham, Feb. 26, 1916, New York City, N.Y.; announcer, newscaster bka commercial spokesman for Manhattan Soap Co.'s Sweetheart cleansing bar starting 1944 via multiple broadcast venues; left Baltimore WITH 1942 to try luck in New York working gigs for CBS, NBC, MBS, becoming CBS newscaster 1945; introduced *The Falcon, Mollé Mystery Theater, Rose of My Dreams, The Strange Romance of Evelyn Winters, We Love and Learn* to 1940s fans.

Edward F. (Eddie) Gallaher, Feb. 26, 1915, Washington, D.C.; disc jockey, emcee, sportscaster bka *On a Sunday Afternoon* live-and-recorded music series host CBS 1953, 1954-ca. 1955, voice of Washington Redskins for hometown radio-TV market 1955–65; launched ethereal duties at Tulsa KTUL 1938 followed by Minneapolis WCCO, Washington WTOP; retired Dec. 22, 2000 after 62 years as broadcaster, more than half-century at four D.C. outlets; d. Nov. 26, 2003.

Death

Harry Bartell, Feb. 26, 2004, Ashland, Ore.; b. Nov. 29, 1913.

February 27

Sound Bite

David Sarnoff, one of two men who will shape broadcasting in 20th century more than contemporaries (other, William S. Paley), is born Feb. 27, 1891 at Uzlian in Russian province of Minsk; classic rags-to-riches tale of Russian emigrant Jew who "probably affected the patterns of the daily lives of more Americans than anyone since Thomas Edison" says biographer; migrates with clan to New York at nine, arriving July 2, 1900, resides in squalor on Manhattan's Lower East Side — yet out of those humble beginnings emerges inquisitive, imaginative, incredibly bright youth possessing unbridled ambition; some day (Jan. 3, 1930) he will be running Radio Corporation of America, thereby NBC.

Debuting

Broadway Is My Beat, Feb. 27, 1949, CBS; crime drama about "the lonesomest mile in the world" assigned to New York plainclothes detective Danny Glover (Anthony Ross, Larry Thor) whose exploits intersected with droll officer Gino Tartaglia (Charles Calvert), city coroner Sergeant Mugowen (Jack Kruschen); one of miniscule handful of series in era (*Dragnet, Twenty-First Precinct*) presenting harsh realities of lawbreaking; working against fans, drama shifted to 16 timeslots, airing every night of week eventually although always on CBS — shortest run one week; final broadcast Aug. 1, 1954.

Canceled

The Crime Files of Flamond, Feb. 27, 1957, MBS; net debut Jan. 7, 1953.

Births

Marian Anderson, Feb. 27, 1897, Philadelphia, Pa.; vocalist (contralto) bka *The Bell Telephone Hour* recurring guest artist 1942–58 (37 appearances followed Jascha Heifetz' 54, Lily Pons' 50, Ezio Pinza's 44); debuted 1924, New York Town Hall; unable to have an active U. S. career due to racial prejudice, she successfully pursued it in England, Germany, Finland, singing steadily 1925–35; 75,000 heard her in person, millions more on radio from Lincoln Memorial on Easter Sunday, April 9, 1939 at concert fostered by Eleanor Roosevelt; Metropolitan Opera performer 1955–65, first Negro to grace its stage; d. April 8, 1993.

Upton Close (Josef Washington Hall), Feb. 27, 1894, Kelso, Wash.; commentator, educator, journalist, newscaster; name change after articles he penned ended with "Up Close" for Shanghai *Weekly Review* in World War I as he lived in Chinese Shantung province during Japanese invasion; correspondent for print media in China, Japan, Siberia; University of Washington lecturer on oriental life, literature; Close, Lowell Thomas partnered as radio's first lecturers 1924; director of American Cultural Expeditions to orient 1926–35, he led hordes to Far East, India, Russia, Middle East, Europe; published multiple volumes; national radio gigs 1942–47; outspoken ultraconservative angered management of NBC, MBS —fired from first, quit second; retired to Mexico; d. Nov. 13, 1960.

Carl Frank, Feb. 27, 1909, Weehawkin, N.J.; actor (film, radio, stage), announcer, entrepreneur-salesman bka *I Remember Mama* figure Uncle Gunnar Gunnerson CBS-TV 1949–57; Broadway credits for *Paths of Glory, Boy Meets Girl, A Sound of Hunting, The Shrike*; silver screen in 1948's *Lady from Shanghai*, Army/Navy training films; radio thespian for *Aunt Jenny's Real Life Stories, Betty and Bob, The Columbia Workshop, Gangbusters, The Shadow, Whispering Streets, Young Doctor Malone*, at least score more; sold real estate insurance in U. S. Virgin Islands late in life; d. Sept. 23, 1972.

David Sarnoff, Feb. 27, 1891, Uzlian, Minsk, Russia; Radio Corporation of America (RCA) staffer, CEO-chairman 1919–70; controlled auxiliary National Broadcasting Co. dual radio (Red, Blue), TV webs; dogmatic, conservative, competitive mogul; video prophet from audio's start turning dream to reality by late 1930s; staunch rival of CBS tycoon William S. Paley, joined him to defend industry against escalating, permeating federal intrusion; d. Dec. 12, 1971.

Death

Hal Neal, Feb. 27, 1980, Darien, Conn.; b. March 25, 1924.

February 28

Deaths

Eddie (Rochester) Anderson, Feb. 28, 1977, Beverly Hills, Calif.; b. Sept. 18, 1905. Charita Bauer, Feb. 28, 1985, New York City, N.Y.; b. Dec. 20, 1923.

February 29

Debuting

Snow Village Sketches (*Soconyland Sketches*), Feb. 29, 1928, NBC; comedy; played in nearly unbroken fashion from inception to May 11, 1935 with *Soconyland* appellation, reprising under *Snow Village* banner Oct. 3, 1936 in trio of segments — to June 26, 1937, Dec. 28, 1942-Nov. 11, 1943, Jan. 13, 1946-June 16, 1946; Arthur Allen, Parker Fennelly leads in *Soconyland* while Fennelly returned with Hiram Neville in second as rural denizens of Snow Village, New Hampshire; bucolic environment depicted life in long-ago, far-away epoch.

Canceled

Valiant Lady, Feb. 29, 1952, ABC; debut March 7, 1938.

Birth

Jimmy Dorsey, Feb. 29, 1904, Shenandoah, Pa.; elder bandleader, sibling of renowned Tommy Dorsey following similar career; pair launched joint band in 1922, separated in 1935 before combining outfits in 1953; Jimmy Dorsey featured on half-dozen net radio series 1928–54 plus myriad big band one-night-stand remotes; d. June 12, 1957.

Death

Melvin Purvis, Feb. 29, 1960, Florence, S.C.; b. Oct. 24, 1903.

March 1

Sound Bite

Emblematic of the incredible power of radio premiums to not only sell merchandise but swell radio audience size, March 1, 1935 issue of trade publication *Broadcasting* reports on what transpired when daytime serial *Today's Children*, airing but short while on NBC Blue, told listeners that — in return for flour label — Pillsbury would send free printed backstory of Moran clan, narrative's central figures; in few weeks 250,000-plus labels arrived, journal witnessing: "The amazing allegiance of hundreds of thousands of women not only to the members of the cast but to Pillsbury products is a constant source of wonderment even among those professional people who for years have been working with radio"; premiums grow in popularity, usefulness as time moves on.

Debuting

Duffy's Tavern, March 1, 1941, CBS; sitcom centered at acclaimed watering hole in seedy section of Manhattan's East Side; included manager-barkeep Archie (Ed Gardner), recurring zany clientele, celebs who were often lampooned during stopovers; final regular broadcast Dec. 28, 1951, pithy syndicated televersion 1954, brief vignettes aired during *Monitor* magazine marathon on weekends NBC mid-to-late 1950s.

Canceled

The Adventures of Superman, March 1, 1951, ABC; debut Feb. 12, 1940 (on nationwide hookup — earlier in limited markets).

Births

Lester Lee (Les) Griffith, March 1, 1906, Union (unverified), Ill.; announcer bka ABC employee 1943–73; left Grand Rapids, Mich. 1935 for NBC New York; introduced radio fans to *Candid Microphone, Dan Harding's Wife, Gangbusters, Girl Alone, The Story of Mary Marlin, The Tom Mix Ralston Straight Shooters*, lots more; d. Nov. 20, 1991.

Cy Harrice, March 1, 1915, Chicago, Ill.; announcer, copywriter, newscaster, program director bka deep voice offering final line after Ernest Chappell's Pall Mall cigarette assertion "Outstanding!" with ending "...and...they are mild!"; linked to other broadcast underwriters E. I. Dupont, General Motors, Miles Laboratories, Procter & Gamble; brought to ether 1930s-50s *The Adventures of the Thin Man, The Big Story, Gabriel Heatter, Cavalcade of America, Ethel and Albert, Grand Central Station, Quick as a Flash, Walter Winchell's Journal, What Makes You Tick?*, more; joined Chicago WLS 1940, rival WGN 1942 as chief newsman; New York freelancer 1945; d. Feb. 14, 2007.

Charles Albert Lyon, March 1, 1903, Detroit, Mich.; actor, announcer, correspondent, newscaster bka *Gene Autry's Melody Ranch* ballads-drama interlocutor CBS late 1940s-1956, narrating one of NBC's last daytime serials *The Woman in My House* 1951–59; pursued stage, Broadway before announcing gig at Cleveland WTAM late 1920s, moving to Chicago NBC 1931 where distinctive voice opened multi features, 1932 political conventions, news spots on WMAQ local NBC staff between shows; summoned fans to 1930s-50s *The Bob Hawk Show, The Curt Massey-Martha Tilton Show, Girl Alone, Life with Luigi, Lum and Abner, Those Websters, Truth or Consequences, Vic and Sade, Wild Bill Hickok*, more; frequent commercial spokesman for Alka-Seltzer acid indigestion reliever, other Miles Labs goods; settled in Hollywood 1940; d. May 11, 1985.

Glenn Miller, March 1, 1904, Clarinda, Iowa; impresario, trombonist; joined Ben Pollack band 1924, started own aggregate twice; played eight ongoing network gigs 1939–44; quit to conduct American Band in European theater during World War II when plane, occupants vanished, never to resurface to date; actor Jimmy Stewart played Miller, June Allyson his wife, in *The Glenn Miller Story* theatrical release 1953; d. Dec. 15, 1944.

Frances Rose "Fannie" (Dinah) Shore, March 1, 1917, Winchester, Tenn.; broadcast entertainer, pop vocalist, recording artist bka hostess of NBC-TV's *The Dinah Shore Show* Nov. 27, 1951-July 18, 1957, *The Dinah Shore Chevy*

Show Oct. 5, 1956-May 12, 1963, *Dinah's Place* Aug. 3, 1970-July 26, 1974, two later daily video ventures; featured singer debuting *The Chamber Music Society of Lower Basin Street* 1940; regular on 17 network audio gigs 1939–55 including trio labeled *The Dinah Shore Show*; d. Feb. 24, 1994.

Deaths

Brace Beemer, March 1, 1965, Oxford, Mich.; b. Dec. 9, 1902. Nadine Connor, March 1, 2003, Los Alamitos, Calif.; b. Feb. 20, 1907. Jack Petruzzi, March 1, 1967, Los Angeles, Calif.; b. May 17, 1907. Dorian St. George, March 1, 2004, Cleveland, Ohio; b. Sept. 16, 1911.

March 2

Canceled

That Brewster Boy, March 2, 1945, CBS; debut Sept. 8, 1941.

Deaths

Stefan Hatos, March 2, 1999, Toluca Lake, Calif.; b. Aug. 20, 1920. Mercedes McCambridge, March 2, 2004, La Jolla, Calif.; b. March 16, 1916. Jack McElroy, March 2, 1959, Santa Monica, Calif.; b. Oct. 21, 1913.

March 3

Debuting

The Mutual Radio Theater, March 3, 1980, MBS; anthology drama; repeated episodes of *The Sears Radio Theater* aired Feb. 5, 1979-Feb. 1, 1980 on CBS; final broadcast Dec. 19, 1980.

Renfrew of the Mounted, March 3, 1936, CBS; juvenile adventure drama; Royal Canadian Mounted Police inspector Douglas Renfrew (House Jameson) chased varmits through snow-capped hills of Dominion provinces as he set stage for even more durable *Sergeant Preston of the Yukon* soon to be bobbing down ether trail 1938–55, doing it all more impressively; animal impersonator Brad Barker provided lonely cry of wolf at start, finish of *Renfrew* episodes; support playing by Joan Baker, Joseph Curtin, Robert Dryden, Carl Eastman, more; show off air 21 months 1937–38; final broadcast Oct. 19, 1940.

Seth Parker (*Sundays at Seth Parker's*, *Sunday Evenings at Seth Parker's*, *The Cruise of the Seth Parker*), March 3, 1929, NBC; serialized melodrama, variety; homespun philosophy, melody in coastal hamlet Jonesport, Maine, launched as hymn-sing but exhibiting serialized narrative; endorsed by leading clergymen Rev. S. Parkes Cadman, Harry Emerson Fosdick, Dr. Daniel Poling; creator-writer-actor-director-producer Phillips H. Lord — recalled for *Gang-busters*, other crime features — vowed boyhood memory of tales his Grandpa told inspired Seth Parker whom he played; other sketch regulars Lizzie Peters (Sophia M. Lord), Ma Parker (Effie Palmer, Barbara Bruce), Cefus Peters and Laith Pettingal (both Bennett Kilpack), more; under sobriquet *The Cruise of the Seth Parker*, gang left on two-year global voyage, airing via shortwave Dec. 5, 1933-March 27, 1934, abruptly ending journey when vessel sank, all returning to shore, show off ether next 15 months; final broadcast March 19, 1939.

Whispering Streets, March 3, 1952, ABC; anthology drama; one of daytime narratives airing on radio's Black Friday, "the day drama died," exhibited closed-end form (everything tidied up neatly at "finish"); initially airing in complete 20-minute features, format changed in 1954 to quarter-hour serialized installments, stories opening Monday, concluding Friday of same week; hostess-narrator "Hope Winslow" impersonated by Gertrude Warner, Cathy Lewis, Bette Davis, Anne Seymour; cast often saw Robert Dryden, Sam Edwards, Barbara Fuller, Robert Readick, Janet Waldo, et al.; final broadcast Nov. 25, 1960.

Canceled

Life with Luigi, March 3, 1953, CBS (last show in primetime though 1954 weekday series persisted); debut Sept. 21, 1948. *Walter Winchell*, March 3, 1957, MBS; debut May 12, 1930.

Birth

John Nelson, March 3, 1915, Spokane, Wash.; actor, announcer, emcee, network program executive (NBC), producer, quizmaster bka *Bride and Groom* host 1945–50, TV manifestation 1951–53; thespian in *The Adventures of Ellery Queen* 1948, presided over giveaways like *Add a Line* 1949, *Know Your NBCs* 1953–54, plus *Breakfast at Sardi's* ca. 1948–49; introduced daily talent audition *Live Like a Millionaire* 1950–53 on radio before succeeding Jack McCoy as emcee; *Your Pet Parade* producer ABC-TV 1951; d. Nov. 3, 1976.

Deaths

Peter Capell, March 3, 1986, Munich, Germany; b. Sept. 3, 1912. Lou Costello, March 3, 1959, Los Angeles, Calif.; b. March 6, 1906. Tobe Reed, March 3, 1988, Rancho Mirage, Calif.; b. Dec. 12, 1911. Ezra Stone, March 3, 1994, Perth Amboy, N.J.; b. Dec. 2, 1917. John Tillman, March 3, 2004, Charlestown, Mass.; b. Nov. 13, 1916. Lew White, March 3, 1955, New York City, N.Y.; b. May 18, 1899.

March 4

Debuting

Junior Miss, March 4, 1942, CBS; teen sitcom derived from Sally Benson novel touting misadventures of Judy Graves (Shirley Temple, Barbara Whiting), "also ran" entry to more enduring *A Date with Judy*, *Meet Corliss Archer* of same genre; at 15 protagonist differentiated from older sister Liz by not yet being boy-crazy as Liz was; father Harry Graves (Elliott Lewis, Gale Gordon), mother Grace (Mary Lansing, Sarah Selby), Lois (K. T. Stevens, Barbara Eiler, Peggy Knudson); feature silent 1942–48, 1950–52; final broadcast July 1, 1954.

Births

Patrick Joseph McGeehan, March 4, 1907, Harrisburg, Pa.; actor, announcer, emcee, voiceover artist; *NBC Comics* animated cartoon finish NBC-TV 1950–51; appeared on three dozen aural ether entries 1940s-80s, primarily as thespian, briefly as host, narrator e.g. *The Abbott and Costello Show*, *Aunt Mary*, *The Bob Hope Show*, *The CBS Radio Mystery Theater*, *Fibber McGee & Molly*, *Gunsmoke*, *The Jack Benny Program*, *Maisie*, *Meet Mr. McNutley*, *The Red Skelton Show*, *Romance of the Ranchos*, *The Roy Rogers Show*, *Stars Over Hollywood*, *Strange as it Seems*, *Suspense*, *The Whistler*; d. Jan. 3, 1988.

Robert Arthur (Bob) Pfeiffer, March 4, 1921, Detroit, Mich.; announcer, newscaster, news editor, producer, sportscaster bka *Ma Perkins* daytime serial final interlocutor CBS late 1950s-Nov. 25, 1960 (popularly acclaimed "day radio drama died"); on air first as Cedar Rapids, Iowa WMT news/sportsman 1946–48, hosted *Operation Success* public service series on Dumont TV 1948; introduced *Choose Up Sides* juvenile stunt show on New York WCBS-TV 1953; arrived on national radio scene late, *The Bickersons* commercial spokesman 1951, *Answer Please* announcer 1958; CBS news editor, special correspondent reporting from western Europe dozen years starting early 1960s; finished career producing news broadcasts for United Nations' public information bureau; d. Dec. 17, 1993.

Death

Verne Smith, March 4, 1978, Seattle, Wash.; b. Nov. 25, 1909.

March 5

Canceled

Ben Bernie, the Old Maestro, March 5, 1943, CBS (although star ill, left show to remainder of cast after Jan. 15, 1943); debut Jan. 17, 1930.

Births

Minerva Pious, March 5, 1903, Russia; actress (stage, radio, film, TV) bka *The Fred Allen Show* comedy-variety entry "Allen's Alley" denizen Mrs. Pansy Nussbaum NBC 1945–49 although she joined Allen's entourage in 1933 as ethnic utility player; reprised celebrated role in 1945 theatrical release *It's in the Bag!*, four more films by 1973; fleeting part in *The Edge of Night* daytime serial CBS-TV 1972; on Broadway three weeks 1964; on air: *Columbia Presents Corwin*, *The Columbia Workshop*, *Duffy's Tavern*, *The Goldbergs*, *The Jack Benny Program*, *Life Can Be Beautiful*, *Snow Village Sketches*; d. March 16, 1979.

Rosemary Rice, March 5, 1932, Montclair, N.J.; actress (radio, stage, TV), commercial spokesperson, recording artist bka prolific daytime serial character thespian (*Life Can Be Beautiful*, *Ma Perkins*, *The Right to Happiness*, *The Second Mrs. Burton*, *Young Doctor Malone*, more); *Archie Andrews* teen sitcom girl-next-door figure Betty Cooper 1946–53; CBS-TV *I Remember Mama* offspring Katrin and narrator (..."When I look back to those days so long ago ... most of all ... I remember Mama") 1949–57; recurring guest performer, vintage radio conventions across America, 1990s-early 2000s.

Deaths

Clarence Hartzell, March 5, 1988, Bella Vista, Ark.; b. Oct. 26, 1910. Grover Kirby, March 5, 1949, Wauconda, Ill.; b. Sept. 6, 1915. Harry Salter, March 5, 1984, Mamaroneck, N.Y.; b. Sept. 14, 1898.

March 6

Debuting

The March of Time, March 6, 1931, CBS; current events anthology drama; "the most important news dramatization program" said one wag; so real that some believed they were hearing actual newsmakers; limited to one or two narratives per show by 1942, straight news filling time; Ted Husing, Westbrook Van Voorhis, Hary Von Zell narrated; Bill Adams, Bill Johnstone, Staats Cotsworth, Art Carney impersonated FDR as Marion Hopkinson, Agnes Moorehead, Nancy Kelly, Jeanette Nolan played wife Eleanor; impersonations offered by topnotch thespians like Ted de Corsia, Kenny Delmar, Arlene Francis, Martin Gabel, Ed Jerome, Myron McCormick, Arnold Moss, Claire Niesen, Everett Sloane, Karl Swenson, Dwight Weist, Orson Welles, more; led to motion picture documentary, ABC-TV edition 1951, 1952; final radiocast July 26, 1945.

Births

Rosario Bourdon, March 6, 1885, Longuereil, Quebec, Canada; accompanist, arranger, cellist, impresario, radio entertainer, recording artist bka first to make fêted cello recordings (Victor Talking Machine Co.), second maestro of *Cities Service Concert* NBC 1927–38; d. April 24, 1961.

Lou Costello (Louis Francis Cristillo), March 6, 1906, Paterson, N.J.; actor, comic bka Abbott and Costello comedy team wisecracker; while performing in vaudeville in 1931 teamed with Bud Abbott, played in burlesque, vaudeville, minstrel, movies; earned acclaim on *The Kate Smith Hour* CBS 1938–40, NBC summer series 1940; *The Abbott and Costello Show* aired on NBC/ABC 1942–49 with syndicated television 1952–53; two appeared in 35 theatrical films 1940–56; act broke up 1957, Abbott sued Costello 1958 for past debts; d. March 3, 1959.

Adelaide Hawley Cumming (Dieta Adelaide Fish), March 6, 1905, Scranton, Pa.; emcee bka "Betty Crocker" on TV 1949–64, nation's "second most recognizable woman" after Eleanor Roosevelt, corporate mascot of General Mills, Inc. personalizing its baking goods with her image on billboards, magazines, newspapers, product literature, commodity packaging; *Adelaide Hawley Show* consultant offering tips, women's issues 1939–46; *The Betty Crocker Show* CBS-TV 1950–51, *The Betty Crocker Star Matinee* ABC-TV 1951–52, plugs on *Bride and Groom*, *The George Burns and Gracie Allen Show*, more TV; when General Mills replaced her with younger model, Cumming returned to school to earn doctorate in speech at 62, teaching English to international students for three decades; d. Dec. 21, 1998.

Virginia Gregg (Virginia Gregg Burket Del Valle), March 6, 1916, Harrisburg, Ill.; actress (radio, film, TV), voiceover artist; pundit dubbed her "radio's female equivalent to William Conrad, Ben Wright and Elliott Lewis"; supported myriad aural sleuths whose monikers topped features — Christopher London, Ellery Queen, Michael Shayne, Philip Marlowe, Barry Craig, Monte Cristo, Richard Diamond, Johnny Dollar — and helped *Confidential Investigator*, *Deadline Mystery*, *Dragnet*, *Gunsmoke*, *Have Gun — Will Travel*, *Nightbeat*, *The Silent Men*, *The Six Shooter*, *T-Man*, *Tales of the Texas Rangers*, more; 39 theatrical films 1946–86, six TV series 1961–81, 20 made-for-TV flicks 1968–82, 220 solo TV shots in dramas/sitcoms/variety shows 1958–83; d. Sept. 15, 1986.

Deaths

Elvia Allman, March 6, 1992, Los Angeles, Calif.; b. Sept. 19, 1904. Nelson Eddy, March 6, 1967, Miami, Fla.; b. June 29, 1901. Cedric Foster, March 6, 1975, Denver, Colo.; b. Aug. 31, 1900.

March 7

Sound Bite

On March 7, 1946, Federal Communications Commission releases policy manual *Public Service Responsibility of Broadcast Licensees* (labeled "Blue Book") directing that licensees "cater to the needs of nonprofit organizations"; request can be satisfied by airing public service announcements combined with plethora of public affairs, other sustained, narrowly-focused programming; in complying, networks, local stations — seeking to renew licenses regularly — will document exposure to service, charitable, academic, governmental agencies on behalf of public welfare (e.g. ecology, education, health, safety, added concerns).

Debuting

Valiant Lady, March 7, 1938, CBS; daytime serial; tale of oppressed heroine Joan Barrett (Joan Blaine, Joan Banks, Florence Freeman) who gave up her vocation to wed plastic surgeon Truman "Tubby" Scott (Charles Carroll, Bartlett Robinson, Martin Blaine); he was insanely jealous (not first male in Hummert sagas to be so!); when blood clot entered his brain, she fought back bravely "to keep his feet planted firmly upon the pathway to success"; empathetic dad Jim Barrett (Richard Gordon, Bill Johnstone, Gene Leonard) provided shoulder to lean on, so did admiring suitor Paul Morrison (Raymond Edward Johnson); Tubby vanished down mine shaft, explosion sealing his fate — Joan's life should have improved but she had troubles galore, running from law to hide from crime Tubby hadn't committed but was accused of (you had to have been there; it was a Hummert drama); off air 1946–51; title reprised for another beleaguered widow CBS-TV 1953–57; final radiocast Feb. 29, 1952.

Canceled

Official Detective, March 7, 1957, MBS; debut Jan. 19, 1947.

Births

Marion Marlowe, March 7, 1929, St. Louis, Mo.; personal appearance/recording artist, vocalist bka *Arthur Godfrey Time* variety revue singer, often in duets with Frank Parker CBS Radio-TV late 1940s-1955, same style on *Arthur Godfrey and His Friends* CBS-TV 1950–55; one of many artists Godfrey terminated in awful six-year reign of "bitchy, bickering strife" critic depicted; he let her go along with Haleloke, Mariners quartet, trio of scribes on April 15, 1955; turned up in guest singing roles in early 1960s TV on *The Perry Como Show, The Ed Sullivan Show.*

Vivian Smolen (Klein), March 7, 1916, New York City, N.Y.; actress (film, radio), commercials voiceover artist (radio, TV) bka *Our Gal Sunday* daytime serial leading lady Sunday Brinthrope 1944–59 ("mistress of Black Swan Hall"), *Stella Dallas* daytime serial heroine's daughter Laurel ("Lolly Baby") Grosvenor (1940s-1955), *Archie Andrews* teen sitcom hero's love interest Veronica Lodge 1943–44; running parts in copious washboard weepers, frequent gigs on *Mr. Keen, Tracer of Lost Persons* 1946–54, other crime features; d. June 11, 2006.

Death

Paula Winslowe, March 7, 1996, Woodland Hills, Calif.; b. March 23, 1910.

March 8

Birth

Franklyn MacCormack, March 8, 1906, Waterloo, Iowa; actor (stage, radio), announcer, disc jockey, poetry reader, producer; in stock, Broadway shows till Depression killed patronage; turned to South Bend, Ind. station reading poetry 1929, moving to St. Louis WIL 1930 where similar gig brought 40,000 listener requests for photo; acting, announcing, producing at Chicago WBBM (CBS affiliate) 1933, expanding base to national audience; opened *Caroline's Golden Store, The Curley Bradley Show, Easy Aces, Hymns of All Churches, Jack Armstrong — the All-American Boy, Myrt and Marge, The Wayne King Show, Woman in White,* more; *Make Believe Ballroom* DJ host on Windy City copycat of popular local New York series 1930s-40s; hosted *Poetic Melodies* on three chains parodying acclaimed Cincinnati WLW *Moon River*; features with like twists followed on Chicago outlets: *Love Letters* WENR, *Great Day for Music* WCPL, *All Night Showcase* WGN; d. June 12, 1971 on air on latter.

Deaths

Parke Levy, March 8, 1993, Los Angeles,

Calif.; b. April 19, 1908. Rhoda Williams, March 8, 2006, Eugene, Ore.; b. July 19, 1930.

March 9

Sound Bite

Edward R. Murrow becomes first media figure to risk career by attacking powerful Sen. Joseph R. McCarthy (R-Wis.) for his sweeping passion in ferreting out those with perceived communist leanings, resulting in blacklists, their being ostracized, separated from livelihoods; Murrow's interrogation of McCarthy, contributing heavily to latter's downfall, occurs on CBS-TV's *Person to Person* March 9, 1954; in no way does it diminish fact Murrow is first, foremost, forever consummate radio newsman whose nightly aural program is priority for legions 1942–44, 1947–59; deposing of McCarthy nets protracted commentary there, too.

Birth

Robert St. John, March 9, 1902, Chicago, Ill.; author, correspondent, newscaster, print journalist (*The Hartford* [Conn.] *Courant, The Oak* [Park, Ill.] *Leaves, The Chicago American, The Chicago Daily News, The Cicero* [Ill.] *Tribune, The Rutland* [Vt.] *Herald* 1927–29, *The Camden* [N.J.] *Courier, The Philadelphia Record* 1920–31), wire journalist (Associated Press 1931–33, 1939–41); joined NBC 1942 for spate of news-oriented features: *Robert St. John and the News* 1943–46, *News of the World* substitute anchor 1943-ca. 1947, *Monitor* correspondent 1959–60, others; labeled by critics "an outspoken liberal," "talented author," "spellbinding lecturer"; worked on 23rd tome at his death — topics often involving Israeli history; d. Feb. 6, 2003.

Deaths

George Burns, March 9, 1996, Beverly Hills, Calif.; b. Jan. 20, 1896. Ned Calmer, March 9, 1986, New York City, N.Y.; b. July 16, 1907. Bob Crosby, March 9, 1993, La Jolla, Calif.; b. Aug. 23, 1913. Ernie Hare, March 9, 1939, Jamaica, N.Y.; b. March 15, 1883. Lawrence Spivak, March 9, 1994, Washington, D.C.; b. June 11, 1900.

March 10

Deaths

E. Power Biggs, March 10, 1977, Boston, Mass.; b. March 29, 1906. Matthew Crowley, March 10, 1983, Clearwater, Fla.; b. June 20, 1905. Irene Tedrow, March 10, 1995, Valley Village, Calif.; b. Aug. 3, 1907.

March 11

Canceled

The American Forum of the Air, March 11, 1956, NBC; debut Dec. 26, 1937 (as *The Mutual Forum Hour*).

National Barn Dance, March 11, 1950, ABC; net debut Sept. 30, 1933.

Births

Daniel Jones (Dan) Donaldson (pseudonym Charlie Warren), March 11, 1915, St. Louis, Mo.; announcer bka *Ma Perkins'* interlocutor-commercial spokesman for Oxydol late 1940s-mid 1950s ("Seeing is believing! For a wash that's deep cleaning ... deep cleaning ... deep cleaning ... use Oxydol"); applied alias to avoid sponsor conflict with competing manufacturer; when a chum bet he couldn't get a "real" radio job (already airing on college station), on a 1939 hiatus to Chicago auditioned at NBC and hired to narrate *two* daytime serials!; his basal timbre introduced 1930s-40s *Clara, Lu 'n' Em, Kitty Keene Inc., The Road of Life, The Trouble with Marriage* while plugging sponsor wares on *Can You Top This?*; d. Dec. 1, 1991.

Philip Leslie, March 11, 1909, Morley, Mo.; freelancing scriptwriter (radio, TV) bka *Fibber McGee & Molly* understudy wordsmith to head writer Don Quinn 1943–50, successor 1950–56; on loan to script *The Marlin Hurt and Beulah Show* spun off from *McGee & Molly* for its inaugural summer run 1945; penned TV lines for *Dennis the Menace, Hazel, The Farmer's Daughter, The Brady Bunch, The Lucy Show* later years; d. Sept. 23, 1988.

Eloise McElhone, March 11, 1921, New York City, N.Y.; emcee, panelist; hostess-narrator of *Modern Romances* ca. 1949–1950s while serving on panels of *Leave It to the Girls* 1945–49, *Think Fast* 1949–50, *S. R. O.* 1953; d. July 1, 1974.

Lawrence Welk, March 11, 1903, Strasburg, N.D.; accordionist, author, emcee, entrepreneur, impresario, recording artist bka *The Lawrence Welk Show* music revue host ABC-TV 1955–71, syndicated TV 1971–82—"Some may have poked fun at the stiff, seemingly uncomfortable bandleader, but Welk gave his fans what they wanted and proved to be an enduring TV icon" a reviewer obsessed; at 13 played accordion for money, at 17 formed three-piece "Biggest Little Band in America" on Yankton, S.D. WNAX; adopted Hotsy Totsy Boys moniker playing ballroom, dance hall circuit, aired radio remotes, by 1947 as Roosevelt (N.Y.) Grill Orchestra; first permanent ethereal gig *Lewrence Welk High Life Revue* ABC 1949–51 followed by other web audio series through 1957; family of regular singers, dancers, instrumentalists drew host of fans; d. May 17, 1992.

Deaths

Gaylord James Avery, March 11, 1996, San Francisco, Calif.; b. July 6, 1918. Radcliffe Hall, March 11, 1997, Nyack, N.Y.; b. Sept. 2, 1914. Joseph Julian, March 11, 1982, New York City, N.Y.; b. June 9, 1910.

March 12

Sound Bite

Fireside Chats inaugurated March 12, 1933 as President Franklin D. Roosevelt addresses nation in informal talk via radio; restores confidence in time of economic, war anxiety; first given in clear English, "An Intimate Talk with the People of the United States on Banking," prevents run on deposits, stabilizes bank system; 30 radio dispatches air in next 11 years; *Fireside Chats* sobriquet inspired by Alexandria, Va. station WJSV honcho Harry Butcher who knew FDR spoke from White House Diplomatic Reception Room by fireplace; Robert Trout, CBS announcer, used epithet introducing FDR March 12; aside from settling nation's nerves, *Chats* solidified viability of reaching citizens with presidential messages via electronic transmission, method never eclipsed but expanded.

Births

Eugene Conley, March 12, 1908, Lynn, Mass.; educator, vocalist (tenor) bka *Voice of Firestone* recurring artist (28 times) 1950s often paired with lyric soprano Nadine Conner in duets; stints with Tampa, Cincinnati, New York City opera entourages in early career; Metropolitan Opera Co. member 1950–56; Texas State University, Denton, professor of voice 1960–78; d. Dec. 18, 1981.

Georgia Ellis (Georgia Hawkins Ellis Puttfarken), March 12, 1917, California; actress (stage, radio, film, TV) bka *Gunsmoke* western drama saloon girl Kitty Russell CBS 1952–61; audio support roles in *The Adventures of Philip Marlowe, Baby Snooks, Crime Classics, Dr. Kildare, Dragnet, Escape, The Great Gildersleeve, The Green Lama, The Modern Adventures of Casanova, Rogers of the Gazette, This Is Your FBI, Yours Truly—Johnny Dollar*, more; *Ziegfeld Follies* girl 1931, three extra Broadway shows 1930–33; four mediocre films 1940–92 plus 1954's *Dragnet*, four *Dragnet* TV episodes 1955–59; d. March 30, 1988.

Mandel Kramer, March 12, 1916, Cleveland, Ohio; actor (film, radio, TV) bka *The Edge of Night* daytime serial character Bill Marceau CBS-TV 1959–79; veteran playing leads, recurring, solo roles in plethora 1940s-50s audio dramas, identifiable nasal-sounding brogue all over dial, nearly 30 ongoing series like *The Adventures of Dick Tracy, The Adventures of Ellery Queen, The Adventures of Superman, Backstage Wife, Call the Police, Casey—Crime Photographer, The Chase, David Harding—Counterspy, The Falcon, Gangbusters, The Light of the World, Mr. and Mrs. North, Perry Mason, The Shadow, Stella Dallas, Terry and the Pirates, True Detective Mysteries, X-Minus One, Yours Truly—Johnny Dollar*; d. Jan. 29, 1989.

Gordon MacRae, March 12, 1921, East Orange, N.J.; actor (stage, film, radio, TV), clarinetist, emcee, pianist, recording artist, saxophonist, vocalist bka *The Railroad Hour* host 1948–54; celluloid versions of *On Moonlight Bay* 1951, *By the Light of the Silvery Moon* 1953, *Oklahoma!* 1955, *Carousel* 1956; routinely subbed for TV showmen Perry Como, Jackie Gleason, Ed Sullivan when away from their gigs; guest on dozens of video venues, occasionally dramatic roles; d. Jan. 24, 1986.

Harlow Wilcox, March 12, 1900, Omaha, Neb.; actor (film, stage, radio, TV), announcer, salesman bka *Fibber McGee & Molly* domestic sitcom interlocutor-commercial spokesman NBC 1935–53 whose mid-show plugs were woven into storyline fabric making messenger akin to star's adversary who habitually groaned at Wilcox's arrival; premier announcer of radio, one of tiny handful everybody thinks of on West Coast in era; presented nearly three dozen web features but is recalled for a few: *Amos 'n' Andy* 1943–48, *The Amos 'n' Andy Music Hall* 1954-ca. 1960, *Suspense* 1948–54; *Truth or Consequences* 1946–54; acted in amateur theatricals, toured Chautauqua circuits; traveling salesman five years; joined Chicago WBBM 1930, New York CBS 1933, Chicago NBC 1934; few fleeting acting roles in Hollywood movies, TV; d. Sept. 24, 1960.

Deaths

Frank Hummert, March 12, 1966, New York City, N.Y.; b. June 2, 1884. Bidu Sayao, March 12, 1999, Rockport, Maine; b. May 11, 1902.

March 13

Sound Bite

Very first broadcast of *CBS World News Roundup* beamed around globe March 13, 1938 with Robert Trout occupying anchor chair, future web news guru Edward R. Murrow reporting as Vienna correspondent; series becomes "longest running news program in broadcasting history," cited for durability on 70th anniversary March 13, 2008 as voices of Trout, Murrow, Walter Cronkite, Dallas Townsend (who occupied anchor chair 25 years), Douglas Edwards, Reed Collins, Christopher Glenn, others heard, replayed for contemporary listeners in reflective walk down memory lane; CBS announcer adds, "And after 70 years, we're just getting warmed up!"; one of few traditions lingering from "those days."

Births

Sammy Kaye, March 13, 1910, Lakewood, Ohio; clarinetist, impresario; collegiate band gained notoriety early on MBS; beyond big band remotes, Kaye held baton for 27 web-based series 1937–56 — his name forming moniker of 20 of those; prominent features *So You Want to Lead a Band* ABC 1946–47, *Chesterfield Supper Club* NBC 1948; d. June 2, 1987.

Louis Bernard Roen, March 13, 1905, Ashland, Wis.; announcer, band promoter, railway telegrapher, station manager, street car operator, vocalist; joined Milwaukee WTMJ 1927 as announcer, soloist; CBS followed for four months before managing Marquette, Mich. WEBO, then Chicago NBC Blue initiating *The Breakfast Club* 1941, ushering in Irna Phillips soap operas *The Guiding Light, Today's Children, We Love and Learn*; d. Feb. 15, 1993.

Richard Wells, March 13, 1905; actor, announcer, engineer, hookup coordinator, producer, program manager; pioneer helping install Chicago KYW 1920, later engineered at Rock Island, Ill., Muscatine, Iowa stations before announcing at Davenport WOC; program manager at Mexican station XER; helped launch Iowa Broadcasting System; interlocutor at Chicago WBBM 1932, presented *Aunt Mary, Ma Perkins*, played in *Kitty Keene Inc., Painted Dreams, The Right to Happiness*, produced *Grandstand Thrills*; d. February 1968.

Deaths

Geoffrey Bryant, March 13, 1982, Springdale, Ark.; b. Oct. 11, 1900. Alex Dreier, March 13, 2000, Rancho Mirage, Calif.; b. June 26, 1916.

March 14

Birth

Les Brown, March 14, 1912, Reinerton, Pa.; impresario bka musical entourage conductor ("Les Brown and His Band of Renown") accompanying comic Bob Hope's broadcasts, films, personal appearances, recordings; numerous global tours with Hope to far-flung military bases; fronted orchestra over MBS 1935; d. Jan. 4, 2001.

Deaths

Frank Blair, March 14, 1995, Hilton Head Island, S.C.; b. May 30, 1915. Carlton KaDell, March 14, 1975, Chicago, Ill.; b. Aug. 21, 1907. Chic Young, March 14, 1973, St. Petersburg, Fla.; b. Jan. 9, 1901.

March 15

Canceled

Betty and Bob, March 15, 1940, NBC (though syndicated version persisted briefly in 1940 beyond network run); debut Oct. 10, 1932. *Hopalong Cassidy*, March 15, 1952, CBS; debut Jan. 1, 1950.

Births

MacDonald Carey, March 15, 1913, Sioux City, Iowa; actor (stage, radio, film, TV), author bka voice delivering epigram for *Days of Our Lives* daytime serial NBC-TV; launched, ended broadcast career as doc, initially as *Woman in White's* Dr. Lee Markham on radio, *Days of Our Lives'* Dr. Tom Horton in video; on Broadway in *Lady in the Dark*, *Shadow of a Doubt*; 1930s-50s radio credits for *The First Nighter*, *Jason and the Golden Fleece*, *John's Other Wife*, *Lights Out*, *Stella Dallas*, *Young Hickory*; earlier toured nation performing Shakespearean roles with Globe Players; in demand for "fresh-scrubbed masculinity" *New York Times* allowed; appeared in movies *Wake Island* 1942, *Suddenly It's Spring* 1946, *Dream Girl* 1948, *Streets of Laredo* 1949, *Bride of Vengeance* 1949, *The Great Missouri Raid* 1950, *Comanche Territory* 1950, more; penned autobiography *Days of My Life*; d. March 21, 1994.

John Frazer, March 15, 1915, Los Angeles, Calif.; announcer; left law school to join Hollywood KEHE 1937; introduced 1930s-40s features *The Bob Hope Show*, *The Chase & Sanborn Hour*, *The Fitch Bandwagon*, *Life Can Be Beautiful*, *The Raleigh and Kool Program with Tommy Dorsey*, *The Signal Carnival*; U. S. Navy in Pacific theater in World War II where he was killed leaving wife, infant daughter, promising broadcasting career; d. May 11, 1945.

Ernie Hare, March 15, 1883, Norfolk, Va.; recording artist, vocalist (bass-baritone) bka singer with Billy Jones as *The Happiness Boys* performing projected 10,000 tunes on 2,000-plus broadcasts; premiered Oct. 18, 1921, Newark WJZ; initially trio (with Larry Briers), when Briers departed 1926 Jones, Hare dubbed selves Happiness Boys after sponsor Happiness Candy Stores signing five-year pact; other underwriters followed, duo altering handle to fit (sox, bug spray, bread, mayonnaise, razors); upon Hare's demise, his daughter sang with Jones a year, Jones persisted solo eight months to his death March 9, 1939.

Billy Jones, March 15, 1887, New York City, N.Y.; recording artist, vocalist (tenor) bka singer with Billy Jones as *The Happiness Boys* performing projected 10,000 tunes on 2,000-plus broadcasts; premiered Oct. 18, 1921, Newark WJZ; initially trio (with Larry Briers), when Briers departed 1926 Jones, Hare named selves Happiness Boys after sponsor Happiness Candy Stores signing five-year pact; as other underwriters followed duo altered handle to fit (sox, bug spray, bread, mayonnaise, razors); upon Hare's demise his daughter sang with Jones one year, Jones persisting solo to his death eight months later; d. Nov. 23, 1940.

David F. Schoenbrun, March 15, 1915, New York City, N.Y.; commentator, correspondent; admired CBS news legend Edward R. Murrow, reveled in his presence, yet never fit parameters of famed "Murrow Boys"—hired in 1947 to report from European outposts, member of "B team" filling "Boys" overseas spots after they went home; served CBS for years at Paris, shifted to Washington 1961 as bureau chief but egoism got in way; CBS shipped him back to Europe in March 1963 as continental news chief yet he quit in three months, leaving chain he professed undying adulation for to be ABC correspondent; d. May 23, 1988.

Deaths

Durward Kirby, March 15, 2000, Fort Myers, Fla.; b. Aug. 24, 1911. Larry Thor, March 15, 1976, Santa Monica, Calif.; b. Aug. 27, 1916.

March 16

Births

Arthur Hale (Arthur W. Glunt), March 16, 1896, Altoona, Pa.; announcer, commentator, newscaster bka late 1930s-late 1940s MBS newsman on multiplicity series: *Calling America*, *Confidentially Yours*, *Your Richfield Reporter*; introduced *Uncle Don* 1930s-40s; left Bridgeport, Conn. WICC 1930 to join New York WOR as announcer, newscaster; d. Oct. 17, 1971.

Betty Johnson, March 16, 1931, Guilford County, N.C.; author, recording artist, vocalist debuting with clan *The Johnson Family Singers* on Charlotte WBT 1940s-50s beamed by CBS; *Arthur Godfrey's Talent Scouts* winner, signed record contract, regular act on Don McNeill's *Breakfast Club*, *The Jack Paar Show*.

Mercedes McCambridge (Charlotte Mercedes Agnes McCambridge), March 16, 1916, Joliet, Ill.; actress (stage, film, radio, TV), author; character actress on radio before strong-willed movie thespian on, off screen; created memorable roles in *I Love a Mystery* while regular in 1930s-40s *Abie's Irish Rose*, *Big Sister*, *Ford Theater*, *The Guiding Light*, *Inner Sanctum Mysteries*, *Murder at Midnight*, *One Man's Family*, *Studio One*, many more plus 1970s *The CBS Radio Mystery Theater*; actor-director Orson Welles dubbed her "the world's greatest radio actress"; among film credits: *All the King's Men* 1949, *Johnny Guitar* 1954, *Giant* 1956, *Suddenly Last Summer* 1959, *The Exorcist* 1973; suffered recurring alcoholism bouts; d. March 2, 2004.

Conrad Nagel, March 16, 1897, Keokuk, Iowa; actor (stage, film, radio, TV), announcer, director, disc jockey, emcee; toured with stock company, acted on Broadway in *The Natural Law*, *Forever After*; performed in 112 B-movies 1918–60, elected president Academy of Motion Picture Arts and Sciences 1933; TV series included *The Conrad Nagel Theater*, dramatic anthology he hosted on Dumont 1955; appeared in 1930s-50s radio plays on *Lux Radio Theater*, *Proudly We Hail*, *Screen Guild Players*, *Treasury Star Parade* while directing *First Love*, *Silver Theater*, introducing *Alec Templeton Time*, hosting *The Passing Parade*, spinning wax on *The Conrad Nagel Show*; d. Feb. 24, 1970.

Deaths

Arthur Godfrey, March 16, 1983, New York City, N.Y.; b. Aug. 31, 1903. Minerva Pious, March 16, 1979, New York City, N.Y.; b. March 5, 1903.

March 17

Debuting

The Kate Smith Show (*Kate Smith Sings*, *Kate Smith and Her Swanee Music*, *Kate Smith's Matinee Hour*, *Kate Smith's New Star Revue*, *Kate Smith's Hour*, *Kate Smith's Coffee Time*, *Kate Smith's A&P Bandwagon*, *The Kate Smith Hour*, *Kate Smith's Column*, *Kate Smith Speaking Her Mind*, *Kate Smith Speaks*, *Kate Smith's Serenade*, *Kate Smith Calling*), March 17, 1931, NBC (initially sang on *Freddy Rich's Rhythm Kings* CBS unnamed dates 1930–31); "The Songbird of the South" came as near universal adulation by adoring American public as any of her epoch for patriotism backed by commanding singing voice; her show was on dial or channel almost incessantly so she never was out of range or vogue; first to perform Irving Berlin's "God Bless America" on air (Nov. 10, 1938), fulfilled calls to repeat it regularly; FDR presented her to British king, queen in 1939 as "This is Kate Smith! *This is America*!"; final radiocast Jan. 2, 1959.

Birth

Karl A. Weber, March 17, 1916, Columbus Junction, Iowa; actor (radio, stage, TV), announcer; intended to be stage actor (got to Broadway later) but distracted by radio, narrated *Cloak and Dagger*, played in 1930s-50s *Arnold Grimm's Daughter*, *Best Plays*, *Dimension X*, *Don Winslow of the Navy*, *Dr. Sixgun*, *The Greatest Story Ever Told*, *Helpmate*, *Lonely Women*, *Lorenzo Jones*, *Mr. Keen—Tracer of Lost Persons*, *The Red Skelton Show*, *The Romance of Helen Trent*, *The Second Mrs. Burton*, *The Strange Romance of Evelyn Winters*, *When a Girl Marries*, more; running roles in TV daytime serials *Search for Tomorrow* CBS 1955–56, *Kitty Foyle* NBC 1958; d. July 30, 1990.

Deaths

Fred Allen, March 17, 1956, New York City, N.Y.; b. May 31, 1894. George Hicks, March 17, 1965, Jackson Heights, Queens, N.Y.; b. Aug. 26, 1905. Charles Peter O'Connor, March 17, 1942, Douglastown, N.Y.; b. June 10, 1910.

March 18

Debuting

The Light of the World, March 18, 1940, NBC; daytime serial; based on narratives in Old Testament, "The Speaker" (Bret Morrison, David Gothard, Arnold Moss) recounted dramatizations with actors playing roles of biblical characters; series built strong following, attracted single sponsor (General Mills) for decade on ether; final broadcast June 2, 1950.

Births

Jody Gilbert (Josephine Gilbert Swartzburg), March 18, 1916, Fort Worth, Texas; actress (stage, film, radio, TV), vocalist bka *Life with Luigi* belly-laughing fat girl Rosa, progeny of immigrant Luigi Basco's pal Pasquale, incessantly trying to marry his daughter to Luigi 1948–54; d. Feb. 3, 1979.

Art Gilmore, March 18, 1912, Tacoma, Wash.; actor, announcer (radio, TV), author, journalist, teacher bka *The Red Skelton Show* interlocutor 1951–71; prolific radio narrator: most durable *Dr. Christian* ca. 1937–38, 1942–54, *Stars Over Hollywood* mid 1940s-1954, flanked by shorter service on 1940s *The Adventures of Frank Race, Amos 'n' Andy, Meet Me at Parky's, Miss Pinkerton Inc., Murder and Mr. Malone, Red Ryder*, many more; *Lux Radio Theater* thespian 1940s-50s; beckoned viewers to 1950s *Captain Midnight, The George Gobel Show, Climax!, Highway Patrol, The Woody Woodpecker Show, The Fred Astair Theater*; narrated 77 movies, shorts 1942–64 while playing in copious TV comedies, dramas; co-author 1946 volume *Television and Radio Announcing*.

Rex S. Koury, March 18, 1911, London, England; composer, impresario, organist, pianist bka *Gunsmoke* signature theme song writer ("The Old Trail" 1952), also penned *The Fugitive, The Amazing Mr. Malone* music; at 14 house organist for silent films at New York's Roxy Theater; staff organist at NBC Hollywood, wrote freelance compositions for CBS Radio, music director at ABC Hollywood; *Fibber McGee & Molly* pianist 1930s; composed church music after 1980 retirement; American Theatre Organ Society president 1983–85; shortly before death regularly played one of Wyoming's largest pipe organs at Casper's First Presbyterian Church; d. May 29, 2006.

Deaths

Jimmy Blaine, March 18, 1967, Wilton, Conn.; b. Dec. 26, 1924. Jessica Dragonette, March 18, 1980, New York City, N.Y.; b. Feb. 14, 1900. Jack McCoy, March 18, 1991 (numerous attempts to establish locality unproductive); b. Nov. 10, 1918. Ed Prentiss, March 18, 1992, Los Angeles, Calif.; b. Sept. 9, 1909.

March 19

Canceled

Seth Parker, March 19, 1939, NBC Blue; debut March 3, 1929. *Space Patrol*, March 19, 1955, ABC; debut Sept. 18, 1950.

Birth

Gayne Whitman (Alfred Vosburgh, alias Alfred Whitman), March 19, 1890, Chicago, Ill.; actor, announcer, emcee; hosted 1930s-40s *Eyes Aloft, Strange as it Seems*, acted in *Chandu the Magician*, introduced *The Arkansas Traveler, The Bell Telephone Hour, Cavalcade of America, The Greatest of These, Lassie, Pacific Story, Paducah Plantation*; d. Aug. 31, 1958.

Death

Diana Bourbon, March 19, 1978; b. Aug. 28, 1900.

March 20

Canceled

A Day in the Life of Dennis Day (*The Dennis Day Show*), March 20, 1955, NBC; debut Oct. 3, 1946. *John's Other Wife*, March 20, 1942, NBC Blue; debut Sept. 14, 1936.

Births

Jack Barry (Jack Barassch), March 20, 1918, Lindenhurst, Long Island, N.Y.; actor, announcer, emcee bka TV game show master of ceremonies-executive; warm-up acts for a surfeit of video games were radio giveaways like *Daily Dilemmas* 1946–48, *Juvenile Jury* 1946–51, 1952–53, *Stars and Starters* 1950; investment payoff included shows he produced or hosted: *The Big Surprise, Blank Check, Break the $250,000 Bank, Classic Concentration, The Generation Gap, High Low Quiz, The Joker's Wild, Juvenile Jury, Play the Percentages, The Reel Game, Tic Tac Dough, Twenty-One, Way Out Games*, more; d. May 2, 1984.

Ray Goulding, March 20, 1922, Lowell, Mass.; comedian (radio, stage, TV), recording and voiceover artist bka *Bob and Ray* comedy figure teamed in late 1940s with Bob Elliott on Boston WHDH where both staffed (*Matinee with Bob and Ray* weekdays) before joining New York NBC; aired on MBS/CBS/PBS 1951–84 plus local New York show, NBC-TV 1951–53; parlayed act into nightclubs, recordings, commercials; d. March 24, 1990.

Jack J. Kruschen, March 20, 1922, Winnipeg, Manitoba, Canada; actor (radio, TV, film, stage) bka ethnic comedy relief, frequently volatile, emotional Italian, Jewish neighbor patriarch, rare occasions villain; radio dramas while in high school, TV dramas on L.A. Don Lee test outlet 1939 seen by 200 three-inch-screen owners; net work: *The Adventures of Philip Marlowe, Broadway Is My Beat, Deadline Mystery, Escape, Frontier Gentleman, Gunsmoke, Lux Radio Theater, One Man's Family, Pete Kelly's Blues, Richard Diamond—Private Detective, Suspense, Tales of the Texas Rangers*, more; 153 solo episodes of TV dramas/sitcoms/variety shows 1953–94, two TV series—*Busting Loose* 1977, *Webster* 1985–87, 15 made-for-TV flicks 1968–94, 73 cinema films 1949–97, Broadway production *I Can Get It for You Wholesale* 1962; d. April 2, 2002.

Stuart Blim Metz, March 20, 1908, Buffalo, N.Y.; announcer, engineer, producer; first job in industry as engineer at Buffalo Broadcasting Corp., transferring in 18 months to programming arm of same outfit, rising to assistant program director-chief announcer; seven years hence hired as staff announcer by New York NBC; opened late 1940s-early 1960s episodes of *The Frankie Laine Show, Grand Central Station, The Light of the World, Mr. Keen—Tracer of Lost Persons, Pepper Young's Family, Suspense, You Are There*; d. Jan. 5, 1994.

Oswald George (Ozzie) Nelson, March 20, 1906, Jersey City, N.J.; actor (stage, film, radio, TV), entrepreneur, impresario, recording artist, saxophonist bka *The Adventures of Ozzie and Harriet* creator, on radio 1944–54, TV 1952–66 playing patriarch in series purportedly personifying family's actual existence—although not really doing so; branded "preeminent sitcom dad of the 50s"; fronted highly popular band in previous career incarnation; d. June 3, 1975.

Lawson Zerbe, March 20, 1914, Oregon; actor, announcer bka *Pepper Young's Family* daytime serial protagonist 1937–45 NBC, *The Adventures of Frank Merriwell* juvenile hero 1946–49 NBC; unlike some peers, Zerbe focused heavily on dozens of daytime radio serials, mysteries, adventures: *Against the Storm, Bandwagon Mysteries, Big Town, Crime and Peter Chambers, David Harding—Counterspy, Dick Tracy, Gangbusters, Murder by Experts, Lora Lawton, Mr. Keen—Tracer of Lost Persons, The Mysterious Traveler, The Mystery Man, The O'Neills, The Road of Life, Roger Kilgore—Public Defender, Treasury Agent, Valiant Lady, Yours Truly—Johnny Dollar*, etc.; entered radio at Cincinnati WLW 1934; d. Aug. 18, 1992.

Deaths

Archie Bleyer, March 20, 1989, Sheboygan, Wis.; b. June 12, 1909. Ted Brown, March 20, 2005, Martin, Fla.; b. May 5, 1921. Don Goddard, March 20, 1944, Sun City, Ariz.; b. July 5, 1904. Chet Huntley, March 20, 1974, Big Sky, Mont.; b. Dec. 10, 1911. J. Anthony Smythe, March 20, 1966, Los Angeles, Calif.; b. Dec. 18, 1885.

March 21

Debuting

Stop the Music!, March 21, 1948, ABC; audience participation quiz, hosts Bert Parks, Bill Cullen, Happy Felton; premise involved telephoning average citizens ostensibly at random (though, in practice, prearranged) asking on air: "Can you tell me the name of the song just played (or sung)?"—huge segment of excited interviewees replied with *previous* melody; show gained such large following, effectively ended NBC comic Fred Allen's enduring career at that hour; final broadcast Feb. 15, 1955 (silent Aug. 10, 1952-Aug. 17, 1954); ABC-TV, emcee Bert Parks, May 5, 1949-April 24, 1952, Sept. 7, 1954-June 14, 1956.

Birth

Vincent J. Pelletier (sometimes Peletier), March 21, 1908, Minneapolis, Minn.; actor, announcer, pianist, station manager, vocalist bka longstanding commercial spokesman for Carnation Co., General Mills, Inc.; debuted on air as amateur soloist at 15 (1923); announced at local station in collegiate years at University of Minnesota, performed as baritone vocalist, piano accompanist with quartet; shifted to rival Minneapolis station as manager; joined Chicago NBC announcing staff 1937; acted in *The Railroad Hour* 1949–54, ushered in *Aunt Mary, The Carnation Contented Hour, Father Knows Best, Grand Hotel, Hymns of All Churches, Masquerade, Today's Children, Vic and Sade*, more while doing same for *The Nat King Cole Show* NBC-TV 1956–57; d. Feb. 25, 1994.

Deaths

MacDonald Carey, March 21, 1994, Beverly Hills, Calif.; b. March 15, 1913. Marlin Hurt, March 21, 1946, Hollywood, Calif.; b. May 27, 1904. Ward Wilson, d. March 21, 1966, West Palm Beach, Fla.; b. May 22, 1903.

March 22

Birth

Donald M. Dowd, March 22, 1905, Philadelphia, Pa.; announcer, host bka *The Breakfast Club* interlocutor-comic foil to emcee Don McNeill ABC 1943–55 (TV simulcast 1954–55); ABC employee 27 years including 1943–56 in Chicago, 1956–70 in New York; earlier radio gigs at Mansfield, Ohio, Philadelphia WLIT, Cincinnati WLW hosting *Moon River* at WLW; joined Chicago NBC to introduce soap operas, other dramas from Windy City 1934; d. Feb. 21, 1977.

Deaths

Ed Fitzgerald, March 22, 1982, New York City, N.Y.; b. Feb. 8, 1893. Harry Sosnik, March 22, 1996, Bronx, N.Y.; b. July 13, 1906. Charles Stark, March 22, 1992 (copious efforts to confirm location futile); b. Sept. 11, 1912. John Wald, March 22, 1988, Los Angeles, Calif.; b. Sept. 6, 1908.

March 23

Debuting

Truth or Consequences, March 23, 1940, NBC; audience participation stunt series, masters of ceremonies Ralph Edwards, Jack Bailey; evolved from vintage parlor game proffering outrageously funny scenarios involving innocent studio participants designed to entice listeners at home to stay by their radios or TVs for next shoe to drop; final broadcast Sept. 12, 1956; NBC televersion May 18, 1954-Sept. 24, 1965, syndicated extensions 1966–75, 1977–78, 1987–88.

Canceled

The Big Story, March 23, 1955, NBC; debut April 2, 1947.

Births

Richard L. Evans, March 23, 1906, Salt Lake City, Utah; announcer, commentator, director, producer bka "the spoken word" homily writer-speaker for *Music and the Spoken Word from the Crossroads of the West* 1930–71; Church of Jesus Christ of Latter Day Saints general officer much of adult life; d. Nov. 1, 1971.

Paula Winslowe (Winifred Reyleck), March 23, 1910, Grafton, N.D.; actress (film, radio, TV), voiceover artist bka *The Life of Riley* matriarch Peg Riley (1944–51); radio audiences heard her on *Arch Oboler's Plays, Broadway Is My Beat, Cavalcade of America, The CBS Radio Workshop, Crime Classics, Escape, The George Burns and Gracie Allen Show, Gunsmoke, The Halls of Ivy, The Lady Esther Screen Guild Theater, Lux Radio Theater, Romance, Silver Theater, Suspense,* more; in video was *Our Miss Brooks* principal's spouse Martha Conklin 1953–58, solo episodes of *The Adventures of Ozzie and Harriet, Climax!, I Love Lucy, The Gale Storm Show, You Are There, Rawhide, Michael Shayne, The Life and Legend of Wyatt Earp, Perry Mason,* others plus speaking parts in *The Flintstones* animated cartoons ABC-TV 1960s; d. March 7, 1996.

Deaths

Peggy Allenby, March 23, 1966, New York City, N.Y.; Feb. 14, 1901. Eileen Farrell, March 23, 2002, Bergen, N.J.; b. Feb. 13, 1920.

March 24

Debuting

Let's Pretend, March 24, 1934, CBS; juvenile fantasy drama; superlative writing, directing, acting, music, din blended to deliver children's fairy tales, other fiction as some of most compelling narratives on ether; creator Nila Mack penned tales, guided cast of juvenile thespians bringing figures to life from pages of favorite tomes of small fry fans; pretenders — some migrating to other audio venues — were Albert Aley, Arthur Anderson, Jack Ayers, Donald Buka, Charita Bauer, Michael Dreyfuss, Gwen Davies, Michael Grimes, Florence Halop, Jackie Kelk, Joan Lazer, Bill Lipton, Jimmy Lydon, Bobby Readick, Walter Tetley, Sybil

Trent, Dick Van Patten, Miriam Wolfe, more; "Uncle" Bill Adams welcomed fans, shilled for sponsor Cream of Wheat; final broadcast Oct. 23, 1954.

Major Bowes' Original Amateur Hour, March 24, 1935, NBC; talent auditions that allowed almost anybody chance to perform onstage on air; grew from *Capitol Family* Bowes launched July 26, 1925 at New York outlet 16 months before NBC operated; final broadcast Jan. 4, 1945, succeeded by *Major Bowes' Shower of Stars* Feb. 8-Aug. 30, 1945 while host lay too ill to continue.

Births

William C. Bivens, March 14, 1915, Wadesboro, N.C.; announcer, publicist bka *The Fred Waring Show* interlocutor 1942–49; introduced *The Harry James Show*, *Vox Pop* both 1943–44 season; early stints in sundry North, South Carolina radio markets led to settling in Charlotte, finishing broadcasting career at WBT-FM; after 1968 retirement became inaugural news director at Central Piedmont Community College, institute he helped establish; d. Jan. 15, 1984.

Julian Funt, March 24, 1906, Brooklyn, N.Y.; scriptwriter bka one of fertile pens of daytime serials in dual media; specialized in medical dramas, 1940s-50s output embraced protracted turns with radio's *Big Sister*, *This Is Nora Drake*, *Young Doctor Malone*—all with medico protagonists, briefer stints on 1950s-60s *Search for Tomorrow*, *Young Doctor Malone* (new plot, cast), *The Guiding Light* teledramas; supplied myriad aural fare for *Big Town*, *Columbia Presents Corwin*, *The Columbia Workshop*, *Hedda Hopper's Hollywood*, *The Henry Morgan Show*, *The Kraft Music Hall*; d. April 8, 1980.

Deaths

Franklin Pearce Adams, March 24, 1960, New York City, N.Y.; b. Nov. 15, 1881. Nelson Case, March 24, 1976, Doylestown, Pa.; b. Feb. 3, 1910. Holland Engle, March 24, 1988, Oakland, Calif.; b. April 26, 1907. Igor Gorin, March 24, 1982, Tucson, Ariz.; b. Oct. 26, 1908. Ray Goulding, March 24, 1990, Manhasset, N.Y.; b. March 20, 1922. Howard Petrie, March 24, 1968, Keene, N.H.; b. Nov. 22, 1906. Richard Widmark, March 24, 2008, Roxbury, Conn.; b. Dec. 26, 1914.

March 25

Debuting

What's My Name?, March 25, 1938, MBS; quiz; hosts Arlene Francis, Budd Hulick (he was replaced by John Reed King, Ward Wilson, Carl Frank) impersonated prominent figures, pitched clues to contestants attempting to learn who those subjects were for small cash prizes; final broadcast July 30, 1949.

Canceled

Break the Bank, March 25, 1955, MBS; debut Oct. 20, 1945. *Pursuit*, March 25, 1952, CBS; debut Oct. 27, 1949.

Births

Edward (Ed) James Begley, March 25, 1901, Hartford, Conn.; actor (radio, stage, film, TV); on radio in teens, then Broadway; most propitious audio role at 48 as agitated homicide Lt. Walt Levinson assisting Dick Powell as *Richard Diamond—Private Detective* NBC/ABC 1949–53; beyond soap operas *Big Sister*, *Life Can Be Beautiful*, *Stella Dallas*, busied self crimefighting most nights in *The Adventures of Charlie Chan* (lead), *The Adventures of Philip Marlowe*, *Casey—Crime Photographer*, *Crime Does Not Pay*, *The Fat Man*, *Let George Do It*, *The Lineup*, *Official Detective* (lead), *The Saint*, *Special Investigator*, *Tales of Fatima*, *Tales of the Texas Rangers*, *Yours Truly—Johnny Dollar*; 42 theatrical films including *It Happens Every Spring* 1949, *Stars in My Crown* 1950, *Twelve Angry Men* 1957, *The Unsinkable Molly Brown* 1964; three TV series 1949–52, five made-for-TV flicks 1953–69, 99 solo parts multi TV series; d. April 28, 1970.

Harold L. (Hal) Neal, Jr., March 25, 1924, Macon, Ga.; announcer, station-network executive bka teenage narrator 1940s of *The Challenge of the Yukon*, *The Green Hornet*, *The Lone Ranger*; joined ABC at Detroit WXYZ 1943, general manager WXYZ 1956 guiding it to Top 40 music format 1958; general manager New York WABC 1960; president ABC-owned radio stations 1963–72; president ABC Radio 1972–80; d. Feb. 27, 1980.

Arturo Toscanini, March 25, 1867, Parma, Italy; impresario, bka maestro of Metropolitan Opera 1908–15, New York Philharmonic Symphony 1928–36, *The NBC Symphony Orchestra*

1937–54 — latter entourage created especially for him; consummate conductor demanding unswerving allegiance at all times, while considered temperamental taskmaster, his music sublime; d. Jan. 16, 1957.

Death

Goodman Ace, March 25, 1982, Manhattan, New York City, N.Y.; b. Jan. 16, 1899.

March 26

Debuting

The Adventures of Frank Merriwell, March 26, 1934, NBC; juvenile mystery-adventure in two distinct runs focused on Yale athlete superstar Merriwell (Donald Briggs in first incarnation, Lawson Zerbe in second), several recurring support players; "one of the most beloved heroes in American fiction" stuck his nose into dark corners trying to help downtrodden, endangered souls; original series ended in three months, resumed 12 years beyond; final broadcast June 4, 1949.

The Woman in My House, March 26, 1951, NBC; daytime serial; some saw this as *One Man's Family*/East for much of its plot adapted from recycled scripts bearing pickles Barbour clan of San Francicso got into, focused on Miami's Carter tribe; dual dramas linked by creator-writer-director-producer Carlton E. Morse who gave Carters five offspring (not unlike Morse's centerpiece narrative) — there was patriarch James (Forrest Lewis), spouse Jessie (Janet Scott), kids Jeff (Les Tremayne), Virginia (Alice Reinheart), Clay (Bill Idelson), Sandy (Peggy Webber, Anne Whitfield), Peter (Jeff Silver); James disapproved of freedoms afforded modern youth while Jessie often took progeny's side — if you knew background of *One Man's Family,* it surely seemed déjà vu; final broadcast April 24, 1959.

Canceled

Front Page Farrell, March 26, 1954, NBC; debut June 23, 1941. *Pot o' Gold,* March 26, 1947, ABC; debut Sept. 26, 1939.

Births

Bob Elliott (Robert Brackett Elliott), March 26, 1923, Boston, Mass.; comedian (radio, stage, TV), recording and voiceover artist bka *Bob and Ray* comedy figure teamed in late 1940s with Ray Goulding on Boston WHDH where both staffed (*Matinee with Bob and Ray* weekdays) before joining New York NBC; eventually aired on MBS/CBS/PBS 1951–84 plus local New York show, NBC-TV 1951–53; parlayed act into nightclubs, recordings, commercials.

Henry (Hank) Sylvern, March 26, 1908, Brooklyn, N.Y.; composer, conductor, organist; d. July 4, 1964.

March 27

Canceled

The Great Gildersleeve, March 27, 1958, NBC; debut Aug. 31, 1941. *The Hallmark Hall of Fame,* March 27, 1955, CBS; debut (as *Hallmark Playhouse*) June 10, 1948. *Myrt and Marge,* March 27, 1942, CBS (syndicated run produced 1946); debut Nov. 2, 1931. *Twenty Questions,* March 27, 1954, MBS; debut Feb. 2, 1946.

Births

Hugh Conover, March 27, 1915, Washington, D.C.; announcer, newscaster bka narrator for handful of 1940s-50s daytime dramas e.g. *Amanda of Honeymoon Hill, Big Sister, The Right to Happiness*; left Columbia, S.C. WIS 1935 for Washington WJSV — reported news there 1939–41; d. Sept. 27, 1992.

Richard Denning (Louis Albert Heindrich Denninger), March 27, 1914, Poughkeepsie, N.Y.; actor (stage, film, radio, TV), executive officer (Boy Scouts of America) bka *My Favorite Husband* masculine spouse George Cooper opposite wacko wife Liz (Lucille Ball) in *I Love Lucy* warm-up 1948–51, *Hawaii 5-O* recurring figure Gov. Philip Grey CBS-TV 1968–80; Paramount Studios demanded he alter birth surname Denninger as it paralleled too closely Chicago gangster John Dillinger's moniker; performed in 91 mostly B theatrical films, 48 produced in five-year span 1937–42; *Mr. and Mrs. North* publisher Jerry North, amateur sleuth TV series 1952–53, 1954, final radio season 1954–55; solo outings on TV's *Cavalcade of America, Cheyenne, Ford Television Theater, General Electric Theater, Lux Video Theater, McCloud, Schlitz Playhouse of Stars, Studio One,* more; d. Oct. 11, 1998.

Fred Foy, March 27, 1921, Detroit, Mich.; announcer bka *The Lone Ranger* interlocutor 1948–56 ("No where in the pages of history can one find a greater champion of justice! Return with us now to those thrilling days of yesteryear! From out of the paths come the thundering hoofbeats of the great horse Silver! The Lone Ranger rides again!"); heard in similar capacity on *The Challenge of the Yukon* 1954–55, *The Green Hornet* 1952, *Theater Five* 1964–65; topped illustrious career introducing *The Generation Gap* ABC-TV 1969, *The Dick Cavett Show* ABC-TV 1969–72, retiring from that web 1985.

Deaths

Milton Berle, March 27, 2002, Los Angeles, Calif.; b. July 12, 1908. Don Gardiner, March 27, 1977, Quoque, Long Island, N.Y.; b. Jan. 10, 1916.

March 28

Canceled

Buck Rogers in the 25th Century, March 28, 1947, MBS; debut Nov. 7, 1932. *Bulldog Drummond*, March 28, 1954, MBS; debut April 13, 1941.

Births

Frank Lovejoy, March 28, 1912, Bronx, N.Y.; actor (stage, radio, film, TV) bka parts in dark movies, *Meet McGraw* crime drama gumshoe NBC-TV 1957–58; when 1929 stock market crash took teen livelihood on Wall Street, turned to acting, touring Northeast prior to Broadway premier 1934; on radio at Cincinnati WLW 1934–35 before *Arch Oboler's Plays, The Blue Beetle, The Damon Runyon Theater, Gangbusters, Manhattan at Midnight, Mr. and Mrs. North, Mr. District Attorney, Murder and Mr. Malone, Nightbeat, We Love and Learn*; 30 theatrical films 1948–58, 45 solo TV roles 1953–62; acclaimed for final Broadway performance in Gore Vidal's *The Best Man* 1960; d. Oct. 2, 1962.

Paul Whiteman, March 28, 1890, Denver, Colo.; impresario bka big band conductor closely identified with network radio although effectively embracing TV late 1940s-mid 1950s; provided accompaniment for 21 aural web-based features 1929–54; one of confirmed deans of epoch; d. Dec. 29, 1967.

Deaths

Dick Haymes, March 28, 1980, Los Angeles, Calif.; b. Sept. 13, 1916. Wendell Niles, March 28, 1994, Toluca Lake, Calif.; b. Dec. 29, 1904.

March 29

Debuting

Our Gal Sunday, March 29, 1937, CBS; daytime serial; epigraph spelled plot: *Once again, we present Our Gal Sunday, the story of an orphan girl named Sunday from the little mining town of Silver Creek, Colorado, who in young womanhood married England's richest, most handsome lord, Lord Henry Brinthrope. The story that asks the question: Can this girl from the little mining town in the West find happiness as the wife of a wealthy and titled Englishman?*; Sunday (Dorothy Lowell, Vivian Smolen) unpretentious, kind, resolute while her beloved Henry (Karl Swenson, Alistair Duncan) was sharp, prosperous, devoted to her, object of bevy of vixens up to no good; at times pair stumbled into darker issues like murder; longest-running soap opera to occupy solo quarter-hour slot (12:45 ET) on one net (CBS); final broadcast Jan. 2, 1959.

Births

E. Power Biggs, March 29, 1906, Westcliff, Essex, England; educator, recording artist, organist bka popularizing pipe organ via weekly CBS concerts 1942–58; d. March 10, 1977.

Clifford Goldsmith, March 29, 1899, East Aurora, N.Y.; actor, playwright, publicist (National Dairy Council), scriptwriter (film, radio, TV) bka *The Aldrich Family* sitcom creator 1939–53, derived from domestic stage play *What a Life!* he penned in mid 1930s; d. July 11, 1971.

Death

Ray Bloch, March 29, 1982, Miami, Fla.; b. Aug. 3, 1902.

March 30

Debuting

Kay Kyser's Kollege of Musical Knowledge,

March 30, 1938, NBC (premiered on Chicago's WGN Feb. 1, 1938); audience participation show hosted by orchestra leader Kay Kyser ("The Old Perfesser"); maestro interviewed studio guests, asked name of tune just rendered for $10 prize; Harry Babbitt, Georgia Carroll, Sully Mason, Ginny Simms supplied vocals with zany antics of Ish Kabibble (Merwyn Bogue) between instrumentals; final broadcast July 29, 1949.

Canceled

Dreft Star Playhouse, March 30, 1945, NBC; debut June 28, 1943. *The Metropolitan Opera Auditions of the Air*, March 30, 1958, ABC; debut Dec. 22, 1935.

Births

Don Hollenbeck, March 30, 1905, Lincoln, Neb.; announcer, analyst, journalist, newscaster bka driven to suicide after hounding by Sen. Joseph McCarthy (R-Wis.) partisans that pursued Communist sympathizers whom Hollenbeck put down on-air for witch hunt resulting in jeopardized reputations, lives of public figures; left U. S. Office of War Information in London 1943 to join NBC London office, then WJZ 1945, ABC flagship outlet (formerly NBC Blue) as newscaster; fired for on-air comments 1946, added at CBS and given news slot ultimately running into McCarthy, terminated again; earlier introduced *Candid Microphone*, moderated *CBS Views the Press*, *We Take Your Word*, reported for *You Are There*, *Hear It Now*; anchored *The Saturday News Special* CBS-TV summer 1950; d. June 22, 1954.

Frankie Laine (Francesco Paolo LoVecchio), March 30, 1913, Chicago, Ill.; actor, author, personal appearance/recording artist, vocalist bka selling 100 million-plus hit records like "That's My Desire," "Mule Train," "Ghost Riders in the Sky," "Jezebel"; sang in clubs, on stages around Windy City in his mid teens, cabarets 15 years; marathon dancer, in one 1932 Atlantic City contest dancing 145 days (3501 hours); hired as $5-weekly soloist by New York WINS; relocated in Hollywood, sang in clubs, recorded "That's My Desire" 1946 which hit charts, fan clubs sprang up in many countries; handful of 1950s film musicals; radio career brief except records spun by DJs millions of times—*The Frankie Laine Show* CBS 1951 lasted three weeks but popular guest on NBC variety series *The Chesterfield Supper Club*, *The Big Show*; impresario Mitch Miller steered him to Columbia label, western-flavored tunes; movie, TV show soundtracks like *Man Without a Star* 1955, *Gunfight at the O.K. Corral* 1957, *3:10 to Yuma* 1957, *Blazing Saddles* 1974; autobiography *That Lucky Old Son* 1993; d. Feb. 6, 2007.

Deaths

Georgia Ellis, March 30, 1988, Los Angeles, Calif.; b. March 12, 1917. Art Hannes, March 30, 1992, Los Angeles, Calif.; b. July 28, 1920. Gabriel Heatter, March 30, 1972, Miami, Fla.; b. Sept. 17, 1890. Hal Peary, March 30, 1985, Torrance, Calif.; b. July 25, 1908. Florence Williams, March 30, 1995, Rockport, Maine; b. Oct. 17, 1910.

March 31

Debuting

The Story of Bess Johnson, March 31, 1941, CBS/NBC; daytime serial; only soap known named for living person, its origins deeply rooted in *Hilltop House* 1937–41 in which actress Bess Johnson ran orphanage; here she ran boarding school; premiered on dual chains same day, yet this dishpan drama persisted on only one web after 13 weeks; final broadcast Sept. 25, 1942.

Canceled

(*The*) *Cavalcade of America*, March 31, 1953, NBC; debut Oct. 9, 1935. *My Favorite Husband*, March 31, 1951, CBS; debut July 23, 1948.

Births

Lester (Les) Damon, March 31, 1908, Providence, R.I.; actor (stage, radio, TV) bka *The Adventures of the Thin Man* mystery hero Nick Charles NBC/CBS 1941–43, 1946–47, *The Falcon* mystery hero NBC/MBS 1951-ca. 1954, *The Guiding Light* daytime serial physician Bruce Banning CBS-TV 1956–60; mediocre parts in 1930s, 1950s Broadway shows; stints in two video serials—*As the World Turns* CBS 1956–57, *Kitty Foyle* NBC 1958; support roles in daytime radio serials *Portia Faces Life*, *The Right to Happiness*, *This Is Nora Drake*, *Young Doctor Malone*, frequently returning to mics at night as leading man on likes of *The Abbott Mysteries*, *The Adventures of Christopher Wells*, *The Lineup*, *Mystery Theater*, *Twenty-First Precinct*, *Under Arrest*; d. July 21, 1962.

Henry Morgan (Henry Lerner von Ost, Jr.), March 31, 1915, New York City, N.Y.; actor, announcer, emcee, scriptwriter bka *Here's Morgan* satirical humor feature host MBS/ABC/NBC 1940–43, 1946–48, 1949–50, *I've Got a Secret* panelist CBS-TV 1952–67, *Monitor* weekend magazine segment host NBC 1966–69; interlocutory assignments on 1940s *Bulldog Drummond*, *The Columbia Workshop*, *Lone Journey*, *Uncle Don*, more, intermittent panelist on *Who Said That?* 1948–50, *The Other Generation* narrator 1969, *The Sears/Mutual Radio Theater* writer-actor 1979; radio "bad boy" for acerbic exclamations on any subject including network management, sponsors — uncontrollably insubordinate though public adored it; debuted on air while New York WMCA page, moved to Philadelphia WCAU, Duluth WEBC, Boston WNAC, New York WOR/national ether, later migrated through Gotham stations WEAF, WHN, WJZ, WMGM; few early TV series; d. May 19, 1994.

Death

Hugh E. Brundage, March 31, 1972, Los Angeles, Calif.; b. Jan. 17, 1915.

April 1

Debuting

Backstage Wife, April 1, 1935, MBS; daytime serial; one of hardiest Frank, Anne Hummert perennials proffering theme of at least 12 washboard weepers — hitching lass from Podunk above her social class, in *this* heroine's case to "one of America's most handsome actors, Larry Noble, matinee idol of a million other women"; Mary (Vivian Fridell, Claire Niesen) quickly learned that Larry (Ken Griffin, James Meighan, Guy Sorel) was object of drooling by every unattached (or attached) starlet/vixen waiting in wings; many males also wished to change Mary's surname to theirs (face it: *everybody* wanted to marry a *Noble*man or woman!); final broadcast Jan. 2, 1959.

Canceled

County Fair, April 1, 1950, CBS; debut July 10, 1945.

Births

Eddy Duchin, April 1, 1909, Cambridge, Mass.; concert and recording artist, impresario, pianist; accompanied Leo Reisman Orchestra late 1920s forming own outfit 1931; linked with dozen web radio series 1934–47, headlined half; d. Feb. 9, 1951.

Robert Dwan, April 1, 1915, San Francisco, Calif.; director; d. Jan. 21, 2005.

Leon Janney, April 1, 1917, Ogden, Utah; actor (film, radio, TV), dialectician, voiceover artist bka *The Parker Family* sitcom teen "Richard the Great" Parker CBS/NBC Blue 1939–42, *The CBS Radio Mystery Theater* anthology drama thespian 80 times CBS 1974–82 (plus repeats); other radio duties: *Charlie Chan*, *The Ethel Merman Show*, *Mr. District Attorney*, *The Eternal Light*, *The Right to Happiness*, *The Shadow*, *Quick as a Flash*, more; at two in vaudeville, film actor as child; 23 theatrical films 1930–68, one made-for-TV flick 1959, six solo TV roles 1961–77, five TV series 1949–79; d. Oct. 28, 1980.

Jane Powell (Suzanne Burce), April 1, 1929, Portland, Ore.; actress, vocalist (soprano) bka screen star in *Three Sailors and a Girl* 1953, *Seven Brides for Seven Brothers* 1954, *The Girl Most Likely* 1957, more; *The Railroad Hour* sixth most enduring costar, appeared with Gordon MacRae nine times 1948–54; nightclubs, provincial theater, TV dramas/specials, Broadway stage, Carnegie Hall followed cinematic pursuits.

Harold J. True, April 1, 1891, Hornell, N.Y.; announcer, emcee, newscaster, radio executive, salesman (real estate, Firestone Tire Co.), sportscaster bka *The Lone Ranger* epic western adventure interlocutor 1933-ca. 1940 (only certified net series); worked in radio advertising at Cleveland, Ohio late 1920s; supplied openings at Detroit WXYZ (which originated *Ranger*) 1930s-ca. 1942, e.g. acting station manager 1932, checking in at rival WWJ ca. 1942–47; embittered by huge profits WXYZ owner George W. Trendle got from *The Lone Ranger* (which Trendle owned) far outstripping cast's pittance; d. Feb. 15, 1973.

Deaths

Jim Jordan, April 1, 1988, Beverly Hills, Calif.; b. Nov. 16, 1896. Lucille Norman, April 1, 1998, Glendale, Calif.; b. June 15, 1926.

April 2

Debuting

The Big Story, April 2, 1947, NBC; bona fide crime tales from newspapers as narrator Robert Sloane hosted print journalists, their exposés parlayed into heavily dramatized half-hour narratives earning huge ratings; televersion 1949–58 (final season syndicated) required quartet of narrators — Sloane, Norman Rose, Ben Grauer, Burgess Meredith; final radiocast March 23, 1955.

Canceled

Grand Central Station, April 2, 1954, ABC; debut Sept. 28, 1937.

Births

Fran Carlon, April 2, 1913, Indianapolis, Ind.; actress (radio, TV) bka *Big Town* newspaper drama society editor-crimebusting sidekick Lorelei Kilbourne CBS/NBC 1943–52; prolific daytime thespian —*Attorney at Law, Girl Alone, Lora Lawton, Ma Perkins, Our Gal Sunday, The Story of Mary Marlin, Today's Children, A Woman of America*— and in *Blackstone — the Magic Detective, The Chicago Theater of the Air, Joan and Kermit*; video credits for *Portia Faces Life* as heroine Portia Manning CBS-TV 1954–55, *As the World Turns* as Julia Burke CBS-TV 1968–75, *The Hamptons* bit part Ada ABC-TV 1983; d. Oct. 4, 1993.

Gertrude (Trudy) Warner, April 2, 1917, West Hartford, Conn.; actress (radio, TV), drama coach bka heroine/leading lady in dozen features (a high?), mostly soap strain: *Against the Storm, Beyond These Valleys, Brownstone Theater, Ellen Randolph, Joyce Jordan, M.D., The Man I Married, Modern Romances, Mrs. Miniver, Perry Mason, The Shadow, Whispering Streets, Young Doctor Malone*; still more running roles —*Big Sister, City Desk, Dangerously Yours, David Harum, Ellery Queen, Ethel and Albert, The Right to Happiness, This Life Is Mine, Valiant Lady, When a Girl Marries*; *As the World Turns* CBS-TV 1960; taught acting at Weist-Barron School, Oberlin College; d. Jan. 26, 1986.

Jack Webb (John Randolph Webb), April 2, 1920, Santa Monica, Calif.; actor, director, producer, scriptwriter bka *Dragnet* realism crime drama Sgt. Joe Friday NBC 1949–57, NBC-TV 1951–59, 1967–70; following brief stint on *The Jack Webb Show* madcap comedy-variety feature on ABC West Coast hookup 1946 he created/starred in trio of radio crime dramas before launching most celebrated work: *Pat Novak for Hire* ABC 1946–47 ABC West Coast hookup, ABC 1949 ... *Johnny Modero — Pier 23* MBS 1947 ... *Jeff Regan — Investigator* CBS West Coast hookup 1948, 1949–50; *Pete Kelly's Blues* added to success string NBC 1951 that integrated drama with star's passion for jazz; linked to 16 theatrical films 1932–73 including *Sunset Boulevard* 1950, *Dragnet* 1954, *Pete Kelly's Blues* 1955, plus half-dozen celluloid short subjects; produced, directed, scripted many TV shows in which he didn't act; d. Dec. 23, 1982.

Death

Jack Kruschen, April 2, 2002, Chandler, Ariz.; b. March 20, 1922.

April 3

Debuting

Mr. District Attorney, April 3, 1939, NBC; crime drama with court defense premise; "champion of the people, defender of our fundamental rights to life, liberty, and the pursuit of happiness," D.A. Paul Garrett (Dwight Weist, Raymond Edward Johnson, Jay Jostyn, David Brian) sported "startling realism" inspired by racket-busting Big Apple D.A. Tom Dewey (whose headline-grabbing carried him to governorship, failed tries for presidency); special investigator Len Harrington (Len Doyle), secretary Edith Miller (Vicki Vola) assisted Garrett; ABC-TV series 1951–52 first to move radio cast to live TV followed by Ziv syndicated version 1954; Ziv also produced transcribed aural series after net show ended — its most popular audio quest reached 201 markets; final net radiocast June 13, 1952.

Palmolive Beauty Box Theater, April 3, 1934, NBC; anthology showcase; pop sound, operettas, Broadway/film musicals appealed to more people (25 million first season) than *Metropolitan Opera* airing two years; *Palmolive* offered familiar music, sprightly arrangements, plots easily absorbed by commoners; artists 1934–36 — Rose Bampton, Jane Froman, James Melton, Lucy Monroe, Frank Parker, Gladys Swarthout, Francia White, more; after 11-month absence, show resumed 1937 with Jessica Dragonette as star (she departed *Cities Service Concerts* under cloud), yet *Palmolive* trimmed sharply, reduced show to half-hour, turned works into figments of originals greatly displeasing Dragonette, dispatching fans, plug pulled few months hence; final broadcast Oct. 6, 1937.

Births

George Jessel, April 3, 1898, Bronx, N.Y.; actor (stage, film, radio, TV), author, comedian, composer, emcee, lyricist, producer, raconteur (dubbed "Toastmaster General of the U. S."), recording artist, vocalist bka *The George Jessel Show* (multiple monikers) variety series headliner CBS/MBS/NBC/NBC Blue/ABC 1934, 1937–40, 1949, 1953–54, 1955, ABC-TV 1953–54; vaudeville, Broadway age 10, onstage with Eddie Cantor 11–16, silent films at 21; key role in *The Jazz Singer* on Broadway 1925 prompted Warner Brothers to adapt as first "talkie" casting Jessel in lead — salary demands gave role to Al Jolson who became overnight star, contenting Jessel with miniscule film parts often targeted at Jews; notorious affairs with starlets detailed in 1975 memoir *The World I Lived In* — spent life surrounded by young show girls; 20th Century–Fox producer 24 times; appeared in 15 theatrical films 1919–76, two made-for-TV flicks 1970, 1977, handful of solo TV episodes; d. May 23, 1981.

Peter Van Steeden, Jr., April 3, 1904, Amsterdam, Noord-Holland, The Netherlands; composer, impresario; *Your Hit Parade* conductor ca. 1937–38; second or third tier maestro during big band epoch; d. Jan. 3, 1990.

April 4

Canceled

The NBC Symphony Orchestra, April 4, 1954, NBC; debut Nov. 2, 1937.

Births

Beatrice (Bea) Benaderet, April 4, 1906, New York City, N.Y.; actress (film, radio, TV), voiceover artist bka *The George Burns and Gracie Allen Show* neighbor Blanche Morton, radio 1940s, CBS-TV 1950s; *The Beverly Hillbillies* cousin Pearl Bodine, CBS-TV 1960s; *Green Acres, Petticoat Junction* hotel operator Kate Bradley, CBS-TV 1960s (same part in both shows — Benaderet starred in *Petticoat Junction*); in 47 Hollywood flicks 1943–62, speaking roles for Warner Brothers animated cartoons mostly; radio repertoire embraced legions of California-based sitcoms: *The Adventures of Ozzie and Harriet* (Gloria, Mrs. Waddington), *The Amos 'n' Andy Show* (single roles), *Duffy's Tavern* (single), *Fibber McGee & Molly* (Millicent Carstairs), *Granby's Green Acres* (Martha Granby), *The Great Gildersleeve* (Eve Goodwin), *The Jack Benny Program* (Gertrude Gearshift), *Maisie* (single), *Meet Millie* (Bertha Bronson), *My Favorite Husband* (Leticia Cooper, Iris Atterbury), *Our Miss Brooks* (single), innumerable others; acted in two dozen more TV series, some ongoing parts; d. Oct. 13, 1968.

John H. Brown, April 4, 1904, Hull, England; actor (radio, stage, TV) bka *The Life of Riley* exuberant mortician Digby "Digger" O'Dell 1944–51, NBC televersion 1949–50 ("Business is a little dead right now ... cherrio, I'd better be shoveling off"); dossier overrun boasting nearly three dozen aural series, 20+ in longrunning roles e.g. *The Adventures of Ozzie and Harriet* (Thorny Tornberry), *The Busy Mr. Bingle* (namesake), *A Date with Judy* (Melvin Foster), *A Day in the Life of Dennis Day* (Mr. Willoughby), *The Fred Allen Show* (John Doe), *Lorenzo Jones* (Jim Barker), *The Saint* (Inspector Fernak); d. May 16, 1957.

John Cameron Swayze, April 4, 1906, Wichita, Kan.; correspondent, emcee, newscaster, print journalist (*The Kansas City Journal*) bka commercial spokesman for Timex wristwatches, purportedly indestructible timepieces kept under water or run over by bulldozer in infamous TV ads ("It takes a licking but keeps on ticking!"); columnist, drama critic at Kansas City paper early 1930s; newscaster at Kansas City KMBC 1935, rival WHB 1937, KMBC 1940 adding game show hosting to inventory; joined New York NBC 1943, acquired berth in radio newscast rotation (*John Cameron Swayze and the News* 1947–48, 1951–53), *Who Said That?* panelist on radio, TV incarnations, *Monitor* correspondent 1955–58; pioneer anchorman of NBC-TV Monday-Friday evening news (trademark sign-off "Glad we could get together"), replaced by Chet Huntley, David Brinkley 1956; linked to 1950s entertainment features at NBC-TV—*Armstrong Circle Theater, Home, The Steve Allen Show*, et al.; joined ABC 1958 hosting evening newscast with others 1961–62; four theatrical flicks 1956–85; d. Aug. 15, 1995.

Robert Venables, April 4, 1907, Chicago, Ill.; announcer, newscaster bka *The Whistler* "strange tale" mystery drama narrator (only established net series); news reporter at Chicago WGN 1941, also staffing Windy City stations WLS, WBBM, Woodstock, Ill. WCLR; after early 1920s voice study in Paris, returned to hometown as assistant stage manager/basso profundo of Civic Opera Co. before breaking into radio as classical music specialist; d. July 30, 1985.

Death

Ginny Simms, April 4, 1994, Palm Springs, Calif.; b. May 25, 1914.

April 5

Sound Bite

Coast-to-coast broadcasting becomes reality April 5, 1927 as NBC launches Orange Network (aka Pacific Coast Network) by recreating Red programming from East Coast at San Francisco KPO where it's dispatched to chain's other West Coast affiliates.

Debuting

Night Watch, April 5, 1954, CBS; crime documentary; whole thing insinuated as authentic as reporter Donn [sic] Reid rode in prowl car with police Sgt. Ron Perkins of Culver City, Calif.; Reid wore hidden wire picking up criminal activity, transpiring repercussions; historian depicted it as "inevitable result of Dragnet's success"; final broadcast April 21, 1955.

Canceled

Camel Caravan (*The Vaughn Monroe Show*), April 5, 1954, CBS; debut Dec. 7, 1933.

Births

William John Andrews, April 5, 1905, Oakland, Calif.; announcer, copywriter, engineer, sportscaster bka *One Man's Family* narrator 1932–1940s; picked as chief announcer for NBC Pacific Coast Network 1933; 1988 paperback by Carlton E. Morse (*The One Man's Family Album*) about people at mics of his legendary epic drama oddly failed to mention Andrews or his better recognized successor Ken Carpenter; d. May 2, 1985.

Marian Jordan (Marian Driscoll), April 5, 1898, Peoria, Ill.; actress (film, radio, stage), pianist, vocalist, bka *Fibber McGee & Molly* sitcom matriarch flanked by eccentric spouse (Jim Jordan) 1935–59; "'Tain't funny, McGee" an identifying exclamation that quickly became part of nation's vernacular; one of the characters she played, neighbor tyke Teeny, was among show's most popular figures; d. April 6, 1961.

Robert Q. Lewis (Robert Goldberg), April 5, 1921, Manhattan, New York City, N.Y.; actor (film, TV), announcer, comic, disc jockey, emcee, nightclub entertainer, raconteur, recording artist, vocalist bka *Arthur Godfrey Time* daily variety series host's surrogate for extended hiatuses 1947–59, headlining radio's *Waxworks*, TV's *The Name's the Same, The Robert Q. Lewis Show, Robert Q's Matinee*; labeled "the quintessential substitute host," filled in for Bud Collyer, Perry Como, Bing Crosby, Faye Emerson, Dave Garroway, Jackie Gleason, Garry Moore, Jack Paar, Ed Sullivan; other aural venues included *The ABCs of Music, The Little Show, The Robert Q. Lewis Show, The Saturday Night Revue, The Show Goes On*; broke into radio on juvenile features, nurtured by DJ assignment at Detroit station while in college; joined Troy, N.Y. WTRY 1941, brief stint on NBC after World War II service, DJ duties at New York WHN that led to "discovery" in 1947 by CBS mogul William S. Paley—signed to long-term CBS contract; ended broadcast career substituting on *To Tell The Truth* game show as emcee CBS-TV 1963–65, DJ gigs on Los Angeles area radio beyond that; d. Dec. 11, 1991.

Lee Stevens (Adolph C. Weinert), April 5, 1924, Baltimore, Md.; announcer, newscaster bka *Big Sister* washboard weeper narrator 1940s (only series noted); began at York, Pa. WSBA 1937 as utility announcer-newscaster; in early video served Baltimore WMAR-TV, one of Ed Sullivan's *Toast of the Town* variety series interlocutors CBS-TV ca. late 1940s-early 1950s.

George S. Stone (George H. Steingoetter), April 5, 1920, Belleville, Ill.; announcer, disc jockey, producer, station official; announcing repertoire included *The Art Van Damme Quintet*, *Crime on the Waterfront*, *Easy Money*, *Grand Marquee*, *Highway Harmonies*, *A Life in Your Hands*, *Lights Out*; began career at Grand Rapids, Mich. WOOD 1941, joined Chicago NBC 1944; later managed Windy City outlet WEFM before producing, hosting local *Through the Night* classical music feature on WFMT 1978–87; d. Aug. 16, 1991.

Deaths

Joseph Curtin, April 5, 1979, Los Angeles County, Calif. (although final residence Belmont, Mass.); b. July 29, 1910. Brian Donlevy, April 5, 1972, Woodland Hills, Calif.; b. Feb. 9, 1901. Guy Sorel, April 5, 1994, New York City, N.Y.; b. Aug. 12, 1914.

April 6

Sound Bite

Daytime cliffhanging begins on NBC Blue April 6, 1931; matinee genre had female as first leading figure, adolescent at that; premiering in 1924 comic strip at about nine or ten, *Little Orphan Annie* reached ether seven years hence looking no older; must have been unnerving to Tom Mix, Sky King, others of ilk that a little child led them — she had no ally for more than year, in fact — when he arrived Nov. 14, 1932, Bobby Benson also pint-sized.

Debuting

Barry Cameron (*The Soldier Who Came Home*), April 6, 1945, NBC; daytime serial; struggles of returning war vet (Spencer Bentley) and young bride Anna (Florence Williams); critics lambasted dishpan drama for "artificial qualities" as nation moved beyond war tales; final broadcast Oct. 11, 1946.

The Jack Berch Show (*Jack Berch and His Boys*), April 6, 1936, MBS; lighthearted musical revue that grew in popularity, particularly with housewives, became daytime quarter-hour ritual Sept. 20, 1943 with almost incessant berth among milady's listening habits in millions of homes; billed as "the friendliest show in radio," featured cheery baritone showman Berch whistling, chatting, singing, reading poetry; unique component "Heart-to-Heart Hookup" included misfortunes of some listeners, dedicated tunes to same; final network broadcast Oct. 15, 1954 although 50 more syndicated five-minute features followed.

Little Orphan Annie, April 6, 1931, NBC Blue; juvenile adventure serial; based on Harold Gray comic strip featuring waif Annie (Shirley Bell, Bobbe Deane, Janice Gilbert) adopted by Simmons Corners denizens Byron Silo (Jerry O'Mera), wife Mary (Henrietta Tedro); input by Annie's chum Joe Corntassel (Allan Baruck, Mel Tormé), prosperous Oliver "Daddy" Warbucks (Henry Saxe, Boris Aplon, Stanley Andrews); trinkets exchanged for sponsor Ovaltine labels proffered so often one wag insisted "plots [were] written around the premiums"; with Frank Hummert, (soon-to-be Mrs. Hummert) Anne Ashenhurst producing, *Annie* surfaced on Chicago WGN 1930, set pattern for glut of kid narratives over aural ether next two decades; Broadway *Annie* musical productions debuted 1977, 1997, theatrical film 1982, TV flick 1999; final radiocast April 24, 1942.

This Is Your FBI, April 6, 1945, ABC; anthology crime drama; nameless characters in show's first couple of years followed by key figure, fabricated special agent Jim Taylor (Stacy Harris) 1948–53 in stories allegedly based on FBI cases (separating it from fictionalized *The FBI in Peace & War* with theme march from "Love for Three Oranges" gripping listeners, pulling them inward); East Coast players to 1947 included Joan Banks, Elspeth Eric, Helen Lewis, Mandel Kramer, Santos Ortega, Karl Swenson, more, while West Coast provided thespians rest of run like Bea Benaderet, Whitfield Connor, William Conrad, Georgia Ellis, Herb Ellis, J. C. Flippen, Carleton Young; final broadcast Jan. 30, 1953.

Births

Mimi Benzell, April 6, 1924, Bridgeport, Conn.; vocalist (lyric coloratura) bka *The Railroad Hour* fifth most enduring costar appearing with Gordon MacRae 11 times 1948–54; "discovered" by Major Edward Bowes on *Original Amateur Hour*; Metropolitan Opera Co. member 1945–49; *Voice of Firestone* guest artist 1950s; cast opposite Robert Weede in enduring Broadway musical *Milk and Honey* 1961; hosted daily two-hour talk show *Lunch with Mimi* on New York WNBC at career close; d. Dec. 23, 1970.

Todd Russell, April 6, 1913, Manchester,

United Kingdom; quizmaster bka *Double or Nothing* 1945–47, *Strike It Rich* 1947–48 master of ceremonies; drifted into TV hosting game shows; d. April 1974 (numerous sources for exact date, place exhausted).

Lowell Jackson Thomas, April 6, 1892, Woodington, Ohio; author, commentator, entrepreneur, freelance writer, lecturer, movie newsreel narrator, newscaster bka *Lowell Thomas and the News* host 1930–76 (*Headline Hunters* 1929–30), last of breed of durable evening newscasters leaving aural airwaves ("Good evening, everybody," "So long until tomorrow!"); history as well-informed surveyor of world events virtually unsurpassed by contemporaries; venerated evening series launched on NBC Blue 1930, shifted to NBC Red 1945, CBS 1947—all in 6:45 p.m. ET slot; globetrotter reporting from diverse spots across run; report put annual income at $2 million in peak years (Procter & Gamble paid him $2,000 per quarter-hour newscast in 1940s, rest from writing, lectures, Movietone newsreels, lucrative sideline ventures); d. Aug. 29, 1981.

Death

Marian Jordan, April 6, 1961, Encino, Calif.; b. April 5, 1898.

April 7

Debuting

The Adventures of Nero Wolfe, April 7, 1943, ABC New England regional hookup; detective drama with eccentric criminologist impersonated by Santos Ortega, Luis Van Rooten, Francis X. Bushman, Sidney Greenstreet as ladies' man, minion Archie Goodwin (Harry Bartell, Lawrence Dobkin, Herb Ellis, John Gibson, Lamont Johnson, Joseph Julian, Elliott Lewis, Wally Maher, Gerald Mohr—nine thespians!) performed legwork in bringing perpetrators to justice (whom brilliant, obese horticulturist Wolfe fingered); series re-branded twice as *The Amazing Nero Wolfe*, *The New Adventures of Nero Wolfe*; origins in 1930s Rex Stout novels, landed briefly on NBC-TV 1981 with William Conrad starring; final American radiocast April 27, 1951 although Canadian reprise aired 1982.

The Robert Q. Lewis Show (*The Little Show*, *The Show Goes On*, *The ABCs of Music*, *Waxworks*), April 7, 1945, NBC; comedy, disc jockey, music, quiz, variety; dubbed "quintessential substitute host," filled for Bud Collyer, Perry Como, Bing Crosby, Faye Emerson, Dave Garroway, Jackie Gleason, Arthur Godfrey, Garry Moore, Jack Paar, Ed Sullivan; madcap brand of humor, often in purportedly serious formats (record-spinning, games, mixture) gained listener—later, viewer—favor, kept star on air as headliner while popular sub for others; snappy asides, droll wit left fans in stitches; final series radiocast Jan. 3, 1959.

Births

Walter (Walt) H. Framer, April 7, 1908, Pittsburgh, Pa.; announcer, director, entrepreneur-businessman, producer (TV quizzes, stage plays), writer, bka *Strike It Rich* human interest audience participation game show originator-executive 1947–57; launched radio career in Pittsburgh airing simple question-and-answer series; *Break the Bank* giveaway co-producer 1945–47; *For Love or Money* game show producer CBS-TV 1958–59; twilight years devoted to Florida tourism, real estate development; d. June 21, 1988.

Walter Winchell (Walter Winchel), April 7, 1897, New York City, N.Y.; actor (stage), columnist, commentator, newscaster, print journalist (*Vaudeville News*, *Billboard*, *The New York Graphic*, *The New York Daily Mirror*) bka *The Jergens Journal*/*Walter Winchell's Journal* ruthless audio gossip columnist aired intermittently NBC/ABC/MBS 1930–57 ("Good evening, Mr. and Mrs. North America and all the ships at sea ... Let's go to press! ... Flash!"), venue paying him $16,000 per quarter-hour weekly, plus syndicated print column; modern radio historian cited newscast as act—"he was an entertainer, too sloppy and careless to be taken seriously by so-called serious journalists, but far too powerful to ignore," another allowed that his impact made him "the most important and powerful reporter in the nation" in 1930s-40s; presided over *The Walter Winchell Show* ABC/NBC-TV 1952–56, *The Walter Winchell File* ABC-TV 1957–58, *The Untouchables* gangster melodrama narrator ABC-TV 1959–63; d. Feb. 20, 1972.

Death

Mary Margaret McBride, April 7, 1976, West Shokan, N.Y.; b. Nov. 16, 1899.

April 8

Debuting

Dimension X, April 8, 1950, NBC; science fiction anthology narrative; premier adult sci-fi drama spawned *X-Minus One* superseding it; large East Coast cast of regulars included Joan Alexander, Peter Capell, Matt Crowley, Joseph Curtin, Les Damon, Roger DeKoven, Jack Grimes, Leon Janney, Ed Jerome, Raymond Edward Johnson, Joseph Julian, John Larkin, Bill Lipton, Jan Miner, Arnold Moss, Santos Ortega, William Quinn, Bryna Raeburn, Alexander Scourby, Luis Van Rooten, Lawson Zerbe, more; final broadcast Sept. 29, 1951.

Birth

Percy Faith, April 8, 1908, Toronto, Canada; arranger, composer, impresario, pianist, recording artist bka conductor for hit single trio — "Delicado" 1952, "Theme from 'Moulin Rouge'" 1953, "Theme from 'A Summer Place'" 1960; film theater pianist, dance orchestra maestro before leading band on Canadian Broadcasting Co. 1931 rising to CBC chief arranger-conductor; moved to U. S., penned "My Heart Cries for You," "'The Virginian' Theme," "Music Through the Night," more; radio conductor 1940s-50s: *The Carnation Contented Hour*, *The Pause That Refreshes on the Air*, *The Woolworth Hour*, others; "his easy listening sounds assured a place on the dial until television pushed aside live music" assessed critic; Columbia Records music director 1950s-60s, produced about 50 albums with own outfit; d. Feb. 9, 1976.

Deaths

Marian Anderson, April 8, 1993, Portland, Ore.; b. Feb. 27, 1897. Julian Funt, April 8, 1980, New York City, N.Y.; b. March 24, 1906. Arthur N. Millet, April 8, 1943, New York City, N.Y.; b. ca. 1907, Chicago, Ill. (announcer without complete birthdate data: began at Dallas WRR 1931 followed by Chicago WIND 1933, WGN 1934, CBS 1935, freelance interlocutor 1937–43; opened *Adopted Daughter*, *Bobby Benson and the B-Bar-B Riders*, *Famous Jury Trials*, *The Goldbergs*, *Our Gal Sunday*, *Valiant Lady*, more). George Arthur Putnum, April 8, 1975, North Hollywood, Calif.; b. Jan. 21, 1914.

April 9

Births

Jim Bannon, April 9, 1911, Kansas City, Mo.; actor (radio, TV), announcer, author; through first wife, humorous actress Bea Benaderet (later divorcing), Bannon linked with Los Angeles KFI, earlier serving Kansas City KCKN, St. Louis KMOX, Hollywood KEHE, Los Angeles KHJ; by 1938 introduced comedians Joe Penner, Edgar Bergen to widespread audiences; announced other major aural series — *The Adventures of Nero Wolfe*, *The Great Gildersleeve*, *I Love a Mystery*, *Stars Over Hollywood*— while acting in *Silver Eagle Mountie*, *The Zane Grey Theater*; Jack Packard in a 1945 trilogy of *I Love a Mystery* movies, series for which he was radio commercial spokesman for Oxydol detergent; *Hawkins Falls* daytime serial drama character Mitch Fredericks NBC-TV 1954–55; *For Better or Worse* half-hour weekly serial anthology host CBS-TV 1959–60; d. July 28, 1984.

Frank Bingman, April 9, 1914, Athens, Ohio; actor (radio, stage, TV), announcer (film trailers, radio), businessman-entrepreneur, disc jockey; staff interlocutor at Cincinnati WLW, WKRC, Hollywood KHJ, Los Angeles KFI; some series introduced: *The Abbott and Costello Show*, *The Cresta Blanca Hollywood Players*, *My Friend Irma*, *Straight Arrow*; thespian for *Cavalcade of America*, *The Joan Davis Show*; product salesman for *The Jack Benny Program*; retired 1972 to devote 13 years to announcing coming attractions in cinemas via 20th Century–Fox trailers followed by critical acclaim playing Henry Drummond in *Inherit the Wind* at Warrenton, Va., community theater 1986; d. Aug. 21, 1988.

George Lowther, April 9, 1913, New York City, N.Y.; announcer, director, narrator, writer bka NBC's first page, at 14; penned scripts for 1930s-40s narratives *The Adventures of Dick Tracy*, *Terry and the Pirates*, *The Shadow*, *The Adventures of Superman*, narrated, directed latter; much later scripted installments of *The CBS Radio Mystery Theater* 1974–75; d. April 28, 1975.

Deaths

Sandy Becker, April 9, 1996, Calverton, N.Y.; b. Feb. 19, 1922. Staats Cotsworth, April 9, 1979, New York City, N.Y.; b. Feb. 17, 1908.

April 10

Debuting

Dr. I. Q., the Mental Banker, April 10, 1939, NBC Blue; quiz show, masters of ceremonies Lew Valentine, Jimmy McClain; final broadcast Nov. 29, 1950; ABC-TV extensions 1953–54, 1958–59.

The (Adventures of the) Falcon, April 10, 1943, NBC; mystery-detective drama with detail-oriented, acerbic-tongued freelance private eye Mike Waring, alias Falcon (Berry Kroeger, James Meighan, Les Tremayne, Les Damon, George Petrie) chasing crooks; sweetheart Nancy sans surname (Joan Alexander) often accompanied him; origins rooted in pulp fiction by Michael Arlen, RKO capitalized with dozen theatrical films 1941–46, trio more 1981–2000, syndicated TV series 1955, print extensions; final radiocast Nov. 29, 1954.

People Are Funny, April 10, 1942, NBC; audience participation stunt series, masters of ceremonies Art Baker, Art Linkletter; original televersion Sept. 19, 1954-April 16, 1961; final radiocast June 10, 1960.

Canceled

Name That Tune, April 10, 1953; debut Dec. 20, 1952.

Births

Bruce Norton Buell, April 10, 1919, Santa Ana, Calif.; announcer, disc jockey (classical music, Los Angeles KFAC); *California Caravan* 1947–52, *Mystery Is My Hobby* 1947–51 his only documented web series; d. April 23, 1996.

Mark Warnow, April 10, 1902, Monastrischt, Russia; CBS staff conductor, violinist; sibling of Raymond Scott, *Your Hit Parade* successor; d. Oct. 17, 1949.

Deaths

John Easton, April 10, 1984, New York City, N.Y.; b. July 10, 1918. Santos Ortega, April 10, 1976, Fort Lauderdale, Fla.; b. June 30, 1899. Jean Vander Pyl, April 10, 1999, Dana Point, Calif.; b. Oct. 11, 1919.

April 11

Sound Bite

First sporting event broadcast occurs April 11, 1921 as KDKA places mics at ringside in Pittsburgh's Motor Square Gardens to air boxing match between Johnny Dundee, Johnny Ray; station beams coverage of baseball game from Forbes Field that August, also first; in time radio athletics fare will include *Baseball Game of the Day, The Bill Stern Sports Newsreel, Gillette Friday Night Fights, It's Sports Time with Phil Rizzuto, Kentucky Derby, NASCAR Racing, NBA Final Four, Rose Bowl Parade/Game, Super Bowl, World Series*, et al.

Debuting

My Friend Irma, April 11, 1947, CBS; sitcom wherein protagonist secretary Irma Peterson (Marie Wilson) deservedly is epitome of dumb blondes; narrated by roommates Jane Stacy (Cathy Lewis) 1947–53, Kay Foster (Mary Shipp) 1953–54; supporting cast capitalizes on Irma's confused mind; final radiocast Aug. 24, 1954, CBS-TV incarnation Jan. 8, 1952-June 25, 1954.

Nick Carter, Master Detective, April 11, 1943, MBS; private eye drama focused on urbane investigator Carter (Lon Clark) who flushed out clues in criminal cases to learn which suspects were culprits; assisted by secretary Patsy Bowen (Helen Choate, Charlotte Manson), newsman Scrubby Wilson (John Kane), police Sgt. "Matty" Mathison (Ed Latimer); *Carter* originated in 1886 dime novel classics, surfaced regularly in Street and Smith-published comics from 1940; radio series bounced around schedule mercilessly — fans struggled to find timeslots; spawned *Chick Carter, Boy Detective* MBS 1943–45 (Chick is Nick's nephew); 1972 made-for-TV flick throwback; final radiocast Sept. 25, 1955.

Canceled

Smilin' Ed McConnell and His Buster Brown Gang, April 11, 1953, NBC; debut (this series) Sept. 2, 1944, star's net career launch Sept. 20, 1932. *The Story of Mary Marlin*, April 11, 1952, ABC; debut Jan. 1, 1935.

Births

Carroll Carroll (Carroll S. Weinschenk), April 11, 1902, New York City, N.Y.; advertising copywriter (J. Walter Thompson), author, magazine scribe, producer, radio continuity writer bka *Kraft Music Hall* wordsmith in Bing Crosby era 1935–46 who literally "dreamed the show up week by week" affirmed wag; while there weren't on-air script credits, "the trademark laid-back Crosby banter and tossed-off asides were largely the work of Carroll" observer allowed, giving Crosby an "urbane, breezy character, an easygoing chatter that ... set the tone for other variety shows that copied its back-fence congeniality"; surprisingly, after Crosby fell out with Kraft and NBC — moving his show from L.A. to San Francisco — he dropped Carroll outright, replacing him sans explanation, prompting tactful Carroll to casually remark: "very complex man"; also penned verbiage for *The Circle, Club Fifteen, Double or Nothing, Meet Corliss Archer, NTG and His Girls* plus series headlined by George Burns and Gracie Allen, Eddie Cantor, Edgar Bergen, Frank Sinatra, Rudy Vallee; produced Al Jolson's feature; d. Feb. 5, 1991.

Robert R. Dixon, April 11, 1911, Stamford, Conn.; announcer, emcee bka tykes' early video star with daily *Chuck Wagon* CBS-TV 1949–51, low-budget rival to NBC's *Howdy Doody*; performed for buckaroos on NY area TV; introduced 1940s-50s radio listeners to newscasters Edward R. Murrow, Larry Lesueur, daytime serials *Life Can Be Beautiful, Perry Mason, Rosemary*, hosted game show *Who Dun It?*; obit named him Murrow's "best friend"; d. Aug. 22, 1998.

Paul Fleischer Douglas, April 11, 1907, Philadelphia, Pa.; actor, announcer, emcee bka silver screen thespian in 30 flicks 1935–59 e.g. *A Letter to Three Wives, It Happens Every Spring, Angels in the Outfield, Executive Suite, The Solid Gold Cadillac, Beau James, The Mating Game*; by late 1940s he didn't give radio thought though his "bombastic personality" alienated many in radio anyway, critic Leonard Maltin wrote; heard on aural musicals, dramas in heyday; d. Sept. 11, 1959.

John W. Larkin, April 11, 1912, Oakland, Calif.; actor (film, radio, TV) bka *The Edge of Night* daytime serial hero-assistant D.A. Mike Karr who evolved into mob's worst nightmare as crusading lawyer battling gangs infiltrating Monticello with vengeance CBS-TV 1956–61, *Perry Mason* crimefighting hero-attorney CBS Radio 1947–55 — that series would have shifted to TV had creator Erle Stanley Gardner permitted — it *did* transfer but re-titled; Larkin premiered on air at Kansas City, Mo. before going to New York to be one of busiest thespians in daytime radio 1930s-50s: *The Adventures of Dick Tracy, Backstage Wife, The Brighter Day, Buck Rogers in the 25th Century, Ever Since Eve, Helpmate, Houseboat Hannah, Kay Fairchild — Stepmother, Lone Journey, Ma Perkins, Mark Trail, Portia Faces Life, The Right to Happiness, The Road of Life, The Romance of Helen Trent*, et al. while acting in boatloads of primetime features e.g. *Candid Microphone, Ford Theater, Special Agent, Under Arrest, X-Minus One*, etc.; TV work in *The Road of Life* 1954–55, *Saints and Sinners* 1962–63, *Twelve O'Clock High* 1964–65; three theatrical films 1964–65; d. Jan. 29, 1965.

Robert West (Bob) Lemond, Jr., April 11, 1913, Hale Center, Texas; announcer; allied with Los Angeles KEHE before brief stint at San Francisco KYA, rejoined KEHE 1938, shifted to rival KNX 1939, introduced score of 1940s-50s Coast-based series e.g. *The Bob Hawk Show, The Hoagy Carmichael Show, Honest Harold, Life with Luigi, Meet Millie, My Friend Irma, Our Miss Brooks, Sweeney and March, The Whistler* — common denominator linking handful of innovative CBS sitcoms aired in timeframe; opened similar fare in 1950s-60s TV: *Life with Father, The Ann Sothern Show, Fibber McGee & Molly, The Nanette Fabray Show, The Farmer's Daughter, And Here's the Show*; d. Jan. 6, 2008.

Paul Owen McGrath, April 11, 1904, Chicago, Ill.; actor (film, radio, TV) bka *Inner Sanctum Mysteries* host Raymond beckoning "come in" to squeaking-door opening; copious roles in 1940s-50s soaps: *The Affairs of Dr. Gentry, Big Sister, Lora Lawton, This Life Is Mine, When a Girl Marries, Young Doctor Malone*, et al.; TV 1955–57 in *First Love, The Edge of Night, The Guiding Light*; 11 cinematic films 1940–69, sundry TV drama guest shots; d. April 13, 1978.

Lee Vines, April 11, 1919, Brantford, Ontario, Canada; actor, announcer, newscaster bka *Hallmark Hall of Fame* anthology interlocutor on trio of video webs — NBC 1952–78, PBS 1979–82, CBS 1983–84; earlier opened *The Robert Q. Lewis Show* variety entry weekdays CBS-TV 1954–56; appeared in numerous TV shows as announcer or actor; played in radio's *Suspense* 1961, *The Sears/Mutual Radio Theater* 1979–81, introduced 1940s-50s aural episodes *The Bob Hawk Show, Cabin B-13, The CBS Radio Workshop, County Fair, Harry James and His Music Makers, The Janette Davis Show, Rate*

Your Mate, Studio One, Up for Parole, Vaughn Monroe Show, more; in 1936 announced at Camden, N.J. station at 17; newsman at Philadelphia WIP 1940.

Death

Ted de Corsia, April 11, 1973, Encino, Calif.; b. Sept. 29, 1905.

April 12

Debuting

The Couple Next Door, April 12, 1937, MBS; daytime comedy; Olan Soule, Elizabeth Harriot as Tom, Dorothy Wright in 1937, Alan Bunch, Peg Lynch in later version as unnamed wedded duo (she was "dear," he "honey bunch"); he was henpecked by overbearing nag; initiated on Chicago WGN 1935, two segments — first ended Sept. 16, 1937 followed by more durable entry two decades later, Dec. 30, 1957-Nov. 25, 1960, departing tarnished "day that drama died."

The Green Hornet, April 12, 1938, MBS; juvenile crimefighting adventure that premiered on Detroit WXYZ Jan. 31, 1936, invading web that WXYZ developed shows for; fantasy saw journalist's son (journalist/nephew of *The Lone Ranger*, aired from WXYZ) playboy Britt Reid (Al Hodge, A. Donovan Faust, Robert Hall, Jack McCarthy), like great uncle before him, wear mask to disguise self from forces of evil, revealed only to companion (in *Ranger* style), oriental valet Kato (Raymond Hayashi, Rollon Parker, Michael Tolan), and driver of Reid's sleek, powerful Black Beauty car; Reid (*Hornet*) hunted "the biggest of all game, public enemies that even the G-Men cannot reach"; final radiocast Dec. 5, 1952, film serials 1939, 1944, ABC-TV series 1966–67.

Guess Who?, April 8, 1944, MBS; quiz; Peter Donald, Happy Felton quizmasters in guessing game involving hidden identities; final broadcast April 30, 1949.

The Perry Como Show (*Columbia Presents Perry Como, The Chesterfield Supper Club*), April 12, 1943, CBS; music variety; on way to selling 100-million-plus recordings with 14 tunes in first place, Grammy winner Como (dubbed "Mr. Nice Guy" by admiring fans) sang heart out on radio features headlining 1943–55, thrusting him before cameras with show bearing his name NBC-/CBS-TV 1948–63, countless Christmas specials followed; final net radiocast July 15, 1955.

Births

Kenneth Williams (Fertig), April 12, 1914, Edmonton, Alberta, Canada; actor, announcer; after introducing *Buck Rogers in the 25th Century* late 1930s, appearing in *David Harum* 1936–51, *Mr. Keen—Tracer of Lost Persons* 1948, others, "town crier" opening daytime/primetime game show *Video Village* CBS-TV 1960–62; assisted emcee Stubby Kaye with *Shenanigans* game show ABC-TV 1964–65; *The Storybook Squares* game show announcer NBC-TV 1969; handled same task on *The Hollywood Squares* in syndication 1972–80; d. Feb. 16, 1984.

Lily Pons, April 12, 1898, Cannes, France; vocalist (coloratura soprano) bka *The Bell Telephone Hour* guest artist with 50 appearances 1942–58 (runner-up to Jascha Heifetz in number with 54); Metropolitan Opera performer 1931–59; countless turns on *Voice of Firestone* ca. 1928–57; d. Feb. 13, 1976.

April 13

Debuting

Bulldog Drummond, April 13, 1941, MBS; crime drama pitted English police inspector Captain Hugh Drummond (George Coulouris, Santos Ortega, Ned Wever, Sir Cedric Hardwicke) against American evildoers of many stripes — murderers, thieves, racketeers, counterfeiters, kidnappers — aided by valet-assistant singly-named Denny (Rod Hendrickson, Everett Sloane, Luis Van Rooten); drawn from figures created by novelist H. C. McNeile, *Drummond* expanded into 19 silent, "talkies" films 1923–52; final broadcast March 28, 1954.

Birth

Larry Keating, April 13, 1899, St. Paul, Minn.; actor (film, radio, TV), announcer, emcee, quizmaster bka *The George Burns and Gracie Allen Show* neighbor Harry Morton ("Dad always said..." repetitious retort to spouse Blanche played by Bea Benaderet) CBS-TV 1953–58, *Mister Ed* neighbor Roger Addison CBS-TV 1961–63; on radio late 1930s-early 1950s welcomed fans to *The Bob Hope Show, County Fair, The First Nighter, The Fitch Bandwagon, Hoagy Carmichael, Murder Will Out, Scramby*

Amby, This Is Your FBI, more while interviewing *Hollywood Startime* guests, hosting *Professor Puzzlewit*; career began at San Francisco KPO, KGO; 40 Hollywood films 1945–64 e.g. *Ma and Pa Kettle Go to Town, My Blue Heaven, The Mating Season, Come Fill the Cup, The Eddy Duchin Story, The Buster Keaton Story*; d. Aug. 26, 1963.

Philip Simon Tonken, April 13, 1919, Hartford, Conn.; announcer, voiceover artist; joined New York WOR, remained with it, WOR-TV to retirement 1989; in 1970s-80s his voice heard on TV station IDs, promos, bumpers, program intros; opened late 1940s-early 1950s aural web shows *High Adventure, Murder by Experts, The Mysterious Traveler, The Private Files of Matthew Bell, Quiet Please, Scotland Yard's Inspector Burke, Sing for Your Supper,* more; Fox Movietone News narrator 1950s-60s; in latter years voice for *Outdoor Life* works recorded by AudioBooks; d. Feb. 4, 2000.

Deaths

William Griffis, April 13, 1998, Chapel Hill, N.C.; b. July 12, 1917. Paul McGrath, April 13, 1978, London, England; b. April 11, 1904.

April 14

Debuting

Believe It or Not, April 14, 1930, NBC; peculiar reality drama; 1940 *Radio Guide* deemed Robert L. Ripley's entry of odd phenomena "consistently the most interesting and thrilling program on the air"; final broadcast Sept. 3, 1948.

Birth

Robert S. Stanton, April 14, 1905, Minneapolis, Minn; NBC staff announcer, program director, sportscaster, vocalist; *Bob Stanton Sports* aired 1942; debuted singing with collegians on Miami WIOD where he announced in 1929, sang with Henry King Orchestra there 1932; New York WMCA announcer mid 1930s, program director at Durham, N.C. WDNC, returned to Gotham as NBC staff announcer/sportscaster at WEAF/WNBC 1939; sports gigs in early TV; Philadelphia WPTZ Radio-TV sportscaster 1955; d. June 17, 1977.

April 15

Births

Hans Georg Conried, Jr., April 15, 1917, Baltimore, Md.; actor (stage, film, radio, TV), dialectician, director, voiceover aritst bka versatile, inexhaustible thespian in myriad mediums; many classical Shakespearean characterizations onstage early in career; in extended radio run late 1930s-early 1980s vast audio arsenal included recurring roles in *Blondie, December Bride, The Gallant Heart, It's a Great Life, Joan Davis Time, The Judy Canova Show, The Life of Riley, Life with Luigi, Maisie, The Mel Blanc Show, My Friend Irma,* occasional solo shots on *The George Burns and Gracie Allen Show, Damon Runyon Theater, Escape, Favorite Story, Orson Welles Theater, Plays for Americans, Romance, The Sears/Mutual Radio Theater, The Whistler* while directing rare episodes of *Stars Over Hollywood*; original Broadway cast of hit *Can-Can* 1953–54; 90 theatrical films (e.g. *I'll See You in My Dreams, You're Never Too Young, Bus Stop, The Big Beat, 1001 Arabian Nights, The Patsy, The Shaggy D. A.*), 22 more made-for-TV, 91 single-shot TV shows, 19 video series; d. Jan. 5, 1982.

Art Ford, April 15, 1921, New York City, N.Y.; disc jockey, emcee, interviewer (radio-TV) bka NBC *Monitor* weekend news-information service host Sunday evening segments late 1960s-early 1970s, *Milkman's Matinee* overnight wax show host over New York's WNEW 1942–54.

Death

Christopher Lynch, April 15, 1994, Worcestershire, England; b. July 23, 1920.

April 16

Debuting

Fibber McGee & Molly, April 16, 1935, NBC; broadly defined family sitcom with wedded actors Jim, Marian Jordan; oddball Fibber fostered grand schemes to be notoriously wealthy, famous while Molly took him in stride; they interacted with peculiar townsfolk who dropped by their domicile at 39 Wistful Vista Tuesday nights; series added colorful idioms to nation's vernacular ("'Tain't funny, McGee," "Heavenly days!," "How do you do, I'm sure");

final broadcast Sept. 6, 1959 on *Monitor*, NBC magazine programming service.

Births

Joan Alexander, April 16, 1918, St. Paul, Minn.; actress, panelist, voiceover artist bka *The Adventures of Superman* character Lois Lane; most memorable of radio queens to play indomitable Della Street, right-hand of *Perry Mason* in durable daytime quarter-hour 1940s to mid 1950s; soap opera specialist turned up regularly in *Against the Storm*, *Bright Horizon*, *David Harum*, *The Light of the World*, *Lone Journey*, *The Open Door*, *Rosemary*, *This Is Nora Drake*, *Young Doctor Malone*, *Woman of Courage*; spots on *Columbia Presents Corwin*, *Dimension X*, *Leave It to Mike*, *The Man from G-2*, *Philo Vance*, *Quick as a Flash*, more; Lois Lane speaker on *Superman* TV cartoon 1966–69.

Milton John Cross, April 16, 1897, New York City, N.Y.; announcer, emcee bka "the voice of the Met," *Metropolitan Opera* broadcast host-commentator missing just two performances 1931–75; with audience of 12–15 million, one of most listened-to men in America; presided over *The Metropolitan Opera Auditions of the Air* 1940s-50s; kept from taking self seriously poking fun at stuffed shirts of highbrow fare on *The Chamber Music Society of Lower Basin Street* 1940-ca. 1944 adding humor "with nothing more than his presence" pundit vowed; hosted durable children's feature *Coast-to-Coast on a Bus* 1927–48 and — from 1920s-50s — *The A&P Gypsies*, *General Motors Concerts*, *Information Please*, *The New York Philharmonic Symphony*, other prestigious features; pursued unattainable career as soloist early, made greater impact on music as speaker; d. Jan. 3, 1975.

Les Tremayne, April 16, 1913, Balham, London, England; actor (stage, film, radio, TV), announcer, emcee bka exceedingly busy, gifted actor who played extensively in four mediums, turning up in four dozen network radio features 1930s-80s principally as thespian, 33 films 1916–2002, five dozen TV series 1954–82 including several with ongoing parts, countless unrecorded onstage venues; with wife actress Alice Reinheart, hosted *The Tremaynes* breakfast chat entry on New York WOR 1940s-50s; d. Dec. 19, 2003.

Dick Wynn (sometimes Winn) (Richard Henry Wynn), April 16, 1909, Fairview, Neb.; announcer bka *The Count of Monte Cristo*, *The Lone Wolf* interlocutor 1940s; d. Aug. 24, 1996.

April 17

Canceled

Manhattan Merry-Go-Round, April 17, 1949, NBC; debut Nov. 6, 1932.

Births

Howard Moorhead Claney, April 17, 1898, Pittsburgh, Pa.; actor (stage), announcer bka narrator with instantly identifiable nasal inflection on daytime serials, primetime mysteries, comedies, musicals, variety hours; acted in stage productions of *A Man of the People*, *Cyrano de Bergerac*, *Juno and the Paycock*, *Liliom*; NBC staff announcer from 1930; in 1940s-50s introduced profuse wares of producers Frank, Anne Hummert including *Amanda of Honeymoon Hill*, *The American Album of Familiar Music*, *Backstage Wife*, *Mr. Chameleon*, *Stella Dallas*, *Waltz Time*; gifted painter, watercolorist, augmented income conducting one-man shows at prestigious art galleries; d. April 30, 1980.

Harry Clark, April 17, 1913, Providence, R.I.; actor, announcer, newscaster, sportscaster; from mid 1930s-early 1950s beckoned listeners to *Backstage Wife*, *The Columbia Workshop*, *The Parker Family*, *The Second Mrs. Burton*, parallel features; CBS newsman 1944–47, performed in *Stoopnagle and Budd* 1930s-40s; sports reporter at Boston WVOM from 1952; d. April 1985 (date, place unsubstantiated; last residence Tucson, Ariz.).

Arthur Lake (Arthur Patrick Silverlake, Jr.), April 17, 1905, Corbin, Ky.; actor (stage, film, radio, TV), circus entertainer bka *Blondie* family sitcom bumbling patriarch-protagonist Dagwood Bumstead 1939–50, derived from enduring comic strip; after 28 *Blondie* films, TV incarnation and 11 radio seasons, Lake allowed "how nice it would be if the show could just go on forever"; joined family in "The Flying Silverlakes" aerial act in road show circus at age five; clan shifted to vaudeville, settling in southern California where Arthur, Jr. premiered in silent film *Jack and the Beanstalk*; led to onscreen collegiate musicals, westerns, namesake role *Harold Teen* 1928, foretaste of things to come; gained radio role after low-budget *Blondie* flick series 1938–50 began; d. Jan. 9, 1987.

Deaths

Dudley Manlove, April 17, 1996, San Bernardino, Calif.; b. June 11, 1914. Frank McGee, April 17, 1974, New York City, N.Y.; b. Sept. 12, 1921. Thomas L. Thomas, April 17, 1983, Scottsdale, Ariz.; b. Feb. 23, 1912.

April 18

Sound Bite

Mutual Broadcasting System ceases operations effective start of Sunday, April 18, 1999; ownership shifts multi times in final decades; California-based syndicated program service Westwood One buys MBS from Amway Corp. September 1985; Westwood One buys NBC Radio 1987, then CBS Radio News, CBS MarketWatch.com Radio Network, Fox News, CNNRadio, giving enterprise possession of three of four national radio chains operating since webs formed, all highly competitive throughout history; at end, MBS chiefly airs newscasts; one wag notes: "Official time of Mutual Radio's death was Midnight 4/17/99. No tribute, no mention it was the last newscast ... it just died"; Mutual moniker remains in Westwood One portfolio, freely applied as corporate trademark.

Canceled

The Affairs of Peter Salem, April 18, 1953, MBS; debut May 7, 1949. *Mr. and Mrs. North*, April 18, 1955, CBS; debut Dec. 30, 1942.

Births

Bob Hastings, April 18, 1925, Brooklyn, N.Y.; actor (film, radio, TV), emcee, recording artist, vocalist, voiceover artist bka *Archie Andrews* lead 1946–53; running parts in dozen televised animated cartoon series 1963–78; ABC-TV *General Hospital* daytime serial character Burt Ramsey 1979–86; recurring guest at vintage radio conventions 1990s, early 2000s.

Bill Hay, April 18, 1887, Dumfries, Scotland; announcer, director, salesman, sales manager (WMAQ, WAMZ), violinist, vocalist bka *Amos 'n' Andy* interlocutor 1928–43; introduced *The Goldbergs* 1934; salesman who fell into radio when show originated from family piano concern on Hastings, Neb. KFKX 1923; shifted to Chicago WGN 1924, met Freeman Gosden, Charles Correll who went on air early 1926 with *Sam 'n' Henry*, precursor to *Amos 'n' Andy* 1928 on rival WMAQ, then NBC 1929, Hay announcing all ("Heah they ah"); created U. S. habit of twice-yearly dental exams via pitches for Pepsodent toothpaste; banished as "old school" when *Amos 'n' Andy* Hollywoodized as sitcom; d. Oct. 12, 1978.

Death

Joan Blaine, April 19, 1949, New York N.Y.; b. April 22, c1900.

April 19

Debuting

Romance, April 19, 1943, CBS; anthology drama; one of most enduring collections of aural plays of adventure, adoration, but inserted into agenda segmentally to plug holes; near inception offered "tender love stories of today, ... memorable love stories of the past"; narratives improved with age, read one assessment; audio thespians, Hollywood icons played: Parley Baer, Bob Bailey, Joan Banks, Harry Bartell, Dick Beals, Humphrey Bogart, Herb Butterfield, Peter Capell, Ronald Colman, William Conrad, Hans Conried, Richard Crenna, Mary Jane Croft, John Dehner, Larry Dobkin, Sam Edwards, Georgia Ellis, Errol Flynn, Henry Fonda, Alice Frost, Van Johnson, Jack Kruschen, Frank Lovejoy, Howard McNear, Santos Ortega, Irene Tedrow, Shirley Temple, Peggy Webber, Betty Winkler, Paula Winslowe, more; final broadcast Jan. 5, 1957.

Canceled

The Aldrich Family, April 19, 1953, NBC; debut July 2, 1939.

Births

Betty Lou Gerson (Lauria), April 19, 1914, Chattanooga, Tenn.; actress (radio, film, TV), voiceover artist; raised in Birmingham, Ala., into radio at Chicago 1934, Hollywood 1947: *The Adventures of the Thin Man*, *Arnold Grimm's Daughter*, *The Chicago Theater of the Air*, *Crime Classics*, *Escape*, *The First Nighter*, *Gangbusters*, *Grand Hotel*, *The Great Gildersleeve*, *The Guiding Light*, *Inner Sanctum Mysteries*, *Lux Radio Theater*, *Ma Perkins*, *Mr. and Mrs. North*, *Mr. President*, *The*

Road of Life, The Saint, Suspense, Tom Mix, The Whistler, Woman in White, Yours Truly—Johnny Dollar, more; 36 solo TV roles 1952–77, 11 cinema films often voice only 1949–97; d. Jan. 12, 1999.

Edward Parke Levy, April 19, 1908, Philadelphia, Pa.; director, producer, scriptwriter (film, radio, TV) bka *My Friend Irma* sitcom head writer 1947–54, CBS-TV; *December Bride* sitcom creator-producer, radio 1952–53, CBS-TV 1954–59; d. March 8, 1993.

Betty Winkler (Keane), April 19, 1914, Berwick, Pa.; actress (radio, stage, TV), author, educator bka *Rosemary* daytime serial heroine Rosemary Dawson Roberts NBC/CBS 1944-ca. early 1950s; leading lady in *Abie's Irish Rose, Girl Alone, Joyce Jordan — Girl Interne, Lone Journey, The Man I Married, This Life Is Mine* qualifying as queen of most soaps; running roles: *Betty and Bob, Just Plain Bill, Masquerade, The O'Neills, Pepper Young's Family, Terry Regan — Attorney at Law*; solo parts: *The Callahans, The Chicago Theater of the Air, Don Winslow of the Navy, Fibber McGee & Molly, Grand Hotel, Inner Sanctum Mysteries, Knickerbocker Playhouse, Romance,* more; Community Theater at age five, Chicago radio in teens; sensory awareness tutor almost 50 years from 1952 — wrote text on subject 1979; d. June 4, 2002.

Death

Russ Hodges, April 19, 1971, San Francisco, Calif.; b. June 18, 1910.

April 20

Sound Bite

Having overrun its allotted time week earlier — cut off air by NBC officials before finish — *The Fred Allen Show* star retaliates on April 20, 1947 broadcast; in opening monologue, Allen proclaims time cut from ends of NBC comedy shows is applied to vice presidents' vacations; Clarence L. Menser, programming veep, orders routine deleted prior to airtime, yet Allen refuses; Menser cuts show off air for half-minute as Allen shares his tale; compounding situation, Menser cuts off Bob Hope, Red Skelton that week for *their* alleged offenses; censorship cries result, Allen affirmed by fans' mail, endorsed by sponsor Standard Brands; before 1947–48 season starts, Menser is quietly spirited away to other duties.

Debuting

Your Hit Parade, April 20, 1935, NBC; pop music; tracked genre based on gauges denoting public preferences; impresarios Lennie Hayton, Al Goodman, Carl Hoff, Ray Sinatra, Freddie Rich, Harry Salter, Harry Sosnik, Abe Lyman, Mark Warnow, Richard Himber, Peter Van Steeden, Leo Reisman, Axel Stordahl, Scott Quintet, Raymond Scott, Don Walker, Dick Jacobs, Johnny Green, Orrin Tucker; vocalists Lanny Ross, Bea Wain, "Wee" Bonnie Baker, Frank Sinatra, Lawrence Tibbett, Johnny Mercer, Dinah Shore, Ginny Simms, Martha Tilton, Dick Haymes, Doris Day, Eileen Wilson, Snooky Lanson, Dorothy Collins, Russell Arms, June Valli, Gisele MacKenzie, Jill Corey, Johnny Desmond, Jerry Wayne, Margaret Whiting, more; final broadcast Jan. 16, 1953, televersion NBC/CBS Oct. 7, 1950-April 24, 1959, unsuccessful comeback CBS-TV Aug. 2–30, 1974.

Canceled

The Big Show, April 20, 1952, NBC; debut Nov. 5, 1950.

Birth

Elena Angela Verdugo, April 20, 1925, Paso Robles, Calif.; actress (stage, film, radio, TV) bka *Meet Millie* sitcom namesake figure Millie Bronson, TV 1952–56, radio ca. 1953–54; *Marcus Welby, M.D.* ABC-TV drama nurse-receptionist Consuelo Lopez 1969–76.

Deaths

Hector Chevigny, April 20, 1965, New York City, N.Y.; b. June 28, 1904. Dresser Dahlstead, April 20, 1998, Las Vegas, Nev.; b. Sept. 19, 1910.

April 21

Debuting

Take It or Leave It, April 21, 1940, CBS; quiz; masters of ceremonies Bob Hawk 1940–41, Phil Baker 1941–47/1951, Garry Moore 1947–49, Eddie Cantor 1949–50, Jack Paar 1950–51/1951–52; segued into *The $64 Question*, netted TV's *The $64,000 Question*, imitators, quiz scandals; final radiocast June 1, 1952.

Canceled

Night Watch, April 21, 1955, CBS; debut

April 5, 1954. *(Maxwell House) Show Boat*, April 21, 1941, NBC; debut Oct. 6, 1932.

Births

H. Jon (Tex) Antoine, April 21, 1923, Texas; announcer; introduced late 1940s features *The Adventures of Frank Merriwell, The Eternal Light* plus *The Jane Pickens Show* 1951–52; inaugurated weather forecasts October 1948 as New York WNBT video operations merged with WNBC Radio to yield WNBC-TV, flagship outlet of NBC chain; d. Jan. 12, 1983.

Max Jordan, April 21, 1895, San Remo, Italy (although German citizen); commentator, correspondent, priest, print journalist (Hearst newspaper syndicate) bka doctorate-toting globetrotter fluently speaking English, French, German, Italian, Spanish — reported on location to newspaper, magazine, radio audiences; hired by NBC 1931 as overseas correspondent, European staff director, news analyst 1930s-40s, net's first religious broadcast director ca. 1944; ordained Catholic priest in Germany 1951, joined Benedictine Order; d. Nov. 28, 1977.

Deaths

Peter Lind Hayes, April 21, 1998, Las Vegas, Nev.; b. June 25, 1915. Gloria Mann, April 21, 1961, Los Angeles, Calif.; b. July 7, 1927. James Melton, April 21, 1961, New York City, N.Y.; b. Jan. 2, 1904.

April 22

Canceled

Casey, Crime Photographer, April 22, 1955, CBS; debut July 7, 1943. *Information Please*, April 22, 1951, MBS; debut May 17, 1938.

Births

Joan Blaine, April 22, ca. 1900, Fort Dodge, Iowa; actress (stage, radio), attorney, author, educator, harpist, vocalist bka *Valiant Lady* daytime serial heroine Joan Barrett CBS/NBC 1938-c1944; prior to showbiz earned livelihood as attorney, educator, touring nation playing harp, singing; performed in brief runs of two Broadway plays 1929; penned short stories, novels; radio — *Silken Strings, The Story of Mary Marlin, A Tale of Today, Welcome Valley*; d. April 18, 1949.

Richard Allen (Dick) Dudley (Casper Bernard Kuhn, Jr.), April 22, 1915, Louisville, Ky.; announcer, disc jockey; NBC page before 1940 elevation to staff announcer, post he filled until 1980 retirement; introduced TV features like *The NBC Symphony Orchestra, Today, The Price Is Right* (sub announcer); radio gigs *The Aldrich Family, Archie Andrews, Believe It or Not*; d. Feb. 2, 2000.

John W. Vandercook, April 22, 1902, London, England; author, commentator, emcee, newscaster, print journalist (*The Columbus Citizen, The Washington News, The Baltimore Post*, Macfadden Publications, *The New York Graphic*) bka globetrotting newsman (to 73 countries across 15 years) dispatching nightly headlines in quarter-hour doses under his moniker over NBC 1940–41, 1945–46, ABC 1953–55, serving MBS in between; dropped out of Yale exclaiming "too damn many Republicans!"; recounted travels via multi pictorial-essay volumes; d. Jan. 6, 1963.

Death

Jane Froman, April 22, 1980, Columbia, Mo.; b. Nov. 10, 1907.

April 23

Debuting

The Adventures of Bill Lance, April 23, 1944, CBS; crime drama aired in twin runs, both with Los Angeles Det. Bill Lance (John McIntire, Pat McGeehan in first embodiment, Gerald Mohr in second) with sharply perceptive mind, often pursuing bad guys at peculiar venues like morgues, North Africa, South America, circuses, waterfronts with partner Ulysses Higgins (Howard McNear); first series concluded Sept. 9, 1945; show resumed on ABC June 14, 1947-Jan. 4, 1948.

Births

James F. Fleming, April 23, 1915, announcer, newscaster, producer bka first newsman on premiering *Today* show NBC-TV 1952–53, *Monitor* inaugural executive producer 1955–57; CBS news correspondent 1938–49; introduced daytime fare in 1940s *The Goldbergs, John's Other Wife, The Light of the World, Vic and*

Sade, plus nighttime features like *Mr. Keen—Tracer of Lost Persons*; *The Morning Show* producer CBS-TV 1956–57 followed by myriad documentaries, specials for TV webs throughout 1960s; d. Aug. 10, 1996.

Edwin Conger Hill, April 23, 1884, Aurora, Ind.; announcer, author, commentator, director, film editor, newscaster, print journalist (Indianapolis, Cincinnati newspapers before joining *The New York Sun* 1904–23); 20th Century–Fox newsreel director, Fox movie editor 1923–27; penned tomes *The Iron Horse* 1925, *The American Scene* 1933, *The Human Side of the News* 1934; joined New York WOR as newscaster 1931, gained MBS analysis entry *The Human Side of the News* (and other appellations) 1933–35, 1936–45, 1946–47, 1950, 1951–52; on 1930s-50s features *The Campbell Playhouse*, *The Mercury Theater on the Air*, *The Realsilk Program*, *This Is London*, more; d. Feb. 12, 1957.

Deaths

Bruce Norton Buell, April 23, 1996, Los Angeles, Calif.; b. April 10, 1919. Vern Carstensen, April 23, 1999, Alhambra, Calif.; b. May 24, 1914. House Jameson, April 23, 1971, Danbury, Conn.; b. Dec. 17, 1902. Al Jarvis, Orange County, Calif., May 6, 1970; b. July 4, 1909.

April 24

Sound Bite

With broadcast of April 24, 2004, Texaco's durable link with Metropolitan Opera Co.'s live Saturday afternoon performances ends, tie-up that began in 1940 with Texas Co. (later Texaco Corp.) underwriting radio tradition debuting 1931; since leaving chains in 1960, seasonal series beamed over global hookup to 360 public, independent radio stations in 42 countries; buying Texaco in 2001, Chevron, Inc. dubbed Met a "world-class cultural treasure" when announcing in spring 2003 renamed ChevronTexaco Corp. no longer had place for Met, deemed by highbrow crowd huge setback for classical music; link may have been most enduring bond in web radio between commercial underwriter, series.

Debuting

Richard Diamond, Private Detective, April 24, 1949, NBC; private eye mystery; in mythical entrepreneurial quest, N.Y.P.D. alumnus Richard Diamond (Dick Powell) carried training, experience, contacts into personal venture, opened rented office on Broadway, base of his challenge against underworld; others in cast: sugar-stick Helen Asher (Virginia Gregg, Frances Robinson), oft-perturbed homicide Lt. Walt Levinson (Ed Begley, Arthur Q. Bryan), dimwitted desk Sgt. Otis Ludlum (Wilms Herbert); 1957–60 TV history disjointed on two webs, two coasts (Diamond moved to Hollywood for part of run), incessant cast changes (Barbara Bain, Mary Tyler Moore in video debut)—all this before going into syndicated repeats under title *Call Mr. D*; final radiocast Sept. 20, 1953.

X-Minus One, April 24, 1955, NBC; sci-fi anthology drama; "From the far horizons of the unknown come transcribed tales of new dimensions in time and space—these are stories of the future, adventures in which you'll live in a million could-be years on a thousand may-be worlds"; outgrowth of NBC's earlier success *Dimension X* (in fact, first 15 shows repeats), yet when it picked up steam *X* and *Gunsmoke* provided "the most interesting dramatic radio of the 1955 season" said one wag: "it blew through NBC like a breath of fresh air"; tales believably chilling with listeners' imaginations running wild; beyond superb scripting, direction, show proffered deluge of seasoned East Coast thespians—Mason Adams, Joan Alexander, Ralph Camargo, Staats Cotsworth, Roger DeKoven, Jack Grimes, Larry Haines, Bob Hastings, Arthur Hughes, Leon Janney, Raymond Edward Johnson, Joseph Julian, Teri Keane, Mandel Kramer, John Larkin, Bill Lipton, Santos Ortega, Bill Quinn, Lawson Zerbe, more; final broadcast Jan. 9, 1958.

Canceled

The Affairs of Dr. Gentry, April 24, 1959, NBC; debut Jan. 14, 1947. *Five Star Matinee*, April 24, 1959, NBC; debut July 30, 1956. *Little Orphan Annie*, April 24, 1942, MBS; debut April 6, 1931. *One Man's Family*, April 24, 1959, NBC; debut April 29, 1932. *Pepper Young's Family*, April 24, 1959, NBC; debut Oct. 2, 1932 (under sundry antecedent monikers). *The Woman in My House*, April 24, 1959, NBC; debut March 26, 1951.

Death

Bud Abbott, April 24, 1974, Woodland Hills, Calif.; b. Oct. 2, 1897. Rosario Bourdon, April 24, 1961, New York City, N.Y.; b. March 6, 1885.

April 25

Canceled

Father Knows Best, April 25, 1954, NBC; debut Aug. 25, 1949. *The Joe Penner Show* (*The Tip Top Show*), April 25, 1940, NBC Blue; debut Oct. 8, 1933.

Birth

Edward R. Murrow (Egbert Roscoe Murrow), April 25, 1908, Pole Cat Creek, N.C.; actor, commentator, correspondent, lumberjack, newscaster, sportscaster bka "the godhead of radio and TV network news" allowed a critic, dispatching world news at critical instants in American life, especially in gruesome years of World War II as London-based newsman colorfully depicted air raids, incendiary fires through eyewitness reports; lumberjack before entering drama, sportscasting on Washington State College KWSC; National Student Federation of America president 1930, other student missions, overseas trips; joined CBS 1935 as director of talks, sent to Europe 1937 to coordinate prewar coverage; over next few years hired handful of protégés popularly labeled "Murrow Boys" who provided CBS coverage from European hot spots; returned to U. S. after war to myriad duties, some on air, reluctantly becoming CBS VP for public affairs, relinquishing post quickly; memorable series *Edward R. Murrow and the News* CBS Radio 1942–44, 1947–59, *See It Now* CBS-TV 1951–58, *Person to Person* CBS-TV 1953–59; aside from war reports, recalled for downfall of Sen. Joseph R. McCarthy (R-Wis.) who crusaded against perceived Communist sympathizers, ruining public figures' lives — Murrow put screws to him on *See It Now* March 9, 1954, by late 1954 McCarthy was finished; President John F. Kennedy appointed Murrow director of U. S. Information Agency 1961; d. April 27, 1965.

Deaths

Janette Davis, April 25, 2005, Naples, Fla.; b. Nov. 2, 1918. Florence Freeman, April 25, 2000, Kankakee, Ill.; b. July 29, 1911. Lanny Ross, April 25, 1988, New York City, N.Y.; b. Jan. 19, 1906. Don Wilson, April 25, 1982, Palm Springs, Calif.; b. Sept. 1, 1900.

April 26

Sound Bite

CBS becomes last of original quartet of national webs to diversify from unitary program concept; on April 26, 1982 it launches Radioradio aimed at youth-oriented market similar to hookups already operated by other chains.

Debuting

Ed Wynn, the Texaco Fire Chief, April 26, 1932, NBC; comedy variety; holdover clown from vaudeville who still dressed part in radio, depicted as "a sad man" by son Keenan for delivering 55 aural gags weekly while visual entertainer; attracted fans with silly costumes, antics, one-liners presiding over variety hours with second-tier performers in slapstick comedy; Wynn aired under several appellations (*Gulliver*, *Ed Wynn's Grab Bag*, *The Perfect Fool*, *Happy Island*) though an analyst said his effectiveness as radio draw ended when he wasn't *The Fire Chief* any more (June 4, 1935); final broadcast Feb. 26, 1945.

Gunsmoke, April 26, 1952, CBS; epic western narrative ushering in adult frontier dramas with like twist; set in Dodge City, Kan. in 1870s where marshal Matt Dillon (William Conrad) spearheaded law, order flanked by townsman Chester Proudfoot (Parley Baer), country doctor Charles Adams (Howard McNear), saloonkeeper Kitty Russell (Georgia Ellis); anthological "story of the violence that moved West with young America and ... of a man who moved with it"; greatest legacy might be 20-year televersion it spawned riding high at CBS 1955–75 with separate cast headed by James Arness (Dillon) evolving into TV's most durable western and primetime series with continuing characters; five made-for-TV flicks 1987–94 recaptured storied past; final radiocast June 18, 1961.

The Life of Riley, April 26, 1941, CBS; family sitcom with lovable, gullible, clumsy blue-collar patriarch, Chester Arthur Riley (memorably William Bendix 1944–51); reactions of kin, comrades to his oddball machinations; company of seasoned thespians in key roles, among them: Conrad Binyon, John Brown, Hans Conried, Sharon Douglas, Barbara Eiler, Bobby Ellis, Jack Grimes, Shirley Mitchell, Alan Reed, Francis "Dink" Trout, Paula Winslowe, more; final radiocast June 29, 1951, NBC-TV Oct. 4, 1949-March 28, 1950, Jan. 2, 1953-Aug. 22, 1958.

Lorenzo Jones, April 26, 1937, NBC; daytime serial; mirth in midst of matinee mayhem as evidenced by epigraph: *We all know couples like lovable, impractical Lorenzo Jones and his devoted wife, Belle. Lorenzo's inventions have made him a character to the town — but not to Belle, who loves him. Their struggle for security Is anybody's story. But somehow with Lorenzo, it has more smiles than tears*; Lorenzo (Karl Swenson), Belle (Betty Garde, Lucille Wall) lived subdued existence to mid 1952 when — with ratings sharply falling — producers Frank, Anne Hummert banished humor, turned tale into melodrama with Lorenzo wandering streets of New York as amnesiac; just before run ended he recovered, walking into arms of beloved Belle; final broadcast Sept. 30, 1955.

Canceled

Amanda of Honeymoon Hill, April 26, 1946, CBS; debut Feb. 5, 1940.

Births

Holland E. Engle, April 26, 1907, Wheeling, W. Va.; announcer, disc jockey, emcee, newscaster; on air at 14, permanent residency at Chicago WGN 1942 with multi shows plus web gigs mid 1940s-mid 1950s: audience participation series *Ladies Fair, Quiz of Two Cities, Variety Fair*; d. March 24, 1988.

John W. McGovern (pseudonym John Wilder), April 26, 1912, Providence, R.I.; actor, announcer; thespian on 1930s-50s features *The Adventures of Maisie, Backstage Wife, California Caravan, The Casebook of Gregory Hood, Columbia Presents Corwin, A Date with Judy, Dimension X, The Eternal Light, Family Theater, Great Plays, Gunsmoke, The Halls of Ivy, Highway Patrol, Ideas That Came True, The Jack Benny Program, The O'Neills, Our Gal Sunday, Radio Guild, Red Ryder, Tennessee Jed, Wild Bill Hickok, X-Minus One*; played Peter Hall in *Today Is Ours* daytime serial NBC-TV 1958; d. July 28, 1985.

Victor Herbert (Vic) Perrin, April 26, 1916; actor, announcer, voiceover artist, writer bka playing in teeming numbers of 1950s "adult western" roles on *Fort Laramie, Frontier Gentleman, Gunsmoke, Have Gun — Will Travel, Luke Slaughter of Tombstone*; surfeit of adult series in other genres e.g. *The CBS Radio Workshop, Dragnet, Heartbeat Theater, One Man's Family, Pete Kelly's Blues, Rogers of the Gazette, Suspense, Yours Truly — Johnny Dollar, The Zane Grey Theater*; mainstream fare *The Adventures of Nero Wolfe, The Adventures of Philip Marlowe, The Clyde Beatty Show, Dr. Paul, Escape, The Roy Rogers Show, The Story of Holly Sloan*, more; junior staff announcer at Hollywood NBC early 1940s, advancing to chief announcer at Blue network; penned one *Gunsmoke* script; *The Outer Limits* sci-fi thriller viewers ABC-TV 1963–65 heard him declare "There is nothing wrong with your television set...."; d. July 4, 1989.

Deaths

Mason Adams, April 26, 2005, Manhattan, New York City, N.Y.; b. Feb. 26, 1919. Lucille Ball, April 26, 1989, Los Angeles, Calif.; b. Aug. 6, 1911. Allan Jackson, April 26, 1976, New York City, N.Y.; b. Dec. 4, 1915. Del Sharbutt, April 26, 2002, Palm Desert, Calif.; b. Feb. 16, 1912.

April 27

Debuting

The NBC Radio Theater, April 27, 1959, NBC; anthology drama; produced-directed by Himan Brown, one of radio's sterling achievers (*Inner Sanctum Mysteries, The CBS Radio Mystery Theater*); complete 55-minute weekday matinee plays about subjects facing "climactic moments in their lives"; alternating thespians Ellie Albert, Lee Bowman, Madeleine Carroll, Gloria DeHaven, Celeste Holm in leading roles; final broadcast Jan. 1, 1960.

Canceled

The Adventures of Nero Wolfe, April 27, 1951, NBC (CBC aired show in Canada Jan. 16-April 10, 1982); debut April 7, 1943. *The Adventures of Sam Spade*, April 27, 1951, NBC; debut July 12, 1946.

Birth

Ned Wever, April 27, 1902, New York City, N.Y.; actor (stage, film, radio, TV), author, composer, scribe bka *Young Widder Brown* daytime serial hero-suitor Dr. Anthony Loring NBC 1940–56; after writing, directing, performing in college productions, cast in multi Broadway roles, composed show tunes, penned lyrics for "Trouble in Paradise," more; joined CBS early 1930s winning handful of male leads: *Angel of Mercy, Bulldog Drummond, Dick Tracy, Lora Lawton, Manhattan Mother, True Detective, True Story Hour, Two on a Clue*— plus guest/running roles: *Betty and Bob, Big Sister, Cavalcade of America, Grand Central Station, Mr. Keen—Tracer of Lost Persons, My True Story, Mystery Theater, Pages of Romance, Perry Mason, Under Arrest, Valiant Lady*, more; performed in 10 theatrical films 1957–63, 70 TV shows; d. May 6, 1984.

Deaths

Alan Bunce, April 27, 1965, New York City, N.Y.; b. June 28, 1902. Edward R. Murrow, April 27, 1965, Pawling, N.Y.; b. April 25, 1908.

April 28

Births

Michael T. Fitzmaurice, April 28, 1908, Chicago, Ill.; actor, acting coach, announcer, emcee, print journalist (*The Los Angeles Times*), voiceover artist bka radio voice of PSAs, commercials for charitable causes (American Cancer Society, Community Chest, March of Dimes), government-backed agencies during World War II; associated in later years with Charles Kebbe training aspiring TV thespians; introduced/played legions of daytime serials: *Joyce Jordan, Lora Lawton, Myrt and Marge, Pepper Young's Family, The Right to Happiness, Rosemary, Stella Dallas, This Life Is Mine, When a Girl Marries*; Broadway productions *The Chocolate Soldier, The Merry Widow*; half-dozen movies; d. Aug. 31, 1967.

Jay Sims, April 28, 1911, New York City, N.Y.; announcer, commentator, newscaster, producer bka Hearst Metrotone *News of the Day* analyst 1945–54; freelance radio-TV interlocutor on *Ask Me Another, Call the Police, Danger Is My Business, High Finance, Stop the Music!, The Walter Winchell Show, Your Hit Parade*; after web radio, reporter/news anchor in New York, for ABC Hollywood/ New York, for *The Stock Market Observer* in Miami which he produced; news director at two stations—San Diego KCBQ, Hemet, Calif. KHYE; d. Aug. 8, 1997.

Deaths

Ed Begley, April 28, 1970, Hollywood, Calif.; b. March 25, 1901. George Lowther, April 28, 1975, Westport, Conn.; b. April 9, 1913.

April 29

Debuting

The Bell Telephone Hour, April 29, 1940, NBC; musical showcase featuring assorted styles from opera to jazz with celebrated guests from disparate genres; maestro Donald Voorhees held baton from first to last performance; final broadcast June 30, 1958, NBC-TV extension Jan. 12, 1959-June 14, 1968, NBC Radio *Encores from The Bell Telephone Hour* Sept. 15, 1968-June 8, 1969.

One Man's Family, April 29, 1932, limited hookup with West Coast NBC outlet trio originating at San Francisco KGO; half-hour primetime drama that ultimately segued into quarter-hour daytime serial; "dedicated to the mothers and fathers of the younger generation and to their bewildering offspring," Carlton E. Morse tale pitted modern attitudes preferred by those bewildering offspring against old-fashioned ideas of father Henry Barbour (J. Anthony Smythe); mother Fanny Barbour (Minetta Ellen, Mary Adams) often pled for leniency from old man, leaning toward Paul (Michael Raffetto, Russell Thorson), Hazel (Bernice Berwin), Claudia (Kathleen Wilson, Floy Margaret Hughes, Barbara Fuller, Laurette Fillbrandt), Clifford (Barton Yarborough), Jack (Page Gilman); forays on NBC-TV into nighttime/daytime versions 1949–55 weren't keepers; final radiocast April 24, 1959.

Births

Edward Kennedy (Duke) Ellington, April 29, 1899, Washington, D.C.; composer, contractor, impresario, pianist; legendary Negro musician headlining mix of net, syndicated shows under banner *A Date with the Duke* mid 1940s; acquired "Duke" sobriquet when adolescent pals took titles of nobility; broadcast locally from New York's Kentucky Club 1923, Cotton Club 1927; considered "best of the predominantly black outfits, overwhelming much of its white competition," though never achieving whites' radio exposure; estimate affirms he composed 2,000+ pieces of music ranging from jazz to orchestral suites, ballets, Broadway shows, sacred numbers; d. May 24, 1974.

John F. MacVane, April 29, 1912, Portland, Maine; author, correspondent, newscaster, print journalist (*The Brooklyn Daily Eagle*, *The New York Sun*, *The London Daily Express*), wire journalist (International News Service); supplied eyewitness accounts from Paris, London, Africa, more European World War II hot spots after leaving print for London NBC staff 1940, war coverage to 1945; reassigned by NBC to UN, transferring late 1940s to ABC in same post to 1977 retirement with varied pithy ABC-TV entries; heard on dozen NBC, ABC radio news, public affairs series 1940s-50s including *John MacVane and the News* 1945–48, 1953–56; penned tome *On the Air in World War II* released 1979; d. Jan. 28 1984.

Frank Parker (Frank Ciccio), April 29, 1903, New York City, N.Y.; recording artist, vocalist (tenor) bka *Arthur Godfrey Time* singer (often with Marion Marlowe) early 1950s, *Arthur Godfrey and His Friends* in same epoch CBS-TV; performed previously with Jack Benny, George Burns and Gracie Allen; early soloist or in groups on *The Eveready Hour*, *The A&P Gypsies*, *Gulf Headliners*, *Cities Service Concert*, *Manhattan Merry-Go-Round*, *American Album of Familiar Music*; publicity blitz by producers Frank, Anne Hummert — behind last two shows — billed him as "America's great romantic tenor"; d. Jan. 10, 1999.

Deaths

Cy Howard, April 29, 1993, Los Angeles, Calif.; b. Sept. 27, 1915. Joe Laurie, Jr., April 29, 1954, New York City, N.Y.; b. Feb. 24, 1891. Bill Quinn, April 29, 1994, Carmarillo, Calif.; b. May 6, 1912.

April 30

Debuting

Arthur Godfrey Time, April 30, 1945, CBS; daytime variety; continuing artists, guests; announcer Tony Marvin introduced star on multi daily segments with "Here's that man himself!"; mainly with this show Godfrey contributed 12 percent of CBS's annual revenues, occupied up to 14 hours' weekly airtime; regular performers (until 1953 when Godfrey began firing most who hadn't left of own volition): Archie Bleyer, Pat Boone, The Chordettes, Janette Davis, Haleloke, Julius LaRosa, Bill Lawrence, The Mariners, Marion Marlowe, The McGuire Sisters, Frank Parker, Carmel Quinn, Lu Anne Simms; portions simulcast on CBS-TV Jan. 7, 1952-April 24, 1959; final radiocast April 30, 1972.

Queen for a Day, April 30, 1945, MBS, weekday human interest feature with emcees Dud Williamson, Jack Bailey; phenomenal prizes for heartbreaking stories; final radiocast June 10, 1957, NBC-TV Jan. 3, 1956-Sept. 2, 1960.

Canceled

The American School of the Air, April 30, 1948, CBS; debut Feb. 4, 1930. *Arthur Godfrey Time*, April 30, 1972, CBS; debut April 30, 1945. *Guess Who?*, April 30, 1949, MBS; debut April 8, 1944.

Births

Eve Arden (Eunice Quedens), April 30, 1908, Mill Valley, Calif.; actress (stage, film, radio, TV) bka *Our Miss Brooks* sitcom Madison High English teacher Connie Brooks 1948–57, TV 1952–56; quit school at 16 joining San Francisco stock company Henry Duffy Players on road, followed by band box repertoire outfit, Pasadena Playhouse revue, movies starting with 1929's *Song of Love*, Ziegfeld Follies girl 1934, promoted in 1936 to Fanny Brice's understudy by Ziegfeld, returned to Hollywood filmdom 1937; on *The Sealtest Village Show* with Jack Haley, Jack Carson NBC 1945–48, turned up spasmodically on *Pabst Blue Ribbon Town* CBS 1945–46; after *Our Miss Brooks*, made more films–*Anatomy of a Murder*, *The Dark at the Top of the Stairs*, *Grease*, *Grease 2*, et al.; *Hello, Dolly!*, *Mame* starring roles onstage 1960s; unsuccessful sitcom *The Eve Arden Show* CBS-TV 1957–58, costar with Kaye Ballard of *The Mothers-in-law* NBC-TV 1967–69; many more single-shot TV features; d. Nov. 12, 1990.

John T. (Jack) Haskell, April 30, 1919, Akron, Ohio; actor, announcer, recording artist, vocalist; sang with bands on Chicago WBBM,

WGN in collegiate music major days at Northwestern; shampoo sponsor's advertising envoy on *Fitch Bandwagon* NBC; sang with vocalist Doris Day, Les Brown Orchestra, joined Dave Garroway on Chicago-, New York-based programming; in Gotham made records, played summer stock, Broadway musicals; vocalized on 1940s-50s radio series *Jack Haskell Show*, *The Jim Backus Show*, *Les Brown Orchestra*, *NBC Bandstand*, *The Peter Lind Hayes Show*, *Stop the Music!*, more; TV gigs *Garroway at Large* 1949–51, *The Dave Garroway Show* 1953–54, *The Jack Paar Show* 1955–56, *Of All Things* 1956, *The Tonight Show* 1962; d. Sept. 26, 1998.

Fulton Lewis, Jr., April 30, 1903, Washington, D.C.; commentator, print journalist (*The Washington Herald* 1925), syndicated columnist (*The Washington Sideshow* 1933–36), wire service journalist (Universal News Service 1928) bka *Top of the News from Washington* analyst 1937-ca. 1957; controversial conservative when nation grew more liberal—"Lewis was loved and hated with equal intensity" said pundit, another observing he was "known for his complete lack of objectivity ... the master of partisan smear who rarely strayed from GOP talking points"; column to 60 newspapers propelled him into radio at Washington WOL 1937, soon aired nationally on MBS, eventually reaching 10 million listeners; incredibly tied to witchhunting Sen. Joseph McCarthy (R-Wis.)—when public turned on McCarthy, it turned on Lewis; d. Aug. 21, 1966.

Orin Tovrov, April 30, 1911, Chicago, Ill.; writer bka *Ma Perkins* daytime serial wordsmith in drama's halcyon epoch NBC/CBS 1939–60—with more than two decades to do it, he turned figures of Ma, Shuffle, Fay, Willie, Evey, Junior into beloved easily-recognized people dropping by millions of American homes for daily visits, raising bar of genre's quality quite a few notches; penned scripts for audio, televersions of *The Brighter Day* plus *The Doctors* anthology serial; d. Aug. 16, 1980.

Deaths

Howard Claney, April 30, 1980, Charlotte, N.C.; b. April 17, 1898. Peter Donald, April 30, 1979, Fort Lauderdale, Fla.; b. June 16, 1918. Agnes Moorehead, April 30, 1974, Rochester, Minn.; b. Dec. 6, 1900. Elmo Roper, April 30, 1971, Norwalk, Conn.; b. July 31, 1900.

May 1

Sound Bite

Mutual Broadcasting System inaugurates Mutual Black Network May 1, 1972, nation's first ethnic-oriented web; MBS sells its controlling shares to Sheridan Broadcasting Corp. in September 1979 which swiftly renames ancillary Sheridan Broadcasting Network; rival operator launches National Black Network July 2, 1973.

Canceled

Man on the Farm, May 1, 1954, MBS; debut Sept. 30, 1939.

Births

Howard Barlow, May 1, 1892, Plain City, Ohio; arranger, CBS staff impresario, vocalist bka *Voice of Firestone* maestro 1943–57 including simulcast 1949–57; "fastidiously attired" on those occasions said one pundit; formed American National Orchestra of native-born Americans 1923; Columbia Symphony Orchestra conductor ca. late 1920s-1930s; *The March of Time* radio musical director 1931–43; stints leading Baltimore Symphony 1939, New York Philharmonic, 1942, 1943, latter airing CBS; d. Jan 31, 1972.

Jack Paar, May 1, 1918, Canton, Ohio; announcer, author, comedian, master of ceremonies, quizmaster (radio, TV), stage entertainer bka *The Tonight Show* aka *The Jack Paar Show* host NBC-TV 1957–62; *The Jack Paar Show* aural variety series aired in segments: NBC June 1-Sept. 28, 1947, ABC Oct. 1-Dec. 24, 1947, ABC July 2-Dec. 28, 1956, latter daytime quarter-hour; *The $64 Question* quizzer 1950–52; penned best-seller *I Kid You Not* 1961; d. Jan. 27, 2004.

Kate Smith (Kathryn Elizabeth Smith), May 1, 1907, Washington, D.C. (despite myth she herself peddled that her birth occurred two years hence at Greenville, Va., which seemed to make her claim "Songbird of the South" legit); vocalist (concert, film, personal appearances, radio, recordings, stage, TV) bka hostess of more than two dozen radio series bearing her moniker 1931–59, plus daily, weekly TV features 1950–54, 1960; cut 3,000 discs over enduring career; evolved into spokesperson for varied causes, gained legions of followers in daily chat sessions with housewives; sold hundreds of millions of dollars of U. S. bonds to assist country in wartime; introduced Irving Berlin's "God Bless America" to nation Nov. 10, 1938, approbation pushing her to repeat it hundreds of times making it signature tune; at White House state visit of Engllsh king, queen 1939, Franklin D. Roosevelt — presenting Ms. Smith — exclaimed: "Your majesties, this is Kate Smith — *this* is America!"; d. June 17, 1986.

Deaths

A. M. Crossley, May 1, 1985, Princeton, N.J.; b. Dec. 7, 1896. Gordon Jenkins, May 1, 1984, Malibu, Calif.; b. May 12, 1910. Henry Neely, May 1, 1963, Elmhurst, N.Y.; b. Nov. 5, 1877.

May 2

Debuting

The Jack Benny Program (and assorted appellations), May 2, 1932, NBC Blue; modified sitcom with stand-up comic Benny as self, recurring cast, guests; most prominent recurring cast included Mary Livingstone (Mrs. Benny), Phil Harris, Eddie Anderson, Dennis Day, Don Wilson, many supporting voices; final new radiocast May 22, 1955, repeats Oct. 28, 1956-July 7, 1957, Sept. 29, 1957-June 22, 1958, TV extension Oct. 28, 1950-Sept. 10, 1965.

Deaths

William John Andrews, May 2, 1985, Contra Costa, Calif.; b. April 5, 1905. Jack Barry, May 2, 1984, New York City, N.Y., b. March 20, 1918. Herb Butterfield, May 2, 1957, Sawtelle, Calif.; b. Oct. 28, 1895. Dud Williamson, May 2, 1948, Lido Beach, Calif.; b. May 4, 1902.

May 3

Sound Bite

All-talk series linking couple of ABC West Coast stations launches on May 3, 1982; on May 10, New York WABC joins; by June 18, hookup of 22 outlets carries service dubbed *Talkradio*; conversational format occupies daily web schedule 10 a.m. to 4 p.m., 12 midnight to 6 a.m. ET.

Debuting

All Things Considered, May 3, 1971, National Public Radio; news-features magazine; initially in 112 markets 90 minutes in early evening soon increasing to two-hour block 5–7 p.m., shifting to 4 p.m. start 1995; still airing daily 2008.

Canceled

This Is Your Life, May 3, 1950, CBS; debut Nov. 9, 1948.

Births

George Hamilton Combs, Jr., May 3, 1899, Lee's Summit, Mo.; attorney, author, bureaucrat, commentator, politician; U. S. Representative from Missouri (Democrat) 1927–29; special assistant to New York state attorney general 1931; simultaneously news director of WHN; founded Radio Press International; named by President Franklin D. Roosevelt as director of National Emergency Council 1936; *George Hamilton Combs News and Commentary* 1937–71 his liberal radio pulpit on NBC Blue, ABC, MBS, plus TV 1952–61; MBS chief U. N. correspondent-news commentator 1961–71; d. Nov. 29, 1977.

Norman Corwin, May 3, 1910, East Boston, Mass.; author, journalist, newscaster, poetry reader, publicity scribe, screenplay wordsmith, scriptwriter bka "America's poet laureate of radio"; at 17 launched career reporting for two Massachusetts newsjournals, projecting him to Springfield WBZA; lasted two weeks in news at Cincinnati WLW 1935, crossing officials on station policy; joined 20th Century–Fox New York as publicist, on air at WQXR 1936, NBC's *The Magic Key of RCA* 1937, hired by CBS as a radio director 1938 at $125 weekly — directed *The Columbia Workshop*, other prestigious anthologies, plus *Norman Corwin's Words Without Music* poetry-reading 1939; brief leave from CBS to pen screenplays for RKO Hollywood 1940 but eagerly returned to CBS to develop, write, direct, produce plays for *26 by Corwin* followed by multiple World War II radio "spectaculars"; continued writing movies, added stage and TV plays; early 2008 persisted in writing, teaching journalism at University of Southern California.

Harry Lillis (Bing) Crosby, May 3, 1903, Tacoma, Wash.; vocalist (pop idol) becoming legend in his time, likely most widely recognized singer of his era through radio, recordings, screen appearances; *Bing Crosby Show* under several appellations an ethereal staple 1931–62 virtually encompassed medium's golden age; d. Oct. 14, 1977.

Curt Massey, May 3, 1910, Midland, Texas; fiddler, pianist, recording artist, trumpeter, vocalist (baritone) bka *Curt Massey Time* musical series host 1943, 1944–45, 1945, 1948, 1949, 1956, *The Curt Massey-Martha Tilton Show* 1949–54 aired concurrently on dual webs; *The Beverly Hillbillies* 1962–70, *Petticoat Junction* 1963–70 both CBS-TV music director, themes composer singing latter series' lyrics on show; d. Oct. 21, 1991.

Oliver Fort Pearson, May 3, 1909, Tennessee; announcer, entrepreneur, newscaster, sportscaster; apprenticeship at Shreveport, La., Port Arthur, Tex., Houston stations before hitting big time at Chicago NBC, affiliates WENR, WMAQ mid 1930s announcing, handling news, sports; lots of athletic events 1936–41; opened 1930s-50s *Beat the Band, The Curt Massey-Martha Tilton Show, Comedy of Errors, The Guiding Light, Hoosier Hot Shots, Lonely Women, Queen for a Day, The Quiz Kids, Terry Regan—Attorney at Law, This Amazing America*; operated sporting goods store at Sherman Oaks, Calif. 1951–56; San Francisco KPIX-TV morning news anchor 1957–60, moved to KFRC Radio briefly between video stints, joined KGO-TV as evening anchor 1961; d. Feb. 19, 1989.

Death

William R. Downs, Jr., May 3, 1978, Bethesda, Md.; b. Aug. 14, 1914.

May 4

Canceled

A Date with Judy, May 4, 1950, ABC; debut June 24, 1941. *The Johnny Olsen Show*, May 4, 1957, MBS; debut June 29, 1946.

Birth

Dudley (Dud) Earle Williamson, May 4, 1902, Alaska; actor, announcer, director, emcee, producer, program creative bka *Queen for a Day* original master of ceremonies; d. May 2, 1948.

Deaths

Norman Brokenshire, May 4, 1965, Hauppauge, N.Y.; b. June 10, 1898. Elaine Carrington, May 4, 1958, New York City, N.Y.; b. June 14, 1891.

May 5

Births

Theodore David (Ted) Brown, May 5, 1921, Collingwood, N.J.; actor, announcer, disc jockey, emcee, quizmaster bka NBC-TV *The Howdy Doody Show* figure Bison Bill 1947–60, *Monitor* host 1970–72, New York area DJ over WMGM, WNEW, WNBC, WVNJ 1948–56, 1962, 1970, 1972–89, 1996; assessing his *Monitor* gig, pundit said he was "brash, opinionated and off-the-wall," at times "a wild man"—he ad-libbed "outrageous remarks, breaking into a foreign accent, and occasionally driving *Monitor* producers crazy because his ravings would put the broadcasts well behind-time"; *Monitor* cohort Jim Lowe termed him "a major talent, with a keen sense of the ridiculous"; d. March 20, 2005.

Alice Faye (Alice Jeanne Leppert), May 5, 1915, New York City, N.Y.; actress (film, radio), recording artist, vocalist bka *The Phil Harris-Alice Faye Show* sitcom costar 1946–54; primarily cast in movie musicals on silver screen, she introduced pop hit parade songs like "You'll Never Know" in 1943's *Hello, Frisco, Hello*; Irving Berlin said he selected Faye over every other vocalist to introduce his songs while in 1937 George Gershwin, Cole Porter dubbed her "the best female singer in Hollywood"; special talent of 20th Century–Fox producer Darryl F. Zanuck till he replaced her with Linda Darnell 1945 causing Faye to quit and Zanuck to blacklist her, keeping her from film work; she said she never missed Hollywood; d. May 9, 1998.

Freeman Fisher Gosden, May 5, 1899, Richmond, Va.; actor (film, radio, stage), director, producer, ukulele strummer bka *Amos 'n' Andy* characters Amos Jones, George (Kingfish) Stevens, Willie (Lightnin') Jefferson, John Augustus (Brother) Crawford, dozens of others; partnership with Charles Correll (Andy) formed 1919 extending rest of lives, briefly commanding largest number of Americans concurrently focused on single amusement; infamous characters launched as *Sam 'n' Henry* over Chicago WGN Jan. 12, 1926, continuing web gigs persisted to *The Amos 'n' Andy Music Hall* final broadcast Nov. 25, 1960, unprecedented for aural comic figures; d. Dec. 10, 1982.

Bret Morrison, May 5, 1912, Chicago, Ill.; actor (stage, film, radio, TV), announcer, commercial artist, emcee, entrepreneur (supplied movie production houses with luxury cars), instructor (stage makeup), voiceover artist (foreign films, animated TV) bka *The Shadow* crime-mystery figure MBS 1943–44, 1945–54; fluency in 14 dialects, co-founded Evanston, Ill. Players Guild, toured dual seasons with Chicago Art Theater Co., three minor Hollywood films; two dozen chain radio series 1930s-70s acting in half, narrating rest e.g. *The Adventures of Superman, Arnold Grimm's Daughter, Carnation Contented Hour, The CBS Radio Mystery Theater, The Chicago Theater of the Air, The First Nighter, The Guiding Light, Heartbeat Theater, The Light of the World* (as "the Speaker"), *The Mysterious Traveler, The Road of Life, The Romance of Helen Trent, The Story of Mary Marlin, Woman in White*, more; d. Sept. 25, 1978.

May 6

Debuting

Straight Arrow, May 6, 1948, MBS-Don Lee West Coast; juvenile adventure; Sheldon Stark, *Straight Arrow* wordsmith, sat under tutelage of Fran Striker, head scribe of radio's most enduring western epic, *The Lone Ranger*— so is it any wonder Stark turned orphaned Comanche (recall *Ranger's* "faithful Indian companion") into hero, now adult warrior posing as rancher Steve Adams (Howard Culver)?; grizzled, faithful white sidekick Packy McCloud (Fred Howard) only guy knowing Adams' identity for sure though housekeeper Mesquite Molly (Gwen Delano) must have wondered why employer vanished as great deeds on great steeds performed for betterment of race relations during his oft absences; Straight Arrow hunted claim-jumpers, swindlers, cattle-rustlers, disturbers of peace just as his "white brothers of the trail" did — with but two folks tops (plus legions tuning in!) realizing who he was; final broadcast June 21, 1951.

Births

Robert Leo Murphy, May 6, 1917, Bismarck, N.D.; announcer, emcee, newscaster, sportscaster bka *The Breakfast Club* interlocutor 1940s (only known net radio show); at St. Paul, Minn. KSTP 1937 read sports scores, moving to news headlines 1940–42; presided over *R.F.D. America* NBC-TV 1949; d. Oct. 25, 1959.

Frank Nelson, May 6, 1911, Denver, Colo.; actor (film, radio, TV), announcer, voiceover artist bka nameless abrasive characters on *The Jack Benny Program* 1934–55, 1956–58 ("Yeeeeeessss? ... Oooooooooooooh, *goodie*! ... Oooooooooooooh, *do* I?!") — his "calling," he said years hence, was "the guy whose sole purpose in life was to annoy the hell out of Jack Benny"; debuted radio on Denver KOA 1926, moved to dramas aired by Los Angeles KFAC 1930, KMTR 1932 qualifying him as reliable, versatile support thespian for aural antics; linked to about three dozen series 1930s-80s, most as actor e.g. *The Abbott and Costello Show, Baby Snooks, The George Burns and Gracie Allen Show, The Eddie Cantor Show, Fibber McGee & Molly, Lux Radio Theater, Maisie, The Phil Harris-Alice Faye Show, The Sears/Mutual Radio Theater*; prolific commercial spokesman, voiced animated figures in video film specials, TV cartoon series, acted on other TV fare, 16 theatrical films 1936–85; d. Sept. 12, 1986.

William T. Quinn, May 6, 1912, New York City, N.Y.; actor (stage, film, radio, TV); support in *The Big Story, The Chase, Cloak and Dagger, Dimension X, Front Page Farrell, Just Plain Bill, The Man Behind the Gun, Mr. Keen — Tracer of Lost Persons, Mrs. Wiggs of the Cabbage Patch, Now Hear This, The Right to Happiness, Stella Dallas, Top Secrets of the FBI, When a Girl Marries*, more; debuted on Broadway at two, film at six, vaudeville next, dozen-plus return trips to Broadway 1923–57, TV series — *The Rifleman* 1958–63, *Archie Bunker's Place* 1979–83, 200 solo TV drama/sitcom episodes 1958–88, four TV mini-series 1976–80, 23 made-for-TV flicks 1969–84, 28 cinema films 1924–89; d. April 29, 1994.

Alice Reinheart, May 6, 1910, San Francisco, Calif.; actress (stage, film, radio, TV) bka *Life Can Be Beautiful* daytime serial ward Chichi Conrad 1938–46, one of two playing durable role; at 12 on Broadway, returned at 14, again at 30, 34; worked radio on *The Adventures of the Abbotts, Casey — Crime Photographer, Gangbusters, John's Other Wife, Her Honor — Nancy James, One Man's Family*, aired six-day-a-week breakfast chatfest with husband-actor Les Tremayne, *The Tremaynes*, over New York WOR 1940s-50s; returned to mic for 1970s *The CBS Radio Mystery Theater*; in between earned theatrical film credits, in casts of TV's *Make*

Room for Daddy 1955–60, *The Donna Reed Show* 1958–66, *Paradise Bay* 1965–66; d. June 10, 1993.

Orson Welles, May 6, 1915, Kenosha, Wis.; actor (stage, radio, film, TV), artist, costume designer, director, editor, music arranger, photographer-cinematographer, producer, set designer, writer bka *The Mercury Theater of the Air* anthology drama producer whose portrayal of H. G. Wells' "The War of the Worlds" on CBS Oct. 30, 1938 threw thousands of East Coast, Midwest listeners into panic believing Martians invading New Jersey; linked to more than three dozen radio series, ties to almost 400 film-TV productions in diverse capacities plus 100 TV appearances as himself; d. Oct. 10, 1985.

Deaths

Don Hancock, May 6, 1980, Anderson, Ind.; b. Oct. 10, 1910. Hugh Studebaker, May 6, 1978 (final address Encino, Calif.); b. May 31, 1900. Lyle Sudrow, May 6, 2006, Los Angeles, Calif.; b. Feb. 19, 1921. Ned Wever, May 6, 1984, Laguna Hills, Calif.; b. April 27, 1902.

May 7

Debuting

The Affairs of Peter Salem, May 7, 1949, MBS; detective-mystery drama; cool, calculating, debonair gumshoe Salem (Santos Ortega) from the hinterlands took passive, non–violent course in capturing urbane varmints, opposite eccentric hero Ortega portrayed in *The Adventures of Nero Wolfe* 1943–44; entry suffered time warp, shifting in-and-out–of seven time periods over disjointed run that saw it airing a few weeks, withdrawn a few months, returning elsewhere on schedule, preventing loyal fans from becoming overly loyal; final broadcast April 18, 1953.

Canceled

The Chicago Theater of the Air, May 7, 1955, MBS; debut Oct. 5, 1940. *Lum and Abner*, May 7, 1954, syndication (final network broadcast May 15, 1953, ABC).

Births

Win Elliot (Irwin Elliot Shalek), May 7, 1915, Chelsea, Mass.; announcer, emcee, sportscaster bka audience participation-game show master of ceremonies who became more prominent as eyewitness to games; quiver filled with former breed on radio (*County Fair, Fish Pond, Musical Mysteries, Quick as a Flash, Walk a Mile*), TV (*It's in the Bag, On Your Account, Tic Tac Dough, Win with a Winner, Make That Spare*); segued into sportscasts for dual media — roundups were ongoing CBS Radio staples 1960s-80s, anchored pre–, post–game World Series radio features while covering New York Rangers hockey team on Gotham WMGM, WINS; d. Sept. 19, 1998.

Gloria Gordon, May 7, 1884, England; actress (stage, film, radio, TV) bka mother of actor Gale Gordon, character thespian in copious broadcast sitcoms; her contributions to radio included recurring characterizations on *The Jack Benny Program* mid–to-late 1940s, *Favorite Story* 1946–49, *My Friend Irma* ca. 1947–54, *The Halls of Ivy* 1950–52, *Doctor Paul* 1951–53; d. Nov. 21, 1962.

Jack Johnstone, May 7, 1906, New York City, N.Y.; announcer, director, writer; working for an ad agency at $32 weekly, engaged to pen few episodes of *Buck Rogers in the 25th Century*; turned into stable work, adding directing, announcing show at $300 weekly; wrote, produced, directed *Yours Truly—Johnny Dollar* 1955–62, penned 1940s installments of *The Adventures of Superman*, directed 1930s-50s *The CBS Radio Workshop, Crime Doctor, Hollywood Star Playhouse, Hollywood Startime, Jack Johnstone's Dramas, Johnny Presents, The Man Called X, Orson Welles' Radio Almanac, The Prudential Family Hour of Stars, Richard Diamond—Private Detective, The Six Shooter, Somebody Knows, The Whistler, Who Knows?*; d. Nov. 16, 1991.

Deaths

Frank Goss, May 7, 1962, Hollywood, Calif.; b. Nov. 20, 1910. George D. Hay, May 7, 1968, Virginia Beach, Va.; Nov. 9, 1908. Don McNeill, May 7, 1996, Evanston, Ill.; b. Dec. 23, 1907.

May 8

Births

Arthur Q. Bryan, May 8, 1899, Brooklyn, N.Y.; actor (film, radio), voiceover artist bka spokesman for animated cartoon figure Elmer Fudd from late 1930s, *Fibber McGee & Molly* irascibly sparring nemesis George (Doc) Gamble 1943–55, *The Great Gildersleeve* barber and Jolly Boys Club cohort Floyd Munson ca. mid 1940s-mid 1950s; d. Nov. 18, 1959.

Eric Hilliard (Ricky/Rick) Nelson, May 8, 1940, Teaneck, N.J.; actor (film, radio, TV), recording artist bka *The Adventures of Ozzie and Harriet* as himself joining radio cast 1949–54, TV 1952–66, teen idol for 18 hits 1957–72 ("I'm Walkin'," "Be Bop Baby," "Poor Little Fool," "It's Late," "There'll Never Be Anyone Else But You," "Travelin' Man," "Hello, Mary Lou," "Young World," "Fools Rush In," "For You," "Garden Party," more); d. Dec. 31, 1985.

Katharine Raht, May 8, 1901, Chattanooga, Tenn.; actress (radio, stage, TV), educator bka *The Aldrich Family* matriarch Alice Aldrich 1939–51; radio second career, having taught school, sought summer employment on air — attaining it, couldn't let it go; d. Dec. 2, 1983.

Death

LaVerne Andrews, May 8, 1967, Brentwood, Calif.; b. July 6, 1911.

May 9

Debuting

The Edgar Bergen and Charlie McCarthy Show, May 9, 1937, NBC; comedy variety; ventriloquist Bergen, puppets McCarthy, Mortimer Snerd, Effie Klinker, Podine Puffington, Lars Lindquist; McCarthy, Snerd most prominent — McCarthy sparred with Bergen/guests, particularly W. C. Fields, while befuddled Snerd belonged in slower group; regulars Don Ameche, Dorothy Lamour, Nelson Eddy, Judy Canova, Bud Abbott, Lou Costello, Frances Langford; headliners at other venues paraded through Bergen portals; final broadcast July 1, 1956.

Births

William Perry Adams, May 9, 1887, Tiffin, Ohio; actor, announcer, bka *Let's Pretend* host-narrator ("Uncle Bill") 1943–54; prolific thespian in recurring parts, anthologies: *Abie's Irish Rose, The Adventures of Mr. Meek, Big Town, Cavalcade of America, The Collier Hour, The Gibson Family, The Light of the World, The March of Time, Pepper Young's Family, Rosemary, Roses and Drums, The Story of Mary Marlin, These Are Our Men, Valiant Lady, Wayside Cottage, Your Family and Mine, Yours Truly—Johnny Dollar*; introduced *The Heinz Magazine of the Air, Saturday Night Serenade*; d. Sept. 29, 1972.

Myron (Mike) Wallace (Myron Leon Wallik), May 9, 1918, Brookline, Mass.; actor, announcer, author, emcee bka *60 Minutes* news documentary investigator 1968–2006 retiring at 88; played in dud radio series but opened stalwarts: *The Green Hornet, The Lone Ranger* both 1940–41, *The Guiding Light, Ma Perkins, The Road of Life* all 1941–42, *Sky King* late 1940s-early 1950s, *The Spike Jones Show* late 1940s, *You Bet Your Life* commercial spokesman 1947–50, *Weekday* 1955–56; many other TV gigs; penned best-selling tome *Between You and Me* 2005.

Deaths

Alice Faye, May 9, 1998, Rancho Mirage, Calif.; b. May 5, 1915. Pauline Frederick, May 9, 1990, Lake Forest, Ill.; b. Feb. 13, 1908. Bill Goodwin, May 9, 1958, Palm Springs, Calif.; b. July 28, 1910. Graham McNamee, May 9, 1942, New York City, N.Y.; b. July 10, 1888. Ezio Pinza, May 9, 1957, Stamford, Conn.; b. May 18, 1892.

May 10

Sound Bite

End of entanglement, May 10, 1943; Federal Communications Commission (FCC) orders Radio Corporation of America — National Broadcasting Co. (NBC) parent — to divest one of two wholly owned divisions (Red, Blue chains) to cease perceived airwaves monopoly; Red dubbed NBC after Blue sold to confection (Life Savers) magnate Edward J. Noble July 1943; FCC approves sale October 1943; Blue labeled American Broadcasting Co. (ABC) 1945.

Births

Louis Buck, May 10, 1910, Bessemer, Ala.; announcer, radio sales executive bka *Grand Ole Opry* interlocutor NBC 1939–46, one of trio of original full-time *Opry* announcers (others David Cobb, Jud Collins); d. May 18, 1971.

Frank Knight, May 10, 1894, St. John's, Newfoundland, Canada; actor, announcer, recording artist bka *Golden Memories of Radio, I Remember Radio* 1960s nostalgia LP records narrator, same duty with *The Longines Symphonette* ca. 1943–57 ("the world's most honored music program presented as a salute to Longines, the world's most honored watch")—Longines Symphonette Society produced nostalgia records; initially on ether at New York WABC 1928; American Academy of Arts and Letters bestowed Diction Award 1930s; a founding father of American Guild of Radio Announcers and Producers; acted in *Arabesque, The Collier Hour, The First National Hour* 1920s-30s radio, introduced 1930s-50s listeners to *The Adventures of Superman, Author Author, The Chesterfield Quarter Hour, The Choraliers, The New York Philharmonic Symphony Orchestra, The Robert Burns Panatella Program, Uncle Don*, more; *Chromoscope* world affairs chat moderator CBS-TV 1951–55; d. Oct. 18, 1973.

Anthony J. La Frano, May 10, 1911, announcer, film-network executive, producer bka RKO-General Corp. VP-exec director/operations for West Coast embracing Hollywood KHJ Radio-TV, San Francisco KFRC; before 1939 ties with KHJ, Santa Barbara program official, VP-program director at Don Lee regional net to 1948; produced *Elsa Maxwell's Party Line* 1943–47, beckoned fans in same era to *California Melodies, Family Theater* (1947–62), *Johnny Modero—Pier 23, The Tommy Dorsey Playstop*, added features; d. Sept. 12, 1961.

Jeff Frank Martin, Jr., May 10, 1914, Oklahoma; actor, announcer; played in 1940s-50s *Hashknife Hartley, Meet Corliss Archer, The Merry Life of Mary Christmas, Tales of the Texas Rangers* while introducing *Alias Jane Doe, The Dick Haymes Show, Everything for the Boys, His Honor—the Barber, Lights Out, Mayor of the Town, Sara's Private Caper, Suspense, Your Lucky Strike*, more, and delivering commercials on *Dimension X*; d. Dec. 22, 1994.

George Allen (Pat) Summerall, May 10, 1930, Lake City, Fla.; NFL player, sportscaster bka *Pat Summerall on Sports* host CBS 1962–93; drafted by Detroit Lions 1952–53, traded to Chicago Cardinals 1954–57, New York Giants 1958–61, mainly place-kicker; when Fox outbid CBS for NFC broadcast rights in 1994, Summerall—as part of announcing package—in deal, remained through 2002; present in Super Bowl broadcast booths 26 times, surpassing all peers.

Deaths

John Lund, May 10, 1992, Coldwater Canyon, Calif.; b. Feb. 6, 1911. Paul Masterson, May 10, 1996, Laguna Beach, Calif.; b. Nov. 11, 1917. Roy Rowan, May 10, 1998, Paw Paw, Mich.; b. Jan. 25, 1920.

May 11

Births

Bidu Sayao, May 11, 1902, Rio de Janeiro, Brazil; vocalist (soprano) bka celebrated Metropolitan Opera diva 1937–51; *The Bell Telephone Hour* guest artist 26 times 1942–58; d. March 12, 1999.

Dorothy Warenskjold, May 11, 1921, San Leandro, Calif.; violinist, vocalist (lyric soprano) bka *The Railroad Hour* second most enduring costar with Gordon MacRae 61 times 1948–54; *Voice of Firestone* frequent recurring guest 1950s; visiting professor of music, University of California at Los Angeles from 1984.

Deaths

Allen C. Anthony, May 11, 1962; b. Aug. 5, 1906. John Frazer, May 11, 1945, Pacific Ocean; b. March 15, 1915. Mark Houston, May 11, 1971, Mansfield, Ohio; b. Oct. 3, 1913. Walter Kinsella, May 11, 1975, Englewood, N.J.; b. Aug. 16, 1900. Charles Lyon, May 11, 1985, Los Angeles, Calif.; b. March 1, 1903.

May 12

Births

Gordon Jenkins, May 12, 1910, Webster Groves, Mo.; accordionist, arranger, banjoist, impresario, lyricist, organist, pianist, recording artist, ukuleleist, vocalist bka soloist on The Weavers' "Goodnight Irene" recording, penned chart-topping "My Foolish Heart," "P.S., I Love You"; arranger for bandleaders Isham Jones, Benny Goodman, Lennie Hayton, Vincent Lopez, Paul Whiteman; NBC West Coast music director 1930s; Decca records music director 1940s showcasing The Andrews Sisters, Louis Armstrong, Dick Haymes, Peggy Lee, The

Weavers; mostly obscure aural series maestro 1935–53; d. May 1, 1984.

Howard Kingsbury Smith, Jr., May 12, 1914, Ferriday, La.; author, commentator, correspondent; regular 1941–61 on *CBS World News Roundup*, *Howard K. Smith News and Comment*, *World News Tonight*; hired for CBS Berlin bureau 1941; despite promise and success, victim of own undoing, falling from grace at CBS, transferring to ABC 1964–79 — part of period as news anchor — leaving ABC under heavy cloud; embittered in old age; d. Feb. 15, 2002.

Death

Perry Como, May 12, 2001, Jupiter Inlet Beach Colony, Fla.; b. May 18, 1912.

May 13

Canceled

Gene Autry's Melody Ranch, May 13, 1956, CBS; debut Jan. 7, 1940.

Death

Jim Kelly, May 13, 1961, Bronx, N.Y.; b. Dec. 14, 1899.

May 14

Canceled

Lowell Thomas and the News, May 14, 1976, CBS; debut Sept. 29, 1930.

Birth

Carlton Brickert, May 14, 1890, Martinsville, Ind.; actor (film, radio, stage), announcer bka soap opera thespian (*Abie's Irish Rose*, *Joyce Jordan*, *Portia Faces Life*, *The Story of Mary Marlin*, *A Tale of Today*, etc.); initial professional experience at 21 with Syracuse, N.Y. stock company followed by work as stage manager; Broadway roles opposite luminaries Mary Boland, Olga Petrova, Florence Reed, Lenore Ulric; silver screen next with half-dozen B-films 1916–23; introduced *Lum and Abner* to 1930s listeners, picking up daytime serial roles, other aural entertainment features as actor or narrator; joined Chicago NBC staff 1938; d. Dec. 23, 1943.

Deaths

Alwyn Bach, May 14, 1993, Portland, Ore.; b. Jan. 24, 1898. Earl J. Glade, Jr., May 14, 2001, Salt Lake City, Utah; b. July 17, 1911.

May 15

Canceled

Mary Margaret McBride, May 15, 1954, ABC; debut Oct. 4, 1937.

Births

Sam G. Edwards, May 26, 1918, Macon, Ga.; actor (stage, radio, film, TV), voiceover artist bka *Meet Corliss Archer* teen sitcom namesake boyfriend Dexter Franklin 1944–56; debuted onstage as infant cradled in actress-mom Edna Park's arms in *Tess of the Storm Country*; on air with showbiz clan in *The Edwards Family* 1937–42; supporting ethereal catalog: *Broadway Is My Beat*, *The CBS Radio Workshop*, *Confession*, *Crime Classics*, *Deadline Mystery*, *Dragnet*, *Escape*, *Father Knows Best*, *The Guiding Light*, *Gunsmoke*, *Have Gun — Will Travel*, *The Lineup*, *One Man's Family*, *Romance*, *The Sears/Mutual Radio Theater*, *The Six Shooter*, *Speed Gibson of the International Secret Police*, *Tales of the Texas Rangers*, *Yours Truly — Johnny Dollar*, more; 134 solo episodes of TV dramas/sitcoms/variety shows 1951–83, three TV series — *Full Circle* 1960, *Red Rocket* 1963, *These Are the Days* 1974 (latter two voice-only), 13 made-for-TV flicks 1969–79, 30 theatrical flicks 1940–81; d. July 28, 2004.

Clifton (Kip) Fadiman, May 15, 1904, Brooklyn, N.Y.; commentator, editor, educator, emcee (radio, TV), writer bka *Information Please* moderator 1938–51; after stints running bookshop, producing community newspaper, penning book reviews for *The Nation* magazine, teaching high school English, joined Simon & Schuster as assistant editor 1927, rose to editor 1929; *The New Yorker* magazine book editor 1933–43, concurrently as Simon & Schuster editor-in-chief, resigning 1935 but persisting as S&S external editorial adviser; Book of the Month Club selection jurist 1945; ties to Famous Writers School mail-order courses; *Information Please* opened doors for stints on *The Pursuit of Happiness* and *The NBC University Theater*, hosted *Conversation* NBC 1954–57, regular on nearly dozen web series plus some on TV; continued literary pursuits with *This Week*, *Holiday*, more periodicals, wrote/edited books; d. June 20, 1999.

Jacques Renard, May 15, 1897, Kiev, Ukraine; impresario, violinist bka handful of sundry primetime series maestro; d. Jan. 30, 1973.

Deaths

Grace Matthews, May 15, 1995, Mt. Kisko, N.Y.; b. Sept. 3, 1910. Frank Sinatra, May 15, 1998, Los Angeles, Calif.; b. Dec. 12, 1915.

May 16

Debuting

True Detective Mysteries, May 16, 1929, CBS; crime drama based on tales in *True Detective* magazine; editor Jack Shuttleworth (Richard Keith)—in time supplanted by unnamed editor (actor John Griggs)—narrated recreations of "a real story of a real crime solved by real people with a real criminal brought to justice"; like *Gangbusters*, added aural "wanted" poster for actual fugitive, offering cash to any locating perpetrators if arrested, convicted; critic branded it "the first network detective series of importance"; final broadcast June 2, 1958 although large gaps in its 29-year run.

The Whistler, May 16, 1942, CBS West Coast regional net; crime drama; accompanied by mournful wavering warble, Whistler (Bill Forman, Gale Gordon, Joseph Kearns, Marvin Miller, Bill Johnstone, Everett Clarke) was narrator that walked by night and knew "many strange tales hidden in the hearts of men and women who have stepped into the shadows ... [and] the nameless terrors of which they dare not speak"; in strange ending twists, culprits revealed guilt—or discovered acts they perpetrated performed for naught; full CBS net run July 3, 1946-Sept. 29, 1948 with West Coast extension to Sept. 8, 1955.

Canceled

The Minute Men (featuring *Stoopnagle and Budd* whose act broke up at end of series though they persisted as solo performers), May 16, 1937, NBC Blue; debut May 24, 1931.

Births

Woody Herman, May 16, 1913, Milwaukee, Wis.; clarinetist, impresario; played clarinet for outfits fronted by Harry Sosnik, Gus Arnheim, Isham Jones—when Jones bowed out, Herman and arranger Joe Bishop replaced him; conducted first outfit held over by Hollywood Palladium 1943; supplied melody to five chain audio series 1942–56 with two brief features under own moniker; admired by his men but some poor business decisions left him owing IRS beyond million dollars when he died; d. Oct. 29, 1987.

Norman D. Ross, May 16, 1886, Portland, Ore.; announcer, athlete, disc jockey, newscaster, print journalist, publicist, sportscaster bka international swimming events competitor (after learning to swim by reading book), set 72 records, surpassed some global aquatic highs, set new marks in Paris 1919, Antwerp 1920, acquired 500 trophies; sportswriter for *The Chicago Daily Journal* before forming publicity firm, joined Chicago WIBO as sportscaster-newscaster-announcer; became Chicago NBC staffer at 47 in 1933; opened net radio series *Talk with Irene Rich*, *Theater Guild on the Air*, etc.; d. June 19, 1953.

Death

John H. Brown, May 16, 1957, West Hollywood, Calif.; b. April 4, 1904.

May 17

Debuting

Information Please, May 17, 1938, NBC Blue; scholarly quiz; queries posed by mainstream Americans—not effusive emcees, anomaly in radio with erudite matter raised not of unsuspecting goons plucked from studio audience but corps of cerebral giants incredibly well-versed in arts-artists-athletes-archives, etc.; far from being staid, mental heavyweights jousted between questions, especially when "dumb" enough to occasionally miss one; incomparable Clifton Fadiman moderated, permanent panelists Franklin P. Adams, John Kieran, Oscar Levant, guests; televersion CBS summer 1952; final radiocast April 22, 1951.

The Jack Kirkwood Show (*Mirth and Madness*, *At Home with the Kirkwoods*, *The Kirkwood Corner Store*), May 17, 1943, NBC; madcap comedy; Kirkwood polished act before San Francisco KFRC audience 1938, took "comic's comic" side-splitting style of slapstick vaudeville routines to national hookup afterward; mercilessly parodied radio detectives, western heroes, anybody he could think of with ludicrously inane material he penned; flanked by wife Lillian Leigh, Herb Sheldon, Ransom Sherman, Steve Dunne, more; "you gotta put something in the pot, boy" he uttered in visits to *The Bob Hope Show*, added to widening lexicon of scads of *Hope* listeners; final broadcast Feb. 20, 1953.

Canceled

The George Burns and Gracie Allen Show, May 17, 1950, CBS; debut as segment of *The Robert Burns Panatella Program*, Feb. 22, 1932.

Births

John Cannon, May 17, 1906, Chicago, Ill.; actor, announcer, cinematic newsreels narrator; opened 1950s TV series *Colgate Comedy Hour*, *I've Got a Secret*, *Strike It Rich!*, *Studio One*, *You Are There*, *Your Hit Parade*; National Academy of Television Arts and Sciences president 1976–2001; d. June 22, 2001.

Jack Petruzzi (Julius Petruzzi, changed to Julian J. Petruzzi), May 17, 1907, Cleveland, Ohio; actor (film, radio), announcer; introduced *Ned Jordan — Secret Agent* late 1930s-early 1940s, played in some aural series that lasted to early 1950s: *The Count of Monte Cristo*, *Escape*, *The Green Hornet*, *Jeff Regan — Investigator*, *The Lone Ranger*, *Lux Radio Theater*, *Ma Perkins*, *Masquerade*, *The Road of Life*, *The Whistler*, *Yours Truly — Johnny Dollar*, more; acted in theatrical films *Tenth Avenue Kid* 1937, *Vertigo* 1958; d. March 1, 1967.

Conway Tearle (Frederick Levy), May 17, 1878, New York City, N.Y.; actor (film, stage), announcer bka *Streamlined Shakespeare* narrator 1937, reprised 1950; in radio two years before death after decades onstage with Shakespearean repertory outfit; also performed in silent, talking B-pictures; d. Oct. 1, 1939.

Jesse Granderson (Grant) Turner, May 17, 1912, Baird, Texas; announcer, guitarist, print journalist (Louisiana, Texas newspapers) bka "voice of the Grand Ole Opry," *Grand Ole Opry* country music-humor show interlocutor on NBC portion 1947–57; performed as "Ike and His Guitar," announced on Abilene, Texas KFYO 1928; pursued newspaper jobs 1930s, joined Longview, Texas KFRO 1940, subsequently moved to stations at Sherman, Texas 1941, Knoxville, Tenn. 1942, hired by Nashville WSM D-Day June 6, 1944, soon assigned to *Opry*; elected to Country Music Hall of Fame 1981; d. Oct. 19, 1991.

Deaths

Roger Bower, May 17, 1979, Sharon, Conn.; b. Jan. 8, 1903. Frank Gallop, May 17, 1988, Palm Beach, Fla.; b. June 30, 1900. Alexander Kendrick, May 17, 1991, Philadelphia, Pa.; b. July 6, 1910. Lawrence Welk, May 17, 1992, Santa Monica, Calif.; b. March 11, 1903.

May 18

Debuting

David Harding, Counterspy (sometimes *Counterspy*), May 18, 1942, ABC; counterintelligence surveillance narrative focused on forces that threatened U. S, security, many fans thinking tales from actual cases, not fiction; under chief agent Harding (Don MacLaughlin), sidekick Peters (Mandel Kramer), global cops unraveled plots to limit our freedoms; their humorless, hard-nosed style, aggressive behavior habitually paid big dividends; final broadcast Nov. 29, 1957.

Births

Perry Como, May 18, 1912, Canonsburg, Pa.; barber, organist, recording artist, trumpeter, vocalist (film, radio, personal appearances, stage, TV) bka TV performer on *The Chesterfield Supper Club* 1948–55, *The Perry Como Show* 1955–59, *Kraft Music Hall* 1959–63, Christmas specials 1948–87; sold in excess of 100 million records with 14 tunes ranked first place; radio venues: *Fibber McGee & Molly* 1936–37, *The Perry Como Show* 1943, 1953–54, *The Chesterfield Supper Club* 1944–49, 1954–55; career began as baritone for outfits fronted by Freddie/Tony/Frank Carlone 1932–37, Ted Weems 1937–43; d. May 12, 2001.

Delmer Randolph (Del) King, May 18, 1908, Kansas City, Mo.; advertising executive, announcer, vocalist bka *Avalon Time* (*The Red Skelton Show*) interlocutor 1938–39 (only documented chain radio gig); sang with Kansas City Opera Co., went on hometown KMBC 1926 as soloist, freelance announcer in Chicago 1927–36, moved to Cincinnati WLW intersecting with comic Red Skelton, went with him to Chicago May 1939, joined advertising agency that packaged show as assistant radio director; d. Aug. 22, 1964.

Raymond Paige, May 18, 1900, Wausau, Wis.; impresario, violinist bka Radio City Music Hall music director 1950–65, similar duties for other venerated entourages — Hollywood Bowl Orchestra, Los Angeles Philharmonic, NBC Symphony, Pittsburgh Symphony; music director at 13-station Don Lee West Coast chain starting 1930; conductor for 17 aural series including *Hollywood Hotel, Stage Door Canteen, Kraft Music Hall*; d. Aug. 7, 1965.

Ezio Pinza (Fortunio Pinza), May 18, 1892, Rome, Italy; vocalist (bass) bka *The Bell Telephone Hour* third most prolific guest artist with 44 appearances 1942–58 (following Jascha Heifetz' 54, Lily Pons' 50); Metropolitan Opera Co. member 1926–48; d. May 9, 1957.

Frederick Shields, May 18, 1904, Kansas City, Mo.; actor, announcer bka *Meet Corliss Archer* sitcom figure Harry Archer in radio 1943–56, reincarnated in TV 1951–52; announced at Kansas City WDAF 1928; on web, acted in *Captain Flagg and Sergeant Quirt, Crime Classics, The Eddie Bracken Show, Honor the Law, Red Ryder, Tarzan* while presenting *Grapevine Rancho*; d. June 30, 1974.

Lew White (Louis P. White), May 18, 1899, Philadelphia, Pa.; composer, educator-entrepreneur; organist, recording artist; entertained at New York's Paramount, Roxy theaters; played for radio's *The Adventures of Dick Cole, The Adventures of Nero Wolfe, Casey — Crime Photographer, Dr. Christian, Grand Central Station, Inner Sanctum Mysteries, Nick Carter — Master Detective, Portia Faces Life*; supplied background themes for Columbia film short subjects; operated New York's School of Hammond Organ late in career; d. March 3, 1955.

Meredith Willson [sic], May 18, 1902, Mason City, Iowa; arranger, composer, disc jockey, flutist, house impresario (NBC), lyricist, piccoloist bka *The Big Show* music conductor NBC 1950–52 (penned finale "May the Good Lord Bless and Keep You"), responded to summons by basal-timbered star Tallulah Bankhead with "Yes, Miss Bankhead, sir?"; *The Music Man* film-stage production composer, librettist, lyricist 1957; maestro two dozen times on radio features 1927–53 (e.g., *Good News of 1937–40, Maxwell House Showboat/Coffee Time, Encore*, eight shows bearing Willson moniker); d. June 15, 1984.

Death

Louis Buck, May 18, 1971, Nashville, Tenn.; b. May 10, 1910. Elmer Davis, May 18, 1958, Washington, D.C.; b. Jan. 13, 1890.

May 19

Canceled

Vox Pop, May 19, 1948, ABC; debut July 7, 1935.

Birth

Wayne Nelson (Theodore C. Nelson), May 19, 1910, Galveston, Texas; announcer, director; career started at Greensboro, N.C. 1929 as announcer-director; from mid 1940s-50s welcomed fans to *Camel Caravan, The New York Philharmonic Symphony Orchestra, The Ted Lewis Show*; d. February 1984 (pervasive searching for exact date futile), Donovan, Ill.

Deaths

Winston Burdett, May 19, 1993, Rome, Italy; b. Dec. 12, 1913. Henry Morgan, May 19, 1994, New York City, N.Y.; b. March 31, 1915.

May 20

Debuting

Peter Potter's Juke Box Jury, May 20, 1954, CBS; audience participation series with studio onlookers, celebrated guest panelists rating pre-released phono discs; aural series followed six-month ABC-TV trial 1953–54; show's arrival perfectly timed with wave of DJs taking over national airwaves occupied by adventure, comedy, drama, mystery, quiz fare; host Potter had earned durable reputation as platter spinner at Hollywood KFWB; final broadcast Oct. 6, 1956.

Canceled

Hedda Hopper, May 20, 1951, NBC; debut Nov. 6, 1939. *The Man Called X*, May 20, 1952, NBC; debut July 10, 1944. *Take a Number*, May 20, 1955, MBS; debut June 5, 1948.

Death

Elliott Lewis, May 20, 1990, Gleneden Beach, Calif.; b. Nov. 28, 1917.

May 21

Canceled

Beulah, May 21, 1954, CBS; debut July 2, 1945.

Births

Cathleen Cordell, May 21, 1915, Brooklyn, N.Y.; actress (radio, TV, film), voiceover artist; radio portfolio of stints on *The Casebook of Gregory Hood, Mr. Keen—Tracer of Lost Persons, The Romance of Helen Trent, Scotland Yard,* The *Second Mrs. Burton*, others of same ilk; appearances 1938–85 in eight theatrical films (often uncredited), 29 solo episodes of sundry TV sitcoms, dramas, nine made-for-TV flicks, one animation-voice series; d. Aug. 19, 1997.

Dennis Day (Owen Patrick Eugene McNulty), May 21, 1916; actor (radio, film, TV, stage), comedian, impressionist, recording artist, vocalist (Irish tenor) bka *The Jack Benny Program* sitcom comic sidekick character (self), soloist NBC/CBS 1939–44, 1946–58, CBS-/NBC-TV 1950–65, *A Day in the Life of Dennis Day* sitcom/music series headliner NBC 1946–55; *The Dennis Day Show* music variety series headliner NBC-TV 1952–54; never sang professionally before *The Jack Benny Program*; prolific recording artist for Columbia, RCA Victor; featured in movies, sporadic guest star on other TV series; d. June 22, 1988.

Horace Heidt, May 21, 1901, Alameda, Calif.; emcee, impresario, pianist, quizmaster, recording artist, talent agent; on national ether almost continually 1932–53; hosted imposing fare like *Pot o' Gold, The Youth Opportunity Program, The Horace Heidt Show, The Swift Show Wagon*; often exhibited aptitude as talent scout as well as maestro; d. Dec. 1, 1995.

Claude Ernest Hooper, May 21, 1898, Kingsville, Ohio; researcher, statistician; with partner co-founded Clark-Hooper, Inc. 1954 selling audience research on magazines, radio to subscribing advertisers; after partner left 1938, outfit renamed C. E. Hooper, Inc. solely focused on monthly ratings of network-sponsored programs, competing with "Crossleys" ratings service; "Hooperatings" heyday 1946–49, embraced TV 1948, sold to rival A. C. Nielsen Co. 1950; Hooper used phone to collect data like "Crossleys" but approached listeners as they heard shows, not afterward, making results more reliable, convincing; d. Dec. 15, 1954.

Lucille Manners (Marie McClinchy), May 21, 1910, Newark, N.J.; vocalist (soprano) bka *Cities Service Concert* subbed for Jessica Dragonette 1936, singing star of that series 1937–47, remaining with program longer than any other celebrity; performed regularly with New York Opera Co.

Deaths

Vinton Hayworth, May 21, 1970, Van Nuys, Calif.; b. June 4, 1906. Dennis King, May 21, 1971, New York City, N.Y.; b. Nov. 2, 1897. Vaughn Monroe, May 21, 1973, Stuart, Fla.; b. Oct. 7, 1911.

May 22

Canceled

Amos 'n' Andy sitcom, May 22, 1955, CBS; network debut Aug. 19, 1929, NBC Blue; spin-off *The Amos 'n' Andy Music Hall* lasted to Nov. 25, 1960. *Armstrong Theater of Today*, May 22, 1954, CBS; debut Oct. 4, 1941. *The Jack Benny Program*, May 22, 1955 final new show, repeats 1956–58, CBS; debut May 2, 1932. *No School Today*, May 22, 1954, ABC; debut Feb. 18, 1950.

Births

Johnny Olson (Johnny Olsen), May 22, 1910, Windom, Minn.; announcer, emcee, radio executive bka *The Price Is Right* CBS-TV interlocutor ("Come on Down!" originator) Sept. 4, 1972-Oct. 12, 1985; breaking into broadcasting on Madison, Wis. outlet as Buttermilk Kid, moved to Mitchell, S.D. KGDA as station manager, announcer, vocalist, preacher (daily devotional series), advertising time salesman; left for Milwaukee WTMJ as chief announcer followed by Hollywood radio a year, returned to Milwaukee to host *Johnny Olson's Rumpus Room* soon-to-be trademark audience participation series, setting future; joined ABC New York 1944 as staff announcer, warmed up studio audiences for exchanges with masters of ceremonies; revived *Rumpus Room* for ABC daytime run through 1951, MBS 1954–57, cohosted with wife Penny Olson, on Dumont TV 1949–52; couple presided over similar daily audio fare *Ladies Be Seated* 1944–49; several more early TV series; Olson presided over *The Jackie Gleason Show* (*Jackie Gleason and His American Scene Magazine*) from Miami Beach CBS-TV 1961–70, flew weekly from live New York game show intros like *Snap Judgment, To Tell the Truth, What's My Line?*; *The Price Is Right* crowning achievement where he welcomed emcee Bob Barker from CBS-TV inception to death; d. Oct. 12, 1985.

Ward Wilson, May 22, 1903, Trenton, N.J.; actor, announcer, emcee, engineer, sportscaster bka *Can You Top This?* host 1945–54, ABC-TV 1950–51; NBC field engineer testing lines, rehearsal mics; initially on-air impressionist, mastering voices of 80 identifiable icons; thespian for *The Aldrich Family* 1946–51, *Philip Morris Playhouse* 1940s, comedies of 1930s-40s headlined by Fred Allen, George Burns and Gracie Allen, Judy Canova; interlocutor for newscasters Fred Vandeventer, Raymond Gram Swing, Walter Winchell; game show inventory: *Stop Me if You've Heard This One, What's My Name?, Winner Take All*; sportscaster at New York WHN 1944–46, WMGM 1952–56, sports director at West Palm Beach WEAT-TV/Radio 1960s; d. March 21, 1966.

Death

Martin Gabel, May 22, 1986, New York City, N.Y.; b. June 19, 1912.

May 23

Sound Bite

On May 23, 1930, Radio Corporation of America buys all shares of stock in National Broadcasting Co.; from chain's inception Nov. 15, 1926, General Electric Corp. owned 30 percent, Westinghouse Corp. owned 20 percent, remainder controlled by RCA; NBC becomes wholly owned subsidiary of RCA at that juncture; ironically, 55 years hence, GE winds up running NBC by itself when it pays $6.3 billion for RCA in 1985, acquiring NBC in deal; while incredible, it probably isn't unprecedented in American commerce.

Canceled

The Fitch Bandwagon, May 23, 1948, NBC (while *The Phil Harris-Alice Faye Show* segment of this umbrella series continued); debut Sept. 4, 1938.

Birth

Rosemary Clooney, May 23, 1928, Maysville, Ky.; recording artist, vocalist (film, nightclubs, personal appearances, stage, radio, TV) bka "Come on-a My House" smash hit recording singer 1951, CBS *The Rosemary Clooney Show, The Bing Crosby-Rosemary Clooney Show* daily audio gigs 1954–62; headlined TV series 1956–58; most memorable film 1954's *White Christmas* with Crosby, Danny Kaye; flagging career rejuvenated with recordings, personal appearances after long bout with alcohol, drug addiction; d. June 29, 2002.

Deaths

George Jessel, May 23, 1981, Los Angeles, Calif.; b. April 3, 1898. David Schoenbrun, May 23, 1988, Manhattan, New York City, N.Y.; b. March 15, 1915.

May 24

Debuting

Stoopnagle and Budd (*The Gloomchasers, The Ivory Soap Program, The Pontiac Program, The Carefree Carnival, The Camel Caravan, The Schlitz Spotlight Revue, The Gulf Headliners, Town Hall Tonight, The Minute Men, Colonel Stoopnagle, Quixie Doodles, Town Hall Varieties, Stoopnagle's Stooperoos*), May 24, 1931, CBS; comedy; labeled radio's first satirists (first to impersonate living people on air, too), Col. Lemuel Q. Stoopnagle (Frederick Chase Taylor), Budd (Wilbur Budd Hulick) opened on Buffalo WMAK 1930, auditioned in New York, pleased brass, failed to connect with common man signified by brief ethereal stints; precursors of *Bob and Ray* with similar stuff but they were embraced by mainstream audience; final broadcast as dual act May 16, 1937 — Taylor, Hulick subsequently heard on other radio features independently.

Births

Vernon (Vern) N. Carstensen, May 24, 1914, Clinton, Iowa; announcer, director, producer; before joining Chicago NBC 1938, on air at Iowa City, Iowa WSUL, Rock Island, Illinois. WHBF; notable net features 1948–49 announcing-directing *Box 13*, producing *The Damon Runyon Theater*; d. April 23, 1999.

Elsa Maxwell, May 24, 1883, Keokuk, Iowa; actress, author, commentator, freelance writer, lyricist, pianist, socialite, syndicated columnist bka *Elsa Maxwell's Party Line* hostess 1938–39, 1942, 1943–46; penned 80 published songs; climbed European social ladder by 1919, threw parties for international dignitaries, celebs; in trio of forgettable American films late 1930s-early 1940s; wrote pieces for *Harper's Bazaar*, *Cosmopolitan*, four books 1951–63; weekly guest on *Tonight* hosted by Jack Paar NBC-TV 1957–62; d. Nov. 1, 1963.

Deaths

Duke Ellington, May 24, 1974, New York City, N.Y.; b. April 29, 1899. John McCarthy, May 24, 1996, Scarsdale, N.Y.; b. Aug. 23, 1914. Carlton E. Morse, May 24, 1993, Sacramento, Calif.; b. June 4, 1901.

May 25

Canceled

The Lone Ranger, May 25, 1956, NBC; ethereal staple launched by WXYZ Detroit Jan. 31, 1933; prompted audio western hero genre; final first-run airing Sept. 3, 1954, ABC.

Births

Joseph Close Harsch, May 25, 1905, Toledo, Ohio; commentator, correspondent, newscaster, print journalist (*The Christian Science Monitor* 1929–43, 1971–74) bka participant in litany of news/analysis entries: *CBS World News Roundup* 1940–41, *Joseph C. Harsch Commentary* 1943, 1955–56, 1967–71, *The Meaning of the News* 1947–49, *Nightline* 1957–59; with Marquis Childs, launched *Washington Report* 1950, commentary aired on Labor-Liberal FM web; penned multiple volumes 1940s-90s pertaining to current events; d. June 3, 1998.

Ginny Simms, May 25, 1914, San Antonio, Texas; entrepreneur-real estate developer, recording artist, vocalist (film, radio, stage, tours) bka songstress with Kay Kyser's band, performed on NBC *Kay Kyser's Kollege of Musical Knowledge* 1938–41, CBS *The Ginny Simms Show* headliner 1941–42, 1945–47; regular on dozen aural series 1937–51; nine RKO B-movies; vanished for years after real estate scandal negatively impacted investors, allegedly engineered by Simms, third spouse Don Eastvold; d. April 4, 1994.

Deaths

Kenneth Banghart, May 25, 1980, Delray Beach, Fla.; b. Sept. 11, 1909. Roger Krupp, May 25, 1987, Ely, Minn.; b. July 31, 1909.

May 26

Debuting

Invitation to Learning, May 26, 1940, CBS; esteemed tome forum; Lyman Bryon moderated roundtable discussion involving erudite, widely-read book scholars like Huntington Cairns, Mason Gross, Quincy Howe, Allen Tate, Mark Van Doren, more; prestigious feature persisted beyond sign-off for most golden age fare; final broadcast Dec. 28, 1964.

Canceled

Poole's Paradise, May 26, 1950, MBS; debut Sept. 28, 1948. *The Red Skelton Show*, May 26, 1953, CBS (although televersion continued to 1971); debut Jan. 7, 1939.

Births

Ben Alexander (Nicholas Benton Alexander), May 26, 1911, Goldfield, Nev.; actor, announcer, emcee, newscaster bka *Dragnet* officer Frank Smith NBC 1952–57, NBC-TV 1952–59; early 1940s introduced listeners to *The Edgar Bergen and Charlie McCarthy Show*, *Everyman's Theater*, *Eyes Aloft*, *The New Old Gold Show*, *Red Ryder*; same decade presided over audience participation features *The Anniversary Club*, *Heart's*

Desire, It Happened in the Service, It's a Living, Lady Be Beautiful, Little Ol' Hollywood, Watch and Win; 1930s-50s exhibited thespianics on *Baby Snooks, Brenthouse, The Great Gildersleeve, I Love a Mystery, The Martin and Lewis Show, This Is Judy Jones*; hosted ABC-TV daytime gamer *About Faces* 1960–61; ended career playing another cop in ABC-TV crime drama *The Felony Squad* 1966–69; d. July 5, 1969.

Wilbur Hatch, May 24, 1902, Moken, Ill.; house musician-impresario (CBS), lyricist, pianist; uncelebrated leader of own outfit, missed public adulation that often marked such groups; still busy conducting music for nearly three dozen aural series, mostly CBS 1933–58: *Suspense, The Whistler, Lady Esther Screen Guild Theater, Meet Corliss Archer, My Favorite Husband, Our Miss Brooks, Escape, December Bride, On a Sunday Afternoon*; d. Dec. 22, 1969.

Al Jolson (Asa Yoelson), May 26, 1886, Srednick, Lithuania; vocalist (film, overseas tours, personal appearances, radio, stage, TV) bka subject of 1946 motion picture *The Jolson Story* starring Larry Parks as venerated singer with Jolson recording soundtrack; appeared on every major headliner's show at $10,000/pop (Fred Allen, Jack Benny, Edgar Bergen, Eddie Cantor, Bing Crosby, Bob Hope, et al.); NBC Radio *Kraft Music Hall* star after Crosby quit series 1947–49; d. Oct. 23, 1950.

Peggy Lee (Norma Dolores Egstrom), May 26, 1920, Jamestown, N.D.; actress (film, radio, TV), author, baker, greeting card designer, painter, philanthropist, poet, recording artist, screenwriter, vocalist (concert tours, nightclubs, personal appearances, radio. stage, TV), voice-over artist bka sultry-voiced singer who recorded over 650 tunes, 60 albums; cast member in nine aural web series 1945–55; earned film credits for *The Jazz Singer, Mr. Music, Pete Kelly's Blues, The Powers Girl, Stage Door Canteen*, more; d. Jan. 21, 2002.

Artie Shaw, May 26, 1910, New York City, N.Y.; clarinetist starting, disbanding bands 10 times 1935–53; talented, restless, unable to make go of much for long time (eight wives); two pithy web-based series—*Melody and Madness* CBS 1938–39, *The George Burns and Gracie Allen Show* NBC 1940–41; d. Dec. 30, 2004.

Carleton G. Young, May 26, 1907, Westfield, N.Y.; actor (film, radio, TV) bka *David Harum* daytime serial namesake hero-banker-philosopher NBC/CBS 1941–44, ca. 1947–50, slightly sinister character thespian in 1930s-60s cinematic productions, role in *The Man Who Shot Liberty Valance* 1962 emblematic; radio credits dominated 1940s-50s with frequently ongoing parts in *Carol Kennedy's Romance, The Count of Monte Cristo, Ellery Queen, Hilltop House, Hollywood Mystery Time, Life Begins, Our Gal Sunday, Portia Faces Life, Second Husband, Society Girl, Stella Dallas, Trouble House*; d. July 11, 1971.

May 27

Debuting

Lone Journey, May 27, 1940, NBC; daytime serial; Frank, Anne Hummert produced; Wolfe Bennett (Les Damon, Staats Cotsworth, Henry Hunter, Reese Taylor, Warren Mills), wife Nita (Claudia Morgan, Betty Ruth Smith, Eloise Kummer, Betty Winkler) had fill of Chicago, relocated to Montana's Judith Mountain, bought ranch — tale focused on restarting their lives in Big Sky country; penned by siblings Sandra, Peter Michael; billed as "the distinguished American radio novel," it was realistic, critics said, raising level of matinee narratives few notches; silent 1943–46, 1947–51; final broadcast June 27, 1952.

Wild Bill Hickok, May 27, 1951, MBS; western juvenile adventure; U. S. marshal James Butler (Wild Bill) Hickok (Guy Madison), sidekick deputy Jingles P. Jones (Andy Devine) rode plains tracking bad guys, bringing them to justice, sometimes traveling undercover; Hickok fast with fists, quick on draw, portly Jones good for laughs, expert marksman; Hickok played in Saturday movie matinees, increasing his aural fascination to adolescents, adding syndicated TV run 1951–58; final radiocast Feb. 12, 1956.

Canceled

The Adventures of Ellery Queen, May 27, 1948, ABC; debut June 18, 1939.

Births

Marlin Hurt, May 27, 1904, DuQuoin, Ill.; actor (radio, stage) bka creator, original actor playing Negro maid Beulah on *The Marlin Hurt and Beulah Show* 1945–46, 1947–54, CBS; character introduced on *Fibber McGee & Molly* Jan.

25, 1944-June 26, 1945, NBC; d. March 21, 1946.

Vincent Leonard Price, Jr., May 27, 1911, St. Louis, Mo.; actor (film, stage, TV), emcee bka thespian in 168 usually low-budget theatrical, TV horror films 1938–95 (last released two years after his death) in which distinctive voice, serio-comic manner combined to typecast him as protégé of older Boris Karloff; on radio, one of five rotating hosts of *The Sears/Mutual Radio Theater* CBS/MBS 1979–81; debuted onstage 1935, 132 TV guest shot appearances, regular on *Pantomime Quiz* stunt game show CBS-TV 1950–52; d. Oct. 25, 1993.

Deaths

Kay Campbell, May 27, 1985, Greenwich, Conn.; b. Aug. 12, 1904. Ted Collins, May 27, 1964, Lake Placid, N.Y.; b. Oct. 12, 1899. Robert Readick, May 27, 1985, Trenton, N.J.; b. Nov. 28, 1925.

May 28

Canceled

Jimmy Fidler in Hollywood, May 28, 1950, ABC; debut Sept. 16, 1934. *The Judy Canova Show*, May 28, 1953, NBC; debut July 6, 1943. *Woman in White*, May 28, 1948, NBC; debut Jan. 3, 1938.

Deaths

Don MacLaughlin, May 28, 1986, Goshen, Conn.; b. Nov. 24, 1906. Frank Singiser, May 28, 1982, Sudbury, Vt.; b. July 16, 1908. Lurene Tuttle, May 28, 1986, Encino, Calif.; b. Aug. 29, 1907.

May 29

Debuting

(*The Private Lives of*) *Ethel and Albert*, May 29, 1944, NBC Blue; sitcom with milquetoast male, opinionated spouse only too happy to express self to him while outlining his course in one-sided exchanges; leads Peg Lynch, Alan Bunce; final broadcast Aug. 28, 1950, triple segment TV extensions 1953–56.

When a Girl Marries, May 29, 1939, CBS; daytime serial; as so many clueless women did in serialdom, heroine picked wrong guy, led to life of misery as she put on happy face many times; Joan Field (Noel Mills, Mary Jane Higby) of affluent family wed penniless Harry Davis (John Raby, Robert Haag, Whitfield Connor, Lyle Sudrow), offering promise while sweeping her off feet — not till later did he emerge as two-timer (thrusting her into years-long numbed depression), accused of murder twice, convicted once, amnesiac, and couple was financially destitute; some of that grief repeated on NBC-TV as creator Elaine Carrington adapted storyline to script *Follow Your Heart* starting Aug. 3, 1953 — viewers not forgiving, however — it was gone Jan. 8, 1954; final radiocast Aug. 30, 1957.

Canceled

Baby Snooks, May 29, 1951, NBC; debut as recurring feature on *Maxwell House Presents Good News* aka *Good News of 1938* on Nov. 4, 1937.

Births

Robert Corley, May 29, 1924, Macon, Ga.; actor (film, radio), director, recording artist, standup comic; *Beulah* namesake in sitcom resurgence about Negro domestic for Anglo-Saxon clan 1947; first Beulah actors men — originated by Marlin Hurt; Corley's career ended as Atlanta TV director; d. Nov. 18, 1971.

Bob Hope (Leslie Townes Hope), May 29, 1903, Eltham, England; actor (stage, film, radio, TV), comedian, vocalist bka *The Bob Hope Show* (multiple monikers) comedy variety series headliner intermittently on radio 1935–58, NBC-TV 1953–56, 1963–67 with specials to 1990s; known for opening monologue with rapid-fire gag delivery, poking fun with guests from entertainment, sports, political realms; widely traveled with Armed Services performing stage shows around globe; spirited rivalry with movie mate Bing Crosby; d. July 27, 2003.

Deaths

Fanny Brice, May 29, 1951, New York City, N.Y.; b. Oct. 29, 1891. George Fenneman, May 29, 1997, Los Angeles, Calif.; b. Nov. 10, 1919. John Gunther, May 29, 1970, New York City, N.Y.; b. Aug. 30, 1901. Rex Koury, May 29, 2006, Casper, Wyo.; b. March 18, 1911. Perry Ward, May 29, 1989, Wichita, Kan.; b. Aug. 18, 1914.

May 30

Debuting

America's Town Meeting of the Air, May 30, 1935, NBC Blue; public affairs discussion; moderated by George V. Denny, Jr. to 1952; "a stupendous innovation for radio" attested *Radio Mirror* 1936; unlike rival *The American Town Meeting of the Air*, series welcomed hecklers, guests restrained from violence on occasion; final broadcast July 1, 1956.

Joyce Jordan, Girl Interne (*Joyce Jordan, M. D.*), May 30, 1938, CBS; daytime serial; took four years (to 1942) for Jordan (Elspeth Eric, Helen Claire, Ann Shepherd, Betty Winkler, Rita Johnson, Gertrude Warner, Fran Carlon) to pass exams qualifying her as surgeon at Preston's Hotchkiss Memorial Hospital, gaining M.D. with it, altering tale's title; courted by suitors like Dr. Henry Powell (Clayton "Bud" Collyer), affluent Neil Reynolds (George Coulouris), more, though she chose poorly, wedding incompatible print journalist Paul Sherwood (Myron McCormick); domestic issues predominated her agenda — patients usually got leftovers; by mid 1940s heroine narrating more than performing; drama silent 1948–51, 1952–55; final broadcast July 1, 1955.

Births

Ben Bernie (Benjamin Anzelevitz), May 30, 1891, New York City, N.Y..; impresario, master of ceremonies, violinist bka entertainer dubbed "the old maestro"; unique blend of verbal expressions endeared showman to audiences in early 1930s, peaking in top 10 programs at 34 rating while headlining net series 1930–43; d. Oct. 20, 1943.

Frank Blair, May 30, 1915, Yemassee, S.C.; actor (stage), announcer, emcee, director, newscaster bka NBC-TV *Today* newsman 1953–75, *Monitor* communicator NBC Radio 1955–59, 1964–66; *Helen Holden — Government Girl* narrator 1941–42; early career took him from Charleston WCSC to Columbia WIS, Greenville WFBC, Washington WOL to New York NBC; d. March 14, 1995.

Mel Blanc (Melvin Jerome Blanc), May 30, 1908, San Francisco, Calif.; actor (radio, film, TV), dialectician, voiceover artist bka cartoon voices of Bugs Bunny, Daffy Duck, Porky Pig, Tweetie Pie, Road Runner, Sylvester, Woody Woodpecker, 400 more, *The Jack Benny Program* sitcom as recurring figures Mexican gardner Sy, violin instructor Monsieur Le Blanc, Benny's Maxwell automobile, petulant polar bear Carmichael; broke into showbiz on *NBC Symphony*, San Francisco, 1928; moved to Portland, Ore. 1933–35 performed with bride Estelle Rosenbaum on KEX music series, augmented act with one-man repertory outfit via multiple inflections; radio regular in 1940s on *The Abbott and Costello Show* (as Botsford Twink), *The George Burns and Gracie Allen Show* (cheery mailman), *The Judy Canova Show* (Pedro, Roscoe E. Wortle), visits to *Blondie*, *The Cisco Kid*, *Fibber McGee & Molly*, *The Great Gildersleeve*, *The Joe Penner Show*, *Tommy Riggs and Betty Lou*, more; TV animated character voices on *The Flintstones*, *The Jetsons*, *Where's Huddles?*; d. July 10, 1989.

Benny Goodman, May 30, 1909, Chicago, Ill.; formed band 1934, on air same year with *Let's Dance*, launched swing craze 1935, featured musician on 13 chain audio series 1928–47; d. June 13, 1986.

Dick Noel, May 30, 1927, Brooklyn, N.Y.; TV personality, vocalist bka *The Breakfast Club* singer ca. late 1940s-50s; after some local TV venues, performed on *The Tennessee Ernie Ford Show* ABC-TV 1962.

Sidney Walton (Sidney Wolpoff), May 30, 1915, Washington, D.C.; announcer, author, commentator, disc jockey, entrepreneur, impresario, newscaster, station owner bka authoritative voice dispatching *Changing Times* infomercial financial tips-advice-commentary NBC/MBS 1955–62 underwritten by periodical of same name ("the nation's first magazine of personal money management") — show went to syndicated TV 1960s-70s; capitalized on success by penning scores of tomes on money matters; 1940s New York gigs newscasting at WOR, WHN, WINS adding DJ spot at latter; on webs opened 1940s-50s *Arthur Tracy — the Street Singer*, *Voice of Experience*, *Whiz Quiz*, dispensed gossip on *Here's Hollywood* — in rare twist, on *Sidney Walton's Music* on NBC Blue 1940 he was emcee, impresario, commercial spokesman, directed singing canaries; purchased Manchester, Conn. WINF Radio; son Mark a founder of CNN, first White House correspondent; d. Sept. 5, 1983.

Deaths

William Hillman, May 30, 1962, New York City, N.Y.; b. Sept 5, 1895. William Spier, May 30, 1973, Weston, Conn.; b. Oct. 16, 1906.

May 31

Debuting

Archie Andrews, May 31, 1943, NBC; family sitcom; Bob Montana-inspired comic book character spawning entrepreneurial merchandise empire including teen-focused comedy with Bob Hastings (Andrews) 1946–53, sidekick-conspirator Harlan Stone (Jughead Jones) 1945–51, 1953; copycat series to *The Aldrich Family* sans avid following, underwriting; nine TV incarnations, eight animated, Sept. 14, 1968-May 6, 1990; final broadcast Sept. 12, 1953.

Lora Lawton, May 31, 1943, NBC; daytime serial; one of dozen dramas with similar themes, that of individuals outside marriage at center of storyline falling for one or other party within it; in this one, Midwestern widow Lawton (Joan Tompkins, Jan Miner) moved to Washington, D.C. as housekeeper for wealthy, handsome shipping magnate, Peter Carver (James Meighan, Ned Wever), one of East Coast's most eligible bachelors; despite legions of damsels hoping to be Mrs. Carver, kindhearted, industrious Lawton selected, starting her own entrepreneurial enterprise as sideline; final broadcast Jan. 6, 1950.

On a Sunday Afternoon, May 31, 1953, CBS; music; eclectic mix of styles performed live by Alfredo Antonini conducting CBS staff orchestra, occasional singing guests, recordings ranging from classical to pop, jazz to waltz, presided over by smooth-talking Eddie Gallaher, Washington WTOP disc jockey; each segment launched with chorus singing stirring "Summertime is Summertime" from Broadway's *Seventeen*; aired one hour first season ending Sept. 6, 1953, second season starting May 9, 1954 aired three hours; persisted beyond second summer in reduced time periods to Nov. 4, 1956 though Gallaher departed before end, conductor replaced, permanent vocalists added.

Stars Over Hollywood, May 31, 1941, CBS' anthology drama; proffered some of Tinseltown's legends as headliners of dramatic fare—Mary Astor, Bonita Granville, Alan Hale, Sr., Phil Harris, Brenda Joyce, Alan Ladd, Anita Louise, Brenda Marshall, Merle Oberon, Basil Rathbone, Ann Rutherford, more; played in light narratives, usually romantic, comedic bent with rare mystery; one of most noble contributions knocking down long-held bias against Saturday daytime programming, getting stars to perform live at 9:30 a.m. local time—by late 1940s perseverance paid off with programming transcribed at other hours, stars shining brightly on Saturday matinees, albeit aural ether; final broadcast Sept. 25, 1954.

Births

Fred Allen (John Florence Sullivan), May 31, 1894, Cambridge, Mass.; actor, comedian, host, TV panelist, writer bka *The Fred Allen Show* star 1932–49; outspoken, opinionated, developed staunchly loyal following; flanked by wife Portland Hoffa, others who tickled America's funnybone via parodies, sarcastic wit; durable series knocked off air by *Stop the Music!* quiz ABC; star returned as regular on radio's purported last hurrah, *The Big Show* NBC 1950–52; *What's My Line?* panelist in twilight years CBS-TV 1954–56; d. March 17, 1956.

Don Ameche (Dominic Felix Amici), May 31, 1908, Kenosha, Wis.; actor, emcee; star roles in *Betty and Bob*, *The Bickersons*, *The First Nighter*, *Grand Hotel*, *Rin-Tin-Tin*; support player for *Jack Armstrong—the All-American Boy*, *The Jimmy Durante Show*, *Lux Radio Theater*, *The National Farm and Home Hour*; presided over *What's New?*, *Your Lucky Strike*; older sibling of radio thespian, interlocutor Jim Ameche; d. Dec. 6, 1993.

Alfredo Antonini, May 31, 1901, Alessandra, Italy; impresario bka CBS staff orchestra conductor 1941–1960s on radio-TV; radio gigs: *Cabin B-13*, *The Eileen Farrell Show*, *Hear it Now*, *Main Street Musicale*, *On a Sunday Afternoon*, *Treasure Hour of Song*, *Yours for a Song*, more; MBS maestro late 1930s; music chairman at Brooklyn's St. John's University; d. Nov. 3, 1983.

John Patrick Michael Joseph (Jack) Costello, May 31, 1908, Sauk Centre, Minn.; actor, announcer, reporter bka dulcet-toned, basal-voiced narrator of *Mr. Keen—Tracer of Lost Persons* 1951–52; *The St. Paul Pioneer Dispatch* scribe in college; announcing grounding at Grand Forks, N.D. KFJN 1932, St. Paul KSTP 1933, joined

New York NBC February 1936, retired there 1976; penned weekly column *From Main Street to Broadway*, peddling to community, county seat newspapers at dollar/installment; opened about 30 NBC features 1930s-50s e.g. *The Bob and Ray Show*, *The Fitch Bandwagon*, *Just Plain Bill*, *Portia Faces Life*, *Stella Dallas*, *X-Minus One*; played in *The Shocking Miss Pilgrim* motion picture 1947, narrated *Amalfi Way* 1955 movie; Bishop Fulton J. Sheen's announcer for dual video vehicles: *Life Is Worth Living* 1952–57, *The Bishop Sheen Program* 1961–68; *Young Doctor Malone* interlocutor NBC-TV 1958–63; d. September 1983 (many sources for date, place exhausted — last residence Flushing, N.Y.).

Albert Mitchell, May 31, 1893, Elsberry, Mo.; commentator, emcee, impresario, lyricist bka *The Answer Man* inquiry series 1937–50; first appearance on radio with Paul Whiteman orchestra where he directed, penned arrangements, announced at performing venues 1919–26; next managed touring segment of *Major Bowes' Original Amateur Hour* talent winners; reached zenith hosting *The Answer Man*, "a hard-core fact-fest" as pundit put it; 2,500 questions arrived daily at peak with 40 assistants answering almost million pieces of mail annually, culling perhaps 200 questions to be aired in five installments weekly; after radio Mitchell joined Marshall Plan, moved to Paris; d. Oct. 4, 1954.

Hugh Studebaker, May 31, 1900, Ridgeville, Ind.; actor, announcer bka *Bachelor's Children* daytime serial protagonist Dr. Bob Graham CBS/NBC 1936–46, *Fibber McGee & Molly* sitcom utility player summoned often as Silly Watson NBC ca. 1937–39, *Midstream* daytime serial male lead Charles Meredith NBC/NBC Blue 1939–41, *That Brewster Boy* sitcom patriarch Jim Brewster CBS 1941–45, *Vic and Sade* sitcom characters Mayor Geetcham, Rishigan Fishigan Blue/CBS/MBS ca. 1943–46, *Beulah* sitcom domestic employer Harry Henderson CBS 1947–52; also straight dramatic roles: *Captain Midnight*, *Deadline Mystery*, *The Guiding Light*, *The Right to Happiness*, *The Road of Life*, *Woman in White*; in pre–net life announced at Kansas City KMBC; d. May 6, 1978.

Deaths

Arlene Francis, May 31, 2001, San Francisco, Calif.; b. Oct. 20, 1907. Ben Grauer, May 31, 1977, New York City, N.Y.; b. June 2, 1908. Michael Raffetto, May 31, 1990, Berkeley, Calif.; b. Dec. 30, 1899.

June 1

Sound Bite

George Foster Peabody Awards ("the Peabodys") begun by Henry V. Grady College of Journalism and Mass Communications at University of Georgia June 1, 1940; prestigious honors of excellence cite stations, nets, producers for illustrious achievements in broadcasting; perpetuate memory of New York financier-philanthropist Peabody (1852–1938), Georgia native, alumnus devoting part of wealth to alma mater and Peabody College for Teachers of Vanderbilt University.

Canceled

The Chesterfield Supper Club, June 1, 1950, NBC; debut Dec. 11, 1944. *Jack Armstrong, the All-American Boy*, June 1, 1950; debut July 31, 1933. *Philco Radio Time*, June 1, 1949, ABC; debut Oct. 16, 1946. *Take It or Leave It*, June 1, 1952, NBC; debut April 21, 1940.

Births

Pat Boone (Charles Eugene Patrick Boone), June 1, 1934, Jacksonville, Fla.; actor, author, personal appearance/recording artist, political activist, vocalist, writer bka 1950s chart topper with "April Love" — title of 1957 film in which he starred — plus "Bernadine," "Ain't That a Shame," "Tutti Frutti," "Long Tall Sally," "At My Front Door (Crazy Little Mama)," "I Almost Lost My Mind," "Chains of Love"; launched emceeing teen talent show on Nashville Radio-TV (where he grew up), won *Ted Mack Original Amateur Hour*, Arthur Godfrey's *Talent Scouts* netting spot on *Arthur Godfrey Time* CBS Radio-TV 1955–57, *Arthur Godfrey and His Friends* CBS-TV 1955–57; list of 16 movies includes *Bernadine* 1957, *Mardi Gras* 1958, *Journey to the Earth* 1959, *State Fair* 1962, *The Greatest Story Ever Told* 1965; actively campaigns for GOP candidates.

Edgar (Cookie) Fairchild, June 1, 1898, New York City, N.Y.; composer, radio-film maestro, stage pianist bka "I Can't Get You Out of My Mind" tunesmith; d. Feb. 20, 1975.

Andrew Samuel (Andy) Griffith, June 1, 1926, Mt. Airy, N.C.; actor (film, TV), educator, narrator, producer (formed own outfit 1972), recording artist, vocalist bka star of dual longrunning TV series: *The Andy Griffith Show* sitcom CBS-TV 1960–68, *Matlock* lawyer-sleuth drama 1986–92 NBC-TV, 1992–95 ABC-TV; *Mayberry R.F.D.* executive producer CBS-TV 1968–71; *The Sears Radio Theater* (*The Mutual Radio Theater*) host Tuesday nights CBS/MBS 1979–81; taught high school music three years, recorded comedy discs, pop songs, hymns.

Kathleen Norris, June 1, 1919, Newark, Ohio; advertising exec, announcer, consumer spokesperson (General Electric, Purina), consumer advocate, emcee, writer; penned web narratives *Bright Horizon* 1945, *By Kathleen Norris* 1939–41, hostess-narrator of *Escape with Me* 1952, *Modern Romances* 1949-early 1950s; background before radio included advertising at Chicago's W. R. Grace Co., directing New York's Better Business Bureau; dispensed tips to housewives on Dumont's *TV Shopper* 1948–50, ran same chain's *Spin the Picture* 1949–50, presided over trio of NBC-TV features: *The Kathi Norris Show* 1950–51, *Today* segment for women 1953, *True Story* drama anthology 1957–61; d. June 15, 2005.

Deaths

Bob Emerick, June 1, 1973, San Diego, Calif.; b. Dec. 9, 1915. Don Lowe, June 1, 1991; b. Jan. 10, 1911, Thomasville, Ala. A. C. Nielsen, Sr., June 1, 1980, Chicago, Ill.; b. Sept. 5, 1897. Dallas Townsend, June 1, 1995, Montclair, N.J.; b. Jan. 17, 1919.

June 2

Debuting

The Jack Carson Show, June 2, 1943, CBS; comedy variety feature; ex-vaudeville celluloid icon Carson played self in blundering fashion alongside nephew Tugwell (Dave Willock, Carson's real-life stage cohort) who routinely deflated star's self–image; others: butler (Arthur Treacher), press agent (Eddie Marr), soloists Anita Ellis, Dale Evans; off air 1949–55 although *The Jack Carson Show* surfaced sporadically NBC-TV 1954–55; final radiocast June 29, 1956.

Canceled

The Light of the World, June 2, 1950, NBC; debut March 18, 1940. *Today's Children*, June 2, 1950, NBC; debut Sept. 11, 1933. *True Detective Mysteries*, June 2, 1955, MBS; debut May 16, 1919, CBS.

Births

Ward Byron, June 2, 1906, Flushing, New York City, N.Y.; announcer, director, film distributor, producer bka *The Fitch Bandwagon* packager, more big band series; short flings with numerous series in varied capacities e.g. *Bughouse Rhythm* creator 1936–37, *The Chamber Music Society of Lower Basin Street* commentator ca. 1950, 1952, *The Chesterfield Supper Club* director ca. 1940s, *The George Jessel Show* director 1937–38, *The Philip Morris Follies of 1946* producer 1946; handful of fleeting TV projects; d. Jan. 28, 1996.

Bennett (Ben) Grauer, June 2, 1908, Staten Island, N.Y.; actor, announcer, emcee, newscaster, voiceover artist; on silver screen at age eight in first of five childhood films; handful of college stage productions; joined NBC as staff announcer 1930 primarily introducing 46 documented series 1930s-50s e.g. *America's Town Meeting of the Air*, *The Battle of the Sexes*, *The Boston Pops Orchestra*, *Grand Central Station*, *Information Please*, *Kay Kyser's Kollege of Musical Knowledge*, *The Magic Key*, *Mr. District Attorney*, *Mr. Keen—Tracer of Lost Persons*, *The NBC Symphony Orchestra*, *The Studebaker Champions*, *The Jergens Journal*, *Your Hit Parade*; played in episodes of *Columbia Presents Corwin* while hosting *Home Is What You Make It*, *Name the Place*, *What Would You Have Done?*; NBC newsman 1940–48, *Monitor* co-communicator 1955, 1957–60; National Academy of Vocal Arts labeled him "the most authoritative [voice] in the world" 1944; introduced/hosted dozen 1950s NBC-TV features, *Big Story* 1955–57 most prominent; retired NBC 1974, persisting on Voice of America, in broadcast commercials; d. May 31, 1977.

Hedda Hopper (Elda Furry), June 2, 1890, Hollidaysburg, Pa.; actress (film, stage, TV), author, columnist, commentator, emcee, voiceover artist bka Hollywood gossip columnist in print, electronic forums—*Hedda Hopper's Hollywood* formidable entry 1939–42, 1944–46, also *Holly-*

wood Showcase 1942, *This Is Hollywood* 1946–47, *The Hedda Hopper Show* 1950–51; acted in late 1930s *The Campbell Playhouse*, *Brenthouse*; *Leave it to the Girls* panelist 1945–49; early occupations: chorus girl, stage-silent screen-"talkies" actress (149 movies), real estate saleslady; newspaper column seen by 30 million readers at peak; pronounced disdain for archrival Louella Parsons, feeling mutual — foes battled in, out of public eye for years (*Life* magazine claimed Hopper "infinitely more liked by the movie colony than her ruthless rival"); d. Feb. 1, 1966.

Frank E. Hummert, Jr., June 2, 1884, St. Louis, Mo.; ad copywriter-executive, journalist, producer bka collaborator with wife Anne in bringing 125+ recurring series to radio, half open-ended soap operas (continued story lines), remainder split in juvenile adventure serials, musicales, mystery features 1931–60; duo branded "most prolific producers in broadcasting," never surpassed; eyes eternally fixed on bottom line, entrepreneurs operated as Air Features, Inc.; employed hundreds of minions to act, announce, direct, edit, play music, supervise, vocalize, write, legal stenography; eccentric Hummerts lived grand lifestyle in opulent Greenwich manor shunning virtually everybody, chauffered to and fro daily, took trips abroad while paying workforce meager sums, linking by typed memos, handing down orders via few trusted sources even in hiring, firing; best remembered for *Backstage Wife*, *David Harum*, *Jack Armstrong — the All-American Boy*, *Little Orphan Annie*, *Lora Lawton*, *Lorenzo Jones*, *Manhattan Merry-Go-Round*, *Ma Perkins*, *Mr. Chameleon*, *Mr. Keen —Tracer of Lost Persons*, *Mystery Theater*, *Our Gal Sunday*, *The Romance of Helen Trent*, *Stella Dallas*, *Waltz Time*, *Young Widder Brown*; d. March 12, 1966.

Gil Stratton, Jr., d. June 2, 1922, Brooklyn, N.Y.; actor (stage, film, radio, TV), sportscaster bka TV voice of Los Angeles Rams professional football team starting mid 1950s; *Life with Luigi* figure Jimmy O'Connor, Luigi Basco's helper at Chicago antiques shop 1948–54; debuted Broadway stage at 19 as Bud Hooper in musical *Best Foot Forward*; 21 cinematic productions; joined casts of *One Man's Family* narrative NBC Radio, *That's My Boy* sitcom CBS-TV 1954–55; numerous single-shot video turns before taking California, Hawaii ethereal gigs.

Walter Tetley (Walter Campbell Tetzlaff), June 2, 1915, New York City, N.Y.; actor (stage, radio, film, TV), voiceover artist bka child actor in vaudeville, seldom in adult roles — *The Great Gildersleeve* sitcom nephew/ward Leroy Forrester NBC 1941–58, *The Fitch Bandwagon*/*The Phil Harris-Alice Faye Show* sitcom grocery delivery boy Julius Abbruzio NBC 1946–54; other mic gigs: *The Alan Young Show*, *The Bob Burns Show*, *Buck Rogers in the 25th Century*, *Coast-to-Coast on a Bus*, *The Cukoo Hour*, *Fibber McGee & Molly*, *The Fred Allen Show*, *Raising Junior*, more; 56 theatrical films 1922–54, most uncredited, voice roles; speaking parts in four animated TV series 1957–69; d. Sept. 4, 1975.

Deaths

Jean Hersholt, June 2, 1956, Hollywood, Calif.; b. June 12, 1886. Sammy Kaye, June 2, 1987, Ridgewood, N.J.; b. March 13, 1910.

June 3

Debuting

The Casebook of Gregory Hood, June 3, 1946, MBS; mystery drama; using curio or artifact as talking points, mythical San Francisco importer Hood (Gale Gordon, George Petrie, Elliott Lewis, Jackson Beck, Paul McGrath, Martin Gabel) wove narrative around it, usually involving globetrotting pursuing wares for sale, along with Sanderson "Sandy" Taylor (Bill Johnstone, Howard McNear, Carl Harper); Hood was debonair, lady-killer, novice composer, amateur sleuth — that perceptibly qualified him for exploits every week; final broadcast Oct. 10, 1951.

Dragnet, June 3, 1949, NBC; police detective drama initiating breed of lifelike crimestoppers; exhibiting cool disposition, L.A. Police Department Sgt. Joe Friday (Jack Webb), enduring partner Ofcr. Frank Smith (Harry Bartell, Vic Perrin, Herb Ellis, Ben Alexander) — accentuating reality noting incongruities, tossing in sporadic splashes of humor — dealt with shoplifting, petty larceny, overdrawn checks, domestic crises, threats seldom carried out, but few rapes, bank robberies, murders — educating public about how "mundane" acts processed in police work; Jack Webb starred in 1954 theatrical film, carried show to NBC-TV 1951–59, 1967–70; 1990–91 syndicated reprise with unknown Jeff Osterhage as Sgt. Vic Daniels failure; final radiocast Feb. 26, 1957.

Winner Take All, June 3, 1946, CBS; quiz; dual players competed for chances to answer queries posed by Bill Cullen, Clayton "Bud" Collyer, Ward Wilson; one player rang bell while other pressed buzzer; vying for merchandise prizes, parties played three matches competitively — one with most correct answers "took all" game's spoils; final broadcast Feb. 1, 1952.

Canceled

Radio Reader's Digest, June 3, 1948, CBS; debut Sept. 13, 1942. *Sky King*, June 3, 1954, MBS; debut Oct. 28, 1946.

Births

Daniel Golenpaul, June 3, 1900, Brooklyn, N.Y.; director, producer bka *Information Please* creator, executive, owner 1938–51; d. Feb. 13, 1974.

Theodore A. (Ted) Mallie, June 3, 1924, Brooklyn, N.Y.; announcer, newscaster; brought late 1940s-mid 1950s features to air: *I Love a Mystery, The Jean Shepherd Show, John Steele—Adventurer, The Shadow, The Sylvan Levin Opera Concert, There's Always a Woman, Wild Bill Hickok*; after MBS faded he survived at New York flagship WOR as announcer, newscaster; d. Jan. 25, 1999.

Charles Francis McCarthy, June 3, 1919, New York City, N.Y.; announcer, newscaster bka newsman on *Charles F. McCarthy and the News* 1946–48, *The Sunday News Desk* 1952; also opened *The NBC Story Shop* 1947–48; launched career delivering headlines over Raleigh WRAL 1939; not to be confused with most infamous marionette of comedian Edgar Bergen; d. July 4, 1988.

Warren Joseph Sweeney, b. June 3, 1909, Arlington, Va.; announcer, newscaster bka inexhaustible interlocutor on mainstay series in golden age waning days: *The Couple Next Door, The FBI in Peace & War, Let's Pretend, Mr. Keen—Tracer of Lost Persons, The Second Mrs. Burton, Yours Truly—Johnny Dollar*; started at Washington WJSV 1931, hoping to be pianist there (music his first love) but instead tapped for announcing; dispatched CBS *News of the World* 1940–44, expanded repertoire opening *The Burl Ives Show, The CBS Radio Workshop, Church of the Air, The Columbia Workshop, Hear It Now, Major Bowes' Original Amateur Hour, The New York Philharmonic Symphony, Our Gal Sunday, The Philadelphia Symphony Orchestra, Radio School of the Air, The Raymond Scott Show, The World Today*, more; d. Oct. 4, 1988.

Deaths

Curley Bradley, June 3, 1985, Long Beach, Calif.; b. Sept. 18, 1910. Joseph C. Harsch, June 3, 1998, Jamestown, R.I.; b. May 25, 1905. Dennis James, June 3, 1997, Palm Springs, Calif.; b. Aug. 24, 1917. Ozzie Nelson, June 3, 1975, Hollywood, Calif.; b. March 20, 1906.

June 4

Debuting

Ladies Be Seated (Ed East and Polly), June 4, 1943, NBC Blue; audience participation stunt show; premiered with cohosts Ed, Polly East, succeeded by Johnny, Penny Olsen, with Tom Moore filling chair in summer 1949, netting him emcee work on MBS successor *Ladies Fair*; studio contestants ate spaghetti in public, pursued gags often blindfolded — kind of subdued matinee replica of *Truth or Consequences, People Are Funny*; final broadcast July 21, 1950.

The Steve Allen Show, June 4, 1950, CBS; comedy variety; launched over Los Angeles KNX 1947, funnyman was innovative wit who connected with fans — not only could he provide impromptu laughs, he could snicker giddily at antics, exhibitions of his guests, other players, unsuspecting goons plucked from studio audiences; as talented composer, pianist, comic, some of best material resulted by combining them; with its initial exposure to talented man via radio, America instantly fell in love with him, turning moniker into household word as first host of *Tonight* show NBC-TV 1954–57; final radiocast Jan. 24, 1953.

Canceled

The Adventures of Frank Merriwell, June 4, 1949, NBC; debut March 26, 1934.

Births

Charles Cummings Collingwood, June 4, 1917, Three Rivers, Mich.; correspondent, newscaster bka "Murrow Boy" making transition from radio to TV; United Press staff in London 1940 hired by Murrow for CBS 1941 (so enamored with Murrow he once remarked "I wanted to *be* Edward R. Murrow"); ongoing aural gigs *CBS World News Roundup, Charles Collingwood and the News, This Is London*; 1940s became first CBS correspondent to U. N.; covered Truman White House; acquired CBS-TV news-based forums starting 1953; at his request, sent to London as chief foreign correspondent 1964 (Murrow's old job); retired from CBS 1982; d. Oct. 3, 1985.

Howard Culver, June 4, 1918, actor, announcer, newscaster bka *Straight Arrow* impersonator 1948–51 transforming self from rancher Steve Adams to great one, righting wrongs proffered by deceitful schemers preying on settlers in old west, war cry "Kaneewah, Fury!" exploding out of echo chamber; as radio faded, Culver signed with CBS-TV's *Gunsmoke*, appearing as hotel clerk Howie Uzzell full run 1955–75; d. Aug. 5, 1984.

Vinton J. Hayworth, June 4, 1906, Washington, D.C.; actor (stage, film, radio, TV), announcer bka aural thespian 1930s-50s in mysteries, soap operas, comedies, anthological dramas e.g. *The Adventures of Michael Shayne, Archie Andrews, Betty and Bob, Chaplain Jim U.S.A., The First Nighter, Life Can Be Beautiful, Lone Journey, Mr. Keen—Tracer of Lost Persons, Myrt and Marge, Second Husband, The Strange Romance of Evelyn Winters*; onstage in nation's capitol 1926, directed first live Chicago TV show 1930, a founder of American Federation of Radio Artists (AFRA); 67 mostly B-film productions (some under pseudonym Stanley Jordan) 1934–66; TV exposure in *Zorro* ABC 1957–59, *Dragnet* NBC 1967–69, *I Dream of Jeannie* NBC 1969–70; d. May 21, 1970.

Carlton E. Morse, June 4, 1901, Jennings, La.; author, director, journalist, producer, scriptwriter bka *One Man's Family* epic clan narrative creator, crafting 27 years on NBC 1932–59, two TV extensions; penned *Adventures by Morse, Family Skelton, His Honor—the Barber, I Love a Mystery, I Love Adventure, The Woman in My House*; newspaperman at *The Sacramento Union, The San Francisco Chronicle, The Seattle Times*; at 28 entered radio, distinguished self from rival scribes by scripting for *specific* actors; after radio, novelist—*Stuff the Lady's Hatbox, A Lavish of Sin, Killer at the Wheel*; d. May 24, 1993.

Deaths

Clem McCarthy, June 4, 1962, New York City, N.Y.; b. Sept. 9, 1882. Betty Winkler, June 4, 2002, Miami, Fla.; b. April 19, 1914.

June 5

Debuting

Live Like a Millionaire, June 5, 1950, NBC; talent audition; with emcee Jack McCoy, family-oriented showcase saw child, parent, sibling, grandparent introduce musical acts cut below Godfrey's *Talent Scouts* in quality; weekday bathtub brigade frequently scheduled dad singing "Million Dollar Baby" as violin virtuoso fiddled "Hot Canary," another family member tickled ivories on "Till the End of Time"—seeming staples of venue; winners, selected by studio applause meter, received week's interest on million dollars, hence show title; televersion CBS/ABC 1951–53; final radiocast Aug. 28, 1953.

Take a Number, June 5, 1948, MBS; quiz; in pattern of aural game shows where building listener involvement was paramount, fans urged to mail in questions asked of contestants—queries used netted gifts to senders; if studio player didn't get it right, submitter got lost prize, too, resulting in harder-to-answer queries; first round champs chose next question by number for grand prize; quizmasters Al "Red" Benson, Happy Felton, Bob Shepherd; final broadcast May 20, 1955.

Canceled

The Adventures of Christopher London, June 5, 1950, NBC; debut Jan. 22, 1950. *The Longines Symphonette*, June 5, 1954, CBS; debut July 5, 1943. *Weekend*, June 5, 1955, NBC; debut Oct. 4, 1955.

Births

William Boyd, June 5, 1895, Hendrysburg, Ohio; actor (film, radio, TV), entrepreneur, personal appearance artist, producer bka Hopalong Cassidy western hero in manifold manifestations; arrived Hollywood 1919, played in more than 100 theatrical films 1920–53, becoming Hoppy 1935, appeared as respected good guy in white hat almost exclusively thereafter, Saturday matinee idol of adolescent set; turned fanatical following into huge merchandising opportunity, branding every trinket, piece of clothing, memento imaginable; NBC-TV series 1949–51, syndicated TV 1952–54, flicks rerun on local stations still; radio series *Hopalong Cassidy* MBS/CBS 1950–52; d. Sept. 12, 1972.

John Raby, June 5, 1916, New York City, N.Y.; actor (radio, TV, film) bka *When a Girl Marries* daytime serial hero Harry Davis CBS/NBC/ABC 1939–42, 1946–1950s; avid daytime thespian on *Amanda of Honeymoon Hill, The Brighter Day, House in the Country, Joyce Jordan — Girl Interne, Our Gal Sunday, Wendy Warren and the News* plus nighttime mysteries *Mr. Keen — Tracer of Lost Persons, Nick Carter — Master Detective*; moved to video serials with fleeting Dumont narrative *A Woman to Remember* 1949, *Concerning Miss Marlowe* NBC-TV 1954, *The Edge of Night* CBS-TV 1956–57 while performing in handful of anthological TV fare; bit part in *That Night* 1957 theatrical movie; d. March 1957 (numerous sources for precise date, place exhausted).

Deaths

Hal Gibney, June 5, 1973, Santa Barbara County, Calif.; b. Aug. 26, 1911. Jeanette Nolan, June 5, 1998, Los Angeles, Calif.; b. Dec. 30, 1911. Rod O'Connor, June 5, 1964, Los Angeles, Calif.; b. Jan. 18, 1914. Mel Torme, June 5, 1999, Los Angeles, Calif.; b. Sept. 13, 1925.

June 6

Debuting

Stella Dallas, June 6, 1938, NBC (premiered Oct. 25, 1937 over New York WEAF); daytime serial; while there were inlaw troubles aplenty in plots of this dishpan drama, Boston seamstress Dallas (Anne Elstner) had a proclivity for mixing it up with thugs, vagrants, thieves, murderers, foreign spies, etc. as often as Johnny Dollar, Sergeant Preston, Tom Mix and Richard Diamond did; what time she wasn't charging after some hood, Stel was fussing over precious Laurel ("Lolly Baby") Grosvenor (Joy Hathaway, Vivian Smolen), grown woman at center of her mom's life, a child who couldn't think for herself without "mummy" to guide her; odd assortment of characters that seemed to take soap opera in a lighter, comical vein, despite all their misfortune; final broadcast Dec. 30, 1955.

Young Widder Brown (premiered as *Young Widder Jones*— to avoid confusion, surname altered when it moved to NBC Sept. 26, 1938 separated from *Lorenzo Jones* by station break), June 6, 1938, MBS; daytime serial; "the age old conflict between a mother's duty and a woman's heart" played out daily for 17 years as widowed tearoom proprietress/mother of "two fatherless children" Ellen Brown (Florence Freeman, Wendy Drew) struggled to keep bread on table and — consequentially — emotions in check as first one suitor, Peter Turner (Clayton "Bud" Collyer), then another, Dr. Anthony Loring (Ned Wever), sought hand — as did every other eligible male who spent a while in Simpsonville; like their *Helen Trent*, producing Hummerts wouldn't allow Ellen to walk aisle for it would blow show's premise, netting angst for her and us; final broadcast June 29, 1956.

Birth

Peter Donald, June 6, 1918, Bristol, England; actor, announcer, emcee, writer, voiceover artist bka one of radio's great dialecticians, exhibiting linguistic agility on *Can You Top This?* 1942–51, 1953–54, ABC-TV 1950–51, *The Fred Allen Show* "Allen's Alley" as jesting Irishman Ajax Cassidy 1945–49; on Broadway at 10 in Noel Coward's *Bittersweet*, soon joining Milton Cross's *Coast-to-Coast on a Bus*; played in/introduced/penned at least 24 series 1930s-50s; *Masquerade Party* host ABC-TV 1954–56; voiceover commercials while narrating industrial film documentaries; late career on south Florida radio-TV; d. April 30, 1979.

June 7

Sound Bite

After very first "network" broadcast Jan. 4, 1923, repeat occurrence doesn't transpire for five months — June 7, 1923 — as Chicago KYW, New York WEAF, Pittsburgh KDKA, Schenectady WGY link via phone line circuitry; first continuous network broadcasting arrives that summer when South Dartmouth, Mass. WMAF programs are transported — for six months — to WEAF; all of this is visionary, of course, projecting far more than miracle being witnessed.

Canceled

Lux Radio Theater, June 7, 1955, NBC; debut Oct. 14, 1934.

Birth

Alois Havrilla, June 7, 1891, Pressov, Czechoslovakia; announcer, emcee, vocalist; 1924–46 on staffs of four New York outlets — WEAF, WJZ, WABC, WOR — joining NBC as baritone soloist, announcer 1926, its formative year; hosted *Strange as It Seems* 1939–40, introduced 1930s-40s *The Campbell Soup Orchestra, The Chevrolet Program, The Colgate House Party, Double or Nothing, Jack Frost Melody Moments, The Palmolive Hour*; narrated Pathe newsreels 1928–46, trio of mini-movies, dozen film shorts; joined Paterson, N.J. WPAT 1946, Newark WNJR 1949–52; d. Dec. 7, 1952.

June 8

Canceled

Let's Dance, June 8, 1935, NBC; debut Dec. 1, 1934.

Births

Charles Frederick Lindsley, June 8, 1894, Higginsport, Ohio; announcer, educator, emcee; *Calling All Cars* narrator 1933–39, *Noah Webster Says* quizmaster 1942–43, 1945–51; Ohio State, University of Minnesota faculties in teens, 1920s, L.A. Occidental College speech prof, dean 1923–58, concurrently Pasadena Playhouse director of radio instruction from 1941; d. Oct. 31, 1960.

Ralph John Locke, June 8, 1877, Bronx, N.Y.; actor (stage, film, radio, TV) bka *Life Can Be Beautiful* daytime serial bookshop proprietor Papa David Solomon CBS/NBC 1938–54 — moral compass for two wards; wasn't Jewish as widely accepted but lifelong Catholic, not linked with Yiddish theater as reported nor born in eastern Europe, all repetitious myths; comic actor on stage 1904–40 in two dozen Broadway, stock company plays; performed in 1915, 1919 silent films, on *One Man's Family* NBC-TV 1950–52; d. Nov. 28, 1954.

Craig S. McDonnell, June 8, 1907, Buffalo, N.Y.; actor, announcer, vocalist; in early 1930s, popular baritone radio singer; later narrated *The NBC Story Shop, The O'Neills* while acting in numerous 1930s-50s dramas: *The Adventures of Dick Tracy, Bobby Benson and the B-Bar-B Riders, Bringing Up Father, Cavalcade of America, The Columbia Workshop, Daddy and Rollo, David Harum, The Eternal Light, Jack and Cliff, Official Detective, The Second Mrs. Burton, Under Arrest, Valiant Lady, X-Minus One*, more; d. Nov. 24, 1956.

Death

Harfield Weedin, June 8, 1993, Boise, Idaho; b. Feb. 15, 1916.

June 9

Canceled

The Abbott and Costello Show, June 9, 1949, ABC; debut July 3, 1940. *The Challenge of the Yukon/Sergeant Preston of the Yukon*, June 9, 1954, MBS; network debut June 12, 1947.

Births

George Bryan, June 9, 1910, New York City, N.Y.; announcer, composer, newscaster, playwright, vocalist bka *Armstrong Theater of Today* 1940s and *Arthur Godfrey's Talent Scouts* interlocutors 1946–56, simulcast 1948–56; presented plethora of 1930s-50s features like *The Helen Hayes Theater, Hit the Jackpot, Let's Pretend, Mr. Chameleon, The Peter Lind Hayes Show, The Road of Life, We the People*; d. June 27, 1969.

Donald Telfer Forbes, June 9, 1912, Camrose, Alberta, Canada; actor, announcer, newscaster, producer bka *The Richfield Reporter* 1940–41; introduced *Ten-Two-Four Ranch* 1941–45; narrated Oscar-winning documentary *The Sea Around Us* 1952; appeared in dozen B-movies 1940–60; occasional episodes of TV's *The Millionaire, Lost in Space*, more; produced popular TV series for Bowles Advertising (*The Andy Griffith Show, Cheyenne, The Dick Van Dyke Show, Perry Mason*); d. Nov. 28, 1995.

Joseph Julian (Joseph Shapiro), June 9, 1910, St. Marys, Pa.; actor (radio, TV, film), author, disc jockey, scribe, sound tech, voiceover artist; acting, sound work Cincinnati WLW; acted, spun records New York WNYC; played in *The Adventures of Nero Wolfe, The Adventures of Superman, Big Sister, Boston Blackie, The Brighter Day, Front Page Farrell, The Goldbergs, Inner Sanctum Mysteries, Life Can Be Beautiful, Lorenzo Jones, Mr. Keen—Tracer of Lost Persons*, more; 1940s articles in *The New York Times, Variety* incensed peers, he claimed they left most radio jobs "unsatisfied," not "serious" acting to most; he "scared the hell out of other cast members" said pundit — urged memorization, performed at times sans script; *Red Channels* blacklisted him — he had little work for years; penned two episodes *The U. S. Steel Hour* ABC-TV 1954–55, *This Was Radio* memoir 1975; dubbed foreign films, voiced radio-TV ads, five theatrical films 1957–62, 15 solo TV roles 1960–67, TV daytime serials *As the World Turns* 1960–63, *The Edge of Night* 1966, *Somerset* 1975–76; d. March 11, 1982.

Fred Waring, June 9, 1900, Tyrone, Pa.; busnessman, concert tour manager, entrepreneur, impresario, recording artist bka *Fred Waring and His Pennsylvanians* maestro 1921–84; lauded by pundit as "man who taught America how to sing"; consummate bandleader, polished perfectionist-showman dominating ethereal rivals in longevity; created glee club-sound trademarking his entourage; part owner of upscale resort, published monthly periodical, launched music publishing concern, established lucrative choral workshops, marketed steam irons/Waring blenders, latter named for him; d. July 29, 1984.

Death

Patrick H. Barnes, June 9, 1969, Milwaukee, Wis.; b. Oct. 26, 1888.

June 10

Debuting

The Abbott Mysteries, June 10, 1945, MBS; crime drama featuring newlywed sleuths Pat, Jean Abbott (series not to confuse with *The Adventures of the Abbotts* NBC entry 1955); summer sub 1945, 1946, 1947 for *Quick as a Flash*; final broadcast Aug. 31, 1947.

The Hallmark Playhouse (successor *Hallmark Hall of Fame*), June 10, 1948, CBS; anthology drama; precursors that spawned some of TV's prestigious moments on *Hallmark Hall of Fame* NBC/CBS/PBS/ABC since Jan. 6, 1952, now Hallmark Channel, occasional new dramas on CBS-TV (2007–08); *Playhouse* tales adapted from literature with Hollywood actors in leads while *Hall of Fame* plays featured same in stories of American life; final radiocast March 27, 1955.

Canceled

Queen for a Day, June 10, 1957, MBS; debut April 30, 1945. *Voice of Firestone*, June 10, 1957, ABC, simulcast ABC-TV (earlier NBC-TV); debut Dec. 3, 1928.

Births

Norman Ernest (Broke) Brokenshire, June 10, 1898, Murcheson, Ont., Canada; actor, announcer, emcee, newscaster, newspaper owner bka *The Theater Guild on the Air, The United States Steel Hour* interlocutors 1945–53; credited self with "inventing" soap opera at New York WJZ 1924 though that's speculative; battled alcoholism across career, losing lots of air gigs to bottle; d. May 4, 1965.

Anne Burr (McDermott), June 10, 1920, Boston, Mass.; actress (stage, radio, TV) bka *City Hospital* anthology drama with connecting backstory as nurse Kate Morrow CBS 1951–58, CBS-TV 1952–53; showbiz start on stage, leads in 1940s Broadway productions *Detective Story, The Hasty Heart*; with deep basal Tallulah Bankhead brogue, often cast in dark, foreboding roles in daytime serials *Backtage Wife, Big Sister, Wendy Warren and the News, When a Girl Marries*, nighttime thrillers *Mr. Keen—Tracer of Lost Persons, Scotland Yard, Studio One*; recurring parts in TV soaps *The Guiding Light* CBS 1952–54, *The Greatest Gift* NBC 1954, *Way of the World* NBC 1955, *As the World Turns* CBS 1956 plus fleeting performances on scattered TV narratives; d. Feb. 1, 2003.

Ernest (Chappie) Chappell, June 10, 1903, Syracuse, N.Y.; announcer, emcee, newscaster, program director, station manager; premiered at Syracuse WFBL 1925, moved to Rochester WHAM as station manager 1927, becoming NBC Blue net voice there; spokesman for American Tobacco Co.'s Pall Mall cigarette brand 17 years (*The Big Story* 1947–55, others); introduced *Eyewitness to History* CBS-TV 1960–63 — chain's coverage of presidential appearances; dozens of radio gigs saw him proffer questions on *Are You a Genius?* 1942–43, deliver sponsor plugs on *Edward R. Murrow and the News* 1945-late 1940s, introduce *Thirty Minutes in Hollywood* 1937–38; d. July 4, 1983.

Lawrence Edward (Larry) Lesueur, June 10, 1909, New York City, N.Y.; announcer, correspondent, newscaster, print/wire service journalist, scriptwriter bka CBS News glory days workhorse; ongoing gigs *CBS World News Roundup* 1942–50s, *Chevrolet Spotlights the News* mid 1950s, *Larry Lesueur and the News* 1946–58 (not continuous), *This Is London* early 1940s, *The World Tonight* 1950s-63; *Women's Wear Daily* reporter 1935, United Press staff 1936; penned scripts, acted in *We the People* CBS 1938–39, chain added him to London staff 1939, later France, Russia, London again (hired by overseas news guru Edward R. Murrow as one of iconic "Murrow Boys"); after World War II, first newsman to air news regularly on New York WCBS-TV predating Douglas Edwards, others; assigned to UN, winning Peabody Award for reportage; *Chronoscope* world issues entry moderator CBS-TV 1953–55; *The U. N. in Action* intermittent public affairs series host CBS-TV 1955–60; transferred to nation's capital, departed CBS 1963, signed with U. S. Information Agency's Voice of America as White House stringer to retirement 1983; major contributor to CBS but never fully appreciated by net, CBS news biographers Stan Cloud, Lynne Olson affirmed; d. Feb. 5, 2003.

Hattie McDaniel, June 10, 1895, Denver, Colo.; actress (film, radio, stage) bka *Gone With the Wind* character Mammy 1939, becoming first of her race to win Oscar — Best Supporting Actress, Feb. 29, 1940; *Beulah* namesake star 1947–51; fostered racial acceptance, change; d. Oct. 26, 1952.

Charles Peter O'Connor, June 10, 1910, Cambridge, Mass.; actor, announcer, correspondent, newscaster, sportscaster; in stock entourage touring East, joined Boston WBZ announcing staff January 1931, moved that year to New York NBC, hired with nine others of 2,500 auditioned; covered Lindbergh baby kidnapping 1932, more events, football scrimmages; beset by alcoholism, chains, sponsors quit hiring him; inability to find job ended in suicide; d. March 17, 1942.

Hal Simms, June 10, 1919, Boston, Mass.; announcer, disc jockey; presented 1950s features *Rate Your Mate*, *The Steve Allen Show*, *Stop the Music!*, *Strike It Rich*; at same time DJ at Philadelphia WIP 1950, introduced *The Jack Paar Show* CBS-TV 1955–56; employed by CBS 1951–93; d. July 2, 2002.

Harold (Harlan/Hal) Stone, Jr., June 10, 1931, Long Island, N.Y.; actor (radio, TV), author, child photo model, director (commercials, TV) bka *Archie Andrews* teen sitcom sidekick-conspirator Forsythe Pendleton (Jughead) Jones 1945–51, 1953; TV advertising director in later life; recurring guest director-performer at vintage radio conventions late 1990s-early 2000s; memoir *Aw ... Relax, Archie! Re-laxx!* 2003; d. Feb. 21, 2007.

Death

Alice Reinheart, June 10, 1993, Avon, Conn.; b. May 6, 1910.

June 11

Canceled

Roadshow, June 11, 1955, NBC; debut Jan. 9, 1954.

Births

Dudley D. Manlove, June 11, 1914, Oakland, Calif.; announcer, newscaster bka *Candy Matson* interlocutor 1949–51 (only series certified); San Francisco KSAN newsman 1939; d. April 17, 1996.

Harry W. Marble, June 11, 1905, Brownville, Maine; announcer, emcee, newscaster; news career launched at Philadelphia WCAU 1938 before relocating to New York CBS 1939, appearing on *Harry Marble and the News* 1939–49, same era's *CBS World News Roundup*, *World News Tonight*; welcomed listeners to *Columbia Presents Corwin*, *Margaret Arlen*, *Up for Parole*, *You Are There*, added public affairs programming into early 1950s; d. Aug. 1, 1982.

Gerald Mohr, June 11, 1914, New York City, N.Y.; actor (radio, stage, film, TV), composer, narrator, newscaster, pianist, vocalist, voiceover artist bka *The Adventures of Philip Marlowe* crime drama namesake CBS 1948–51 ("Get this and get it straight — crime is a sucker's road and those who travel it wind up in the gutter, the prison or the grave"); in 1930s joined Gotham station as junior reporter, Orson Welles repertory company, stage in Broadway productions; narrated radio-TV episode intros for *The Lone Ranger*; radio work embraced *The Adventures of Bill Lance*, *The Adventures of Nero Wolfe*, *Bandwagon Mysteries*, *Dan Dunn — Secret Operative 48*, *Hopalong Cassidy*, *Lux Radio Theater*, *Rogue's Gallery*, *The Six Shooter*, *Suspense*, *Tales of the Texas Rangers*, *The Whistler*, more; numerous TV series, solo appearances, motion pictures; d. Nov. 10, 1968.

Lawrence E. Spivak, June 11, 1900, Brooklyn, N.Y.; emcee, producer bka *Meet the Press* panelist/moderator/producer 1945–50, 1952–75, NBC-TV 1947–75 (show persisted after his 1975 retirement); d. March 9, 1994.

Risë Stevens (Risë Steenberg), June 11, 1913, New York City, N.Y.; author, educator, fundraiser, recording artist, vocalist (mezzo-soprano) (concert tours, film, opera, radio, TV) bka *Voice of Firestone* fourth most frequently recurring artist (58 appearances) 1940s, 1950s intermittently singing in same era on two more NBC "Monday Night of Music" epic features — *The Bell Telephone Hour, The Railroad Hour*; won *The Metropolitan Opera Auditions of the Air* 1936 semifinals; Metropolitan Opera Co. member 1938–61; New York's Mannes College of Music president, Met charitable giving enlistment officer in later years.

Deaths

John Milton Kennedy, June 11, 1006, Los Angeles, Calif.; b. June 23, 1912. Vivian Smolen, June 11, 2006, Lake Worth, Fla.; b. March 7, 1916.

June 12

Sound Bite

Monitor, most pervasive programming innovation in broadcasting history, launched on NBC June 12, 1955; inspired by network president/resident program mastermind Sylvester L. (Pat) Weaver (creator of NBC-TV's *Today, Tonight, Home*); format consists of "nuggets of information or entertainment long enough to grab the audience's interest but short enough not to bore them" historian says, marking "radio's increasing strength as a portable medium — something TV was not"; initial 40-hours-per-weekend "programming service" carries listeners globally wherever newsmaking occurs/stars perform/extraordinary events happen in common peoples' lives; stellar list of hosts preside over multi-hour segments — Mel Allen, Morgan Beatty, Frank Blair, Ted Brown, Bill Cullen, Hugh Downs, Art Ford, Frank Gallop, Joe Garagiola, Dave Garroway, Ben Grauer, Monty Hall, Walter Kiernan, Jim Lowe, Frank McGee, Ed McMahon, Henry Morgan, Barry Nelson, Gene Rayburn, Don Russell, Ted Steele, John Bartholomew Tucker, Big Wilson; scores of luminaries appear every weekend like Steve Allen, Jack Benny, Milton Berle, Perry Como, Bill Cosby, Bob Hope; regulars' staff features — Bob (Elliott) and Ray (Goulding), Dr. Joyce Brothers, Al Capp, Bob Considine, Phyllis Diller, Fibber McGee & Molly, Arlene Francis, Betty Furness, Joe Garagiola, Graham Kerr, Ernie Kovacs, Ann Landers, Mike Nichols and Elaine May, Gene Shalit, Jonathan Winters; later in run 40-hour format is trimmed but NBC innovation persists; final broadcast Jan. 26, 1975.

Debuting

The Challenge of the Yukon (*Sergeant Preston of the Yukon*), June 12, 1947, ABC; juvenile adventure premiering nearly decade before on Detroit WXYZ (Feb. 3, 1938), third of acclaimed web trilogy (*The Lone Ranger, The Green Hornet*) WXYZ originated; Sgt. William Preston (Paul Sutton, Brace Beemer) — pulled by sled of lead dog King — combed snowy wilds of Canadian Yukon territory to ferret out lost, often pursuing desperadoes in skilled display of tracking deduction; premium bonanza for little tykes tuning in like certificates for square inch of Yukon land; CBS-TV 1955–58; final radiocast June 9, 1955.

Births

Archie Bleyer, June 12, 1909, Corona, N.Y.; impresario, CBS staff musician, recording artist-executive bka *Arthur Godfrey Time* virtuoso originating unique identifying resonance late 1940s-early 1950s; instrumental accompaniment for all Godfrey radio-TV shows (*Arthur Godfrey and His Friends, Arthur Godfrey Digest, Arthur Godfrey's Talent Scouts*); dismissed Oct. 19, 1953 for perceived disloyalty at start of mass singer, musician firings that tarnished public's trust of pervasive entertainer Godfrey; d. March 20, 1989.

Roger Forster, June 12, 1915, New York City, N.Y.; announcer; enduring voice introducing web radio fare late 1940s-late 1950s: *The CBS Radio Workshop, The Couple Next Door, The Guiding Light, Mystery Theater, Twenty-First Precinct*; opened *To Tell the Truth* game show CBS-TV 1960; d. Nov. 15, 2003.

Jean Hersholt, June 12, 1886, Copenhagen, Denmark; actor (stage, film, radio) bka *Dr. Christian* lead CBS 1937–54; played many Hollywood flicks, some with radio-sounding titles e.g. *Abie's Irish Rose, The Country Doctor, Grand Hotel, Meet Doctor Christian, Stage Door Canteen, Stella Dallas, The Student Prince*; founded Motion Picture Relief Fund to aid industry personnel suffering economic setbacks; Oscar panel designated Jean Hersholt Humanitarian Award, presented to him for compassionate, philanthropic exploits; d. June 2, 1956.

Mary Lee Taylor (Erma Perham Proetz), June 12, 1891, Denver, Colo.; ad agency staffer, culinary artist, home economist bka *The Mary Lee Taylor Program* cooking hints CBS/NBC 1933–54 (when she died, others impersonated mythical gastronomic expert); on air for Pet Milk Co., how-to feature in 1933 for American homemaker featured Pet recipes "designed to help mothers give their families the most wholesome diet possible under rationing limitations"; advertising copywriter, account executive, director, executive VP at Gardner Advertising (latter office at time of death)—created Taylor, test kitchens, recipes; won Harvard Advertising Award three times, first to do so; d. Aug. 7, 1944.

Deaths

David Brinkley, June 12, 2003, Houston, Texas; b. July 10, 1920. Ted Cott, June 12, 1973, New York City, N.Y.; b. Jan. 1, 1917. Jimmy Dorsey, June 12, 1957, New York City, N.Y.; b. Feb. 29, 1904. Franklyn MacCormack, June 12, 1971, Chicago, Ill.; b. March 8, 1906.

June 13

Canceled

Mr. District Attorney, June 13, 1952, ABC (popular syndicated version circulated later in 1950s); debut April 3, 1939.

Births

Robert (Bob) Bailey, June 13, 1913, Toledo, Ohio; actor (radio, film, TV) bka *Let George Do It* detective drama private eye George Valentine MBS-Don Lee West Coast regional hookup 1946–54, *Yours Truly—Johnny Dollar* crime drama insurance investigator-sleuth Dollar CBS 1955–60; support roles on *Aunt Mary, Girl Alone, Kitty Keene Incorporated, Knickerbocker Playhouse, Mortimer Gooch* (namesake), *One Man's Family, Romance, The Story of Holly Sloan, Today's Children*; dozen theatrical films 1943–62, seven solo TV dramatic series episodes 1954–84; d. Aug. 13, 1983.

Carl Eastman, June 13, 1908, New York City, N.Y.; actor, announcer, broker, director, personal manager (commercial talent), producer; acted in *Abie's Irish Rose, Big Story, Cavalcade of America, Gangbusters, The Right to Happiness, Under Arrest, Woman of Courage*, more; directed *The Adventures of M. Hercule Poirot, Perry Mason, Rosemary, We Love and Learn*; clients included Mason Adams, Dane Clark, Don Morrow, Arnold Moss, Santos Ortega; d. Jan. 16, 1970.

Ralph Livingstone Edwards, June 13, 1913, Merino, Colo.; actor, announcer, director, emcee, producer, program creator-owner bka *Truth or Consequences* 1940–51, 1952–54, *This Is Your Life* 1948–50 master of ceremonies with televersion extensions; TV game-audience participation show producer for *Place the Face* 1953–55, *It Could Be You* 1956–61, *Crosswits* 1975–80/1986–87, *The People's Court* 1981–93/1997–; d. Nov. 16, 2005.

("Senator") Ed Ford, June 13, 1887, Brooklyn, N.Y.; humorist, illustrator, monologist, raconteur, writer bka *Can You Top This?* panelist 1940–54; d. Jan. 27, 1970.

William D. (Bill) Lipton, June 13, 1926, Brooklyn, N.Y.; actor (radio, stage, TV); ethereal premier on New York WOR *Rainbow House*, added to *Let's Pretend* cast CBS 1938, starred on *Gasoline Alley* as Skeezix, originated title role of *Chick Carter—Boy Detective*; frequently on *The Columbia Workshop, The March of Time*, other anthologies, serial workaholic with continuing parts on *Mrs. Miniver, The Right to Happiness, The Road of Life, Young Doctor Malone*; reprised role of John Brent in *The Road of Life* CBS-TV 1954–55 after fleeting stint on *Tom Corbett—Space Cadet* CBS-TV 1950; d. Oct. 29, 2001.

Edwin R. Wolfe, b. June 13, 1893, Rochester, N.Y.; actor, freelance program director, producer; called shots on daytime serials *The Brighter Day, Hilltop House, Ma Perkins, Pepper Young's Family* (also acted in it), *The Road of Life*; when thespian Charles Egleston died in 1958 after 25 years as *Perkins* business partner Shuffle Shober, Wolfe filled role "temporarily"—until drama canceled Nov. 25, 1960; produced

Break the Bank quiz 1945–55; also directed *Madame Sylvia of Hollywood, The Parker Family*, more; d. Sept. 22, 1983.

Deaths

Fran Allison, June 13, 1989, Sherman Oaks, Calif.; b. Nov. 20, 1907. Benny Goodman, June 13, 1986, New York City, N.Y.; b. May 30, 1909. Charles Nobles, June 13, 1977, Reno, Nev.; b. Oct. 22, 1908.

June 14

Births

Jon Arthur (Jonathan Arthur Goerss), June 14, 1918, New Kensington, Pa.; actor, announcer bka creator-host-impersonator of dual juvenile series *Big Jon and Sparkie* ABC 1950–58, *No School Today* ABC 1950–54; with cast of fantasy figures, most inspired by innovative turntable/speech trickery (voice of 200+ characters), shows featured appeals for better hygiene, singing, storytelling, serialized narratives, exchanges with pals of Sparkie, "the little elf from the land of make-believe, who wants more than anything else ... to be a real boy"; on air at Beckley, W. Va. WJLS 1939, Cincinnati WSAI 1940s where his guttural sounds were welcomed by small fry in 1948, nationally in 1950; matinee show aired over Cincinnati WKRC 1960s; transferred to New York, Korea, San Francisco — heard in latter on KEAR, Christian Family Radio outlet; d. Feb. 24, 1982.

Major Edward Bowes, June 14, 1874, San Francisco, Calif.; emcee, entrepreneur, producer, talent scout, theater manager bka *The Original Amateur Hour* creator/host/producer; "the Ziegfeld of bird-whistlers and spoon-players" said one wag; Bowes held talent auditions that drew anybody capable of blowing harmonica, tapping wine glass — ridiculous to sublime; d. June 14, 1946.

Elaine Sterne Carrington, June 14, 1891, New York City, N.Y.; writer bka creator-scribe for trio of major daytime serials airing simultaneously — *Pepper Young's Family* (quadruple monikers) NBC Blue/MBS/NBC 1932–59, *When a Girl Marries* CBS/NBC/ABC 1939–57, *Rosemary* NBC/CBS 1944–55; she held third most fertile pen in daytime radio (surpassed by Frank/Anne Hummert, Irna Phillips) — but only one writing every word of every script among trio; plausible situations, figures her hallmark; also penned radio's *Trouble House* 1936–37, *Marriage for Two* 1949–50/1951–52, tepid soap *Follow Your Heart* NBC-TV 1953–54 lasting five months; before radio, authored steady stream of fiction for women's slicks — *Collier's, Good Housekeeping, Harper's, Ladies' Home Journal, Redbook, Woman's Home Companion*, more; scripted acclaimed Broadway play *Nightstick* reprised twice on big screen as *Alibi*; d. May 4, 1958.

John Scott Trotter, June 14, 1908, Charlotte, N.C.; perfectionist orchestral maestro who made pop idol Bing Crosby "sound like Crosby" on air, recordings, film; worked with crooner 1936 through most gigs; succeeded it conducting *George Gobel Show* music NBC-/CBS-TV 1954–60; d. Oct. 29, 1975.

Deaths

Major Edward Bowes, June 14, 1946 (his birthday), Rumson, N.J.; b. June 14, 1874. H. V. Kaltenborn, June 14, 1965, New York City, N.Y.; b. July 9, 1878. Betty Mandeville, June 14, 2001, Henderson, N.C.; b. June 18, 1910. Alan Reed, June 14, 1977, Los Angeles, Calif.; b. Aug. 20, 1907.

June 15

Sound Bites

Broadcasting reports in June 15, 1938 issue that 56 percent of all network series integrate premium offers: "In 'merchandising' tie-ups the faces of radio characters smiled from cereal packages, comic strips, pencil boxes, shirts, hats, glassware, guns, holsters, lunch boxes, games, dolls," trade periodical observes; premiums involve listeners in programs while providing feedback to clients on fans' depth of commitment; before ratings services furnish extensive data, that interaction is fairly suggestive about how shows are received by whom, at same time netting maximum commercials exposure.

Blue Network officially rebranded with American Broadcasting Co. (ABC) nomenclature June 15, 1945; in interim period — since web's divestiture by NBC — chain often dubbed "the Blue Network of the American Broadcasting Company."

Debuting

The Dave Garroway Show (*Reserved for Garroway, Dial Dave Garroway, Fridays with Dave Garroway*), June 15, 1947, NBC; conversation, music; scintillating laid-back style first noticed by listeners within reach of 50,000-watt Chicago WMAQ 1946 airing *The 11:60 Club*; one of most illustrious voices in broadcasting during golden age radio's last decade, TV's first; moved to New York, in right spot for hosting premiering *Today* on NBC-TV, chair occupied 1952–61; final radiocast heard (under multiple sobriquets) June 17, 1955.

Juvenile Jury, June 15, 1946, MBS; adolescent issues panel; ongoing five-member unit of articulate five-to-12-year-olds fielded few of 5,000 questions submitted to show weekly on topics ranging from kissing, makeup, allowances to spanking, study habits, attire; New York WOR personality Jack Barry proposed idea, launched station feature May 11, 1946, moved to web next month; video versions for NBC/CBS/syndication 1947–55, 1970; final radiocast Feb. 15, 1953.

Canceled

The Texaco Star Theater (*The Milton Berle Show*), June 15, 1949, ABC; debut Sept. 6, 1936.

Births

Lucille Norman, June 15, 1926, Lincoln, Neb.; vocalist bka *The Railroad Hour* most enduring costar, appearing with Gordon MacRae 73 times 1948–54; few undistinguished onscreen, added radio roles; d. April 1, 1998.

David Rose, June 15, 1910, London, England; arranger, composer, impresario, net music director (MBS), pianist bka *The Red Skelton Show* music conductor, radio 1947–51, TV 1951–71, composer of *Skelton* theme "Holiday for Strings"; maestro of nearly dozen more aural series 1936–52; d. Aug. 23, 1990.

Deaths

Kathleen Norris, June 15, 2005, London, England; b. June 1, 1919. Meredith Willson [sic], June 15, 1984, Santa Monica, Calif.; b. May 18, 1902.

June 16

Canceled

Snow Village Sketches, June 16, 1946, MBS; debut (as *Soconyland Sketches*) Feb. 29, 1928.

Births

Peter (Carson) Donald, June 16, 1918, Bristol, England; actor (radio, stage, TV), comedian, emcee, dialectician, narrator, voiceover artist bka *The Fred Allen Show* "Allen's Alley" character Ajax Cassidy, *Can You Top This?* quipmeister 1940–54; versatile range of voice inflections for audio, video applications in programming, commercials; myriad radio duties for *The Benny Goodman Show, Coast-to-Coast on a Bus, Columbia Presents Corwin, The Grummits, Into the Light, The Lady Next Door, Manhattan at Midnight, The March of Times Quiz, Second Husband, Stella Dallas, The Story of Mary Marlin, Talk Your Way Out of It, Terry and the Pirates, Treasury Star Parade, Your Family and Mine*; 1950s TV game show staple with *Ad Libbers, Can You Top This?, Masquerade Party, Prize Performance, Where Was I?, Pantomime Quiz*; narrated industrial film documentaries later; d. April 20, 1979.

Helen Traubel, June 16, 1899, St. Louis, Mo.; actress (film), author, nightclub performer, part owner of major league sports team (St. Louis Browns), vocalist (soprano) bka diva of Metropolitan Opera 1939–53; 23 guest artist appearances on *The Bell Telephone Hour* 1940–58; infrequent singing stints on *Voice of Firestone* 1928–57; d. July 28, 1972.

Death

Mel Allen (Melvin Allen Israel), June 16, 1996, Greenwich, Conn.; b. Feb. 14, 1913.

June 17

Debuting

The Adventures of Philip Marlowe, June 17, 1947, NBC; detective drama; L.A. private-eye investigator (Van Heflin, Gerald Mohr) worked in tandem with professional law enforcement unlike some peers; "Get this and get it straight" he admonished at inception of half-hour: "crime is a sucker's road and those who travel it wind up in the gutter, the prison or the grave"; inspired by Raymond Chandler fiction; final radiocast Sept. 15, 1951, ABC televersion Sept. 29, 1959-March 29, 1960 with Philip Carey portraying hard-boiled detective.

Suspense, June 17, 1942, CBS; mystery anthology drama; "radio's outstanding theater of thrills" was that — one of most universally admired anxiety-driven narratives gracing ether offering superlative writing, direction, acting by sterling names of stage, screen, radio, TV; production in hands of tested veterans Elliott Lewis, Norman Macdonnell, William N. Robson, William Spier, Bruno Zirato, Jr.; among headliners: Desi Arnaz and Lucille Ball, Jack Benny, Milton Berle, Humphrey Bogart, Henry Fonda, Cary Grant, Jim and Marian Jordan (*Fibber McGee & Molly*), Danny Kaye, Cathy Lewis, Frederic March, Agnes Moorehead, Red Skelton, Orson Welles, Richard Widmark, et al.; "tales well calculated to keep you in suspense"; most celebrated — Lucille Fletcher's "Sorry, Wrong Number" with Moorehead — aired eight times; anthological CBS-TV incarnations 1949–54/1964; final radiocast Sept. 30, 1962.

Canceled

The American Album of Familiar Music, June 17, 1951, ABC; debut Oct. 11, 1931. *Bobby Benson and the B-Bar-B Riders*, June 17, 1955, MBS; debut Nov. 14, 1932. *Fridays with Dave Garroway*, June 17, 1955, NBC; debut June 15, 1947.

Birth

Jerry Fielding (Joshua Feldman), June 17, 1922, Pittsburgh, Pa.; arranger, composer (film, TV), impresario, recording artist; d. Feb. 17, 1980.

Deaths

Jeff Chandler, June 17, 1961, Los Angeles, Calif.; b. Dec. 15, 1918. Hy Gardner, June 17, 1989, Miami, Fla.; b. Dec. 2, 1902. Hugh James, June 17, 2001, Madison, Conn.; b. Oct. 13, 1915. Kate Smith, June 17, 1986, Raleigh, N.C.; b. May 1, 1907. Bob Stanton, June 17, 1977, Miami, Fla.; b. April 14, 1905.

June 18

Sound Bite

NBC launches all-news radio hookup (forerunner of CNN, MSNBC, rivals) June 18, 1975 to 33 affiliates; web claims it must have 150 outlets to turn profit; service withdrawn May 29, 1977 when beamed to 62 stations.

Debuting

The Adventures of Ellery Queen, June 18, 1939, CBS; crime drama featuring professional New York scribe Queen (Hugh Marlowe, Carleton Young, Sidney Smith, Lawrence Dobkin, Howard Culver) with avocation of solving murder, mayhem assisted by spirited secretary-love interest Nikki Porter (Kaye Brinker, Virginia Gregg, Charlotte Keane, Helen Lewis, Marian Shockley, Barbara Terrell, Gertrude Warner); Queen viewed his sleuthing pursuits as book research, didn't charge clients for services; over protracted run, show shifted between CBS, NBC twice winding up last season at ABC with final performance May 27, 1948; televersions seen on various networks Oct. 19, 1950-Sept. 19, 1976; grew to seven theatrical films 1940–42, two made-for-TV flicks 1971/1975, countless tomes.

Canceled

The Adventures of Ozzie and Harriet, June 18, 1954, ABC; debut Oct. 8, 1944. *Gunsmoke*, June 18, 1961, CBS; debut April 26, 1952. *The Phil Harris-Alice Faye Show*, June 18, 1954, NBC; debut as *The Fitch Bandwagon* Sept. 29, 1946.

Births

Melville S. Brandt, June 18, 1919, Brooklyn, N.Y.; actor, announcer, emcee bka NBC-TV spokesman informing viewers "The following program is brought to you in living color on NBC" 1962–75, elected national president AFTRA 1967; introduced *The Adventures of Frank Merriwell* 1947–49 replayed by some outlets 1970s, *When A Girl Marries* 1947-ca. 1951; *Monitor* magazine co-communicator ca. 1957–58; *The Bell Telephone Hour* interlocutor NBC-TV incarnation 1959–68, *G. E. College Bowl* NBC-TV 1963–67; *Saturday Night Live* announcer NBC-TV 1981–82; moved to New Port Richey, Fla. in retirement.

Clayton (Bud) Collyer (Clayton Johnson Heermance, Jr.), June 18, 1908, New York City, N.Y.; actor, announcer, emcee bka *To Tell the Truth* moderator CBS-TV 1956–67; one of radio's most indefatigable, turned up all over dial in 1930s-40s as host, narrator or thespian: *The Adventures of Superman, Big Sister, Break the Bank, Cavalcade of America, Chick Carter—Boy Detective, The Goldbergs, The Guiding Light, Joyce Jordan, Just Plain Bill, Pretty Kitty Kelly, Truth or Consequences, Winner Take All, Young Widder Brown*; commercial spokesman for Duz detergent on multi audio runs for Procter & Gamble ("Duz does everything!"); fixture of early TV game shows, presiding over 1940s-60s *The Missus Goes a-Shopping, Winner Take All, Break the Bank, Talent Jackpot, Beat the Clock, Say It with Acting, Masquerade Party, On Your Way, Quick as a Flash, Feather Your Nest, Number Please, To Tell the Truth*; d. Sept. 8, 1969.

Russell Patrick Hodges, June 18, 1910, Dayton, Tenn.; sportscaster; joined Covington, Ky. WCKY as rookie announcer 1931, sportscaster calling Cincinnati Reds baseball games 1933; moved to Gary, Ind. WIND 1935 as sports director, aired Chicago Cubs games; moved to Charlotte WBT 1939, Washington, D.C. WOL 1941 gaining MBS sports feature, became net's chief sportscaster 1944; joined New York WINS 1946, rival WMCA 1948; collaborated with Mel Allen airing New York Yankees games on WINS, New York Giants games on WMCA; *Russ Hodges' Scoreboard* host quarter-hour weeknights Dumont TV 1948–49; *International Boxing Club Bouts* ringside announcer CBS-TV 1948–50, 1951–55; presided over *NCAA Football* NBC-TV 1951–53, 1955; moved with Giants to San Francisco 1958 to 1970 retirement; d. April 19, 1971.

Kay Kyser (James Kern Kyser), June 18, 1897, Rocky Mount, N.C.; actor (film), emcee, impresario (personal appearances, radio, TV), pharmacist, quizmaster, recording artist, religious executive (Christian Science broadcast-film ministry) bka *Kay Kyser's Kollege of Musical Knowledge* audience participation show host-maestro March 30, 1938-July 29, 1949; as "The Old Perfesser" Kyser developed unique band-leading style by interviewing studio guests, offering small cash gifts for naming tunes just played; d. July 23, 1985.

Betty Mandeville, June 18, 1910, Minneapolis, Minn.; director, producer bka *The FBI in Peace & War* executive ca. 1949–58; d. June 14, 2001.

E. G. Marshall (Everett Eugene Grunz), June 18, 1914, Owatonna, Minn.; actor (film, stage, TV), emcee bka *The CBS Radio Mystery Theater* host 1974–81, securing one of most venerated names of large, small screens for "dramatic" comeback feature on aural airwaves two decades after golden age heyday passed; performed in 92 theatrical, TV movies 1945–98, turned up on TV dramatic series 1949–95 in 138 guest shots; defense attorney in *The Defenders* CBS-TV 1961–65, physician in *The Bold Ones* NBC-TV 1969–73; d. Aug. 24, 1998.

Death

Charles H. Mullen, June 18, 2002, Darien, Conn.; b. Oct. 28, 1927.

June 19

Sound Bite

Federal Communications Commission is established by Congress June 19, 1934 to take effect July 1, 1934, superseding Federal Radio Commission created in 1927; FCC mandates that airwaves must be regulated to responsibly provide for public's benefit; FCC gets powerful oversight assignment to achieve it.

Canceled

The Rudy Vallee Show, June 19, 1955, CBS; debut Oct. 24, 1929.

Births

Martin Gabel, June 19, 1912, Philadelphia, Pa.; actor (stage, film, radio, TV), director, panelist, producer bka *Big Sister* daytime serial leading man Dr. John Wayne CBS Radio 1936–1940s, *What's My Line?* sporadic guest panelist CBS-TV 1950s-60s; habitual radio thespian on *The Casebook of Gregory Hood, Columbia Presents Corwin, Everyman's Theater, The March of Time, The Mercury Theater on the Air*; on Broadway in 1933—many ensuing performances; directed/produced stage shows, films; silver screen 1930s-80s; d. May 22, 1986.

Guy Lombardo, June 19, 1902, London, Ontario, Canada; impresario fronting Royal Canadians band with four musical brothers, others proffering "The Sweetest Music This Side of Heaven"; entourage labeled *Guy Lombardo Orchestra* in 21 of 27 chain, syndicated audio series 1928–56; band's "Auld Lang Syne" rendition linked with New Year's Eve from late 1920s; d. Nov. 5, 1977.

Virginia Payne, June 19, 1910, Cincinnati, Ohio; actress (radio, stage) bka *Ma Perkins* daytime serial namesake 1933–60; "mother of the airwaves" only 23 when lifetime achievement duty began, earlier portraying *Honey Adams* in serial about Southern diva (singing by Jane Froman) over Cincinnati WLW; when WLW trial domestic comedy *The Puddle Family* didn't bring local soapmaker Procter & Gamble desired sales of Oxydol detergent, P&G gambled with tale of rural widow with three kids, hired Payne to play her; resulting sales growth phenomenal — thrust series, Payne to Chicago NBC; tremolo in her voice made her sound convincingly older; while part became identifying hallmark, she played feminine lead in *The Carters of Elm Street*, recurring roles in *The Brighter Day*, *Cavalcade of America*, *Cloak and Dagger*, *The First Nighter*, *The Light of the World*, *Lonely Women*, *Today's Children*, finished with *The CBS Radio Mystery Theater*; performed in half-dozen stage shows (tours, Broadway) 1960s-70s; elected American Federation of Television and Radio Artists local president in Chicago, New York, first feminine national president 1958; d. Feb. 10, 1977.

Edward Thorgersen, June 19, 1902, Elizabeth, N.J.; announcer, emcee, sportscaster bka first to present Lowell Thomas weeknight newscasting gig 1930; Fox Movietone newsreels sports narrator 1930s; six 15-minute newscasts weekly on New York WOR early 1940s; late 1920s-30s net series *The A&P Gypsies*, *B. A. Rolfe and His Lucky Strike Dance Orchestra*, *Cities Service Concert*, *Happy Wonder Bakers*, *Planters Pickers*, etc.; presided on *The Elgin Football Revue* 1936–37, *Ed Thorgersen Sports Commentary* 1939; d. Dec. 22, 1997.

Deaths

Lester O'Keefe, June 19, 1977, Midland Park, N.J.; b. Aug. 25, 1896. Norman Ross, June 19, 1953, Evanston, Ill.; b. May 16, 1896. Ed Wynn, June 19, 1966, Beverly Hills, Calif.; b. Nov. 9, 1886.

June 20

Birth

Matthew D. Crowley, June 20, 1905, New Haven, Conn.; actor, announcer bka dramatist turning up in 1930s-50s juvenile adventure, daytime serial fare: *The Adventures of Superman*, *Buck Rogers in the 25th Century*, *Hop Harrigan*, *Jungle Jim*, *Mark Trail* among the former; *John's Other Wife*, *Myrt and Marge*, *Perry Mason*, *Pretty Kitty Kelly*, *The Road of Life* among latter; surfaced on Broadway in *Lady of Letters*, *The Front Page*; d. March 10, 1983.

Deaths

Robert Armbruster, June 20, 1994, Santa Monica, Calif.; b. Oct. 9, 1897. James Meighan, June 20, 1970, Huntington, N.Y.; b. Aug. 22, 1906. Lew Valentine, June 20, 1976, Los Angeles, Calif.; b. Aug. 5, 1912.

June 21

Canceled

The Adventures of Charlie Chan, June 21, 1948, MBS; debut Dec. 2, 1932. *The Railroad Hour*, June 21, 1954, NBC; debut Oct. 4, 1948. *Straight Arrow*, June 21, 1951, MBS; debut May 6, 1948.

Death

Walt Framer, June 21, 1988, Miami Beach, Fla.; b. April 7, 1908.

June 22

Canceled

The Adventures of Christopher Wells, June 22, 1948, CBS; debut Sept. 28, 1947.

Louella Parsons, June 22, 1954, CBS; debut Dec. 23, 1945.

Births

Paul Frees (Solomon Hersh Frees), June 22, 1920, Chicago, Ill.; actor (film, radio, stage, TV), author, composer, lyricist, voiceover artist; launched career in vaudeville as comic Buddy Green, then linked to 250+ theatrical motion pictures, animated cartoons (for nine production houses), TV shows (e.g. *The Millionaire's* John Beresford Tipton), often uncited; gave speech to animatronic figures at Walt Disney theme parks; radio work embraced *The Adventures of Philip Marlowe, The Adventures of Sherlock Holmes, Crime Classics, Dangerous Assignment, Escape, The Green Lama, Gunsmoke, The Player, Pursuit, Romance, Suspense*, more; Pillsbury Co. paid him $50,000 annually in early 1970s for his voice in Pillsbury Doughboy commercials; d. Nov. 2, 1986.

Johnny Jacobs, June 22, 1916, Milwaukee, Wis.; announcer; arrived at webs late 1940s, hung on for decade welcoming fans to *Beulah, December Bride, The Doris Day Show, Earn Your Vacation, Frontier Gentleman, The Jo Stafford Show, The Johnny Mercer Show, Juke Box Jury, Junior Miss, My Friend Irma, Our Miss Brooks, Rosemary Clooney, Steve Allen*, more; in another half of career in TV late 1950s-mid 1970s, beckoned viewers to *The Betty White Show, Mr. Smith Goes to Washington, Dream Girl of '67, The Newlywed Game, The Joker's Wild, Blank Check, Spin-Off, Give-N-Take*, more; d. Feb. 8, 1982.

Deaths

John Cannon, June 22, 2001, Cologne, Germany; b. May 17, 1906. Dennis Day, June 22, 1988, Bel Air, Calif.; b. May 21, 1917. Don Hollenbeck, June 22, 1954, New York City, N.Y.; b. March 30, 1905.

June 23

Debuting

The Breakfast Club, June 23, 1933, NBC Blue; weekday audience participation (initially *The Pepper Pot*); emcee Don McNeill welcomed apprenticing volley of entertainers, among them: singers Dick Teela, "Curley" Bradley, Johnny Desmond, Alice Lon, Betty Johnson, Dick Noel, Ilene Woods; impresarios Walter Blaufuss, Eddie Ballantine; comics Jim and Marian Jordan, Bill Thompson, Fran Allison, Sam Cowling, Homer and Jethro; final broadcast Dec. 27, 1968, disappointing ABC-TV exposure Feb. 22, 1954-Feb. 25, 1955.

Boston Blackie, June 23, 1944, NBC; detective drama about ex-thief who plied background pursuing, capturing bad guys; Blackie (Chester Morris, Richard Kollmar) flanked by atypical assortment of companions who dialogued with him between action scenes — nurse/sugarstick Mary Wesley (Jan Miner, Lesley Woods), ex-con-sans-surname Shorty (Tony Barrett) supplying Blackie with underworld tips, inept New York police homicide inspector Faraday (Richard Lane, Frank Orth, Maurice Tarplin); Blackie originated in early 1900s pages of *Cosmopolitan, Redbook*; next in silent films 1918, 1923, 11 "talkies" 1941–49, 58 syndicated TV installments 1951–53; final radiocast Sept. 3, 1950.

Front Page Farrell, June 23, 1941, MBS; daytime serial; billed as "the exciting, unforgettable radio drama ... of a crack newspaperman and his wife"; tale of mythical *Brooklyn Eagle* reporter David Farrell (Richard Widmark, Carleton Young, Staats Cotsworth), spouse Sally (Florence Williams, Virginia Dwyer); David's nose for news often carried him to darker stories while flanked by managing editor George Walker (Frank Chase), homicide Lt. Carpenter (Robert Donley); series began in typical washboard weeper fashion emphasizing domestic issues involving principals plus Sally's mom — David's work seemed like sideline at times; refocus in late 1940s shifted concerns from home to job, serial equaling nighttime thrillers as it pursued murderers, kidnappers, etc.; new heinous crimes introduced Mondays with David chasing culprits all week, revealing identities, seeing them nailed Fridays; final broadcast March 26, 1954.

Wendy Warren and the News, June 23, 1947, CBS; daytime serial with dark tinges; in unique format, soap opera heroine Wendy Warren (Florence Freeman) was chic print-electronic journalist — reporter for mythical *Manhattan Gazette* in fictional two-thirds of quarter-hour, revealing tips to milady in succinct "news reports from the women's world" after headlines dispatched by respected CBS newsman Douglas Edwards; drama in Cold War era encountered plethora of espionage agents, spies, undercover operatives, seditious informants laboring for foreign interests to bring our country down; while running domestic tale persisted, sinister tone attracted legions of men to midday audience; final broadcast Jan. 3, 1958.

Canceled

The Henry Morgan Show, June 23, 1950, NBC; debut Oct. 28, 1940.

Births

Arthur (Art) Hanna, June 23, 1906, Milton, Mass.; director; production guru chiefly of daytime serials with no fewer than 11, most for creators Frank, Anne Hummert: *The Brighter Day, David Harum, Front Page Farrell, Joyce Jordan, M.D., Just Plain Bill, Lora Lawton, Our Gal Sunday, Perry Mason, The Right to Happiness, Stella Dallas, This Is Nora Drake*; only freelance director in golden age with trio of concurrent daily dramas on dual chains plus primetime shows; produced five Broadway plays before radio — stage protégés Peter Falk, Hal Holbrook, Jack Klugman, Jack Lemmon, Christopher Plummer, Jimmy Stewart; directed, managed theaters in summer stock while in radio; after 25 years, with radio fading, turned to teaching, coaching aspiring thespians at Valley Forge Military Academy and Junior College for two decades; d. Nov. 17, 1981.

John Milton Kennedy, June 23, 1912, Farrell, Pa.; announcer bka *Lux Radio Theater* interlocutor 1940s; *Armchair Detective* figure Mr. Crime Interrogator CBS-TV 1949; *Letter to Loretta* announcer NBC-TV 1953–54; d. June 11, 2006.

Edward P. Morgan, June 23, 1910, Walla Walla, Wash.; newscaster, print journalist, wire journalist (United Press International) bka *Edward P. Morgan and the News* commentator 1955–67; hired by Seattle journal 1930s as reporter, UPI next as wire correspondent; after World War II joined *Collier's* editorial staff, CBS 1951, ABC 1954 relocated to nation's capital, remained rest of life — nearly two decades with ABC; bent markedly liberal, won multiple prestigious news awards; active in handful of ABC-TV features, hosted National Educational Television *PBL* (Public Broadcasting Laboratory) newsmagazine 1967–69; d. Jan. 27, 1993.

Norman Rose, June 23, 1917, Philadelphia, Pa.; actor (film, stage), announcer, drama coach, host, newscaster bka narrator *The CBS Radio Mystery Theater, Dimension X*; peers labeled him "voice of God"; d. Nov. 12, 2004.

June 24

Sound Bite

NBC attempts to capitalize on nostalgia craze by returning to air one of its most popular transcribed fare June 24, 1973, *X-Minus One*, sci-fi thriller off ether since Jan. 9, 1958 (origins in *Dimension X* from April 8, 1950); web nixes hope of groundswell following by failing to assign permanent home, thwarting fans seeking it: broadcast monthly, *X-Minus One* routinely moves in, out of Saturday, Sunday timeslots; narrator Fred Collins begs listeners to register their loyalty by writing NBC but few do so; show is axed March 22, 1975; frustration doesn't fall on deaf ears at CBS — by 1974, net returns drama to air with original tales seven nights weekly at same hour on *The CBS Radio Mystery Theater*, prevailing nine years; NBC experiment may be viewed as both testing, learning ground.

Debuting

A Date with Judy, June 24, 1941, NBC; teen sitcom, prime example of 1940s Radioland strain featuring trials, tribulations of Judy Foster (Ann Gillis, Dellie Ellis, Louise Erickson) flanked by parents, sibling, boyfriend, peers, added characters; web's answer to *The Aldrich Family, Archie Andrews* which majored on adolescent boys; final broadcast May 4, 1950.

Canceled

Bob and Ray (*Presents the CBS Radio Network*), June 24, 1960, CBS; principals' net debut July 2, 1951 (act took root at Boston WHDH in late 1940s). (*The Rise of*) *The Goldbergs*, June 24, 1950, CBS; debut Nov. 20, 1929. *The Romance of Helen Trent*, June 24, 1960, CBS; debut Oct. 30, 1933. *The Six Shooter*, June 24, 1954, NBC; debut Sept. 20, 1953.

Births

Phil Harris (Wonga Philip Harris), June 24, 1904, Linton, Ind.; actor (film, radio, TV), impresario, philanthropist, recording/voiceover artist bka *The Jack Benny Program* modified sitcom maestro-wisecracking sidekick 1936–52, *The Phil Harris-Alice Faye Show* sitcom costar with spouse playing selves, *The Thing* top-selling recording 1950; loud, brassy, flamboyant demeanor; d. Aug. 11, 1995.

Arthur Hughes, June 24, 1893, Bloomington, Ill.; actor (stage, radio) bka *Just Plain Bill* daytime serial namesake 1932–55; deemed by peers "an actor's actor," memorized lines for broadcasts though he could read them; a favorite of producers Frank, Anne Hummert (whose social contacts lagged); Hughes filled in for ailing Bennett Kilpack as *Mr. Keen, Tracer of Lost Persons*, turned up in casts of *The Collier Hour* (as Fu Manchu), *East of Cairo*, *I Love Linda Dale*, *Jungle Jim*, *The Orange Lantern*, *Stella Dallas*; began, ended professional career on stages including Broadway shows playing to adoring fans; d. Dec. 28, 1982.

Deaths

Paul Lavalle, June 24, 1997, Harrisonburg, Va.; b. Sept. 6, 1908. Barbara Weeks, June 24, 2003, Las Vegas, Nev.; b. July 4, 1913.

June 25

Debuting

It Pays to Be Ignorant, June 25, 1942, MBS; academic quiz parody; "board of experts" (Lulu McConnell, Harry McNaughton, George Shelton) tried to decipher what questions were interspersed with sprawling non-pertinent discourses, frequently curtly interrupting each other, quizmaster Tom Howard; Groucho Marx's oft-asked "Who was buried in Grant's tomb?" on *his* show would have been classic fodder here for queries were inane — yet listeners loved it and show continued nearly decade; spawned pithy televersions on CBS 1949, NBC 1951, syndication 1973; final radiocast Sept. 26, 1951.

Canceled

Big Town, June 25, 1952, CBS; debut Oct. 19, 1937. *The Halls of Ivy*, June 25, 1952, NBC; debut Jan. 6, 1950. *Life Can Be Beautiful*, June 25, 1954, NBC; debut Sept. 5, 1938. *Pat Novak for Hire*, June 25, 1949; debut Feb. 13, 1949.

Births

Peter Lind Hayes (Joseph Conrad Lind), June 25, 1915, San Francisco, Calif.; actor (stage, radio, film, TV), emcee, writer bka *The Peter Lind Hayes Show* variety series headliner CBS 1954, *Arthur Godfrey Time* substitute host 1950s; with wife Mary Healy (ex-Miss New Orleans beauty queen) cohosted *The Peter Lind Hayes-Mary Healy Show* NBC-/ABC-TV 1950–51, 1958–59; performed with her in *Peter Loves Mary* sitcom NBC-TV 1960–61; vaudeville, nightclubs, 25 theatrical films 1936–82, two made-for-TV flicks 1959/1987, 37 TV series appearances, hosted other TV series 1949/1951–52/1963; d. April 21, 1998.

Mary Livingstone (Benny) (Sadie Marks), June 25, 1905, Seattle, Wash.; actress (stage, radio, TV) bka *The Jack Benny Program* sitcom figure Mary Livingstone NBC Blue/NBC/CBS 1932–58; suffered mic fright, never overcame it; guest shots on *The Fred Allen Show*, *The George Burns and Gracie Allen Show*, *Lux Radio Theater*; d. June 30, 1983.

Arthur Tracy (Abba Tracovutsky), June 25, 1899, Kamenetz-Podolsk, Moldavia; vocalist (film, nightclubs, radio, stage, TV) bka "The Street Singer" billing as identity hidden few years; popularity waned after secret acknowledged; *The Street Singer* prevailed eratically on trio of chains 1932–42; d. Oct. 5, 1997.

Deaths

Owen Miller Babbe, June 25, 1996, Mason City, Iowa; b. Dec. 19, 1916. Gary C. Breckner, June 25, 1945, Redlands, Calif.; b. Nov. 10, 1891. Jack Farren, June 25, 1997, Los Angeles, Calif.; b. Nov. 17, 1922. Frank Hemingway, June 25, 1989, Los Angeles, Calif.; b. Jan. 22, 1903. Jay Jostyn, June 25, 1976 (last residence Los Angeles, Calif.); b. Dec. 13, 1901.

June 26

Debuting

Kraft Music Hall, June 26, 1933, NBC; variety series featuring at diverse times headliners Paul Whiteman, Bing Crosby, Edward Everett Horton, Eddie Foy, Eddy Duchin, Nelson Eddy, Al Jolson, Dorothy Kirsten; Kraft, NBC sued Crosby in highly publicized clash when he didn't meet contract obligations after decade at show's helm in 1945; final broadcast Sept. 22, 1949.

Mr. President, June 26, 1947, ABC; historical anthology drama; Edward Arnold impersonated different U. S. president weekly whose name wasn't revealed until narrative's close (figure simply addressed as "Mr. President" in conversations); generic secretary "Miss Sarah" (Betty Lou Gerson) answered to him weekly; final broadcast Sept. 23, 1953.

Canceled

Arnold Grimm's Daughter, June 26, 1942, NBC; debut July 5, 1937. *The Fred Allen Show*, June 26, 1949, NBC; debut Oct. 23, 1932. *My Little Margie*, June 26, 1955, CBS; debut Dec. 7, 1952.

Births

Richard Crooks, June 26, 1900, Trenton, N.J.; recording artist, vocalist (tenor) (concert tours, operas, radio, symphonies) bka *Voice of Firestone* regular 1932–45, most visible personality in epoch (115 appearances); familiarized *Firestone* audiences with "In My Garden" initially July 25, 1932, later "If I Could Tell You"—both penned by Idabelle Firestone (Mrs. Harvey S., Sr.) that ultimately became show's dual themes; Metropolitan Opera Co. member 1933–43; music critic alleged Crooks could "sing any kind of music with exquisite taste" as another credited him with "impeccable phrasing and musical dignity" and third claimed his voice was "by far the most attractive among the American tenors of his generation"; d. Oct. 1, 1972.

Alex Dreier, June 26, 1916, Honolulu, Haw.; actor, commentator, correspondent, newscaster, wire journalist bka possessing uncanny ability to make political, world predictions seemingly right on target; analysis under multi sobriquets (*Alex Dreier News and Comments*, *Skelly News*, *Alex Dreier—Man on the Go*) NBC staple 1942–56; pacesetter's weekday newscast at 8 a.m. ET 1951–56 intersected with second daily quarter-hour at 7 P.M. ET 1953–56; he turned to celluloid thereafter, appeared in six films, three made-for-TV flicks, occasional parts in dozen TV dramas; d. March 13, 2000.

Deaths

Walter O'Keefe, June 26, 1983, Torrance, Calif.; b. Aug. 18, 1900. Michael Roy, June 26, 1976, Los Angeles, Calif.; b. July 18, 1913.

June 27

Debuting

Best Seller, June 27, 1960, CBS; anthology drama; five-a-week installment narratives in 10-minute doses purportedly taken from pages of popular novels; distinctive as last new daytime serial on web radio; final broadcast Nov. 25, 1960.

Canceled

Against the Storm, June 27, 1952, ABC; debut Oct. 16, 1939. *Lone Journey*, June 27, 1952, ABC; debut May 27, 1940. *Mark Trail*, June 27, 1952, ABC; debut Jan. 30, 1950. *The Strange Romance of Evelyn Winters*, June 27, 1952, ABC; debut Nov. 20, 1944. *Tarzan*, June 27, 1953, CBS; debut Sept. 12, 1932.

Births

Edward J. Fleming, June 27, 1918, Baraboo, Wis.; announcer, broker, newscaster bka *Our Gal Sunday* interlocutor 1941–43, 1946-ca. 1956 ("Once again, we present *Our Gal Sunday* ... the story that asks the question: Can this girl from the little mining town in the West find happiness as the wife of a wealthy and titled Englishman?"); introduced *Front Page Farrell* 1950–54 for *Sunday* sponsor American Home Products (Anacin, Bi-So-Dol, Kolynos, Kriptin, et al.); joined New York WCBS as reporter 1941, then chain newsman; returned from World War II to take news tasks with WCBS-TV, left for WPIX-TV early 1950s; anchorman at Los Angeles KNXT 1958–64, San Francisco KRON-TV 1964–67, departed broadcasting to become broker; retired outside San Francisco.

Willard A. (Bill) Kennedy, June 27, 1912, Cleveland, Ohio; actor (film), announcer, broker, newscaster, trucker bka *Nobody's Children* interlocutor 1939–41 (only substantiated net series); appeared in solo film *Winning Your Wings* 1942; 1950s-70s at Detroit WKBD-TV, Windsor, Ontario CKLW-TV reporting on movies, stars; d. Jan. 27, 1997.

John Herrick McIntire, June 27, 1907, Spokane, Wash.; actor (film, radio, TV), announcer, emcee bka cinema thespian 1947–89 appearing in 70 theatrical releases e.g. *The Asphalt Jungle*, *Walk Softly Stranger*, *Psycho*, *Elmer Gantry*, *Herbie Rides Again* plus 16 made-for-TV flicks; prolific performer in TV episodes of *Naked City*, *Wagon Train*, *The Virginian*, *The Innocent and the Damned*, *Shirley*, *American Dream*; launched career late 1920 announcing at Beverly Hills KEJK (since renamed KMPC); freelance announcing from 1934; radio acting credits late 1930s-late 1980s for *The Adventures of Mr. Meek*, *The Adventures of Sam Spade*, *Crime Doctor*, *Dragnet*, *Gunsmoke*, *The Lineup*, *The*

March of Time, The Philip Morris Playhouse, The Sears/Mutual Radio Theater, Suspense, Tarzan, We the Abbotts, The Whistler, dozen more; d. Jan. 30, 1991.

Deaths

George Bryan, June 27, 1969, Stamford, Conn.; b. June 9, 1910. Howard Hoffman, June 27, 1969, Hollywood, Calif.; b. Nov. 4, 1893.

June 28

Debuting

Dreft Star Playhouse (premiered as *Hollywood Theater of the Air*), June 28, 1943, NBC; film anthology drama; budgeting $3,000 for talent weekly, Procter & Gamble Co. launched quarter-hour weekday morning version of rival Lever Brothers' popular CBS Monday night *Lux Radio Theater*; dubbed "noble experiment," draws Hollywood headliners for adaptations of major movies, sans live audience *Lux* style; American homemakers largely unimpressed — soap bust scrubbed in 21 months; final broadcast March 30, 1945.

The Quiz Kids, June 28, 1940, NBC; quiz; hosted by Joe Kelly, quartet of pint-sized scholars comprised panel, showcased adolescent intellect, comparing favorably with erudite adults on *Information Please* panel; audiences observed in disbelief how rapidly smart youngsters got right answers; show silent 1951–52; fostered intermittent video series NBC/CBS 1949–56; final radiocast Jan. 3, 1954.

Births

Alan Bunce, June 28, 1908, Westfield, N.J.; actor (stage, film, radio, TV) bka henpecked husbands in dual audio series, *The Private Lives of Ethel and Albert* ABC 1944–50 with extensions to three TV chains 1953–56, *The Couple Next Door* CBS 1957–60; 35 stock productions, Broadway; radio credits for *David Harum, Hello Peggy, Home of the Brave, John's Other Wife, Joyce Jordan — Girl Interne, Pepper Young's Family, Young Widder Brown*; five movies with key role in *Sunrise at Campobello* 1960, two dozen parts in TV anthologies 1950–65 — *Studio One, Kraft Television Theater, The U. S. Steel Hour*, etc., d. April 27, 1965.

Hector Chevigny, June 28, 1904, Missoula, Mont.; novelist, scriptwriter bka *The Second Mrs. Burton* daytime serial wordsmith in halcyon era CBS 1950s; shortly after arriving in New York City in 1943 lost sight from bilateral retina detachment — lived in Manhattan's Gramercy Park with wife, two kids, seeing eye dog; returned *Burton* to roots previous scribe diminished, borrowed heavily from comedy to segue into laid-back family narrative — nourished roles for specific actors (as peer Carlton E. Morse did in *One Man's Family*); successively wrote TV plays, passel of published works e.g. *Adjustment of the Blind, Lord of Alaska, My Eyes Have a Cold Nose, Woman of the Rock*; d. April 20, 1965.

Kelvin Kirkwood Keech, June 28, 1895, Punahou, Hawaii; announcer, ukulelist, vocalist; joined NBC twice as announcer — 1929–35, 1937-?, freelancing in between; welcomed fans to 1930s *Billy and Betty, The Eveready Hour, Heart-throbs of the Hills, Popeye the Sailor, Terry and the Pirates* (also sang, strummed ukulele), *Twenty Thousand Years in Sing Sing*; d. May 1977, Jackson Heights, N.Y.

Dan Seymour, June 28, 1914, New York City, N.Y.; ad exec, announcer, emcee, producer bka J. Walter Thompson Co. CEO 1967–72, filled leadership posts there 1955–74 after Young and Rubicam stint 1949–55; went on air Boston WNAC 1935; joined New York CBS 1936, left to freelance announce, produce 1940–49; narrated H. G. Welles' science fiction thriller "The War of the Worlds" on *The Mercury Theater on the Air* Oct. 30, 1938 that threw many panic-struck listeners into chaos; although heard on nearly three dozen net series 1935–49 — *The Aldrich Family, Bulldog Drummond, Meet Mr. Meek, The Mollé Mystery Theater, Tex and Jinx* — two stand out: *Aunt Jenny's Real Life Stories* daytime serial where he effusively pitched culinary treats made at home with sponsor's shortening ("For all you bake or fry ... rely on Spry!") 1939–49, hosted human interest feature *We the People* 1943–49; appeared on few pithy early TV entries; d. July 27, 1982.

Peter Thomas, June 28, 1924, Pensacola, Fla.; announcer, voiceover artist; prolific commercial pitchman still airing, introducing Tru TV channel *Forensic Files*, other features; in radio's golden age ushered *Dream Time, Young Doctor Malone* onto air; one of last web announcers narrating soap operas on "day radio drama died" Nov. 25, 1960: "This is Peter Thomas... As the current series of *Young Doctor Malone* comes to a close, we leave Jill on the eve of her wedding day happy in the knowledge that Scotty's mother at last has given her blessing... As for Jerry, the weeks that lie ahead will be challenging ones as he must resume the responsibilities of directing the clinic. But with the encouragement and support of Tracy, Jerry will go forward in new paths of service"—Organ up, out.

Death

José Iturbi, June 28, 1980, Los Angeles, Calif.; b. Nov. 28, 1895.

June 29

Debuting

The Johnny Olsen Show (*Johnny Olsen's Rumpus Room, Johnny Olsen's Get-Together, Johnny Olsen's Luncheon Club*), June 29, 1946, ABC; audience participation; denoted by affable disposition, bespectacled, balding, smiling voice; at times along with wife, Penny, hosted freewheeling daytime shows for ladies—chit-chat, contests, giveaways, recognitions; all dress rehearsal for Olsen's famed later gigs as Jackie Gleason's announcer, pièce de résistance yelling "Come on down!" to *The Price Is Right* contestants; final broadcast May 4, 1957.

Strike It Rich, June 29, 1947, CBS; human interest cash-prize giveaway, masters of ceremonies Todd Russell, Warren Hull; doted on unfortunates in dire extremes; final broadcast Dec. 27, 1957; televersion May 7, 1951-Jan. 3, 1958.

Vic and Sade, June 29, 1932, NBC; pithy homespun comical skits that ultimately evolved into sitcom starring Art Van Harvey (Victor Gook), Bernardine Flynn (spouse Sade); "best American humor of its day" poet Edgar Lee Masters branded slightly offbeat world Gooks occupied; final broadcast Sept. 19, 1946.

Canceled

The Guiding Light, June 29, 1956, CBS (televersion persists); debut Jan. 25, 1937. *The Jack Carson Show*, June 29, 1956, CBS; debut June 2, 1943. *The Life of Riley*, June 29, 1951, NBC; debut April 26, 1941. *Portia Faces Life*, June 29, 1951, NBC; debut Oct. 7, 1940, CBS. *Quick as a Flash*, June 29, 1951, ABC; debut July 16, 1944. *The Screen Guild Theater*, June 29, 1952, CBS (spinoffs *Hollywood Soundstage, Stars in the Air* departed April 3, 1952, June 30, 1952 respectively, both with similar themes, CBS); debut Jan. 8, 1939. *Young Widder Brown*, June 29, 1956, NBC; debut June 6, 1938.

Births

Thomas Clinton (T. Tommy) Cutrer, June 29, 1924, Tangipahoa Parish, La.; announcer, commercial spokesman (Martha White Mills, Inc.), disc jockey, drummer, emcee, entrepreneur, politician, producer, recording artist, station owner (Jackson, Miss. WJQS) bka *Grand Ole Opry* interlocutor 1954–64 filling NBC portion on rare occasions 1955–57; voted nation's top DJ 1957 by *Billboard* readers; Democrat losing primary to Al Gore, Jr. for U. S. Congress 1976, elected to Tennessee state Senate 1978–82; from McComb, Miss. WSKB, career moved to stations in New Orleans, Little Rock, Memphis, Jackson, Houston, Shreveport—first DJ spinning Johnny Cash wax 1952; d. Oct. 11, 1998.

Nelson Eddy, June 29, 1901, Providence, R.I.; vocalist (baritone) bka *The Bell Telephone Hour* fifth most prolific guest artist (27 appearances following Jascha Heifetz' 54, Lily Pons' 50, Ezio Pinza's 44, Marian Anderson's 37), half of "America's Singing Sweethearts" in 1930s MGM celluloid musical releases paired wiith Jeanette MacDonald; d. March 6, 1967.

Ed Gardner (Edward Fredrick Poggenburg), June 29, 1901, Astoria, Long Island, N.Y.; actor (stage, film, radio, TV), ad agency rep (J. Walter Thompson), creative, director, producer, promoter, writer bka *Duffy's Tavern* sitcom barkeep-manager Archie 1941–51; extensions: movie 1945, syndicated televersion 1954, *Monitor* vignettes weekends mid to late 1950s; notorious tightwad reining in expenses on legendary series; d. Aug. 17, 1963.

Mary Jane Higby (Sorel), June 29, 1909, St. Louis, Mo.; actress (film, radio), author bka *When a Girl Marries* daytime serial heroine Joan Field Davis CBS/NBC/ABC 1939–57, *This Is Nora Drake* title role CBS 1957–59, *The Romance of Helen Trent* figure Cynthia Carter Swanson Whitney CBS 1940s-50s; silent films; on radio in *Hollywood Hotel, Lux Radio Theater, Parties at Pickfair, Shell Chateau* before soap opera, bonding with *David Harum, John's Other Wife, Joyce Jordan — Girl Interne, Linda's First Love, Perry Mason, Stella Dallas, The Story of Mary Marlin, Thanks for Tomorrow* with sideline operations in *Five Star Matinee, Mr. Keen — Tracer of Lost Persons, The Mysterious Traveler, Nick Carter — Master Detective*, etc.; penned 1966 behind-the-mic exposé *Tune in Tomorrow*; key role 1970 theatrical film *The Honeymoon Killers*; d. Feb. 1, 1986.

Ruth Warrick, June 29, 1916, St. Joseph, Mo.; actress (stage, radio, film, TV), author, model bka *The Guiding Light* daytime serial R.N. Janet Johnson CBS Radio/TV 1953–54, *As the World Turns* serial's Aunt Edith Hughes CBS-TV 1956–60, 1963, *True Story* anthology drama NBC-TV 1960, *All My Children* serial haughty matriarch Phoebe Tyler ABC-TV 1970–2005; college plays, trip to New York led to *Vox Pop* interview, modeling, theatrical plays, opened gates to radio's *Grand Central Station, Great Plays, The Guiding Light, Joyce Jordan, M.D., Myrt and Marge*; personal appeals as Ruth Warrick for Prom home permanents on *Stella Dallas, Young Widder Brown* early 1950s; radio pushed her onto silver screen, pivotal role in 1940's *Citizen Kane* netting RKO contract; Broadway, stock "first love"; penned *The Confessions of Phoebe Tyler* memoir; d. Jan. 15, 2005.

Death

Rosemary Clooney, June 29, 2002, Beverly Hills, Calif.; b. May 23, 1928.

June 30

Sound Bite

The Guiding Light daytime serial adds live televised embodiment June 30, 1952 on CBS; same storyline initially airing via audio transcription at 1:45 P.M. ET repeated in live video version at 2:30 P.M. (latter shifts to 12:45 P.M. six months hence); radio cast acts Irna Phillips scripts on tube; sponsoring Procter & Gamble Co. shuts down aural format June 29, 1956, convinced sufficient number of homemakers willing to stop their work, watch 15-minute episodes, exists.

Debuting

Club Fifteen, June 30, 1947, CBS; music variety; host (for most of run) Bob Crosby traded snappy ripostes with *The Andrew Sisters* between numbers adding lighthearted frivolity while singing included soft ballads, bouncy polkas, spirited jazz, pop standards of bygone, present eras; more regulars were Margaret Whiting, The Modernaires, Jo Stafford, Gisele MacKenzie plus rare guests; Dick Haymes presided Aug. 29, 1949-June 30, 1950; final broadcast Jan. 16, 1953.

Lights Out, June 30, 1934, NBC Blue; horror drama; chilling, bone-crushing tales of macabre, cannibalism, brain spatter, stuff that goes bump in night — and many worse dastardly deeds — were corralled in dramas for terrified, appreciative audiences; film icon Boris Karloff among favored leads, support contributed by Mason Adams, Murray Forbes, Vinton Hayworth, Raymond Edward Johnson, Mercedes McCambridge, Arch Oboler, Harold Peary, Arthur Peterson, Earle Ross, Alexander Scourby, Irene Tedrow, Willard Waterman, Betty Winkler, others; final broadcast Aug. 6, 1947.

Welcome Travelers, June 30, 1947, ABC; human interest interviews, masters of ceremonies Tommy Bartlett, Les Lear; final broadcast Sept. 24, 1954; televersion at intervals Sept. 8, 1952-Oct. 28, 1955.

Canceled

Barry Craig, Confidential Investigator, June 30, 1955, NBC; debut Oct. 3, 1951. *The Bell Telephone Hour*, June 30, 1958, NBC (*Encores from The Bell Telephone Hour* on ether Sept. 15, 1968-June 8, 1969, NBC); debut April 29, 1940. *The Jimmy Durante Show*, June 30, 1950, NBC; debut Sept. 10, 1933. *Our Miss Brooks*, June 30, 1957, CBS; debut July 19, 1948. *Terry and the Pirates*, June 30, 1948, ABC; debut Nov. 1, 1937.

Births

Phillips Carlin, June 30, 1894, New York City, N.Y.; announcer, newscaster, programming executive (NBC, Blue, MBS), sportscaster bka pioneer New York WEAF interlocutor 1920s-30s fare *The A&P Gypsies, The Chilquot Club Eskimos, Dixie Circus, The Goodrich Silvertown Orchestra, Major Bowes' Original Amateur Hour, Roxy and His Gang*, more; touted by NBC as "the voice with a smile"; originated web's identifying chimes December 1926; d. Aug. 27, 1971.

Frank Gallop, June 30, 1900, Boston,

Mass.; actor, announcer, broker, emcee bka bass voice exploding from abyss (as if from echo chamber) on *The Perry Como Show* NBC-TV 1955–63 invoking "Oh, Mr. C...."; heavy hitter of golden age radio, on premises late 1930s-end of age welcoming fans to *Amanda of Honeymoon Hill, An Evening with Romberg, Hilltop House, The Hour of Charm, Kaltenborn Edits the News, The New York Philharmonic Symphony, The Prudential Family Hour, Quick as a Flash, Stella Dallas, Texaco Star Theater, When a Girl Marries, A Woman of America*; co-communicator for *Monitor* 1955–60; listeners often mistook him for Englishman due to princely inflections; myriad TV series *Broadway Open House, What Happened, The Buick Circus Hour, Kraft Mystery Theater, Cartoonies*; d. May 17, 1988.

Santos Ortega (Santos Edward Ortego), June 30, 1899, New York City, N.Y.; actor (radio, stage, TV) bka *As the World Turns* daytime serial figure Grandpa Hughes CBS-TV 1956–76; anthology, running roles in 55 net radio series 1930s-70s: *The Adventures of Ellery Queen, Big Sister, Bulldog Drummond, The CBS Radio Mystery Theater, City Hospital, Dimension X, Gangbusters, Mr. and Mrs. North, Myrt and Marge, Our Gal Sunday, Perry Mason, Romance, Valiant Lady, Yours Truly—Johnny Dollar*, more; d. April 10, 1976.

Carl Webster Pierce, June 30, 1898, Quincy, Mass.; announcer bka *Breakfast at Sardi's/Breakfast with Breneman/Breakfast in Hollywood* interlocutor Blue/ABC 1942-ca. 1948 (only series certified); d. Aug. 16, 1962.

Deaths

Galen Drake, June 30, 1989, Long Beach, Calif.; b. July 26, 1906. Gale Gordon, June 30, 1995, Escondido, Calif.; b. Feb. 20, 1906. Mary Livingstone, June 30, 1983, Los Angeles, Calif.; b. June 25, 1905. Fred Shields, June 30, 1974, North Hollywood, Calif.; b. May 18, 1904.

July 1

Sound Bite

Federal Communications Commission begins operating July 1, 1934; although broadcasting industry with National Association of Broadcasters opposes it, fearing increased governmental intrusion into airwaves, Congress sends provision to President Franklin D. Roosevelt for signature; FCC replaces Federal Radio Commission begun in 1927; separates radio, telegraph sectors.

Canceled

America's Town Meeting of the Air, July 1, 1956, ABC; debut May 30, 1935. *The Dinah Shore Show*, July 1, 1955, NBC; debut Aug. 6, 1939. *The Edgar Bergen and Charlie McCarthy Show*, July 1, 1956, CBS; debut May 9, 1937. *Joyce Jordan, M.D.*, July 1, 1955, NBC; debut May 30, 1938. *Junior Miss*, July 1, 1954, CBS; debut March 4, 1942. *Rosemary*, July 1, 1955, CBS; debut Oct. 2, 1944. *Show Business Old and New* (*The Eddie Cantor Show*), July 1, 1954, NBC; debut Sept. 13, 1931.

Births

John Lair, July 1, 1894, Livingston, Ky.; announcer, director, emcee, entrepreneur bka *Renfro Valley Sunday Mornin' Gatherin'* hymn-singing host CBS 1940s–50s, *Renfro Valley Barn Dance* country shindig master of ceremonies on four chains 1938–51, *National Barn Dance* chief 1927–37; Chicago WLS program director-music librarian 1927–37; joined Cincinnati WLW 1937; with Benjamin "Whitey" Ford, bought rural roadside tract at Renfro Valley, Ky., erected country music theater drawing 10,000 patrons annually; d. Nov. 13, 1985.

Henry William (Bill) Stern, July 1, 1907, Rochester, N.Y.; commentator, sportscaster bka *The Colgate Sports Newsreel* (multiple appellations) sports commentary host 1937–56; late 1930s–early 1940s net duties on *The Army Hour, Boxing Bouts, Four Star News, Goodrich Sports Review, Sports Scraps*; called football games over Rochester WHAM at 18, later for Austin, Birmingham, Cincinnati, New Orleans stations; managed New York Roxy Theater before filling similar capacity at Radio City Music Hall, Center Theater 1932–late 1950s; hired by NBC 1936 as sportscaster, joined ABC 1953, MBS 1960s; many TV venues in medium's early days; d. Nov. 19, 1971.

Deaths

James Doyle, July 1, 1980, Lynnwood, Wash.; b. Oct. 4, 1910. Eloise McElhone, July 1, 1974, New York City, N.Y.; b. March 11, 1921.

July 2

Debuting

The Adventures of the Thin Man, July 2, 1941, NBC; blithe mystery restored after 1948 hiatus as *The New Adventures of the Thin Man*, precedent set by other sleuths; based on Dashiell Hammett's novel, aired via four chains, centered on ex-private eye turned Gotham publisher's mystery editor Nick Charles (Les Damon, Les Tremayne, David Gothard, Joseph Curtin), trouble-prone spouse Nora (Claudia Morgan)—all five lead thespians veterans of daytime soaps; are there enough parallels to *Mr. and Mrs. North* here?; Dick Powell, Myrna Loy starred in half-dozen *Thin Man* flicks 1934–47, Peter Lawford, Phyllis Kirk reprised leads on NBC-TV 1957–59; final radiocast Sept. 1, 1950.

The Aldrich Family, July 2, 1939, NBC, teen-centered sitcom; leads with Ezra Stone, Norman Tokar, Dickie Jones, Raymond Ives, Bobby Ellis (Henry Aldrich), Jackie Kelk, Johnny Fiedler, Jack Grimes, Michael O'Day (Homer Brown); focus on adolescent foibles, amusing complications; copied by manifold successors; final radiocast April 19, 1953; NBC–TV Oct. 2, 1949–May 29, 1953.

Beulah, July 2, 1945, CBS (initially *The Marlin Hurt and Beulah Show*); definitive domestic sitcom with Negro cook-housekeeper as protagonist; Hurt, Bob Corley, Hattie McDaniel, Lillian Randolph, Amanda Randolph in title role; Caucasian employers played by Hugh Studebaker, Jess Kirkpatrick (Harry Henderson), Mary Jane Croft, Lois Corbett (Alice), Henry Blair, Sammy Ogg (Donnie); Beulah's beau Bill Jackson impersonated by Marlin Hurt, Ernie "Bubbles" Whitman, with Ruby Dandridge as nextdoor domestic Oriole; final radiocast May 21, 1954, ABC televersion Oct. 3, 1950–Sept. 22, 1953.

Bob and Ray, July 2, 1951, NBC; comedy satire; first of multi series with zany offbeat comedians Bob Elliott, Ray Goulding capitalizing on charming ability to turn ordinary occasions/conversations into extraordinary with oddball characterizations, ostensibly think-on-your-feet zingers that convulsed America; pair met as staffers at Boston WHDH where daily *Matinee with Bob and Ray* 1946–51 colossal hit; exchanges spawned showbiz careers, venturing into nightclubs, added personal appearances, advertising, PBS, local New York radio, NBC–TV 1951–53; final commercial net radiocast June 24, 1960.

Meet Millie, July 2, 1951, CBS; sitcom involving single-but-looking working-girl Millie Bronson (Audrey Totter 1951–ca. 1953, Elena Verdugo ca. 1953–54) in madcap feature complicated by mother, neighbors, work associates; final radiocast Sept, 23, 1954, CBS televersion Oct. 25, 1952–Feb. 28, 1956.

Talent Scouts, July 2, 1946, CBS; talent audition competition; master of ceremonies Arthur Godfrey; CBS–TV simulcast Dec. 6, 1948 to end of radio run, final radiocast Oct. 1, 1956, televersion extension to July 21, 1958.

Birth

Barry Gray (Bernard Yaroslaw), July 2, 1916, Red Lion, N.J.; announcer, emcee bka host of 1940s comments shows—*Author Meets the Critics*, *Barry Gray on Broadway*, *Scout about Town*—while introducing *Uncle Don*; radio debut on West Coast handling live remotes at supermarket openings; New York WOR 1945–47, Miami Beach WKAT 1947–50, New York WMCA 1951; maintained radio talk show until late in life; *Winner Take All* master of ceremonies CBS–TV 1952, *Songs for Sale* panelist CBS Radio 1952; d. Dec. 21, 1996.

Death

Hal Simms, July 2, 2002, Brookline, Mass.; b. June 10, 1919.

July 3

Debuting

The Abbott and Costello Show, July 3, 1940, NBC; comedy-variety feature starring Bud Abbott, Lou Costello; seasonal fill-in for vacationing comic Fred Allen but returned two years hence (Oct. 8, 1942) as permanent schedule entry seven seasons, switching to ABC last two; final broadcast June 9, 1949.

Blondie, July 3, 1939, CBS; family sitcom 1939–50; centered on bumbling Dagwood Bumstead (Arthur Lake), spouse Blondie (Penny Singleton most durably 1939–46); originated in newspaper strip, spawning comic books, novel, merchandise, 28 films, dual TV series, postage stamp, Library of Congress exhibit, signature sandwich, restaurant chain, website, projected stage musical; newspaper strip still produced in 2008; final broadcast July 6, 1950, NBC–TV extension Jan. 4–Sept. 27, 1957, CBS–TV extension Sept. 26, 1968–Jan. 9, 1969.

Canceled

Mayor of the Town, July 3, 1949, MBS; debut Sept. 6, 1942.

Deaths

Jim Backus, July 3, 1989, Santa Monica, Calif.; b. Feb. 25, 1913. Jack Smith, July 3, 2006, Westlake Village, Ventura, Calif.; b. Nov. 16, 1913. Rudy Vallee, July 3, 1986, North Hollywood, Calif.; b. July 28, 1901.

July 4

Births

Fielden Farrington, July 4, 1909, Clinton, Ind.; announcer, author, newscaster bka *The Romance of Helen Trent* interlocutor 1944–60 ("...the real-life drama of Helen Trent who—when life mocks her ... breaks her hopes ... dashes her against the rocks of despair—fights back bravely ... successfully ... to prove what so many women long to prove in their own lives: that because a woman is 35—or more—romance in life need not be over ..."), lines he delivered more than 4,000 times; introduced *The Armstrong Theater of Today*, *The Green Hornet*, *Just Plain Bill*, *We Love and Learn*; network newscaster penning tales of macabre for *The CBS Radio Mystery Theater* 1974–76; wrote novels *A Little Game* 1968, *The Strangers in 7A* 1972; d. July 1977, Bayville, N.Y.

Al Jarvis, July 4, 1909, Russia; eminently enduring disc jockey at Hollywood KFWB, ruling West Coast ether platter-spinning 1930s, 1940s; credited self with originating *Make Believe Ballroom* concept/handle though Martin Block—who made it famous—assigned label to himself; d. May 6, 1970.

Barbara Weeks, July 4, 1913, Boston, Mass.; actress (film, radio); in 44 theatrical B-movies, none memorable, often uncredited 1930–56; radio work in *Her Honor—Nancy James*, *Meet the Dixons*, *The Open Door*, *Philip Morris Playhouse*, *The Road of Life*, *We Love and Learn*; d. June 24, 2003.

Deaths

Morgan Beatty, July 4, 1975, St. John's, Antigua and Barbuda; b. Sept. 6, 1902. Ernest Chappell, July 4, 1983, North Palm Beach, Fla.; b. June 10, 1903. Bob Hawk, July 4, 1989, Laguna Hills, Calif.; b. Dec. 15, 1907. Charles Kuralt, July 4, 1997, New York City, N.Y.; b. Sept. 10, 1934. Charles McCarthy, July 4, 1988, New Bern, N.C.; b. June 3, 1919. Tyler McVey, July 4, 2003, Rancho Mirage, Calif.; b. Feb. 14, 1912. Vic Perrin, July 4, 1989, Los Angeles, Calif.; b. April 26, 1916. Henry Sylvern, July 4, 1964, New York City, N.Y.; b. March 26, 1908.

July 5

Debuting

Arnold Grimm's Daughter, July 5, 1937, CBS; daytime serial; for a while, namesake hero (Don Merrifield) couldn't accept offspring Connie's (Margarette Shanna, Betty Lou Gerson, Luise Barclay) nuptials to childhood sweetheart Dal Tremaine (Ed Prentiss, Robert Ellis)—but Dal's parents *never* accepted her!; when Dal died suddenly and son born to Connie, premise shifted, pointedly focused on grandpa and tot; final broadcast June 26, 1942.

The Longines Symphonette, July 5, 1943, MBS; maestros Macklin Marrow 1943–49, Mishel Piastro 1949–54 held baton flanked by scholarly-sounding host Frank Knight, who took delight in reminding listeners: "This is the world's most honored music program presented as a salute to Longines, the world's most honored watch.... These beautiful melodies and Longines watches have this in common: throughout the world, where there is an appreciation of things fine and beautiful, *both* are held in the highest esteem"; final broadcast June 5, 1954.

Maisie (*The Adventures of Maisie*), July 5, 1945, CBS; lighthearted narrative following "career" of down-on-her-luck entertainer, Maisie Revere (Ann Sothern), and questionable hangers-on she attracted; support cast included familiar names—Joan Banks, Bea Benaderet, Hans Conried, Sheldon Leonard, Marvin Miller, Frank Nelson, Lurene Tuttle, etc.; final broadcast Dec. 26, 1952.

Birth

Don G. Goddard, July 5, 1904, Binghamton, N.Y.; announcer, consultant, emcee, newscaster, print journalist (*The New York World*) bka NBC staff newsman at times headlining own series *Don Goddard and the News* 1940–41, 1944–45; introduced band remotes ca. late 1930s–1940s; supplemented chain newscasting stints with news duties for New York WEAF 1942, WMCA 1946, WINS 1947–48; *Watch the World* juvenile current events entry host NBC-TV 1950; shifted to ABC–TV presiding over *Medical Horizons* documentary 1955–57; ABC-TV early evening news anchor 1958–60; hosted *Focus on America* documentary including film footage shown earlier by local affiliates ABC-TV 1963; in "second career" became well known for labors in geriatric drug abuse, consulting for Mile High Council on Alcoholism, St. Luke's Chemical Dependency Program fostering similar efforts elsewhere; d. March 20, 1994.

Deaths

Ben Alexander, July 5, 1969, Hollywood, Calif.; b. May 26, 1911. Anne Hummert, July 5, 1996, New York City, N.Y.; b. Jan. 19, 1905.

July 6

Debuting

The Judy Canova Show, July 6, 1943, CBS; comedy variety; singer-comedienne played self, pigtails-and-calico hillbilly (image never able to shake) in premise, having arrived in Hollywood from"Rancho Canova" at Cactus Junction; flanked by some figures with equally colorful names: landlady Aunt Aggie (Verna Felton, Ruth Perrott), boyfriend-taxi operator Joe Crunchmiller (Sheldon Leonard), nonsensical Benchley Botsford (Joseph Kearns, George Dietz), housekeeper Geranium (Ruby Dandridge), gardener-chauffeur Pedro (Mel Blanc), cranky houseguest Mr. Hemingway (Hans Conried), beefy Humphrey Cooper (Gerald Mohr) — and other recognizable players Elvia Allman, Jim Backus, Sharon Douglas, Gale Gordon; final broadcast May 28, 1953.

The Lineup, July 6, 1950, CBS; police drama; in strain of cop dramas emerging at mid–century omitting glamour of crime, focused on stringency of law enforcement/tab for illegal activity; Lt. Ben Guthrie (William Johnstone), Sgt. Matt Grebb (Joseph Kearns, Wally Maher), Sgt. Peter Carter (John McIntire, Jack Moyles) pursued realistic crimes most listeners had never heard — strangling spinsters, contract murders, attacking police, residence bombings of figures in public eye; Guthrie, others investigated cases of lineup subjects — "under the cold, glaring lights pass the innocent, the vagrant, the thief, the murderer" said a voice; CBS–TV series 1954–60 had different cast, repackaged as *San Francisco Beat*, shipped to local stations following net run; final radiocast Feb. 20, 1953.

A Prairie Home Companion (*American Radio Company*), July 6, 1974, PBS; variety; Minnesota homespun radio entertainer Garrison Keillor inspired to create-host-produce feature by likes of several vintage radio series, notably *Arthur Godfrey Time, Fibber McGee & Molly, Gene Autry's Melody Ranch, Grand Ole Opry, Smilin' Ed McConnell and His Buster Brown Gang*; country singers performed on series still running in 2008; silent 1986–89; prompted books, 2006 theatrical film billed as "Radio like you've never seen it before."

Canceled

Blondie, July 6, 1950, ABC; debut July 3, 1939.

Births

LaVerne Andrews, July 6, 1911, Mound, Minn.; vocalist (contralto)—film, public appearances, radio, recordings, stage bka one of infamous Andrews Sisters trio; recorded 1,800 songs, sold 90 million platters; *The Andrews Sisters Eight-to-the-Bar Ranch* ABC 1944–46, *Club Fifteen* CBS 1947–53 notable audio gigs; d. May 8, 1967.

Gaylord James Avery, July 6, 1918, Minnesota; announcer; Omaha WOW, Lincoln, Neb. KFAB staffs 1930s–40s; narrated 1950s net radio gigs *Gangbusters, My Son Jeep* persisting as CBS interlocutor through 1960s; introduced 39 classic syndicated episodes *The Honeymooners* that Jack Lescoulie originally did on live TV — opening was re–cut for local, cable distribution; *The Entertainers* announcer CBS–TV 1964–65; d. March 11, 1996.

Alexander Kendrick, July 6, 1910, Philadelphia, Pa.; author, correspondent, print journalist (*The Chicago Sun*) bka biographical author of CBS News mentor: *Prime Time—The Life of Edward R. Murrow* 1969 though he joined corps too late to be one of infamous "Murrow Boys"; hired from *Sun* 1947, reported from Vienna awhile; *CBS News, CBS World News Roundup, Edward R. Murrow and the News, The World Tonight* contributor; d. May 17, 1991.

Dorothy Kirsten, July 6, 1910, Montclair, N.J.; vocalist (lyric soprano) bka *The Railroad Hour* third most enduring costar, appearing with Gordon MacRae 39 times 1948–54; unprecedented three-decade run with Metropolitan Opera Co. 1945–75; performed with Mario Lanza onscreen in *The Great Caruso*, Bing Crosby in *Mr. Music*; 1950s guest artist stints intermittently on *Voice of Firestone*; d. Nov. 18, 1992.

Myra Marsh, July 6, 1894, Maine; actress (film, radio, TV); bit character role in *My Friend Irma* as mom of investment counselor Richard Rhinelander III, Jane Stacy's employer-boyfriend; continuing turns on *A Date with Judy, Junior Miss, That's Rich*; performances in 37 B-movies, solo outings half-dozen times on mostly dramatic TV fare; d. Oct. 29, 1964.

Death

Roy Rogers, July 6, 1998, San Bernadino, Calif.; b. Nov. 5, 1911.

July 7

Debuting

Casey, Crime Photographer, July 7, 1943, CBS; mystery-detective drama tied to journalist shutterbug, theme re-branded often: *Flashgun Casey* 1943, *Casey, Press Photographer* 1944, *Crime Photographer* 1945, *Casey, Crime Photographer* 1947, *Crime Photographer* 1954; in another tale of amateur sleuthing, photojournalist for fictitious *Morning Express* Jack Casey (Jim Backus, Matt Crowley, Staats Cotsworth) loitered at Blue Note Café with reporter-romantic distraction Annie Williams (Jone Allison, Alice Reinheart, Lesley Woods, Betty Furness, Jan Miner) between action, dialogued with bartender-sans-surname Ethelbert (John Gibson); live CBS videocast 1951–52 with Richard Carlyle, Darren McGavin starring; final radiocast April 22, 1955.

Escape, July 7, 1947, CBS; anthology adventure drama; heard in 18 time periods over seven years, stepchild of later radio surmounted its handicaps by becoming what one historiographer labeled audio's "greatest series of high adventure"—so good were some of its chilling classic tales they were reprised on sister series *Suspense*, one of radio's sterling anthology showcases; major names in superlative West Coast acting company included Parley Baer, Joan Banks, Harry Bartell, Ed Begley, Gloria Blondell, Herb Butterfield, William Conrad, Hans Conried, John Dehner, Sam Edwards, Laurette Fillbrandt, Paul Frees, Virginia Gregg, Joseph Kearns, Elliott Lewis, Frank Lovejoy, Jeanette Nolan, Vic Perrin, Jack Webb, Paula Winslowe, more; final broadcast Sept. 25, 1954.

The Parker Family, July 7, 1939, CBS; domestic sitcom; dubbed "Richard the Great" by sisters, teen adolescent Richard Parker (Leon Janney, Michael O'Day) recalled "misunderstanding of the week" in clan tale that included patriarch Walter (Jay Jostyn), matriarch Helen (Linda Carlon-Reid, Marjorie Anderson), siblings Nancy (Mitzi Gould), Elly (Patricia Ryan), Grandpa Parker (Roy Fant); final broadcast Nov. 10, 1944.

Twenty-First Precinct, July 7, 1953, CBS; police drama, one of new breed of crime narratives in early 1950s aimed at mature subjects, audiences; offering "a factual account of the way police work in the world's largest city," anthology presented grim sketch of law enforcement in urban context, under command of Capt. Frank Kennelly (Everett Sloane, James Gregory, Les Damon) assisted by Lt. Matt King (Ken Lynch), Sgt. Waters (Harold J. Stone), Sgt. Collins (Jack Orrisa); daily events within confines of police substation incidental to main plot of solo case pursued per episode following step-by-step investigations—some of vivid, brutal crimes; without attracting permanent sponsor, for three years drama presented dynamic pic of hard-core police work; final broadcast July 26, 1956.

Vox Pop (*Sidewalk Interviews, Voice of the People*), July 7, 1935, NBC Blue; human interest quiz; launched on Houston KTRH late 1932, radio salesmen Parks Johnson, Jerry Belcher took mics streetside to interview passersby about Roosevelt-Hoover political campaigns in full swing, spontaneity netting series; infamy spread, projected show to New York–based chains; Johnson owned feature outright by 1936 — Belcher replaced successively by Wally Butterworth, Neil O'Malley, Warren Hull; final broadcast May 19, 1948.

Canceled

American Melody Hour, July 7, 1948, CBS; debut Oct. 22, 1941.

Births

Gloria Mann (Zipser) (Gloria Mostman), July 7, 1927, New York City, N.Y.; actress (radio, stage, TV) bka *Archie Andrews* teen sitcom stuck-up girlfriend Veronica Lodge 1943–51 ("Hi-y'all, Ah-cheekins ... It's awful nice to see y'all, Ah-cheee ... dee-aaaaah! Ah-ha-ha-ha-ha-ha-ha-ha-ha"); on Broadway at age eight in Pulitzer-winning *The Old Maid*; at 12 one of twin offspring of CBS soap opera heroine on *The Life and Love of Dr. Susan*; successive radio roles in *Real Stories from Real Life, The Johnny Morgan Show, My True Story*; intermittently on NBC–TV's *Robert Montgomery Presents* early 1950s; d. April 21, 1961.

Terry O'Sullivan, July 7, 1915, Kansas City, Mo.; actor (radio, stage, TV), announcer bka *Search for Tomorrow* figure Arthur Tate, second spouse (one of many) of heroine Jo Ann Barron on longrunning (1951–86) daytime serial CBS–TV — O'Sullivan was in role 1952–55, 1956–68 (to scripted demise); prolific soap opera thespian in other TV dramas while playing Tate: *Valiant Lady* CBS 1955–56, *Days of Our Lives* NBC 1966–68, *The Secret Storm* CBS 1968–69; welcomed daytime viewers to *Dollar a Second* game on Dumont, *Leave It to the Girls* panel chatfest on ABC, both 1953–54; launched career in Midwest tent shows; interlocutor for 1940s radio features *Anchors Aweigh, Dreft Star Playhouse, The General Mills Hour* while acting in *Make-Believe Town — Hollywood*, dispatching commercials on *Glamour Manor*; d. Sept. 14, 2006.

David Ross (David Rosenthan), July 7, 1894, New York City, N.Y.; actor, announcer, emcee, poet (published in *The New Republic, The Nation*), recording artist (poetry), writer; New York WABC announcer 1926; American Academy of Arts and Letters diction award recipient 1932; 1920s–50s opened *Chesterfield Presents, The Coke Club, The Columbia Workshop, The Fred Waring Show, Lombardoland U.S.A., Myrt and Marge, The Street Singer, The Studebaker Champions, Take It or Leave It*, others while acting in *The Curiosity Shop* (which he wrote), *The True Story Hour*, hosted *Breezin' Along*; *Time for Reflection* poetry-reading series on Dumont TV 1950–51, *Where Was I* game show panelist Dumont TV 1952–53; retired as freelance announcer 1972; d. Nov. 12, 1975.

Deaths

Bill Cullen, July 7, 1990, Bel Air, Calif.; b. Feb. 18, 1920. Peter Kalischer, July 7, 1991, New Orleans, La.; b. Dec. 25, 1914. Gladys Swarthout, July 7, 1969, Florence, Italy; b. Dec. 25, 1900.

July 8

Debuting

Blind Date, July 8, 1943, NBC; human interest game; forerunner of TV's *The Dating Game* pitting six servicemen against sight-unseen trio of stunning female models (partition separated genders), men vying for chaperoned night-on-town with one — three losers got $15, tickets to Broadway shows, peck on cheek from hostess Arlene Francis who spat out double entendres unknowingly; final radiocast Jan. 18, 1946, telecast ABC/NBC/Dumont erratically 1949–53.

Joan Davis Time (*The Sealtest Village Store, Joanie's Tea Room, Leave It to Joan*), July 8, 1943, NBC; comedy, music, sitcom; honing comedic craft as she, Jack Haley filled for Rudy Vallee as Coast Guard beckoned 1943, ex-vaudevillian Davis thrust into own show; pursued one figure on handful of aural ventures, projecting her to NBC-TV's domestic sitcom *I Married Joan* 1952–55; audio support cast: Hans Conried, Mary Jane Croft, Verna Felton, Sharon Douglas, Shirley Mitchell, Willard Waterman, more; final radiocast Aug. 28, 1950.

Tales of the Texas Rangers, July 8, 1950, NBC; western narrative; ranger-hero Jace Pearson (Joel McCrea), superior Captain Stinson (Tony Barrett) interacted in tales hinging on true cases of select 50-member Rangers, "most famous and oldest law enforcement body in North America" dating to 1820s; Pearson's car pulled horse trailer that bore Charcoal, steed he rode on trails tracking cold-blooded killers, thieves, kidnappers, etc. where car couldn't go; narrator revealed sentences meted to perpetrators at chapter's end;

CBS-TV incarnation 1955–57, ABC-TV repeats 1957–59; final radiocast Sept. 14, 1952.

Canceled

Dangerous Assignment, July 8, 1953, CBS; debut July 9, 1949.

Births

Melville Ruick, July 8, 1898, Boise, Idaho; actor, announcer bka *City Hospital* anthology with continuing threads where he played Dr. Barton Crane, on CBS in early 1950s, adding televersion on ABC/CBS 1951–53; resided in front of cameras on *Doorway to Danger* Cold War adventure as John Randolph NBC 1951, *The Guiding Light* soap opera as Rev. Dr. Paul Keeler CBS 1952–54; also introduced *Dear John*, *Lux Radio Theater* on aural ether; d. Dec. 24, 1972.

William (Bill) Thompson, July 8, 1913, Terre Haute, Ind.; actor, dialectician-animal imitator, PR executive, vocalist, voiceover artist bka *Fibber McGee & Molly* regulars Horatio K. Boomer, Mr. Old Timer (Rupert Blasingame), Nick DePopolous, Wallace Wimple 1936–53; working knowledge of 19 languages, dialects; first player added to *FM&M* cast; running gigs with *The Sinclair Weiner Minstrels* (singer), *The Breakfast Club* (meek, mush-mouthed figure resembling Mr. Wimple few years hence), *The Story of Mary Marlin* (parrot parody); film impersonations: white rabbit Dodo (*Alice in Wonderland*), pirate Mr. Smee (*Peter Pan*), five dialects (*Lady and the Tramp*), more to late 1960s; community relations official with Los Angeles' Union Oil Corp. from 1957; d. July 15, 1971.

Deaths

Wayne Howell, July 8, 1993, Pompano Beach, Fla.; b. Feb. 16, 1921. John Reed King, July 8, 1979, Woodstown, N.J.; b. Oct. 25, 1914.

July 9

Debuting

Dangerous Assignment, July 9, 1949, NBC; international espionage drama; global troubleshooter Steve Mitchell (Brian Donlevy, Lloyd Burrell) pursued criminals in glittering spots, narrating tales in first person; unnamed fed bureau propelled him to foreign soil; easy for fans to figure out denoument, critic said, turning it into "just another spy show" with few transfixing reasons to tune in; Donlevy starred in 39-week syndicated TV series 1952; final net radiocast July 8, 1953 although transcribed audio series with Burrell lasted to 1954.

Canceled

Can You Top This?, July 9, 1954, NBC; debut Dec. 9, 1940.

Births

Hans Von Kaltenborn, July 9, 1878, Milwaukee, Wis.; author, commentator, correspondent, newscaster, print journalist (*The Merrill* [Wis.] *Advocate*, *The Brooklyn Eagle*) bka one of most reliably authoritative voices spanning nation's Great Depression–World War II–postwar prosperity–Korean conflict eras with evening commentaries on dual hookups; *H. V. Kaltenborn Comments* (*Kaltenborn Edits the News*) debuted on New York WOR 1927 with minor break to 1930 when "dean of American commentators" joined CBS, part of daily reporting landscape to 1940, shifting to NBC in similar capacity, retiring 1955; fluent in German, Italian, French; staccato clipped speech quickly branded him, parodied by comics; typical 15.9 Hooper rating in war years topped only by Walter Winchell among radio commentators, underscoring depth of following; Association of Radio News Analysts first president 1942; authored seven tomes including memoir *Fifty Fabulous Years, 1900–1950*; *Who Said That?* panelist NBC Radio 1948, 1949, 1950, NBC-TV 1954; d. June 14, 1965.

Joan Tompkins (Swenson), July 9, 1915, Westchester County, N.Y.; actress (stage, radio, TV), author, educator, entrepreneur bka *This Is Nora Drake* daytime serial heroine CBS 1949–57, *Lora Lawton* title role NBC 1943–46, *Young Widder Brown* chum Norine Temple 1940s-56; onstage opposite Henry Fonda at White Plains, N.Y. 1938, Broadway plays later; ongoing aural credits: *Against the Storm*, *Big Sister*, *David Harum*, *Our Gal Sunday*, *Your Family and Mine*, occasional guest shots on *Call the Police*, *Mr. Keen—Tracer of Lost Persons*; many TV parts in *Little House on the Prairie*, *Barnaby Jones*, *Bonanza*, *Mannix*, *Dr. Kildare*, more; with spouse-radio thespian Karl Swenson, formed Beverly Hills acting enterprise; after his death (1978) she corralled writing troupe that published several volumes (Tompkins avid author, too); d. Jan. 29, 2005.

Dorothy Thompson, July 9, 1894, Lancaster, N.Y.; author, columnist ("On the Record" 200 papers 1936–58, *The Ladies' Home Journal*), commentator, freelance writer (Jewish Correspondence Bureau), lecturer, print journalist (*The Chicago Daily News, The Philadelphia Public Ledger, The New York Evening Post, The New York Tribune*), publicist (New York Woman Suffrage Party, National Social Unit Organization, American Red Cross) bka *Dorothy Thompson Commentary* hostess 1937–41, 1942, 1943, 1944, 1945 NBC/NBC Blue/MBS (only certified net gig); issues crusader; first of her gender to be foreign bureau chief (Berlin 1924 for New York, Philadelphia papers), Nobel Prize literature recipient 1930; penned 10 tomes; life parodied in 1942 film *Woman of the Year* starring Katharine Hepburn; d. Jan. 30, 1961.

Death

Eric Sevareid, July 9, 1992, Washington, D.C.; b. Nov. 26, 1912.

July 10

Debuting

County Fair, July 10, 1945, Blue/ABC; audience participation game show; masters of ceremonies Jack Bailey, Peter Donald, Win Elliot trotted out contestants drawn from studio audience who played games traditionally found on fair midways to incessant tune of calliope; final broadcast April 1, 1950.

The Man Called X, July 10, 1944, CBS; international mystery drama; globetrotter Ken Thurston (Herbert Marshall), covert U. S. agent, dispatched to foreign territory to expose spies, more subversives intent on bringing down America, traveling with peculiar lightfingered figure Pagan Zeldschmidt (Leon Belasco) at times leaving latter's contributions to ambiguity beyond giving X somebody to dialogue with; Joan Banks, William Conrad, Barbara Fuller, Peter Leeds, Carleton Young, other Hollywood players routinely turned up in support; syndicated televersion appeared 1956–57; final radiocast May 20, 1952.

Canceled

The Adventures of Michael Shayne, July 10, 1953, ABC; debut Oct. 16, 1944.

Births

David Brinkley, July 10, 1920, Wilmington, N.C.; newscaster, writer bka *The Huntley-Brinkley Report* evening newscast teammate partnered with Chet Huntley NBC-TV 1956–70, *David Brinkley's Journal* public affairs series host NBC-TV 1961–63, *This Week with David Brinkley* news-commentary forum host ABC-TV 1981–96; joined NBC Radio 1943 as newswriter—said one source: "His talent for strong and clear writing became evident as he continually struggled to write for announcers who read only the words and seemed to miss the meaning"; also delivered 10-minute radio newscasts, D.C. reporter for John Cameron Swayze's *The Camel News Caravan* NBC-TV 1949–56; d. June 12, 2003.

John Easton, July 10, 1918, New York City, N.Y.; announcer, copywriter bka busy commercial scribe for multi brands—Arnold (bread), Avon, Beechnut (coffee), Betty Crocker, Buick, Dentyne, E. I. Dupont, El Producto (cigars), General Motors, Ipana (toothpaste), Johnson & Johnson, Reynolds (metals), Tareyton (cigarettes), Texaco, U. S. Steel; presented *The Adventures of Maisie, The Great Gildersleeve, Let George Do It* 1945–54; d. April 10, 1984.

Harry Golder, July 10, 1908, Detroit, Mich.; announcer, newscaster, sportscaster bka *The Lone Ranger* interlocutor ca. 1930s, early 1940s; Detroit WXYZ jack of all trades—narrating, news, sports; d. Oct. 16, 1968.

Graham McNamee, July 10, 1888, Washington, D.C.; announcer, author, clerk (Rock Island Railroad), emcee, salesman (Armour & Co.), sportscaster, syndicated columnist (*Graham McNamee Speaking*), vocalist bka "first announcer superstar" hosting NBC inaugural gala Nov. 15, 1926; while pursuing business lines, sang on Broadway, performed with opera outfit, solo concerts; hired by New York WEAF 1923 as announcer-baritone vocalist; media critic allowed "within a year McNamee would be the most famous man in radio—without question the most influential and hardest-worked announcer in the medium's first decade"; another labeled him "the father of sportscasting"—he covered baseball, basketball, boxing, football, horse racing, other events; pursued political campaigns, conventions from 1924; introduced legions of 1920s-40s features like *The Atwater-Kent Hour*, *The Cities Service Orchestra*, *Ed Wynn — the Texaco Fire Chief*, *Elsa Maxwell's Party Line*, *The Rudy Vallee Show*, *Voice of Firestone*; 1928 tome *You're on the Air* among first on topic; d. May 9, 1942.

Death

Mel Blanc, July 10, 1989, Los Angeles, Calif.; b. May 30, 1908.

July 11

Debuting

The Mercury Theater on the Air (*Mercury Theater*, *The Campbell Playhouse*), July 11, 1938, CBS; anthology drama; under watchful eye of skilled craftsman Orson Welles, presented what is ostensibly best recalled broadcast in vintage radio, H. G. Wells' "War of the Worlds"; millions of listeners convinced selves Martians landed at Grovers Mill, N.J. and about to pillage U. S. East Coast, so believable was production despite disclaimers it was only play; celebrated repertory company included Ray Collins, Joseph Cotton, Kenny Delmar, Alice Frost, Martin Gabel, Agnes Moorehead, Everett Sloane, Karl Swenson, more; silent 1938–46; final broadcast Sept. 13, 1946.

Births

Thomson (Tommy) Bartlett, July 11, 1914, Milwaukee, Wis.; announcer, emcee, entrepreneur bka *Welcome Travelers* master of ceremonies 1947–54; at 14, announced at Milwaukee WISN (his first role that of barking dog), moved to Chicago WBBM at 19, opened *Meet the Missus*, *The Missus Goes to Market*, both regional entries; brief stint with CBS series *News and Rhythm* 1939, introduced selections by *Carl Hohengarten's Orchestra*; narrated radio remote from Chicago Rail Fair 1950, positioned next to Cypress Gardens booth inspiring him to develop own venue, luring thousands of summer vacationers to Tommy Bartlett's Ski, Sky and Stage Show, Robot World and Exploratory at nearby Wisconsin Dells, Wis., all-consuming passion for many years; d. Sept. 6, 1998.

Lu Ann Simms (Luanne Ciminelli), July 11, 1932, Rochester, N.Y.; personal appearance/recording artist, vocalist bka *Arthur Godfrey Time* variety revue singer CBS Radio-TV 1952–55, *Arthur Godfrey and His Friends* CBS-TV 1952–55; one of many artists Godfrey dismissed in awful six-year "bitchy, bickering strife" era (critic); in handful of Godfrey's *Talent Scouts* winners (Pat Boone, The Chordettes, Carmel Quinn, etc.) he liked so well, made permanent members of troupe, thereby "Little Godfreys"; sang on CBS-TV's *The Jackie Gleason Show*, *The Ed Sullivan Show* (latter four times); d. Sept. 22, 2003.

Harry Von Zell, July 11, 1906, Indianapolis, Ind.; actor, announcer, emcee, producer, program director, ukuleleist, vocalist, writer bka *George Burns and Gracie Allen* domestic sitcom as inept sidekick-interlocutor, periodically on radio 1942–50, permanently on CBS-TV 1951–58, plus successor *George Burns Show* NBC-TV 1958–59; sang, strummed ukulele on Inglewood, Calif. KMIC 1926 snagging announcer-vocalist-producer-writer slot, San Diego KGB program director 1928, joined Los Angeles KTMR 1929; impresario Paul Whiteman's announcer, moved with him to Gotham 1930, joined CBS, presented crooner Bing Crosby first time on air 1931; hired by Young & Rubicam ad agency for radio production 1935; returned to chains in "performing" capacities bantering with headliners Fred Allen, Phil Baker, Ben Bernie, Burns and Allen, Eddie Cantor, Joan Davis, Dinah Shore; same on *The George Gobel Show* CBS-TV 1959–60; 27 B-movies 1935–75, made-for-TV flick *Ellery Queen* 1975; d. Nov. 21, 1981.

Deaths

Clifford Goldsmith, July 11, 1971, Tucson, Ariz.; b. March 29, 1899. Sam Taub, July 11, 1979, Brooklyn, N.Y.; b. Sept. 10, 1886. Lucille Wall, July 11, 1986, Reno, Nev.; b. Jan. 18, 1899, Chicago, Ill. Carleton Young, July 11, 1971, Santa Monica, Calif.; b. May 26, 1907.

July 12

Debuting

The Adventures of Sam Spade, July 12, 1946, ABC; crime detective drama with Spade

(Howard Duff, Steve Dunne) of San Francisco as epitome of strain of case-hardened cynical sleuths, dictating "capers" to girl Friday Effie Perrine (Lurene Tuttle) whose air-headed responses nevertheless allowed flirtatious tease between them; based on figures inspired by Dashiell Hammett novels; mid-century Red scare prompted end of Duff's services (blacklisted six years) as sponsor substituted *Charlie Wild, Private Detective*— new investigator on the opposite coast (New York) with Effie Perrine as steno (go figure!); *Wild* made it to TV on three webs 1950–52 but *Spade* didn't; final radiocast April 27, 1951.

Births

Milton Berle (Milton Berlinger), July 12, 1908, New York City, N.Y.; actor (film, stage, radio, TV), comedian bka *The Milton Berle Show* (myriad monikers) comedy variety series headliner with intermittent radio runs 1936–49, NBC-TV 1948–56, 1958–59; on silent screen at age five, career embraced Ziegfeld Follies, vaudeville, Broadway, nightclubs, movies, broadcasting; first radio comic to jump from radio to TV, setting course for peers; possibly accountable for sales of more early TV sets in U. S. than anyone; facial contortions, outlandish garb, physical antics cemented appeal to video crowd; branded "Uncle Miltie," "Mr. Television"; radio series equally zany with sidekicks Jack Albertson, Jackson Beck, Ed Begley, Arthur Q. Bryan, John Gibson, Jack Gilford, Charles Irving, Al Kelly, Pert Kelton, Billy Sands, Mary Shipp, Arnold Stang, Roland Winters; d. March 27, 2002.

Charles William Griffis, July 12, 1917, Beverly Hills, Calif.; actor (stage, film, radio, TV), announcer bka *All My Children* figure Harlan Tucker ABC-TV 1977–81, 1983; on Broadway 1950 in plethora of stage productions, joining PlayMakers Repertory company at Chapel Hill, N.C. few years before death; dubbed foreign films into English, performed in *It Came Upon a Midnight Clear* perennial holiday hit with Mickey Rooney; TV episodes of *Newhart, Designing Women, Remington Steele*; on 1940s-50s radio introduced *Believe It or Not* while acting in *The Adventures of Father Brown, Archie Andrews, Chick Carter — Boy Detective, Crime and Peter Chambers, Dimension X, Dr. Sixgun, The Road of Life, Roger Kilgore — Public Defender* and — much later — The *CBS Radio Mystery Theater* 1974–82, *Adventure Theater* 1977–78; d. April 13, 1998.

Death

Ted Mack, July 12, 1976, Tarrytown, N.Y.; b. Feb. 24, 1904.

July 13

Births

Joseph Bell, July 13, 1912, California; actor, announcer, director, producer; from 1920s-50s, acted in *The Big Guy, The Collier Hour, David Amity, My True Story, The New Penny, The Right to Happiness, X-Minus One*; narrated *The Adventures of Sherlock Holmes, The Gulf Headliners, Twenty Thousand Years in Sing Sing, Uncle Jim's Question Bee*; directed *Big Town, The Bishop and the Gargoyle, East of Cairo, The Orange Lantern*; produced *House in the Country*; d. March 1987, Centralia, Mo.

Harry Sosnik, July 13, 1906, Chicago, Ill.; advertising agency executive (Ted Bates), impresario, network executive (ABC late 1960s), pianist, record executive (Decca); conductor *Your Hit Parade* inaugural (1936), final (TV 1958–59) performances; formed own band early 1930s, frequented Chicago's Edgewater Beach Hotel, played Windy City's World's Fair; directed music for two dozen aural web series 1928–54 including *The Joe E. Brown Show, The Gracie Fields Show, The Adventures of the Falcon, Hildegarde, The Danny Kaye Show, The Danny Thomas Show*; d. March 22, 1996.

Dave Garroway, July 13, 1913, Schenectady, N.Y.; announcer, emcee, sportscaster bka *Today* (*The Dave Garroway Today Show*) magazine series inaugural host NBC-TV 1952–1961, *Wide Wide World* documentary host NBC-TV 1955–58, *The Dave Garroway Show* (*Garroway at Large*, et al.) musical variety series NBC Radio 1947, 1949–53, 1954–55; easygoing commentary style refreshing for audiences to hear, watch, making him instantly popular with masses; launched radio career as NBC page in New York followed by on-air stints at Pittsburgh KDKA, Chicago WMAQ, branching out to stream of broadcast hits with NBC; regular contributor to *Monitor* 1950s-60s; d. July 21, 1982.

Dorothy May Kilgallen (Kollmar), July 13,

1913, Chicago, Ill.; actress (film, radio), author, commentator, emcee, panelist, screenwriter, syndicated newspaper columnist bka *What's My Line?* paneist CBS-TV 1950–65, CBS Radio 1952–53, "Voice of Broadway" newspaper gossip columnist 1938–65 reaching 20 million readers at 1950 peak; collegiate cub reporter for *The New York Evening Journal* (later *The New York Journal American*); with husband Richard Kollmar (*Boston Blackie* on radio) launched breakfast chat *Dorothy and Dick* on New York WOR 1945–63 rivaling *The Fitzgeralds* (Ed, Pegeen), *Tex* (McCray) *and Jinx* (Falkenburg), other Gotham duos; national 1940s radio gigs *Chandu— the Magician, Leave It to the Girls, Star Time with Dorothy Kilgallen, The Voice of Broadway*; d. Nov. 8, 1965.

Deaths

Grantland Rice, July 13, 1954, New York City, N.Y.; b. Nov. 1, 1880. Westbrook Van Voorhis, July 13, 1968, New Milford, Conn.; b. Sept. 21, 1903.

July 14

Debuting

The Stan Freberg Show, July 14, 1957, CBS; mocking humor; purportedly last live big-scale show of breed on chain radio with headliner using satire to spoof windbags, smug, weak-minded; Billy May conducted full orchestra; despite show's brevity (15 weeks), Freberg proclaimed himself "the last network radio comedian"; observed May: "I think everybody realized that we were kind of closing down a chapter of some sort of history"; final broadcast Oct. 20, 1957.

Births

Douglas Edwards, July 14, 1917, Ada, Okla.; announcer, newscaster bka pioneer CBS-TV anchorman (*Douglas Edwards with the News* 1947–62); major radio newscaster (*CBS World News Roundup* 1945–48, *Wendy Warren and the News* 1947–58, *Douglas Edwards and the News* ca. 1958–88); 5-minute weekday newscast CBS-TV April 16, 1962-May 30, 1980; author Gary Paul Gates affirmed: "All the other TV anchormen ... are the direct descendants of Douglas Edwards"; d. Oct. 13, 1990.

George Frederick Putnam (at times identified as George Carson Putnam to sidestep mixup with separate announcing-newscasting George Putnam); July 14, 1914, Breckenridge, Minn.; announcer (film, radio), emcee, newscaster, sportscaster, TV editor bka NBC second tier newsman, though more active in that arena than other Putnam; hosted five chain news programs 1939–51: *Campbell Condensed News, George Putnam and the News, Humanizing the News, Salute to Saturday, Sunday News Highlights*; presented *The Army Hour*, narrated *Spotlight on America* same epoch; introduced Lawrence Welk troupe in North Dakota same year (1937) went on ether sportscasting at St. Paul, Minn. KSTP before hire by New York NBC 1939 as newscaster; after World War II joined New York MBS 1946, news anchorman at Los Angeles KTTV television 1951, later moving to KTLA, local radio stations KHJ, KCOP, KIEV/KRLA, KPLS; Movietone newsreel narrator 1941–44; several short-term early network TV projects.

Death

Kenny Delmar, July 14, 1984, Stamford, Conn.; b. Sept. 5, 1910.

July 15

Debuting

Music and the Spoken Word from the Crossroads of the West (*The Mormon Tabernacle Choir, The Salt Lake City Tabernacle Choir*), July 15, 1929, NBC Blue; blended voices of mammoth choral group, pipe organ performing recognized hymns and obscure spiritual melodies coupled with three-minute midpoint homily to encourage global audience; colossal instrument played in pervasive runs by Frank Asper, Clay Christiansen, Richard P Condie, Richard Elliott, John Longhurst, Jerrold Ottley, Alexander Schreiner; "the Spoken Word" by Richard L. Evans, Spencer Kinnard, Lloyd Newell; syndicated series still airs making it second-longest running U. S. radio series (following *Grand Ole Opry*).

Canceled

The Frank Sinatra Show (under sundry monikers), July 15, 1955, NBC; debut Oct. 20, 1942. *The Perry Como Show*, July 15, 1955, CBS; debut April 12, 1943.

Deaths

Florence Halop, July 15, 1986, Los Angeles, Calif.; b. Jan. 23, 1923. Bill Thompson, July 15, 1971, Los Angeles, Calif.; b. July 8, 1913.

July 16

Debuting

Quick as a Flash, July 16, 1944, MBS; quiz; quizmasters Ken Roberts, Win Elliot, Bill Cullen presided as six contestants from studio audience vied for cash prizes in horserace-themed competition, trying to be first giving correct answers to questions; final broadcast June 29, 1951.

Canceled

Dick Tracy, July 16, 1948, ABC; net debut Feb. 4, 1935. *Waltz Time,* July 16, 1948, NBC; debut Sept. 27, 1933.

Births

Edgar (Ned) Calmer, July 16, 1907, Chicago, Ill.; newscaster (radio, TV), novelist, overseas correspondent, print journalist, scriptwriter bka CBS foreign, domestic reporter 1940–67; *Backstage Wife* soap opera scribe ca. late 1930s; *Ned Calmer and the News* 1943–44; correspondent for 1940s-50s *CBS World News Roundup, World News with Robert Trout, You Are There*; d. March 9, 1986.

Charles Egleston, July 16, 1882, Covington, Ky.; actor (radio, film, TV) bka *Ma Perkins* daytime serial confidante-business partner Shuffle Shober NBC/MBS/NBC Blue/CBS 1933–58; in role shaping his life from day one (Aug. 14, 1933 on Cincinnati WLW), branded to death by it, moved with narrative to Chicago 1933, New York 1947; in *Backstage Wife, The First Nighter, Gateway to Hollywood, Grand Hotel, Grand Marquee, Just Plain Bill, Portia Faces Life, Uncle Ezra's Radio Station*; bit part in 1946 cinematic film *The Well-Groomed Bride*; performed in half-dozen solo roles in TV dramas 1952–56; d. Oct. 31, 1958.

Raphael Floyd Phillips Gibbons, July 16, 1887, Washington, D.C.; announcer, author, commentator, emcee, print journalist (*The Minneapolis Daily News, The Milwaukee Free Press, The Minneapolis Tribune, The Chicago World, The Chicago Tribune*), wire journalist (International, Universal News services) bka "restless, unorthodox roving reporter ... brought high excitement, courage, and ingenuity ... to earn his reputation as premier war correspondent of his generation" a critic allowed; reported on half-dozen chain radio series, most memorable likely *The Headline Hunter* 1929–33; subject of two biographies; d. Sept 24, 1939.

Joe O'Brien, July 16, 1915, Yonkers, N.Y.; announcer, disc jockey, sportscaster; *Rosemary* soap opera narrator 1940s, *Jack and Cliff* cast 1948; New York WMCA staff 1940–68, rival WNBC 1968–86, retired from full time work but persisted part time to 2000 on Peekskill, N.Y. WHUD; d. July 24, 2005.

Frank Singiser, July 16, 1908, Montevideo, Minn.; announcer, director, newscaster, writer; applying at Schenectady's General Electric Co. for work in 1928 was directed to WGY subsidiary, hired as announcer, director, writer; moved to NBC 1929 as announcer—*The A&P Gypsies, Cavalcade of America, G. E. Circle, General Motors Concerts*; joined New York WOR 1937, a flagship outlet of MBS; gained web news births—*Mutual News* 1938–39, *The Sinclair Headliner* 1944–46; persisted as MBS announcer to 1971 retirement; d. May 28, 1982.

William Woodson, July 16, 1917, Los Angeles, Calif.; actor, announcer, voiceover artist bka animated cartoon voices in *The C. B. Bears* NBC-TV 1977–78, *Super Friends* ABC-TV 1977–83; acted in 1940s-50s installments of *Just Plain Bill* while narrating *Douglas of the World, This Is Your FBI.*

Deaths

Wayne King, July 16, 1985, Paradise Valley, Ariz.; b. Feb. 18, 1901. Margaret Speaks, July 16, 1977, Blue Hill, Maine; b. Oct. 23, 1904. Jo Stafford, July 16, 2008, Centuy City, Calif.; b. Nov. 12, 1917. Dwight Weist, July 16, 1991, Block Island, R.I.; b. Jan. 16, 1910.

July 17

Births

William Dennis Gargan, July 17, 1905, Brooklyn, N.Y.; actor (stage, film, radio, TV), author, producer bka *Murder Will Out* crime drama Inspector Burke ABC 1945–46, *I Deal in*

Crime drama gumshoe Ross Dolan ABC/MBS 1946–48, *Martin Kane, Private Detective* crime drama gumshoe MBS 1949–51, NBC-TV 1949–51, syndicated TV 1958, *Barry Craig, Confidential Investigator* crime drama gumshoe NBC 1951–55; before playing private eyes, Gargan worked as PI—and poked fun at ethereal bungling by radio detectives; eight Broadway shows 1925–32, 95 theatrical films 1928–56, five solo episodes of TV series 1949–58; autobiography *Why Me?* recounted cancer battle that saw larynx removal ending his career 1960; d. Feb. 16, 1979.

Earl J. Glade, Jr., July 17, 1911, Provo, Utah; announcer, broadcasting executive, educator, producer, writer bka *Music and the Spoken Word from the Crossroads of the West* early interlocutor-producer 1933–47; after Salt Lake City, moved to Boise, Idaho managing KDSH Radio, purchasing KBOI-TV; Brigham Young University director of broadcast services 1966–76 launching KBYU-TV, teaching communications while there; d. May 14, 2001.

Arthur (Kelly) Linkletter, July 17, 1912, Moose Jaw, Saskatchewan, Canada; announcer, author, emcee bka *House Party* 1945–67, *People Are Funny* 1943–60 master of ceremonies; *The Art Linkletter Show* prevailed as hidden camera primetime game entry seven months on NBC-TV 1963; new venture under same moniker, cohosed by Art's daughter Diane, aired on CBS-TV six months 1969; Linkletter's best seller *Kids Say the Darndest Things* prompted CBS-TV feature of same name 1998–2000 hosted by Bill Cosby, Linkletter.

Eleanor Steber, July 17, 1914, Wheeling, W. Va.; author, concert and recording artist, educator, vocalist (soprano) bka *Voice of Firestone* regular 1944–57, second most visible artist (107 appearances), sole Christmas concert soloist 1945–57; The *Metropolitan Opera Auditions of the Air* 1940 winner with Met contract, debuting there in more premiers than other artists, performing with company 404 times; "one of the most important sopranos in the USA during the 1940s and 1950s with a sweet and yet full voice, and outstanding versatility" said music critic; personality clash with new Met executive Rudolph Bing caused her to quit Met in 1961; taught music later at Cleveland, Julliard, New England Conservatory and American Institute of Music Studies, Graz; d. Oct. 3, 1990.

Deaths

Dizzy Dean, July 17, 1974, Reno, Nev.; b. Jan. 16, 1910. Larry Haines, July 17, 2008, Delray Beach, Fla.; b. Aug. 3, 1917.

July 18

Debuting

The Columbia Workshop (*Twenty-Six by Corwin, Columbia Presents Corwin, The CBS Radio Workshop* under expanding nomenclature), July 18, 1936, CBS; anthology drama; plays of superlative writing, acting, directing signified entries; East Coast thespians in casts included Joan Alexander, Burgess Meredith, Arnold Moss, Minerva Pious, Karl Swenson, Orson Welles, others; West Coast actors in final season composed of Parley Baer, William Conrad, Sam Edwards, Joseph Kearns, Jack Kruschen, Lurene Tuttle, Vic Perrin, etc.; final broadcast Sept. 22, 1957.

The Howard Miller Show, July 18, 1955, CBS; daytime quarter-hour record-spinning entry majoring on forthcoming discs just before they hit record stores; hosted by venerable, authoritative Chicago personality who made career appearing on Windy City aural outlets almost five decades; final broadcast Jan. 9, 1959, possibly rivaled in longevity only by *Make Believe Ballroom* among daily network DJ series.

Births

Harriet Hilliard (Peggy Lou Snyder), July 18, 1909, Des Moines, Iowa; actress (stage, film, radio, TV), vocalist, recording artist bka *The Adventures of Ozzie and Harriet* costar on radio 1944–54, TV 1952–66; d. Oct. 2, 1994.

Marvin Miller (Marvin Mueller), July 18, 1913, St. Louis, Mo.; actor, announcer, newscaster, voiceover artist bka *The Millionaire* human interest drama's Michael Anthony CBS-TV 1955–60, possibly on more radio series than anyone else (88 network, syndicated documented including 20 soap operas, masculine record); radio gigs included *Backstage Wife, The Bickersons, Dragnet, Duffy's Tavern, The First Nighter, The George Burns and Gracie Allen Show, The Guiding Light, Jack Armstrong—the All-American Boy, Lassie, Louella Parsons, Ma Perkins* (pseudonym Charlie Warren), *One Man's Fam-*

ily (20 roles), *The Railroad Hour, The Romance of Helen Trent, Stars Over Hollywood, That Brewster Boy, The Whistler*; apprenticeship at St. Louis KWK, WIL, KMOX; freelance Chicago announcer on 40 net shows weekly; moved to West Coast early 1940s; legions of 1950s-80s TV features beyond *The Millionaire*, many animated with voiceover parts; 76 mostly B theatrical movies 1945–85; d. Feb. 8, 1985.

John Rayburn, July 18, 1927, Anna, Ill.; announcer, author, emcee, newscaster, sportscaster; hired by Cape Girardeau, Mo. KFVS 1946 — initial basketball/football play-by-plays; Big 10 football/Missouri Valley basketball followed; shift to video at Peoria, Ill. WTVH-TV early 1950s, Denver KOA 1959 — sports to news anchor early 1960s; contributed to *The CBS Evening News, The Huntley-Brinkley Report, Monitor, NBC News on the Hour, Today*, more net series; in 21st century, conducted Internet Big Band show, sports podcast for journalists; penned memoir *Cat Whiskers and Talking Furniture* 2008.

Joseph S. Ripley, July 18, 1913, Bluefield, W. Va.; announcer, director, producer, publicist; 1940s-early 1950s interlocutor of *Dorothy Dix on the Air, Nick Carter — Master Detective, Troman Harper — the Rumor Detective, Walk a Mile*, others; airtime career began at Roanoke, Va. 1930s, then Hartford, Conn. WTIC, New York WCBS, WNCN, WOR — produced quiz shows at latter like *Guess Who?* while directing *Real Stories from Real Life* both 1944; *Armstrong Circle Theater* announcer NBC-TV 1950-ca. mid 1950s; produced radio commercials for New York Yankees 1955–66 followed as promoter with *Holiday on Ice*; final broadcast years at Patchogue, N.Y. WALK 1973–83; d. Feb. 3, 1993.

Michael Roy, July 18, 1913, Hannaford, N.D.; actor, announcer, author, celebrity chef, disc jockey bka scribe of nine cookbooks 1966–78 that substantiated authenticity, notoriety for culinary expertise dispensed since initial TV cooking show *Secrets of a Gourmet* on Los Angeles W6XAO (later named KTSL, KNXT) 1944–50; *Mike Roy's Kitchen* aired on KNX Radio, CBS 1950–62 followed by *At Your Service* 1962–72; introduced fans to 1940s *The Abbott and Costello Show, The Alan Young Show, Duffy's Tavern, The Martin and Lewis Show, The Spike Jones Show, Tommy Riggs and Betty Lou, The Vaughn Monroe Show*, others while acting in *All-Star Western Theater*; Burbank KWIK DJ 1947; played in *The Forgotten Faces* theatrical film 1961, episode of *Emergency!* paramedic drama NBC-TV 1975; d. June 26, 1976.

Red Skelton (Richard Bernard Skelton), July 18, 1913, Vincennes, Ind.; actor (stage, film, radio, TV), artist, author, comedian, composer, producer, voiceover artist, writer bka *The Red Skelton Show* comedy variety series headliner NBC/CBS 1939, 1941–53, NBC-/CBS-TV 1951–71; circus showbiz start, at 10 on road in burlesque, medicine/minstrel shows, showboats, vaudeville; *The Rudy Vallee Show* 1937 led to movies, NBC; portrayed figures audiences loved — Bolivar Shagnasty, Cauliflower McPugg, Clem Kadiddlehopper, Freddie the Freeloader, George Appleby, Gertrude and Heathcliffe, Junior the Mean Widdle Kid, San Fernando Red, Willy Lump-Lump; 39 cinema films 1938–65 — standout *The Fuller Brush Man* 1948, three made-for-TV flicks 1970–81, seven TV solo roles 1955–60; bitter, outspoken after CBS canceled him 1970; d. Sept. 17, 1997.

Death

Ron Rawson, July 18, 1994, Cohasset, Mass.; b. Oct. 28, 1917.

July 19

Debuting

Our Miss Brooks, July 19, 1948, CBS; sitcom with wisecracking high school English teacher Connie Brooks (Eve Arden) mixing it up with pompous windbag principal Osgood Conklin (Gale Gordon); complications added by recurring support team of students, teachers, associates; final broadcast June 30, 1957, CBS-TV incarnation Oct. 3, 1952-Sept. 21, 1956.

Births

Thomas B. Grandin, July 19, 1907, Cleveland, Ohio; correspondent, FCC official, salesman, rancher bka reporter CBS News 1939–40, ABC News 1944–45; brief member infamous "Murrow Boys" picked by CBS overseas news guru Edward R. Murrow to report from Europe in World War II; Federal Communications Commission foreign-broadcast monitoring assistant editor between CBS-ABC terms; left radio after war to be sales exec, Arizona rancher; d. October 1977 (last residence Phoenix, Ariz.—many sources to pinpoint exact date, place exhausted).

Rhoda Elaine Williams, July 19, 1930, Denver, Colo.; actress (stage, film, radio, TV), educator bka *Father Knows Best* family sitcom eldest daughter Betty Anderson 1949–54; at nine appeared on *I Want a Divorce!* succeeded by exposure on *Dr. Christian, One Man's Family, The Life of Riley, Lux Radio Theater*, more; 14 theatrical motion pictures including *National Velvet* 1944, *House of Strangers* 1949, *Cinderella* 1950, *The Heart Is a Rebel* 1958, *The Sergeant Was a Lady* 1961; *Mixed Doubles* fleeting sitcom costar NBC-TV 1949 plus 21 more turns in single-shot video comedic, dramatic fare; d. March 8, 2006.

July 20

Debuting

Gangbusters (premiered as *G-Men* three months), July 20, 1935, NBC Blue; crime anthology drama billed as "the only national program that brings you authentic police cases"; actor impersonated real lawman ("by proxy") outlining via flashbacks case he worked on; as culprits apprehended, bulletin-style advisory on miscreants at large aired; drama engaged biggest contingent of sound techs, equipment, turntables in radio, practitioner allowed; televersion on NBC 1952 canceled in nine months, replaced by *Dragnet*; final radiocast Nov. 27, 1957.

Births

Verna Felton (Millar), July 20, 1890, Salinas, Calif.; actress (stage, radio, film,TV),voice-over artist bka incredible, inimitable guttural yet velvet voice in varied venues—Disney animated cartoons on big, small screens plus broadcast series in identifying character parts e.g. *The Red Skelton Show* comedy-variety feature as Junior, "the mean widdle kid's" grandma NBC/CBS 1945–53, NBC-/CBS-TV 1951-ca. 1966, *December Bride* sitcom protagonists' comrade Hilda Crocker CBS 1952–53, CBS-TV 1954–59, reprised in spinoff *Pete and Gladys* CBS-TV 1960–61; aural ether support duty in *The Adventures of Ozzie and Harriet, The Adventures of Philip Marlowe, Fibber McGee & Molly, The George Burns and Gracie Allen Show, The Jack Benny Program, The Judy Canova Show, My Little Margie, Point Sublime, Tommy Riggs and Betty Lou*; stage actress—brief Broadway stint 1929, debut on big screen 1917 silent film, 27 "talkies" pictures released 1950–67 (often voice-only roles), played 19 solo episodes of TV sitcoms/dramas/variety shows 1951–63; d. Dec. 14, 1966.

Murray Forbes, July 20, 1906, Chicago, Ill.; actor (radio, film), writer bka *Ma Perkins* daytime serial heroine's son-in-law Willie Fitz NBC/MBS/NBC Blue/CBS 1933–60; career launched on *The General Tire Show* 1931, figured in Chicago-based series *Aunt Jenny's Real Life Stories, The First Nighter, Fu Manchu, Foxes of Flatbush, Grand Hotel, Joe Palooka, Just Plain Bill, Knickerbocker Playhouse, Lonely Women, The Story of Mary Marlin, Today's Children*; moved to L.A. after enduring radio run ended in New York, theatrical film *The Big Catch* 1967; novelist of *Hollow Triumph* 1948; d. Jan. 28, 1987.

July 21

Debuting

Mr. Chameleon, July 21, 1948, CBS; police detective narrative; "the man of many faces," Chameleon (Karl Swenson) was born sans given name in production factory of Frank, Anne Hummert where his dramatic moments were scripted by minions dedicated to concealing his identity until he trapped killers or other miscreants into guilty admissions; assisted by Det. Dave Arnold (Frank Butler), pair put away vilest offenders relying on Chameleon's deductive powers, shrewd disguises; Swenson was master dialectician—there is strong suggestion Hummerts created that role specifically for him; final broadcast Aug. 7, 1953.

Canceled

Ladies Be Seated, July 21, 1950, ABC; debut June 4, 1943. *The Roy Rogers Show*, July 21, 1955, NBC; debut Nov. 21, 1944.

Births

Frank D. Barton, July 21, 1909, Alameda County, Calif.; actor, announcer, emcee; briefly ed *The Open House* music variety series from San Francisco with Helen Morgan 1941; NBC career employee in L.A. 1942–74, rising to web's chief Hollywood announcer; interlocutor for *A Day in the Life of Dennis Day, Dr. I. Q.—the Mental Banker, The James and Pamela Mason Show, One Man's Family* while in bit parts on *Official Detective*; d. Jan. 11, 1995.

Himan Brown, July 21, 1910, New York City, N.Y.; actor, director, educator, lecturer, producer bka *The CBS Radio Mystery Theater* anthology drama producer-director CBS 1974–82; read poetry on air 1927, pushed NBC to air *The Rise of the Goldbergs* (he acted in it) 1929; radio arsenal: *Adventure Theater, The Adventures of the Thin Man, The Affairs of Peter Salem, Barry Craig—Confidential Investigator, Bulldog Drummond, City Desk, David Harum, Dick Tracy, Dr. Friendly, Flash Gordon, Grand Central Station, Green Valley USA, The Gumps, Hilda Hope, M.D., Inner Sanctum Mysteries, International Airport, John's Other Wife, Joyce Jordan—Girl Interne, Little Italy, Marie—the Little French Princess, The NBC Radio Theater, Terry and the Pirates, Way Down East*; produced two 1957 films, one made-for-TV flick 1959, two episodes *The Inner Sanctum* syndicated TV 1954; created creaking door, menacing farewell "Pleasant dreams..." that embroidered *Inner Sanctum, Mystery Theater*; in 21st century produced dramas at City University of New York for Brooklyn WBCR.

Gene Kirby, July 21, 1909; announcer, director, sportscaster bka *Game of the Day* play-by-play announcer 1951-?; before joining New York WINS as sports reporter, affiliated with ABC, NBC, MBS 1940s-50s for *America's Town Meeting of the Air, Claude Thornhill and His Orchestra, The Clock, The Fat Man, Johnny Olsen's Rumpus Room*, more while directing *Big Moments in Sports, Greatest Sports Thrills*, appearing on 1961's *Tops in Sports*; d. March 1985 (copious efforts to obtain precise date, place thwarted).

Irna Phillips, July 21, 1901, Chicago, Ill.; creator, educator, writer bka daytime serials developer who fruitfully transcended dual broadcast mediums; launched first matinee serial, *Painted Dreams*, on Chicago WGN Oct. 20, 1930; from humble beginnings sprang many descendants of her fertile pen (and of pens held by wordsmiths she paid to flesh out her plots) including *Today's Children, The Guiding Light, The Road of Life, Woman in White, The Right to Happiness, Lonely Women, Masquerade, The Brighter Day*—on TV *These Are My Children, The Road of Life, The Guiding Light, The Brighter Day, Another World, As the World Turns*, also directly/indirectly influencing *Young Doctor Malone, Peyton Place, A World Apart, All My Children, Loving, One Life to Live, Days of Our Lives, The Young and the Restless, The Bold and the Beautiful*; demanding, difficult to work with, yet left indelible imprint on industry; d. Dec. 22, 1973.

Deaths

Pierre Andre, July 21, 1962, Evanston, Ill.; b. Nov. 25, 1899. Les Damon, July 21, 1962, Los Angeles, Calif.; b. March 31, 1908. Dave Garroway, July 21, 1982, Swarthmore, Pa.; b. July 13, 1913. Vicki Vola, July 21, 1985, New York City, N.Y.; b. Aug. 27, 1911. Robert Young, July 21, 1998, Westlake Village, Calif.; b. Feb. 22, 1907.

July 22

Deaths

John B. Kennedy, July 22, 1961, Toronto, Canada; b. Jan. 16, 1895. Jack Lescoulie, July 22, 1987, Memphis, Tenn.; b. Nov. 17, 1911. Lyle Van, July 22, 1997, Clearwater, Fla.; b. Sept. 10, 1904.

July 23

Debuting

My Favorite Husband, July 23, 1948, CBS; wedded couple sitcom about normal bank VP George Cooper (Richard Denning), conniving spouse Liz (Lucille Ball); she was given to outlandish schemes in attempts to be noticed, playing one-upwomanship in situation of week; in every sense show was precursor to far better acclaimed CBS-TV's *I Love Lucy* costarring Ball and hubby Desi Arnaz, applying same scatter-brained tactics; final radiocast March 31, 1951, CBS-TV extension Sept. 12, 1953-Dec. 27, 1955 (starring Barry Nelson, Joan Caulfield).

Births

Jackson Beck, July 23, 1912, New York City, N.Y.; actor (radio, film, TV), announcer, panelist, voiceover artist bka audio thespian for more than 50 series like *The Adventures of Superman, Big Sister, Calling All Cars, Casey—Crime Photographer, The CBS Radio Mystery Theater, The Cisco Kid, Columbia Presents Corwin, Death Valley Days, Easy Aces, The FBI in Peace & War, Grand Central Station, Life Can Be Beautiful, The March of Time, The Milton Berle Show, Myrt and Marge, The Shadow, You Are There, Yours Truly—Johnny Dollar, X-Minus One*; concurrently opened *Believe It or Not, Mark Trail, Tom Corbett—Space Cadet*, handful more; New York airman on WINS, WHN, WBNX, WNEW; *Tom Corbett—Space Cadet* televersion interlocutor 1950–55; speaking roles in 1960s TV animations *King Leonardo and His Short Subjects, Tennessee Tuxedo, Batman, Superman*, nearly 150 theatrical cartoons; d. July 28, 2004.

Christopher Gerard Lynch, July 23, 1920, Rathkeale, County Limerick, Ireland; vocalist (Irish tenor) bka *Voice of Firestone* singer picked by Harvey S. Firestone, Sr. to succeed retired Richard Crooks; first of Lynch's 69 gigs there Sept. 30, 1946, Carnegie Hall, at gala *Firestone* fête; Lynch, Eleanor Steber key artists that season; with summers in homeland, Lynch "stopped by" *Firestone* sporadically 1950s; predecessor, peers' fame incessantly elusive; with heart elsewhere, returned to Europe permanently; d. April 15, 1994.

Karl Swenson, July 23, 1908, Brooklyn, N.Y.; actor (radio, stage, TV) bka *Lorenzo Jones* namesake hero 1937–55, *Our Gal Sunday* leading man Lord Henry Brinthrope 1937-mid 1950s (both daytime serials) plus *Mr. Chameleon* namesake crime detective 1948–53, role crafted by producers Frank, Anne Hummert based on his wide dialectical capacity; on stage 1930 in summer stock followed by Broadway musical revues, plays; on air in *The March of Time* 1935 succeeded by *Aunt Jenny's Real Life Stories, Cavalcade of America, Ford Theater, Grand Central Station, Inner Sanctum Mysteries, Linda's First Love, Mrs. Miniver, Portia Faces Life* (radio, TV), *Rich Man's Darling, The Whisper Men*, scads more; solo TV shots, multi theatrical films; d. Oct. 8, 1978.

Deaths

Kay Kyser, July 23, 1985, Chapel Hill, N.C.; b. June 18, 1897. Leith Stevens, July 23, 1970, Los Angeles, Calif.; b. Sept. 13, 1909.

July 24

Births

Milton Biow, July 24, 1892, New York City, N.Y.; advertising packager extraordinaire, program creative bka commercial-pitching bellman Johnny Roventini's employer ("Callllllll for Philip Morraissse"); *Take It or Leave It, The $64,000 Question* instigator; d. Feb. 1, 1976.

Raymond Edward Johnson, July 24, 1911, Kenosha, Wis.; actor (radio, stage, film, TV) bka *Inner Sanctum Mysteries* crime drama host "Raymond" ("Pleasant dreeeeaaaammmmssss ... hummmmmm?") NBC Blue/CBS 1941–45; stereotyped as foreboding character, winning presiding duties, ominous figures for fare like *Arch Oboler's Plays, Crime Club, Cloak and Dagger, Dimension X, Gangbusters, Lights Out, Mr. District Attorney, Tales of Tomorrow*, more plus romantic male leads in soap opera quartet—*Brave Tomorrow, The Guiding Light, Kate Hopkins—Angel of Mercy, Valiant Lady*; performed on Broadway in *The Patriots* 1943, as Alexander Graham Bell in 1947 motion picture *Mr. Bell*, narrated made-for-TV flick *The Night of the Auk* 1960; d. Aug. 16, 2001.

Lawrence M. (Larry) Klee, July 24, 1914, Manhattan, New York City, N.Y.; gagwriter, script editor, scriptwriter bka *Mr. Keen, Tracer of Lost Persons* crime-detective drama scribe NBC Blue/CBS/NBC 1942–51, 1952–55; workhorse in Air Features trenches, assembly-line production unit of Frank, Anne Hummert—Klee churned out reams of dialogue for their *Backstage Wife, Chaplain Jim U.S.A., Front Page Farrell, Mystery Theater, The Romance of Helen Trent, Stella Dallas, Valiant Lady, Young Widder Brown* plus other producers' wares: *Aunt Jenny's Real Life Stories, The Clock, The Fat Man, Hearts in Harmony, Mr. and Mrs. North*; originated thesis of radio-TV's *The Lineup*; wrote screenplay for *The Roosevelt Story* 1947 documentary movie; scripted *Man Against Crime* mystery-detective series starring Ralph Bellamy in live simulcast 1949–56; d. Jan. 1, 1957.

Glenn Riggs, July 24, 1907, East McKeesport, Pa.; actor (stage), announcer bka *My True Story* daytime anthology drama interlocutor 1943-early 1950s; purchased mine supplies for Pittsburgh firm while working sideline jobs in showbiz, onstage at Nixon Theater, touring with stock troupe; seeking work at Westinghouse making appliances, instead thrust before microphone at outfit's KDKA, serving as announcer-newscaster 1929–38; left for New York NBC—when Red, Blue parted in 1943, Riggs went to Blue (ABC), retiring 1972; radio intros for *The Adventures of the Thin Man*, *The Bing Crosby Show* (Kraft/Philco), *Hop Harrigan*, *Jungle Jim*, *Ladies Be Seated*, *The Private Lives of Ethel and Albert*, *True or False*, *Vic and Sade*, more; d. Feb. 19, 1985.

Basil Ruysdael, July 24, 1888, Jersey City, N.J.; actor (stage, film, radio, TV), announcer, educator, producer, vocalist, voiceover artist, writer bka 1930s-50s commercial spokesman for American Tobacco Co. Lucky Strike cigarettes on *Your Hit Parade*, *Information Please*, *The Jack Benny Program*, others ("From men who know tobacco best, it's Luckies, two to one!" flanked by rapid-delivery tobacco auctioneer spiel); toured with Henry W. Savage in Gilbert and Sullivan operettas, comic operas, voice training in Europe, sang in Bohemian opera two seasons; leading Met Opera basso 1910–18; California voice instructor 1920s, appeared in B-movies—33 times 1929–61; joined Newark WOR 1929 writing, narrating, acting, introducing *Cavalcade of America*, *The Jack Paar Show*; 1950s TV character actor in *The General Electric Theater*, *Science Fiction Theater*, *Black Saddle*, *Perry Mason* while working newsreels, transcriptions, narrating program pictures/slide films; d. Oct. 10, 1960.

Death

Joe O'Brien, July 24, 2005, Pittsfield, Mass.; b. July 16, 1915.

July 25

Birth

Harold (Hal) Peary (Harold José Pereira de Faria), July 25, 1908, San Leandro, Calif.; actor (radio, TV), vocalist, voiceover artist bka *The Great Gildersleeve* pompous windbag-Summerfield water commissioner Throckmorton P. Gildersleeve 1941–50; brought most famous characterization to life in cast of *Fibber McGee & Molly* 1939 (joined show as utility player 1937) netting series of motion pictures; lead in pithy *Honest Harold* sitcom 1950–51 after leaving NBC for CBS; two dozen visits to running TV shows; portrayed *Fibber McGee & Molly* Mayor LaTrivia in quick reprise NBC-TV 1959; voiceovers for Christmas movies 1976, 1979; d. March 30, 1985.

Death

Martin Agronsky, July 25, 1999, Washington, D.C.; b. Jan. 12, 1915.

July 26

Canceled

The March of Time, July 26, 1945, ABC; debut March 6, 1931. *Twenty-First Precinct*, July 26, 1956, CBS; debut July 7, 1953.

Births

Gracie Allen (Grace Ethel Cecil Rosalie Allen), b. July 26, 1895, San Francisco, Calif.; actress (stage, film, radio, TV), bka *The George Burns and Gracie Allen Show* family sitcom matriarch wowing everybody with unassuming, riotous deductions 1932–50, CBS-TV extension 1950–58; "Gracie Allen for President" campaign waged in 1940 on their show, others resulted in write-in votes in U. S. general election; d. Aug. 27, 1964.

Galen Drake (Foster Rucker), July 26, 1906, Kokomo, Ind.; commentator, newscaster bka authoritative-sounding expert with observations, opinions on variety of household, daily living encounters that resonated with America's homemakers 1944-ca. 1960 in which he dispensed tips, advice in folksy style (*The Galen Drake Show*, *Housewives Protective League*, *This Is Galen Drake*); newscaster 1960s-ca. 1971; began reading Bible aloud to New York WOR listeners Oct. 17, 1960 in succinct installments; d. June 30, 1989.

Donald Voorhees, July 26, 1903, Allentown, Pa.; music prodigy in right place at right time, moving with *The Atwater Kent Hour* after Oct. 4, 1925 inception on New York WEAF to NBC as web launched, late 1926; unprecedented as net impresario, culminating in *The Bell Telephone Hour*, holding baton first to final performances April 29, 1940-June 30, 1958, NBC-TV extension Jan. 12, 1959-June 14, 1968, NBC Radio *Encores from the Bell Telephone Hour* Sept. 15, 1968-June 8, 1969; d. Jan. 10, 1989.

July 27

Debuting

Lum and Abner, July 27, 1931, NBC (actually began earlier same year on Hot Springs, Ark. KTHS); sitcom featuring Lum Edwards (Chester Lauck), Abner Peabody (Norman Goff), proprietors of backwater general store; cornpone dialogue as they interacted with clientele, largely their voices in myriad rural dialects; final broadcast May 7, 1954.

Canceled

Meet the Press, July 27, 1986, NBC (NBC televersion persists); debut Dec. 1, 1946. *Weekday*, July 27, 1956, NBC; debut Nov. 7, 1955.

Deaths

Larry Elliott, July 27, 1957, Port Chester, N.Y.; b. Aug. 31, 1900. Bob Hope, July 27, 2003, Toluca Lake, Calif.; b. May 29, 1903. Dan Seymour, July 27, 1982, New York City, N.Y.; b. June 28, 1914.

July 28

Debuting

Under Arrest, July 28, 1946, MBS; crime drama; inner-workings of local police department exploited; initial protagonist Capt. John Drake (Joe DeSantis, Craig McDonnell) succeeded by Capt. Jim Scott (Joe DeSantis, Ned Wever); critic branded it "an undistinguished show"; final broadcast Oct. 4, 1954.

Births

William Nettles (Bill) Goodwin, July 28, 1910, San Francisco, Calif.; actor (film, radio, stage), announcer, emcee, hotelier-entrepreneur, voiceover artist; after appearing in 1929 stage production, pre–law student Goodwin turned focus to show biz, joining Henry Duffy Players at Portland, Ore.; led him to radio, jobs succession — Sacramento KFVK, San Francisco KFRC, Los Angeles KHJ 1932, New York CBS 1934; decade later he picked up $1,000 weekly introducing *The Burns and Allen Show*, another $1,000 introducing *Songs by Sinatra*, plus added features: *Al Pearce and His Gang, Blondie, A Date with Judy, The Edgar Bergen and Charlie McCarthy Show, The Camel Caravan, Louella Parsons, The Park Avenue Penners, The Bob Hope Show*, more; *The Bill Goodwin Show* Tuesday, Thursday afternoons NBC-TV 1951–52; master of ceremonies for audience participation features on dual webs 1955 —*Penny to a Million* ABC-TV, *It Pays to Be Married* NBC-TV; voiced animated figures on *The Boing Boing Show* CBS-TV 1956–58; 30 motion pictures e.g. *Wake Island* 1942, *The Jolson Story* 1946, *The Life of Riley* 1949, *Jolson Sings Again* 1949, *Tea for Two* 1950, *The Big Beat* 1958; bought, operated Palm Springs' Nooks Hotel 1956–58; d. May 9, 1958.

Arthur R. (Art) Hannes, July 28, 1920, Newport, Ky.; announcer, newscaster bka *Studio One* narrator CBS-TV 1948–58, CBS staffer 1947–67; dispatched news at Olean, N.Y. WHDL 1940; familiar to web radio fans of 1940s-60s *The CBS Radio Workshop, The Couple Next Door, Funny Side Up, Gangbusters, Hearthstone of the Death Squad, The Show Goes On, Sing it Again, Twenty-First Precinct, Whispering Streets, Yours Truly—Johnny Dollar*; d. March 30, 1992.

Rudy Vallee (Hubert Prior Vallee), July 28, 1901, Island Pond, Vt.; actor (film, radio), disc jockey, impresario, saxophonist, vocalist bka *How to Succeed in Business Without Even Trying* smash hit Broadway star 1961–65, movie release 1967; headliner on half-dozen national radio series 1929–55; considered "original crooner" predating Bing Crosby; industry colleagues cited him as "most difficult taskmaster of all"; played in 35 movies; d. July 3, 1986.

Deaths

Jim Bannon, July 28, 1984, Ojai, Ventura, Calif.; b. April 9, 1911. Jackson Beck, July 28, 2004, New York City, N.Y.; b. July 23, 1912. Truman Bradley, July 28, 1974, Los Angeles, Calif.; b. Feb. 8, 1905. Sam Edwards, July 28, 2004, Durango, Colo.; b. May 26, 1918. John McGovern, July 28, 1985, Brooklyn, N.Y.; b. April 26, 1912. Helen Traubel, July 28, 1972, Santa Monica, Calif.; b. June 16, 1899.

July 29

Canceled

The Brighter Day, June 29, 1956, CBS;

debut Oct. 11, 1948. *Kay Kyser's Kollege of Musical Knowledge*, July 29, 1949, ABC; debut March 30, 1938.

Births

Joseph J. Curtin, July 29, 1910, Cambridge, Mass.; actor (stage, radio) bka *Mr. and Mrs. North* crime melodrama publisher-amateur sleuth Jerry North NBC/CBS 1942–54; on Broadway early 1930s in *The Merchant of Venice*; ethereal initiation on *Roses and Drums* 1934 followed by prolific recurring daytime roles in *Backstage Wife*, *David Harum*, *Her Honor—Nancy James*, *Hilltop House*, *Myrt and Marge*, *Second Husband*, *Stella Dallas*, *The Story of Bess Johnson*, *Young Widder Brown* plus *The Thin Man* lead; d. April 5, 1979.

Florence Freeman (Berman), July 29, 1911, New York, N.Y.; actress, educator, newscaster bka queen of dual daytime serials airing concurrently: *Young Widder Brown* tearoom proprietress Ellen Brown NBC 1938–54, *Wendy Warren and the News* electronic-print newswoman Wendy Warren CBS 1947–58; feminine lead in third soap opera—*Dot and Will* 1935–37—while in recurring roles on 1930s-50s *Aunt Jenny's Real Life Stories*, *John's Other Wife*, *Pepper Young's Family*, *Valiant Lady*; primetime dramas included *Mr. Keen—Tracer of Lost Persons*, *The Paul Whiteman Show*, *Show Boat*; high school English teacher prior to entering radio at New York WMCA 1933; d. April 25, 2000.

Veola Vonn (Nelson) (sometimes identified as Viola Vonn, Vyola Von, Vyola Vonn), July 29, 1918, New York City, N.Y.; actress (radio, film, TV); support roles: *The Adventures of Ozzie and Harriet*, *Blondie*, *Chandu the Magician*, *The Charlotte Greenwood Show*, *The Eddie Cantor Show*, *The George Burns and Gracie Allen Show*, *The Jack Benny Program*, *My Favorite Husband*, *Presenting Charles Boyer*; 19 theatrical films 1935–59 mostly uncredited or bit parts; half-dozen TV appearances 1952–57; d. Oct. 28, 1995.

Niles Welch (sometimes Welsh), July 29, 1888, Hartford, Conn.; actor (film, radio, stage), announcer bka movie thespian playing in 121 silent, "talkies" celluloid productions 1913–40; stage shows prior to film; introduced 1930s radio fans to *American School of the Air*, *The Campbell Playhouse* while performing in *Columbia Workshop*, *The Road of Life* episodes; d. Nov. 21, 1976.

Deaths

Tex McCrary, July 29, 2003, New York City, N.Y.; b. Oct. 13, 1910. William Todman, July 29, 1979, New York City, N.Y.; b. July 31, 1916. Fred Waring, July 29, 1984, Danville, Pa.; b. June 9, 1900.

July 30

Sound Bite

Radio Corporation of America, parent firm of National Broadcasting Co., announces sale of Blue Network July 30, 1943 to American Broadcasting System, Inc. controlled by Edward J. Noble, Life Saver candy magnate, ex-U. S. undersecretary of commerce, for $8 million—largest sale in broadcasting history; sale approved by FCC Oct. 12, 1943; new owner renamed American Broadcasting Co., Blue nomenclature replaced with ABC June 15, 1945.

Debuting

Five Star Matinee, July 30, 1956, NBC; anthology drama; transcribed tales of romance, adventure, comedy, mystery featuring East Coast thespians in whole 30-/25-minute weekday narratives though not continuous (interrupted by *Monitor* some days); final broadcast April 24, 1959.

Canceled

Hilltop House, July 30, 1957, NBC; debut Nov. 1, 1937, CBS. *What's My Name?*, July 30, 1949, ABC; debut March 25, 1938.

Birth

Charles Irving (Irving Zipperman), July 30, 1912, St. Paul, Minn.; actor (film radio, TV), announcer, director, emcee, newscaster, producer bka *Search for Tomorrow* daytime serial debuting producer-director CBS-TV 1951–57, setting course for much of what followed in matinee video drama for decade; newscaster at Chicago WGN 1942, acted in 1940s web fare *Bobby Benson and the B-Bar-B Riders*, *The Joe Dimaggio Show*, *Tales of Willie Piper*, *The Texaco Star Theater*, *Young Doctor Malone*; in same epoch introduced *The Breakfast Club*, *Exploring the Unknown*, *The Fat Man*, *Here's Morgan*, *The Morey Amsterdam Show*, *Those Websters*, *Vic and Sade* while hosting *Coronet Quick Quiz*, directing 1950s *A Crime Letter from Dan Dodge, This Is Nora Drake*; appeared in half-dozen movies late 1950s-late 1960s, *A Face in the Crowd* most prominent; at same time directed or played in TV series *Bewitched, The Andy Griffith Show, The Wackiest Ship in the Army*, more; d. Feb. 15, 1981.

Deaths

Myron McCormick, July 30, 1962, New York City, N.Y.; b. Feb. 8, 1907. Robert Venables, July 30, 1985, Woodstock, Ill.; b. April 4, 1907. Karl Weber, July 30, 1990, Boston, Mass.; b. March 17, 1916.

July 31

Debuting

Jack Armstrong, the All-American Boy, July 31, 1933, CBS; juvenile adventure serial, possibly most prominent of glut of late-afternoon features aimed at tykes, adolescents, highly persuasive in convincing moms to buy cereals, breakfast foods, drinks sponsoring; persisted 17 years under own moniker plus extra season under *Armstrong of the SBI* extension; Hudson High star athlete, honor student Armstrong (Jim Ameche, St. John Terrell, Stanley Harris, Frank Behrens, Charles Flynn, Michael Rye) led compatriots Billy Fairfield (John Gannon, Roland Butterfield, Milton Guion, Murray McLean, Dick York), Betty Fairfield (Shaindel Kalish, Sarajane Wells, Loretta Poynton, Naomi May, Patricia Dunlap), pilot Uncle Jim Fairfield (Jim Goss), later criminal investigator Vic Hardy (Ken Griffin); they snuffed out crime ranging from espionage, fascists, communists to more conventional thugs like counterfeiters, thieves, gangsters; 15 chapters of 1947 theatrical serial produced, 1947 comic books ended with 13 issues, syndicated comic strip died early death, two Big Little Books issued 1937, 1939; final radiocast under main title June 1, 1950.

The Shadow, July 31, 1930, CBS (six monikers before *The Shadow* starting with *Detective Story Hour*); mystery-crime drama rooted in eccentricity; affluent playboy with social conscience Lamont Cranston (James LaCurto, George Earle, Robert Hardy Andrews, Jr., Frank Readick, Jr., Orson Welles, Bill Johnstone, Bret Morrison, John Archer, Steve Courtleigh) shared alias identity ("The Shadow") only with constant companion "the lovely Margo Lane" (Agnes Moorehead, Marjorie Anderson, Judith Allen, Laura Mae Carpenter, Lesley Woods, Grace Matthews, Gertrude Warner); rooted in *The Shadow* magazine from 1931, figure applied hypnotic powers to cloud minds so evildoers could hear — but not see — him, reminding them "weed of crime bears bitter fruit ... crime does not pay ... the Shadow knows," mocking miscreants with creepy laughter; movies released 1937, 1940 (15-episode serial), 1946, 1994 (latter starred Alec Baldwin); comics, magazines, books, premiums in profusion; final broadcast Dec. 26, 1954.

Canceled

Jungle Jim, July 31, 1954, syndicated; debut Nov. 2, 1935.

Births

Barbara (Barbra) Fuller, July 31, 1921, Nahant, Mass.; actress (radio, film, TV) bka *One Man's Family* daytime serial as impetuous twin Claudia Barbour NBC 1945–59; joined Chicago NBC 1932; radio repertoire: *Armstrong Theater of Today, His Honor — the Barber, The Light of the World, Lux Radio Theater, Madame Courageous, Manhattan at Midnight, Painted Dreams, The Road of Life, Scattergood Baines, Stars Over Hollywood, Stepmother*, more; 15 theatrical films 1949–73, 12 solo episodes of sundry TV dramas 1953–70; produced, marketed metaphysical instruction audiotapes, radio talks.

Roger Thurston Krupp, July 31, 1909, Minneapolis, Minn.; actor (film, radio), advertising agency staffer, announcer, newscaster; apprenticeship prior to NBC San Francisco 1932 at Minneapolis WRHM 1930, St. Paul KSTP, Oakland KTAB; first announcer to appear as one in theatrical film — MGM's *Are You Listening* 1932; to Los Angeles KFI 1933, then Post Broadcasting System in Hawaii, J. Walter Thompson ad agency in New York, rejoined radio locally at WNEW 1934, moving to Chicago WBBM, Hollywood KMTR 1939, New York WHN early 1940s; freelanced for multiple chains introducing 1930s-50s fare *The Adventures of Ellery Queen, The American Album of Familiar Music, Arnold Grimm's Daughter, Backstage Wife, Bing Crosby, David Harding — Counterspy, Famous*

Jury Trials, Jungle Jim, Just Plain Bill, Lowell Thomas and the News, Lum and Abner, The Manhattan Merry-Go-Round, Mr. Chameleon, The Quiz Kids, Scattergood Baines, Stella Dallas, Vic and Sade, dozen more while playing in *Kelly's Courthouse*, dispensing news on *The Kemtone Hour*; d. May 25, 1987.

Elmo Roper, July 31, 1900, Hebron, Neb.; commentator, entrepreneur. jewelry salesman, marketing researcher bka public opinion collector-publisher divulging fascinating details about populace on series *Elmo Roper* CBS 1948–50; intrigued as 1930s employer asked him to process customer surveys; co-founded Cherington, Wood, and Roper 1933, early marketing research firm; initiated *Fortune Survey*, country's first poll applying scientific sampling techniques 1935–50; founded Roper Center for Public Opinion Research at Williams College 1946, since relocated to University of Connecticut; d. April 30, 1971.

William R. (Bill) Shadel, July 31, 1908, Milton, Wis.; correspondent, educator, print journalist (*The American Rifleman* editor); hired by revered CBS chief foreign guru Edward R. Murrow late 1943 as European reporter though never member of famed "Murrow Boys" picked earlier; postwar duty at Washington, D.C. outlet WTOP Radio-TV, New York in 1947; radio gigs from 1944 *CBS World News Roundup, This Is London, World News Roundup/World News Tonight*; some early CBS-TV features; resigned 1954 to join ABC anchoring chain's evening TV newscast 1960–62; after retiring 1975 University of Washington communications prof; d. Jan. 29, 2005.

William Todman, July 31, 1916, New York City, N.Y.; director, program creative, producer bka Goodson and Todman Productions co-owner, radio-TV game show originator extraordinaire; d. July 29, 1979.

August 1

Canceled

Broadway Is My Beat, Aug. 1, 1954, CBS; debut Feb. 27, 1949.

Births

Alice Frost, Aug. 1, 1905, Minneapolis, Minn.; actress (stage, film, radio, TV) bka *Mr. and Mrs. North* mystery melodrama leading lady sleuthing Pamela North whose high-pitched voice sounded like airhead yet exhibited brains to figure out who-done-it on NBC/CBS 1942–54, *Big Sister* daytime serial heroine Ruth Evans Wayne CBS 1936–42, *Woman of Courage* queen Martha Jackson CBS ca. 1941–42; habitually all over dial in repeating roles: *Bright Horizon, Buck Rogers in the 25th Century, The Columbia Workshop, David Harum, Famous Jury Trials, Lorenzo Jones, Maverick Jim, The Mercury Theater on the Air, Mrs. Wiggs of the Cabbage Patch, Stoopnagle and Budd, Suspense, Town Hall Tonight*; Broadway thespian in *Green Grow the Lilacs* 1931; ongoing part in *I Remember Mama* CBS-TV 1949, played in more TV dramas 39 times 1952–79, three made-for-TV flicks, parts in four cinematic films 1963–65; d. Jan. 6, 1998.

Bill Shipley, Aug. 1, 1918, Ottawa, Kan.; announcer, newscaster; delivered news at Kansas City WDAF 1945 before landing at webs where he introduced *Look Your Best* 1947–48, *The Jimmy Dorsey Show* 1950; d. Nov. 25, 1996.

John Ernest Storm, Aug. 1, 1912, Ware, Neb.; announcer; at Los Angeles NBC 1937–69 presented 1940s-50s *Dangerous Assignment, Hawthorne's Adventures, The Man Called X, The New Adventures of Nero Wolfe, Richard Diamond—Private Detective, The Roy Rogers Show, Thirteenth Juror*, more.

Death

Harry Marble, Aug. 1, 1982, Damariscotta, Maine; b. June 11, 1905.

August 2

Canceled

The Chamber Music Society of Lower Basin Street, Aug. 2, 1952, NBC; debut Feb. 11, 1940.

Births

John Kieran, Aug. 2, 1892, Bronx, N.Y.; educator, journalist (author, columnist, editor), lecturer, linguist, TV emcee bka *Information Please* panelist 1938–51; *The New York Times* sports reporter 1915, contributed first bylined column daily 1927; covered Gov. Franklin D. Roosevelt at state capital 1932, coined *brain trust* in Roosevelt's first presidential bid, depicting sages steering campaign; after World War II stint, joined *The New York Herald Tribune* followed by Hearst syndicate, *The New York Sun*; launched *Information Please Almanac* 1947 as editor; hosted NBC-TV's *John Kieran's Kaleidoscope* 1948, *Treasures of New York* 1951; college lecture circuit, myriad newspapers, tomes — literary works sold 350,000 volumes by 1969; possessed "predilection for collecting knowledge and was considered a walking encyclopedia" pundit affirmed; d. Dec. 9, 1981.

Macklin Marrow, Aug. 2, 1900, Mecklenberg, Va.; impresario, violinist bka *The Longines Symphonette* conductor 1943–49; active interest beyond radio in community/religious projects embracing music, performed on violin, conducted Gotham entourages; d. Aug. 8, 1953.

Deaths

Ralph Bell, Aug. 2, 1998; b. Nov. 27, 1915. David Gothard, Aug. 2, 1977, Los Angeles County, Calif.; b. Jan. 14, 1911. Lesley Woods, Aug. 2, 2003, Los Angeles, Calif.; b. Aug. 22, 1910.

August 3

Canceled

Death Valley Days, Aug. 3, 1944, CBS (although show in essence persisted under refocused premises, titles — *Death Valley Sheriff*, *The Sheriff*); debut Sept. 30, 1930.

Births

Ray Bloch, Aug. 3, 1902, Alsace-Lorraine, France; impresario, musical director, pianist bka *The Jackie Gleason Show* maestro ("flower of the musical world") CBS-TV 1950s, 1960s; during network radio career starting 1930 to mid 1950s, music conductor for *Crime Doctor*, *Gay Nineties Revue*, *Hollywood Opera House*, *Johnny Presents*, *The Milton Berle Show*, *Model Minstrels*, *The Philip Morris Playhouse*, *Pick and Pat*, *Quick as a Flash*, *Sing It Again*, *Songs for Sale*, *Stop the Music!*, *Take It or Leave It*, *What's My Name?*; bandmaster for *Toast of the Town* hosted by Ed Sullivan CBS-TV 1950s; d. March 29, 1982.

Hugh Douglas (Henry Dorf), Aug. 3, 1915, Chicago, Ill.; announcer, disc jockey, newscaster; Chicago WCFL staff 1945; bid fans "hello" to *The First Nighter*, *The CBS Radio Workshop*, *Have Gun — Will Travel*, *Hollywood Soundstage*, *Romance*; d. Sept 1, 1993.

A. Larry Haines (Lawrence Hecht), Aug. 3, 1917, Mt. Vernon, N.Y.; actor (stage, film, radio, TV) bka *Search for Tomorrow* TV daytime serial character Stu Bergman (1951–86) winning three Emmys for it; aside from 80 guest star roles in *The CBS Radio Mystery Theater* 1970s-80s, resilient commodity in golden age of dramatic audio 1930s-60s at prestigious addresses: *Big Town*, *David Harding — Counterspy*, *David Harum*, *Dimension X*, *The Falcon*, *The FBI in Peace & War*, *Gangbusters*, *Mr. District Attorney*, *Pepper Young's Family*, *Rosemary*, *The Second Mrs. Burton*, *Young Doctor Malone*, et al.; on Broadway in *Generation*, *Last of the Red Hot Lovers*, *Promises — Promises*, *A Thousand Clowns*; movie support roles in *The Odd Couple* 1968, *The Seven-Ups* 1973, *Tank* 1984; running TV parts: *Maude*, *Phyl and Mikhy*, *Loving*; d. July 17, 2008.

Irene Tedrow, Aug. 3, 1907, Denver, Colo.; actress (stage, radio, film, TV) bka *Meet Corliss Archer* teen sitcom matriarch Janet Archer CBS/ABC 1953–56, CBS-TV 1952; onstage as teen, returned often in major shows like *Hamlet*, *Richard III*, *Our Town*, *Pygmalion*; radio support in *The Adventures of Philip Marlowe*, *Baby Snooks*, *Broadway Is My Beat*, *Chandu the Magician*, *Crime Classics*, *Defense Attorney*, *The George Burns and Gracie Allen Show*, *The Great Gildersleeve*, *Gunsmoke*, *The Saint*, more; 44 theatrical films 1940–81, one TV mini-series 1978, six TV series 1949–75, 19 made-for-TV flicks 1964–89, 149 solo shots in TV dramas/sitcoms; d. March 10, 1995.

August 4

Debuting

Crime Doctor, Aug. 4, 1940, CBS; crime drama; psychiatrist Benjamin Ordway (Ray Collins, House Jameson, John McIntire, Hugh Marlowe, Brian Donlevy, Everett Sloane), amnesiac, woke up to find — in other life — he was crime lord, now pursued straight/narrow focused on war on corruption; useful to police Inspector Ross (Walter Greaza), D. A. Miller (Edgar Stehli); series spawned 10 theatrical films starring Warner Baxter 1943–49; final broadcast Oct. 19, 1947.

Births

Philip Norman Clarke, Aug. 4, 1904, London, England; actor (stage, film, radio) bka *Mr. Keen, Tracer of Lost Persons* crime-mystery detective CBS/NBC 1950–55; scion of celebrated Brit thespianic clan, presented to U. S. audiences in biblical stage play *Joseph and His Brethren*, later on Broadway in *Macbeth, On Whitman Avenue*; played in *The Lure* British motion picture 1933; on air by 1937 in first of 10,000 broadcasts: *Against the Storm, The Light of the World, The Sealed Book* (cackling "keeper of the book" hermit), more; d. Sept. 27, 1985.

Alan Bradley Kent, Aug. 4, 1909, Chicago, Ill.; announcer, copywriter, emcee bka *Pepper Young's Family* interlocutor mid 1940s-1950s; penned lyrics 1941 to one of earliest, most memorable singing jingles for Newell-Emmett ad agency ("Pepsi-Cola hits the spot, 12 full ounces, that's a lot..."); broke into radio without pay weekends on New York WOV 1931 while selling sporting goods for real; full time job at NBC that year at half sales pay airing on WEAF, WJZ; joined New York WNEW 1938, returned to NBC 1940; opened 1930s-40s *Blackstone—the Magic Detective, The Career of Alice Blair, Hobby Lobby, Jane Arden, The Old Gold Hour, Perry Mason*, more while hosting *Cosmo Tune Time*, scripting *Duffy's Tavern*; d. Dec. 4, 1993.

Frank Luther (Frank Luther Crow), Aug. 4, 1899, Kansas City, Mo.; actor (film), announcer, author, emcee, recording artist, vocalist bka having brought "more stories in song to children than anyone else on radio and records" said pundit (alias Bud Billings); 1920s-40s singing radio credits: *Five Star Theater, The Frank Luther Show, Happy Wonder Bakers Trio, Heartthrobs of the Hills, Luncheon at the Waldorf, Manhattan Merry-Go-Round*, more; d. Nov. 16, 1980.

August 5

Debuting

Backstage Wife, Aug. 5, 1935, MBS, daytime serial; epigraph: *Now we present once again, Backstage Wife, the story of Mary Noble, a little Iowa girl who married one of America's most handsome actors, Larry Noble, matinee idol of a million other women ... the story of what it means to be the wife of a famous star*; tale of dashing Broadway thespian chased by legions of wily females, whose spouse accepted it—yet, when another male looked at her, actor became enraged with jealousy; most durably on NBC 1936–55, though final broadcast Jan. 2, 1959.

Births

Allen C. Anthony, Aug. 5, 1906, Buffalo, N.Y.; announcer bka *Dr. I. Q., the Mental Banker* interlocutor 1939–50; splendid plugging Mars confections, sponsor hired him for same on *Dr. I. Q. Junior, Inner Sanctum*; d. May 11, 1962.

Parley Edward Baer, Aug. 5, 1914, Salt Lake City, Utah; actor (radio, film, TV), announcer, voiceover artist (commercials) bka *Gunsmoke* western narrative townsman Chester Proudfoot CBS 1952–61, elf spokesman Ernie Keebler in cookie plugs; bit parts in films by 1949 like *The Young Lions* 1957, *Gypsy* 1963, *Counterpoint* 1993, *Dave* 1993; familiar in aural support spots: *The Adventures of Philip Marlowe, The Count of Monte Cristo, Crime Classics, Dragnet, Escape, Fibber McGee & Molly, Granby's Green Acres, Honest Harold, Lux Radio Theater, The Six Shooter, Suspense, Tales of the Texas Rangers, Yours Truly—Johnny Dollar*, more; *The Adventures of Ozzie and Harriet* neighbor Herb Darby ABC-TV 1955–61, *The Andy Griffith Show* Mayor Stoner CBS-TV 1962–63, *The Double Life of Henry Phyfe* Mr. Hamble ABC-TV 1966; d. Nov. 22, 2002.

Al Goodman, Aug. 5, 1890, Nikopol, Russia; impresario, recording artist; conducted music on 18 audio series e.g., *Gulf Headliners, Palmolive Beauty Box Theater, Your Hit Parade, The Maxwell House Showboat, Texaco Star Theater, The Prudential Family Hour*; d. Jan. 10, 1972.

Don Stanley (Donald Stanley Uglum), Aug. 5, 1917, Stoughton, Wis.; announcer; from 1944–90 at Los Angeles NBC; 1940s-50s opened *Mr. and Mrs. Blandings, The NBC University Theater, The New Adventures of Nero Wolfe, Out of the Deep, Richard Diamond—Private Detective, Your Radio Theater*, more; began radio broadcasting late 1930s at Madison, Wis. WHA, WIBA, WTMJ-FM followed by Chicago ABC, Los Angeles NBC; finished with 46 years at Hollywood-Burbank NBC-TV as staff announcer; d. Jan. 20, 2003.

Lew Valentine, Aug. 5, 1912, San Benito, Texas; announcer, emcee bka *Dr. I. Q., the Mental Banker* quizmaster 1939–42, 1946–50; career launched as actor, announcer, producer, vocalist at San Antonio WOAI; *Sing for Your Dough* host 1942; d. June 20, 1976.

Deaths

Judy Canova, Aug. 5, 1983, Hollywood, Calif.; b. Nov. 20, 1916. Fred C. Collins, Aug. 5, 2006, New York City, N.Y.; b. Oct. 7, 1925. Howard Culver, Aug. 5, 1984, Hong Kong; b. June 4, 1918.

August 6

Debuting

The Dinah Shore Show, Aug. 6, 1939, NBC Blue; music variety; feminine pop recording icon hosted shows under several appellations e.g. *Songs by Dinah Shore, In Person—Dinah Shore, The Birdseye Open House, The Ford Show*; sang with others on *Call for Music, The Jack Smith Show*; multi TV series; radio runs ended with simulcast of NBC-TV show headlined March 23, 1953-July 1, 1955.

Canceled

Lights Out, Aug. 6, 1947, ABC; debut June 30, 1934.

Births

Jim Ameche (James Amici), Aug. 6, 1915, Kenosha, Wis., sibling of busy radio vet Don Ameche; actor, announcer, emcee bka *Jack Armstrong—the All-American Boy* lead 1933–37; samples of bulging radio repertoire embraced playing, introducing, hosting *The Adventures of Ellery Queen, The Amos 'n' Andy Music Hall, Big Sister, Grand Central Station, Grand Hotel, The First Nighter, Here's to Romance, Lux Radio Theater, Philip Morris Playhouse, Silver Eagle—Mountie, Texaco Star Theater, Welcome Travelers*; 11 years with Chicago WJJD handling 150-minute insert daily, weekday morning show New York WHN 1963–69; late in career opened Ameche Academy of Broadcasting institute on Los Angeles' Wilshire Boulevard; moved to Nashville to record commercials next, joined Tucson KCEE as DJ 1975; d. Feb. 4, 1983.

Lucille Ball (Lucille Désirée Ball), Aug. 6, 1911, Jamestown, N.Y.; actress (film, radio, TV), panelist, producer bka *My Favorite Husband* wacko wife Liz Cooper opposite Richard Denning (George Cooper) 1948–51, *I Love Lucy* wacko wife Lucy Ricardo opposite Desi Arnaz (Ricky Ricardo) CBS-TV Oct. 15, 1951-June 24, 1957, more wacko characterizations in multi TV series—*The Lucy-Desi Comedy Hour* 1957–60, *The Lucy Show* 1962–68, *Here's Lucy* 1968–74, *Life with Lucy* 1986; 92 largely B-films 1932–74, some memorable treats: *Fancy Pants* 1950, *The Fuller Brush Girl* 1950, *The Long, Long Trailer* 1954, *A Guide for the Married Man* 1967, *Mame* 1974; d. April 26, 1989.

John Daly (Jackie) Kelk, Aug. 6, 1921, Brooklyn, N.Y.; actor (stage, film, radio, TV), advertising director, literary agent bka *The Aldrich Family* teenage sidekick-conspirator (alongside Henry Aldrich) Homer Brown 1939–51, *The Adventures of Superman* cub reporter Jimmy Olsen 1940s; Broadway stage in *Bridal Wise* at nine followed by bit parts in B-film trio in adolescence; same era in company of kids riding airwaves' *Coast-to-Coast on a Bus*, Milton Cross driving; added 1930s-40s aural credits: *Hello Peggy, Dick Tracy, The Gumps, Hilltop House, Terry and the Pirates, Valiant Lady, Mother o' Mine, Amanda of Honeymoon Hill, Rosemary, The Chesterfield Supper Club, Hildegarde's Radio Room, Theater Guild on the Air*; major flicks *Somebody Up There Likes Me* 1956, *The Pajama Game* 1957; left entertainment 1960s as casting director at New York's Compton Advertising, engaging Jane Withers as "Josephine the Plumber" there; hired by Louise Shary Literary Agency; d. Sept. 5, 2002.

Louella Parsons (Louella Rose Oettinger), Aug. 6, 1880, Freeport, Ill.; author, commentator, emcee, print journalist, screenplay writer, syndicated columnist bka Hollywood gossip reporter, shows named for self 1945–51, 1952–54, biography *The First Lady of Hollywood*, "prima donna of the gossipmongers"; most formidable of breed divulging secrets of stars, studios, "ruthless rival" (*Life*) fought resolutely to protect turf against archrivals Hedda Hopper, Walter Winchell; first job as *The Dixon* (Ill.) *Morning Star* drama editor in high school, later scripted screenplays, tome *How to Write for the "Movies"* 1915; launched nation's first movie gossip column in *The Chicago Record-Herald* 1914, her second in *The New York Morning Telegraph* 1914, third in *The New York American* 1922, fourth in *The Los Angeles Examiner*, then Hearst Syndicate with 600-paper distribution; hostess of chain radio entries *Hollywood Hotel* 1934–38, *Hollywood Premiere* 1941; eight B-movie credits 1928–51; d. Dec. 9, 1972.

Death

Everett Sloane, Aug. 6, 1965, Brentwood, Calif.; b. Oct. 1, 1909.

August 7

Canceled

Mr. Chameleon, Aug. 7, 1953, CBS; debut July 21, 1948.

Deaths

Raymond Paige, Aug. 7, 1965, Larchmont, N.Y.; b. May 18, 1900. Mary Lee Taylor, Aug. 7, 1944, St. Louis, Mo.; b. June 12, 1891.

August 8

Births

Eddie Fisher, Aug. 10, 1928, Philadelphia, Pa.; recording artist, vocalist (personal appearances, radio, stage, TV) who waxed string of 22 hits after labeled by U. S. DJs "America's Most Promising Male Vocalist"; classic Coca-Cola-backed radio series 1953–56 seamlessly transferred to NBC-TV 1953–59; bad press, public disfavor stirred by divorce of Debbie Reynolds to wed Elizabeth Taylor 1959, fleeting marriages to three more wives including Connie Stevens; unsuccessful comeback 1970s, publicized gambling/alcohol addiction treatment.

Ross Graham, Aug. 8, 1905, Benton, Ark.; banker, baritone-bass vocalist, public utility official; Arkansas entry in national talent hunt 1931, joined *Roxy and His Gang* next year; headlined NBC series 1935–36, sang with The Revelers on *Cities Service Concert* 1930s; professional retirement 1947; d. Jan. 5, 1986.

Edward John Noble, Aug. 8, 1882, Gouveneur, N.Y.; industrial magnate, philanthropist, U. S. Undersecretary of Commerce, bka founder Life Savers, Inc., growing from failing mint confectioner to global enterprise of $20 million sales in 1950s, spurring $8 million 1943 buyout of NBC Blue after FCC ordered NBC to shed one of dual chains, ensuing merger with United Paramount forming competitive American Broadcasting Co. radio-TV net; d. Dec. 29, 1958.

Deaths

Jack Brinkley, Aug. 8, 1972, Chicago, Ill.; b. Nov. 30, 1907. Macklin Marrow, Aug. 8, 1953, New York City, N.Y.; b. Aug. 2, 1900. Jay Sims, Aug. 8, 1997, Escondido, Calif.; b. April 28, 1911.

August 9

Birth

Robert K. McCormick, Aug. 9, 1911, Danville, Ky.; author, newscaster bka not to confuse with *The Chicago Tribune* publisher-WGN owner Robert McCormick; hosted *Robert McCormick and the News* from Washington NBC 1947–49; *Current Opinion* facilitator NBC-TV 1947, *Battle Report* moderator on Korean conflict NBC-TV 1950–52; NBC staffer 1942–76, managed Washington bureau, subsequently embodied web in Europe, based in Paris; after retiring, penned *Facing Alcoholism*, tome about cause he championed; d. Sept. 4, 1985.

Death

Jimmy Fidler, Aug. 9, 1988, Westlake, Calif.; b. Aug. 24, 1900.

August 10

Births

Franklyn Ferguson, Aug. 10, 1902, Texas (precise location elusive); actor, announcer, director; radio baptism 1933 with Southwest Broadcasting System as program director followed by air stints at Grand Rapids, Mich., Detroit, Chicago; in Windy City 1948 introduced *The Breakfast Club*, *Jack Armstrong—the All-American Boy*, *The Tom Mix Ralston Straight Shooters*, *The Quiz Kids*; TV acting 1956–69 in *My Friend Flicka*, *Temple Houston*, *Peyton Place*; d. Sept. 1969, Tampa, Fla.

Jack Lester (Jack L. Swineford), Aug. 10, 1915, Enid, Okla.; actor (film, radio, TV), announcer, disc jockey, emcee, sportscaster, voiceover artist; radio at New Orleans WNOE 1946 (sports), Chicago WENR 1949 (DJ); 1940s opened *Jack Armstrong—the All-American Boy*, hosted *Junior Junction* 1946–52, acted in *Masquerade*, *Silver Eagle—Mountie*, *Sky King*, *The World's Great Novels*; introduced *Majority Rules*

ABC-TV 1949–50, played in NBC-TV daytime sudsers *The Bennetts* 1953–54, *A Time to Live* 1954; voice of *McDuff—the Talking Dog* animated cartoon NBC-TV 1976; 15 B-movies 1933–82; d. Sept. 18, 2004.

Jane Pickens, Aug. 10, 1908, Macon, Ga.; civic leader, philanthropist, recording artist, socialite, vocalist (soprano) bka *The Jane Pickens Show* NBC Radio 1948–49, ABC-TV 1954, *Pickens Party* NBC Radio 1955–57; in clan act with sibs Patti, Helen as Three Little Maids from Pixie; NBC hired trio to compete with CBS's Boswell Sisters; when sisters wed, Jane went solo in *Ziegfeld Follies of 1936*; fruitless Manhattan GOP congressional candidate 1972; d. Feb. 21, 1992.

Deaths

James F. Fleming, Aug. 10, 1996, Princeton, N.J.; b. April 23, 1915. Ted Husing, Aug. 10, 1962, Pasadena, Calif.; b. Nov. 27, 1901. John Nesbitt, Aug. 10, 1960, Carmel, Calif.; b. Aug. 23, 1910.

August 11

Death

Phil Harris, Aug. 11, 1995, Rancho Mirage, Calif.; b. June 24, 1904.

August 12

Births

Kay Campbell (Catherine Frances Campbell Hibben), Aug. 12, 1904, Kansas City, Mo.; actress (radio, TV), hostess, publisher bka *Ma Perkins* daytime serial whiny-voiced nagging daughter Evey Perkins Fitz NBC/CBS 1945–60; more radio running roles on *Backstage Wife, Front Page Farrell, Just Plain Bill, Myrt and Marge, Painted Dreams, The Romance of Helen Trent, The Story of Mary Marlin*; as radio livelihood faded, segued into enduring characterizations on video soaps *The Guiding Light* 1957–64, *The Edge of Night* 1964–69, *All My Children* 1970–85; *The Armstrong Circle Theater* hostess NBC-TV 1950–54; *New York Athletic Club Magazine* publisher 1962–70; d. May 27, 1985.

Guy Sorel, Aug. 12, 1914, Paris, France; actor (film, radio, TV) bka *Backstage Wife* daytime serial male lead Larry Nobel — last in strain NBC/CBS 1951–59; ongoing audio parts: *The Adventures of Superman, Just Plain Bill, The Road of Life, Twenty Thousand Years in Sing Sing, You Are There*; wed soap heroine Mary Jane Higby; big screen: *The 13th Letter* 1951, *The Honeymoon Killers* 1970, *Tell Me That You Love Me Junie Moon* 1970; multi shots in TV e.g. 1950s *Hallmark Hall of Fame, The Lone Ranger, Naked City*; d. April 5, 1994.

August 13

Deaths

Bob Bailey, Aug. 13, 1983, Lancaster, Calif.; b. June 24, 1913. Joseph Reeves Bolton II, Aug. 13, 1986, Santa Monica, Calif.; b. Sept. 8, 1910. Tom Reddy, Aug. 13, 1961, Fenton, Mich.; b. Sept. 30, 1917. Phil Rizzuto, Aug. 13, 2007, West Orange, N.J.; b. Sept. 25, 1917.

August 14

Births

William R. Downs, Jr., Aug. 14, 1914, Kansas City, Mo.; correspondent, newscaster, novelist, wire service journalist bka *CBS World News Roundup* reporter 1942–62, one of legendary "Murrow Boys" hired by Edward R. Murrow; career began with United Press: Kansas City, Denver, New York, London, intercepted by Murrow at latter; resigned CBS 1962 to be a novelist but after 20 months without success joined ABC News to finish career; d. May 3, 1978.

Ed Herlihy, Aug. 14, 1909, Dorchester, Mass.; actor (film, stage, TV), announcer, emcee, newscaster bka commercial spokesman for Kraft Foods Co. 42 years (*The Great Gildersleeve, Kraft Music Hall, Kraft Television Theater*, more venues in dual mediums), voice of Universal-International newsreels screened in cinema houses 25 years; from Boston WLOE 1932 moved to rivals WHDH, WEEI 1933, NBC New York 1935 retiring 63 years later; dubbed "studio workhorse with the versatility to handle a broad spectrum of general utility chores";

chores included three dozen radio series e.g. *The Big Show*, *Ed Herlihy and the News*, *Grand Central Station*, *Information Please*, *Inner Sanctum Mysteries*, *Just Plain Bill*, *Life Can Be Beautiful*, *Mr. District Attorney*, *The O'Neills*, *People Are Funny*, *Truth or Consequences*, *Vic and Sade*, *Weekend*; performed in five silver screen features, four made-for-TV flicks; d. Jan. 30, 1999.

Ken Nordine, Aug. 14, 1911, Cherokee, Iowa; actor, announcer, emcee; dozen-plus 1940s–50s series as narrator—*Biography in Sound*, *The Breakfast Club*, *Armstrong of the SBI*, *Silver Eagle—Mountie*, *Welcome Travelers*, others — and acting on *Sky King*, *World's Great Novels*; d. Sept. 15, 1993.

Deaths

Eugene Lock Baker, Aug. 14, 1981, Burbank, Calif.; b. Jan. 11, 1910. Oscar Levant, Aug. 14, 1972, Beverly Hills, Calif.; b. Dec. 27, 1906.

August 15

Sound Bite

CBS Radio affiliates hammering web officials for years to sharply reduce chain schedule so they (local stations) can sell time more profitably at home; threat of mutiny dissipates Aug. 15, 1960 when radio president Arthur Hull Hayes announces that — effective Nov. 25, 1960 — net will drastically pare down its offerings to handful of daytime/primetime features, mostly five-minute variety, plus 10 minutes of news on hour starting Nov. 28, 1960; if anybody hasn't suspicioned which medium is expendable already, here's final confirmation.

Birth

Johnny Roventini, Aug. 15, 1910, Brooklyn, N.Y.; bellhop, commercial mascot for Philip Morris Co. bka pint-sized man in signature red usher's jacket with gold trim, striped trousers, black pillbox hat, white gloves "stepping out of thousands of store windows" where life-sized cardboard figure advertised Philip Morris cigarettes for sale within, or cheerily bidding on radio-TV broadcasts: "Callllllll for Phillllllllip Morraisseeeeeeee!"; in stroke of genius, four-foot bellhop at New Yorker Hotel hired 1933 to put Philip Morris on map on series like *Johnny Presents* (diverse musical, variety, drama shows) CBS/NBC 1937–46, *The Philip Morris Playhouse* CBS/NBC 1941–44, 1948–49, 1951–53; TV, too (*Candid Camera*, *I Love Lucy*, etc.) though Johnny replaced in some early 1950s TV spots by dancing girls wearing oversized cigarette packs; persisted, however, to 1974 retirement, paid $50,000 annually at peak; d. Nov. 30, 1998.

Deaths

Ford Bond, Aug. 15, 1962, St. Croix, U. S. Virgin Islands; b. Oct. 23, 1904. Jack Mather, Aug. 15, 1966, Wauconda, Ill.; b. Sept. 21, 1907. Will Rogers, Aug. 15, 1935, Point Barrow, Alas.; b. Nov. 4, 1879. John Cameron Swayze, Aug. 15, 1995, Sarasota, Fla.; b. April 4, 1906.

August 16

Sound Bite

American Federation of Radio Artists (AFRA), forerunner of present American Federation of Television and Radio Artists (AFTRA), is formed Aug. 16, 1937; Actors' Equity Association, loosely organized predecessor union dating from 1936, renounces its authority, allowing AFRA to become first coalition to foster serious clout in representing working radio performers in U. S.; as time elapses, AFRA will grow in numerical strength as well as pervasive influence.

When radio time sales decline five percent in 1954 from previous year—first dip since 1938 — and purveyors of doom profess dark assessments of radio's viability for future in array of areas, on Aug. 16, 1954 CBS announces it's combining radio, TV news operations, until then totally distinct; TV news chief Sig Mickelson named net's news guru, given VP status, staff of 376 (formerly 13); ominous sign that industry isn't pinning fortunes on radio any longer.

Birth

Walter Kinsella, Aug. 16, 1900, New York, N.Y.; actor (stage, film, radio, TV); support roles in *Abie's Irish Rose*, *Dick Tracy*, *Joe and Mabel*, *Leave It to Mike*, *The Mighty Casey*, *Mr. and Mrs. North*, *Mr. District Attorney*, *Stella Dallas*, *That's My Pop*, more; eight Broadway plays 1927–59, two cinematic films 1930/1950, 15 TV dramas/sitcoms/variety shows 1951–66; d. May 11, 1975.

Deaths

Jay Jackson, Aug. 16, 2005, Jupiter, Fla.; b. Nov. 4, 1918. Raymond Edward Johnson, Aug. 16, 2001, Wallingford, Conn.; b. July 24, 1911. Carl Webster Pierce, Aug. 16, 1962, Los Angeles, Calif.; b. June 30, 1898. George Stone, Aug. 16, 1991, Traverse City, Mich.; b. April 5, 1920. Orin Tovrov, Aug. 16, 1980, Boston, Mass.; b. April 30, 1911.

August 17

Canceled

Silver Theater, Aug. 17, 1947; debut Oct. 3, 1937.

Births

Walter F. Herlihy, Aug. 17, 1914, Dorchester, Mass.; announcer bka first staff man at ABC Radio moved to television where he presented multi pioneering series headlined by entertainers Gloria DeHaven, Lisa Ferraday, early 1950s *Blind Date, Dr. I. Q.—the Mental Banker, Kraft Television Theater*; 1940s radio intros included *The Best Bands in the Land, Dorothy Kilgallen's Diary, Police Woman, Powers Charm School*; d. Oct. 6, 1956.

Quincy Howe, Aug. 17, 1900, Boston, Mass.; author, commentator, educator, freelance writer, newscaster; joined New York WQXR 1939–42 followed by nightly news commentaries MBS, CBS, ABC; fired by CBS for making sponsor unhappy 1947, exited radio to teach journalism, returned 1953 to ABC; narrated local series in epoch on New York WCBS; extensive yet fleeting TV stints 1940s–60s CBS, ABC; wrote more about radio commentary than peers e.g. *The News and How to Understand It* (Simon & Schuster, 1940); d. Feb. 19, 1977.

Deaths

Ed Gardner, Aug. 17, 1963, Los Angeles, Calif.; b. June 29, 1901. William Redfield, Aug. 17, 1976, New York City, N.Y.; b. Jan. 26, 1927.

August 18

Births

Tom Moore, Aug. 18, 1912; announcer, emcee, vocalist bka master of ceremonies of mid 20th century MBS daytime audience participation features *Ladies Be Seated, Ladies Fair*; interlocutor of 1940s *Captain Midnight, The Quiz Kids*, few more, hosted primetime *Meet Your Match*; emanated from vaudeville clan, sang with bands before going on Chicago radio 1939 understudying with Tommy Bartlett at WBBM on audience participation entries *Meet the Missus, The Missus Goes to Market* (Bartlett ultimately shined on *Welcome Travelers*); presided over few pithy TV shows; d. April 1986 (precise date elusive despite many efforts), San Antonio, Texas.

Walter O'Keefe, Aug. 18, 1900, Hartford, Conn.; actor, emcee, stage show entertainer, quizmaster bka *Double or Nothing* master of ceremonies 1947–54; went on radio mid 1920s—early ethereal gigs *The Lucky Strike Magic Carpet, The Jack Pearl Show, The Saturday Night Party, The Tuesday Night Party, The Walter O'Keefe Show, Town Hall Tonight, The Al Jolson Show, The Packard Hour*; *Battle of the Sexes* 1942–44, temporarily replaced Don McNeill presiding over *The Breakfast Club* mid 1940s leading to *Double or Nothing*; *The Wizard of Odds* emcee 1949–54, played self in video series *Mayor of Hollywood* 1952, *Two for the Money* TV quizmaster 1954; frequently on NBC weekend radio marathon *Monitor* 1957–59; shortly before death said conquering alcohol greatest single achievement of life; d. June 26, 1983.

Perry Ward, Aug. 18, 1914, Tulsa, Okla.; announcer, emcee; hosted *Expectant Father* 1946, *Scramby Amby* intermittently 1943–47, *What's Doin', Ladies?* 1945–46, same decade opened *Aunt Mary, Duffy's Tavern, Gaslight Gaieties, Gene Autry's Melody Ranch, Jimmy Wakeley's Western Song Parade, Strange Wills, The Theater of Famous Radio Players*; d. May 29, 1989.

Deaths

Bennett Kilpack, Aug. 18, 1962, Santa Monica, Calif.; b. Feb. 6, 1883. Lawson Zerbe, Aug. 18, 1992 (final residence Franklin, N.J.); b. March 20, 1914.

August 19

Sound Bite

Amos 'n' Andy network premier, Aug. 19, 1929, NBC Blue, epic archetypical sitcom instituting conversational dialogue between familiar figures; leads posed as blacks by whites in lively comedic exchanges — Freeman Gosden (Amos Jones), Charles Correll (Andrew H. Brown); proffered rudimentary soap opera elements; inadvertently sold radios to millions as home entertainment devices; final broadcast under moniker CBS May 22, 1955, principals prevailed in *The Amos 'n' Andy Music Hall* Sept. 13, 1954-Nov. 25, 1960, CBS.

Births

Don Carney (Howard Rice), Aug. 19, 1886, St. Joseph, Mich.; actor, announcer, emcee, pianist, recording artist, vocalist bka *Uncle Don* juvenile series host New York WOR ca. 1926–47, MBS 1938–39; d. Jan. 14, 1954.

Katherine Elizabeth (Marie) Wilson, Aug. 19, 1916, Anaheim, Calif.; actress (stage, film, radio, TV) bka *My Friend Irma* sitcom ditzy blonde Irma Peterson 1947–54, CBS-TV 1952–54; Broadway dancer initially, at 18 returned to West Coast to appear in 51 primarily B-films 1934–62, mired in parts similar to Irma Peterson's character, expressing some dismay; later played in two made-for-TV movies, 11 guest shots on tube, summer stock, dinner theater, commercials, nightcubs; d. Nov. 23, 1972.

Deaths

Cathleen Cordell, Aug. 19, 1997, Los Angeles, Calif.; b. May 21, 1915. Groucho Marx, Aug. 19, 1977, Los Angeles, Calif.; b. Oct. 2, 1890.

August 20

Births

Andre Baruch, Aug. 20, 1908, Holland; announcer, pianist bka *Your Hit Parade* interlocutor 1936–47, NBC-TV 1950–57, with wife-singer Bea Wain on syndicated reprise of original radio version; introduced 1930s-50s listeners to *The American Album of Familiar Music, The Andrews Sisters Eight-to-the-Bar Ranch, Bobby Benson and the B-Bar-B Riders, Guy Lombardo Time, Just Plain Bill, The Kate Smith Show, Little Orphan Annie, Marie — the Little French Princess, Myrt and Marge, Second Husband, The Shadow,* many others; major commercial spokesman for American Tobacco Co. (Lucky Strike) 22 years; he, Wain had record music gigs New York WMCA 1950s, West Palm Beach WPBR 1970s; d. Sept. 15, 1991.

Theodore (Ted) Donaldson, Aug. 20, 1933, New York City, N.Y.; actor (stage, film, radio, TV), bookseller, dialectician, recording artist, vocalist bka *Father Knows Best* family sitcom son Bud Anderson 1949–54.

Stefan Hatos, Aug. 20, 1920, Aurora, Ill.; ad agency broadcast exec (Foote, Cone & Belding), announcer, director, English horn player, oboeist, producer, saxophonist, writer; hired at Detroit WJLB 1939, in three months shifted to rival WXYZ as staff announcer with NBC Blue ties; penned episodes *The Green Hornet, The Lone Ranger* at WXYZ, *The Hermit's Cave* at rival WJR; *The March of Time* regional producer-director-scribe; CBS New York producer-director-scribe on *Beulah, The Curt Massey Show, David Harding — Counterspy, David Harum, The Green Hornet, It Pays to Be Married, Ladies Be Seated, Meet Corliss Archer, Nick Carter — Master Detective, Treasury Agent, Welcome Travelers, Your Hit Parade,* more; by 1948, assisted FCB bringing to TV fare like *Al Pearce and His Gang, The Bob Hope Show, Fun for the Money, It Could Be You, It Pays to Be Ignorant, Let's Make a Deal, Masquerade Party, Split Second, The Tony Martin Show, Three for the Money*; enduring partnership with Monty Hall led to creation, production of myriad game shows; d. March 2, 1999.

Floyd Neal, Aug. 20, 1906, Plymouth County, Iowa; announcer bka 1930s-40s opener for *Uncle Don, Viennese Nights* (only substantiated series though he narrated *Tribute to George Gershwin* MBS July 15, 1937); d. Dec. 22, 1985.

Theodore Alan Reed (Herbert Theodore "Teddy" Bergman), Aug. 20, 1907, New York City, N.Y.; actor (stage, film, radio, TV), dialectician, voiceover artist bka *Life with Luigi* conniving cohort Pasquale 1948–54, Fred Flintstone in successive TV animated cartoon series 1960–66, 1967–70, 1972–74; d. June 14, 1977.

John ("John R") Richbourg, Aug. 20, 1910, Manning, S.C.; actor, disc jockey, newscaster bka "patron saint" of rhythm and blues below Mason-Dixon line with nightly record show over Nashville's extensive 50,000-watt WLAC 1947–73; exposed numerous performers to vast audience leading to national acclaim: Chuck Berry, James Brown, Bo Diddley, Aretha Franklin, Marvin Gaye, B. B. King, Gladys Knight, Little Richard (Penniman), Wilson Pickett, Otis Redding, Ike and Tina Turner, Jackie Wilson, others; Richbourg won dramatic parts in *Gang-busters, Lorenzo Jones, Our Gal Sunday, Second Husband*, similar fare 1929–41; d. Feb. 15, 1986.

Death

Vivian Fridell, Aug. 20, 1998, Wilmette, Ill.; b. Oct. 15, 1912.

August 21

Births

Kenneth L. Carpenter, Aug. 21, 1900, Avon, Ill.; announcer (radio, TV), commercial spokesman, voiceover artist, sportscaster bka interlocutor for copious prestigious 1930s to 1950s series—*The Bing Crosby Show* (multiple appellations), *The Edgar Bergen and Charlie McCarthy Show, The Great Gildersleeve, The Life of Riley, Lux Radio Theater, Meet Corliss Archer, One Man's Family, Truth or Consequences*, TV *Lux Video Theatre* 1950–57; Crosby's permanent announcer on five successive audio series; legions video commercials; d. Oct. 16, 1984.

Carlton KaDell, Aug. 21, 1907, Danville, Ill.; actor, announcer, emcee, vocalist, writer; toured with thespians on a Chautauqua circuit before playing in stock; at 23 hired by Chicago WJJD to act, announce, sing, write; three months hence a freelance thespian, interlocutor on West Coast 1932–39, returning to Windy City for recurring role in *The Romance of Helen Trent*; making way back to Coast, came "home" to Chicago early 1950s to stay, acting in *Hawkins Falls* daytime serial NBC-TV 1953-ca. 1955; hired by local KEFM Radio late in career; from late 1930s-early 1950s linked to *Amos 'n' Andy, Armstrong of the SBI, Backstage Wife, Big Town, The Dorothy Lamour Show, The Edgar Bergen and Charlie McCarthy Show, The Jack Carson Show, Kay Fairchild—Stepmother, Masquerade, Mayor of the Town, Red Ryder, The Right to Happiness, The Road of Life, The Saint, Sky King, Tarzan*, dozen or so more; d. March 14, 1975.

Deaths

Frank Bingman, Aug. 21, 1988, Warrenton, Va.; b. April 9, 1914. Jean Paul King, Aug. 21, 1965, Los Angeles, Calif.; b. Dec. 1, 1904. Fulton Lewis, Jr., Aug. 21, 1966, Washington, D.C.; b. April 30, 1903.

August 22

Canceled

Rocky Jordan, Aug. 22, 1951, CBS; debut (*A Man Named Jordan*) Jan. 8, 1945.

Births

Ray Douglas Bradbury, Aug. 22, 1920, Waukegan, Ill.; prolific fantasy-horror-mystery-science fiction book author, wordsmith (film, radio, stage, TV dramas) bka *Dimension X, X-Minus-One* original playwright.

James Meighan, Aug. 22, 1906, New York City, N.Y.; actor (stage, radio) bka prolific aural thespian 1930s-50s, perennial masculine lead in daytime serials—*Alias Jimmy Valentine, Backstage Wife, Dot and Will, I Love Linda Dale, Lora Lawton, Marie—the Little French Princess, Orphans of Divorce*—while hero in *The Falcon, Flash Gordon*, more; running parts-guest roles repertoire: *Against the Storm, Death Valley Days, Hearthstone of the Death Squad, Just Plain Bill, Mr. Keen—Tracer of Lost Persons, The Romance of Helen Trent*, many others; in stock, Broadway productions earlier; nephew of silent screen star-Paramount matinee idol Thomas Meighan (1879–1936); d. June 20, 1970.

Lesley Woods, Aug. 22, 1910, Berwick, Iowa; actress (radio, film, TV, stage) bka girlfriend-confidante of aural sleuth trio—*Boston Blackie, Casey—Crime Photographer, The Shadow*; daytimer on *Backstage Wife, Bright Horizon, The Guiding Light, Joyce Jordan—Girl Interne, The Road of Life, The Romance of Helen Trent, Rosemary, This Is Nora Drake, We Love and Learn, Woman in White*; shifted to TV easily in dozen-plus primarily soap sagas 1959–2001: *Young Doctor Malone, The Secret Storm, The Edge of Night, A Flame in the Wind, The Nurses, Search for Tomorrow, Bright Promise, Return to Peyton Place, General Hospital, Days of Our Lives, Dear Detective, All My Children, The Bold and the Beautiful*, 40 one-time roles in sundry TV dramas, 16-made-for TV flicks, six theatrical films, on Broadway in *A Case of Libel* 1963–64; d. Aug. 2, 2003.

Deaths

Robert R. Dixon, Aug. 22, 1998, Bethel, Conn.; b. April 11, 1911. Helen Hiett (Waller), Aug. 22, 1961, Chamonix, France; b. Sept. 23, 1913. Del King, Aug. 22, 1964, St. Louis, Mo.; b. May 18, 1908.

August 23

Births

Bob Crosby, Aug. 23, 1913, Spokane, Washing ton; impresario (Bob Crosby's Bobcats ensemble), recording artist, vocalist (personal appearances, radio, TV) bka headliner of CBS Radio *Club Fifteen* 1947–49, 1950–53, CBS-TV *The Bob Crosby Show* 1953–57; frequently in shadow of more renowned nine-years-senior sibling Bing; d. March 9, 1993.

John J. McCarthy, Aug. 23, 1914, New York City, N.Y.; bka NBC staff announcer, linking there March 13, 1936; d. May 24, 1996.

John Booth Nesbitt, Aug. 23, 1910, Victoria, British Columbia, Canada; actor (radio, stage), announcer, commentator, print journalist (Seattle, Spokane newspapers); toured with Northwest stock company, managed road shows for New York troupe; following brief foray into print, signed with Spokane station as announcer, joined San Francisco NBC 1933; local feature *Headlines of the Past* gained acclaim, shifting between three chains as *The Passing Parade* intermittently 1937–51; MGM engaged him to produce movie shorts under same moniker; brought *So the Story Goes*, *Treasury Star Parade* to radio fans while playing in *Family Theater*, *Fibber McGee & Molly*, *Radio Reader's Digest*, delivering bulletins with *John Nesbitt and the News*; d. Aug. 10, 1960.

J. Olin Tice, Jr., Aug. 23, 1919, Savannah, Ga.; announcer; ethereal pilgrimage carried him from Anderson, S.C. WAIM to Greenville, S.C. WFBC, Columbia, S.C. WIS, WCOS, Durham, N.C. WDNC, Charlotte WBT 1943, Washington, D.C. WTOP 1943; ephemeral list of 1950s CBS programs included *The Galen Drake Show*, *Mr. Keen—Tracer of Lost Persons* (relief announcer), *There's Music in the Air*; d. Jan. 8, 1998.

Deaths

David Rose, Aug. 23, 1990, Burbank, Calif.; b. June 15, 1910. Wilmer Walter, Aug. 23, 1941, New York City, N.Y.; b. Feb. 9, 1881.

August 24

Canceled

My Friend Irma, Aug. 24, 1954, CBS; debut April 11, 1947.

Births

Don Douglas (Douglas Kinleyside), Aug. 24, 1905, London, England; actor (film, radio), announcer, played all roles for *The Black Castle* 1942–44; acted in same era's *Kelly's Courthouse*, *Scattergood Baines*; career ended when he died after appendectomy; d. Dec. 31, 1945.

James M. (Jimmy) Fidler, Aug. 24, 1900, St. Louis, Mo.; commentator, journalist, publicist bka *Jimmy Fidler in Hollywood* gossipmongering series under multi appellations via networks, syndication 1933–1970s; Fidler hoped to be screen idol but failed, edited *The Hollywood News* 1920, press agent for Sid Grauman/studios/stars; pursued scandalous tidbits for fanzines, newspapers, penned syndicated column hitting 360 journals at peak; contributed gossip to Fox Movietone newsreels in cinema houses; on ether with own show competing with Louella Parsons, Hedda Hopper—"He was more feared by some studios and stars than Hopper or Parsons" author John Dunning averred; d. Aug. 9, 1988.

Dennis James, Aug. 24, 1917, Jersey City, N.J.; actor, announcer, emcee, sportscaster—Dumont hired him in those capacities for fledgling New York-based service to 300 TV set owners 1938; worked Jersey City WATT Radio to 1940, shifted to New York WNEW; late 1940s *Lawyer Q* master of ceremonies while introducing *The Peter Donald Show*, *Ted Mack's Original Amateur Hour*; returned to TV making mint with score of audience participation features mid 1940s-80 e.g. *Cash and Carry*, *Stop the Music!*, *The Dennis James Show*, *Chance of a Lifetime*, *Judge for Yourself*, *The Name's the Same*, *On Your Account*, *Two for the Money*, *High Finance*, *Your First Impression*, *Can You Top This?*, *The Price Is Right*, *Name That Tune*, et al.; d. June 3, 1997.

Durward Kirby, Aug. 24, 1911, Covington, Ky.; actor, announcer, author, commercial spokesman, dancer, disc jockey, emcee, newscaster, vocalist bka proverbial "second banana," sidekick on string of radio, TV variety features under *The Garry Moore Show* moniker CBS Radio 1950, 1959–61, CBS-TV 1950–58 (daytime), 1958–64, 1966–67 (primetime); on radio at Indianapolis WFBM 1934, Cincinnati WLW 1935, Chicago 1937 on NBC, WENR, WMAQ; led listeners into 1940s-50s *Herb Shriner Time*, *Break the Bank*, *The Breakfast Club*, *Club Mati-*

nee (hosted by Moore), *The Fred Waring Show, Here's to Romance, Hilltop House, Li'l Abner, Lone Journey, The Quiz Kids, Sunday Dinner at Aunt Fanny's, Two for the Money*, more; dispensed news on *Crisco Radio Newspaper, Press Radio News;* presided on *Honeymoon in New York*; *Candid Camera* with Allen Funt CBS-TV 1961–66; penned three tomes; d. March 15, 2000.

Deaths

Mary Jane Croft, Aug. 24, 1999, Los Angeles, Calif.; b. Feb. 15, 1916. E. G. Marshall, Aug. 24, 1998, Bedford N.Y.; b. June 18, 1914. Amanda Randolph, Aug. 24, 1967, Duarte, Calif.; b. Sept. 2, 1896. Dick Wynn, Aug. 24, 1996, Gardena, Calif.; b. April 16, 1909.

August 25

Debuting

Father Knows Best, Aug. 25, 1949, NBC; billed as "Radio's Most Typical Family" sitcom; household featuring patriarch Jim Anderson (Robert Young), matriarch Margaret Anderson (Jean Vander Pyl), three offspring, interaction in daily life depicting predominant moral values; final radiocast April 25, 1954; televersion — Robert Young with different cast, 1954–60, network repeats 1960–67, syndication 1967–80, unlimited reruns thereafter by cable.

Give and Take, Aug. 25, 1945, CBS; quiz; players chose gifts, tried to win them in question rounds as John Reed King hosted; mainstay of CBS Saturday matinee schedule though aired briefly in summers 1946, 1947 late weekday afternoons in addition to Saturdays; final broadcast Dec. 26, 1953.

Birth

Lester Anthony O'Keefe (pseudonym Allan Stuart), Aug. 25, 1896, St. Louis, Mo.; announcer, director, disc jockey, lyricist, producer, vocalist, writer bka text scribe for "La Rosita," Paul Dupont composition enjoying success in film by same name in 1923 starring Mary Pickford, recorded by several renowned artists 1920s-50s like Tommy Dorsey, Benny Goodman, Jimmy Dorsey, Four Aces; penned many more songs 1920s, one heard in 1952 film *Stars and Stripes Forever*; debuted as tenor soloist Newark WJZ early 1920s; opened Dorothy Kilgallen's *Voice of Broadway* aural newspaper gossip column CBS 1941–42, announced/directed/produced plethora of NBC Radio features 1940s, DJ at WJZ early 1950s; national president Radio Actors Guild 1950; d. June 19, 1977.

August 26

Births

Phil Baker, Aug. 26, 1896, Philadelphia, Pa.; accordionist, author, comedian, emcee, lyricist, quizmaster, stage entertainer bka *Take It or Leave It* (*The $64 Question*) master of ceremonies 1941–47, 1951; d. Nov. 30, 1963.

Jack Berch, Aug. 26, 1907, Sigel, Ill.; door-to-door salesman, impresario, vocalist (baritone) bka ebullient showman combined whistling, chatting, singing, poetry in *The Jack Berch Show* (*Jack Berch and His Boys*) 1936–54, daytime quarter-hour billed as "friendliest show in radio"; unique component "Heart-to-Heart Hookup" shared incidents of less-fortunate listeners, earmarked tunes for them; d. Dec. 10, 1992.

Harold T. (Hal) Gibney, Aug. 26, 1911, Woodland, Calif.; announcer, emcee bka *Tales of the Texas Rangers* interlocutor 1950–52 whose stentorian-toned delivery memorably compelling: "Texas! More than 260,000 square miles! And 50 men who make up the most famous and oldest law enforcement body in North America!"; before joining NBC Hollywood 1936 career in previous five years spanned San Francisco KSFO, KTAB, Portland KGW; presented enduring favorites *Dr. I. Q.— the Mental Banker, Dragnet, Hawthorne House, Irene Rich Dramas, The Magic Key of RCA, Walter Winchell*; d. June 5, 1973.

George Francis Hicks, Aug. 26, 1905, Tacoma, Wash.; announcer, newscaster bka taping German bombing mission D-Day June 6, 1944 which became classic bit of wartime drama, confirmed Hicks' credentials as major newsman; beat 100 candidates auditioning to announce at Washington, D.C. WRC 1928, joined New York WEAF/NBC 1929, created light features, covered 1936 political campaigns; Blue web's sole foreign correspondent (London) 1942–45; linked to 1930s-50s *Death Valley Days, The Jack Benny Program, Seth Parker*, more; tapped by U. S. Steel

Co. as spokesman on *The U. S. Steel Hour* 1945–53 radio, 1953–63 TV—18 years' employment; hosted other video ventures like public affairs series *The U.N. in Action* CBS-TV 1955–59; d. March 17, 1965.

Irving R. Levine, Aug. 26, 1922, Pawtucket, R.I.; commentator, correspondent, newscaster, print/wire journalist bka first full-time network TV reporter covering economy ("pioneer of economics reporting on TV" said *Time*), NBC News financial guru, then delivered *Nightly Business Report* commentaries PBS; NBC reporter more than 35 years including four in Moscow, 10 in Rome, two in Tokyo, year in London before nasal-sounding dateline at end of stories: "Irving R. Levine...NBC News... Washington"; dispatches on NBC top-of-the-hour news, *Monitor*, NBC-TV *Today*, *NBC Nightly News*; started at *The Providence Journal-Bulletin*, then International News Service bureau chief at Vienna.

Deaths

Art Baker, Aug. 26, 1966, Los Angeles, Calif.; b. Jan. 7, 1898. Larry Keating, Aug. 26, 1963, Hollywood, Calif.; b. April 13, 1899. Knox Manning, Aug. 26, 1980, Woodland Hills, Calif.; b. Jan. 17, 1904. Julie Stevens, Aug. 26, 1984, Wellfleet, Mass.; b. Nov. 23, 1916.

August 27

Births

George Archibald (Arch) Presby, Aug. 27, 1907, Sherbrooke, Quebec, Canada; announcer, emcee bka Froggy the Gremlin who plunked magic twanger when summoned by host on *Smilin' Ed and His Buster Brown Gang* NBC 1944–53, NBC-TV 1950–54, 1957–58 (latter season *Andy's Gang*), materialized onstage, turning studio of precocious tykes into unbridled raucous adolescents; on air at hometown station 1925, joined Portland, Ore. KEX 1929, shifted to rival outlet KGW 1930, San Francisco NBC staff 1937, rose to web's chief L.A. announcer, retiring 1972; *Bughouse Rhythm* music commentator 1937, opened late 1940s-early 1950s *The Cass Daley Show*, *The Truitts*, *Your Crossword Quiz*, hosted *Breakfast in Hollywood*, local juvenile TV show *Uncle Archie*; d. Jan. 22, 2007.

Larry Thor (Arnleifur Lawrence Thorsteinson), Aug. 27, 1916, Lundar, Manitoba, Canada; actor, announcer, film narrator, newscaster, vocalist, writer; on air singing, writing at Flin Flon, Manitoba CFAR, announcing at Timmins, Ontario CKGB, newscasting at Toronto CKCL, reporting for CBS at Montreal, narrating industrial films, short subjects; joined Hollywood KFAC as announcer, moved to rival KMPC as newscaster, announced CBS shows 1948–1950s—*The Carnation Family Party*, *The Clyde Beatty Show*, *The Green Lama*, *Rocky Jordan*, *Suspense*; acted in *Broadway Is My Beat* 1949–54; d. March 15, 1976.

Vicki (Wilkinson) Vola, Aug. 27, 1911, Denver, Colo.; actress; premiered on hometown KLZ 1933 before brief Hollywood stint acting in radio drama, putting roots down in New York City 1938; beyond principals' duties 1939–40 CBS soap operas *Brenda Curtis*, *Manhattan Mother*, portfolio bulged with *The Adventures of Christopher Wells*, *Backstage Wife*, *Buck Rogers in the 25th Century*, *The Cisco Kid*, *Crime Doctor*, *The Fat Man*, *Ford Theater*, *Foreign Assignment*, *Jungle Jim*, *The Man I Married*, *Manhunt*, *Mr. District Attorney*, *The Mystery Man*, *Our Gal Sunday*, *The Road of Life*, *Under Arrest*, *Yours Truly—Johnny Dollar*; housekeeper-murderer Harriet Baxter in *Search for Tomorrow* CBS-TV 1959–60; d. July 21, 1985.

Deaths

Gracie Allen, Aug. 27, 1964, Hollywood, Calif.; b. July 26, 1895. Phillips Carlin, Aug. 27, 1971, New York City, N.Y.; b. June 30, 1894. Jinx Falkenburg, Aug. 27, 2003, Long Island, N.Y.; b. Jan. 21, 1919.

August 28

Sound Bite

Although multiple experimental broadcasting stations advertised for years (see *Sold on Radio* by this author), a plug for residential apartment living over New York WEAF Aug. 28, 1922 captured imagination of most radio historians who cited it as "first commercial aired in America"; underwriter Queensborough Corp. put $50 in WEAF coffers for 10-minute diatribe on joys of residing at rental properties in Jackson Heights; pitched by H. M. Blackwell, plug turned out to be radio's first informercial, airing in "drive time" at 5 o'clock — long before radios affixed as extras in cars (or horse-driven buggies).

Canceled

The Bickersons, Aug. 28, 1951, CBS; debut Sept. 8, 1946. *Leave It to Joan* (*The Joan Davis Show*), Aug. 28, 1950, CBS; debut July 8, 1943. *Live Like a Millionaire*, Aug. 28, 1953, ABC; debut June 5, 1950. (*The Private Lives of*) *Ethel and Albert*, Aug. 28, 1950, ABC; debut May 29, 1944.

Births

Diana Bourbon, Aug. 28, 1900, New York City, N.Y.; director, producer; d. March 19, 1978.

John F. Holbrook, Aug. 28, 1910, Cameron, Wis.; announcer, director; served dual key stations — Chicago WGN, Hollywood KHJ later; 1931 recipient radio diction award of American Academy of Arts and Letters; presented 1930s-50s fans *The Bickersons, Chicago Theater of the Air, Dinah Shore, Double or Nothing, The Horace Heidt Show, Little Known Facts About Well Known People, Newspaper of the Air, The Philip Morris Playhouse, The Red Skelton Show, This Is Your Life*; directed *Moon Dreams* 1946–47; d. Sept. 20, 1978.

H. Norman Schwarzkopf, Sr., Aug. 28, 1895, Newark, N.J.; announcer, state police chief (New Jersey 1921–36) bka *Gangbusters* narrator 1938–42 — producer Phillips Lord capitalized on notoriety of Lindbergh kidnapping, execution of Bruno Hauptman for it during chief's watch; d. Nov. 25, 1958.

August 29

Births

Arthur Anderson, Aug. 29, 1922, Staten Island, N.Y.; actor (stage, radio, TV) bka *Let's Pretend* juvenile narrative thespian in plethora of make-believe parts CBS 1936–54; portfolio expanded to *American School of the Air, Aunt Jenny's Real Life Stories, Big Sister* (product spokesman), *Hotel for Pets, Lawyer Tucker, Mercury Theater, Tony and Gus*, more; multi TV roles; penned *Let's Pretend: A History of Radio's Best Loved Children's Show by a Longtime Cast Member* 1994, reprised as *Let's Pretend and the Golden Age of Radio* 2004; performs at Friends of Old Time Radio conventions annually at Newark, N.J.

Lurene Tuttle, Aug. 29, 1907, Pleasant Lake, Ind.; actress (film, radio, stage); originated part of Marjorie Forrester, niece of *The Great Gildersleeve*, left after three seasons 1941–44 to appear in 44 theatrical motion pictures, 12 made-for-TV films, five running parts on TV series, 114 solo performances on tube; d. May 28, 1986.

Willard Lewis Waterman, Aug. 29, 1914, Madison, Wis.; actor (stage, film, radio, TV), commercial spokesman bka *The Great Gildersleeve* pompous windbag-Summerfield water commissioner Throckmorton P. Gildersleeve 1950–58; entered national Chicago radio hub 1935 (*The Romance of Helen Trent, Ma Perkins, The Chicago Theater of the Air*), sometimes paired with Hal Peary in *The Tom Mix Ralston Straightshooters*— Peary's successor as Gildy years hence; later gigs *Kay Fairchild — Stepmother, Those Websters, The Guiding Light, The Damon Runyon Theater, The Amos 'n' Andy Show, My Friend Irma, Lux Radio Theater, The Halls of Ivy*; 35 B-films 1949–73, more than score TV guest shots; nearly 2000 Broadway performances in *Mame* from 1966, continued in London; 1980 radio commercial for Sony won coveted CLIO trophy; d. Feb. 2, 1995.

Deaths

Kathryn C. Cravens, Aug. 29, 1991, Burkett, Texas; b. Oct. 27, 1898. Lowell Thomas, Aug. 29, 1981, Pawling, N.Y.; b. April 6, 1892.

August 30

Debuting

Walter Winchell (*The Jergens Journal, Walter Winchell's Journal*), May 12, 1930, CBS; gossipmonger; syndicated columnist who — like rivals Jimmy Fidler, Hedda Hopper, Louella Parsons, others — jumped to radio with startling revelations gained by snooping among fêted Hollywood idols; in heyday Winchell print column reached 2000 papers giving maximum exposure to Sunday night ethereal diatribes; fought tenaciously like contemporaries to air juicy tidbits first; declared modern wag: "Today, looking back at the period of Winchell's greatest popularity in the 1930s and 1940s, it is hard to imagine the power he possessed and the ruthlessness with which he used it"; less-than-acclaimed TV exponents ABC/NBC/syndication 1952–60; final radiocast March 3, 1957.

Canceled

Terry Regan, Attorney at Law, Aug. 30, 1938, NBC; debut Jan. 3, 1938. *When a Girl Marries*, Aug. 30, 1957, ABC; debut May 29, 1939.

Births

Shirley Booth (Thelma Marjorie Ford), Aug. 30, 1898, New York City, N.Y.; actress (film, radio, stage) bka *Duffy's Tavern* figure Miss Duffy 1941–43; costar 1952 film *Come Back, Little Sheba* as drab housewife Lola Delaney; *Hazel* TV sitcom as irrepressible housekeeper Hazel Burke 1961–66 ; d. Oct. 16, 1992.

John Joseph Gunther, Aug. 30, 1901, Chicago, Ill.; author, commentator, correspondent, print journalist (*The Chicago Daily News*), bka author, string of *Inside* volumes 1930s-60s (*Inside Africa, Asia, Europe, Latin America*, etc.), three dozen more — most prolific ex-electronic journalist in print; *NBC News* reporter 1939–41, *John Gunther Comments* host 1941, 1943–44; U. S. War Department stringer 1942–44; *Information Please* guest panelist 1930s-40s; *John Gunther's High Road* travelogue host ABC-TV 1959–60; d. May 29, 1970.

August 31

Debuting

The Great Gildersleeve, Aug. 31, 1941, NBC (figure initiated on *Fibber McGee & Molly* Sept. 26, 1939, spun off); sitcom involving unmarried Springfield water commissioner Throckmorton P. Gildersleeve (Hal Peary 1941–50, Willard Waterman 1950–58) fancying self as ladies' man; two wards in care, Negro housekeeper, plethora of chums interacting; final radiocast March 27, 1958; fleeting syndicated TV extension 1955.

Hop Harrigan, Aug. 31, 1942, NBC Blue; juvenile adventure serial with aerial themes; bombing missions, dogfights with America's adversaries part of day's work for 18-year-old air ace Harrigan (Albert Aley, Chester Stratton), copilot Tank Tinker (Jackson Beck, Ken Lynch), Hop's honey Gail Nolan (Mitzi Gould); youthful trio risked lives for nation — captured, held in concentration camps, yet beat odds by sheer wit, agility; originated DC comics; final broadcast Feb. 6, 1948.

The Prudential Family Hour (*The Prudential Family Hour of Stars*), Aug. 31, 1941, CBS; concert music, drama; music ranging from pop to opera over seven seasons alongside pithy composer narrative; Metropolitan Opera artists Eileen Farrell, Patrice Munsel, Risë Stevens, Gladys Swarthout supported by vocalists Ross Graham, Sterling Holloway, Jack Smith, comments by music critic Deems Taylor; after two seasons, Prudential offered dramas headlined by Hollywood legends Humphrey Bogart, Bette Davis, Gregory Peck, Ginger Rogers, Barbara Stanwyck, Robert Taylor, special guests; final broadcast Feb. 26, 1950.

Canceled

The Abbott Mysteries, Aug. 31, 1947, MBS; debut June 10, 1945.

Births

Lawrence K. (Larry) Elliott, Aug. 31, 1900, Washington, D.C.; actor, announcer, newscaster bka *Mr. Keen—Tracer of Lost Persons* most durable interlocutor 1943–51 ("It's time now for Mr. Keen, Tracer of Lost Persons"); CBS's chief White House reporter mid 1930s, fill-in for Arthur Godfrey when Godfrey late for wakeup program at Washington WJSV; transferred to New York CBS October 1938, later became freelance announcer beckoning listeners to daytime serials (*Barry Cameron, Front Page Farrell, The Strange Romance of Evelyn Winters*), primetime features (*The American Melody Hour, The Bob Hawk Show, Boston Blackie, The Texaco Star Theater, Treasury Star Parade*); performed in *Kraft Theater* NBC-TV 1956; d. July 27, 1957.

Cedric W. Foster, Aug. 31, 1900 (copious sources futile in confirming place); commentator, newscaster, print journalist, publicist bka news analyst *Cedric Foster News and Commentary* 1940–67, one of most durable of breed though never major player, heard largely in matinee spots; *The Hartford Times* reporter before joining WTHT as station manager developing weeknight commentary on international affairs picked up by Yankee network; 50 transatlantic crossings in World War II; after national radio stint, relocated to Denver airing over local stations, Intermountain chain beaming him regionally; left broadcasting for PR 1970; d. March 6, 1975.

Arthur Godfrey, Aug. 31, 1903, New York City, N.Y.; announcer, disc jockey, emcee, showman extraordinaire bka *Arthur Godfrey Time, Talent Scouts* host on CBS, same for *Arthur Godfrey and His Friends* CBS-TV Jan. 12, 1949-April 28, 1959 including break, title change; broke into radio on dare in Baltimore late 1920s, subsequently moved to Washington, D.C., New York outlets with early morning DJ show; offered listeners moving eyewitness account of President Franklin D. Roosevelt's funeral cortege 1945; advertisers stood in line for spots on his show even as he poked fun at them; public acclaim, respect instantly evaporated when he turned on performing staff, firing many beginning 1953; comeback attempted but adulation he enjoyed forever eroded; d. March 16, 1983.

Daniel Schorr, Aug. 31, 1916, New York City, N.Y.; author, columnist (*The Des Moines Register-Tribune* Syndicate 1977–80), commentator, correspondent, educator (University of California — Berkeley 1977); freelance writer 1948–53, print journalist (*The Bronx Home News, The Jewish Daily Bulletin, The New York Journal-American* 1940), wire journalist (Jewish Telegraphic Agency 1939, Dutch news agency ANETA 1941–43, 1945–48); joined CBS bureaus 1953: Latin America/Europe 1953–55, Moscow 1955–58, U.S./European roving reporter 1958–60, Germany/Central Europe 1960–66, Washington, D.C. 1966–76; CNN senior Washington correspondent 1980–85, NPR senior analyst 1985- (still working fall 2008); five volumes 1970–2001; radio gigs 1953–76: *CBS Morning News, Edward R. Murrow and the News, Washington Week, The World Is Our Beat, World News Roundup/ World News Tonight.*

Deaths

Michael Fitzmaurice, Aug. 31, 1967, New York City, N.Y.; b. April 28, 1908. Guy Savage, Aug. 31, 1981, Fort Worth, Texas; b. Jan. 22, 1906. David P. Stone, Aug. 31, 1995, Minneapolis, Minn.; b. Oct. 27, 1901. Gayne Whitman, Aug. 31, 1958, Hollywood, Calif.; b. March 19, 1890.

September 1

Sound Bite

On Sept. 1, 1938, NBC is comprised of 154 affiliates; with 48 outlets in its portfolio in 1928, chain's station outreach increased by 221 percent in a decade.

Canceled

The Adventures of the Thin Man, Sept. 1, 1950, ABC; debut July 2, 1941.

Births

Ray Barrett, Sept. 1, 1907, New York City, N.Y.; actor (stage, TV), announcer, educator, newscaster, sportscaster, writer; *Talent Search Country Style* 1951, *Monitor* mid 1950s-ca. 1960s; joined Hartford, Conn. WDRC 1930s after teaching English/public speaking in New York; summer stock a sideline; between horse runs on *Trotting Races* NBC-TV 1950 he, Bill Stern conducted quizzes; Barrett on NBC-TV *Gillette Summer Sports Reel* 1953/1955, *The Gillette Cavalcade of Sports,* opened *Robert Montgomery Presents* NBC-TV 1950–57, at intervals in plays on *Goodyear Playhouse* NBC-TV 1951–60; reported Russian space craft Sputnik I launch to NBC-TV viewers Oct. 4, 1957; d. Jan. 16, 1973.

Don Harlow Wilson, Sept. 1, 1900, Lincoln, Neb.; actor, announcer, emcee, sportscaster bka *The Jack Benny Program* modified sitcom (sundry sobriquets) interlocutor-commercial spokesman 1934–55, 1956–58, televersion 1950–65, mid-show sponsor plugs inserted within storyline; acted in, hosted or introduced 30 net series e.g. *The Aldrich Family, The Al Jolson Show, Baby Snooks, Chance of a Lifetime, The Lanny Ross Show, The Joe E. Brown Show, The Frank Sinatra Show, Tarzan*; debuted in singing trio on San Francisco KFRC 1927, moved to Los Angeles KHJ 1928; NBC sportscaster 1929–37; more TV gigs; 27 theatrical B-movies 1932–53; d. April 25, 1982.

Deaths

Hugh Douglas, Sept. 1, 1993, Los Angeles, Calif.; b. Aug. 3, 1915. Drew Pearson, Sept. 1, 1969, Washington, D.C.; b. Dec. 13, 1897.

September 2

Debuting

The Bing Crosby-Rosemary Clooney Show, Sept. 2, 1957, CBS; two pop idols combine talents in daily 10-minute morning songfest to 1958, returning to nighttime microphones for quarter-hour Feb. 29, 1960; final broadcast Sept. 28, 1962, that weekend marking virtual end of web-based entertainment.

Dr. Sixgun, Sept. 2, 1954, NBC; western drama; Dr. Ray Matson (Karl Weber) practiced medicine at Frenchman's Fork, claiming to put "healing before killing" but prowess/reputation with sixgun diminished medico credentials for at times he exhibited passion to right wrongs of vigilantes, bushwhackers; sidekick Pablo (William Griffis) traveled alongside; one of strain of mature-themed westerns appealing to adults in 1950s; final broadcast Oct. 13, 1955.

Fifteen Minutes with Crosby (*Presenting Bing Crosby*), Sept. 2, 1931, CBS; vocal music; Crosby's network premier, first of many successive ventures (*Bing Crosby—the Cremo Singer*, *Music That Satisfies*, *Kraft Music Hall*, *Philco Radio Time*, *This Is Bing Crosby*, *The Bing Crosby Show*, *The Bing Crosby-Rosemary Clooney Show*) as superstar crooned in inimitable style; final broadcast Oct. 31, 1931 though Crosby aired incessantly to Sept. 28, 1962.

Births

Radcliffe Hall, Sept. 2, 1914, New York City, N.Y.; announcer, newscaster, sportscaster; left Schenectady WGY as sportscaster 1939 for NBC New York where he introduced features like *Dough Re Mi* 1942, *Hildegarde* ca. 1944–45, reported for *NBC News* beginning 1945; d. March 11, 1997.

Amanda Randolph, Sept. 2, 1896, Louisville, Ky.; actress (stage, film, radio, TV), comic thespian bka *Amos 'n' Andy* mother-in-law figure Ramona ("Mama") Smith CBS 1951–54, CBS-TV 1951–53, *Beulah* namesake CBS 1952–54, *Make Room for Daddy* maid Louise NBC-TV 1955–64; d. Aug. 24, 1967.

Henry Junior Taylor, Sept. 2, 1902, Chicago, Ill.; ambassador, author, columnist, commentator, wire journalist (North American Newspaper Alliance, Scripps-Howard, United Features) bka *Your Land and Mine* news analyst MBS/ABC/NBC 1945–56 (only certified credit); joined New York WHN 1942, affiliated with Blue chain (future ABC) 1943; arch conservative vigorously protesting government spending, socialism; named by President Dwight D. Eisenhower ambassador to Switzerland 1957–62, returned to produce United Features column, pen tomes; d. Feb. 24, 1984.

Death

Frank Graham, Sept. 2, 1950, Hollywood, Calif.; b. Nov. 22, 1911.

September 3

Canceled

Believe It or Not, Sept. 3, 1948, NBC; debut April 14, 1930. *Boston Blackie*, Sept. 3, 1950, CBS; debut June 23, 1944.

Births

Peter Capell, Sept. 3, 1912, Berlin, Germany; actor (radio, film, TV) bka foreign-sounding subjects in sundry parts, media; voice familiar to listeners of *Casey—Crime Photographer*, *Confidentially Yours*, *Front Page Farrell*, *Mr. Keen—Tracer of Lost Persons*, *Portia Faces Life*, *The Right to Happiness*, *Secret Missions*, *Tom Corbett—Space Cadet*, *Wendy Warren and the News*, *When a Girl Marries*; played in 27 TV features (many made/aired in Germany), two TV series, 27 solo episodes of TV anthology dramas, 44 theatrical movies largely filmed in Germany for German-speaking audiences; d. March 3, 1986.

Grace Matthews, Sept. 3, 1910, Toronto, Canada; actress bka *Big Sister* daytime serial heroine Ruth Evans Wayne CBS Radio 1946–52, feminine leads in 1940s-50s soap sagas *The Brighter Day*, *Hilltop House*, *Soldier's Wife*, *The Story of Dr. Susan*; *Just Plain Bill* cast, played *The Shadow* confidante Margo Lane, returned to mic as occasional star of 1970s *The CBS Radio Mystery Theater*; *The Guiding Light* figure Claudia Dillman CBS-TV 1968–69; d. May 15, 1995.

Death

Len Sterling, Sept. 3, 1995, Los Angeles, Calif.; b. Jan. 11, 1924.

September 4

Debuting

The Carol Burnett-Richard Hayes Show, Sept. 4, 1961, CBS; comedy, music; Arthur Godfrey's *Talent Scouts* champ Hayes holdout (singer Godfrey *didn't* fire) with Old Redhead as 30-year daytime series ended April 30, 1972 (Hayes there about 14 years); in 1961 Burnett on *The Garry Moore Show* CBS-TV 1958–64, 1966–67; Hayes, Burnett sang, joked 20 minutes weeknights as relics of golden age radio played out; with broadcast of Jan. 25, 1962, Burnett replaced by Peggy King, feature renamed *The Richard Hayes Show*, aired through end 1962.

The Fitch Bandwagon, Sept. 4, 1938, NBC; music/music variety/sitcom; trio of motifs: 1938–45 — band music featuring pop standards, orchestras fronted by Tommy Dorsey, Jimmy Grier, Harry James, Freddy Martin, Jan Savitt, Harry Sosnik; 1945–46 — music variety, visiting bands, songstress Cass Daley playing in sketches with Francis "Dink" Trout; 1946–48 — The *Phil Harris-Alice Faye Show* domestic sitcom that lasted to 1954 began, featuring Elliott Lewis, Walter Tetley, Robert North, impresario Walter Scharf; final broadcast May 23, 1948.

Canceled

(*The Adventures of*) *Sherlock Holmes*, Sept. 4, 1956, ABC; debut Oct. 20, 1930.

Birth

Paul Harvey (Paul Harvey Aurandt), Sept. 4, 1918, Tulsa, Okla.; author, commentator, entrepreneur, newscaster bka *Paul Harvey News and Comments* reporter-analyst since 1950, *The Rest of the Story* narrator from 1970s; most enduring national newsman; jack-of-all-trades at Tulsa KVOO, stations at Salina, Kan., Abilene, Tex., Oklahoma City, St. Louis, Kalamazoo, Mich., Chicago WENR 1944; *Speak Your Mind* weeknights WGN 1948; beamed to 600 outlets on ABC, 18 million listeners 2008; "Despite his stylized delivery, he never achieved the dramatic impact produced by the timing of Edward R. Murrow" critic noted.

Deaths

John Conte, Sept. 4, 2006, Indian Wells, Calif.; b. Sept. 15, 1915. Robert McCormick, Sept. 4, 1985, New York City, N.Y.; b. Aug. 9, 1911. Walter Tetley, Sept. 4, 1975, Woodland Hills, Calif.; b. June 2, 1915.

September 5

Debuting

Life Can Be Beautiful, Sept. 5, 1938, CBS; daytime serial; owner of Slightly Read Book Shop, "Papa David" Solomon (Ralph Locke), takes in two street urchins — Carol (Chichi) Conrad (Alice Reinheart, Teri Keane), Stephen Hamilton (John Holbrook, Earl Larrimore) — who become his wards, fall in love, wed; Stephen dies but security of old man's love pervades drama with touching, satisfying encounter depicting life in slower lane, complete with moral bromides and — above all — eternal optimism; final broadcast June 25, 1954.

Births

Kenneth H. (Kenny) Delmar, Sept. 5, 1910, Boston, Mass.; actor, announcer, voiceover artist bka *Fred Allen Show* "Allen's Alley" blowhard windbag Senator Beauregard Claghorn 1945–49 ("Somebody, ah say, somebody knocked? That's a joke, son, that's a joke!"); on at least two dozen aural series including dramatic anthologies, comedies, variety features 1930s-50s, shows often headlined by celebs (Danny Kaye, Henry Morgan, Jack Benny); few film credits; prolific voice roles in TV animated cartoons 1960s; d. July 14, 1984.

William Hillman, Sept. 5, 1895, New York City, N.Y.; author, correspondent, newscaster, print/wire services journalist; took overseas newspaper appointment 1926 to Paris, Berlin, London; chief of Hearst papers' foreign correspondents 1934–39; King Features Syndicate official at London, directed British News Service Ltd., *Collier's Weekly* European manager 1939–40; returned to U. S., joined Washington, D.C. WMAL 1941; he, Ernest K. Lindley collaborated on nightly quarter-hour newscast NBC Blue/ABC chain 1942; joined Washington WOL 1946, soon winning solo newscast at MBS; North American Newspaper Alliance roving correspondent mid 1940s-1962; produced volume of memorabilia on Harry S [sic] Truman 1952, assisted Truman composing memoirs, more literary/TV projects related to ex-chief; d. May 30, 1962.

Arthur Charles Nielsen, Sr., Sept. 5, 1897, Chicago, Ill.; electrical engineer, researcher, statistician; founded A. C. Nielsen Co. 1923 to appraise suitability of industrial machinery for manufacturers, moving into retail sales in Depression era, measured radio audiences by late 1930s, added TV 1950 buying rival C. E. Hooper, Inc. ("Hooperatings" eclipsed "Crossleys" 1946); introduced Audimeter 1942, gadget recording every twist of radio dial with most effective data to date; Nielsen's global research behemoth now The Nielsen Co.; d. June 1, 1980.

James Wallington, Sept. 5, 1907, Rochester, N.Y.; announcer, emcee, vocalist, voiceover artist (commercials); went on air singing, announcing at Schenectady WGY 1928; American Academy of Arts and Letters diction award 1933, 1935; introduced President Franklin D. Roosevelt to NBC audiences; linked to three dozen 1930s-50s series e.g. *Ben Bernie — the Old Maestro, The Big Show, The Carnation Contented Hour, Duffy's Tavern, The Eddie Cantor Show, The Thomas Melton Show, The Jimmy Durante Show, Philco Hall of Fame, Screen Director's Playhouse*; ended career at Voice of America; d. Dec. 22, 1972.

Deaths

Mitchell Ayers, Sept. 5, 1969, Las Vegas, Nev.; b. Dec. 24, 1910. Allen Funt, Sept. 5, 1999, Monterey, Calif.; b. Sept. 16, 1914. Mark Hawley, Sept. 5, 1986, San Jacinto, Calif.; b. Feb. 17, 1910. Jackie Kelk, Sept. 5, 2002, Rancho Mirage, Calif.; b. Aug. 6, 1921. Bob Stephenson, Sept. 5, 1970, Los Angeles, Calif.; b. Feb. 7, 1901. Sidney Walton, Sept. 5, 1983, Avon, Conn.; May 30, 1915.

September 6

Sound Bite

Nation with musical tastes dominated by big bands, ballads in 1930s-40s jolted from its comfort zone by disc jockey Alan ("Moondog") Freed; hired away from Cleveland WJW where he revolutionized musical landscape spinning rock 'n' roll records, Freed goes on New York WINS Sept. 6, 1954 wiith hour at 4 p.m., three hours at 11 p.m. M-F, taking Gotham by storm and altering listening habits in 60 more markets by syndication; by early 1956 Freed, impresario Count Basie *Rock 'n' Roll Dance Party* Saturday nights on CBS-TV; day of crooner, brassy instrumentals over — radio (and Freed) critical in transformation.

Debuting

The Milton Berle Show (*Community Sing, Summer Hotel, Stop Me if You've Heard This One, Three Ring Time, Let Yourself Go, Kiss and Make Up, At Home with the Berles, The Texaco Star Theater*), Sept. 6, 1936, CBS; comedy, music, variety, quiz; never huge success in radio, Berle became "Mr. Television" by jumping ship to Videoland 1948, his antics there from vaudeville training persuading millions of Americans to go out and buy first TVs, blazing trail for other radio performers; aural cast: Arthur Q. Bryan, Ed Begley, Pert Kelton, Arnold Stang, Mary Shipp, more; *The Milton Berle Show* (multi titles) NBC-/ABC-TV 1948–56, 1958–59, 1966–67; final radiocast June 15, 1949.

Mayor of the Town, Sept. 6, 1942, NBC; lighthearted drama; actor Lionel Barrymore as Springfield executive in warm tale of rural Americana, alongside housekeeper Marilly (Agnes Moorehead), ward Butch (Conrad Binyon), granddaughter Holly-Ann (Priscilla Lyon), Butch's sweetheart Sharlee Bronson (Gloria McMillan); Springdale was life in slow track, one wag's depiction "not unlike Dr. Christian's River's End or Gildersleeve's Summerfield"; bred syndicated televersion 1954 starring Tomas Mitchell; final radiocast July 3, 1949.

Canceled

Chandu the Magician, Sept. 6, 1950, ABC; debut Oct. 10, 1932.

Fibber McGee & Molly, Sept. 6, 1959, on *Monitor* NBC where pithy vignette exchanges persisted following departure as primetime halfhour June 30, 1953, daytime/nighttime quarterhour March 23, 1956; debut April 16, 1935.

Births

Morgan Beatty, Sept. 6, 1902, Little Rock, Ark.; commentator, emcee bka NBC *News of the World* newscaster 1946–67; while brief profile might point elsewhere, reliance as evening commentator for two decades kept him in key slot at NBC, particularly beyond departure of H. V. Kaltenborn; d. July 4, 1975.

Grover Cleveland Kirby (aka Cleve Conway), Sept. 6, 1915; actor, announcer, newscaster, sportscaster; New Orleans WWL newscaster 1938–39, moved to sportscasting for Chicago WENR/newscasting for WMAQ/announcing for NBC April 1939; identified as Kleve Kirby until then — to eliminate confusion with already on-air Chicagoan Durward Kirby, handle altered to Cleve Conway, persisting to late 1943 when Blue, Red nets separated, Durward going with Blue, Cleve with Red — Cleve adopting old appellation; *The Sheaffer Parade, Stories of Escape, Today's Children, The Tommy Dorsey Show* in his ethereal repertoire; died in car wreck injuring WMAQ announcer George Stone; d. March 5, 1949.

Paul Lavalle (Joseph Usifer), Sept. 6, 1908, Beacon, N.Y.; arranger, clarinetist, conductor, bka *Cities Service Band of America* (*Highways in Melody, Band of America*) most durable, memorable impresario 1944–56; *The Chesterfield Supper Club, Club 15* musical arranger; directed Radio City Music Hall Orchestra seven years; retired early 1980s; d. June 24, 1997.

Billy Mills, Sept. 6, 1894, Flint, Mich.; arranger, house impresario (CBS, NBC), pianist, vocalist bka *Fibber McGee & Molly* music conductor 1938–53; CBS Chicago general music supervisor 1932–37 before shift to NBC when hired by *McGee* sponsor S.C. Johnson & Son; maestro for added trio of NBC Johnson features (*Alec Templeton Time, Hap Hazard, The Victor Borge Show*), then *The Great Gildersleeve, The Amos 'n' Andy Show* for other sponsors; d. Oct. 20, 1971.

Jay Cleve Stewart (Jay Fix), Sept. 6, 1918, Summitville, Ind.; announcer, emcee, producer bka sidekick to host Monty Hall on TV wildly exciting costumed studio audience stunt show *Let's Make a Deal* NBC/ABC 1964–76; produced, presided over juvenile stunt feature *Fun Fair* ABC-TV 1950–51; flanked hosts of other TV game series 1977–88: *It's Anybody's Guess, The Joker's Wild, Joker! Joker!! Joker!!!, Sale of the Century*; announcer at Terre Haute WBAW 1939, Cincinnati WLW 1940, Hollywood CBS 1943; intros for 1940s-50s *Duffy's Tavern, The Great Gildersleeve, June's My Girl, Take It or Leave It, Truth or Consequences*, more; emcee of half-dozen quiz/stunt entries — *The Carnation Family Party, Jay Stewart's Fun Fair, Meet the Missus, Surprise Package, What's Doin', Ladies?, The Wizard of Odds*; d. Sept. 17, 1989.

John R. Wald, Sept. 6, 1908, Hastings, Minn.; announcer, newscaster bka interlocutor of NBC's *The Great Gildersleeve* 1947–49, *Fibber McGee & Molly* 1953–56; dispatched news as *The Richfield Reporter* 1939-early 1940s; other 1940s-50s intros: *Confession, The Eddie Bracken Show, Frontier Gentleman, NBC Presents Short Story, The Six Shooter, Summerfield Bandstand*; appeared on *The National Lampoon Radio Hour* 1972–76; d. March 22, 1988.

Deaths

Tommy Bartlett, Sept. 6, 1998, Wisconsin Dells, Wis.; b. July 11, 1914. Johnny Desmond, Sept. 6, 1985, Los Angeles, Calif.; b. Nov. 14, 1920. William Spargrove, Sept. 6, 1984, Mission Hills, Calif.; b. Dec. 10, 1908. Dick Willard, Sept. 6, 2000, Taos, N.M.; b. Jan. 22, 1914.

September 7

Debuting

Mystery Theater (*Mollé Mystery Theater, Hearthstone of the Death Squad*), Sept. 7, 1943, NBC; crime drama; "crime connoisseur" Geoffrey Barnes (Bernard Lenrow) narrated tales of mayhem, murder; in 1948, with producers Frank, Anne Hummert running show, Barnes gave way to Inspector Hearthstone (Alfred Shirley) as resident criminologist who played in narratives instead of introducing them, hunting miscreants like ill-fated prey, assisted (as always in Hummert detective dramas) by dim bulb sidekick posing dumb questions to make hero appear brilliant — in Hearthstone's case, detective Sam Cook (James Meighan); new moniker (*Hearthstone of the Death Squad*) aired 1951–52; final broadcast latter nomenclature Sept. 17, 1952.

Canceled

The A&P Gypsies, Sept. 7, 1936, NBC; debut Jan. 3, 1927.

September 8

Debuting

The Bickersons (and assorted monikers), Sept. 8, 1946, NBC; sitcom highlighting squabbling couple John (Don Ameche, Lew Parker),

Blanche (Frances Langford) Bickerson peppering every exchange with put-down zingers; final broadcast Aug. 28, 1951.

That Brewster Boy, Sept. 8, 1941, NBC; teen sitcom evocative of Henry (*The Aldrich Family*) exploiting adolescent pitfalls of Joey Brewster (Eddie Firestone, Jr., Arnold Stang, Dick York); tactics separated it from similar shows including pal Chuck (Billy Idelson) often landing Joey into jeopardy before scramming, and Joey's sis's boyfriend — each boy detesting other; final broadcast March 2, 1945.

The Jack Pearl Show (*Peter Pfeiffer, The Raleigh-Kool Program, Jack and Cliff, The Baron and the Bee*), Sept. 8, 1932, NBC; madcap comedy variety; Pearl as Baron von Munchhausen, tall tales teller with thick German accent, straight man Charlie (Cliff Hall) played stooge to baron prompting habitual inqury: "Vass you dere, Sharlie?"; music directed by Abe Lyman, Tommy Dorsey, vocalists, guests; barrage of one-liners audiences loved in initial season yet turned elsewhere thereafter, star making multi failed comeback tries; off air 1937–48; final broadcast of format Sept. 25, 1951 though comedy spelling match *The Baron and the Bee* aired with Pearl, Hall July 21, 1953 to Sept. 8, 1953.

Canceled

The Whistler, Sept. 8, 1955, CBS West Coast region; debut May 16, 1942.

Birth

Joseph Reeves Bolton II, Sept. 8, 1910, Flushing, N.Y.; announcer, educator, emcee, government broadcaster, instrumentalist, newsreel sportscaster bka New York WPIX-TV personality 1955–76; listeners heard him welcome them to *The 1937 Radio Show, Go Get It* 1941–43, *Uncle Don* 1939–40; d. Aug. 13, 1986.

Deaths

Clayton (Bud) Collyer, Sept. 8, 1969, Greenwich, Conn.; b. June 18, 1908. Harry Holcombe, Sept. 8, 1987, Valencia, Calif.; b. Nov. 11, 1906.

September 9

Sound Bite

Chain naissance, Sept. 9, 1916; National Broadcasting Co. (NBC) formed; Radio Corporation of America (50% ownership), General Electric Corp. (30%), Westinghouse Corp. (20%); RCA subsequently buys out GE, Westinghouse on May 23, 1930; shortly before inaugural broadcast on Nov. 15, 1926, NBC pays $1 million for telephone company "network" that includes New York WEAF, to be designated NBC flagship station (Red chain).

Birth

Clem McCarthy, Sept. 9, 1882, East Bloomfield, N.Y.; print journalist (San Diego journal, racing sheets *The Morning Telegraph, The Daily Racing Form*), sportscaster bka notably linked to equestrian competitions (originally hoped to be jockey) including posting from Churchill Downs (Kentucky Derby), other venerated venues; discussed figures, delivered scores, gave eyewitness accounts late 1930s-early 1950s on *All Sports Program, The Clem McCarthy Sports Show, The Eddie Bracken Show, Krueger Sports Reel, Racing Scratches, Sports, NBC Takes You to the Races*; went on air at Chicago KYW, then earned simultaneous paychecks in 1930s from NBC, New York WINS, WMCA, plus WHN from 1944; *Gillette Summer Sports Reel* commentator NBC-TV 1953; d. June 4, 1962.

Ed Prentiss, Sept. 9, 1909, Chicago, Ill.; actor (radio, TV), announcer bka *Bonanza* epic western figure sporadically appearing as banker NBC-TV 1959–73, "glue" binding soap opera experimental trilogy under umbrella moniker "The General Mills Hour" NBC mid 1940s (narrated intertwined storylines of *The Guiding Light, Today's Children, Woman in White*); acted in 1930s-50s episodes *Arnold Grimm's Daughter, Captain Midnight, Painted Dreams, The Romance of Helen Trent, A Tale of Today*, more while presenting *The Air Adventures of Jimmy Allen, Armstrong of the SBI, Dave Garroway* (multiple appellations), *The First Nighter, Jack Armstrong — the All-American Boy, Silver Eagle — Mountie*, more; linked to handful forgettable early TV shows before stints in mid 1960s NBC daytime serials *Morning Star, Days of Our Lives*; d. March 18, 1992.

Death

Burgess Meredith, Sept. 9, 1997, Malibu, Calif.; b. Nov. 16, 1907.

September 10

Debuting

The Jimmy Durante Show (*The Chase & Sanborn Hour, The Jumbo Fire Chief Program, The Jimmy Durante-Garry Moore Show, The Camel Caravan*), Sept. 10, 1933, NBC; comedy variety; a premier singing funnyman of vintage radio known already via stage/screen, caught second wind on ether, rejuvenated faltering career; regulars Elvia Allman, Don Ameche, Candy Candido, Hope Emerson, Florence Halop (Hotlips Houlihan), Garry Moore, Victor Moore, Arthur Treacher, Alan Young, more; vocalists Georgia Gibbs, Peggy Lee with impresarios Roy Bargy, Xavier Cugat, Dave Rubinoff; two TV segments — *The Jimmy Durante Show* NBC 1954–56, *Jimmy Durante Presents the Lennon Sisters Hour* ABC 1969–70; final radiocast June 30, 1950.

The Zero Hour, Sept. 10, 1973, MBS; suspense drama; hosted by Rod Serling, MBS's attempt to capitalize on nostalgia craze that swept America in epoch, on heels of returning *X-Minus One* June 24, 1973 at NBC, ahead of *The CBS Radio Mystery Theater* Jan. 6, 1974; *Zero* aired 13 weeks of half-hour tales weeknights to Dec. 7, 1973, resumed with second batch April 29-July 26, 1974.

Births

Charles Bishop Kuralt, Sept. 10, 1934, Wilmington, N.C.; author, commentator, copywriter, correspondent, emcee, print journalist (*The Charlotte News*), sportscaster bka *On the Road with Charles Kuralt* traveling journalist visiting, interviewing populace of American backwaters on CBS Radio-TV 1967–78, *Sunday Morning* newsmagazine host CBS-TV 1979–94; at 14 dispatched sports scores on Charlotte WAYS, reported for Charlotte's afternoon daily 1955, on air at WBT 1956, copy rewrite man at New York CBS 1957, head of web's Latin American bureau, chief West Coast correspondent 1963, roving reporter; three George Foster Peabody awards, 10 Emmys over 37-year career; penned half-dozen volumes, mostly of road exploits, beloved South; "his voice, his inflection, his delivery — everything was just pure art" said rival; d. July 4, 1997.

Sam Taub (Samuel Sidney Life), Sept. 10, 1886, Brooklyn, N.Y.; print journalist (*The New York Morning Telegraph*), sportscaster bka *Madison Square Boxing Bouts* ringside broadcaster 1944–45; on air with sports on Newark WOR 1922, first boxing gig on rival WJZ 1929, sports commentator on New York WHN 1937, rival WMGM 1948–52; announced 7,000 career bouts; Taub's NBC series originated 1940 on WHN, persisted to 1945; d. July 11, 1979.

Lyle Van (Lyle Dennison Van Valkenburgh), Sept. 10, 1904, Troy, N.Y.; newscaster, program director, vocalist bka *Lyle Van and the News* host 1943–44, 1945, 1948–51; went on air singing over Atlanta WSB, then program director at rival WGST, moved to New York NBC as newscaster 1934, shifted to MBS 1940s staying put into 1950s; d. July 22, 1997.

Deaths

George Baxter, Sept. 10, 1976, New York City, N.Y.; b. Dec. 13, 1904. Edwin Jerome, Sept. 10, 1959, Pasadena, Calif.; b. Dec. 30, 1885.

September 11

Debuting

Today's Children, Sept. 11, 1933, NBC Blue; daytime serial; ran in dual sections separated by six years (1933–37, 1943–50); with roots in origins of soap opera, tale sprang from *Painted Dreams*—first of genre to air (1930), fell into trouble as scribe Irna Phillips claimed rights, fighting Chicago WGN in court over ownership, war she lost decade later; nonplussed Phillips moved to rival station WMAQ, altered title, characters' names in original narrative, continued as *Today's Children*; widowed Irish-American matriarch Mother Moran (Phillips) shepherded daughters Eileen (Ireene Wicker, Fran Carlon), Frances Moran Matthews (Bess Johnson, Sunda Love); final broadcast June 2, 1950.

Births

Charles Kenneth Banghart, Sept. 11, 1909, Paramus, N.J.; announcer, emcee, newscaster; widely recalled as prominent NBC daily newsman late 1940s though he introduced boatload of series unrelated to news like *Archie Andrews*,

Home Is What You Make It, Katie's Daughter, Lora Lawton, Meredith Willson's [sic] *Music Room, The Private Files of Rex Saunders, RCA Victor Show, Robert Q. Lewis, The Robert Show Chorale, The Bell Telephone Hour, When a Girl Marries, The World's Great Novels*; narrated U. S. Navy instruction films during World War II; *Gillette Summer Sports Reel* commentator NBC-TV 1953; DJ on New York WRCA 1957; thespian in regional theater co-producing several plays at Olney (Md.) Summer Playhbouse; joined New York WCBS Radio 1962 to finish broadcast career; d. May 25, 1980.

Anne Seymour (Anne Eckert), Sept. 11, 1909, New York City, N.Y.; actress (stage, radio, TV, film) bka *The Story of Mary Marlin* daytime serial protagonist who quit Iowa housewifery to succeed missing amnesiac spouse as U. S. Senator NBC/NBC Blue 1937–43; seventh generation theatrical clan, roots in Ireland 1740, she began with outfit touring New England, took mom's maiden name; on Broadway in *Mr. Moneypenny* 1928, others; entered radio 1932, source affirmed: "her distinctively warm style and vocal timbre were perfect for playing some of radio's noblest, self-sacrificing heroines"; in *The Magnificent Montague* sitcom as Lily NBC 1950–51, turns in *Bulldog Drummond, The FBI in Peace and War, Grand Hotel, Mr. Keen—Tracer of Lost Persons, The Romance of Helen Trent, My Secret Story, Our Gal Sunday, Portia Faces Life, The Private Files of Rex Saunders, A Woman of America*, more; on *Studio One* CBS-TV 1948, first of multi video dramas (*Cagney and Lacey, Gunsmoke, Perry Mason*, etc.); debuted on silver screen as Lucy Stark in *All the King's Men* 1949, few more; Broadway again as Sara Delano Roosevelt in *Sunrise at Campobello* 1958; d. Dec. 8, 1988.

Charles Stark, Sept. 11, 1912, Reading, Pa.; announcer, disc jockey, emcee, newscaster, voiceover artist bka workhorse in mid 1930s-mid 1950s radio given to opening drainboard dramas—*Claudia and David, Mother o' Mine, My Son and I, Our Gal Sunday, Scattergood Baines, When a Girl Marries*—while proffering *The Bob Hawk Show, Can You Top This?, Mr. and Mrs. North, The Rudy Vallee Show*, more, plus *Odd Side of the News* reports; career began at Reading WEEU 1927 followed by Philadelphia KYW, WCAU, WIP; joined New York WMCA 1936, hosted *Charlie Stark Music Shop* DJ entry at WINS 1948–52; couple of fleeting ABC-TV ventures in video early days, recorded spot-promotions announcements until mid 1980s retirement; d. March 22, 1992.

Deaths

Paul Douglas, Sept. 11, 1959, Hollywood Hills, Calif.; b. April 11, 1907. Louise Fitch, Sept. 11, 1996, Los Angeles, Calif.; b. Oct. 18, 1914. Lorne Greene, Sept. 11, 1987, Santa Monica, Calif.; b. Feb. 12, 1915. Hanley Stafford, Sept. 11, 1968, Hollywood, Calif.; b. Sept. 22, 1899.

September 12

Debuting

Tarzan, Sept. 12, 1932, syndicated by New York WOR, flagship outlet of soon-to-be-formed MBS; juvenile adventure with jungle venue; in early aural runs under trio of longer monikers, returning March 22, 1952 on CBS after 16-year absence under *Tarzan* handle; "lord of the jungle" bare-chested, vine-swinger Tarzan (James H. Pierce, Carlton KaDell, Lamont Johnson) revolted against evildoers invading his turf, protected environment as much as *Red Ryder, Sky King, Buck Rogers* did theirs—Tarzan accompanied by background din of elephant roars, bird chirps, monkey chatter; in excess of 70 full-length or serialized film yarns screened in theaters; TV series aired NBC 1966–68, reprised CBS 1969; new syndicated TV series 1991–92; final net radiocast June 27, 1953 although some syndicated shows repeated in limited markets beyond date.

Canceled

Archie Andrews, Sept. 12, 1953, NBC; debut May 31, 1943. *Truth or Consequences*, Sept. 12, 1956, NBC; debut March 23, 1940.

Birth

Doctor Frank McGee, Sept. 12, 1921, Monroe, La.; emcee, interviewer, news executive bka *Today* newsmagazine host NBC-TV 1971–74—"McGee was not well liked by the *Today* staff" said TV historian Alex McNeil: "McGee insisted on opening and closing the show himself and also reserved the right to ask the first question of any guest slated to be interviewed by [Barbara] Walters. Whether the rift between the two would have widened will never be known ... McGee died of bone cancer ... after only two and one-half years"; NBC top-of-the-hour newscast correspondent, *Monitor* weekend magazine segment host 1961–64; began career at Oklahoma City WKY-TV, successively moved to Montgomery, Ala. WSFA-TV as news director, Washington, D.C. NBC, New York NBC; d. April 17, 1974.

Deaths

William Boyd, Sept. 12, 1972, Laguna Beach, Calif.; b. June 5, 1895. Tony La Frano, Sept. 12, 1961, Los Angeles, Calif.; b. May 10, 1911. Frank Nelson, Sept. 12, 1986, Hollywood, Calif.; b. May 6, 1911. Lillian Randolph, Sept. 12, 1980, Los Angeles, Calif.; b. Dec. 14, 1898. Glenn Riggs, Sept 12, 1875, Malaga, Spain; b. July 24, 1907.

September 13

Debuting

The Amos 'n' Andy Music Hall, Sept. 13, 1954, CBS; disc jockey feature with humorous banter between principals (Freeman Gosden, Charles Correll) whose legendary characterizations extended from 1920s—with occasional headlining guests; final broadcast Nov. 25, 1960.

The Eddie Cantor Show, Sept. 13, 1931, NBC; comedy variety; star heard under multiple monikers (*The Chase & Sanborn Hour*, *Texaco Town*, *Time to Smile*, *Town Hall Tonight*, *Show Business Old and New*, *Ask Eddie Cantor*); classic vaudeville showman vocalist-comedian, master of one-liners, segueing easily before mic, presented top-draw talent in glitzy showcase of icons with regulars that included violinist Dave Rubinoff, comic Bert Gordon ("The Mad Russian"), juvenile performers Bobby Breen and Deanna Durbin, vocalists Dinah Shore, Margaret Whiting, acting company playing humorous parts—Elvia Allman, Gerald Mohr, Frank Nelson, Herb Vigran, Veola Vonn, et al.; final net broadcast July 1, 1954 although syndicated repeats circulated 1956, 1961–63.

Radio Reader's Digest, Sept. 13, 1942, CBS; real life anthology drama; with Conrad Nagel narrating, stories drawn from pages of magazine came to life in buoyant dramatizations; sponsored by Hallmark, led to *Hallmark Hall of Fame* on radio, TV; final broadcast June 3, 1948.

The Road of Life, Sept. 13, 1937, CBS; daytime serial; creator Irna Phillips maintained strong affinity for professionals—this was exhibit A in her medic arsenal; male protagonist unusual: surgeon Dr. Jim Brent (Matt Crowley, Ken Griffin, Don MacLaughlin, David Ellis, Howard Teichmann) practiced medicine in hamlet of Merrimac where, in distant future, he would be hospital administrator; Brent had other dilemmas to pacify first including attempts to satisfy tormenting wife number one, Carol Evans (Lesley Woods, Barbara Luddy, Louise Fitch, Marian Shockley); after she died—late in run—Jim remarried, to Jocelyn McLeod (Barbara Becker, Virginia Dwyer), finding how good marriage could be; solid soap saga intertwined patients' crises with homefront issues; went to CBS-TV briefly in 1954–55 grooming MacLaughlin for pivotal role as Chris Hughes on *As the World Turns* CBS-TV 1956–86; final radiocast Jan. 2, 1959.

Canceled

The Mercury Theater on the Air, Sept. 13, 1946, CBS; debut July 11, 1938.

Births

Dick Haymes, Sept. 13, 1916, Buenos Aires, Argentina; actor (film, stage, TV), recording artist, vocalist (nightclubs, radio) bka baritone crooner rivaling Perry Como, Bing Crosby, Frank Sinatra though never equal; cosmopolitan entertainer living in Argentina, France, Ireland, Switzerland, United States; sang with bands fronted by Ray Bloch, Tommy Dorsey, Benny Goodman, Harry James, Gordon Jenkins; appeared in more than dozen movie musicals (1944's *Irish Eyes Are Smiling*, 1945's *State Fair*, 1953's *Crusin' Down the River*, et al.); beset by personal troubles—alcohol addiction, alimony payments (seven spouses, among them Joanne Dru, Rita Hayworth, Fran Jeffries), back tax troubles, fought feds' bid to deport him for draft-dodging; d. March 28, 1980.

Leith Stevens, Sept. 13, 1909, Mount Moriah, Mo.; composer (film, radio), house arranger-impresario (CBS), pianist; CBS company man devoting bulk of professional career to chain as arranger 1930, staff conductor 1934, composer of many *Columbia Workshop* scores 1936–47; music director of 30 aural series 1932–58 (*Death Valley Days*, *Ford Sunday Eve-*

ning Hour, *The Adventures of Ellery Queen*, *Rogue's Gallery*, *Escape*, *Pursuit*, *Yours Truly Johnny Dollar*, *Biography in Sound*, et al.); *The George Burns and Gracie Allen Show* maestro CBS-TV 1950–58; d. July 23, 1970.

Mel Torme, Sept. 13, 1925, Chicago, Ill.; actor (film, radio, TV), arranger, author, composer, drummer, pianist, vocalist bka husky-voiced sensual singer penning more than 300 tunes, most famous 1947's "The Christmas Song"; *Little Orphan Annie* pal Joe Corntassel in juvenile adventure radio serial, also acted in *Jack Armstrong—the All-American Boy*, *The Romance of Helen Trent*; lent moniker to pithy NBC Radio *Torme Time* 1947, *The New Mel Torme Show* 1948, *The Mel Torme Show* daily variety series CBS-TV 1951–52; d. June 5, 1999.

September 14

Debuting

Big Sister, Sept. 14, 1936, CBS; daytime serial; one of soap opera's leading helping-hand figures, Ruth Evans Wayne (Alice Frost, Nancy Marshall, Marjorie Anderson, Mercedes McCambridge, Grace Matthews) not only was mentor to her orphaned younger siblings Ned (Michael O'Day), Sue Evans Miller (Fran Carden, Peggy Conklin, Helen Lewis, Dorothy McGuire, Haila Stoddard) but coddled her mental lightweight spouse Dr. John Wayne (Martin Gabel, Paul McGrath, Staats Cotsworth), dependent of counselor-in-residence, too; trio's foibles kept nurse Ruth busy plus advances of dashing Dr. Reed Bannister (David Gothard, Berry Kroeger, Ian Martin, Arnold Moss) playing her heartstrings; in 1946, drama gained impetus as first soap televised albeit one episode with cast standing before mics reading scripts, yet signaling future; final broadcast Dec. 26, 1952.

John's Other Wife, Sept. 14, 1936, NBC; daytime serial; insecure wife with suspicions about her spouse's clerical helper—plus his knockout aide—kept plot boiling as romantic triangle (foursome?) misery; included Perry Department Store proprietor John Perry (Hanley Stafford, Matt Crowley, Luis Van Rooten, William Post, Jr., Joseph Curtin, Richard Kollmar), his wife Elizabeth (Adele Ronson, Erin O'Brien-Moore), secretary Annette Rogers (Franc Hale), aide Martha Curtis (Phyllis Welch, Rita Johnson); final broadcast March 20, 1942.

Canceled

Tales of the Texas Rangers, Sept. 14, 1952, NBC; debut July 8, 1950.

Births

Cecil B. Brown, Sept. 14, 1907, New Brighton, Pa.; author, educator, foreign correspondent, newscaster, TV news-public affairs director bka *Cecil Brown and the News* MBS headliner 1942–56 following controversial departure from CBS; distant "Murrow Boys" cohort; d. Oct. 25, 1987.

Harry Salter, Sept. 14, 1898, Bucharest, Romania; impresario, producer, violinist bka ABC music director 1940s-70s; *Your Hit Parade* bandmaster 1936–37; *Stop the Music!* premiering maestro 1948–52; d. March 5, 1984.

Deaths

Gertrude Berg, Sept. 14, 1966, New York City, N.Y.; b. Oct. 3, 1899. Warren Hull, Sept. 14, 1974, Waterbury, Conn.; b. Jan. 17, 1903. Terry O'Sullivan, Sept. 14, 2006, St. Paul, Minn.; b. July 7, 1915.

September 15

Canceled

The Adventures of Philip Marlowe, CBS, Sept. 15, 1951; debut June 17, 1947. *Bride and Groom*, Sept. 15, 1950, ABC; debut Nov. 26, 1945.

Births

Jack Bailey, Sept. 15, 1907, Hampton, Iowa; announcer, disc jockey, emcee, instrumentalist, voiceover artist bka *Queen for a Day* master of ceremonies 1945–57, television 1956–64; broke into show biz delivering spoken lines for Goofy in Donald Duck animated cartoons screened in cinema houses 1939–40; introduced national radio audiences to *Glamour Manor*, *Silver Theater*, *Duffy's Tavern*; by 1944 presided over audio game shows *Meet the Missus*, *Potluck Party*, *Stop That Villain*, *County Fair*, *Comedy of Errors*; success with audience participation fare led to interim host *Place the Face* 1953–54, succeeded

Ralph Edwards hosting *Truth or Consequences* 1954–56 — both TV entries; d. Feb. 1, 1980.

John Conte, Sept. 15, 1915, Palmer, Mass.; actor, announcer, emcee, vocalist; climbed CBS ladder to Hollywood chief announcer before freelancing 1937; road shows, myriad California little theater productions, later Broadway musicals (*Allegro*, *Carousel*); presented radio listeners with *Al Pearce and His Gang*, *Baby Snooks*, *The Frank Morgan Show*, *Silver Theater*, more while acting in *Philco Radio Hall of Fame*, *Sherlock Holmes*, hosting others; *Your Show of Shows* guest singer NBC-TV 1950–54; presided over own NBC-TV quarter hour Tuesday, Thursday evenings 1950–51; added TV gigs; 14 mostly B-films 1932–64; daily matinee feature New York WABC Radio 1953; d. Sept. 4, 2006.

Elspeth Eric (Dora Elsbeth Thexton), Sept. 15, 1907, Chicago, Ill.; actress (stage, radio), scriptwriter bka *The CBS Radio Mystery Theater* anthology scribe, thespian CBS 1974–82; Woodstock, Mount Kisco summer stock 1931–32, toured in 1930s plays, appeared on Broadway; 1940s-50s acted on radio crime dramas e.g. *The Abbott Mysteries*, *The Adventures of the Falcon*, *The FBI in Peace & War*, *Gangbusters*, *Mr. and Mrs. North*, *Suspense*, *True Detective Mysteries*, *Yours Truly — Johnny Dollar*, more while in recurring roles on *Big Sister*, *Front Page Farrell*, *Rosemary*, *The Second Mrs. Burton*, *This Is Nora Drake*, *Young Doctor Malone*; solo performances in TV dramas, joined casts of daytime serials *The Road of Life* CBS-TV 1954–55, *The Secret Storm* CBS-TV 1968, scripted *Another World* NBC-TV 1969–71; d. 1993, New York City.

Harry Fleetwood, Sept. 15, 1917, Laurel Springs, N.J.; announcer, disc jockey, vocalist bka *Music through the Night* classical melody series host New York WNBC 1954–75, WNCN 1975-late 1980s; d. Jan. 18, 2004.

Sheilah Graham (Lily Shiel), Sept. 15, 1904, Leeds, England; author, columnist, commentator, dancer, vocalist bka 1930s mistress of writer F. Scott Fitzgerald; Hollywood gossipmonger with syndicated newspaper column to 178 newspapers at peak, radio series *Heinz Magazine of the Air*, *Sheilah Graham*, *Three City Byline*, *Vanity Fair*, *Yours for a Song* where she doled out intimate details on stars, studios 1930s-1950s; never equaled eminence of contemporaries Jimmy Fidler, Hedda Hopper, Louella Parsons, Walter Winchell; *The Sheilah Graham Show* NBC-TV 1951, *Hollywood Today* NBC-TV 1955; *Girl Talk* recurring guest on syndicated TV 1963–70; hid Jewishness; d. Nov. 17, 1988.

Penny Singleton (Mariana Dorothy Agnes Letitia McNulty), Sept. 15, 1908, Philadelphia, Pa.; actress (film, radio, stage), vocalist, voiceover artist bka *Blondie* family sitcom namesake matriarch (Blondie Bumstead) 1939–46; *The Jetsons* TV animated cartoon matriarch (Jane Jetson) 1962–67, 1969–76, 1979–81, 1982–83, 1985, 1987; elected president American Guild of Variety Artists 1969, first woman to head AFL-CIO union; d. Nov. 12, 2003.

Peggy W. Webber (McClory), Sept. 15, 1925, Laredo, Texas; actress (stage, radio, TV, film), director, producer, voiceover artist, writer bka *Dragnet* crime drama matriarch Ma Friday, sundry other figures (100+ episodes) NBC 1949–57, NBC-TV 1952–59, 1967–70; adept early: performed onstage in silent cinemas at two-and-a-half, on air at 11, wrote/directed/produced early TV shows at 18, won Emmy for drama anthology series *Treasures of Literature* at 21; radio coups: *The Cases of Mr. Ace*, *Cathy and Elliott Lewis Onstage*, *Escape*, *Have Gun — Will Travel*, *I Love Adventure*, *Nightbeat*, *Pete Kelly's Blues*, *Romance*, *The Saint*, *The Sears/Mutual Radio Theater*, *Tales of the Texas Rangers*, *The Woman in My House*, more; eight theatrical B-movies 1946–58, voices in two TV animated series 1981–83, appeared in 39 solo dramatic parts beyond *Dragnet* 1946–2005.

Deaths

Andre Baruch, Sept. 15, 1991, Los Angeles, Calif.; b. Aug. 20, 1908. Virginia Gregg, Sept. 15, 1986, Encino, Calif.; b. March 6, 1916. Ken Nordine, Sept. 15, 1993, Jamestown, N.Y.; b. Aug. 14, 1911.

September 16

Debuting

Jimmy Fidler in Hollywood (sundry designations), Sept. 16, 1934, NBC; gossipmonger; alleged to have premiered on unknown 1933 date as *Hollywood on the Air;* first substantiated gig this as his tell-all brand of hearsay revealed scandalous details in personal lives of Tinseltown figures, studios hiring them; historian suggested that — unlike contemporaries Hedda Hopper,

Louella Parsons who supposedly treated subjects with respect — Fidler dubbed radio's "most threatening menace to movies and movie people," labeling lousy flicks "stinkers," reading open memos to icons from "little black book" while condemning for affairs, divorce, shady dealings; persisted in radio, TV half-century source claimed although final certifiable net radiocast series ended May 28, 1950.

Canceled

The Mysterious Traveler, Sept. 16, 1952, MBS; debut Dec. 5, 1943.

Births

Lawrence S. (Larry) Dobkin, Sept. 16, 1919, New York City, N.Y.; actor (radio, TV), announcer bka radio series vet — one (*Rocky Jordan*) he introduced, 26 he played in ongoing or sporadic roles: *Broadway Is My Beat*, *Escape*, *Gunsmoke*, *Have Gun — Will Travel*, *Lux Radio Theater*, *One Man's Family*, *The Roy Rogers Show*, *Suspense*, *Yours Truly — Johnny Dollar*; impersonated Gen. George Patton in ABC-TV miniseries *War and Remembrance* 1988, 1989; d. Oct. 28, 2002.

Allen Funt, Sept. 16, 1914, Brooklyn, N.Y.; emcee, writer, producer bka *Candid Microphone* 1947–48, 1950, *Candid Camera* 1948–90 creator ("Remember ... sometime ... somewhere ... when you least expect it ... someone will step up to you and say ... 'Smile, you're on *Candid Camera*!'"); still circulates in syndication; scripted Eleanor Roosevelt's 1940–41 dialogue show, prepared stunts for 1940s *Truth or Consequences*; *The Garry Moore Show* regular CBS-TV 1959–60; *Tell It to the Camera* producer CBS-TV 1963–64; d. Sept. 5, 1999.

Dorian St. George, Sept. 16, 1911, New York City, N.Y.; actor, announcer; presented 1930s-50s installments of *The Adventures of Charlie Chan*, *Candid Microphone*, *Hollywood Airport* while playing in *Fish Pond*; d. March 1, 2004.

Death

Alan Courtney, Sept. 16, 1978, Miami, Fla.; b. Nov. 29, 1912.

September 17

Canceled

Hearthstone of the Death Squad, Sept. 17, 1952, CBS; debut Aug. 30, 1951 (though lineage can be traced to *Mystery Theater* as early as June 29, 1948).

Births

Gabriel Heatter, Sept. 17, 1890; actor, commentator, emcee, newscaster, print journalist (*The New York Record*, *The Brooklyn Times*, *The New York Journal*, *Forest and Stream*, *The Nation*, *The Miami Beach Sun*) bka ad-libbing announcer at Bruno Richard Hauptmann's execution 1936 for kidnapping, killing Lindbergh baby, making Heatter household word; as "boy orator," warmed up street-corner audiences 1906 for journalist William Randolph Hearst running for governor; seven-night-a-week quarter-hour analyst for New York WMCA 1932, moved to rival WOR 1933, pushed onto national stage 1935–65 peaking as 196 MBS affiliates beamed him six nights weekly ("Ah, there's good news tonight!"); other 1930s-50s gigs: *America Today*, *Behind the Front Page*, *Borden's Home News*, *Cavalcade of America*, *NBC Bandstand*, *Of All Things*, *We the People*; bit parts in two films — *Champagne for Caesar* 1950, *The Day the Earth Stood Still* 1951; Miami WIOD late in career; d. March 30, 1972.

Mary Shipp, Sept. 17, 1915, Los Angeles, Calif.; actress (stage, film, radio, TV); replacement for *My Friend Irma* character Jane Stacy played by Cathy Lewis who departed 1953, though Shipp played new roommate Kay Foster — show ran one more season; she also was Miss Spaulding in same era on *Life with Luigi*; both series went to TV with Shipp reprising radio roles.

Alice (Anderson Thorpe) Yourman, Sept. 17, 1907, Oregon, Ill.; actress (stage, film, radio, TV), announcer (*Two on a Clue* 1944–46), commercials voiceover artist bka *Archie Andrews* teen sitcom matriarch Mary Andrews 1945–53; prolific daytime serials thespian (*The Guiding Light*, *Myrt and Marge*, *The Right to Happiness*, *Young Widder Brown*, more) late 1930s-mid 1950s; active in Mt. Vernon, Ohio community theater guild before New York; as radio faded, in theatrical film *Dirtymouth* 1970, made-for-TV film *Luke Was There* 1976, durable Laura Grant in *The Guiding Light* CBS Radio-TV 1953–62, concurrently Anita Borkowitz in same web's *The Edge of Night* 1957; d. Oct. 28, 2000.

Deaths

Claudia Morgan, Sept. 17, 1974, New York City, N.Y.; b. Nov. 12, 1911. Red Skelton, Sept. 17, 1997, Rancho Mirage, Calif.; b. July 18, 1913. Jay Stewart, Sept. 17, 1989, Los Angeles, Calif.; b. Sept. 6, 1918.

September 18

Sound Bite

CBS premiers Sunday, Sept. 18, 1927 as Columbia Phonograph Broadcasting System; chain VP Maj. J. Andrew White master of ceremonies for inaugural with 22-piece symphony conducted by Howard Barlow, Metropolitan Opera Co. cast in "The King's Henchman"; New York Philharmonic, Philadelphia Symphony Orchestra featured same day; 16-station hookup originated at Newark WOR (replaced by New York WABC in 15 months); hookup went east to Boston, west to Council Bluffs, north to Detroit, south to St. Louis.

Debuting

Space Patrol, Sept. 18, 1950, ABC; intergalactic juvenile adventure; 30th century police-keeping force charged with protecting five worlds from evildoers across universe — Earth, Jupiter, Mars, Mercury, Venus ("United Planets"); Space Patrol based on man-made planet Terra under command of chief officer Buzz Corey (Ed Kemmer) who — accompanied by sidekick Cadet Happy (Lyn Osborne) with incessant annonying expression "Smokin' rockets, Commander!" — frequently shot off via spaceship to far-flung remote spots to rope in another celestial evilmonger; villains didn't die on made-for-tykes drama — once hit with Corey's ray gun, they were rendered immobile, shown error of ways on brainograph that convicted them of misdeeds, turned them around; televersion ABC 1950–55; final radiocast March 19, 1955.

Canceled

Ted Mack's Original Amateur Hour, Sept. 18, 1952, ABC; debut Sept. 29, 1948.

Births

Eddie (Rochester) Anderson, Sept. 18, 1905, Oakland, Calif.; actor (film, radio, TV) bka *The Jack Benny Program* gravelly-voiced valet whose witty jibes highlighted Benny's tightwad character 1937–55, TV 1950–65; at 14 appeared with circus artist parents in all-black revue; performed in vaudeville with brother prior to landing in films, answering open call for Benny tryout 1937; d. Feb. 28, 1977.

Joseph (Curley) Bradley (Raymond George Courtney), Sept. 18, 1910, Colgate, Okla.; actor (film, radio), rodeo prodigy, stuntman, vocalist (cowboy-Western ballads) bka *Tom Mix and the Ralston Straightshooters* lead 1944–51; d. June 3, 1985.

Death

Jack Lester, Sept. 18, 2004, Canoga Park, Calif.; b. Aug. 10, 1915.

September 19

Debuting

Just Plain Bill, Sept. 19, 1932, CBS; daytime serial launched with five-night-a-week quarter-hour installments, matinee rendering added 1933; one of hardiest perennials of flowering breed setting model for durable soaps not eclipsed until it left air — by *Ma Perkins*, *The Romance of Helen Trent* (both premiered 1933) nipping at *Bill's* heels; Bill Davidson (Arthur Hughes), "barber of Hartville," homespun philosopher who took others' troubles to himself, righted wrongs, put criminals behind bars; daughter Nancy Donovan (Ruth Russell, Toni Darnay), son-in-law Kerry Donovan (James Meighan) assets to plots; final broadcast Sept. 30, 1955, scrubbed from ether to allow for dismal failure *Weekday*.

Canceled

Vic and Sade, Sept. 19, 1946, MBS; debut June 29, 1932. *You Bet Your Life*, Sept. 19, 1956, NBC; debut Oct. 27, 1947.

Births

Elvia Allman (Elvia Beatrice Bayler), Sept. 19, 1904, Spencer, N.C.; actress (radio, film, TV); ex-vaudeville vocalist, dancer, on Los Angeles KHJ 1930 in monologues, reading poems; supporting roles in boatload of aural comedies, sitcoms, variety series 1930s-50s: *The Abbott and Costello Show, Al Pearce and His Gang, The Bob Hope Show, Fibber McGee & Molly, The Fred Allen Show, The George Burns and Gracie Allen Show, The Jimmy Durante-Garry Moore Show, Kraft Music Hall, The Life of Riley, The Ray Bolger Show*, more; regular on CBS-TV's *The Beverly Hillbillies, Petticoat Junction*; d. March 6, 1992.

Dresser Dahlstead, Sept. 19, 1910, Springville, Utah; announcer on 1930s-40s series like *Death Valley Days, The Fitch Bandwagon, I Deal in Crime, I Love a Mystery, I Love Adventure*; worked for Ogden, Utah station to pay for college; in radio full time at San Francisco 1931, joined NBC there 1932; d. April 20, 1998.

Betty Garde, Sept. 19, 1905, Philadelphia, Pa.; actress (stage, film, radio, TV); after lesser stage shows, burst onto Broadway as Aunt Eller in 1940s original version of *Oklahoma!*; on radio in *The Aldrich Family, Big Story, The Columbia Workshop, The Fat Man, Front Page Farrell, Gangbusters, Here's Morgan, Inner Sanctum Mysteries, Lorenzo Jones, Mr. and Mrs. North, Mrs. Wiggs of the Cabbage Patch, Perry Mason, The Phil Silvers Show, The Thin Man*, score more; 11 theatrical films 1929–62; TV credits 1949–71 for ongoing roles in *Kobb's Corner, Easy Aces, The World of Mr. Sweeney, The Edge of Night, As the World Turns*, 29 performances in solo episodes of scattered TV fare; d. Dec. 25, 1989.

Blanche Thebom, Sept. 19, 1915, Monessen, Pa.; vocalist (mezzo-soprano) bka Metropolitan Opera diva 1941–63; *The Bell Telephone Hour* 26 guest artist appearances 1940–58, *The Railroad Hour* infrequent costar 1948–54, *Voice of Firestone* singing guest 1928–57.

Deaths

Martin Block, Sept. 19, 1967, Englewood, N.J.; b. Feb. 3, 1903. Win Elliot, Sept. 19, 1998, Norwalk, Conn.; b. May 7, 1915.

September 20

Sound Bite

On Saturday night Sept. 20, 1952 at 11:59 p.m., two parallel organizations operating almost independently of one another but sharing common themes — American Federation of Radio Artists (AFRA) dating from 1937, Television Authority (TvA) from 1950, latter embodying talent on tube — combine to form American Federation of Television and Radio Artists (AFTRA); at inception, new union represents more than 25,000 working performers: actors, comedians, emcees, quizmasters, disc jockeys, vocalists, dancers, freelance/staff announcers, sportscasters, specialty acts, sound effects techies, walk-ons, extras, puppeteers, reporters, news/policy analysts, models, moderators, panelists; today AFTRA wields huge stick in electronic performance negotiations.

Debuting

The Six Shooter, Sept. 20, 1953, NBC; western drama appealing to adults (mature-themed frontier narratives early 1950s species); transient gunslinger Britt Ponset (James Stewart) preferred helping people to crimefighting, righting wrongs but at times he, six shooter, reputation pressed into service; premiered April 13, 1952 on *The Hollywood Star Playhouse* as one-time folksy frontier play but in due course netted series; final broadcast June 24, 1954.

Smilin' Ed McConnell and His Buster Brown Gang (*Aladdin Lamp Program, Ballard's Oven-Ready Biscusit Time*), Sept. 20, 1932, CBS; juvenile variety; jolly old fat man sang, played piano, laughed heartily, narrated adventure dramas, dispensed moral bromides to small fry ("Don't forget to attend Sunday school and church tomorrow") as he kept order amid rowdy crowd of boisterous preteens in studio audience; years of practice on net air (1932–41) before Saturday morning jamboree launch Sept. 2, 1944 netting instant recognition (by viewers, too — NBC/CBS/ABC 1950–55); characterizations of Squeeky the Mouse, Midnight the Cat, Grandie the Piano, Froggy the Gremlin turned raucous adolescents into ecstatic rebel-rousers; final broadcast April 11, 1953.

Canceled

Richard Diamond, Private Detective, Sept. 20, 1953, ABC; debut April 24, 1949.

Birth

Joseph King, Sept. 20, 1915, Birmingham, Ala.; announcer, emcee bka interlocutor for 1940s-50s features *Claudia, The Eileen Barton Show, Here's to Vets, Mr. and Mrs. North, The*

Philip Morris Playhouse, Songs By Morton Downey, Spotlight Revue, The Toni Arden Show, Walk a Mile; CBS affiliate staff at Washington WJSV before shift to New York, heard on web's *A Report to the Nation* 1942, D-Day coverage 1944; joined New York WOR-TV in 1950s announcing, hosting weekday juvenile fare as "Sheriff Joe."

Deaths

John Holbrook, Sept. 20, 1978, Sapphire, N.C.; b. Aug. 28, 1910. Vincent Lopez, Sept. 20, 1975, North Miami, Fla.; b. Dec. 30, 1894.

September 21

Debuting

Life with Luigi, Sept. 21, 1948, CBS; sitcom with ethnic twist focused on Italian immigrant Luigi Basco (J. Carrol Naish) desperately hoping to be contributing U. S. citizen — funny things happened to Chicago antique emporium operator, often at hands of conniving pal Pasquale (Alan Reed); Hans Conried, Joe Forte, Jody Gilbert, Ken Peters, Mary Shipp, Gil Stratton, Jr. other key players; final primetime radiocast March 3, 1953; fleeting CBS televersions bombed twice — Sept. 22-Dec. 29, 1952, April 9-June 4, 1953.

Births

John E. (Jack) Mather, Sept. 21, 1907, Chicago, Ill.; actor (film, radio), announcer bka 1930s-50s juvenile western adventure thespian in *The Cisco Kid, Gene Autry's Melody Ranch, Speed Gibson of the International Secret Police, Wild Bill Hickok*; though typecast, turned up in myriad added dramatic, comedic entries: *Cavalcade of America, Dr. Christian, The Edgar Bergen and Charlie McCarthy Show, Fibber McGee & Molly, The Jack Benny Program, Lux Radio Theater, The Phil Harris-Alice Faye Show*, more; opened *Radio Almanac, Tommy Riggs and Betty Lou*; played in three 1950s movies; d. Aug. 15, 1966.

Westbrook Van Voorhis (Hugh Conrad), Sept. 21, 1903, New Milford, Conn.; announcer, commentator bka "voice of doom" for sober style opening *The March of Time* documentary 1937–39, 1942–45; *Westbrook Van Voorhis* commentary feature 1943–45, later narrated *The Great Adventure* 1951 on radio; hired by New York CBS 1930s, affiliated with NBC Blue 1937, remained with it in transition to ABC; filled slots with half-dozen forgettable video series 1949–58 but recalled for narrating movie documentaries for *Time* magazine about 15 years, likewise armed forces instructional films; d. July 13, 1968.

September 22

Canceled

The CBS Radio Workshop, Sept. 22, 1957, CBS; debuted as *The Columbia Workshop* July 18, 1936 followed in strain by *Twenty-Six by Corwin, Columbia Presents Corwin, The CBS Radio Workshop. Kraft Music Hall*, Sept. 22, 1949, NBC; debut June 26, 1933.

Births

Richard C. Hottelet, Sept. 22, 1917, Brooklyn, N.Y.; author, commentator, correspondent, newscaster, wire journalist (United Press) bka POW held in German concentration camps, only U. S. reporter (for UP) detained four months in 1941 for condemning Hitler's preparation for global conflict which he observed (released in exchange for German held by Allies); next worked for U. S. Office of War Information/London before CBS overseas news guru Edward R. Murrow hired him 1944, final member of infamous "Murrow Boys" to report from Europe; 1940s radio gigs *CBS Morning News Roundup, CBS World News Roundup* (*The World Tonight*) ca. 1944-ca. 1985, *Crisco Radio Newspaper, Richard C. Hottelet News, The World Is Our Beat, You Are There*; sent to UN by CBS 1956, presided over dual daily CBS-TV news shows 1957–61; retired 1985, then spokesman for U. S. envoy to U. N.; moderated *America and the World* NPR 1993.

Hanley Stafford (Alfred John Austin), Sept. 22, 1899, Hanley, Staffordshire, England; actor (stage, film, radio, TV) bka *Baby Snooks* family sitcom patriarch Lancelot ("Daddy") Higgins, kindhearted foil to Snooks, brat taking full advantage of his leniency, at last pushing him over edge of despair 1938–51; d. Sept. 11, 1968.

Elizabeth (Betty) Wragge (Brooke), Sept. 22, 1917, New York City, N.Y.; actress (stage, radio, TV) bka *Pepper Young's Family* sibling Peggy Young Trent (Carter's spouse) appearing in precursor drama *Red Adams* NBC Blue 1932–33 before it segued into *Forever Young*, *Pepper Young's Family* both 1936 aired intermittently on NBC/MBS/NBC Blue/CBS till 1959, relieved of duty — never replaced — two years while in Broadway play; at three in silent films, at nine in *Gold Star Pals* on NBC 1927, first net commercial series employing child actors; subsequently acted in *Mary and Bob's True Stories* 1928–32, other series netted "more than 10,000 live radio broadcasts"; performed in off-Broadway plays, summer stock, dinner theater, toured in musicals, dubbed Italian films into English, TV commercials, industrial/training videos; d. Oct. 6, 2002.

Deaths

Lu Ann (Luanne) Simms, Sept. 22, 2003, Hollywood, Calif.; b. July 11, 1932. Edwin R. Wolfe, Sept. 22, 1983 (last residence Holmes, N.Y.); b. June 13, 1893.

September 23

Canceled

Meet Millie, Sept. 23, 1954, CBS; debut July 2, 1951. *Mr. President*, Sept. 23, 1953, ABC; debut June 26, 1947. *Two for the Money*, Sept. 23, 1956, CBS; debut Sept. 30, 2952.

Birth

Helen Hiett, Sept. 23, 1913, Tazewell, Ill.; correspondent, newscaster, print journalist bka early 1940s feminine reporter, some of her reportage from Europe (*Helen Hiett News* 1941–42, *News Roundup* 1940 from Paris, *Sunday Evening News Roundup* 1941 from Madrid); after resigning from NBC Blue chain, directed forums of *The New York Herald Tribune*; returned overseas to live after wedding U. S. envoy Theodore Waller 1948; d. Aug. 22, 1961.

Elliott Roosevelt, Sept. 23, 1910, New York City, N.Y.; author, commentator, emcee, station owner; son of Franklin D. Roosevelt who was U. S. president 1933–45; managed Hearst radio chain from 1933; on-air gigs *Elliott Roosevent Commentary* 1939, *Information Please* guest panelist 1940s, *At Home with Faye* [Emerson] *and Elliott* 1946; *Eleanor and Elliott Roosevelt* 1950–51; bought trio of Texas radio stations, launched Texas State Network linking 26 outlets with MBS; penned more than score of books, mostly fiction; Miami Beach, Fla. mayor 1965–69; aleniated self from parents, siblings personally, politically much of life through widely publicized missteps; d. Oct. 27, 1990.

Deaths

Carl Frank, Sept. 23, 1972, St. John, U. S. Virgin Islands; b. Feb. 27, 1909. Earl Godwin, Sept. 23, 1956, Rehoboth Beach, Del.; Jan. 24, 1881. Phil Leslie, Sept. 23, 1988, Tarzana, Calif.; b. March 11, 1909.

September 24

Debuting

What's the Name of That Song?, Sept. 24, 1944, MBS (premiered Don Lee chain 1943); musical quiz with object akin to *Kay Kyser's Kollege of Musical Knowledge*, *Name That Tune*, *Stop the Music!* but never equal; emcees Dud Williamson, Bob Bence, Bill Gwinn; final broadcast Dec. 16, 1948.

Canceled

Welcome Travelers, Sept. 24, 1954, NBC; debut June 30, 1947.

Deaths

Floyd Gibbons, Sept. 24, 1939, Saylorsburg, Pa.; b. July 16, 1887. Jerry Lawrence, Sept. 24, 2005, Los Angeles, Calif.; b. Dec. 18, 1911. Harlow Wilcox, Sept. 24, 1960, Hollywood, Calif.; b. March 12, 1900.

September 25

Sound Bite

Amalgamated Broadcasting System, spearheaded by entertainer Ed Wynn, Hungarian native violinist Ota Gygi, launches Sept. 25, 1933 with four-hour gala from New York flagship station WBNX, handful of primarily East Coast outlets; Wynn sinks personal fortune into it, misguidedly allows Gygi to run it — latter alienates most of press, diminishes potential financial recoup boasting that ABS's limited commercialization "necessary but distasteful evil" while tales of fraud, graft surface; five weeks into it, Oct. 28, 1933, bankrupt ABS is eternally off air, experiencing $300,000 indebtedness; loss, end of

Fire Chief series concurrently running at NBC, marital discord take Wynn to nervous breakdown by decade end; Mutual Broadcasting System emerges Sept. 29, 1934 out of ABS's surplus inspiration, theories, practices.

Debuting

The Tom Mix Ralston Straight Shooters, Sept. 25, 1933, NBC; juvenile western adventure serial, aired at times under sobriquets of diverse incarnations: *Tom Mix*, *The Curley Bradley Show*, *The Singing Marshal*; derived from exploits of hyped "greatest western film star of the silent era"; namesake star (Artells Dickson, Jack Holden, Russell Thorson, Joe "Curley" Bradley) colorful plainsman who — with sheriff Mike Shaw (Leo Curley, DeWitt McBride) — tracked bank robbers, bushwhackers, cattle rustlers, stagecoach bandits, murderers, saboteurs, myriad evilmongers, bringing them to justice; final broadcast Dec. 16, 1951.

Canceled

Escape, Sept. 25, 1954, CBS; debut July 7, 1947. *The Jack Pearl Show*, Sept. 25, 1951, NBC; debut Sept. 8, 1932. *Nick Carter, Master Detective*, Sept. 25, 1955, MBS; debut April 11, 1943. *Night Beat*, Sept. 25, 1952, NBC; debut Feb. 6, 1950. *Stars Over Hollywood*, Sept. 25, 1954, CBS; debut May 31, 1941. *The Story of Bess Johnson*, Sept. 25, 1942, NBC; debut March 31, 1941.

Birth

Philip Francis ("Scooter") Rizzuto, Sept. 25, 1917, Brooklyn, N.Y.; sportscaster bka New York Yankees shortstop who helped team win 10 pennants, eight World Series in 13 seasons 1941–42, 1946–56 — All-Star five times, American League MVP 1950, Baseball Hall of Famer 1994; retired from playing field as Yankee play-by-play broadcaster four decades (adding expression "Holy cow!" to American vernacular) ; *Phil Rizzuto's Sports Caravan* NBC, CBS 1952-ca. 1960s faithfully followed by true believers.

Deaths

Bob Considine, Sept. 25, 1975, New York City, N.Y.; b. Nov. 4, 1906. Bret Morrison, Sept. 25, 1978, Hollywood, Calif.; b. May 5, 1912. Emily Post, Sept. 25, 1960, New York City, N.Y.; b. Oct. 27, 1873.

September 26

Sound Bite

William S. Paley becomes president of United Broadcasters while Major White remains president of the Columbia Phonograph Broadcasting System on Sept. 26, 1928; in January 1929, Paley merges dual units, renames it Columbia Broadcasting System, assumes presidency; says critic Francis Chase, Jr. in 1942: "From the day he took over the reins of CBS, Paley has been driven by an unquenchable ambition to overtake and exceed NBC as the nation's greatest network ... While he hasn't achieved this end from a physical property or program standpoint, he has passed NBC in time sales, the core of broadcasting"; seven years hence via raids on NBC's longstanding talent, he achieves remainder of it.

Debuting

Pot o' Gold, Sept. 26, 1939, NBC; quiz; from embryonic era of aired game shows, one of earliest to telephone listeners with chance to win money, leading to "bank nights" at many cinemas — if *Pot o' Gold* called movie patron while in theater, he earned $1,000 cash for missed call; bandleader Horace Heidt original emcee to 1941, show returned 1946-March 26, 1947 with Happy Felton presiding.

Canceled

The Fat Man, Sept. 26, 1951, ABC; debut Jan. 21, 1946. *It Pays to Be Ignorant*, Sept. 26, 1951, NBC; debut June 25, 1942. *Mr. Keen, Tracer of Lost Persons*, Sept. 26, 1955, CBS; debut Oct. 12, 1937.

Deaths

Charles Correll, Sept. 26, 1972, Chicago, Ill.; b. Feb. 2, 1890. Jack Haskell, Sept. 26, 1998, Englewood, N.J.; b. April 30, 1919.

September 27

Debuting

Fun for All, Sept. 27, 1952, CBS; audience participation smorgasbord; Bill Cullen, Arlene Francis cohost mirth-filled feature integrating lively contests with studio audience, comedy, music; final broadcast Dec. 26, 1953.

Waltz Time, Sept. 27, 1933, NBC; one of multiple Frank, Anne Hummert-produced series focused on ballads, waltzes, classical, semiclassical tunes; Abe Lyman impresario; Frank Munn, Evelyn MacGregor, Bob Hannon featured leads; vocalists Lois Bennett, Bernice Claire, Mary Eastman, Lucy Monroe, Vivienne Sega, The Amsterdam Chorus ensemble; final broadcast July 16, 1948.

Cancelled

Bachelor's Children, Sept. 27, 1946, CBS; debut Sept. 28, 1936. *The First Nighter*, Sept. 27, 1953, NBC; debut Nov. 27, 1930.

Births

William Conrad, Sept. 27, 1920, Louisville, Ky.; actor (radio, film, TV), composer, director, lyricist, producer, voiceover artist bka *Gunsmoke* western narrative sheriff Matt Dillon CBS 1952–61; embraced aural crimefighting features e.g. *The Adventures of Sam Spade, Crime Classics, Hawk Larabee, Johnny Madero—Pier 23, The Man Called X, Meet Miss Sherlock, Pete Kelly's Blues, The Saint, The Six Shooter, Tales of the Texas Rangers, This Is Your FBI*, more; rapacious appetite for screen work linked to acting, directing, production, music of 60 theatrical films 1954–91, 30 made-for-TV flicks 1975–87, two TV miniseries 1977–78, guest-solo roles in 169 TV shows/episodes 1955–93, 11 TV series 1950–92 producing one show, voicing three animated cartoons, narrating four features (109 episodes of *The Fugitive* 1963–67 alone), starring in three more (*Cannon* 1971–76, *Nero Wolfe* 1981, *Jake and the Fatman* 1987–92); d. Feb. 11, 1994.

Cy Howard, Sept. 27, 1915, Milwaukee, Wis.; actor, director, producer, program creative, scriptwriter (film, radio, stage) bka *My Friend Irma* sitcom originator 1947–54, *Life with Luigi* sitcom originator 1948–54; d. April 29, 1993.

Edward Tomlinson, Sept. 27, 1892, Stockton, Ga.; author, columnist (Scripps-Howard papers), commentator, correspondent (*The New York Herald Tribune*), freelance writer (*Colliers, Cosmopolitan, Reader's Digest*), lecturer bka *Edward Tomlinson News and Comments* host NBC 1940–45, 1946–49; earlier series *The Other Americans* 1935–36, *What's New in South America?* 1938; NBC South American correspondent 1936–43; used platforms to advocate strong ties linking Pan America, U. S.; d. Dec. 29, 1973.

Deaths

Philip Clarke, Sept. 27, 1985 (final residence Dothan, Ala.); b. Aug. 4, 1904. Hugh Conover, Sept. 27, 1992, Morgan Hill, Calif.; b. March 27, 1915. Laurette Fillbrandt, Sept. 20, 2000, Fairfax, Va.; b. Oct. 22, 1915.

September 28

Sound Bites

William S. Paley, one of two men to shape much of broadcasting in 20th century (other, David Sarnoff), is born Sept. 28, 1901 in Chicago, Ill.; Jewish parents emigrate from Ukraine, meet, wed in Windy City; young Paley never proud of clan's hardships, claims dad "probably a millionaire" opening cigar-making Samuel Paley & Co. 1896 at 21—Ogden Ave. hovel they lived in doubled as pop shop; Paley, chief rival Sarnoff—Jewish, 10 years his senior—know sting of poverty; by 27th birthday, Paley runs one of most powerful broadcasting regimes in world (CBS), for more than half-century, far cry from starting point.

Columbia Broadcasting System dates to Sept. 28, 1928; unable to sell enough air time to advertisers, existing Columbia Phonograph Broadcasting System is purchased by Philadelphia cigar manufacturer-advertiser Sam Paley, partners; Paley installs son William S. (Bill) Paley, 27, as operating director—younger Paley will become web's destiny for about five decades, ultimately turning fledgling chain into powerful broadcast empire; outfit renamed CBS.

Debuting

The Adventures of Christopher Wells, Sept. 28, 1947, CBS; intercontinental crime drama; crusading journalist hero (Myron McCormick, Les Damon) traipsed earth seeking tales for his Big Apple tabloid; inspired by writer-producer Ed Byron who introduced *Mr. District Attorney* eight years earlier, farce wasn't comparable; pitted in half-hour against NBC's *Fibber McGee & Molly* at mid-season, *Wells* shot down in flames; final broadcast June 22, 1948.

Bachelor's Children, Sept. 28, 1936, CBS; daytime serial; trial premier on Chicago WGN Sept. 9, 1935-Sept. 25, 1936; Bob Graham (Hugh Studebaker), 35, single doctor accepted dying comrade's twin daughters, 18 — one rebellious, angry (Janet, actress Patricia Dunlap), other kindly, calm (Ruth Ann, actresses Marjorie Hannah, Laurette Fillbrandt); at last Graham's pal Sam Ryder (Olan Soule) wed Janet while Graham married Ruth Ann, none of it signaling eternal bliss; final broadcast Sept. 27, 1946.

Grand Central Station, Sept. 28, 1937, NBC Blue; anthology drama; one of most memorable ethereal starts: "As a bullet seeks its target, shining rails in every part of our great country are aimed at Grand Central Station, heart of the nation's greatest city. Drawn by the magnetic force of the fantastic metropolis, day and night great trains rush toward the Hudson River, sweep down its eastern bank for 140 miles, flash briefly by the long red row of tenement houses south of 125th Street, dive with a roar into the two-and-one-half-mile tunnel which burrows beneath the glitter and swank of Park Avenue, and then ... [*bell clangs, engine hisses*] Grand Central Station!"; fans followed an arriving traveler, what transpired with him next with little allusion to journey just ended; Jim Ameche, Helen Claire, Roger DeKoven, Hume Cronyn, Arnold Moss, others of ilk performed; final broadcast April 2, 1954.

Poole's Paradise (*Presenting Poole*, *Poole's Parlor*, *Bob Poole Show*), Sept. 28, 1948, MBS; recordings; for a while Bob Poole may have cornered more web time than any other disc jockey in nation; in early postwar era New Orleans insomniacs tuned in *Poole's Paradise* on WWL accompanied by Spike Jones-type sound effects; ascended to prominence on New York WOR not long afterward, at mid century Poole aired morning, afternoon weekday slots, Saturday matinees; show marked by witty banter ("Hi out there all my little chickadees"), evocative of tantalizingly cheery Raymond of *Inner Sanctum Mysteries*; waxworks punctuated by telephone quizzes, patchy guests, snappy asides, classic din; after New York, Poole aired on local Chicago ether; final net broadcast May 26, 1950.

Canceled

The Bing Crosby-Rosemary Clooney Show, Sept. 28, 1962, CBS; debut Sept. 2, 1957. *The FBI in Peace & War*, Sept. 28, 1958, CBS; debut Nov. 25, 1944. *Screen Directors' Playhouse*, Sept. 28, 1951, NBC; debut Jan. 9, 1949.

Births

Harold Thomas Henry (Boake) Carter, Sept. 28, 1903, Baku, Azerbaijan; author, commentator, newscaster, print editor-reporter, syndicated columnist known for covering Lindbergh baby kidnap 1932; controversial, highly partisan ultraconservative; CBS fired star newsman after 1933–38 tenure, he soon joined MBS 1940–44; d. Nov. 16, 1944.

Jack Meakin, Sept. 28, 1906, Salt Lake City, Utah; composer, impresario, pianist; *The Chamber Music of Lower Basin Street* most recognizable gig bearing baton 1940; d. Dec. 30, 1982.

Edward Vincent Sullivan, Sept. 28, 1901, Harlem, New York City, N.Y.; emcee, print journalist bka *The Ed Sullivan Show* (multiple monikers) variety series host CBS/NBC Blue 1932, 1941, 1943–44, 1946, *The Ed Sullivan Show* (*Toast of the Town*) variety series master of ceremonies CBS-TV 1948–71; after sportswriting, was theater-gossip columnist of *The New York Graphic*, *The New York Daily News*, syndicated to others; awkward mannerisms, little acting ability, dubbed "Old Stone Face" on TV as comics spoofed his stage presence; nevertheless, huge following attracted by diverse acts that made show — him — powerful in CBS lineup; among radio "finds" was Jack Benny; d. Oct. 13, 1974.

William S. Paley, Sept. 28, 1901, Chicago, Ill.; advertising executive, broadcasting czar bka CBS corporate president-chairman 1928–90 who thrived on job, won spirited competitions with big-league rival David Sarnoff, chairman at RCA, titular head of NBC; protected industry from federal intrustion where possible; his word often final "say" though outwardly he seemed less stiff than Sarnoff; held out allegiance to radio in face of emerging TV; d. Oct. 26, 1990.

September 29

Sound Bites

Last of breed of nationwide commercial chains on air with stable moniker as of Sept. 29, 1934; influential broadcasting quartet with independent program departments (Chicago WGN, Cincinnati WLW, Newark WOR, Detroit WXYZ) earlier merged as provisional Quality Network, sharing ethereal features, now altering nomenclature to form Mutual Broadcasting System (MBS); it differs from rivals NBC Red, NBC Blue (later ABC), CBS by having no central ownership (WGN, WOR technically own all limited stock), no owned-and-operated outlets nor contractual affiliates; in 1936 New England-based Colonial Network (13 stations), West Coast-based Don Lee Network (10 stations) join MBS netting national hookup; promoting itself as "network for all America," MBS watches member stations peak at 950 in 1979; operations cease April 18, 1999.

Lowell Thomas goes nationwide Sept. 29, 1930 on NBC Blue/CBS West Coast hookup with daily newscast outlasting all peers but Paul Harvey when Thomas quits May 14, 1976 at CBS; NBC exclusively dispatches his voice 1931–47.

Debuting

Double or Nothing, Sept. 29, 1940, MBS; primetime, daytime (1947ff) quiz; masters of ceremonies Walter Compton, John Reed King, Todd Russell, Walter O'Keefe; final broadcast Jan. 15, 1954; CBS-TV host Bert Parks 1952–54.

The Phil Harris-Alice Faye Show (premiered as *The Fitch Bandwagon*), Sept. 29, 1946, NBC; situation comedy starring bandleader and ex-vocalist stay-at-home mom as selves; zany regular figures impacted their lives, complicating plots; final broadcast June 18, 1954.

Ted Mack's Original Amateur Hour, Sept. 29, 1948, ABC; Mack hosted talent auditions in vein of predecessor "institution" created by Major Edward Bowes, *The Original Amateur Hour* March 24, 1935-Jan. 4, 1945; final broadcast Sept. 18, 1952, televersions embrace four webs Jan. 18, 1948-Sept. 27, 1970.

Canceled

Dimension X, Sept. 29, 1951, NBC; debut April 8, 1950.

Births

Gene Autry (Orvon Gene Autry), Sept. 29, 1907, Tioga, Texas; actor (film, radio, TV), baseball franchise owner (California Angels), broadcasting stations' owner, entrepreneur, personal appearance entertainer (events, parades, rodeos, stage), recording artist, vocalist (cowboy-western music), bka *Gene Autry's Melody Ranch* headliner 1940–43, 1945–56, plus star of 90-plus shoot-'em-up western films aimed at juvenile set 1934–53; sold boatloads of recordings of "Here Comes Santa Claus," "Rudolph the Red-Nosed Reindeer" late 1940s; CBS-TV *The Gene Autry Show* July 23, 1950-Aug. 7, 1956; d. Oct. 2, 1998.

Ted de Corsia, Sept. 29, 1905, Brooklyn, N.Y.; actor (stage, radio, film, TV); apart from brief leads in *McGarry and His Mouse*, *Pursuit*, *That Hammer Guy*, radio resume mainly sprinkled with support roles in felony escapism: *The Adventures of Christopher London*, *The Adventures of Ellery Queen*, *Big Town*, *Bulldog Drummond*, *Casey— Crime Photographer*, *Crime Classics*, *I Deal in Crime*, *One Man's Family*, *Richard Diamond— Private Detective*, *The Shadow*, *The Six Shooter*, *T-Man*, *Terry and the Pirates*, *True Detective Mysteries*; acted on Broadway 1929/1935, 60 theatrical films 1943–72, made-for-TV flick 1960, 164 solo appearances in tube dramas/sitcoms/variety series; d. April 11, 1973.

Richard C. Harkness, Sept. 29, 1907, Artesian, S.D.; correspondent, newscaster, print/wire service journalist (United Press), publicist bka *Monitor* newscaster 1955–72, *NBC News on the Hour* newscaster mid 1950s-1972, *Richard Harkness and the News* 1944–45, 1947–53, *NBC News Roundup* correspondent 1945; served UP Kansas City, Oklahoma City, Dallas, Jefferson City, Mo., Washington, D.C. (White House rep), joining *The Philadelphia Inquirer* 1937 in D.C. bureau; NBC Washington news staff 1942 with series simultaneously airing on New York WNBC, Washington WRC several years apart from other NBC work; interviewed current events figures for *The Richard Harkness Show* NBC-TV 1948–49; linked to more news, public affairs ventures in TV's early epoch; following 1972 retirement, press agent 1974–77 for drug abuse effort created by President Gerald R. Ford; d. Feb. 16, 1977.

Deaths

William Perry Adams, Sept. 29, 1972, New York City, N.Y.; b. May 9, 1887. Tom Hanlon, Sept. 29, 1970, Hollywood, Calif.; b. Nov. 7, 1907. Robert Latting, Sept. 29, 1983, San Jose, Calif.; b. Dec. 29, 1921.

September 30

Debuting

Death Valley Days, Sept. 30, 1930, NBC; frontier anthology drama; Old Ranger (Jack MacBryde, Tim Daniel Frawley, George Rand, Harry Humphrey) narrated tales of Old West frequently including Old Prospector (Harvey Hays), Lonesome Cowboy (John White), company of seasoned actors; covered wagons, sagebrush, cactus, saloon gals, bartenders, outlaws, prospectors, blacksmiths, Indians part of passing scene; syndicated TV series 1952–70, 1974, final radiocast Aug. 3, 1944; spinoff *Death Valley Sheriff* 1944–45, successor *The Sheriff* 1945–51.

Man on the Farm, Sept. 30, 1939, MBS; agricultural-livestock issues forum; final broadcast May 1, 1954.

National Barn Dance, Sept. 30, 1933, NBC Blue; country music jamboree; originated April 19, 1924 Chicago WLS — predating legendary *Grand Ole Opry*— by man who created *Opry* in 1925, George D. Hay; performers included Arkansas Woodchoppers, Pat Buttram, The Dinning Sisters, George Gobel, Bob Hastings, Hoosier Hot Shots, Lulu Belle and Skyland Scotty, more; off network 1946–49; ABC-TV 1949; though it lasted to 1970 locally, never drew idolatrous esteem of *Opry* fans as latter persisted to today; final net broadcast March 11, 1950.

The National Farm and Home Hour, Sept. 30, 1929, NBC Blue; variety, rural features; "the farmer's bulletin board" offered agricultural community news, music, hints for growing crops/livestock, politics, forums to help farmers prosper; Everett Mitchell hosted, H. R. Baukhage reported news, forgettable singers, comedians, actors performed in sketches, musical interludes; with one six-month abandonment, series endured three decades from inception on Pittsburgh KDKA 1928; final broadcast Jan. 25, 1958.

Two for the Money, Sept. 30, 1952, NBC; quiz; always able to think on feet, keen wit Herb Shriner ideal as comic quizmaster (think Groucho Marx) with snappy asides in diverse situations; before challenging three player teams with questions for cash gifts, Shriner offered humorous monologue exhibiting strong suit; successful first round teams tried for jackpot payoff; TV incarnations featured hosts Shriner, Walter O'Keefe, Dennis James, Sam Levenson NBC/CBS 1952–57; final radiocast Sept. 23, 1956.

Canceled

Cathy and Elliott Lewis Onstage, Sept. 30, 1954, CBS; debut Jan. 1, 1953. *Just Plain Bill*, Sept. 30, 1955, NBC; debut Sept. 19, 1932. *Lorenzo Jones*, Sept. 30, 1955, NBC; debut April 26, 1937. *Meet Corliss Archer*, Sept. 30, 1956, CBS; debut Jan. 7, 1943. *Suspense*, Sept. 30, 1962, CBS; debut June 17, 1942. *Yours Truly, Johnny Dollar*, Sept. 30, 1962, CBS; debut Feb. 11, 1949.

Birth

Tom Reddy (Merrill Thomas Mulready), Sept. 30, 1917, Eagle Grove, Iowa; announcer, emcee, station executive; welcomed listeners to mid 1940s-early 1950s *The Chesterfield Supper Club*, *The Fitch Bandwagon*, *Guest Star*, *Theater U.S.A.*; master of ceremonies on forgettable 1950s daytime CBS-TV series *Journey through Life*, *How Do You Rate*; following airtime, co-owned Flint, Mich. WTAC Radio; d. Aug. 13, 1961.

Deaths

Edgar Bergen, Sept. 30, 1978, Las Vegas, Nev.; b. Feb. 16, 1903. Freddy Martin, Sept. 30, 1983, Newport Beach, Calif.; b. Dec. 9, 1906.

October 1

Sound Bite

Philco Radio Time starring crooner Bing Crosby breaks barrier of prerecording programs for national hookups; first show ABC Oct. 1, 1947 sets trend reforming industry, deletes archaic chain rule against taping; pattern quickly copied, eliminates need for "second" live performances with time-friendly concern for West Coast audiences.

Canceled

Talent Scouts, Oct. 1, 1956, CBS; debut July 2, 1946.

Birth

Everett Sloane, Oct. 1, 1909, Manhattan,

New York City, N.Y.; actor (stage, radio, film, TV), director, lyricist, voiceover artist bka *Citizen Kane* theatrical movie figure Mr. Bernstein 1941; onstage at age seven, poor reviews of collegiate acting sent him to Wall Street as runner; turned to radio after 1929 stock market debacle, landed on Broadway in *Boy Meets Girl* 1936; with exception of daytime serials *Big Sister, This Is Nora Drake, Today's Children,* habitually worked most all West Coast crimefighting series: *The Adventures of the Falcon, The Affairs of Peter Salem, Buck Rogers in the 25th Century, Bulldog Drummond, Crime and Peter Chambers, Crime Doctor, Crime Does Not Pay, Flash Gordon, The Private Files of Rex Saunders, The Shadow, Treasury Agent, Twenty-First Precinct,* etc.; 26 theatrical releases 1941–64, four made-for-TV flicks 1956–65, 140 appearances in TV drama episodes 1955–65; failing eyesight led to suicide; d. Aug. 6, 1965.

Deaths

Richard Crooks, Oct. 1, 1972, San Mateo, Calif.; b. June 26, 1900. Frank Munn, Oct. 1, 1953, Queens Village, N.Y.; b. Feb. 2, 1894. Conway Tearle, Oct. 1, 1939, Los Angeles, Calif.; b. May 17, 1878.

October 2

Debuting

The Cisco Kid, Oct. 2, 1942, MBS; juvenile western adventure, Latin adaptation of tenderhearted Robin Hood in O. Henry classics that stole from haves, shared with have-nots; Cisco (Jackson Beck, Jack Mather), sidekick Pan Pancho dubbed "Chico" (Louis Sorin, Harry Lang, Mel Blanc) captured Mexican banditos, U. S. desperadoes; ladies' man Cisco kissed señoritas in storyline; Duncan Renaldo, Leo Carillo played dual leads in syndicated televersion (156 episodes starting 1950); daily comic strip 1950–68, made-for-TV flick TNT 1994; final net radiocast Feb. 14, 1945 though transcribed aural run aired 1947–56.

Pepper Young's Family (premiered with trio of antecedents—*Red Adams, Red Davis, Forever Young* before seguing into *PYF* June 29, 1936), Oct. 2, 1932, NBC Blue; daytime serial; developed into profound tale of life in typical post–Depression home, markedly relying upon authenticity, detail to make storyline, characters believable; narrative focused on son Larry "Pepper" Young (Curtis Arnall, Lawson Zerbe, Mason Adams), clan included father Sam (Bill Adams, Thomas Chalmers, Jack Roseleigh), mother Mary (Marion Barney), daughter Peggy (Elizabeth Wragge); domestic crises aplenty but still far more reality than found in most drainboard dramas; final broadcast April 24, 1959.

Births

Bud Abbott (William Alexander Abbott), Oct. 2, 1897, Asbury Park, N.J.; actor (stage, film, radio, TV), comedian bka Abbott and Costello comedy team straight man; quit school at 14, worked in Brooklyn burlesque, gravitated to vaudeville as straight man, teamed with rising comic Lou Costello 1931 in burlesque, vaudeville, minstrel, cinema; national exposure on *The Kate Smith Hour* CBS 1938–40, NBC summer 1940; *The Abbott and Costello Show* NBC/ABC 1942–49, syndicated TV 1952–53, 1967 (latter antimated); 35 theatrical films 1940–56; act dissolved 1957, Abbott sued Costello for uncollected sums 1958 but Costello died 1959 before resolution; IRS demanded $750,000 back taxes—Abbott sold two residences, jewelry, furs, surrendered movie profits; revival of old stage routines with Candy Candido 1961 didn't pan out; d. April 24, 1974.

Mary Marvin Breckinridge, Oct. 2, 1905, New York City, N.Y.; congressional intern, Democratic National Committee attaché, newscaster, photojournalist bka only feminine affiliate of "Murrow Boys" overseas correspondents hired by CBS sage Edward R. Murrow 1939–40, later U. S. diplomat Jefferson Patterson's spouse, globetrotter, Washington socialite, philanthropist; d. Dec. 11, 2002.

Julius Henry (Groucho) Marx, Oct. 2, 1890, New York City, N.Y.; actor (film, radio, stage), comedian, emcee, quizmaster bka *You Bet Your Life* master of ceremonies 1947–56, televersion extension to 1961; extensive vaudeville, stage, film work with brothers' act in early years of career; d. Aug. 19, 1977.

Deaths

Gene Autry, Oct. 2, 1998, Los Angeles, Calif.; b. Sept. 29, 1907. Harriet Hilliard (Nelson), Oct. 2, 1994, Laguna Beach, Calif.; b. July

18, 1909. Frank Lovejoy, Oct. 2, 1962, New York City, N.Y.; b. March 28, 1912.

October 3

Debuting

Barry Craig, Confidential Investigator, Oct. 3, 1951, NBC; crime detective drama; working independently from Madison Avenue digs while narrating his own adventures so fans could follow, hero (William Gargan) pledged to keep patrons' business classified (hence show's title); clientele often couldn't involve professional law officers in pursuits for sundry reasons, although Craig relied on exchanges with Lt. Travis Rogers (Ralph Bell); final broadcast June 30, 1955.

A Day in the Life of Dennis Day (*The Dennis Day Show*), Oct. 3, 1946, NBC; sitcom featuring Jack Benny vocalist Day in mythical storyline about his quests pursuing girl of his dreams, typically interposed between vocal numbers by singing star; final broadcast March 20, 1955.

Rosemary, Oct. 2, 1944, NBC; daytime serial; secretary Rosemary Dawson, (Betty Winkler, Virginia Kaye) age 20, struggled at inception of this saga to provide sustenance for herself, widowed mother, teen sis; it wasn't till she met, wed journalist Bill Roberts that real tragedy struck, however — he came home amnesiac from war, beyond dabbled in affairs, alcoholism, they lost baby, were estranged, separated — enough misery to mark her as one of daytime drama's most beleaguered heroines; fnal broadcast July 1, 1955.

Silver Theater, Oct. 3, 1937, CBS; anthology drama; named for sponsoring International Silver Co. (sometimes summer sub for its leading show, *The Adventures of Ozzie and Harriet*), hosts Conrad Nagel, John Loder presenting legends of silver screen in original dramatic, sporadic comic fare, plus rare movie adaptations; featured Clark Gable, Cary Grant, Helen Hayes, Ginger Rogers, Rosalind Russell, Jimmy Stewart, more; star formula discarded in final summer with leading radio actors performing — Staats Cotsworth, Anne Elstner, Mary Jane Higby, Jay Jostyn, Virginia Payne, et al.; final broadcast Aug. 17, 1947.

Births

Gertrude Berg, Oct. 3, 1899, New York City, N.Y.; actress (radio, TV, stage, film), writer bka *The Goldbergs* daytime serial/sitcom heroine Molly Goldberg 1929–34, 1936, 1937–45, 1949–50, televersion 1949–51, 1952–53, 1954–56; created humorous slice-of-life mesadventures of Bronx Jewish family with gossipy, big-hearted materfamilias Molly with signature greeting "Yoo-hoo, is anybody?"; Berg won Emmy 1950; *Molly and Me* in Broadway, theatrical film productions; Berg returned to Broadway in *Majority of One* 1959; d. Sept. 14, 1966.

Mark E. Houston, Oct. 3, 1913, Cleveland, Ohio; announcer bka *Queen for a Day* interlocutor ca. 1945-ca. 1950s, only certified web series; d. May 11, 1971.

Deaths

Charles Collingwood, Oct. 3, 1985, New York City, N.Y.; b. June 4, 1917. Eleanor Steber, Oct. 3, 1990, Langhorne, Pa.; b. July 17, 1914.

October 4

Debuting

Armstrong Theater of Today, Oct. 4, 1941, CBS; anthology melodrama; "It's high noon on Broadway!" shouted announcers George Bryan, Tom Shirley at top of show, enumerating events scheduled around country that day or weekend, ending with "...and all over America it's time for Armstrong's *Theater of Today*" (underwritten until 1953 by flooring manufacturer Armstrong Cork Co.); final broadcast May 22, 1954.

Mary Margaret McBride (*Martha Deane*), Oct. 4, 1937, MBS; women's issues forum-interviews; journalism background, hostess was instant fave with chatfest on topics for distaff audience that often included legendary guests; parlayed it into new career as hers faltered — dual decades on air including New York WOR 1934–40, four chains 1937–54; final broadcast May 15, 1954.

The Railroad Hour, Oct. 4, 1948, ABC; pop, semiclassical feature airing operettas, Broadway/film musicals, narratives of famous authors/musicians, mixed cabaret exhibitions; cited by critic as "best show of its kind" in epoch; starred movie, recordings singing icon Gordon MacRae, multitude of harmonizing guests, some returning frequently; final broadcast June 21, 1954.

We, the People, Oct. 4, 1936, NBC Blue; human interest drama; launched as sketch on *The Royal Gelatin Hour* (Rudy Vallee), it prospered, leading to own run; narratives focused on both common, celebrated man; hosted by Phillips H. Lord, Gabriel Heatter, Milo Boulton, Dwight Weist, Dan Seymour, Burgess Meredith, Eddie Dowling; Weist, Seymour emceed televersion CBS/NBC 1948–52; final radiocast Jan. 25, 1951.

Weekend, Oct. 4, 1953, NBC; magazine; one of two NBC precursors (other *Roadshow* starting Jan. 9, 1954) to eminently acclaimed, durable *Monitor* 1955–75 (plus failed *Weekday* 1955–56); smorgasboard approach provided comment on current topics, interviews wirh influential newsmakers, news, book reviews, like features—snippets to flow freely on *Monitor*, setting new program trend for NBC; early regulars Fannie Hurst, Leon Pearson, Elmo Roper, Tex (McCrary) and Jinx (Falkenburg McCrary), John Mason Brown; originally two hours, reduced to one in 1955; final broadcast June 5, 1955.

Canceled

The Fred Waring Show, Oct. 4, 1957, ABC (syndicated series persisted three more years); debut Jan. 4, 1931. *Honolulu Bound* (*The Phil Baker Show*), Oct. 4, 1939, CBS; debut Dec. 6, 1931. *Under Arrest*, Oct. 4, 1954, MBS; debut July 28, 1946.

Birth

James Doyle, Oct. 4, 1910, St. Paul, Minn.; announcer, newscaster, union official bka Seattle executive secretary, American Federation of Television and Radio Artists 1966–77; announcer at Los Angeles KHJ 1937, joined NBC 1940; 1940s-50s assignments *The Abbott and Costello Show, Louella Parsons, The Wizard of Odds*; *Dr. I. Q.—the Mental Banker* roving questioner; d. July 1, 1980.

Deaths

Fran Carlon, Oct. 4, 1993, New York City, N.Y.; b. April 2, 1913. Albert Mitchell, Oct. 4, 1954, Paris, France; b. May 31, 1893. Claire Niesen, Oct. 4, 1963, Encino, Calif.; b. Oct. 14, 1922. Warren Sweeney, Oct. 4, 1988, Stamford, Conn.; b. June 3, 1909.

October 5

Debuting

The Chicago Theater of the Air, Oct. 5, 1940, MBS (premiered May 9, 1940 over Chicago's WGN); hour Saturday matinee broadcast sans commercials of leading operettas, operatic vignettes, other classics; similar fare to ABC/NBC feature *The Railroad Hour* with celebrated artists (e.g., Igor Gorin, Virginia Haskins, Lauritz Melchoir, James Melton, Conrad Thibault, Thomas L. Thomas); final broadcast May 7, 1955.

Easy Aces (*Mr. Ace and Jane*), Oct. 5, 1931, CBS (introduced in 1929 over Kansas City, Mo. KMBC); sitcom proffering cynical husband, dimwitted wife (Goodman, Jane Ace) who never met malaprop they didn't apply to ludicrous extent; billed as "radio's distinctive laugh novelty"; final broadcast Dec. 31, 1948.

Canceled

Inner Sanctum Mysteries, Oct. 5, 1952, CBS; debut Jan. 7, 1941.

Birth

Anthony (Tony) Marvin, Oct. 5, 1912, New York City, N.Y.; announcer, disc jockey, emcee, newscaster, commercial voiceover artist bka *Arthur Godfrey Time* daytime variety series interlocutor CBS 1945-ca. 1957 ("And now, here's that man himself!"), same duty for *Arthur Godfrey and His Friends* CBS-TV 1949–59, *Casey—Crime Photographer* mystery CBS 1946–48, headline reader on *Tony Marvin and the News* 1942-mid 1940s, 1959–1960s; introduced some key 1940s-50s CBS entries: *The Arthur Godfrey Digest/Roundtable, The Charlie Ruggles Show, The Columbia Workshop, Major Bowes' Original Amateur Hour, This Life Is Mine*; announced at New York WNYC at career start, proclaimed "official voice" of 1939 New York World's Fair, joined CBS same year; *The Tony Marvin Show* DJ daily matinee feature began on New York WABC 1958; supplied original voice of Tony the Tiger for 1950s Kellogg's cereal commercials; left CBS berth after two decades, joined MBS as newscaster 1959; d. Oct. 10, 1998.

Death

Arthur Tracy, Oct. 5, 1997, Manhattan, New York City, N.Y.; b. June 25, 1899.

October 6

Debuting

City Hospital, Oct. 6, 1951, CBS; anthology drama with linking storyline; medical director Dr. Barton Crane (Santos Ortega, Melvin Ruick), nurse Kate Morrow (Anne Burr) have issues as often as patients at "City Hospital, where life begins and ends, where around the clock — 24 hours a day — men and women are dedicated to the war against suffering and pain"; ABC-/CBS-TV 1951–53, final radiocast Nov. 8, 1958.

Show Boat (*The Maxwell House Show Boat, Show Boat Matinee, Home Town Unincorporated*), Oct. 6, 1932, NBC; variety; "one of the giant hits of early network radio musical variety" critic surmised, passing Rudy Vallee to rank just behind Eddie Cantor with 45.9 rating; amiable skipper Captain Henry (Charles Winninger, Frank McIntyre)—final season Captain Barney (Carlton Brickert)— steered ship of myriad musicmakers/comics/actors: Victor Arden, Jules Bledsoe, Winifred Cecil, Nadine Conner, Annette Hanshaw, Irene Hubbard, Marlin Hurt ("Beulah"), Mabel Jackson, Wright Kramer, Pick Malone and Pat Padgett ("Molasses and January"), Hattie McDaniel, Lucy Monroe, Adele Ronson, Lanny Ross, Mark Smith, Conrad Thibault, Thomas L. Thomas, Ned Wever, Muriel Wilson, more; orchestras of Donald Voorhees, Gus Haenschen, Al Goodman, plus choirs, ensembles; final broadcast April 21, 1941.

Canceled

Palmolive Beauty Box Theater, Oct. 6, 1937, CBS; debut April 8, 1934. *Peter Potter's Juke Box Jury*, Oct. 6, 1956, ABC; debut May 20, 1954.

Deaths

Walter Herlihy, Oct. 6, 1956, Forest Hills, N.Y.; b. Aug. 17, 1914. Betty Wragge, Oct. 6, 2002, New York City, N.Y.; b. Sept. 22, 1917.

October 7

Debuting

Modern Romances, Oct. 7, 1936, NBC Blue; anthology drama; part of unique, miniscule segment of matinee sagas with storylines defying conventional open-end formats exhibited by most in strain with tales reaching denouements at regular intervals; *Aunt Jenny's Real Life Stories, Modern Romances* prevailed longer than others; Gertrude Warner, Eloise McElhone, Kathi Norris narrated latter serial by impersonating Helen Gregory, "editor" of *Modern Romances* slick, early tales drawn from its pages; pundit called them "confession stories in a third-person style which exchanged secret sharing for keyhole peeping"; casts changed with new narratives; off air 1937–49, 1951–53; five-part dramas seen weekly NBC-TV Oct. 4, 1954-Sept. 19, 1958; final radiocast Feb. 25, 1955.

Portia Faces Life, Oct. 7, 1940, CBS; daytime serial; first day, serial's heroine Portia Blake (Lucille Wall, Anne Seymour) was widowed, left with young son to raise; she took over late spouse's legal practice, launched sterling law career of own though faced domestic crises en masse largely at hands of newspaperman Walter Manning (Myron McCormick, Bartlett Robinson); she wed him, subsequently bringing her lifetime of heartache that ended — on last show — with her headed for slammer — but that's another story; televersion April 5, 1954-July 1, 1955 CBS; final radiocast June 29, 1951.

Births

Frederick C. Collins, Oct. 7, 1925, Fort Wayne, Ind.; announcer, emcee, newscaster, voiceover artist bka TV "voice of NBC peacock," narrator of NBC Radio sci-fi thrillers of golden, post-golden eras —*Dimension X* 1950–51, *X-Minus One* 1955–58, 1973–75; pled with listeners tuning in latter transcription reprise to urge local outlets to continue it, write chain if they wanted more — unfortunately, not enough did to retain it but repeats never enjoyed permanent timeslot so fans had trouble staying connected; from Lafayette, Ind. WASK, progressed to Fort Wayne WOWO to New York NBC as staff announcer 1948–69; other 1950s radio gigs: *Best Plays, The Big Guy, The Chase, Crime and Peter Chambers, Dr. Sixgun, My Son Jeep, Radio City Playhouse, Spend a Million, Top Secret, Wanted*; voiced scads of local, national radio/TV commercials; d. Aug. 5, 2006.

Vaughn Monroe, Oct. 7, 1911, Akron, Ohio; impresario, recording artist, restaurateur, trombonist, trumpeter, vocalist (nightclubs, personal appearances, radio, stage, TV) bka *Camel Caravan* star 1946–54 partially on dual radio chains concurrently, CBS-TV 1950–51; principal electronic, print media advertising spokesperson for R. J. Reynolds Tobacco Co.; d. May 21, 1973.

Donald Newton Rickles, Oct. 7, 1927, Portland, Ore.; announcer bka late 1940s-early 1950s interlocutor of *Nightbeat, The Whisperer, The Whistler* (only substantiated net series); not to be confused with contemporary sultan of insult comedy born in New York City May 8, 1926; Vancouver, Wash. KVAN newscaster before vaulting to chains; d. Feb. 19, 1985.

October 8

Debuting

The Adventures of Ozzie and Harriet, CBS, domestic sitcom starring Ozzie, Harriet Hilliard Nelson ("America's Favorite Young Couple"), David, Ricky Nelson; perpetuated mythical idealism that resonated with fans; final broadcast June 18, 1954; ABC-TV Oct. 3, 1952-Sept. 3, 1966.

The Joe Penner Show (*The Baker's Broadcast, Park Avenue Penners, The Tip Top Show*), Oct. 8, 1933, NBC Blue; comedy variety; critic panned Penner's try to replicate Jack Benny's rise to radio stardom as one-dimensional, couched in bizarre vaudeville line "Wanna buy a duck?"; fans soon tired of it, vanished (Penner died of heart attack at 36 never realizing goal); along with star as "black sheep," other sitcom sketch Park Avenue Penner players were Margaret Brayton, Gay Seabrook, Martha Wentworth; final broadcast April 25, 1940.

Deaths

Ted Pearson, Oct. 8, 1961, Eastchester, N.Y.; b. Nov. 3, 1902. Karl Swenson, Oct. 8, 1978, Torrington, Conn.; b. July 23, 1908.

October 9

Debuting

(*The*) *Cavalcade of America*, Oct. 9, 1935, CBS; anthology drama with history theme; early shows of bygone vignettes in national life gave way to bio narratives, special projects, historical book adaptations, current events, modern issues, plausible charades of earlier epochs; in 1940 Hollywood stars headlined shows with superior radio dramatists moved to support parts — Ted de Corsia, Kenny Delmar, Ed Jerome, Raymond Edward Johnson, William Johnstone, Agnes Moorehead, Jeanette Nolan, Everett Sloane, Karl Swenson, Orson Welles, et al.; NBC-/ABC-TV Oct. 1, 1952-June 4, 1957, final radiocast March 31, 1953.

Canceled

The Mary Lee Taylor Show, Oct. 9, 1954, NBC; debut Nov. 7, 1933.

Births

John Robert Sommers Armbruster, Oct. 9, 1897, Philadelphia, Pa.; film musician (MGM), house impresario (NBC), pianist; accompanied NBC inaugural Nov. 15, 1926; frequently directed NBC Hollywood Orchestra; maestro for dozens of aural series (*The Chase & Sanborn Hour, The Judy Canova Show, Cavalcade of America, A Day in the Life of Dennis Day, The Great Gildersleeve*, et al.); Hollywood Bowl recurring guest conductor; d. June 20, 1994.

Walter Compton (Walter Knobeloch), Oct. 9, 1912, Charleston, S.C.; announcer, director, emcee, newscaster, writer, TV station executive bka *Double or Nothing* originator-host 1940–43; d. Dec. 9, 1959.

John Guedel, Oct. 9, 1913, Portland, Ind.; director, producer, program developer, writer bka *House Party, People Are Funny, You Bet Your Life* creator-executive; d. Dec. 15, 2001.

October 10

Debuting

Betty and Bob, Oct. 10, 1932, NBC Blue; daytime serial; one of earliest of breed with traction (7.5 years) while also espousing premise typifying countless Hummert dramas on way — wedding simpletons from sticks way above their stations; man-hungry vamps chased fortune heir Bob Drake (Don Ameche, Les Tremayne, Vinton Hayworth, Onslow Stevens, Spencer Bentley, Carl Frank, J. Anthony Hughes, Van Heflin) as mistrust, jealousy, bickering alienated him from Betty (Elizabeth Reller, Beatrice Churchill,

Alice Hill, Mercedes McCambridge, Arlene Francis); their infant died (to improve ratings — it didn't help) as die cast for legions of like-minded domestic tales; final net broadcast March 15, 1940.

Chandu the Magician, Oct. 10, 1932, MBS-Don Lee; juvenile adventure with San Francisco covert agent Frank Chandler dubbed "Chandu" (Jason Robards, Sr., Gayne Whitman, Howard Hoffman, Tom Collins) — having mastered secrets of Hindu yogi — roaming earth in search of despots that hoped to enslave universe; villainous Egyptian Roxor (Luis Van Rooten) archenemy, tenacious, determined to win over Chandu; show silent 1936–48; series mired in profusion of kid-friendly premiums, magic tricks frequently; final broadcast Sept. 6, 1950.

Painted Dreams, Oct. 10, 1933, CBS; daytime serial; widely accepted by scholars as first of genre on premier Oct. 20, 1933 over Chicago WGN where it ran into trouble in 1931 when wordsmith Irna Phillips claimed it was her property (in order to carry it to national chain), WGN officials insisting drama was aired by them, thus they owned it; in decade-long lawsuit Phillips lost, but well before that she reprised idea under moniker *Today's Children* over rival WMAQ which beamed it nationally; in intermittent spurts *Painted Dreams* returned to air after WGN relented and Phillips was no longer factor; final broadcast Nov. 20, 1940.

Canceled

The Casebook of Gregory Hood, Oct. 10, 1951, ABC; debut June 3, 1946.

Births

Don Hancock, Oct. 10, 1910, Anderson, Ind.; announcer, newscaster, voiceover artist bka commercial spokesman for American Home Products Corp. (brand names Heet, Anacin, Aerowax, Black Flag, Wizard Wick, Easy-Off, Kriptin, Bi-So-Dol, Freezone, et al.) in plugs on two live CBS-TV 1950s daytime serials —*Love of Life, The Secret Storm*— two or three spots per quarter-hour episode; P.A. announcer at Indiana Symphony summer concerts 1977–79; presented 1930s -50s radio fans with *The Adventures of Ellery Queen, Believe It or Not, The Children's Hour, Front Page Farrell, The Goldbergs, Grand Central Station, The Jack Smith Show, Life Can Be Beautiful, The Romance of Helen Trent, The Shadow, Stop the Music!*, more; CBS newsman 1940s; d. May 6, 1980.

Marian Shockley (Collyer), Oct. 10, 1911, Kansas City, Mo.; actress (stage, film, radio, TV); appeared in first of 20 theatrical B-movies 1930, often bit, uncredited parts; Broadway in 1936 with George M. Cohan in *Dear Old Darling*, other shows followed —*Abie's Irish Rose, Two Time Mary, Reno, Censored*; repetitive roles in radio's *Abie's Irish Rose, The Adventures of Ellery Queen* (daring secretary Nikki Porter 1939), *The Guiding Light, Mystery Theater, The Road of Life* (feminine lead Carol Brent) — worked with future spouse Clayton (Bud) Collyer at latter serial, wed him on *Bride and Groom*; d. Dec. 14, 1981.

Deaths

Eddie Cantor, Oct. 10, 1964, Beverly Hills, Calif.; b. Jan. 31, 1892. Tony Marvin, Oct. 10, 1998, Boynton Beach, Fla.; b. Oct. 5, 1912. Basil Ruysdael, Oct. 10, 1960, Hollywood, Calif.; b. July 24, 1888. Cesar Saerchinger, Oct. 10, 1971, Washington, D.C.; b. Oct. 23, 1884. Orson Welles, Oct. 10, 1985, Hollywood, Calif.; b. May 6, 1915.

October 11

Debuting

The American Album of Familiar Music, Oct. 11, 1939, NBC; one of several Frank and Anne Hummert-produced series focused on ballads, waltzes, classical, semi-classical tunes; impresarios Gustav Haenschen, Abe Lyman; vocalists Bernice Claire, Donald Dame, Margaret Dunn, Vivian Della Chiesa, Jean Dickenson, Felix Knight, Elizabeth Lennox, Daniel Lieberfeld, Evelyn MacGregor, Lucy Monroe, Virginia Rea; final broadcast June 17, 1951.

The Brighter Day, Oct. 11, 1948, NBC; daytime serial; widower with four daughters, one son, Rev. Richard Dennis (Bill Smith) accepted ministry to nonsectarian flock at Three Rivers where his family lived fishbowl existence with personal foibles aired before congregation as he tried to steer parishioners along straight, narrow — not easy when some of his clan exhibited rebellion, jealousy, obsessions, materialism, alcohol addiction, immoral behavior — pastor eventually voted out as undershepherd; persisted on CBS-TV Jan. 4, 1954-Sept. 28, 1962; final radiocast June 29, 1956.

Canceled

Barry Cameron, Oct. 11, 1946, NBC; debut April 16, 1945.

Births

Jane (Sherwood) Ace, Oct. 11, 1897, Kansas City, Mo.; actress, comedienne bka *Easy Aces, Mr. Ace and Jane* spouse playing self to real-life husband-scribe Goodman Ace 1932–45, 1948, syndication 1945–46; nasal-tongued delivery of malaproprisms Goodman put in her mouth ("Home wasn't built in a day"); *Jane Ace — Disc Jocey* humor/waxworks hostess NBC 1951–52; d. Nov. 11, 1974.

Forrest E. Boone, Oct. 11, 1893, Winchester, Ky.; advertising pitchman, tobacco auctioneer bka one of two American Tobacco Co. commercial spokesmen (other, L.A. "Speed" Riggs) for Lucky Strike cigarettes with fast-paced auction-imitating spiel starting "Hey TWENTY NINE nine nine nine nine nine nine, roundem roundem roundem roundem roundem, am I right at thirty thirty thirty..." ending "Sol-l-l-d to A-merican!" on *Information Please* ca. 1940–44, *The Jack Benny Program* 1944–55, *Your Hit Parade* ca. late 1930s-1953, more; d. Feb. 24, 1982.

Geoffrey Bryant, Oct. 11, 1900, Houston, Texas; actor (radio, stage), announcer; *Aunt Jenny's Real Life Stories, City Desk, Death Valley Days, Just Plain Bill, Meyer the Buyer, Mystery in the Air, This Is Your FBI* regular while narrating *Central City, Mr. District Attorney* 1930s-40s; performed in London, New York, touring company revues before radio initiation; d. March 13, 1982.

Ralph D. Paul, Jr., Oct. 11, 1920, Denver, Colo.; announcer, educator, emcee bka *Strike It Rich* human interest interlocutor, commercial spokesperson ("mar-*vel*-ous" Vel dishwashing powder, "*fab*-u-lous" Fab laundry detergent plugs interspersed with welcoming hard-luck tale contestants) CBS/NBC Radio 1947–57, CBS-TV/NBC-TV 1951–58; when teary-eyed emcee Warren Hull — moved by markedly upsetting story — unable to proceed, Paul replaced star until composure returned; welcomed fans to 1940s–50s *The Aldrich Family, Mother Knows Best, Seven Front Street, True Detective Mysteries, Walk a Mile,* others; cohosted *Second Honeymoon* with Bess Meyerson late 1940s; introduced viewers to *The Ed Sullivan Show* 1959–61, 1964–71; warm-up man traveling with singer Vaughn Monroe; on air at 16 at Denver KVOD, later El Paso KTSM, Baltimore WBAL, New York WOR late 1940s; finished career 1971-early 1980s directing radio-TV at WHPC, Long Island Nassau Community College; d. Nov. 28, 1987.

Jean Vander Pyl, Oct. 11, 1919, Philadelphia, Pa.; actress (film, radio, TV), voiceover artist bka *Father Knows Best* family sitcom matriarch Margaret Anderson 1949–54; *The Flintstones* TV animation character Wilma Flintstone 1960–74, supplied voices to score of similar cartoon series, animated TV films 1960s-1990s; d. April 10, 1999.

Eleanor Roosevelt, Oct. 11, 1884, New York City, N.Y.; commentator, emcee bka America's First Lady 1932–45, wife of FDR; beyond innovations, accomplishments, often in guest shots on chain series while hostessing more "firsts": *Eleanor and Anna Roosevelt* 1948–49, *Eleanor and Elliott Roosevelt* 1950–51, *Eleanor Roosevelt* 1934, 1937, 1940, *Over Our Coffee Cups* 1941–42, *Today with Mrs. Roosevelt* 1950–51, *Vanity Fair* 1933–34; d. Nov. 7, 1962.

Deaths

Connee Boswell, Oct. 11, 1976, New York City, N.Y.; b. Dec. 3, 1907. T. Tommy Cutrer, Oct. 11, 1998, Gallatin, Tenn.; b. June 29, 1924. Richard Denning, Oct. 11, 1998, Escondido, Calif.; b. March 27, 1914.

October 12

Debuting

The Jack Smith Show (*The Oxydol Show, The Tide Show*), Oct. 12, 1943, CBS; pop music; dubbed by critic Deems Taylor "man with the smile in his voice," Smith sang nightly with costars Dinah Shore, Margaret Whiting, rare guests backed by Frank DeVol's orchestra; final broadcast Dec. 26, 1952.

Mr. Keen, Tracer of Lost Persons, Oct. 12, 1937, NBC Blue; private eye investigative drama; for 18 years — longer than anybody else in radio or TV—"kindly old investigator" Westrel Keen (Bennett Kilpack, Philip Clarke) plus Irish buffoon partner Mike Clancy (Jimmy Kelly) unraveled mysteries in dual formats: for six years, searched for missing persons who vanished of own free will or otherwise, then tracked cold-blooded killers via simple-minded, hokey-sounding deduction, interviewed handful of suspects, followed clues to finger murderers; missed few (or no) new episodes in 52-week cycles, weekly half-hours, nightly serialized versions airing concurrently at times; final broadcast Sept. 26, 1955.

Birth

Joseph Martin (Ted) Collins, Oct. 12, 1899, New York City, N.Y.; announcer, emcee, newscaster bka *The Kate Smith Show* sidekick; entrepreneurial-minded, projected Smith from obscurity to America's forefront, turning her into singing legend; ex–Columbia Records scout became her personal manager, producer, newsman on plethora of shows, conversationalist exchanged pleasantries, substantive stuff with her 1931–64; pair never signed contract—shook hands on business deal immensely profitable to both; d. May 27, 1964.

Deaths

Bill Hay, Oct. 12, 1978, Santa Monica, Calif.; b. April 18, 1887. Johnny Olsen, Oct. 12, 1985, Santa Monica, Calif.; b. May 22, 1910.

October 13

Canceled

Dr. Sixgun, Oct. 13, 1944, NBC; debut Sept. 2, 1954. *House Party*, Oct. 13, 1967, CBS; debut Jan. 15, 1945.

Births

Harry Hershfield, Oct. 13, 1885, Cedar Rapids, Iowa; humorist, raconteur bka *Can You Top This?* panelist 1940–54; d. Dec. 15, 1974.

Hugh James (Hugh McIlrevey), Oct. 13, 1915, Bronxville, N.Y.; announcer bka *Voice of Firestone* interlocutor sharply attired in tux, white shirt, tie for NBC/ABC simulcasts 1949–57, earlier NBC Radio (from ca. late 1930s; familiar to listeners of handful 1940s-50s daytime serials: *House in the Country, The Right to Happiness, The Second Mrs. Burton, Wendy Warren and the News* (using pseudonym Bill Flood), *When a Girl Marries*—at one point narrated four soaps daily; also heard on *Call the Police, Famous Jury Trials, The Parker Family, Three Star Extra, True Detective Mysteries, Walter Winchell's Journal*, more; began career as NBC page, tour guide, Philadelphia announcer, NBC operations in Washington, D.C., New York 1937 as lead-in for Lowell Thomas' nightly newscast; freelance announcer 1940s navigating varied chains; d. June 17, 2001.

John Reagan (Tex) McCrary, Oct. 13, 1910, Calvert, Texas; author, commentator, print journalist bka *Meet Tex and Jinx* breakfast chat series (afternoons starting 1954) with spouse Jinx Falkenburg over New York WEAF/WNBC 1946–58, among handful in breed; interviewees included Bernard Baruch, Margaret Truman, Ethel Waters, "name" figures; expanded to TV via intermittent pithy features 1947–58; McCrary filled menial tasks at *The New York World-Telegram* in initial job, transferred to *The New York Daily Mirror* 1936; contributed to 1944 volume *The First of Many*; d. July 29, 2003.

Deaths

Bea Benaderet, Oct. 13, 1968, Los Angeles, Calif.; b. April 4, 1906. Douglas Edwards, Oct. 13, 1990, Sarasota, Fla.; b. July 14, 1917. Lud Gluskin, Oct. 13, 1989, Palm Springs, Calif.; b. Dec. 16, 1898. Ed Sullivan, Oct. 13, 1974, Manhattan, New York City, N.Y.; b. Sept. 28, 1901.

October 14

Debuting

Grand Ole Opry, Oct. 14, 1939, NBC (launched on Nashville WSM Nov. 28, 1925); still running, most enduring broadcast feature in history, never missed weekly performance; initially perpetuated rustic sounds appealing to mountain folk, turned hillbilly into country music that developed robust following globally; founded industry with proliferating tentacles, signified Nashville as recording Mecca branded "Music City, U.S.A.," home to country legends; half-hour web portion of 4.5-hour live show headlined by Roy Acuff 1939–46, Red Foley 1946–57; final network broadcast Dec. 28, 1957.

Lux Radio Theater, Oct. 14, 1934, NBC; anthology drama, comedy, music; originally drawn in reticent fashion from Broadway stage, most prestigious hour in radio after shifting to West Coast 1936, presented abbreviated storylines of prominent theatrical motion pictures with top Hollywood stars, glitz, glamour, budget of magnificent proportions; film shooting schedules briefly disrupted at time for stars to rehearse for *Lux*, attesting to high perception within industry; Cecil B. DeMille, William Keighley, Irving Cummings principal hosts, augmented by fill-ins; spawned *Lux Video Theater* anthology CBS-/NBC-TV 1950–57; final radiocast June 7, 1955.

Birth

Claire Niesen (Ruick), Oct. 14, 1922, New York City, N.Y.; actress (radio, stage) bka *Backstage Wife* daytime serial heroine Mary Noble 1945–59; on stage at 15, gained rave reviews for *Empress of Destiny, My Heart's in the Highlands, All for Passion, The Talley Method, A Star Is Born*; audio leading lady in *The Second Mrs. Burton, We Who Dream*, roles (most recurring) in *Her Honor—Nancy James, Life Can Be Beautiful, The Light of the World, The March of Time, Mr. Keen—Tracer of Lost Persons, The O'Neills, The Right to Happiness*; as radio faded, career did too—she hoped for showbiz comeback when stricken by cancer, hospitalized 40 weeks, death; d. Oct. 4, 1963.

Deaths

Hyman J. (Hy) Averback, Oct. 14, 1997, Los Angeles, Calif.; b. Oct. 21, 1920. Bing Crosby, Oct. 14, 1977, Madrid, Spain; b. May 3, 1903.

October 15

Sound Bite

The inaugural issue of *Broadcasting*, periodical that will possess a commanding influence on trade, appears Oct. 15, 1931; at inception magazine pertains almost totally to radio but before decade is out *Broadcasting* will progressively hint at video's potential.

Canceled

The Jack Berch Show, Oct. 15, 1954, ABC; debut April 6, 1936.

Births

Vivian N. Fridell (Solomon), Oct. 15, 1912, Milwaukee, Wis.; actress, drama coach bka *Backstage Wife* daytime serial heroine Mary Noble MBS/NBC 1935–45; broke into radio in college, graduated to Chicago radio 1930s to gain repeating roles in soap operas *The Road of Life, The Romance of Helen Trent*, etc.; when they located to New York, she exited radio to teach dramatics to junior, senior high school students in Glencoe, Ill. home; d. Aug. 20, 1998.

Jan Miner, Oct. 15, 1917, Boston, Mass.; actress (commercials, film, radio, stage, TV) bka *Lora Lawton* namesake socialite heroine 1946–50, *Hilltop House* orphanage superintendent "Miss Julie" Erickson, ca. 1948–55, 1956–57; manicurist Madge, Palmolive dishwashing liquid TV ads 1960s; d. Feb. 15, 2004.

Robert Rockwell, Oct. 15, 1920, Chicago, Ill.; actor (stage, film, radio, TV), commercial spokesman, voiceover artist bka TV thespian with more than 350 appearances in medium; d. Jan. 25, 2003.

Robert Trout (Robert Albert Blondheim), Oct. 15, 1908, Washington, D.C.; commentator, correspondent, newscaster bka premier CBS newscaster in era before arrival of Edward R. Murrow (1935–61) whom he tutored, Trout credited with contributions to more than two dozen CBS series, most in news; began by introducing President Franklin D. Roosevelt's fireside chats for CBS 1933; inaugurated *The World Today/The World Tonight* 1940; filled prestigious quarter-hour nightly radio newscast slot when Murrow elevated to VP-news-public affairs 1946 but when Murrow returned to mic following year (detesting his new job), Trout pushed out, departing for NBC; couple of TV series there; rejoined CBS 1952, CBS-TV co-anchor at Democratic convention 1964 with Roger Mudd, though pair fell on their faces, Trout seeing last try for coveted prize of evening news anchorman evaporate; retired 1996; d. Nov. 14, 2000.

October 16

Debuting

The Adventures of Michael Shayne, Oct. 16, 1944, MBS-Don Lee; detective melodrama that—in multiple reincarnations—was re-branded twice, launched as *Michael Shayne, Private Detective* then *The New Adventures of Michael Shayne* before moniker simplified; literature, film origins; namesake handled by Wally Maher, Jeff Chandler, Donald Curtis, Robert Sterling, Vinton Hayworth; girl Friday, Phyllis (Phyl) Knight — doubling as Shayne's blonde bombshell honey — impersonated by Louise Arthur, Cathy Lewis, Judith Parrish; sleuth played by Richard Denning extended to NBC-TV 1960–61; final radiocast July 10, 1953.

Against the Storm, Oct. 16, 1939, NBC; daytime serial; one of two winning Peabody Award (1942 — other *One Man's Family*), highbrow narrative focused on mythical Harper College prof Jason McKinley Allen (Roger DeKoven) warning of fascist totalitarianism as global conflagration erupted; ended Dec. 25, 1942, returned 11:30 P.M. as half-hour drama April 25, 1949 MBS, on hiatus Oct. 21, 1949; resumed as daytime quarter-hour serial Oct. 1, 1951-June 27, 1952 ABC.

Philco Radio Time, Oct. 16, 1946, ABC; musical variety feature headlined by crooner Bing Crosby after he walked from decade-long contract with NBC's *Kraft Music Hall* over passion to violate longstanding network rule against prerecording shows, Crosby reaching landmark goal in second season Oct. 1, 1947; final broadcast June 1, 1949 though star persisted on CBS through Sept. 28, 1962, virtual end of audio web entertainment.

The Right to Happiness, Oct. 16, 1939, NBC Blue; daytime serial; first true spinoff drama, deeply rooted in storyline of *The Guiding Light* (began NBC Jan. 25, 1937) as creator Irna Phillips multiplied her wares in cupboard of drainboard dramas; protagonist Carolyn Allen (Eloise Kummer, Claudia Morgan) ultimately became Carolyn Allen Walker Kramer Nelson MacDonald — most married heroine in aural soapdom (whom Joanne Barron topped with her trips down aisle as leading lady on TV's *Search for Tomorrow*); Carolyn experienced continuous domestic crises at hands of men she wed (one she was charged with killing), also by son who — as teen — gave her fits aplenty; one of four open-end dramas languishing to fateful "day radio drama died" Nov. 25, 1960.

Births

Douglas Browning, Oct. 16, 1910, Norwood, Ohio; actor, announcer, engineer bka *Terry and the Pirates* interlocutor ca. 1937–48; other introductions often of 1940s audience participation fare like *Ed East and Polly, Go for the House, Ladies Be Seated, The Old Gold Hour, The Sea Hound, Stop the Music!*; finished career at Charleston, W. Va. WKAZ as night engineer.

William Spier, Oct. 16, 1906, New York City, N.Y.; director, producer, writer bka *Suspense* producer-director CBS 1942–50, *The Adventures of Sam Spade* same duty ABC/CBS/NBC 1946–51; until late in runs Spier refused to let names of Hollywood icons on air except at ends of shows — Howard Duff (Sam Spade) raged bitterly as Spier liberally marketed himself in opening-closing billboards ("radio's master of suspense"), fought Duff two years till he, Lurene Tuttle got upfront credit; at 19, on *Musical Drama* magazine staff, moved to Batten, Barton, Durstine & Osborn ad agency at 20, joined CBS West Coast unit 1941, produced-directed *The Atwater-Kent Hour, The General Motors Family Hour, The March of Time, The Philip Morris Playhouse*, etc.; directed theatrical film 1952, wrote 1970 screenplay plus two made-for-TV flicks 1960, penned solo TV episodes 17 times 1956–61, produced trio of TV series 1952–54; d. May 30, 1973.

Deaths

Shirley Booth, Oct. 16, 1992, North Chatham, Mass.; b. Aug. 30, 1898. Harry Golder, Oct. 16, 1968, Los Angeles, Calif.; b. July 10, 1908.

October 17

Debuting

Captain Midnight, Oct. 17, 1939, transcribed by Chicago WGN (where it premiered Oct. 10, 1938) for Midwest, Southwest stations where Skelly Oil Co. goods sold; flying themed juvenile adventure serial; into hands of World War I aerial ace Capt. Jim (Red) Albright aka Captain Midnight (Bill Bouchey, Ed Prentiss, Paul Barnes) much of nation's peacekeeping entrusted though superiors in secret government agency didn't know who he was (hokey?); sailed across skies with adolescent accomplices Chuck Ramsey (Billy Rose, Jack Bivens, Johnny Coons),

Joyce Ryan (Angeline Orr, Marilou Neumayer), Ichabod "Ikky" Mudd (Art Hearn, Sherman Marks); America could rest, aware quartet defended shores from ancient terrorists; movie serials, novels, TV series (CBS, 1954–56) waved flag, too; prompted by *The Air Adventures of Jimmie Allen* 1933–36 for same sponsor, same scribes; MBS, NBC Blue beamed to U. S.; final radiocast Dec. 15, 1949.

Birth

Florence Williams (Marshall), Oct. 17, 1910, St. Louis, Mo.; actress (stage, radio) bka *Front Page Farrell* reporter David Farrell's wife Sally NBC ca. mid 1940s-1954 — after drama turned from domestic to deadly, she routinely accompanied her crack newspaperman spouse on chilling culprit chases that put both in peril on frequent occasions; supplied 1930s-50s radio roles in *Barry Cameron* (heroine again), *Great Plays, Hearthstone of the Death Squad, The Light of the World, The Magic Key, Mr. Keen—Tracer of Lost Persons* (copious cases 1947–54), *Romance, Roses and Drums, X-Minus One*, more; prolific stage thespian on Broadway 1932–57 in *The Little Foxes, You Can't Take It with You, Inherit the Wind*, other Great White Way plays, plus regional theater productions like *The Belle of Amherst, The Madwoman of Chaillot*; d. March 30, 1995.

Deaths

Arthur Hale, Oct. 17, 1971, Harrisburg, Pa.; b. March 16, 1896. Mark Warnow, Oct. 17, 1949, New York City, N.Y.; b. April 10, 1902.

October 18

Sound Bite

NBC launches Gold Network (aka Pacific Gold Network) Oct. 18, 1931— NBC Blue programming beamed from East Coast to Blue affiliates on West Coast, similar to sending Red programming to west via newly-formed Orange Network four years earlier; monikers of dual West Coast links abandoned in 1936 as Red programming is designated Red, Blue marked Blue, same as elsewhere.

Debuting

Perry Mason, Oct. 18, 1943, CBS; daytime serial with dark undertones, chilling plots; infamous defense attorney (first appearing in Erle Stanley Gardner pulp fiction 1920s-30s) focused outside courtroom on chasing rapscallions or their prey in relentless efforts to put bad guys away before diabolical schemes matured; Mason (Bartlett Robinson, Santos Ortega, Donald Briggs, John Larkin) was dapper, brilliant with mental tenacity countering equally sharp criminals; assisted by secretary Della Street (Gertrude Warner, Jan Miner, Joan Alexander), private investigator Paul Drake (Matt Crowley, Chuck Webster), police Lt. Tragg (Mandel Kramer, Frank Dane); unlike CBS-TV series 1957–66, NBC made-for-TV flicks 1980s-90s (formats starring Raymond Burr, Barbara Hale) with revelations of killers on witness stands, daytime listeners usually *knew* who-done-it — real joy was in pursuits instead of convictions; final radiocast Dec. 30, 1955.

Canceled

Adventures by Morse, Oct. 18, 1945, syndication; debut Oct. 26, 1944.

Births

Helen Claire, Oct. 18, 1911, Union Springs, Ala.; actress (radio, stage), fashion analyst; running parts in *Backstage Wife, The O'Neills* (only heroine of a daytime drama dying in childbirth), *Stella Dallas* (durable "Mad" Ada Dexter), *The Strange Romance of Evelyn Winters*; sporadic visits to *Death Valley Days, Great Plays, Dr. Christian, The Sheriff, Stories of the Black Chamber, David Harding— Counterspy*, others; *Mr. Keen— Tracer of Lost Persons* character roles dozens of times; Broadway, touring company stage shows; Fox Movietone News fashion commentator 1937–49; d. Jan. 12, 1974.

Louise A. Fitch (screen pseudonym Louise Lewis), Oct. 18, 1914, Council Bluffs, Iowa; actress (radio, TV, film); radio thespian in soap opera, sitcom, anthology drama mix, often as leading lady: *Arnold Grimm's Daughter, Backstage Wife, Big Sister, Joyce Jordan — Girl Interne, Kitty Keene Incorporated, The Light of the World, Lux Radio Theater, Ma Perkins, Mortimer Gooch, The Road of Life, Scattergood Baines, That Brewster Boy, Two on a Clue, We Love and Learn, The Whistler, Woman in White*; between 1955 and 1994 in eight theatrical films, two TV series (*General Hospital, Paradise Bay*), six made-for-

TV flicks, 45 solo roles on assorted TV anthology dramas; d. Sept. 11, 1996.

Adele Ronson, Oct. 18, 1906, New York City, N.Y.; actress (radio, stage), announcer, voiceover artist (radio, TV commercials into 1990s); community theater, Broadway productions before radio work 1930–76 (webs, syndication); *As the Twig Is Bent* narrator, *The Coty Playgirl* hostess, prolific impact as audio thespian: *Buck Rogers in the 25th Century*, *The Eno Crime Club*, *The Goldbergs*, *Inner Sanctum Mysteries*, *John's Other Wife*, *The March of Time*, *Mr. Keen—Tracer of Lost Persons*, *My True Story*, *Perry Mason*, more; d. Oct. 31, 2000.

Deaths

Nancy Dickerson, Oct. 18, 1997, Manhattan, New York City, N.Y.; b. Jan. 27, 1927. Frank Knight, Oct. 18, 1973, New York City, N.Y.; b. May 10, 1894.

October 19

Sound Bite

Nation "shocked" Oct. 19, 1953 as millions tuning in to CBS's *Arthur Godfrey Time* hear host fire one of his favored minions, pop singer Julius LaRosa; adulation for Godfrey instantly turns sour, many angry; star begins long downhill career descent, never recovering; loses audience, advertisers, associates, aircast industry respect; instead of learning, ironically he blindly perseveres on destructive path, firing almost all artists in troupe off-air, most in bunches (e.g. nine tossed April 15, 1955), in so doing dismantling one of nation's idolized entertainment entourages while damaging self beyond repair with some ex-fans.

Debuting

Big Town, Oct. 19, 1937, CBS; crime drama; crusading against denizens of underworld, *The Illustrated Press* managing editor Steve Wilson (Edward G. Robinson, Edward Pawley, Walter Greaza), society editor Lorelei Kilbourne (Claire Trevor, Ona Munson, Fran Carlon) acted in fictional accounts drawn from genuine newspaper revelations; televersion added 1950–56 on trio of nets, in syndication under quartet of sobriquets; final radiocast June 25, 1952.

Canceled

Crime Doctor, Oct. 19, 1947, CBS; debut Aug. 4, 1940. *Renfrew of the Mounted*, Oct. 19, 1940, NBC Blue; debut March 3, 1936.

Births

Charles Robert Douglas Hardy Andrews, Oct. 19, 1903, Effingham, Kan.; author, journalist, scriptwriter bka producer Frank, Anne Hummert's original workhorse prior to instituting assembly-line methods netting scripts for 20-plus concurrent audio series; penned Hummerts' early creations *The Stolen Husband*, *Betty and Bob*, *Judy and Jane*, *Easy Aces*—prototypes of proliferating stable of serialized melodrama ultimately reaching 70 features—before focusing skills on first of breed with staying power, *Just Plain Bill* (Andrews preferred title *Bill the Barber* but overridden by future Mrs. Hummert, Anne Ashenhurst); for decade ex-reporter for *The Minneapolis Journal*, *The Chicago Daily News* ground out dialogue for 4–7 daily radio shows, typing in excess of 100,000 words weekly noon-midnight seven days a week while consuming 40 cups of coffee, chain-smoking 100 cigarettes daily; simultaneously wrote countless novels, scripted movie screenplays solo or with partners until he "got tired" dialoguing *Just Plain Bill*, *Ma Perkins*, *The Romance of Helen Trent*, others; randomly wrote *Death Valley Days* episodes, other TV series installments 1958–70; d. Nov. 11, 1976.

Bern Bennett (Bernard Blume), Oct. 19, 1921, Rochester, N.Y.; announcer (radio, TV) bka TV *Tournament of Roses Parade* interlocutor 1962–1999, similar duty for *The Young and the Restless* 1973–2003, *The Bold & the Beautiful* 1987–2004; radio introductions included *Winner Take All* ca. 1946–52 (TV 1948–50), *Rock 'n' Roll Dance Party* 1956; more gigs announcing TV fare including *Beat the Clock* 1950–58, *The Steve Allen Show* 1952, *The Phil Silvers Show* 1955–59, *To Tell the Truth* 1956–60, *The Clear Horizon* 1960–61/1962, *The Verdict Is Yours* 1960–62, *Your Surprise Package* 1961–62, *The Danny Kaye Show* 1963–67, *The Jonathan Winters Show* 1967–69; officially retired CBS 2003 after 59 years.

Death

Grant Turner, Oct. 19, 1991, Nashville, Tenn.; b. May 17, 1912.

October 20

Sound Bite

Irna Phillips writes, produces, directs, stars in first true soap opera embodiment Oct. 20, 1930 as Chicago WGN airs *Painted Dreams* by installment six days weekly at debut; persists without sponsorship for year until Windy City meatpacker underwrites it; Ireene [sic] Wicker only other player in trailblazing narrative of Irish-American clan — two women take all roles; after Phillips falls out with WGN over series' ownership, she departs in huff early 1934, offers same idea to rival WMAQ, soon back on ether with original premise under banner *Today's Children*; gains national exposure 1933–37, 1943–50 while losing WGN lawsuit; force to be reckoned with in soap opera, nevertheless, to 1973 death.

Debuting

Break the Bank, Oct. 24, 1945, MBS; quiz; ether's first "big money" quiz with escalating cash prizes habitually reached four figures fostering appetite for increasingly larger payoffs; devised for erudite contestants that read widely and retained knowledge, proffering questions on sundry topics delivered by dynamic personality quizmasters Bert Parks, Clayton (Bud) Collyer; "wishbowl" feature let home audience play by sending post cards — those drawn got all-expense-paid trips to show; series aired weekday matinee, weekly evening primetime formats; final radiocast March 25, 1955, televersion ABC/NBC/CBS 1948–57.

The Frank Sinatra Show, Oct. 20, 1942, CBS; music; pop singer often with entourage of screaming teenyboppers in tow belted out standards from present, past epochs under handful of sobriquets: *Frank Sinatra in Person*, *Songs by Sinatra*, *Light-Up Time*, *Meet Frank Sinatra*, *Here's Frank Sinatra*, *To Be Perfectly Frank*; vocalist idolized as *Your Hit Parade* headliner 1943–44, 1947–49; many gigs guest performing elsewhere; series radiocasts ended July 15, 1955; unconfirmed report he starred in successor weekday radio run ABC 1956–58.

(*The Adventures of*) *Sherlock Holmes*, Oct. 20, 1930, NBC; detective mystery; "world's most famous detective" — seen as perhaps "most universally recognized fictional character in history" — Sherlock Holmes (William Gillette, Clive Brook, Richard Gordon, Louis Hector, Basil Rathbone, Tom Conway, John Stanley, Ben Wright, John Gielgud) eccentric but possessed extraordinarily clever brain for solving crimes, especially when contrasted with dimmer associate Dr. John H. Watson (Leigh Lovel, Harold West, Nigel Bruce, Alfred Shirley, Ian Martin, Wendell Holmes, Eric Snowden, Ralph Richardson); while entry seems to have aired 26 years, silent 10 years plus summer hiatuses, diminishing but not erasing durable run; NPR, PBS aired BBC *Holmes* feature 1970s; at least 50 English theatrical films exist, 15 made-for-TV flicks; final radiocast Sept. 4, 1956.

Cancelled

The Stan Freberg Show, Oct. 20, 1957, CBS; debut July 14, 1957.

Birth

Arlene Francis (Gabel) (Arline Francis Kazanjian), Oct. 20, 1907, Brookline, Mass.; actress (stage, film, radio, TV), emcee, hostess, interviewer, panelist, quizmistress, writer bka *What's My Line?* game show jurist CBS-TV 1950–67, syndicated TV 1968–75, NBC/CBS Radio 1952–53, *Home* magazine hostess NBC-TV 1954–57, *Blind Date* game show quizmistress-writer NBC/ABC 1943–46, *The Affairs of Ann Scotland* crime drama private eye ABC 1946–47, *Monitor* magazine interviewer NBC 1955–60s; radio debut at New York WOR 1935 led to *Amanda of Honeymoon Hill*, *The Beatrice Lillie Show*, *Betty and Bob*, *Big Sister*, *Cavalcade of America*, *Central City*, *Family Living*, *Forty-Five Minutes in Hollywood*, *Fun for All*, *Helpmate*, *The Hour of Charm*, *It Happens Every Day*, *The March of Time*, *Mr. District Attorney*, *My Good Wife*, *Second Husband*, *What's My Name?*, more; premier on Broadway 1928, films 1932, on TV in *Answer Yes or No*, *By Popular Demand*, *Comeback Story*, *Prize Performance*, *Suspense*, *Talent Patrol*, *Tonight*, *Who's There?*; d. May 31, 2001.

Deaths

Ben Bernie, Oct. 20, 1943, Beverly Hills, Calif.; b. May 30, 1891. Billy Mills, Oct. 20, 1971, Glendale, Calif.; b. Sept. 6, 1894.

October 21

Births

Hyman J. (Hy) Averback, Oct. 21, 1920,

Minneapolis, Minn.; actor (film, radio, TV), announcer, director, producer; introduced listeners to 1940s-50s shows headlined by Bob Hope, Jack Carson, Jack Paar, Ray Noble as well as *Hollywood Calling, Let's Talk Hollywood, The Sealtest Village Store, Sweeney and March, Take It or Leave It*; in same epoch exhibited thespianic talents on *The Advetures of Maisie, The Adventures of Philip Marlowe, Broadway Is My Beat, Crime Classics, Suspense, The Lineup, Presenting Charles Boyer, Richard Diamond—Private Detective, The Saint, Tales of the Texas Rangers, The Whistler*; Los Angeles radio gigs KHJ, KMPC, KFWB; in eight movies, produced handful of others, directed one or more episodes of 21 TV series, produced 10, performed in handful; produced 15 TV movies, one miniseries; d. Oct. 14, 1997.

Jack McElroy (Erwin Faust McElroy), Oct. 21, 1913, Cherokee County, Kan.; announcer, emcee, vocalist; introduced *Bride and Groom* 1945–50, *Breakfast at Sardi's/Breakfast in Hollywood* master of ceremonies 1949–50, 1952–54; d. March 2, 1959.

Deaths

Maxene Andrews, Oct. 21, 1995, Hyannis, Mass.; b. Jan. 3, 1916. Happy Felton, Oct. 21, 1964, New York City, N.Y.; b. Nov. 30, 1907. Curt Massey, Oct. 21, 1991, Rancho Mirage, Calif.; b. May 3, 1910.

October 22

Debuting

American Melody Hour, Oct. 22, 1941, NBC Blue; one of multiple Frank and Anne Hummert-produced features focused on ballads, waltzes, classical, semiclassical tunes; Vivian Della Chiesa featured soloist flanked by Eileen Farrell, Bob Hannon, Evelyn MacGregor, Stanley McClelland, Conrad Thibault, Jane Pickens, The Knightsbridge Chorus ensemble; final broadcast July 7, 1948.

Births

Roger DeKoven, Oct. 22, 1906, Chicago, Ill.; actor (stage, radio, TV, film) bka *Days of Our Lives* daytime serial figure James Spencer NBC-TV 1968–86, *Against the Storm* protagonist prof Jason Allen NBC/MBS/ABC 1939–42, 1949, 1951–52; beyond male lead on *Brave Tomorrow* played support roles on *ABC Mystery Time, Best Plays, Casey—Crime Photographer, The CBS Radio Workshop, Chandu the Magician, The Chase, Crime and Peter Chambers, Famous Jury Trials, Gangbusters, Grand Central Station, Life Can Be Beautiful, The Mysterious Traveler, This Is Nora Drake, X-Minus One, Yours Truly—Johnny Dollar*, more; stage plays, Broadway, four theatrical films 1951–86, one made-for-TV flick 1973, 16 solo TV dramas 1943–69; d. Jan. 28, 1988.

Parker Fennelly, Oct. 22, 1891, Northeast Harbor, Maine; actor (radio, TV, film), commercial spokesman bka *The Fred Allen Show* sitcom "Allen's Alley" crusty, whimsical New Englander Titus Moody ("Howdy bub!") NBC 1945–49; more aural credits, often lead/ongoing roles e.g. *The Adventures of the Thin Man, Barry Craig—Confidential Investigator, Crime Does Not Pay, House in the Country, Lawyer Tucker, Mr. Feathers, Scattergood Baines, Snow Village Sketches, The Story of Ellen Randolph, Valiant Lady, Your Family and Mine*; 10 theatrical films 1949–71 including *Angel in My Pocket* 1969; custodian in pithy 1970 CBS-TV comedy-drama *Headmaster*; performed 37 solo TV drama episodes 1947–63; drove Pepperidge Farm wagon in TV ads in Northeast; d. Jan. 22, 1988.

Laurette Fillbrandt (Hipple), Oct. 22, 1915, Zanesville, Ohio; actress bka prolific daytime serial player; broke into radio Cincinnati 1934, Chicago 1935 in *The Affairs of Anthony, Bachelor's Children, The Chicago Theater of the Air, Girl Alone, The Guiding Light, Dan Harding's Wife, I Love a Mystery, Lone Journey, Ma Perkins, Midstream, One Man's Family, The Private Practice of Dr. Dana, A Tale of Today, Today's Children, Woman in White*, more; d. Sept. 27, 2000.

Charles A. Nobles, Oct. 22, 1908, Holyoke, Mass.; announcer, dance-drama instructor, impresario, saxophonist bka *Wake Up America* interlocutor 1940–43 (only substantiated net series); on air at Springfield, Mass. 1935, shifted to Boston WBZ, joined New York NBC September 1937; one of 16 announcers aligned with Blue chain as it separated from NBC 1942; June 13, 1977.

Deaths

Walter Lanier (Red) Barber, Oct. 22, 1992, Tallahassee, Fla.; b. Feb. 17, 1908. Roland Winters, Oct. 22, 1989, Engelwood, N.J.; b. Nov. 22, 1904.

October 23

Debuting

The Fred Allen Show (*The Linit Bath Club Revue, The Salad Bowl Revue, The Sal Hepatica Revue, The Hour of Smiles, Town Hall Tonight, Texaco Star Theater*), Oct. 23, 1932, CBS; comedy variety; consummate entertainer in radio's earliest days whose showcase included barrage of topical one-liners between acerbic-tongued humorist, show regulars, venerated guests in exchanges, rib-tickling sketches interspersed with music; opinionated Allen parodied everything he could get laughs out of as legions spent part of Sunday nights with him in 1930s-40s; "Allen's Alley" sketch 1945–49 kept fans holding sides; prolonged "feud" with comedian Jack Benny earned high ratings for both shows; regulars Kenny Delmar, Peter Donald, Parker Fennelly, Portland Hoffa, Minerva Pious, more; Allen victim of *Stop the Music!* tune-filled contest at ABC whose ratings did him in although he didn't leave quietly; final broadcast June 26, 1949.

Canceled

Let's Pretend, Oct. 23, 1954, CBS; debut March 24, 1934.

Births

David Ford Bond, Oct. 23, 1904, Louisville, Ky.; announcer, lecturer, media political consultant, producer, real estate developer, vocalist bka veteran interlocutor of crime detective dramas, musicals, serialized narratives fostered by Frank and Anne Hummert while prominent commercial spokesman for trio of firms: Cities Service Oil Co.—*Cities Service Band of America* (other titles) 1930–53; B. T. Babbitt, Inc. ("Beeee-aaaa-beeee ... Ohhhh!")—*David Harum, Lora Lawton, Nona from Nowhere*; Sterling Drugs, Inc.—*The American Album of Familiar Music, American Melody Hour, Backstage Wife, Hearthstone of the Death Squad, Manhattan Merry-Go-Round, Mark Sabre, Stella Dallas*; debuted at Louisville WHAS July 19, 1922 at 17, elevated to chief announcer later; joined New York NBC 1929; produced/packaged/distributed transcribed features to radio-TV stations 1942; radio-TV consultant to Gov. Thomas E. Dewey (R-New York), President Dwight D. Eisenhower; developed resort hotel in Virgin Islands after quitting radio 1953; d. Aug. 15, 1962.

Floyd Mack (Floyd MacLaughlin), Oct. 23, 1912, Ava, Ohio; announcer, entrepreneur-businessman, newscaster bka *The Bell Telephone Hour* interlocutor NBC Radio 1940–58, NBC-TV 1959–68, *Encores for the Bell Telephone Hour* NBC Radio 1968–69; *Floyd Mack and the News* reporter 1942-ca. 1944; operated recording venture in years on air, moving later to Newark, Ohio supplying transportation services to local seniors; d. Jan. 3, 1983.

Bob Montana, Oct. 23, 1920, Stockton, Calif.; comic book-newspaper illustrator bka progenitor of entrepreneurial empire inspired by Montana's drawings of *Archie Andrews*, pals, netting broadcast, print, screen, stage, merchandise reproductions ad infinitum; d. Jan. 4, 1975.

Cesar Victor Saerchinger, Oct. 23, 1884, Aachen, Germany; commentator, emcee, print journalist (*The New York Evening Post*) bka key figure formulating basics of radio overseas reporting; hired by CBS 1930 to dispatch reports from London (in pre–Edward R. Murrow epoch) became "dean of this esoteric profession of foreign radio reps" inaugurating transatlantic aircasting; in an ill-conceived notion—convinced by May 1937 there was no future in European newscasting—Saerchinger resigned post, succeeded by soon-to-be-venerated Murrow; joining NBC, he went on air with weekly quarter-hour commentary *The Story Behind the Headlines* 1938–44; d. Oct. 10 1971.

Margaret Speaks, Oct. 23, 1904, Columbus, Ohio; vocalist bka *Voice of Firestone* mainstay mid 1930s-mid 1940s (40 appearances); earlier in Humming Birds trio with "Whispering" Jack Smith over New York WJZ; debuted with San Francisco Opera 1941; d. July 16, 1977.

Death

Al Jolson, Oct. 23, 1950, San Francisco, Calif.; b. May 26, 1886.

October 24

Debuting

The Rudy Vallee Show (*The Fleischmann Hour, The Sunshine Hour, The Royal Gelatin*

Hour, Vallee Varieties, Sealtest Village Store, Villa Vallee), Oct. 24, 1929, NBC; variety; premiered on New York WABC 1928, became one of radio's foremost performers; his was — said one reviewer — "the most important show on the air" in early 1930s, adding "Vallee's discoveries of people who later joined the front ranks of the entertainment world has never been equaled"; reputed taskmaster, difficult to work with, yet public fawned over "original crooner" predating Crosby, Sinatra; legendary guests of stage, screen radio on his show — John Barrymore sidekick early 1940s; by 1950s glitz, glamour mostly gone as he spun records for livelihood between chitchat; final broadcast June 19, 1955.

Births

Teri Keane, Oct. 24, 1925, New York City, N.Y.; actress (radio, stage, TV) bka *The Edge of Night* daytime serial figure Martha Marceau CBS-TV 1964–75, *The Second Mrs. Burton* heroine Terry Burton CBS Radio ca. early 1950s-1960, *Life Can Be Beautiful* leading lady Carol "Chichi" Conrad 1946–54; Broadway player; feminine lead in radio's *Marriage for Two*, recurring/guest shots in 1940s-50s *Adventure Theater, Big Sister, Gangbusters, Inner Sanctum Mysteries, Just Plain Bill, Mr. Keen—Tracer of Lost Persons, Mr. Mercury, The Road of Life, Show Boat, Somerset Maugham Theater, X-Minus One*, still more plus *The CBS Radio Mystery Theater* 1970s-80s; daytime runs in *The Guiding Light* CBS-TV 1957, *One Life to Live* ABC-TV 1976–77, *Loving* ABC-TV 1983–84.

David Oswald Nelson, Oct. 24, 1936, New York City, N.Y.; actor (film, radio, TV), director-producer (commercials, film, TV), bka *The Adventures of Ozzie and Harriet* as himself joining radio cast 1949–54, TV 1952–66.

Melvin Purvis, Oct. 24, 1903, Timmonsville, S.C.; announcer, FBI agent bka *Top Secrets of the FBI, True Adventures of Junior G-Men* host-narrator late 1930s (only credited series); following FBI career joined radio; never firing shot, yet present at Chicago slaying of notorious criminal John Dillinger July 22, 1934, perpetuating legend (refuted by FBI) that he took Dillinger out; d. Feb. 29, 1960.

Death

Walter Woolf King, Oct. 24, 1984, Beverly Hills, Calif.; b. Nov. 2, 1896.

October 25

Canceled

Al Pearce and His Gang, Oct. 25, 1947, ABC; debut Jan. 13, 1934.

Births

John Reed King, Oct. 25, 1914, Atlantic City, N.J.; actor, announcer, emcee, newscaster, quizmaster; broke into radio as newsman in hometown, presented big band remotes; with CBS news vets Robert Trout, Ed Murrow, supplied weekly summary in French beamed to occupied France in World War II; ran game shows in carload lots: *Break the Bank, Chance of a Lifetime, Give and Take, Go for the House, The Great Day, Missus Goes a-Shopping* on 1940s radio, more on 1950s TV: *Battle of the Ages, Chance of a Lifetime, Give and Take, Missus Goes a-Shipping, On Your Way, There's One in Every Family, What's Your Bid?, Where Was I?*, more; opened added aural series e.g. *American School of the Air, The Columbia Workshop, Death Valley Days, Duffy's Tavern, Grand Central Station, The Heinz Magazine of the Air, The Mel Torme Show, Our Gal Sunday, The Sheriff, The Stu Erwin Show, Texaco Star Theater, The Victor Borge Show, The Ziegfeld Follies of the Air*; portrayed *Sky King*; d. July 8, 1979.

Albert Lewis, Oct. 25, 1912; director, scriptwriter (film, radio, TV) bka *Our Miss Brooks* director-chief scribe 1948–57; contributed to trio of screenplays—*Ziegfeld Follies* 1946, *Ma and Pa Kettle* 1949, *Our Miss Brooks* 1956, later penned occasional episodes of unrelated TV series until landing permanent gig scripting *Julia* NBC-TV 1968–71; d. Feb. 3, 2002.

Deaths

Cecil B. Brown, Oct. 25, 1987, Los Angeles, Calif.; b. Sept. 14, 1907. Morton Downey, Oct. 25, 1985, Palm Beach, Fla.; b. Nov. 14, 1901. Bob Murphy, Oct. 25, 1959, Wilmette, Ill.; b. May 6, 1917. Vincent Price, Oct. 25, 1993, Los Angeles, Calif.; b. May 27, 1911.

October 26

Debuting

Adventures by Morse, Oct. 26, 1944, syndication; spine-tingling chiller anthology drama wherein principals San Francisco detective Capt. Bart Friday (Elliott Lewis, David Ellis, Russell Thorson) with geographical base reaching ends of earth, sidekick Skip Turner (Jack Edwards) brushed against supernatural themes; Carlton E. Morse escapade exhibiting lots of parallel to *I Love a Mystery* aired by NBC, CBS, MBS; final broadcast Oct. 18, 1945.

Births

Patrick H. Barnes, Oct. 26, 1888, Sharon, Pa.; announcer, emcee, producer; on air at embryonic Pittsburgh KDKA 1921, moved to Chicago WHT as chief announcer 1925, produced *Henry Adams and His Book* that year, one of earliest recorded shows on ether, managed WHT 1927; transitioned to Windy City's WGN, WENR, shifted to New York City 1930s to affiliate with WOR, WINS, WNBC; introduced national audiences to forgettable 1930s-40s *I'll Never Forget, Let's Be Charming, Those Good Old Days, Musical Cruise, Pleasure Island*; headlined trio of 1930s shows under own moniker; after radio gigs, relocated to Milwaukee 1954 as WISN-TV public affairs director until death; d. June 9, 1969.

Igor Gorin, Oct. 26, 1908, Grodek, Ukraine; composer, educator, film actor, vocalist (baritone) bka *Voice of Firestone* regular with 33 guest shots, intermittent visits to *The Bell Telephone Hour*; debuted Metropolitan Opera Feb. 10, 1964; University of Arizona voice teacher afterward; d. March 24, 1982.

Clarence L. Hartzell, Oct. 26, 1910, Huntington, W. Va.; actor, announcer, entrepreneur; narrated *Secret City* 1941–42, aural actor 1930s-50s: *Author's Playhouse, Li'l Abner, Lum and Abner, One Man's Family, The Road to Danger, The Silver Eagle, Those Websters, Today's Children, Uncle Ezra, Vic and Sade*, more; NBC-TV as *Cactus Jim* 1949–51, *Those Endearing Young Charms* sitcom 1951–52; after airtime, operated Arkansas antique emporium; d. March 5, 1988.

Edwin W. Reimers, Oct. 26, 1912, Moline, Ill.; actor (film, TV), announcer, newscaster, program/special events director bka commercial spokesman for Sears, Roebuck & Co. Allstate Insurance unit — people recalled *his* voice assuring "You're in good hands ... with Allstate," durable plugger for Procter & Gamble's Crest toothpaste; *Matinee in Rhythm, Milton Cross Opera Album* 1940s radio credits; acted, announced, newscasted at Des Moines WHO 1932–36, program director at Buffalo WBEN 1936–42, after World War II special events director of WBEN-TV 1946–47, New York ABC Radio-TV announcer 1948–49, Los Angeles KTTV television actor, announcer 1950; five B-movies 1951–71; introduced TV series *The Crusader, Do You Trust Your Wife?, Kaiser Aluminum Hour, Mr. Adams and Eve, Pantomime Quiz, Wire Service* 1949–70; d. Jan. 28, 1986.

Deaths

Hattie McDaniel, Oct. 26, 1952, Woodland Hills, Calif.; b. June 10, 1895. William S. Paley, Oct. 26, 1990, New York City, N.Y.; b. Jan. 28, 1901.

October 27

Debuting

Pursuit, Oct. 27, 1950, CBS; mystery detective drama; Scotland Yard inspector Peter Black (Ted de Corsia, John Dehner, Ben Wright) conducted "relentless, dangerous pursuit, when man hunts man" after crime; support cast William Johnstone, Joseph Kearns, Raymond Lawrence, Jeanette Nolan, more; series silent mid 1950-mid 1951; final broadcast March 25, 1952.

This Is Nora Drake, Oct. 27, 1947, NBC; daytime serial; is there a woman in serialdom more put upon than nurse Drake (Charlotte Holland, Joan Tompkins, Mary Jane Higby)?; she chose intended mate, bachelor Dr. Ken Martinson (Alan Hewitt), who was coerced into wedding Peggy King (Lesley Woods, Mercedes McCambridge, Joan Alexander), making his life hell from first day; when she assured Ken he'd get divorce over her dead body, not only did he, Nora have to wait it out, so did fans — premonition of things to come, taking five years to resolve; Nora became Peggy's object of scorn — made Nora's life agony, despite latter's failed tries to link with other lovers; final broadcast Jan. 2, 1959.

You Bet Your Life, Oct. 27, 1947, ABC; audience participation comedy quiz; host Groucho Marx; final broadcast Sept. 19, 1956; NBC-TV Oct. 5, 1950-Sept. 21, 1961, TV syndication 1980, 1992.

Births

John (Jack) Carson, Oct. 27, 1910, Carman, Manitoba, Canada; actor (stage, film, radio, TV), comedian, emcee bka *The Jack Carson Show* (*Everybody Loves Jack*) comedy variety series headliner CBS 1943–47, also *The Sealtest Village Store* NBC 1947–49, *Jack Carson* CBS 1954/1955–56; more than 100 movies 1937–60, frequent TV roles, guest shots; vanished few times for weeks in 1940s to appear as clown with Ringling Brothers and Barnum and Bailey Circus, never recognized; d. Jan. 2, 1963.

Kathryn C. Cravens, Oct. 27, 1898, Burkett, Texas; actress, author, commentator, newscaster bka first feminine radio commentator on national hookup; launched career at 15 as 20th Century–Fox silent film actress under alias Kitty O'Dare; acted in dramas she penned for St. Louis KWK 1929, then KMOX where she was on air four times daily labeled "Voice of St. Louis"; interviewer on *News Through a Woman's Eyes* CBS 1936–38, *Kathryn Cravens Broadcasts the News* MBS 1945; in two years at CBS, flew 50,000 miles pursuing story material; authored novel *Pursuit of Gentlemen* 1951; d. Aug. 29, 1991.

Leif Erickson (William Anderson), Oct. 27, 1911, Alameda, Calif.; actor (film, radio, TV), vocalist; *My Friend Irma* recurring figure Richard Rhinelander III 1947–54; appeared in 77 mostly B theatrical motion pictures; performed in nine made-for-TV films, hero in NBC-TV hour-long western *The High Chapparal* 1967–71 plus single visits 71 times to sundry TV series; d. Jan. 29, 1986.

Emily Post (Emily Price), Oct. 27, 1873, Baltimore, Md.; author, etiquette consultant, lecturer, print journalist (newspapers, *The Century, Harper's, Scribner's*, et al.), syndicated columnist (200 newspapers) bka "nation's most famous authority on how to behave graciously in society and business"; aural advice, tip-giving talk series on CBS, NBC Red, Blue under several monikers: *Emily Post* 1930–33, 1934, *How to Get the Most Out of Life* 1937–38, *The Right Thing to Do* 1938–39; freelance articles in sundry periodicals, five fiction volumes 1904–10, yet her course set with 1922's *Etiquette: The Blue Book of Social Usage*, tome updated 10 times, in 89th printing at death (many added volumes on manners, social graces); established Emily Post Institute 1946 persisting beyond her demise studying issues of gracious living; d. Sept. 25, 1960.

David P. Stone, Oct. 27, 1901, Savannah, Ga.; announcer, producer bka *Grand Ole Opry* country music show interlocutor (only net series); on air at Nashville WLAC 1920s; moved to rival WSM, by 1928 announcer, co-producer of future legendary *Opry*; joined St. Paul KSTP 1940, hired to launch-produce-host country music/comedy feature, *Sunset Valley Barn Dance*; remained as KSTP farm director to retirement at 85 in 1986; d. Aug. 31, 1995.

Deaths

Xavier Cugat, Oct. 27, 1990, Barcelona, Spain; b. Jan. 1, 1900. Elliott Roosevelt, Oct. 27, 1990, Scottsdale, Ariz.; b. Sept. 23, 1910. Herb Sheldon, July 21, 1964, Manhasset, N.Y.; actor, announcer, emcee; 1940s-1950s web inventory *Ethel and Albert, Honeymoon in New York*, more as announcer, hosted *The Herb Sheldon Show*, acted in *The Jack Kirkwood Show*, cast member of *Mirth and Madness, The Robert Q. Lewis Show*; b. 1913 (numerous sources seeking exact date exhausted), Brooklyn, N.Y. Rex Stout, Oct. 27, 1975, Danbury, Conn.; b. Dec. 1, 1886.

October 28

Debitomg

The Henry Morgan Show (*Here's Morgan*), Oct. 28, 1940, MBS; comedy; acerbic-tongued jester who dissed everything, everybody — loved nothing more than giving needle to those deserving it, especially own sponsors, some dropping him as result though audiences ate it up; launched as *Meet Mr. Morgan* on New York WOR 1940; built following but never sold goods like Arthur Godfrey, never as funny as Fred Allen, two entertainers who also took jaundiced sponsor views; final broadcast June 23, 1950.

Sky King, Oct. 28, 1946, ABC; juvenile adventure serial with aerial theme; "America's favorite flying cowboy" Schuylar J. King (Roy Engel, Jack Swineford, Earl Nightingale, Carlton KaDell, John Reed King) owned Flying Crown ranch near Grover, Ariz., two planes — Songbird, Flying Arrow — used to investigate crimes, chase culprits; assisting were teenage niece Penny King (Beryl Vaughn, Beverly Younger), nephew Clipper King (Jack Bivens,

Johnny Coons), ranch foreman (Uncle) Jim Bell (Cliff Soubier); video series on NBC-/ABC-TV 1951–54, rerun multiple times on CBS-TV 1959–66; newspaper comic strip early 1950s, single 1964 comic book proved hero better liked in electronic media; final radiocast June 3, 1954.

Births

Herbert (Herb) Butterfield, Oct. 28, 1895, Providence, R.I.; actor (radio, film, TV) bka support thespian in ongoing roles favoring "name" crimefighters e.g. Ellery Queen, Philip Marlowe, Jack Armstrong, Jeff Regan, Pete Kelly, Richard Diamond, Roy Rogers; expanded niche to encompass *Broadway Is My Beat, Confession, Crime Classics, Dangerous Assignment, Dragnet, The Man from Homicide, Pursuit, The Silent Men, Tales of the Texas Rangers*; handful of dishpan dramas—*Kitty Keene Incorporated, Ma Perkins, One Man's Family, Today's Children*; uncredited in half-dozen theatrical flicks 1949–56 including *The Ten Commandments*; 21 spots on solo TV dramas 1953–57; d. May 2, 1957.

Charles H. Mullen, Oct. 28, 1927, Brooklyn, N.Y.; actor (radio, stage, TV), salesman (tobacco) bka American Tobacco Co. president-CEO 1986–92; succession of radio series including *Coast-to-Coast on a Bus, Dick Tracy, Believe It or Not, Archie Andrews* (in latter played title role 1945–46); brief exposure on *Robert Montgomery Presents* NBC-TV, hosted multiplicity of pithy early CBS-TV kids' features; d. June 18, 2002.

Ronald W. (Ron) Rawson, Oct. 28, 1917, Clear Lake, Iowa; announcer bka daytime interlocutor presenting late 1930s-50s *The Brighter Day, Joyce Jordan, Life Can Be Beautiful, Portia Faces Life, The Right to Happiness, The Road of Life, Young Doctor Malone*, others plugging Procter & Gamble goods—one of key commercial spokespersons (with Nelson Case, Bud Collyer) employed to pitch Procter & Gamble wares (Cheer, Crisco, Dreft, Ivory, Joy, Spic 'n' Span, etc.)—persisting in early CBS-TV serials *The Guiding Light, The Road of Life, Search for Tomorrow, The Seeking Heart*; added radio intros: *The Adventures of the Thin Man, Can You Top This?, The Hour of Charm, Radio Reader's Digest, Speed Gibson of the International Secret Police, Topper*, more; linked to NBC-TV's *Colgate Comedy Hour* 1950s; Screen Actors Guild-New York president; managed John Drew Theater, East Hampton, N.Y., prior to executive producer of South Shore Music Circus, Cohasset, Mass., 1968–88; d. July 18, 1994.

Deaths

Peter G. Cranford, Oct. 28, 2000, Thomson, Ga.; b. Nov. 9, 1908. Larry Dobkin, Oct. 28, 2002, Los Angeles, Calif.; b. Sept. 16, 1919. Leon Janney, Oct. 28, 1980, Guadalajara, Mexico; b. April 1, 1917. Veola Vonn, Oct. 28, 1995, Orange County, Calif.; b. July 29, 1918. Alice Yourman, Oct. 28, 2000, Columbus, Ohio; b. Sept. 17, 1907.

October 29

Births

Fanny Brice (Fania Borach), Oct. 29, 1891, New York City, N.Y.; actress (film, radio, stage), recording artist, vocalist bka *Ziegfeld Follies* entertainer 1910–23; *Baby Snooks* impish miscreant practicing devilment to bewilder longsuffering pop (usually actor Hanley Stafford) 1937–51; d. May 29, 1951.

Virginia Clark (Virginia Bowers), Oct. 29, 1908, Peoria, Ill.; actress, vocalist bka *The Romance of Helen Trent* daytime serial initial heroine 1933–44, airing from Chicago; in childhood/youth lived in Little Rock, chosen Miss Little Rock, Miss Arkansas, appeared in 1925 Miss America pageant; first radio job on Chicago WJJD 1931 as *Personality Girl* singer; after *Helen Trent*, had morning show as Virginia Gale on Chicago WGN early 1950s; trail grows cold after she "moved East" (newspaper clipping) by 1960s with spouse #3—totally vanished from OTR historiographers' radar.

Deaths

Woody Herman, Oct. 29, 1987, Los Angeles, Calif.; b. May 16, 1913. Bill Lipton, Oct. 29, 2001, Portland, Ore.; b. June 13, 1926. Myra Marsh, Oct. 29, 1964, Los Angeles, Calif.; b. July 6, 1894. Jack Slattery, Oct. 29, 1979, Lancaster, Calif.; b. Feb. 18, 1917. John Scott Trotter, Oct. 29, 1975, Los Angeles, Calif.; b. June 14, 1908.

October 30

Sound Bite

Oct. 30, 1938—most alarming program in

vintage radio history airs as CBS offers Orson Welles' production of H. G. Wells' play "War of the Worlds" on *The Mercury Theater on the Air*; uninformed listeners missing sporadic disclaimers that it's "only a play" have fear of God put into them, convinced menacing Martians arrived in spacecraft at Grovers Mill, N.J. prepared to overtake America; some who realize later they have been duped, not knowing truth at time of airing, furious; nevertheless, it's surely night to gather around family radio receiver, still signified by hordes as audio "panic broadcast."

Debuting

The Romance of Helen Trent, Oct. 30, 1933, CBS (premiered on Chicago WGN July 24, 1933); daytime serial; oft-quoted epigraph said it all: *And now The Romance of Helen Trent, the real-life drama of Helen Trent who — when llife mocks her, breaks her hopes, dashes her against the rocks of despair—fights back bravely, successfully, to prove what so many women long to prove in their own lives: That because a woman is 35, or more, romance in life need not be over, that the romance of youth can extend into middle life, and even beyond*; widowed Hollywood fashion dress designer Trent (Virgina Clark, Betty Ruth Smith, Julie Stevens) was epitome of saintliness, on pedestal out of reach though many tried to deter her purity (fact she was widowed seemed unrelated to such a virtuous creature); her most persistent suitor, Gil Whitney (Marvin Miller, William Green, David Gothard) never got to first base — producers Frank, Anne Hummert made sure of it for if she remarried their title, premise would be done for; after 27 years, 7,222 episodes — more than any other radio soap — Trent was still 35, still charming legions of boy toys; final broadcast June 24, 1960.

Births

Joan Banks (Lovejoy), Oct. 30, 1918, Petersburg, W. Va.; actress (stage, radio, film, TV), voiceover artist bka prolific daytime serial thespian corralling leads, support roles; insisted "radio was always my first love"; audio work on *Boston Blackie, Bright Horizon, Bringing Up Father, Gangbusters, Gunsmoke, Her Honor — Nancy James, Hollywood Star Theater, House in the Country, Joyce Jordan, M.D., Lux Radio Theater, Maisie, The Man Called X, Manhattan at Midnight, Mary and Bob's True Stories, Mr. Keen — Tracer of Lost Persons, My Friend Irma, The O'Neills, Portia Faces Life, The Saint, Stoopnagle and Budd, Suspense, This Day Is Ours, Today's Children, Valiant Lady, A Woman of America, Young Doctor Malone, Young Widder Brown*, more; performed in half-dozen theatrical films 1951–61 while making 45 mostly single appearances in TV dramas, sitcoms 1957–67; d. Jan. 18, 1998.

Carl Warren (Carleton Weidenhammer), Oct. 30, 1905, Bridgeport, Conn.; announcer, disc jockey bka *Bobby Benson and the B-Bar-B Riders* interlocutor Cactus MBS 1949-mid 1950s; from 1930s-50s introduced *Dick Kuhn and His Orchestra, Guest Time* (DJ), *Hit That Ball, News Tester, Red Benson's Movie Matinee, Songs of the B-Bar-B, Tex Fletcher — the Singing Cowboy, Treasury Agent*; after New York WOR separated from MBS in 1959, Warren stayed with WOR — often heard on WOR-TV; d. Feb. 10, 1968.

Death

Steve Allen, Oct. 30, 2000, Los Angeles, Calif.; b. Dec. 26, 1921.

October 31

Canceled

Fifteen Minutes with Crosby, Oct. 31, 1931, CBS; debut Sept. 2, 1931.

Deaths

Charles Egleston, Oct. 31, 1958, New York City, N.Y.; b. July 16, 1882. Arthur Gary, Oct. 31, 2005, New York City, N.Y.; b. Jan. 28, 1914. Dick Joy, Oct. 31, 1991, Medford, Ore.; b. Dec. 28, 1915. Charles Frederick Lindsley, Oct. 31, 1960, Pasadena, Calif.; b. June 8, 1994. Kenneth Niles, Oct. 31, 1988, Los Angeles, Calif.; b. Dec. 9, 1906. Arthur Peterson, Oct. 31, 1996, Los Angeles, Calif.; b. Nov. 18, 1912. Adele Ronson, Oct. 31, 2000, New York City, N.Y.; b. Oct. 18, 1906.

November 1

Debuting

Hilltop House, Nov. 1, 1937, MBS; daytime serial; storyline focused on children at orphanage; incarnated thrice, original narrative ended March 28, 1941, resumed May 17, 1948-July 1,

1955, reprised Sept. 3, 1956-July 30, 1957; superintendent Bess Johnson (real name) called shots first time around with "Miss Julie" Erickson (Jan Miner, Grace Matthews) in charge thereafter; story not limited to peculiar problems with kids, inadequate funding, difficulties with overseers — Julie had love life that netted domestic complications.

Terry and the Pirates, Nov. 1, 1937, NBC; juvenile adventure serial; heir to oriental gold mine Air Corps Col. Terry Lee (Jackie Kelk, Cliff Carpenter, Owen Jordan, Bill Fein), buddy Patrick Ryan (Clayton Collyer, Warner Anderson, Bob Griffin, Larry Alexander), plus some adolescents worked to keep world safe in face of nemesis Dragon Lady Lai Choi San (Agnes Moorehead, Adelaide Klein, Marion Sweet), other rapscallions trying to control earth; concept born in Milton Caniff comic strip, serialized in TV 1952; final radiocast June 30, 1948.

Birth

Grantland Rice, Nov. 1, 1880, Murfreesboro, Tenn.; emcee, print journalist sportscaster, syndicated columnist ("The Sportlight") bka originating cliché "It doesn't matter whether you win or lose, but how you play the game" (1946 poem *Alumnus Football*), pioneered athletic electronic media coverage; career embraced sports reporting at Nashville's *The Tennessean*, *The Atlanta Journal & Constitution*, *The New York Tribune* 1911, column; play-by-play commentator for baseball's first World Series broadcast Oct. 5, 1921 on Westinghouse group station hookup; continued Series 1922, 1923 (shared mic with Graham McNamee 1923, grooming him for greater tasks); offered capsule football commentaries on *Cities Service Concert* 1933, *Information Please* guest panelist ca. 1938-ca. 1951, *Sports Stories* host NBC 1943–44; single-reel sports films; gave golfing exposure as middle class sport — attention it had never enjoyed before; d. July 13, 1954.

Deaths

Dale Carnegie, Nov. 1, 1955, Queens, N.Y.; b. Nov. 24, 1888. Richard L. Evans, Nov. 1, 1971, Salt Lake City, Utah; b. March 23, 1906. William Johnstone, Nov. 1, 1996, New York City, N.Y.; b. Feb. 7, 1908. Elsa Maxwell, Nov. 1, 1963, New York City, N.Y.; b. May 24, 1883.

November 2

Sound Bites

The unofficial "beginning of radio" occurs Nov. 2, 1920 as Pittsburgh KDKA airs widely heralded Harding-Cox presidential election returns in evening; singular episode permits virtually all radio historiographers to label KDKA nation's "pioneer station," signifying broadcast as modest start of something grand; KDKA grew from experimental station 8XK operated by Westinghouse engineer Dr. Frank Conrad — his test model converted to KDKA earlier in 1920.

NBC jumps into all-night world of words with *Nighttalk* Nov. 2, 1981; for two hours at 10 p.m. ET Bruce Williams addresses financial concerns of callers followed by three hours of banter about listeners' psychological issues with Sally Jessy Raphael (eventually leading to Raphael's daytime TV feature); *Nighttalk* prompts NBC to institute *Talknet* in September 1982 with same experts airing plus more with shows transported by satellite, now cutting-edge technology.

Debuting

Jungle Jim, Nov. 2, 1935, syndicated (Saturday airing dominant); juvenile adventure serial; Jungle Jim Bradley (Matt Crowley, Gerald Mohr), Kolu (Juano Hernandez), Shanghai Lil (Franc Hale)— regulars in tales based on Sunday comic strip working off same storyline; spawned syndicated TV feature 1955 starring Johnny Weissmuller as African guide (not to be mistaken for syndicated *Ramar of the Jungle* 1952–53); final radiocast transcription July 31, 1954.

Myrt and Marge, Nov. 2, 1941, CBS; daytime serial; key subjects included hard-boiled stage actress-chorus girl vet Myrtle Spear (Myrtle Vail), novice thespian Marge Minter (Donna Dammerel Fick, Helen Mack, Alice Goodwin, Lucy Gilman); while Marge tried to protect pretty fresh face from pressures, anxiety rose between them as they craved same parts, men; Marge had multiple suitors, wedded attorney Jack Arnold (Vinton Hayworth) who became crimefighting assistant D.A.; in real life, Donna — Myrtle's daughter — died in childbirth Feb. 15, 1941, giving way to offstage tragedy; final net broadcast March 27, 1942 although drama returned in five-month syndicated reprise 1946.

The NBC Symphony Orchestra, Nov. 2,

1937, NBC; for most of run, large entourage of impressive staff musicians conducted by famed no-nonsense impresario Arturo Toscanini performed; final broadcast April 4, 1954.

Births

Janette Davis (Dorothy Janette Marguerite Davis Musiello), Nov. 2, 1918, Memphis, Tenn.; producer, recording artist, vocalist bka foremost singer on *Arthur Godfrey Time* CBS 1946–57, CBS-TV 1952–57, *Arthur Godfrey Digest/Roundtable* CBS 1950–55, *Arthur Godfrey and His Friends* CBS-TV 1949–57; *Arthur Godfrey's Talent Scouts* producer 1956–58, privately coached aspirants — at cancellation, retired to private life; childhood in Pine Bluff, Ark. where at 14 won amateur contest, awarded Memphis radio contract; proceeded to stations in Quincy, Ill., Shreveport, La., WLW Cincinnati working with Red Skelton, WBBM Chicago on *Petrillo Janette and MacCormack* CBS series 1944 followed by net features *The King's Jesters and Janette, Serenade and Swing, Jobs for GI Joe, Victory Matinee*; *The Janette Davis Show* went on CBS from New York late weeknights 1946–47, Sunday afternoons 1948; "She works hard and gets better all the time" vowed *Time* magazine in 1950, classifying her — like every other female winning Godfrey's favor — "wholesome"; d. April 25, 2005.

Dennis King, Nov. 2, 1897, Coventry, Warwickshire, United Kingdom; actor (radio, stage, TV), announcer, vocalist; sang on early 1930s series *Dennis King, The Paramount-Publix Radio Hour, Swift Garden Party*, introduced 1940s *When a Girl Marries*, acted in *Somerset Maugham Theater* 1951–52; played in 1959–61 syndicated TV dramatic anthology *The Play of the Week*; d. May 21, 1971.

Walter Woolf King, Nov. 2, 1896, San Francisco, Calif.; actor (film, radio, stage), announcer, emcee, vocalist; performing history encompassed vaudeville, Gilbert & Sullivan operettas, Broadway musicals, more than two dozen cinematic features; in 1930s radio, acted in *The Fleischmann Yeast Hour, Lux Radio Theater* while singing on *Paul Whiteman's Musical Varieties*, presiding over *The Flying Red Horse Tavern*, introducing *The Eddie Cantor Show*; d. Oct. 24, 1984.

Death

Paul Frees, Nov. 2, 1986, Tiburon, Calif.; b. June 22, 1920.

November 3

Sound Bite

After 12-year run under banner *Nightcap* on Salt Lake City KSL, on Nov. 3, 1975 nation's first all-night web call-in feature, *The Herb Jepko Show*, debuts on MBS; before it goes nationwide, however, in early 1970s ad hoc hookup carries it to listeners in Baltimore, Denver, Los Angeles, Louisville, Seattle; instead of dealing with controversial topics as most successor talk shows will, Jepko engages callers in chatting about events happening at that juncture in their lives.

Birth

Ted Pearson (Theodore Anders Pehrson [*sic*]), Nov. 3, 1902, Arlington, Neb.; actor, announcer, vocalist; first radio gig at Gary, Ind. WJKS 1920s involved 12-hour days announcing, singing, reading monologues; NBC talent scout took him to Chicago to open net features late 1920s-late 1950s: *The Adventures of the Thin Man, The Armour Hour, Cavalcade of America, The CBS Radio Workshop, The Empire Builders, Florsheim Frolics, The King Cole Trio, The Studebaker Champions, Young Doctor Malone*, more; bit parts 1937–51 in seven theatrical films, *The Day the Earth Stood Still* likely best recalled; d. Oct. 8, 1961.

Deaths

Alfredo Antonini, Nov. 3, 1983, Clearwater, Fla.; b. May 31, 1901. John Nelson, Nov. 3, 1976, Palm Springs, Calif.; b. March 3, 1915.

November 4

Debuting

Baby Snooks, Nov. 4, 1937, NBC, integrated into *Maxwell House Presents Good News* aka *Good News of 1938*, renamed *The Baby Snooks Show* Sept. 17, 1944, CBS; sitcom with monster juvenile Snooks Higgins (actress Fanny Brice), patriarch Lancelot ("Daddy") Higgins (Hanley Stafford most of run); premiered as one-time feature on *The Ziegfeld Follies of the Air* Feb. 29, 1936, CBS; after pithy breaks, final broadcast May 29, 1951.

Canceled

On a Sunday Afternoon, Nov. 4, 1956, CBS; debut May 31, 1953.

Births

Courtney (Court) Benson, Nov. 4, 1914, Vancouver, Canada; actor (film, radio, TV), announcer, educational and industrial film narrator; thespian 1940s-80s on *Adventure Theater, Backstage Wife, Big Sister, Big Town, Cavalcade of America, The Falcon, Lux Radio Theater, Suspense, The CBS Radio Mystery Theater, Theater Five, Wendy Warren and the News, Young Widder Brown*; interlocutor for *Gangbusters, Tennessee Jed*; running roles in 1950s-60s TV: *Young Mr. Bobbin, First Love, The Doctors, The Edge of Night, The Guiding Light*; performed in theatrical motion picture *Dirtymouth* 1970; d. Feb. 5, 1995.

Arthur W. (Art) Carney, Nov. 4, 1918, Mt. Vernon, N.Y.; actor (film, stage, TV) bka CBS-TV *The Jackie Gleason Show* character Ed Norton 1952–57, 1966–70; *Archie Andrews* figure Uncle Herman Jones, *Joe and Ethel Turp* castmate Billy Oldham in 1940s; *Search for Tomorrow* gangster bit part CBS-TV early 1950s; serious roles in motion pictures subsequently; d. Nov. 9, 2003.

Robert Bernard Considine, Nov. 4, 1906, Washington, D.C.; announcer, columnist, newscaster bka "On the Line with Considine" host with signature marking radio, TV features growing out of "On the Line" syndicated newspaper column 1933–75; *The Washington Herald* first print job succeeded by *The Washington Post, The New York Daily Mirror*; introduced *The Fred Waring Show* ca. 1930s-40s though major aural contributions *On the Line* 1947–68/1971–75, *Monitor* ca. 1968–71; same moniker on NBC-TV 1951–54, ABC-TV 1954; author, co-author or editor of 25 books including bios of Jack Dempsey, Armand Hammer, Robert L. Ripley, Babe Ruth, Toots Shor; d. Sept. 25, 1975.

Howard Ralph Hoffman, Nov. 4, 1893, Ohio; actor (stage, film, radio, TV), announcer; introduced 1940s-50s *Magic Rhythm, Silver Eagle — Mountie, Sweet River*, acted in 1930s *Chandu the Magician*; left vaudeville for Broadway stage; took initial radio job at Chicago WEGM; when radio started to fade, moved to West Coast, winning parts in large, small screen productions: five films 1958–64, cast in myriad TV dramas mid 1950s-mid 1960s; d. June 27, 1969.

Jay Jackson, Nov. 4, 1918, Stockdale, Ohio; actor (radio, TV), announcer, emcee; apprenticed at two Columbus, Ohio stations — WCOL 1937, WBNS 1942; mid 1940s-early 1950s acted in *The Philip Morris Playhouse on Broadway*, presided over *Twenty Questions*, introduced fans to *The Beatrice Kay Show, Broadway Talks Back, David Harding — Counterspy, The Falcon, Gangbusters, Information Please, The Radio Reader's Digest, The Sammy Kaye Show*, pitched commercials for *The Bickersons*; moved with *Twenty Questions* to Dumont TV 1953–54, ABC-TV 1954–55, hosting *Tic Tac Dough* in primetime NBC-TV 1957–58; welcomed 1950s tube viewers to *Father Knows Best, Masquerade Party, The Perry Como Show*, narrated 1960s Laurel and Hardy video retrospectives; d. Aug. 16, 2005.

Will Rogers, Nov. 4, 1879, Oolagah, Okla.; actor (film, stage, radio), emcee bka the cowboy laureate; wild west shows 1903 carrying rope tricks to vaudeville, earned top billing at Ziegfeld Follies, played on silent screen, in talkies — 54 Hollywood features 1918–35; acted in radio 1928–35 on *The Eveready Hour, Gulf Headliners, The Will Rogers Program, The Ziegfeld Follies of the Air*, humorist on live NBC inaugural gala Nov. 15, 1926; d. Aug. 15, 1935.

November 5

Debuting

The Big Show, Nov. 5, 1950, NBC; dazzling variety colossus proffering venerated "name" guests; with Tallulah Bankhead as hostess, Meredith Willson's orchestra, chorus, big-budgeted extravaganza intended to stem TV's tide while retaining NBC's traditionally huge Sunday night audience after most of its comedians defected to CBS; while moments of glory occurred, despite attempts at grandeur with likes of Eddie Cantor, Jimmy Durante, Judy Garland, Bob Hope, Groucho Marx, Ethel Merman, Rudy Vallee, other Hollywood icons, aims never attained — it died before close of second season; final broadcast April 20, 1952.

Hedda Hopper (*Hedda Hopper's Hollywood,*

This Is Hollywood), Nov. 6, 1939, CBS; gossip-mongering; one of handful of premier insiders transmitting transgressions of Tinseltown from personal lives of rich/glamorous/famous to secrets of studios employing them; Hopper was fierce competitor in ongoing battle, trying to outwit rivals like Jimmy Fidler, Louella Parsons, Walter Winchell by being first to reveal scandalous tidbits; final broadcast May 20, 1951.

Births

Henry Milton Neely (sometimes Neeley), Nov. 5, 1877, Philadelphia, Pa.; actor, announcer, author, editor-publisher (*Radio in the Home* fanzine), emcee, opera society-radio executive, lecturer, print journalist (*The Philadelphia Evening Ledger*) bka originator of daily newspaper radio column; early career as film, theater critic of local paper before launching own periodical; Philadelphia Opera Society founder, inaugural secretary before 1921 appointment directing Philadelphia WIP; brief radio span (ending 1946 when he lectured, wrote on astronomy for Hayden Planetarium), opened *The Fitch Bandwagon*, *General Motors Concert*, *Green Valley U.S.A.*, *Philco Radio Hour*, others while scripting *Maxwell House Show Boat*, acting in *As the Twig Is Bent*, *The Greatest Story Ever Told*, *Hilltop House*, *Just Plain Bill*, *This Life Is Mine*, *Orphans of Divorce*, *Stella Dallas*; wrote two astronomy tomes released after death; d. May 1, 1963.

Roy Rogers (Leonard Slye), Nov. 5, 1911, Cincinnati, Ohio; actor (film, radio, TV), entrepreneur-businessman, personal appearance entertainer (events, parades, rodeos, stage), recording artist, vocalist (cowboy/western ballads) bka singing star of countless Saturday matinee "good guy vs. bad guy" western frontier movies; dubbed "King of the Cowboys" by publicists; *The Roy Rogers Show* 1944–53 with interruptions; d. July 6, 1998.

Deaths

Buddy Cole, Nov. 5, 1964, Hollywood, Calif.; b. Dec. 15, 1916. Guy Lombardo, Nov. 5, 1977, Houston, Texas; b. June 19, 1902.

November 6

Debuting

Manhattan Merry-Go-Round, Nov. 6, 1932, NBC Blue; one of multiple Frank, Anne Hummert-produced series, it "brings you the bright side of life ... that whirls you in music to all the big nightspots of New York town ... to hear the top songs of the week"; Victor Arden, Andy Sannella impresarios; vocalists Rachel Carlay, Glenn Gross, Rodney McClennan, Marian McManus, Lucy Monroe, Dick O'Connor, Barry Roberts, Dennis Ryan, Conrad Thibault, Thomas L. Thomas; The Boys and Girls of Manhattan, The Jerry Mann Voices, The Men About Town ensembles; Jimmy Durante, Bert Lahr, Beatrice Lillie featured artists; final broadcast April 17, 1949.

November 7

Debuting

Buck Rogers in the 25th Century, Nov. 7, 1932, CBS; juvenile sci-fi serial with explicit bent toward crime, injustice; World War I fighter pilot Rogers (Curtis Arnall, Matt Crowley, Carl Frank, John Larkin) trapped in suspended animation 500 years awoke to escort Space Corps lieutenant Wilma Deering (Adele Ronson, Virginia Vass) on spaceship missions to preserve universe; control bold goal of nemesis, Killer Kane (Bill Shelley, Dan Ocko); Rogers, Deering thwarted him, accomplice Ardala Valmar (Elaine Melchior); capitalized on premium hysteria ad nauseam; two televersions: ABC 1950–51, NBC 1979–81; final radiocast March 28, 1947.

Dr. Christian, Nov. 7, 1937, CBS; anthology drama; recurring figures Dr. Paul Christian (Jean Hersholt), nurse Judy Price (Helen Claire, Rosemary DeCamp, Lurene Tuttle, Kathleen Fitz) interacted with patients, medicos in rural River's End; fans submitted scripts for cash awards; final broadcast Jan. 6, 1954.

The Mary Lee Taylor Show (*Pet Milky Way*), Nov. 7, 1933, CBS; culinary forum; gastronomic connoisseur Taylor provided cooking tips — shortcuts in kitchen as well as purchasing, serving, preserving food — while answering fans' queries in 21-year run of whipping up something for one or many to consume; occasional guest experts contributed points between dispensing recipes, reading slowly, repeating so milady could jot them down; final broadcast Oct. 9, 1954.

Weekday, Nov. 7, 1955, NBC; magazine;

"What were they thinking?" might be asked of NBC brass killing off venerated soap operas, quiz shows that held sacrosanct timeslots for decades; impinging on milady's daytime listening habits, moguls substituted chats with well-known figures, tips for running homes, news, music, advice, etc. in marathon occupying five-hour span; built on laid-back *Monitor* scheme that successfully took over NBC weekend schedule previous summer, *Weekday* heard by different audience, flopped instantly — housewives didn't respond; sparkling teams (Walter Kiernan-Martha Scott, Mike Wallace-Margaret Truman), yet NBC loath to admit mistake, quietly removing show from docket after 38 weeks; to its dismay, long-held ties irretrievably boken, audience having fled, never recouped; final broadcast July 27, 1956.

Births

William Franklin (Billy) Graham, Jr., Nov. 7, 1918, Charlotte, N.C.; evangelist, minister bka "nation's spiritual counselor ... Pope of Protestant America" said *Time*; conducted hundreds of spiritual crusades since 1949, evolving into *Hour of Decision* evangelical preaching services CBS 1951–57, NBC 1955–61, ABC-TV 1951–54, syndicated TV 1954-present; led thousands to receive Jesus Christ as personal savior; friend, confidant of every U. S. president since Eisenhower; consistently identified by Gallup Poll as "One of Ten Most Admired Men in World"; Baptist pastor; ministry persists under Graham son William III.

Thomas Hanlon, Jr., Nov. 7, 1907, Fort Scott City, Kan.; actor, announcer, disc jockey, newscaster, sportscaster; replaced Ken Carpenter as chief announcer at Los Angeles KFI 1936 (Carpenter freelanced on *Kraft Music Hall*); in 1939 Hanlon was announcer, DJ, news/sportscaster at CBS-KNX reporting network news early 1940s, introducing myriad series 1930s-40s e.g. *Escape*, *The Ford Show*, *Gene Autry's Melody Ranch*, *The Gulf Headliner*, *Hallmark Playhouse*, *Jane Endicott— Reporter*, *Paducah Plantation*, *Red Barber Sports*, *Theater of Romance*, *We the People*; 1926–54 in 64 primarily B-films though few memorable ones: *It Happens Every Spring* 1949, *Kill the Umpire* 1950, *The Pride of St. Louis* 1952, *The Bob Mathias Story* 1954; d. Sept. 29, 1970.

Richard S. (Dick) Stark. Nov. 7, 1911, Grand Rapids, Mich.; announcer bka familial workhorse sibling (including brother Charles) in mid 1930s-mid 1950s radio given to opening washboard weepers — in *his* case *Against the Storm*, *Lone Journey*, *Pepper Young's Family*, *Perry Mason*, *When a Girl Marries* in addition to *Hit the Jackpot*, *Hour of Charm*, *It Pays to be Ignorant* (radio, TV), *The Perry Como Show*, *Walter Winchell's Journal*; made it big on early CBS-TV, sitting before camera on smoke-filled set calmly narrating chilling tales of *Danger*, plugging Remington razors "that cut so close they can shave a peach" on *What's My Line?* in live demonstrations, opening *The Perry Como Show* quarter-hour three nights weekly; d. Dec. 12, 1986.

Death

Eleanor Roosevelt, Nov. 7, 1962, New York City, N.Y.; b. Oct. 11, 1884.

November 8

Canceled

City Hospital, Nov. 8, 1958, CBS; debut Oct. 6, 1951.

Births

Jerome Hines (Jerome Albert Link Heinz), Nov. 8, 1921, Hollywood, Calif.; author, chemist, composer, educator, vocalist (bass), voice coach bka *Voice of Firestone* regular whose 37 appearances placed him seventh on show's most frequent guest list late 1940s-late 1950s plus TV extension to 1963; concurrent appearances sporadically on *The Bell Telephone Hour*; Hines altered surname in World War II to curtail anti-German sentiment; Metropolitan Opera Co. member for unprecedented 868 performances 1946–87; reviewer said he was known not only for "rich timbre" but "research he conducted into the historical and psychological background of the roles he portrayed"; deeply religious, produced opera about Jesus Christ, *I Am the Way*; d. Feb. 4, 2003.

Edmund Birch (Tiny) Ruffner, Nov. 8, 1899, Crawfordsville, Ind.; advertising agency exec, announcer, emcee, prizefighter (at 6'4" dubbed "Tiny"), producer, salesman, vocalist, writer; joined New York WEAF December 1927, flagship outlet of month-old NBC; left for Benton & Bowles ad agency as radio department supervisor where he placed-penned-produced-proffered shows like *The Better Half*, *Fred Allen*, *Palmolive Beauty Box Theater*, *Show Boat*; narrated 1942 theatrical film *Double Talk Girl*; d. Feb. 23, 1983.

Deaths

Dorothy Kilgallen, Nov. 8, 1965, New York City, N.Y.; b. July 13, 1913. Howard Miller, Nov. 8, 1994, Naples, Fla.; b. Dec. 17, 1912.

November 9

Debuting

This Is Your Life, Nov. 9, 1948, NBC; human interest feature; Ralph Edwards shifted hosting duties from durably successful *Truth or Consequences* to his newest creation; element of surprise characterized show as stunned celeb or public figure surrounded by family, friends, associates in walk down memory lane signifying icon's record; moved to NBC-TV 1952–71, brief syndicated televersions 1970, 1983; final radiocast May 3, 1950.

Canceled

My Son Jeep, Nov. 9, 1956, CBS; debut Jan. 25, 1953.

Births

Peter Gordon Cranford, Sr., Nov. 9, 1908, Brooklyn, N.Y.; author, columnist (*The Atlanta Journal*), educator, psychologist, researcher, talk show host bka *Take It or Leave It* (1940–52) conceptualist seguing into *The $64 Question*, *The $64,000 Question*, imitators, TV quiz show scandals; penned half-dozen tomes; Central State Hospital, Milledgeville, Ga., chief clinical psychologist before quitting 35-year practice in discipline at Augusta, Ga.; d. Oct. 28, 2000.

George Dewey Hay, Nov. 9, 1895, Attica, Ind.; announcer, commercial spokesman, emcee, journalist, showman, talent scout bka "The Solemn Old Judge," WSM *Grand Ole Opry* founder 1925 (NBC 1939–57), coincidentally giving venerated series its moniker 1927; introduced all acts early years, assigned portions of multi–hour show later; emotional collapse reduced appearances fall 1947; d. May 7, 1968.

Ed Wynn (Isaiah Edwin Leopold), Nov. 9, 1886, Philadelphia, Pa.; actor (stage, radio, film, TV), clown, director, emcee; one pundit observed Wynn never was comedian but clown, *visual* performer who died slow death on radio stage even outfitted in traditional clown garb before studio audience because his best gags sight-oriented; came out of vaudeville, radio money so tempting he couldn't refuse ($5,000 weekly at start); biggest hit on ether his debuting one, *Ed Wynn — the Texaco Fire Chief* 1932–35, followed by four more though bloom was off rose, Wynn faded fast; there were still some bright spots as he was nominated for Academy Award for *The Diary of Anne Frank* 1959 plus powerful performance in "Requiem for a Heavyweight" on *Playhouse 90* CBS-TV Oct. 11, 1956; variety feature *The Ed Wynn Show* ran one season CBS-TV 1949–50; d. June 19, 1966.

Death

Art Carney, Nov. 9, 2003, Chester, Conn.; b. Nov. 4, 1918.

November 10

Sound Bite

Singer Kate Smith introduces Irving Berlin's "God Bless America" to millions on CBS's *The Kate Smith Hour* Nov. 10, 1938; "electrified the nation" critic claims; at debut, Smith says Berlin tune "will be timeless ... it will never die ... others will thrill to its beauty long after we are gone"; repetitious on-air performances, recordings prove her right — anthem achieves immortality.

Canceled

The Parker Family, Nov. 10, 1944, Blue; debut July 7, 1939.

Births

Gary C. Breckner, Nov. 10, 1891, Illinois (city unsubstantiated); actor (stage), announcer, sportscaster; staffs of Los Angeles outlet trio 1932–40: KHJ, KNX, KMPC; introduced listeners to *Al Pearce and His Gang*, *The Army Hour*, *Breakfast in Hollywood*, *Jimmy Fidler in Hollywood*, *Maxwell House Coffee Time*, *The Phil Baker Show*, more; d. June 25, 1945.

George Fenneman, Nov. 10, 1919, Beijing, China; actor, announcer bka right hand to two entertainment legends, Jack Webb (*Dragnet, Pat Novak for Hire, Pete Kelly's Blues*), Groucho Marx (*You Bet Your Life*)—"The story you're about to hear is true ... the names have been changed to protect the innocent," "Say the secret word and divide a hundred dollars"; commercial spokesman for Liggett & Myers Tobacco Co.'s Chesterfield cigarettes (*Gunsmoke*); nine motion pictures, hosted pithy TV games *Anybody Can Play* 1958, *Your Surprise Package* 1961–62, *Your Funny—Funny Films* 1963; d. May 29, 1997.

Jane Froman, Nov. 10, 1907, St. Louis, Mo.; recording artist, vocalist (concert tours, film, nightclubs, radio, stage) bka subject of 1952 theatrical picture *With a Song in My Heart* starring Susan Hayward as Froman for which Froman recorded soundtrack; toured with Paul Whiteman's entourage before Broadway debut in *Ziegfeld Follies of 1934*; critically injured in 1943 USO plane crash enroute to entertain servicemen; regular on score of aural web series 1931–49, several she headlined (*The Jane Froman Show* five times); d. April 22, 1980.

Billy May, Nov. 10, 1916, Pittsburgh, Pa.; actor, composer, impresario (film, radio, TV), recording artist bka *Fibber McGee & Molly* maestro 1938–53; d. Jan. 22, 2004.

Jack E. McCoy, Nov. 10, 1918, Akron, Ohio; announcer, emcee, producer bka *Live Like a Millionaire* daytime talent audition master of ceremonies NBC, ABC 1950–53, CBS-TV 1951, simultaneously presiding over daily *Breakfast at Sardi's/Breakfast in Hollywood* ABC 1952–54; *Glamour Girl* daytime makeover contest executive producer, host NBC-TV 1953–54, *Pinky Lee Show* cast NBC-TV 1955–56; introduced mid 1940s-50s radio fans to *Escape, The Hardy Family, It's a Great Life, Kay Kyser's Kollege of Musical Knowledge, Maisie, My Mother's Husband*; d. March 18, 1991.

Robert L. Shepard, Nov. 10, 1915, New York City, N.Y.; announcer, emcee; in addition to quizmaster for *Take a Number*, opened 1940s-50s *Break the Bank, David Harding—Counterspy, Jack Bundy's Carnival, Mr. District Attorney, Pot o' Gold, You Can't Take It with You, Your Home Beautiful*; d. Dec. 19, 1993.

Death

Gerald Mohr, Nov. 10, 1968, Stockholm, Sweden; b. June 11, 1914.

November 11

Sound Bite

Use of radio in presidential politics begins Nov. 11, 1921 as Warren G. Harding's Armistice Day address is beamed across ether; during his brief tenure, Harding heartily endorses broadcasting as numerous successive speeches air; it's widely publicized that he owns a radio, positively boosting medium's fascination.

Births

Harry John Holcombe, Nov. 11, 1906, Malta, Ohio; actor (stage, film, radio, TV), announcer, director, producer, writer bka grandfather in Country Time lemonade TV commercials 1970s-80s; toured with Stuart Walker Stock Co. across Midwest 1920s; went on Cincinnati WLW 1930 in serial *Judge Perkins*, expanding into programming, writing, producing, announcing, hosting *Moon River* music-poetry feature; to New York directing 1930s-50s *Curtain Time, Dr. I. Q.—the Mental Banker, Judy and Jane, Lux Radio Theater, Tena and Tim*, presenting headliners Benny Goodman, Bob Crosby, Joe Penner; bit parts in movies *The Purple V* 1943, *Matilda* 1978; running roles, sporadic parts 1950s-70s TV episodes *The Wonderful John Acton, The Road of Life, Search for Tomorrow, Bonanza, Barefoot in the Park*; d. Sept. 8, 1987.

Paul C. Masterson, Nov. 11, 1917, Hardin, Mont.; announcer, newscaster bka interlocutor for 1940s *The Adventures of Ellery Queen, Tommy Riggs and Betty Lou*; broke into radio at Phoenix KOY 1940 as newscaster; d. May 10, 1996.

Jess Oppenheimer (Jessurun James Oppenheimer), Nov. 11, 1913, San Francisco, Calif.; director, producer, scriptwriter (Young & Rubicam advertising agency) bka *My Favorite Husband* sitcom head writer 1948–51, CBS-TV *I Love Lucy* sitcom head writer 1951–56; Teleprompter inventor; d. Dec. 27, 1988.

Deaths

Jane Ace, Nov. 11, 1974, New York City, N.Y.; b. Oct. 11, 1897. Robert Hardy Andrews, Nov. 11, 1976, Santa Monica, Calif.; b. Oct. 19, 1903.

November 12

Births

Claudia Morgan, Nov. 12, 1911, Brooklyn, N.Y.; actress (radio, stage, TV) bka *The Adventures of the Thin Man* character Nora Charles 1941–50, *The Right to Happiness* protagonist Carolyn Allen Walker Kramer Nelson MacDonald 1942–60; acclaimed as Maggie Cutler in *The Man Who Came to Dinner* on Broadway, with touring companies, many more stage roles; running parts in 1930s-40s aural series *The Adventures of the Abbotts, Against the Storm, David Harum, Lone Journey*; visits to 1940s-70s narratives *The CBS Radio Mystery Theater, Dimension X, The Falcon, Radio City Playhouse, Quiet Please*; stint in *Way of the World* dramatic anthology NBC-TV early 1955; d. Sept. 17, 1974.

Jo Stafford, Nov. 12, 1917, Coalinga, Calif.; philanthropist, recording artist, vocalist bka Capitol, Columbia disc singer in 1940s, 1950s with string of solo hits ("I'll Never Smile Again," "Jambalaya," "Make Love to Me," "Shrimp Boats," "Tennessee Waltz," "You Belong to Me," more); launched career with siblings, trio billed as The Stafford Sisters, singing country music on Los Angeles KHJ; joined Tommy Dorsey outfit late 1930s; routinely sang with audio headliners Dorsey, Al Jolson, Johnny Mercer, Bob Crosby, Paul Weston (her spouse), plus *The Jo Stafford Show* CBS 1945, 1953, ABC 1948–49; d. July 16, 2008.

Deaths

Eve Arden, Nov. 12, 1990, Los Angeles, Calif.; b. April 30, 1908. Donald Baker, Nov. 12, 1968, Hollywood, Calif.; b. Feb. 26, 1903. Norman Rose, Nov. 12, 2004, Upper Nyack, N.Y.; b. June 23, 1917. David Ross, Nov. 12, 1975, New York City, N.Y.; b. July 7, 1894. Penny Singleton, Nov. 12, 2003, Sherman Oaks, Calif.; b. Sept. 15, 1908. Grace Valentine, Nov. 12, 1964, New York City, N.Y.; b. Feb. 14, 1994.

November 13

Births

Frederick B. Bate, Nov. 13, 1886, Chicago, Ill.; newscaster; living in Paris hired by NBC September 1932 as chain's European rep, London bureau chief for web 1936; highly competitive with CBS: Bate once observed "CBS had something we didn't have — Ed Murrow" referring to CBS's dominance in London reportage in World War II; Bate moved to New York as director of NBC short-wave broadcasting 1942; retired 1949, promoted educational TV under Ford Foundation grant 1950–54; d. Dec. 25, 1970.

Jack (John) Narz, Nov. 13, 1922, Louisville, Ky.; announcer, emcee, sportscaster bka TV game show host 1958–75: *Dotto* (quiz exposing tainted scandal leading to cancellation of TV big money contests, though Narz never implicated); *Top Dollar, Video Village, Seven Keys, I'll Bet, Beat the Clock, Concentration, Now You See It*; launched career sportscasting at Burbank KWIK 1947, welcomed chain radio listeners to mid 1950s on *Curt Massey Time, Meet Corliss Archer, Space Patrol, The Tennessee Ernie Ford Show* before TV where, in 1950s, opened *Space Patrol, Life with Elizabeth, The Bob Crosby Show, Kay Kyser's Kollege of Musical Knowledge*; following showbiz retirement 1975 played in celebrity golf tourneys raising dollars for charity.

John Stephen Tillman, Nov. 13, 1916, Clio, Ala.; announcer, emcee; on air at 16 singing to studio organ played by mom at Dothan, Ala. WAFG, became staff announcer; Emory College studies supplemented by Atlanta WSB income; left school, hired as newscaster-emcee at Louisville WHAS 1938; joined New York CBS announcers 1939, Army 1943–46, back to radio, finished elusive degree at N.Y. University; opened *The Columbia Workshop, The Danny O'Neil Show, Marriage for Two, The Story of Mary Marlin, Winner Take All*, more; New York WPIX-TV news anchor-reporter 1948–67, then radio-TV-public affairs chief, Port of New York Authority; indicted on defrauding charges 1978, restitution paid, criminal accusations removed, guilty of three misdemeanors, fined; remained at agency to 1983 or beyond; d. March 3, 2004.

Deaths

Upton Close, Nov. 13, 1960, Guadalajara, Mexico; b. Feb. 27, 1894. John Lair, Nov. 13, 1985, Lexington, Ky.; b. July 1, 1894.

November 14

Debuting

Bobby Benson and the B-Bar-B Riders, Nov.

14, 1932, CBS; western juvenile adventure relying on narratives, campfire singing; 12-year-old orphaned ranch-owner Benson (Richard Wanamaker, Billy Halop, Ivan Cury, Clive Rice, Herbert C. Rice, Charles Irving, Bob Haig, Al Hodge, Neil O'Malley, Tex Ritter), with hands working ranch, stumbled onto exploits far beyond typical adolescents' reach; rustlers, smugglers, bank/stagecoach robbers were their usual quarry; show was re-branded half-dozen times; one of few durable preteen shows that never made it to video; final broadcast June 17, 1955.

Births

Rosemary DeCamp, Nov. 14, 1910, Prescott, Ariz.; actress (stage, film, radio, TV) bka *Dr. Christian* character Judy Price late 1940s-early 1950s; surfeit of radio credits in 1930s-40s *Blondie, The Columbia Workshop, Dot and Will, The Dreft Star Playhouse, Easy Aces, Gangbusters, The Goldbergs, I Want a Divorce, One Man's Family, Tom Mix*, more; TV roles in *The Life of Riley* 1949–50, *Death Valley Days* 1952–75, *The Bob Cummings Show* 1955–59, *That Girl* 1966–70; more than two dozen mostly B-film parts yet some memorable musicals (e.g. *By the Light of the Silvery Moon, Look for the Silver Lining, On Moonlight Bay, Yankee Doodle Dandy*); d. Feb. 20, 2001.

John (Johnny) Desmond, Nov. 14, 1920, Detroit, Mich.; actor, vocalist (baritone) bka *The Breakfast Club* audience participation series singer 1940s-50s; as teen, sang with outfits fronted by Gene Krupa, Bob Crosby, later with Glenn Miller, Jerry Gray; hosted near-dozen pithy audio musicales, several bearing his name in monikers (*The Johnny Desmond Follies, Johnny Desmond Goes to College, The Johnny Desmond Show*, et al.); TV gigs *The Don McNeill TV Club* 1950–51, *Face the Music* 1948, *Glenn Miller Time* 1961, *The Jack Paar Show* 1954, *Music on Ice* 1960, *Tin Pan Alley TV* 1950, *Your Hit Parade* 1958–59; acted in brief TV sitcoms *Sally* 1958, *Blansky's Beauties* 1977; d. Sept. 6, 1985.

Morton Downey, Nov. 14, 1901, Wallingford, Conn.; entrepreneur-capitalist, recording artist, vocalist (cruise ships, film, nightclubs, personal appearances, political rallies, stage, radio, TV) bka perhaps only artist to host series on four aural chains in brief span for single sponsor (Coca-Cola); recurring cast member of dozen radio series 1930–51, five bearing singer's name in titles; d. Oct. 25, 1985.

Martha Ellen Tilton (Brooks), Nov. 14, 1915, Corpus Christi, Texas; actress, recording artist, vocalist bka "Sweetheart of Swing" billing in 1930s; radio singer in Los Angeles during high school; performed with bands headlined by Hal Grayson, Benny Goodman, Artie Shaw, Billy Mills; rave reviews for inaugural all-jazz concert at Carnegie Hall Jan. 16, 1938; early soloist on Capitol, recording hits like "I'll Walk Alone"; known as Liltin' Martha Tilton, aired weekly on *Martha Tilton Time* NBC 1940–41, subbed for Jo Stafford on *The Chesterfield Supper Club* NBC ca. 1944–49, sang twice daily on dual webs' *Curt Massey-Martha Tilton Time* CBS 1949–54, MBS 1952–54; played self in silver screen's *The Benny Goodman Story* 1955, acted in other films, dubbed singing in flicks for stars Anne Gwynne, Martha O'Driscoll, Barbara Stanwyck; TV guest shots; d. Dec. 8, 2006.

Death

Robert Trout, Nov. 14, 2000, New York City, N.Y.; b. Oct. 15, 1908.

November 15

Sound Bite

First "national" network broadcast, Nov. 15, 1926; National Broadcasting Co. airs $50,000 four-hour inaugural gala with comedy teams, orchestras, vocalists from Waldorf Astoria Hotel with 1,000 guests, live pickups from multiple points east of Kansas City; Merlin H. Aylesworth, NBC president 1926–36, master of ceremonies; celebration beamed by 21 affiliates, four extra outlets via 3,600-mile special telephone cable line.

Birth

Franklin Pearce Adams (FPA), Nov. 15, 1881, Chicago, Ill.; journalist, instigator Algonquin Hotel Round Table discussions bka *Information Please* permanent panelist 1938–51 (considered "expert-in-residence in matters literary"); Chicago newspaperman before World War I, returning to publish volumes of short prose, poetry; launched personal forum "The Conning Tower" in *The New York Tribune* 1913, column persisting 35 years; only added radio attempt, *The Word Game*, premiered six nights before *Information Please* withdrawn; *Biography in Sound* profile subject NBC Sept. 17, 1955; d. March 24, 1960.

Death

Roger Forster, Nov. 15, 2003, Charlotte, N.C.; b. June 12, 1915.

November 16

Canceled

Aunt Jenny's Real Life Stories, Nov. 16, 1956, CBS; debut Jan. 18, 1937.

Births

James Edward (Jim) Jordan, Nov. 16, 1896, Peoria, Ill.; actor (film, radio, stage), entrepreneur-salesman, vocalist (tenor) bka *Fibber McGee & Molly* sitcom patriarch, eccentric harboring delusions of fame, wealth as spouse (Marian Jordan) supported him 1935–59; career began as singer, advanced to vaudeville, cracked radio in 1923, led to Chicago WIBO recurring all-music gig *The Jordans, Marian and Jim* 1925; multiple series followed with two most influential warm-ups to their future success on Chicago outlets: *The Smith Family* WENR 1929–32, *Smackout* WMAQ, WENR, KYW 1931–35; d. April 1, 1988.

Mary Margaret McBride, Nov. 16, 1899, Paris, Mo.; author, commentator, freelance writer, print journalist, publicist, syndicated columnist bka *Mary Margaret McBride* chatfest hostess 1937–54 — six million listeners (mostly housewives) tuned in daily to hear "first lady of radio" dispense cooking tips, common sense, perceptive insights on diverse topics padded by more than 1,200 interviews with "colorful plumbers," public figures (Eleanor Roosevelt, Harry S Truman were two); launched career as collegiate newspaper reporter, then *The Cleveland Press* 1919, assistant publicist at Interchurch World Movement in New York City 1920, *The New York Evening Mail* feature writer 1920, freelance writer 1924–34 selling scads of articles to *Cosmopolitan*, *Good Housekeeping*, *The Saturday Evening Post*, other periodicals while penning dozen volumes; won on-air hostess job at New York WOR 1934, initially identified as Martha Deane; bombed on NBC-TV 1948; syndicated column 1953–56; d. April 7, 1976.

Burgess Meredith, Nov. 16, 1907, Cleveland, Ohio; actor (stage, radio, film, TV) bka major star of sliver screen, TV with remarkable output; on stage in Maxwell Anderson play *Winterset* adding film in 1936, first of 173 screen portrayals in combined media; trouble in lead of NBC Blue's *Red Davis* (preceded by *Red Adams*, forerunners of *Pepper Young's Family*) when, in 1934, he forgot to return to studio for live West Coast repeat aired earlier to East — fired from weekly $350 Depression-era slot; *Cavalcade of America*, *Inner Sanctum Mysteries*, *We the People*, others tied him over; d. Sept. 9, 1997.

George O. Petrie, Nov. 16, 1912, New Haven, Conn.; actor (stage, radio, film, TV) bka *The Jackie Gleason Show* (aka *The Honeymooners*) comedy-variety utility player in myriad characterizations CBS-TV 1952–57, 1966–69, *Search for Tomorrow* daytime serial attorney Nathan Walsh 1954–58, *Dallas* serial drama figure Harv Smithfield CBS-TV 1979–91; support player primarily except fleeting leads in radio's *The Adventures of Superman*, *The Adventures of the Falcon*, *The Amazing Mr. Malone*, *Backstage Wife*, *Big Town*, *Call the Police*, *The Casebook of Gregory Hood*, *Charlie Wild — Private Detective*, *The FBI in Peace & War*, *Philo Vance*, *Tennessee Jed*, *Twenty-First Precinct*, more; Broadway performer eight times 1938–46, 16 feature-length movies 1944–92, 19 made-for-TV flicks 1975–90, one TV miniseries 1982, eight TV series 1951–96, solo appearances 98 times in TV drama/sitcom/variety fare; d. Nov. 16, 1997.

John Ward (Jack) Smith, Nov. 16, 1913, Bainbridge Island, Seattle, Wash.; recording artist, vocalist (tenor), TV personality bka *The Jack Smith Show* host CBS 1945–52; branded by opera critic Deems Taylor "man with the smile in his voice" (it was true); early in career singer with bands fronted by Gus Arnheim, Jimmie Grier, Anson Weeks, Phil Harris; in early TV, full time or fill-in emcee for handful of audience participation shows (*Place the Face*, *Welcome Travelers/Love Story*, *Queen for a Day*, *You Asked for It*), hosted syndicated TV travelogue *The American West* 1966–71; d. July 3, 2006.

Deaths

Boake Carter, Nov. 16, 1944, Hollywood, Calif.; b. Sept. 28, 1903. Ralph Edwards, Nov. 16, 2005, West Hollywood, Calif.; b. June 13, 1913. Jack Johnstone, Nov. 16, 1991, Santa Barbara, Calif.; b. May 7, 1906. Frank Luther, Nov. 16, 1980, New York City, N.Y.; b. Aug. 4, 1899. George Petrie, Nov. 16, 1997, Los Angeles, Calif.; b. Nov. 16, 1912.

November 17

Births

Jack Farren, Nov. 17, 1922, New York City, N.Y.; announcer, producer; *Under Arrest* narrator ca. late 1940s; switched to TV early 1950s producing *Howdy Doody, Winky Dink and You*; executive producer with Barry & Enright, Goodson-Todman game show outfits; produced motion picture *Fuzz* 1972, made-for-TV flicks *Mafia Princess* 1986, *Fatal Judgment* 1988; d. June 25, 1997.

Jack Lescoulie, Nov. 17, 1911, Sacramento, Calif.; actor (stage, film), announcer, disc jockey, emcee, producer bka *Today* newsmagazine on NBC-TV handling announcing, news, sports, features, interviews (he spoke opening words at debut Jan. 14, 1952, lasted to 1961), *The Jackie Gleason Show* comedy hour interlocutor CBS-TV 1952–59, *The Grouch Club* host-"grouchmaster" 1938–40, *Meet the Champions* sports interview host NBC-TV 1956–57; radio history included Los Angeles KGFJ 1932 as DJ, rival KFAC before joining New York-based stock company followed by San Francisco station—debuting *The Grouch Club* locally there; New York WMCA 1938, rival WNEW 1942 conducting overnight DJ feature *Milkman's Matinee*, after World War II joined rival WOR with Gene Rayburn conducting morning DJ entry *The Jack & Gene Show*, returning to all-night DJ work at WOR 1947; several pithy early TV gigs; d. July 22, 1987.

William (Bill) Rogers, Nov. 17, 1916, Thompsonville, Mich.; announcer bka spokesman for American Cancer Society—chose his voice for glut of syndicated 1950s aural features about cancer awareness, giving: *Songs for America, Can Baseball Be Made an Even Better Game?, A Tribute to ..., The Cancer Quack, Listening to Jazz, Music as You Like It, Of These We Sing, Let Freedom Sing, This Is Our Music, Music America Loves, The Music We Love*; "regular" same era audio shows *The Brighter Day, Charlie Wild—Private Detective, The Columbia Workshop, David Harding—Counterspy, Hoot'nanny*; d. Jan. 27, 1996.

Deaths

Bill Baldwin, Nov. 17, 1982, Los Angeles, Calif.; b. November 26, 1913. Sheilah Graham, Nov. 17, 1988, West Palm Beach, Fla.; b. Sept. 15, 1904. Art Hanna, Nov. 17, 1981, Paoli, Pa.; b. June 23, 1906. Ireene Wicker, Nov. 17, 1987, West Palm Beach, Fla.; b. Nov. 24, 1900.

November 18

Debuting

Presenting Al Jolson, Nov. 18, 1932, NBC; musical variety; infamous vocalist became legendary star, aired under multi successive program monikers (*Kraft Music Hall, Shell Chateau, Lifebuoy/Rinso Program, Tuesday Night Party*, plus his own name); invariably linked to "My Mammy," "April Showers" trademark themes; ended series broadcasts with *Kraft* again May 26, 1949 (though *Kraft* persisted one more summer with Nelson Eddy, Dorothy Kirsten).

Births

Arthur H. Peterson, Jr., Nov. 18, 1912, Mandan, N.D.; actor (stage, film, radio, TV) bka *The Guiding Light* daytime serial protagonist Dr. John Ruthledge, minister of rural Five Points flock, NBC 1937–46; thespianic debut 1930s with original Federal Theater Project; intertwined radio, theater, movies including stage plays, touring company, spotty screen inventory—10 cinematic films 1948–77, three made-for-TV flicks 1972–77; Chicago-based radio narratives *Bachelor's Children, The Barton Family, Girl Alone, The First Nighter, Silver Eagle—Mountie, The Story of Mary Marlin, Tom Mix, Woman in White*; fleeting parts in TV: *That's O'Toole* sitcom ABC 1949, *The Crisis* current events NBC 1949, *Hawkins Falls* daytime serial NBC 1952, *Soap* sitcom ABC 1977–81, performances in 65 scattered episodes TV dramas, sitcoms 1959–83; founded Los Angeles' Actors Alley Repertory Theater 1971; showbiz retirement 1991; d. Oct. 31, 1996.

Don Quinn, Nov. 18, 1900, Grand Rapids, Mich.; cartoonist, gagwriter, scriptwriter bka *Fibber McGee & Molly* sitcom head writer

1935–50, *The Halls of Ivy* drama head writer 1950–52; d. Dec. 30, 1967.

Deaths

Arthur Q. Bryan, Nov. 18, 1959, Hollywood, Calif.; b. May 8, 1899. Bob Corley, Nov. 18, 1971, Atlanta, Ga.; b. May 29, 1924. Louis G. Cowan, Nov. 18, 1976, New York City, N.Y.; b. Dec. 12, 1909. Dorothy Kirsten, Nov. 18, 1992, Los Angeles, Calif.; b. July 6, 1910.

November 19

Births

Tommy Dorsey, Nov. 19, 1905, Shenandoah, Pa.; younger bandleader-sibling of less renowned Jimmy Dorsey following similar pursuits; pair launched combined band 1922, separated 1935 before re-combining outfits 1953; Tommy Dorsey featured on 19 network series 1928–54 plus myriad of big band one-night-stands; d. Nov. 26, 1956.

Charles (Chuck) Webster, Nov. 19, 1901, England; actor (stage, radio, film, TV), telegraph operator bka Abraham Lincoln impersonator in 300-plus radio performances starting 1926 (*Believe It or Not, Roses and Drums*, more); raised in Montreal, preceded acting as telegraph operator; in Broadway productions before radio became source of livelihood, mainly in daytime serial casts: *The Abbott Mysteries, Backstage Wife, Big Sister, The Falcon, I Love Linda Dale, Life Can Be Beautiful, The Light of the World, Mr. Keen—Tracer of Lost Persons, Pepper Young's Family, Perry Mason, Pretty Kitty Kelly, The Right to Happiness, Rosemary, The Story of Mary Marlin, Young Doctor Malone*; big screen roles in *Good Morning, Miss Dove* 1955, *Tea and Sympathy* 1956; played several times in trio of early TV anthologies 1957–61: *Alcoa Presents, Alfred Hitchcock Presents, Gunsmoke*; d. February 1965, Los Angeles, Calif.

Death

Bill Stern, Nov. 19, 1971, Rye, N.Y.; b. July 1, 1907.

November 20

Debuting

(The Rise of) The Goldbergs, Nov. 20, 1929, NBC Blue; daytime serial initiated as evening drama with advancing storyline; creator-writer-heroine Gertrude Berg "created an image of herself ..., then found it nationally accepted as a true reflection of an entire ethnic group" pundit allowed; branded "the quintessential Jewish mama" by another reviewer; with believable domestic setting/figures, tale proffered by critics as "best-crafted ethnic soap opera on the air"; spawned Broadway production *Molly* netting theatrical film, spiraled onto three TV chains, syndication 1949–55; final radiocast June 24, 1950.

The Strange Romance of Evelyn Winters, Nov. 20, 1944, CBS; daytime serial; dashing playwright Gary Bennett, 38 (Martin Blaine, Karl Weber), became guardian of orphaned Ms. Winters, 23 (Toni Darnay)—who needs a sentinel at 23?; pair ultimately fell in love, wed; reactions of chums prompted compelling storyline; silent 1948–51, eeked out another year; final broadcast June 27, 1952.

Young Doctor Malone, Nov. 20, 1939, NBC Blue; daytime serial; another of myriad medico dramas, featured Jerry Malone (Alan Bunce, Carl Frank, Charles Irving, Sandy Becker) as leading Three Oaks physician running local clinic, employed by New York medical research institute in between; wife Ann Richards Malone (Elizabeth Reller, Barbara Weeks) succeeded professionally, too, as another clinic's superior, though they lived split lives in separate towns by 1950s when Ann died; Jerry remarried, to Tracy Adams (Joan Alexander, Jone Allison, Gertrude Warner), godsend for him; in time as much counselor-in-residence as bodily physician; with different cast/script, show played on NBC-TV Dec. 29, 1958-March 29, 1963; final radiocast on proverbial "day radio drama died" Nov. 25, 1960.

Canceled

Painted Dreams, Nov. 20, 1940, NBC Blue; net debut Oct. 10, 1933.

Births

Fran Allison, Nov. 20, 1907, La Porte City, Iowa; actress, comedienne, TV star bka *Breakfast Club* Aunt Fanny 1937–68, *Kukla, Fran and Ollie* TV juvenile marionette series live character Fran 1948–57, 1961–62, 1969–71, 1975–76; *Sunday Dinner at Aunty Fanny's* variety show hostess 1938–39; regular on *Clara, Lu 'n' Em, Club Matinee, Meet the Meeks, National Barn Dance, The National Farm and Home Hour; The Peabodys, Smile Parade, Uncle Ezra's Radio Station, Vic and Sade, Wee Gags*; d. June 13, 1989.

Judy Canova (Julietta Canova), Nov. 20, 1913, Starke, Fla.; actress (stage, film, radio, TV), comedienne, recording artist bka *The Judy Canova Show* (originally *Rancho Canova*) sitcom headliner in which she played singing hayseed CBS 1943–44, NBC 1945–53; gifted vocalist also performed grand opera selections; launched career with sis on Jacksonville WJAX 1928; later at Village Barn in Greenwich Village, gained exposure in *Ziegfeld Follies of 1936*, air dates with Rudy Vallee, Paul Whiteman; TV guest shots: *The Colgate Comedy Hour, Love American Style*; d. Aug. 5, 1983.

Margaret Draper, Nov. 20, 1922, Salt Lake City, Utah; actress (film, radio, TV) bka *The Brighter Day* daytime serial eldest daughter Liz Dennis in drama's formative era NBC/CBS 1948-ca. early 1950s, *Ma Perkins* daughter Fay as tale wound to end CBS 1950s-60; in five scattered TV episodes, cinematic film 1950s.

Frank B. Goss, Nov. 20, 1910, Washington, D.C.; announcer, newscaster, publicist; Long Beach, Calif. KFOX hired him as announcer-publicity director 1937; joined Hollywood KFWB 1938, Los Angeles KNX 1940–62 as announcer-newscaster with daily morning, evening series while introducing CBS network shows *Escape, The Hallmark Hall of Fame, Hollywood Showcase, Irene Rich Dramas, Somebody Knows, Stars Over Hollywood*, more; Associated Press bestowed Best Radio Award 1957, Southern California Radio-TV News Club conferred Golden Mic Award 1958; d. May 7, 1962.

Frank Waldecker (Franz H. Waldecker), Nov. 20, 1909, Douglass, Kan.; actor (stage), announcer; stage manager traveling with performing Dead End Kids, appeared in several plays; opened multiple 1940s-50s series: *A Date with Duchin, Gabriel Heatter and the News, Pitching Horseshoes, Postcard Serenade, Treasury Varieties, Twenty Questions*; worked local stations: Boston WBZ early 1940s, New York WOR/WQXR, Los Angeles KFAC mid 1960s; d. Jan. 13, 1995.

Deaths

Les Griffith, Nov. 20, 1991, New York City, N.Y.; b. March 1, 1906.

Cathy Lewis, Nov. 20, 1968, Hollywood, Calif.; b. Dec. 27, 1916.

November 21

Debuting

The Roy Rogers Show, Nov. 21, 1944, MBS; cowboy-Western tunes featuring Rogers (touted "King of the Cowboys"), wife Dale Evans ("Queen of the West"), ensembles Sons of the Pioneers, Riders of the Purple Sage, humor with Pat Brady, Pat Buttram, Gabby Hayes, plus dramatic adventure shoot-'em-up tale of old West reminiscent of legions of Saturday matinee films aimed at small fry; never as celebrated as rival *Gene Autry's Melody Ranch* partially due to incessant shifts to different timeslots, days of week, denying potential fans long-term continuity; NBC-TV Dec. 30, 1951-June 23, 1957, reruns CBS-TV January 1961-September 1964; final radiocast July 21, 1955.

Deaths

Harry Von Zell, Nov. 21, 1981, Calabasas, Calif.; b. July 11, 1906. Niles Welch, Nov. 21, 1976, Laguna Niguel, Calif.; b. July 29, 1888.

November 22

Births

Frank Graham, Nov. 22, 1911, Detroit, Mich.; actor (film, radio, stage), announcer, emcee; after ephemeral gig with Los Angeles Theatre Guild, joined Seattle Repertory Theatre becoming its leading man; Seattle station hired him offering visibility past local confines; hired by CBS Hollywood outlet KNX 1937, increasing exposure, earning billing as "man with a thousand voices" playing in *Armchair Adventures, The Adventures of Bill Lance, Cavalcade of America, Jeff Regan—Investigator, Lum and Abner, The Man Called X* while introducing shows headlined by Ginny Simms, Jim Backus, Judy Canova, Rudy Vallee; *The Three Caballeros* gave film exposure 1945; d. Sept. 2, 1950.

Howard Petrie, Nov. 22, 1906, Beverly, Mass.; actor (film, TV), announcer; junior announcer at Boston-Springfield WBZ-WBZA 1929 moving to New York NBC 1930, among 10 hired of 2,500 auditioned; career took three turns: in first, opened radio's *Abie's Irish Rose, Big Sister, Blondie, The Garry Moore Show* (varied monikers), *The Jimmy Durante Show, The Judy Canova Show, The Man I Married, The O'Neills,* more; in second, played in 31 motion pictures 1947–57 e.g. *Fancy Pants, Walk Softly Stranger, Seven Brides for Seven Brothers, The Bob Mathias Story*; in third, running part on *The Edge of Night* daytime serial CBS-TV 1964–65 while acting in solo episodes 26 other video series (*Alcoa Theater, Bat Masterson, Bonanza, Cheyenne, Death Valley Days, Maverick, Perry Mason, Rawhide,* etc.); d. March 24, 1968.

Roland Winters, Nov. 22, 1904, Boston, Mass.; actor (film, radio, TV), announcer, emcee, panelist bka early TV character thespian on *Mama, Doorway to Danger, Meet Millie, The Smothers Brothers Show*; played in 1960 made-for-TV flick *The Iceman Cometh*, 39 largely B-movie films 1947–70; acted in radio's *The Greatest Story Ever Told, Lorenzo Jones, The Milton Berle Show, My Best Girls,* opened *Bright Horizon, The Goodwill Hour,* hosted lesser known entries, panelist on *The Fishing and Hunting Club of the Air*; d. Oct. 22, 1989.

Deaths

Parley Baer, Nov. 22, 2002, Los Angeles, Calif.; b. Aug. 5, 1914. Gene Hamilton, Nov. 22, 2000, Nassau, N.Y.; b. Dec. 12, 1910.

November 23

Debuting

Have Gun, Will Travel, Nov. 23, 1958, CBS; western adventure among spate of 1950s frontier dramas focused toward grown-ups; eccentricity in programming, one of handful of shows launched on TV (CBS Sept. 14, 1957-Sept. 21, 1963 starring Richard Boone) defying usual order of radio aircast first; solo-dubbed college-educated high-priced gun-for-hire protagonist Paladin (John Dehner) resided at San Francisco hotel, sought perilous tasks others could/would not perform — sometimes crimefighting for law; final radiocast Nov. 27, 1960.

Births

John Dehner (John Dehner Forkum), Nov. 23, 1915, Staten Island, N.Y.; actor (stage, radio, film, TV), animator, announcer, disc jockey, newscaster, pianist bka *Have Gun — Will Travel* western drama hero Paladin CBS Radio 1958–60; Walt Disney Studio animator, DJ, pianist, at Los Angeles KFWB announcer-newscaster; movies began 1947, in 30+ films; audio thespian: *The Adventures of Philip Marlowe, The Black Book, The CBS Radio Workshop, The Count of Monte Cristo, Escape, Family Skelton, Frontier Gentleman, Gunsmoke, The Hermit's Cave, Pursuit, Rogers of the Gazette, Romance, Smilin' Ed and His Buster Brown Gang, The Truitts, The Whistler,* more; moved seamlessly to TV on *The Andy Griffith Show, Bailey's of Balboa, Big Hawaii, The Doris Day Show, The Roaring Twenties*; *Temperatures Rising, The Virginian*; d. Feb. 4, 1992.

Don Gordon, Nov. 23, 1906, Los Angeles, Calif.; actor (radio, TV), announcer; radio duty succession led him from Milwaukee WTMJ to St. Louis KMOX 1934, returning in eight months to WTMJ, to Chicago WBBM 1940 where he introduced *Bachelor's Children, Captain Midnight, Curtain Time, Ladies Fair, The Tom Mix Ralston Straight Shooters,* acting in *Wings of Destiny*; after radio exhibited thespianic talent in 1960s *The Blue Angels* on syndicated TV, on *Lucan* ABC-TV 1977–78, *The Contender* CBS-TV 1980.

Julie Stevens (Underhill) (Harriet Foote), Nov. 23, 1916, St. Louis, Mo.; actress (stage, radio, film, TV) bka *The Romance of Helen Trent* daytime serial heroine CBS 1944–60, *Kitty Foyle* title role CBS 1942–44; on Broadway then radio in *The Abbott Mysteries, Abie's Irish Rose, Big Town, Ethel and Albert, Gangbusters, The Light of the World, Mr. Keen — Tracer of Lost Persons, The Road of Life, Stella Dallas, Quick as a Flash*; after radio in TV commercials, occasional *Big Story* episode NBC-TV 1950s; in retirement cohosted *Ted and Julie* with Ted Bell on Orleans, Mass. WVLC while acting at Cape Cod community theater; d. Aug. 26, 1984.

Death

Billy Jones, Nov. 23, 1940, New York City, N.Y.; b. March 15, 1887.

November 24

Births

Dale Carnegie, Nov. 24, 1888, Maryville, Mo.; author, entrepreneurial salesman, self-help motivational guru who launched an industry bka *How to Win Friends and Influence People* scribe (Simon & Schuster, 1936); dispensed advice via national ether 1930s, early 1940s; d. Nov. 1, 1955.

Don MacLaughlin, Nov. 24, 1906, Webster, Iowa; actor (radio, stage, TV) bka *As the World Turns* daytime serial patriarch Chris Hughes CBS-TV 1956–86, *The Road of Life* daytime serial patriarch Dr. Jim Brent NBC/CBS Radio ca. late 1940s-mid 1950s, CBS-TV 1954–55; taught, coached, at 26 went to New York to try out as thespian, performed on Broadway, won leads in 1940s radio series — *Chaplain Jim U.S.A.*, *David Harding— Counterspy*, *Tennessee Jed*, *The Zane Grey Theater*— repeated often in *The Adventures of Superman*, *Ethel and Albert*, *Gangbusters*, *The Witch's Tale*, *You're in the Army Now*, ongoing roles in *Buck Private and His Girl*, *Lora Lawton*, *The Romance of Helen Trent*, *The Story of Mary Marlin*, *We Love and Learn*, *Young Widder Brown*; d. May 28, 1986.

Ireene (Seaton) Wicker (Hammer), Nov. 24, 1900, Quincy, Ill.; actress (stage, radio, TV), author, recording artist, vocalist bka *The Singing Lady* juvenile series storyteller NBC Blue/MBS/NBC/ABC 1932–39, 1940–41, 1945, ABC-TV 1948–50, 1953–54, continued intermittently PBS to 1975; assisted Drama Mama Irna Phillips with soap opera's original opus *Painted Dreams* over Chicago WGN 1930–31, leading to copycat serial *Today's Children* in which both again acted; other Wicker radio stops: *Deadline Dramas*, *Harold Teen*, *Judy and Jane*, *Song of the City*; "Lady with a Thousand Voices" characterizations on kids' shows (using marionettes in video); penned children's books, made recordings; won Peabody Award 1958 for contributions to youngsters; d. Nov. 17, 1987.

Margaret Worrall (Pegeen) Fitzgerald, Nov. 24, 1904, Norcatur, Kan.; commentator bka *The Fitzgeralds* wedded couple breakfast chat 1945–47, show airing locally New York WOR 1940–82, solo by her on WNYC 1984–88; d. Jan. 30, 1989.

Death

Craig McDonnell, Nov. 24, 1956, New York City, N.Y.; b. June 8, 1907.

November 25

Sound Bite

End of era, Nov. 25, 1960; CBS cancels daytime drama remnants (*The Couple Next Door*, *The Right to Happiness*, *Whispering Streets*, *Ma Perkins*, *Young Doctor Malone*, *The Second Mrs. Burton*, *Best Seller*), primetime *The Amos 'n' Andy Music Hall* while reducing *Arthur Godfrey Time*, *House Party* five more minutes (inserting 10 minutes of news at top of each hour); action signals virtual conclusion of network features, widely dubbed "Black Friday," also "day radio drama died."

Debuting

The FBI in Peace & War, Nov. 25, 1944, CBS; crime drama based on Fred Collins tome; stories of racketeering, swindles, carjacking, crime against business sounding so real many fans thought they were actual cases; heading weekly chase was FBI field agent Adam Sheppard (Martin Blaine) with cluster of disciplined cohorts helping round up quarry under dispatch of field supervisor Andrews (Donald Briggs); for six years show opened with drum-pounding as deep baritone voice allowed "L-A-V-A, L-A-V-A" for P&G cleanser segueing into memorable march from Prokofiev's *Love for Three Oranges*; final broadcast Sept. 28, 1958.

Canceled

The Amos 'n' Andy Music Hall, Nov. 25, 1960, CBS; debut Sept. 13, 1954. *Best Seller*, Nov. 25, 1960, CBS; debut June 27, 1960. *The Couple Next Door*, Nov. 25, 1960, CBS; debut April 12, 1937. *Ma Perkins*, Nov. 25, 1960, CBS; debut Dec. 4, 1933, NBC. *The Right to Happiness*, Nov. 25, 1960, CBS; debut Oct. 16, 1936. *The Second Mrs. Burton*, Nov. 25, 1960, CBS; debut Jan. 7, 1946. *Whispering Streets*, Nov. 25, 1960, CBS; debut March 3, 1952. *Young Doctor Malone*, Nov. 25, 1960, CBS; debut Nov. 20, 1939.

Births

Pierre Andre, Nov. 25, 1899, Duluth, Minn.; announcer, dancer, emcee bka *Captain Midnight* interlocutor 1940–49, CBS-TV 1954–56; for more than two decades starting early 1930s introduced boatload of mostly soap operas, juvenile adventures like *Arnold Grimm's*

Daughter, Backstage Wife, Betty and Bob, The Carters of Elm Street, The Couple Next Door, Harold Teen, How's the Family?, Little Orphan Annie, The Romance of Helen Trent, Sky King, Tena and Tim, more; early radio career at Duluth WEBC, St. Paul KSTP, Chicago WGN, WLS; danced in three 1946–47 films—*Tangier, The Gay Cavalier, My Wild Irish Rose*; hosted daily *Pierre Andre Show* WGN to his death; d. July 21, 1962.

Verne Smith, Nov. 25, 1909, New York City, N.Y.; actor, announcer; thespian in *Arnold Grimm's Daughter*, commercial spokesman on *The Great Gildersleeve*, introduced score of 1930s-1950s web series e.g. *The Adventures of Ozzie and Harriet, The Bob Burns Show, The Judy Canova Show, Kay Kyser's Kollege of Musical Knowledge, Louella Parsons, The Roy Rogers Show*; d. March 4, 1978.

Deaths

Ted Meyers, Nov. 25, 1996, Pasadena, Calif.; b. Dec. 31, 1913. Norman Schwarzkopf, Nov. 25, 1958, West Orange, N.J.; b. Aug. 28, 1895. Bill Shipley, Nov. 25, 1996, Sedona, Ariz.; b. Aug. 1, 1918.

November 26

Debuting

Bride and Groom, Nov. 26, 1945, ABC; weekday audience participation series, host John Nelson; final broadcast Sept. 15, 1950; segmented televersion (one interval three years) Jan. 25, 1951-Jan. 10, 1958.

Births

William (Bill) Baldwin, Sr., Nov. 26, 1913, Pueblo, Colo.; actor, announcer, newscaster; beyond late 1930s-40s big band remotes, introduced 1950s series *The Edgar Bergen and Charlie McCarthy Show, Golden Days of Radio, Here's Morgan, The Jack Kirkwood Show, The Mario Lanza Show, Night Editor*; microphone-groomed at Grand Junction, Colo. KSSC, Omaha WOW, Chicago WGN; plethora of outlets followed Windy City, in order: Shreveport KWKH, Omaha KOIL, San Francisco KFSO, Omaha KOIL (again), Salt Lake City KDYL, Hollywood KFWB, San Francisco KGO becoming Blue network's Bay Area news director there; bit part in motion picture *Champion* 1949; trio of NBC-TV announcing duties: *The Bob Cummings Show* 1956–59, *The Thin Man* 1957–59, *The Flintstones* 1960–66; used own name 1962–71 announcing arrival, departure of *The Beverly Hillbillies* CBS-TV, feat few peers realized; American Federation of Television and Radio Artists board 1949, president 1970; d. Nov. 17, 1982.

Arnold Eric Sevareid, Nov. 26, 1912, Velva, N.D.; author, correspondent, newscaster, print journalist (*The Minneapolis Star, The Minneapolis Journal, The New York Herald Tribune*), wire journalist (United Press), writer; hired by Edward R. Murrow at CBS August 1939 signifying him as one of legendary "Murrow Boys"; numerous capacities at CBS with ongoing appearances on 1940s-70s *Capitol Cloakroom, CBS World News Roundup, Eric Sevareid and the News, Report to the Nation, This Is London, World News Roundup/World News Tonight, World News with Robert Trout*; penned 10 volumes 1935–83; numerous CBS-TV gigs—regular talking head on *The CBS Evening News* with Walter Cronkite until 1977 retirement; d. July 9, 1992.

Deaths

Tommy Dorsey, Nov. 26, 1956, Greenwich, Conn.; b. Nov. 19, 1905. Eddie Gallaher, Nov. 26, 2003, Washington, D.C.; b. Feb. 26, 1915.

November 27

Debuting

The First Nighter, Nov. 27, 1930, NBC Blue; anthology drama; Mr. First Nighter (Charles P. Hughes, Macdonald Carey, Bret Morrison, Marvin Miller, Donald Briggs, Rye Billsbury) beckoned patrons to "little theater off Times Square" for performances of original light romantic plays that coincided with growing American appetite for theaters starting at time when not many could afford frivolous entertainment; stalwart thespians like Don Ameche, Betty Lou Gerson, Barbara Luddy, Olan Soule, Cliff Soubier, Les Tremayne, others graced stage for three-act productions; final broadcast Sept. 27, 1953.

The Hormel All-Girl Band and Chorus, Nov. 27, 1949, ABC; music; beginning with dozen feminine ex-military musical artists in 1947, performing promotional unity formed for Hormel Foods, Inc.; troupe expanded to 60-member orchestra-glee club that sponsor put on ether to push wares to larger audience through aural entertainment gig; began as Sunday evening feature, evolving into Saturday matinee staple; final broadcast Feb. 13, 1954.

Canceled

Gangbusters, Nov. 27, 1957, MBS; debut July 20, 1935. *Have Gun, Will Travel*, Nov. 27, 1960, CBS; radio debut Nov. 23, 1958.

Births

Ralph Bell, Nov. 27, 1915, New York City, N.Y.; actor bka whiny, nasal-voiced thespian specializing in copious gangster roles, other baddie figures across medium's golden age on *Barry Craig— Confidential Investigator, Casey— Crime Photographer, Cloak and Dagger, Dick Tracy, The FBI in Peace & War, Gangbusters, Treasury Agent, True Detective Mysteries, Under Arrest, Yours Truly—Johnny Dollar*, et al., running parts (again with sinister connections) in daytime dramas *Big Sister, This Is Nora Drake*; d. Aug. 2, 1998.

George Hogan, Nov. 27, 1909, Kansas City, Mo.; actor, announcer, producer, station official, writer, vocalist; began radio career as part owner of station, sponsor, producer, announcer, occasional actor; moved to other outlets at St. Louis, Fort Worth, Chicago, Detroit, Philadelphia, New York in varied capacities—writer, producer, actor, vocalist, announcer—eventually stopping at New York WOR (MBS features); net gigs included introducing *High Adventure, Luncheon at Sardi's, The Saturday Night Swing Club, Snow Village Sketches*.

Edward Britt (Ted) Husing, Nov. 27, 1901, Bronx, N.Y.; announcer, author, disc jockey, sportscaster; overwhelmed 600 applicants for announcing slot at New York WJZ, moved to Boston WBET 1927, returned to New York WHN in weeks joining CBS Dec. 25, 1927, leaving mid 1940s for WHN as quarter-million-dollar DJ, DJ-sports reporter at rival WMGM 1948–54; brain tumor sidelined him though futile attempts to return in 1957 at Los Angeles KFI, by then blind invalid; over career introduced two dozen chain series e.g. shows topped by George Burns and Gracie Allen, Jane Froman, Fred Allen, Henry Morgan, Paul Whiteman while providing sports commentary to *The Oldsmobile Program, The Studebaker Champions, Ted Husing, Ted Husing's Sportslants*; d. Aug. 10, 1962.

Charles Wood, Nov. 27, 1911, Pittsburgh, Pa.; announcer bka interlocutor 1936–37 *The Green Hornet, The Lone Ranger* adventure dramas; briefly on Cleveland WTAM 1934, joining Pittsburgh station afterward, then Detroit WXYZ as news commentator 1936, Cincinnati WLW 1937 late-night music-poetry feature *Moon River*, New York ABC 1949–76.

Death

Cameron Prud'homme, Nov. 27, 1967, Pompton Plains, N.J.; b. Dec. 16, 1892.

November 28

Sound Bite

The Grand Ole Opry launched Nov. 28, 1925 over Nashville WSM; intervening years proved history's hardiest broadcasting enterprise, with little sign of signing off; half-hour portion of globally renowned music talent showcase on NBC 1939–57; "mother church of country music" exploded into stage shows, recordings, broadcasting, merchandising mania unimaginable in 1925—or since.

Births

Frank Black, Nov. 28, 1894, Philadelphia, Pa.; impresario, musical arranger, pianist, piano roll manufacturing executive bka radio maestro-arranger for myriad features including *Cities Service Concert, Happy Wonder Bakers, The Jack Benny Program, The NBC Symphony Orchestra, NBC String Symphony, The Palmolive Hour, The Jane Pickens Show*, more; d. Jan. 29, 1968.

José Iturbi, Nov. 28, 1895, Valencia, Spain; concert pianist, guest artist 22 times on *The Bell Telephone Hour* 1940–58; d. June 28, 1980.

Elliott Lewis, Nov. 28, 1917, New York City, N.Y.; actor (film, radio, TV), director, producer, recording artist, script consultant, writer (mystery novelist, script wordsmith) bka *The Phil Harris-Alice Faye Show* sitcom guitarist Frankie Remley 1946–54, *Cathy and Elliott Lewis Onstage* dramatic anthology actor-director-producer 1953–54, more; d. May 20, 1990.

Robert (Bob) Readick, Nov. 28, 1925, New York City, N.Y.; actor (radio, film) bka *Rosemary* daytime serial leading man, faltering Bill Dawson who needed his feet planted firmly on pathway to success, wed to woman who tried, CBS ca. late 1940s-1955; audio support role credits on *The Adventures of Father Brown, Aunt Jenny's Real Life Stories, Let's Pretend, The Second Mrs. Burton, Space Patrol, This Is Nora Drake, Time for Love, Twenty-First Precinct, Whispering Streets* briefly with title role in *Yours Truly—Johnny Dollar* 1960–61; appeared in two B-movies, *Harrigan's Kid* 1943, *The Canterville Ghost* 1944; d. May 27, 1985.

Deaths

Donald Forbes, Nov. 28, 1995, West Hollywood, Calif.; b. June 9, 1912. Max Jordan, Nov. 28, 1977, Illgau, Switzerland; b. April 21, 1895. Ralph Locke, Nov. 28, 1954, Bronx, N.Y.; b. June 8, 1877. Garry Moore, Nov. 28, 1993, Hilton Head, S.C.; b. Jan. 31, 1915. Ralph Paul, Nov. 28, 1987, Amityville, Long Island, N.Y.; b. Oct. 11, 1920.

November 29

Canceled

David Harding, Counterspy, Nov. 29, 1957, MBS; debut May 18, 1942. *Dr. I. Q., the Mental Banker*, Nov. 29, 1950, ABC; debut April 10, 1939. *The Falcon*, Nov. 29, 1954, MBS; debut April 10, 1943.

Births

Harry Bartell, Nov. 29, 1913, New Orleans, La.; actor, announcer, disc jockey; pundit estimates Bartell appeared in more than 10,000 radio shows on no less than 182 series putting him at forefront of contemporaries; broke into show biz in Houston early 1930s in pithy audio film adaptations, prelude to later *Lux Radio Theater* exhibitions; local DJ on West Coast 1937 concurrently appearing at Pasadena Playhouse; performed 77 TV series; radio standouts: *Broadway Is My Beat* 1949–54, *A Date with Judy* 1940s, *Escape* 1947–54, *Gunsmoke* 1952–61, *Yours Truly—Johnny Dollar* 1950s-1962, 177 more; d. Feb. 26, 2004.

Alan Courtney, Nov. 29, 1912, New York City, N.Y.; announcer, disc jockey, emcee; DJ at 17 persisting at trade most of career, initially on New York outlets WOV, WNEW, WMCA, WOR while hosting *Stoopnagle and Budd* 1938–39, introducing *The Korn Kobblers* 1942–43, 1946–47, presiding on *Courtney Record Carnival* 1947–50 to national audience; in next life was DJ, controversial, often stormy Miami talk show host leading to multiple job shifts between WGBS, WQAM, WIOD, WINZ; d. Sept. 16, 1978.

Vin Scully (Vincent Edward Scully), Nov. 29, 1927, Bronx, N.Y.; sportscaster bka play-by-play voice of Brooklyn/Los Angeles Dodgers baseball teams—58-year tenure (2008) with Dodgers longest of any broadcaster with single club in professional sports history (salary $3 million annually); California Sportscaster of Year 28 times, Ford Frick Award given by Baseball Hall of Fame 1982, inducted into Radio Hall of Fame 1995, named Broadcaster of Century by American Sportscasters Association 2000; Fordham University student broadcaster, hired by Washington WTOP as sub, recruited by CBS Radio sports director Red Barber for college football coverage, joined Barber/Connie Desmond in Dodger radio-TV booth 1950, set yet unbroken record as youngest person to air World Series 1953 at 25; lead announcer for CBS' World Series coverage 1979–82, 1990–97—between those mediums, called 28 Series, more than any other; called NFL games for CBS-TV 1975–82; transferred to NBC as web's foremost baseball announcer 1983–89 including Saturday *Game of the Week*.

George Walsh, Nov. 29, 1917, Cleveland, Ohio; announcer bka memorable voice introducing *Gunsmoke* epic western drama CBS 1952–61, CBS-TV 1955–75 (only radio figure moved to televersion); in final years of radio *Suspense* thriller mystery Walsh's basso profundo beckoned fans ("And nowwwwww ... another tale well-calculated ... to keep you in ... Susssspense ...!"); on air at Roswell, N.M. KSWS 1946, moved to Hollywood KNX 1952, stayed 34 years!; introduced 1950s aural features *Cathy and Elliott Lewis Onstage, The CBS Radio Workshop, Escape, Scattergood Baines, Whispering Streets*, more; d. Dec. 5, 2005.

Deaths

George Hamilton Combs, Jr., Nov. 29,

1977, West Palm Beach, Fla.; b. May 3, 1899. Gene Rayburn, Nov. 29, 1999, Gloucester, Mass.; b. Dec. 22, 1917.

November 30

Births

John D. (Jack) Brinkley, Nov. 30, 1907, Oxford, N.C.; actor, announcer, disc jockey bka daytime serials thespian (*Betty and Bob, The Couple Next Door, Judy and Jane, Kitty Keene Incorporated, Ma Perkins,* et al.); radio pilgrimage carried him from Hartford WTIC to New York WINS to Chicago WLS where he freelanced as announcer for Chicago-based CBS, NBC series; d. Aug. 8, 1972.

Richard Donald (Dick) Crenna, Nov. 30, 1927, Los Angeles, Calif.; actor (film, radio, TV) bka *A Date with Judy* sitcom — Judy Foster's boyfriend Oogie Pringle 1946–50, *Our Miss Brooks* sitcom — student-conspirator Walter Denton 1948–57, TV 1952–56, TV *The Real McCoys* sitcom — grandson Luke McCoy 1957–63, CBS-TV *Judging Amy* sitcom — fiancée of Amy's mom Jared Duff 2000–03; d. Jan. 17, 2003.

Francis J. (Happy) Felton, Jr., Nov. 30, 1907, Bellevue, Pa.; emcee, impresario, stage performer; inherited host duties in final weeks of radio's *Stop the Music!* early 1955; primarily children's entertainer presiding over *Happy Felton's Spotlight Gang* NBC-TV 1954–55, multiple local shows on New York TV in same epoch; d. Oct. 21, 1964.

Deaths

Phil Baker, Nov. 30, 1963, Copenhagen, Denmark; b. Aug. 26, 1896. Jim Brown, Nov. 30, 2004; announcer, *Give and Take* 1945–53, only verifiable series; b. ca. 1927 (myriad attempts to attain specific data futile). Merrill Mueller, Nov. 30, 1980, Los Angeles, Calif.; b. Jan. 27, 1916. Johnny Roventini, Nov. 30, 1998, Suffern, N.Y.; b. Aug. 15, 1910.

December 1

Debuting

Let's Dance, Dec. 1, 1934, NBC; most enduring (in hours) sponsored radio series thus far, three-hour coast-to-coast extravaganza repeated three more hours for Western listeners before live audience; Benny Goodman, Kel Murray, Xavier Cugat outfits performed for 20 minutes hourly; final broadcast June 8, 1935.

Meet the Press, Dec. 1, 1946, MBS; public affairs forum; most enduring program in NBC history still airing — while starting on another web!; launched by *Amercian Mercury* editor Lawrence Spivak, freelance scribe Martha Rountree, reviewing issues of current day (then, now) with scintillating newsmakers guesting; Spivak's inviolable rule "never take anyone who withholds info" netted show making own headlines for its candor (now quoted on rival webs); televersion added 1947, simulcast 1952; final radiocast July 27, 1986.

Births

Johnny Johnston, Dec. 1, 1915, St. Louis, Mo.; actor (film, stage), impresario, recording artist, vocalist; nightclub singer joining Art Kassel's band Castles in the Air, on radio late 1930s; signed with Capitol Records 1942, recording "That Old Black Magic," "Dearly Beloved," "Laura," more; performed in movie musicals *Star Spangled Rhythm* 1942, *This Time for Keeps* 1947; played lead opposite Shirley Booth in Broadway musical *A Tree Grows in Brooklyn* 1951; wed six times, to actress/singer Kathryn Grayson 1947–51; d. Jan. 6, 1996.

Jean Paul King, Dec. 1, 1904, North Bend, Neb.; actor (film, radio, stage), announcer, disc jockey, educator, newscaster, production manager, recording artist, voiceover artist; performing history in vaudeville, stock with Henry Duffy Players, silent pictures, musical comedy, light opera, San Francisco Theater Guild; arrived Cincinnati late 1920s as production manager WLW, WSAI; joined NBC as staff announcer Chicago 1934, New York 1935; acted in 1920s-30s *Death Valley Days, Famous Jury Trials,* more, introduced 1930s *Clara, Lu 'n' Em, The Goldbergs, The Lanny Ross Show, Myrt and Marge, The Palmolive Beauty Box Theater,* more, dispatched headlines on *Hecker's Information Service*; narrated *News of the Day* newsreels late 1930s while working local station gigs; made commercial photos, recordings, slide films, broadcast instructor at Provincetown (Mass.) Wharf Theatre; local DJ New York WABC 1942, Las Vegas KENO 1952, Hollywood KABC 1955; d. Aug. 21, 1965.

Rollon Parker (Rollin W. Parker), Dec. 1, 1907, Rutland, Vt.; actor bka *The Green Hornet* juvenile adventure serial oriental sidekick Kato ca. late 1930s-late 1940s — Black Beauty driver, personal valet to crusader Britt Reid who hunted "biggest of all game, public enemies that even the G-men cannot reach"; at originating Detroit WXYZ, Parker appeared in similar adolescent fare: *The Lone Ranger*, *The Challenge of the Yukon* (latter in pre–net era), *Ned Jordan — Secret Agent*, 1934 syndicated *Green Valley Line*; performed in *The Hermit's Cave* horror anthology drama circulated by Detroit WJR mid 1930s-mid 1940s, played in WWJ dramas through late 1940s; Chicago Mummers member afterward; death July 1967 unverified — attempts to isolate precise date, place to no avail.

Tom Shirley, Dec. 1, 1899, Chicago, Ill.; actor (film, radio, TV), announcer, voiceover artist; premiered in 1907 silent film *East Lynne*; assistant to Hollywood producer Cecil B. DeMille 1921; entered radio in Los Angeles, San Francisco, Salt Lake City, Chicago WBBM 1932 — as actor at WBBM but soon narrated CBS series moving to New York 1940s; played in *The Aldrich Family*, *The Court of Missing Heirs* while opening *The Adventures of the Thin Man*, *Armstrong Theater of Today*, *The Bell Telephone Hour*, *Grand Central Station*, *Jack Armstrong — the All-American Boy*, *Just Plain Bill*, *Myrt and Marge*, *The Vaughn Monroe Show*; zenith with running parts in late 1950s daytime serials, *From These Roots* NBC, *Love of Life* CBS; d. Jan. 24, 1962.

Rex Stout, Dec. 1, 1886, Noblesville, Ind.; commentator, emcee; inspired mystery novels of Nero Wolfe starting in 1934 netting *The Adventures of Nero Wolfe*; hosted *Our Secret Weapon* 1942–43, visiting scholar on *People's Platform* 1943; d. Oct. 27, 1975.

Deaths

Dan Donaldson, Dec. 1, 1991, Chapel Hill, N.C.; b. March 11, 1915. Horace Heidt, Dec. 1, 1995, Los Angeles, Calif.; b. May 21, 1901.

December 2

Debuting

The Adventures of Charlie Chan, Dec. 2, 1932, NBC Blue; detective series presenting tales of tenacious investigator Chan (Walter Connolly, Ed Begley, Santos Ortega) employed by Honolulu Police Department, assisted by Lee Chan (Rodney Jacobs, Leon Janney), most trusted Number One Son; senior Chan quoted ancient Chinese proverbs at opportune moments, gifted with astounding deductive powers, impeccable manners; reached MBS, NBC, ABC before signing off June 21, 1948.

Births

Hy Gardner, Dec. 2, 1902, Manhattan, New York City, N.Y.; gossipmonger, celebrity interviewer bka host of *Hy Gardner Calling* NBC 1952–53, persisted on local TV, *The Hy Gardner Show* syndicated TV 1965; heard on radio's *Celebrity Party*, *Three City By-Line*, *Twin Views of the News*; *The New York Herald Tribune* Broadway columnist 1951–66; rival to Dorothy Kilgallen, others in trade; *To Tell the Truth* game show panelist CBS-TV late 1950s; with wife Marilyn co–penned syndicated "Glad You Asked That" column 1967–89; d. June 17, 1989.

Ezra Stone (Ezra Chaim Feinstone), Dec. 2, 1917, New Bedford, Mass.; actor (stage, film, radio, TV), author, director, educator, scriptwriter bka *The Aldrich Family* teen sitcom star Henry Aldrich 1939–42, 1945–51; on stage at age six in Philly production *Phosphorous and Suppressed Desires*; toured with Washington, D.C. National Junior Theater 1931–32, premiering on New York stage 1935 in musical revue *Parade* playing seven roles followed by string of comedies, lead in Clifford Goldsmith's *What a Life!* (author-blueprint for *The Aldrich Family* bowing April 13, 1937 at Biltmore Theater with 538 consecutive performances); *The Boys from Syracuse*, *See My Lawyer* followed as he played on radio features headlined by Kate Smith, Rudy Vallee culminating in Henry Aldrich role; American Theater instructor 1946–58 while penning sketches for *The Aldrich Family*, series topped by comics Danny Thomas, Milton Berle, Fred Allen, Martha Raye; performed in couple of 1940s flicks plus two made-for-TV in 1970s-80s, more stage shows, acted in half-dozen TV dramas, directed countless single TV episodes, series, made-for-TV movies; d. March 3, 1994.

Deaths

Katharine Raht, Dec. 2, 1983, Chattanooga, Tenn.; b. May 8, 1901.

Cal Tinney, Dec. 2, 1993, Tulsa, Okla.; b. Feb. 2, 1908.

December 3

Sound Bite

Longest running voice in net radio newscasts, Paul Harvey, launches coast-to-coast broadcast with Sunday night quarter-hour at 10:15 p.m. ET Dec. 3, 1950; while not heard continually (microphone supplied by countless guest reporters during frequent absences), show is mainstay on U. S. radio; beamed with signature "Paul Harvey ... good day!" in 2008; surpasses second most enduring web newsman Lowell Thomas (1930–76) by more than decade.

Debuting

Voice of Firestone, Dec. 3, 1928, NBC; classical, semiclassical music ranged from operatic selections to show tunes, pop standards, spirited marches performed by Firestone orchestra, chorus with guests from spotlighted forms; impresarios Hugo Mariani 1928–30, William Daly 1931–36, Alfred Wallenstein 1936–43, Howard Barlow 1943–57, Wilfred Pelletier partial 1955; cornerstone of NBC "Monday Night of Music" from late 1940s that included *The Railroad Hour*, *Voice of Firestone*, *The Bell Telephone Hour*, *Cities Service Band of America* in back-to-back half-hours, collectively raising America's musical culture level; Hugh James longstanding interlocutor; show aired same day (Monday) at same hour (8:30 p.m.) Sept. 7, 1931 till it left air, NBC until chain no longer offered accustomed 30-minute slot, shifting to ABC; final broadcast June 10, 1957, TV simulcast Sept. 5, 1949 to end of radio run, TV only extension to June 16, 1963.

Birth

Connee Boswell, Dec. 3, 1907, New Orleans, La.; instrumentalist, vocalist (film, stage, radio, TV); on her own after she, siblings Martha and Vet (Helvetia) disbanded Boswell Sisters act in late 1930s that they formed in early 1920s, played vaudeville, toured, recorded, performed on radio; paralyzed at age four, wheelchair-bound Connee related well to disabled military in World War II; versatile artist played cello, guitar, piano, saxophone, trombone, violin; appeared on more than dozen audio shows regularly 1927–46, habitually singing with crooner Bing Crosby 1940s; d. Oct. 11, 1976.

December 4

Sound Bite

The Eveready Hour debuting Dec. 4, 1923 over New York WEAF allowed people well beyond confines of Gotham to be exposed to dazzling dance music (by Browning King Orchestra — King was local clothier; countless shows, figures, entities named for advertisers during early epoch, somewhat akin to naming facilities for enterprises now); "Judged even by today's standards," pundit wrote, "it [the series] would not be found wanting"; one of first shows picked up by NBC, aired to Dec. 16, 1930.

Debuting

Ma Perkins, Dec. 4, 1933, NBC (began on Cincinnati WLW Aug. 14, 1933); daytime serial; "mother of the airwaves" Perkins (Virginia Payne) doubtlessly was most beloved figure of soap opera, helping-hand soul running Rushville Center lumberyard while raising three offspring after death of her late spouse; Ma dealt with more domestic crises in loss of son John (Gilbert Faust) in World War II, good-natured Fay (Rita Ascot, Cheer Brentson, Margaret Draper, Laurette Fillbrandt, Marjorie Hannan) who wed men that died young, trouble-finding Evey (Laurette Fillbrandt, Dora Johnson, Kay Campbell), her husband Willie Fitz (Murray Forbes) and — so critical to plot — Shuffle Shober (Charles Egleston, Edwin Wolfe), Ma's business partner-confidante; was there washboard weeper personifying form any better?; final broadcast on "day radio drama died" Nov. 25, 1960.

Canceled

Clara, Lu 'n' Em, Dec. 4, 1942, CBS; network debut Jan. 27, 1931.

Births

Allan Harry Jackson, Dec. 4, 1915, Hot Springs, Ark.; announcer, newscaster bka first radio newsman informing listeners of President John F. Kennedy's death Nov. 22, 1963 quarter-hour ahead of rivals; early part time radio apprenticeship at Urbana, Ill. WILL, Hot Springs, Ark. KTHS before full time work at Kalamazoo, Mich. WKZO 1936, KTHS 1937, Cincinnati WLW, Louisville WHAS, Texas State Network 1939, Memphis WMC, New York CBS 1943 joining elite news staff, staying 32 years; gigs: *Allan Jackson and the News* 1950–56, *CBS Morning News Roundup* mid 1940s-1975, *CBS News* 1940s-1975, *Chevrolet Spotlights the News* mid 1950s, *Crisco Radio Newspaper* mid 1940s, *The New York Philharmonic Symphony Orchestra* 1950, *News of the World* 1943–44, *The World Tonight* 1940s-1975; *Youth Takes a Stand* public affairs moderator CBS-TV 1953–54; d. April 26, 1976.

Isabel Randolph (Ryan), Dec. 4, 1889, Chicago, Ill.; actress (stage, film, radio, TV), vocalist bka *Fibber McGee & Molly* sitcom socialite Mrs. Abigail Uppington whom McGee labeled "Uppie" ca. 1937–43; support roles on 1940s-50s sitcoms *A Day in the Life of Dennis Day, The George Burns and Gracie Allen Show, Maisie, My Favorite Husband*; on stage at five, in stock company at 14, at 21, depicted by journalist as "one of the youngest and most popular leading ladies of that metropolis [Chicago] ... fortunate possessor of good looks, and magnetic personality and a rich soprano voice"; leading lady with Iowa-based stock outfit 1917–18; relocated to L.A. for films, broadcasting in 1930s; d. Jan. 11, 1973.

Death

Alan Kent, Dec. 4, 1993 (copious searches for death place to no avail); b. Aug. 4, 1909.

December 5

Debuting

The Mysterious Traveler, Dec. 5, 1943, MBS; horror anthology drama; host-traveler Maurice Tarplin aboard phantom train beckoned listeners into "strange and terrifying," trip sure to "thrill you a little and chill you a little" as he urged fans to "get a good grip on your nerves, and be comfortable ... if you can!"; tales ranged from heart-stopping murders to science fiction thrillers; East Coast thespians played regularly — Jackson Beck, Roger DeKoven, Elspeth Eric, William Johnstone, Joseph Julian, Jan Miner, Santos Ortega, Bryna Raeburn, Lyle Sudrow, Lawson Zerbe, more; silent 1945–46; final broadcast Sept. 16, 1952.

Canceled

The Green Hornet, Dec. 5, 1952, ABC; net debut April 12, 1938.

Death

George Walsh, Dec. 5, 2005, Monterey Park, Calif.; b. Nov. 29, 1917.

December 6

Debuting

The Phil Baker Show (*The Armour Star Jester, The Gulf Headliner, Honolulu Bound*), Dec. 6, 1931, CBS; comedy variety; comic, accordion virtuoso ex-vaudevillian Baker was timid before microphone, overcame it instituting heckling stooge Beetle (Hank Ladd, Sid Silvers, Ward Wilson) never seen by studio audience — offstage voice interrupted Baker routines dozen times per show — relaxing his nervous condition in process; other parts played by Elvia Allman, Harry McNaughton, Agnes Moorehead, more; singing by The Andrews Sisters, Al Garr; most of troupe entertained when show resumed in 1939 for Dole Packing under rebranded *Honolulu Bound*; final broadcast Oct. 4, 1939.

Births

Agnes Moorehead, Dec. 6, 1900, Clinton, Mass.; actress (radio, film, TV) bka *Suspense* crime drama figure Mrs. Elbert Stevenson who overheard murder plot without realizing she was intended victim in Lucille Fletcher's chilling tale "Sorry, Wrong Number" aired eight times CBS 1943–62 — actor Orson Welles dubbed it "greatest show of all time," *Bewitched* sitcom character Endora ABC-TV 1964–72; played numerous added aural roles, primetime crimetime to drainboard daytime dramas; 109 screen productions (combined Hollywood theatrical, TV work) with 20 more TV appearances as herself; d. April 30, 1974.

Jane Morgan, Dec. 6, 1880, England; actress, violinist bka *Aunt Mary* daytime serial philosopher-protagonist Mary Lane 1942–51, *Our Miss Brooks* sitcom aged landlady Mrs. Margaret (Maggie) Davis 1948–57; in mid 1940s she,

Gloria Gordon (Gale Gordon's mom) turned up on *The Jack Benny Program* as Martha and Emily, aging broads Benny found irresistible; played Mrs. O'Reilly, rooming house proprietress where Irma Peterson, Jane Stacy were roomies in *My Friend Irma* 1947 (soon replaced by Gloria Gordon so she could be Connie Brooks' landlady); Mother Hemp to *Honest Harold* 1951, scores of *Lux Radio Theater* gigs, *Suspense*, *Cavalcade of America*, *The Great Gildersleeve*, *The Bob Hope Show*, *The Adventures of Philip Marlowe*, *Richard Diamond—Private Detective* plus couple of movies including 1956's *Our Miss Brooks* as Maggie Davis; d. Jan. 1, 1972.

Death

Don Ameche (Dominic Felix Amici), Dec. 6, 1993, Scottsdale, Ariz.; b. May 31, 1908.

December 7

Debuting

Camel Caravan, Dec. 7, 1933, CBS; variety, including music, comedy; first of manifold segments under banner headlined by diverse entertainers e.g. impresarios Glen Gray, Benny Goodman, Bob Crosby, Xavier Cugat, Freddie Rich; singers Martha Tilton, Johnny Mercer, Connie Haines, Lanny Ross, Vaughn Monroe; comics/hosts Walter O'Keefe, F. Chase Taylor, Budd Hulick, Jack Oakie, Herb Shriner, Bud Abbott, Lou Costello, Jimmy Durante, Garry Moore, Jack Carson, Elvia Allman, Mel Blanc, Bob Hawk; Vaughn Monroe sang under *Camel Caravan* label CBS-TV 1950–51 while on radio; final radiocast April 5, 1954.

My Little Margie, Dec. 7, 1952, CBS; sitcom; featured twentysomething single daughter Margie Albright (Gale Storm), widowed dad Verne Albright (Charles Farrell)—with whom she lived—plus countless women pursuing him as she torpedoed most; in unique twist for genus, show premiered on TV (June 16, 1952—Aug. 24, 1955) in advance of radio embodiment; final aural broadcast June 26, 1955.

Births

Robert Vahey (Bob) Brown, Dec. 7, 1905, New York City, N.Y.; actor, announcer, director, emcee, producer, vocalist, writer bka Cincinnati WLW *Moon River* inaugural host 1930-ca. 1932, *The Breakfast Club* interlocutor 1936–41, same for 1930s Chicago-based daytime serials (*Backstage Wife*, *Girl Alone*, *Ma Perkins*, *The Story of Mary Marlin*, *Vic and Sade*); d. Feb. 14, 1988.

Archibald Maddock Crossley, Dec. 7, 1896, Fieldsboro, N.J.; columnist, researcher, statistician; sizeable aid to radio audience measurement, devised scheme to apply scientifically selected random sample to proportionately signify widespread opinions; (don't confuse with Cincinnati industrialist/WLW owner Powel Crosley, Jr.—note spelling); Crossley, Inc. (*Crossley Surveys*) founded 1926 focusing on radio audience numbers 1929; Cooperative Analysis of Broadcasting launched 1930, nation's first national ratings service soon dubbed "Crossleys" figured by phone calls to U. S. homes; system outdistanced competitors to 1946 when eclipsed by Hooperatings; Crossley penned syndicated newspaper column starting 1936, political pollster late 1940s-52, retired 1962; d. May 1, 1985.

Death

Alois Havrilla, Dec. 7, 1952, Englewood, N.J.; b. June 7, 1891.

December 8

Deaths

Anne Seymour, Dec. 8, 1988, Los Angeles, Calif.; b. Sept. 11, 1909. Martha Tilton, Dec. 8, 2006, Brentwood, Calif.; b. Nov. 14, 1915.

December 9

Sound Bite

Across long tenure, President Franklin D. Roosevelt reaches audience peak with war message broadcast December 9, 1941, two days after Japanese attack on Pearl Harbor; crowd of 62.1 billion tunes in for his peak Hooperating of 79.0, possibly making it highest rating in radio history, outperforming what ostensibly may be commercial radio's all-time watermarks: 53.4 C.A.B. (Crossley) in early 1931 by *Amos 'n' Andy*, 58.4 C.A.B. in January 1933 by *The Chase & Sanborn Hour* with Eddie Cantor; perhaps to date, highest numbers for commercial broadcast ever occurred Oct. 19, 1948 as ex-radio showman Milton Berle — in first season on TV — earned 63.2 Hooperating in metro New York City, translating into 92.4 share of audience; recall not many homes were equipped with TV sets, not many cities could get reception, competition almost nil.

Debuting

Can You Top This?, Dec. 9, 1940, MBS; audience participation series; hosts Roger Bower, Ward Wilson, quipster panel; final broadcast July 9, 1954.

Births

Bruce Bill (Brace) Beemer, Dec. 9, 1902, Mount Carmel, Ill.; actor, announcer bka legendary voice of venerated masked rider of plains *The Lone Ranger* ("Hi-yo Silver!") 1941–56; in 1932 Detroit WXYZ staffer heard him reading poetry over Indianapolis station where he was announcer, actor since 1922; summoned to WXYZ as interlocutor for growing stable of dramas, Beemer briefly playing lead in *The Challenge of the Yukon*; stentorian tone introducing *The Lone Ranger* stepped in to fill void on death of actor Earl Graser in traffic accident, remained commandingly authoritative accent of iconic figure rest of run; in millions of U. S. homes Beemer and unmistakable inflection synonymous with West's most celebrated mythical crimefighter; toured fairs, rodeos across nation adorned with trappings of infamous role although never involved with movie, TV manifestations; distinguished voice worked against him after series left air — producers wouldn't hire him for sounding "too much like *The Lone Ranger*"; thus raised racehorses on his farm outside Detroit; d. March 1, 1965.

Robert E. Emerick, Dec. 9, 1915, Tacoma, Wash.; announcer (film, radio, TV), educator, voiceover artist (commercials); credits for *Bobby Benson and the B-Bar-B Riders, The Mysterious Traveler, Scattergood Baines, Top Secrets of the FBI*; worked stations at San Francisco, Los Angeles before New York WOR, later to ABC-TV; narrated TV documentaries, motion picture films; director of speech, drama at Litchfield (Conn.) Preparatory School 1971–73; d. June 1, 1973.

Freddy Martin, Dec. 9, 1906, Cleveland, Ohio; drummer, tenor saxophonist who formed band in 1931 in smooth, sweet, syrupy manner of Guy Lombardo yet copied by jazz musicians enamored with Martin's style; kept durable ties with Cocoanut Grove in L.A.; accompanied dozen network series 1933–56, seven identified by Martin moniker; d. Sept. 30, 1983.

Kenneth L. Niles, Dec. 9, 1906, Livingston, Mont.; actor, announcer, producer, voiceover artist; debuted at Seattle KJR late 1920s, joined Los Angeles KHJ 1930, designated chief announcer 1933; 14 B-flicks 1937–51 playing radio announcer in most; ties to about 30 aural series 1930s-50s, mostly as announcer e.g. *Big Town, The George Burns and Gracie Allen Show, A Date with Judy, Hollywood Hotel* (also co-produced), *Lady Esther Serenade, Maisie, The Marlin Hurt and Beulah Show, Parties at Pickfair*; *Top Cat* primetime animated show narrator ABC-TV 1961–62, busy commercial voiceover speaker; d. Oct. 31, 1988.

Deaths

Walter Compton, Dec. 9, 1959, Washington, D.C.; b. Oct. 9, 1912. John Kieran, Dec. 9, 1981, Rockport, Mass.; b. Aug. 2, 1892. Louella Parsons, Dec. 9, 1972, Santa Monica, Calif.; b. Aug. 6, 1880.

December 10

Births

Morton Gould, Dec. 10, 1913, Richmond Hill, N.Y.; composer, impresario, pianist (film, radio, stage), recording artist; conductor-arranger at MBS from 1936; orchestra leader on 100 record albums; penned scores for renowned maestro Meredith Willson's [sic] radio shows, for ballets, Broadway productions, movies, symphonies; musical director of half-dozen aural series; American Society of Composers, Authors & Publishers (ASCAP) president 1986–94; d. Feb. 21, 1996.

Chet Huntley, Dec. 10, 1911, Cardwell, Mont.; announcer, entrepreneur, newscaster bka partner with newsman David Brinkley on competitive weeknight *Huntley-Brinkley Report* NBC-TV 1956–70; joined Spokane KHQ 1934 shifted to Portland, Ore. KGW 1936, Los Angeles KFI 1937, Hollywood KNX 1939 — heard by

CBS West Coast hookup to 1951; affiliated with ABC Los Angeles 1951–55, joined NBC New York 1955 beaming *Chet Huntley and the News* 1956 on radio; retired 1970 to develop Montana recreation complex Big Sky; d. March 20, 1974.

William Spargrove (William Sparrougrove), Dec. 10, 1908, Belle Plaine, Iowa; announcer bka *Hollywood Byline* interlocutor 1949–50; worked several Midwestern stations before joining New York NBC early 1938; anchored weekly *Esso Television Reporter* NBC-TV spring 1940; stayed with Blue net 1942; d. Sept. 6, 1984.

Deaths

Jack Berch, Dec. 10, 1992, Jamaica, N.Y.; b. Aug. 26, 1907. Freeman Gosden, Dec. 10, 1982, Los Angeles, Calif.; b. May 5, 1899. Peter Grant, Dec. 10, 1990, Cincinnati, Ohio; b. Dec. 13, 1906. Jascha Heifetz, Dec. 10, 1987, Los Angeles, Calif.; b. Feb. 2, 1901.

December 11

Debuting

The Chesterfield Supper Club, Dec. 11, 1944, NBC; music variety; Perry Como, Jo Stafford, Peggy Lee headlining alternate nights with iconic guests like Frankie Laine, Mel Blanc, King Cole Trio, Arthur Godfrey, Buddy Clark, Johnny Mercer, et al., orchestra impresarios Ted Steele, Sammy Kaye, Lloyd Shaffer, Tex Beneke, Mitchell Ayers, Paul Weston, Dave Barbour; final broadcast June 1, 1950.

Birth

Dick Tufeld, Dec. 11, 1926, Los Angeles, Calif.; actor (film TV), announcer, voiceover artist bka *Lost in Space* science fiction thriller robot voice CBS-TV 1965–68, same part in *Lost in Space* movie 1998, *The Simpsons* sitcom solo installment Fox TV February 2004; while he opened late 1940s-early 1950s radio episodes of *The Amazing Mr. Malone*, *Falstaff's Fables*, *Space Patrol*, Tufeld's broadcast impact was on tube — from 1960–84 he presented *Surfside 6*, *The Judy Garland Show*, *Hollywood Palace*, *Celebrity Sweepstakes*, *People Are Funny* plus multi animated cartoon series; narrated 1976 theatrical film *Tunnel Vision*.

Deaths

Mary Marvin Breckinridge (Patterson), Dec. 11, 2002, Washington, D.C.; b. Oct. 2, 1905. Robert Q. Lewis, Dec. 11, 1991, Los Angeles, Calif.; b. April 5, 1921.

December 12

Sound Bite

Actress Mae West creates uproar in nine-minute sketch penned by Arch Oboler with actor Don Ameche on *The Edgar Bergen and Charlie McCarthy Show* Dec. 12, 1937; tale focuses on Adam, Eve's discharge from Garden of Eden suited to West's bawdy sensuality image; not only does it infringe on religious values of many, West's love-groans, promiscuity in depicting Eve's seduction of Adam exceeds radio's sexual bounds; many offended, Catholic Church takes special umbrage, protests vehemently, threatens boycott of sponsoring Standard Brands' Chase & Sanborn coffee; upshot is FCC inquiry as NBC prohibits West's name on all future shows — and West won't return to aural air until 1973, possibly precedent in evolution of modern conservative syndicated talk-show syndrome.

Births

Winston Mansfield Burdett, Dec. 12, 1913, Buffalo, N.Y.; newspaper stringer, overseas-UN radio journalist bka "Murrow Boys" clansman, reporter *CBS World News Roundup* 1940–78, *The World Tonight* 1956–78, avowed pre–CBS Communist-Soviet spy, banished 1956 to Rome to finish tenure as correspondent; d. May 19, 1993.

Louis G. Cowan (Louis G. Cohen), Dec. 12, 1909, Chicago, Ill.; CBS-TV president 1950s, professor, program creator, producer, publisher bka *The $64,000 Question* executive, proverbial quiz show scandal sacrificial lamb; d. Nov. 18, 1976.

Gene Hamilton, Dec. 12, 1910, Toledo, Ohio; announcer, dancer, emcee, guitarist, vocalist; left Columbus, Ohio WAIU as vocalist, guitarist 1929 for Cleveland WTAM, joining NBC there as announcer, master of ceremonies, working web features at Chicago Merchandise Mart 1931, moving to New York Radio City 1933, retiring from chain 1975; introduced radio fans to *Biography in Sound*, *The Boston Pops Orchestra*, *The Chamber Music Society of Lower Basin Street*, *Dr. Gino's Musicale*, *The First Nighter*, *General Motors Concert*, *Kaltenborn Edits the News*, *Lum and Abner*, *The NBC Symphony Orchestra*, *Professor Quiz*, *Sammy Kaye*, *Voice of Firestone*, more; d. Nov. 22, 2000.

Tobe Reed (Howard E. Reed), Dec. 12, 1911, Seattle, Wash.; d. announcer, quizmaster; 1940s portfolio: *The Baby Snooks Show*, *Birds Eye Open House*, *Club Good Cheer*, *Don't You Believe It*, *The Drene Show*, *Duffy's Tavern*, *The Fitch Bandwagon*, *The George Burns and Gracie Allen Show*, *The Lifebuoy Show*, *Mail Call*, *The Maxwell House Summer Show*, *Revere All-Star Revue*, *The Star and the Story*; *Top Dollar* quiz series emcee CBS-TV 1958; d. March 3, 1988.

Frank Sinatra, Dec. 12, 1915, Hoboken, N.J.; actor (radio, film, TV), personal appearances, recording artist, vocalist bka "old blue eyes" headlining multi radio, TV series; bobbysoxers' idol on *Your Hit Parade* 1940s; "widely held to be the greatest singer in American pop history" claimed *New York Times* reviewer, citing him as "first modern pop superstar ... he defined that role ... when his first solo appearances provoked the kind of mass pandemonium that later greeted Elvis Presley and the Beatles"; sang with Harry James, Tommy Dorsey, Kay Kyser near career start, radio following with *Broadway Bandbox*, *The Frank Sinatra Show*, *The Ginny Simms Show*, *Light Up Time*, *Reflections*, *The Pause That Refreshes*, *Rocky Fortune*, *Songs by Sinatra*; movies, nightclubs, records, TV kept him before doting fans; d. May 15, 1998.

Deaths

Tallulah Bankhead, Dec. 12, 1968, New York City, N.Y.; b. Jan. 31, 1902. David Sarnoff, Dec. 12, 1971, New York City, N.Y.; b. Feb. 27, 1891. Dick Stark, Dec. 12, 1986, Stogrande, Spain; b. Nov. 7, 1911.

December 13

Births

George Baxter, Dec. 13, 1904, Paris, France; actor (film, TV), announcer; d. Sept. 10, 1976.

Peter Grant (Melvin M. MaGinn), Dec. 13, 1906, St. Louis, Mo.; announcer, newscaster; though earning law degree 1930, gave it up for radio, joined St. Louis KMOX 1930, Cincinnati WLW 1932, rose to chief announcer 1937, presided over venerated *Moon River* late night show, handled newscasts, introduced Red Skelton's *Avalon Time* 1939 to nationwide audience; surprised some when it was revealed typical announcers read 2,200 words per quarter-hour — Grant read 2,600; transitioned to WLWT TV 1948, retired 1968, returned to WLWT as news commentator; staffed WLW/WLWT 33 years before taking Sundays off; rival newsman depicted him as "pioneer in gaining public respect for newscasting as a major and dependable source of information"; d. Dec. 10, 1990.

Jay Jostyn (Eugene J. Josten), Dec. 13, 1901, Milwaukee, Wis.; actor (film, radio, TV) bka *Mr. District Attorney* crime drama unnamed lead NBC/ABC 1939–52 possessing recognized voice in resilient run — so real to fans habitually he got requests for legal advice on marital impasses, boundary disputes, etc.; *Mr. District Attorney* only radio mystery shifting to live video with original cast intact, including Jostyn, two sidekicks — ABC-TV every other Monday where he was Paul Garrett 1951–52; other radio: *Famous Jury Trials*, *Foreign Assignment*, *Hilltop House*, *Mr. Keen—Tracer of Lost Persons*, *The Mystery Man*, *Our Gal Sunday*, *The Parker Family*, *Second Husband*, *The Top Guy*; launched showbiz career as Hollywood stock actor, radio followed in New York 1936; seven theatrical films 1954–60, added solo episode TV work; d. June 25, 1976.

Andrew Russell (Drew) Pearson, Dec. 13, 1897, Evanston, Ill.; author, commentator, educator (University of Pennsylvania, Columbia University), emcee, entrepreneur (directed illicit Irish Sweepstakes), newscaster, syndicated columnist, print journalist (*The Baltimore Sun* plus *United States Daily*, precursor to *U. S. News & World Report*) bka news analyst under myriad monikers 1939–53 —*Drew Pearson*, *Drew Pearson Comments*, *Listen America*, *Calling America*, *Sunday Evening News of the World*, *Washington Merry-Go-Round* (hosting latter); unpopular in quarters, rankled presidents Franklin D. Roosevelt, Harry S [sic] Truman, other public figures without favoring either political party; globetrotter with continual wanderlust; gained notoriety by predictions about world affairs claiming

84% accuracy; penned 10 tomes 1935–74; forays into early TV without lasting consequence; d. Sept. 1, 1969.

December 14

Births

Jim Kelly (James Charles Kelly III), Dec. 14, 1899, Manhattan, New York City, N.Y.; actor (stage, film, radio, TV) bka *Mr. Keen, Tracer of Lost Persons* crime-detective drama as Mike Clancy, bumbling sidekick ("partner" but questionably so) to "kindly old tracer"—gifted, brawn sans brains ("Saints preserve us, boss! He's got a gun!")—NBC Blue/CBS/NBC 1937–55; heard on thousands of local aircasts in New York; on stage in *Arsenic and Old Lace, As You Like It, Seventeen*, nearly score more; 18 films (*A Face in the Crowd, Twelve Angry Men, Twenty-First Precinct, West Point*, etc.); countless early TV anthologies, daytime serials like *Big Story, Camera Three, The Guiding Light, Hallmark Hall of Fame, Kraft Theater, Love of Life, Omnibus*, dozens more; d. May 13, 1961.

Lillian Randolph, Dec. 14, 1898, Louisville, Ky.; actress (film, radio, TV) bka *The Great Gildersleeve* cook-housekeeper Birdie Lee Coggins 1941–54, *Amos 'n' Andy* character Madam Queen 1943–55, *Beulah* namesake 1951–52; only performer in trilogy of *Gildersleeve* formats (film, radio, TV); often confused with elder sister Amanda Randolph playing similar venues, Lillian more prolific on screen in 50+ movies 1938–79 (*It's a Wonderful Life* 1946, *Hush Hush, Sweet Charlotte* 1964 stand out among chiefly B-fare); played more than dozen TV roles plus 1977 miniseries *Roots* as Sister Sara; d. Sept. 12, 1980.

Deaths

William Bendix, Dec. 14, 1964, Los Angeles, Calif.; b. Jan. 14, 1906. Verna Felton, Dec. 14, 1966, North Hollywood, Calif.; b. July 20, 1890. Marian Shockley, Dec. 14, 1981, Los Angeles, Calif.; b. Oct. 10, 1911.

December 15

Sound Bite

Flagship affiliate/originating station of Columbia Broadcasting System transfers from Newark WOR to New York WABC (which will ultimately be renamed WCBS 18 years hence, in 1946) effective Dec. 15, 1928.

Canceled

Captain Midnight, Dec. 15, 1949, MBS; debut Sept. 30, 1940 (although transcribed version aired to selected Midwest, Southwest cities via Chicago WGN Oct. 17, 1939-March 27, 1940).

Births

Jeff Chandler (Ira Grossel), Dec. 15, 1918, Brooklyn, N.Y.; actor (film, radio, stage) bka *Our Miss Brooks* bashful biology instructor Philip Boynton 1948–53, virile leading man in sundry Hollywood celluloid productions 1950s; d. June 17, 1961.

Edwin LeMar (Buddy) Cole, Dec. 15, 1916, Irving, Ill.; actor, impresario, jazz pianist, organist, recording artist, theater instrumentalist, vocalist; first time in two decades big orchestras traditionally backing crooner Bing Crosby on multi aural series yanked to pare costs, replaced by Buddy Cole Trio in daily gig 1954–57, troupe playing behind Crosby, Rosemary Clooney vocals; pianist Cole said: "I'd go in and record a basic track with Bing or Rosie with rhythm backing ... I've done as many as 20 tunes a day ... a few days later we'd play them back and add electric guitars, organ, kettle drums, chimes, whatever"; at peak Cole had 300 Crosby, 200 Clooney songs, 40 duets in can; d. Nov. 5, 1964.

Alan "Moon Dog" Freed, Dec. 15, 1922, Johnstown, Pa.; disc jockey commanding Northeast teens' respect after debut over New York WINS Sept. 6, 1954, bka CBS-TV *Rock 'n' Roll Dance Party* (with Count Basie) starting March 1956; ultimately disfavored by radio, TV outlets employing him (plus payola scandal); powerful perch with teens evaporated; d. Jan. 20, 1965.

Bob Hawk, Dec. 15, 1907, Creston, Iowa; announcer, disc jockey, emcee, quizmaster; baptized into radio on Chicago outlet at 18 as announcer, DJ, interviewer, poetry reader; picked to run two fleeting game shows—*Foolish Questions, Fun Quiz* followed by two 1938 successes—*The People's Rally, Quixie Doodle Quiz* setting his future; *Take It or Leave It* original emcee CBS 1940–41; money dispute, Hawk left to preside over *How'm I Doin'?* 1942 (dismal failure lasting few months); snagged another quiz, *Thanks for the Yanks* (renamed *The Bob Hawk Show*) 1942–53; waning net years as NBC DJ 1951–54; d. July 4, 1989.

Ray Daniel Morgan, Dec. 15, 1917, Spring City, Utah; actor, announcer, newscaster, producer, sportscaster; handful of fleeting early TV series; some syndicated radio gigs; on Atlantic City, N.J. WPG 1939, Boston WCOP 1940, Atlantic City WBAB 1940, Washington, D.C. WWDC 1946; latter 1940s-early 1950s produced *Chandu—the Magician*, acted in *The Greatest Story Ever Told*, opened *Murder at Midnight*, *Coke Club*, more; d. Jan. 18, 1975.

Deaths

Frank Behrens, Dec. 15, 1986, Brooklyn, N.Y.; b. Feb. 15, 1919. John Guedel, Dec. 15, 2001, West Hollywood, Calif.; b. Oct. 9, 1913. Harry Herschfield, Dec. 15, 1974, New York, N.Y.; b. Oct. 13, 1885. C. E. Hooper, Dec. 15, 1954, Salt Lake City, Utah; b. May 21, 1898. Glenn Miller, Dec. 15, 1944, English Channel; b. March 1, 1904. Arnold Moss, Dec. 15, 1989, New York City, N.Y.; b. Jan. 28, 1910. Murray Wagner, Dec. 15, 1993, Westlake Village, Calif. (SSDI affirms he died Jan. 3, 1994, California Death Index displays date shown here); b. Dec. 17, 1914.

December 16

Canceled

The Tom Mix Ralston Straight Shooters, Dec. 16, 1951, MBS; debut Sept. 25, 1933. *What's the Name of That Song?*, Dec. 16, 1948, MBS; debut Sept. 24, 1944.

Births

Lud(wig) Gluskin, Dec. 16, 1898, New York City, N.Y.; drummer, house impresario-music director at CBS Radio starting 1936, CBS-TV 1948–58; conducted music for three dozen aural series: *Columbia Presents Corwin*, *Campana Serenade*, *The Amos 'n' Andy Show*, *Suspense*, *My Friend Irma*, *The Philip Morris Playhouse*, *The Adventures of Sam Spade*, *Life with Luigi*, *My Little Margie*, *Cathy and Elliott Lewis Onstage*, et al.; d. Oct. 13, 1989.

Cameron Prud'homme, Dec. 16, 1892, Auburn, N.Y.; actor (stage, film, radio, TV), writer bka enduring namesake thespian in *David Harum* 1944–47, 1950–51; running parts in *Backstage Wife*, *Life Can Be Beautiful*, *One Man's Family*, *Stella Dallas*, *A Woman of America*, *Young Widder Brown* in sunshine hours, *Cavalcade of America*, *Theater Guild on the Air* as sun departed; penned *Hawthorne House* scripts, NBC West Coast 1930s-40s serial; d. Nov. 27, 1967.

Deaths

Robert Dryden, Dec. 16, 2003, Englewood, N.J.; b. Feb. 8, 1917. Haleloke Kahauolopue, Dec. 16, 2004, Union City, Ind.; b. Feb. 2, 1923.

December 17

Births

House Jameson, Dec. 17, 1902, Austin, Texas; actor (stage, film, radio, TV), public service announcement pitchman bka *The Aldrich Family* patriarch Sam Aldrich 1939-ca. 1951, TV incarnation 1949–53; dozen Broadway productions 1925–68, with touring companies; *Renfrew of the Mounted* first radio gig as Inspector Douglas Renfrew 1936–37, 1938–40, soap opera roles: *Young Widder Brown*, *This Day Is Ours*, *Hilda Hope, M.D.*, *By Kathleen Norris*, *Brave Tomorrow*, *Marriage for Two*; fleetingly supplanted Raymond Edward Jones 1941 as chilling voice of "Raymond" beckoning terrified fans to *Inner Sanctum Mysteries*; 1940s-50s anthologies *The Columbia Workshop*, *Cavalcade of America*, *Philip Morris Playhouse*, *Columbia Presents Corwin*, *Philco Radio Playhouse*, *X-Minus One*, *Suspense*; lead as Dr. Benjamin Ordway in *Crime Doctor* CBS 1940–47; 1956–69 in 39 episodes of video fare e.g. *Goodyear Television Playhouse*, *Robert Montgomery Presents* (14 times), *Studio One*, *The U. S. Steel Hour*, *Naked City* (8 times), *Hallmark Hall of Fame*, others; miniseries *The Sacco-Vanzetti Story* 1960, made-for-TV flick *The Borgia Stick* 1967, running parts in trio daytime TV serials: *The Edge of Night* 1957–58, *Another World* 1965–66, *Dark Shadows* 1967; five theatrical motion pictures—nude in final film *The Swimmer* 1968; d. April 23, 1971.

Howard Miller, Dec. 17, 1912, Galesburg, Ill.; announcer, disc jockey, multiple stations owner, program director, sportscaster, talk show host bka *The Howard Miller Show* platter spinner, daily introducing soon-to-be-released discs, CBS July 18, 1955-Jan. 9, 1959; rose to fame at Chicago WIND where his DJ legacy exceeded two decades; d. Nov. 8, 1994.

Murray Wagner (Murray Ivan Ginsberg), Dec. 17, 1914, Bronx, N.Y.; announcer; opened handful of mid 1940s-early 50s shows like *Double or Nothing, Meet Miss Sherlock, Tell It Again*; handing reins of *Double or Nothing* to Walter O'Keefe daily, exuberantly depicted star as "man of the half-hour," added "here he is — your paymaster of ceremonies," bellowed "OK, O'Keefe!" prior to thunderous applause by studio audience on cue; suspended by AFTRA July 21, 1953 for failing to disclose possibility of present/past communist affiliation; d. Dec. 15, 1993 or Jan. 3, 1994.

Deaths

Arthur Kohl, Dec. 17, 1972, Tampa, Fla.; b. Jan. 26, 1908. Bob Pfeiffer, Dec. 17, 1993, New York City, N.Y.; b. March 4, 1921.

December 18

Sound Bite

CBS ended one of its last connections to radio's golden age Dec. 18, 1971 as once-popular remote broadcasts of band concerts abandoned; dated to 1930s, webs/stations filled hours of time with pickups from live bandstands; most were dropped late 1940s but CBS continued to feed few to diminishing handful of outlets — just 40 still airing Saturday morning concerts when broadcasts pulled.

Canceled

Sam 'n' Henry, Dec. 18, 1927, WGN Chicago, Ill.; debut Jan. 12, 1926.

Births

Jerry Lawrence, Dec. 18, 1911, Rochester, N.Y.; actor (film, TV), announcer, disc jockey, quizmaster bka *Truth or Consequences* audience participation stunt show interlocutor NBC-TV 1954–56; radio work at New York WOR, WNEW, CBS net, introduced *The Frank Sinatra Show* 1944; hosted DJ entry *Moonlight Savings Time* 2:30 to 5 a.m. weekdays in World War II for troop ships, war industry hands; aired Los Angeles radio-TV from 1945 on KTLA, KCOP, KFWB developing local quiz shows, opened aural series *The Spade Cooley Show*; bit parts in flicks *The Hitch-Hiker* 1953, *X-15* 1961, solo shots on *The Donna Reed Show, Dragnet*, other TV fare; d. Sept. 24, 2005.

J. Anthony Smythe, Dec. 18, 1885, San Francisco, Calif.; actor (radio, stage, TV), director, writer bka *One Man's Family* narrative/daytime serial patriarch Father Henry Barbour ("Oh, Fanny! Fanny! Fanny!") NBC 1932–59, NBC-TV 1954–55; launched stage career in college shows, regional theater, stock company, leads lasted two decades; went on *Split Second Tales* NBC 1930 while writing, directing, speaking on *Carefree Carnival* 1933–36; d. March 20, 1966.

Deaths

Eugene Conley, Dec. 18, 1981, Denton, Texas; b. March 12, 1908. Mark Goodson, Dec. 18, 1992, Los Angeles, Calif.; b. Jan. 14, 1915.

December 19

Canceled

The Mutual Radio Theater, Dec. 19, 1980, MBS; debut March 3, 1980 (repeating episodes broadcast Feb. 5, 1979-Feb. 1, 1980 as *The Sears Radio Theater* on CBS).

Births

Paul Luther, Dec. 19, 1908, Aylesbury, Saskatchewan, Canada; actor, announcer, columnist, scriptwriter; kicked off career as Canadian announcer; mid 1930s-mid 1940s in Chicago he opened *The Adventures of Dick Cole, Bright Horizon, Don Winslow of the Navy, Vic and Sade* while acting in *Backstage Wife, The Man Behind the Gun, Our Secret Weapon* (which he scripted), more; penned "Inside Radio" column 1947–48 for *The Portland* [Maine] *Press Herald* that also ran in some other newspapers; d. November 1978, Harrison, N.Y.

Owen Miller Babbe, Dec. 19, 1916, Council Bluffs, Iowa; announcer, entrepreneur; introduced 1940s episodes *The Adventures of Sherlock Holmes*; staff of Los Angeles KMTH 1939, Beverly Hills KMPC 1940 as announcer, newscaster; left radio mid-century to open Jones Piano House, Fort Dodge, Iowa, adding second store at Mason City 1962, retiring 1984; d. June 25, 1996.

Dennis Clark, Dec. 19, 1911, Roscommon, Mich.; vocalist (tenor) (attempts to locate additional facts fruitless).

Cicely Tyson, Dec. 19, 1933, Harlem, New York City, N.Y.; actress (film, TV), emcee, fashion model bka *The Sears/Mutual Radio Theater* narrator-hostess CBS/MBS 1979–81, one of five personalities presiding over weeknight anthology drama; 82 theatrical, TV films 1961–2005 with guest shots in 25 TV series.

Deaths

Bob Shepard, Dec. 19, 1993, Los Angeles, Calif.; b. Nov. 10, 1915. Les Tremayne, Dec. 19, 2003, Santa Monica, Calif.; b. April 16, 1913.

December 20

Debuting

Name That Tune, Dec. 20, 1952, NBC; audience participation series with object similar to that of *Kay Kyser's Kollege of Musical Knowledge*, *Stop the Music!*, *What's the Name of That Song?*; emcees Red Benson, Bill Cullen, George de Witt, Tom Kennedy had short runs; show prevailed 17 weeks while sporadic TV incarnations persisted 1950s-1970s; final broadcast April 10, 1953.

Births

Charita Bauer, Dec. 20, 1923, Newark, N.J.; actress (radio, stage, TV), model bka *The Guiding Light* "matriarch" Bertha (Bert) Bauer on CBS Radio 1950–56, CBS-TV 1952–84; acting debut at nine on Broadway, entered radio in 1930s *Let's Pretend* ensemble; soap opera ingénue with ongoing roles in *David Harum*, *Front Page Farrell*, *Lora Lawton*, *Orphans of Divorce*, *Our Gal Sunday*, *The Right to Happiness*, *Rose of My Dreams*, *Second Husband*, *Stella Dallas*, *Young Widder Brown*; turned up often on *The FBI in Peace & War*, *Johnny Presents*, *Maudie's Diary*, *Mr. Keen—Tracer of Lost Persons*, plus regular in radio, TV versions of *The Aldrich Family*; one TV movie 1983; d. Feb. 28, 1985.

Audrey Totter, Dec. 20, 1918, Joliet, Ill.; actress (stage, film, radio, TV) bka *Meet Millie* (Bronson) sitcom star 1951-ca. 1953; earlier joined touring ensemble performing *My Sister Eileen* on stages across nation; in her early 20s, landed recurring role in daytime soap *Bright Horizon* CBS 1941–45 while honing craft before footlights at Gotham venues; signed with MGM 1945, later with Columbia, 20th Century–Fox completing 43 motion pictures, possibly most prominent *Main Street After Dark* 1945, *The Postman Always Rings Twice* 1946, *Lady in the Lake* 1947, *Any Number Can Play* 1949; in face of burgeoning TV on heretofore sacred turf, film studio wouldn't permit Totter to perform in video rendition of *Meet Millie* though it ok'd her continuance on aural airwaves; Totter so disgusted, quit series altogether, winning continuing roles on trio of video entries: *Cimarron City* NBC 1958–59, *Our Man Higgins* ABC 1962–63, *Medical Center* CBS 1972–76; she turned up in single TV dramatic episodes 50 times.

December 21

Deaths

Adelaide Cumming, Dec. 21, 1998, Bremerton, Wash.; b. March 6, 1905. Barry Gray, Dec. 21, 1996, Manhattan, New York City, N.Y.; b. July 2, 1916.

December 22

Debuting

The Metropolitan Opera Auditions of the Air, Dec. 22, 1935, NBC; venerable *Metropolitan Opera* broadcaster Milton J. Cross succeeded Met general manager Edward Johnson as *Auditions* host-commentator 1947; final broadcast March 30, 1958.

Births

Don McNeill, Dec. 23, 1907, Galena, Ill.; announcer, emcee, bka *The Breakfast Club* master of ceremonies 1933–68; early radio career took him from Milwaukee WTMJ to Louisville WHAS (worked for local newspapers in both cities) to West Coast comedy act billed as "Don and Van, the Two Professors" which fell on hard times in nation's economic depression; auditioned to host *The Pepper Pot* at NBC Blue, won, turned it into network cash cow as *The Breakfast Club*, garnered devoted following; showcased regulars on morning show on *The Don McNeill TV Club* over ABC-TV Sept. 13, 1950-Dec. 19, 1951, ABC-TV version of *The Breakfast Club* lasted even shorter span Feb. 22, 1954-Feb. 25, 1955; much more durable on radio than most peers in similar capacities; d. May 7, 1996.

Gene Rayburn (Eugene Rubessa), Dec. 22, 1917, Christopher, Ill.; announcer, disc jockey, emcee, newscaster bka NBC Radio *Monitor* weekend entertainment-information service's most enduring, perhaps most gregarious host 1961–74, and *The Match Game* racy panel quiz emcee NBC-TV Dec. 31, 1962-Sept. 20, 1969, CBS-TV July 2, 1973-April 20, 1979, syndicated 1979–81, NBC-TV Oct. 31, 1983-July 27, 1984, syndicated 1985; second career after radio running TV game shows — *The Sky's the Limit* 1954, *Make the Connection* 1955, *Choose Up Sides* 1966, *Dough Re Mi* 1958–60, *Tic Tac Dough* 1959, *Play Your Hunch* 1962, *Snap Judgment* 1969, *The Amateur's Guide to Love* 1972, *Break the $250,000 Bank* 1985; d. Nov. 29, 1999.

Deaths

Wilbur Hatch, Dec. 22, 1969, Los Angeles, Calif.; b. May 24, 1902. Jeff Frank Martin, Jr., Dec. 22, 1994, Solvang, Calif.; b. May 10, 1914. Floyd Neal, Dec. 22, 1985, Los Angeles, Calif.; b. Aug. 20, 1906. Irna Phillips, Dec. 22, 1973, Chicago, Ill.; b. July 21, 1901. Ed Thorgersen, Dec. 22, 1997, Wolfeboro, N.H.; b. June 19, 1902. Jimmy Wallington, Dec. 22, 1972, Arlington, Va.; b. Sept. 5, 1907.

December 23

Sound Bite

NBC introduces fully functional coast-to-coast chain Dec. 23, 1928; while net has recreated Red web's East Coast-originated programming since April 5, 1927 for Orange (West Coast) affiliates, not until now has it technically possessed capability to send programming to whole country concurrently if it chooses to.

Debuting

Louella Parsons (*Hollywood News*), Dec. 23, 1945, ABC; gossipmonger; first to inaugurate enduring Hollywood newspaper gossip column in *The Chicago Record-Herald* 1914, became permanently entrenched with similar aural column, usually topping major rivals as first to reveal filmdom's most appalling secrets; one scholar allowed "Parsons established herself as the social and moral arbiter of Hollywood ... her disfavor was feared more than that of movie critics"; while she aired locally by 1928, some historians claim she had network exposure in 1931; 1934, 1944, late 1945 can be confirmed; final broadcast June 22, 1954.

Deaths

Mimi Benzell, Dec. 23, 1970, Manhasset, N.Y.; b. April 6, 1924. Carlton Brickert, Dec. 23, 1943, New York City, N.Y.; b. May 14, 1890. Jack Webb, Dec. 23, 1982, West Hollywood, Calif.; b. April 2, 1920.

December 24

Sound Bite

On December 24, 1926, singing jingle commercials arrive on ether as food processing pioneer Washburn-Crosby Co., owner of Minneapolis WCCO and forerunner of General Mills, Inc., puts barbershop quartet before mic to harmonize: *Have you tried Wheaties? The best breakfast food in the land!* It's sound of much more that will soon be coming down the pike all across that land.

Births

Herb Allen, Dec. 24, 1913, San Francisco, Calif.; actor, announcer, producer; career embraced San Francisco KFRC, Hollywood KLAC-TV, Chicago WENR-TV plus web-based work introducing 1940s chapters of *Dear John*, *The Guiding Light*, *The Hardy Family*, *I Want a Divorce*, *People Are Funny*, *Sherlock Holmes*; produced *The Johnny Carson Show* CBS-TV 1955–56, associate producer *The Bob Crosby Show* NBC-TV 1958.

Mitchell Ayers, Dec. 24, 1910, Milwaukee, Wis.; impresario, music executive bka vocalist, Perry Como's radio, recording, stage, TV musical conductor from 1948 for many years after disbanding his own outfit; music maestro Columbia Records; d. Sept. 5, 1969.

Death

David Roberts, Dec. 24, 1996, Sacramento, Calif.; b. Feb. 25, 1912. Melville Ruick, Dec. 24, 1972, Sherman Oaks, Calif.; b. July 8, 1898.

December 25

Sound Bite

The Metropolitan Opera inaugural broadcast, Dec. 25, 1931, NBC; overcoming longtime resistance of Met management to airing concerts, economic chaos dictated otherwise; premier featured Humperdinck's *Hansel and Gretel* carried by 129 NBC affiliates; luminary Met stars, host Milton J. Cross — legendary "voice of the Met" 1931–75 — persisted to 1960 as web-generated series, since aired by "special network" linking stations globally.

Births

Peter Kalischer, Dec. 25, 1914, New York City, N.Y.; correspondent, print journalist (*Collier's*), scriptwriter, wire journalist (United Press) bka *The World Tonight* reporter 1957–78; other radio gigs *CBS News* 1957–78, *CBS World News Roundup* 1957–78, *Edward R. Murrow and the News* 1957–59, penned scripts for *Cavalcade of America* 1952; from 1957 CBS leaned heavily on him for coverage from Orient, transferred him to Paris 1966 where he stayed until leaving CBS 1978; taught communications at Loyola University 1978–82; d. July 7, 1991.

Nat Shilkret (Nathaniel Schildkraut), Dec. 25, 1889, Queens, N.Y.; house impresario (NBC) as well as for film, recordings, record industry executive; member of bands fronted by E. F. Goldman, Arthur Pryor, John Philip Sousa; RCA Victor music director 1913, later headed label's operations in 35 nations overseas; *The Eveready Hour* maestro Nov. 16, 1926, day after NBC's inaugural, first conductor of continuing nationally aired musicale; recurring member music entourages for 15 network series, often director 1926–44; led broadcast orchestras in Baltimore, Boston, Harrisburg, Providence, Washington 1935–39; conducted multiple Hollywood celluloid studio bands; d. Feb. 18, 1982.

Gladys Swarthout, Dec. 25, 1900, Deepwater, Mo.; film actress, vocalist (mezzo-soprano) bka Metropolitan Opera Co. member 1929–45; *Voice of Firestone* regular (34 appearances) plus intermittent visits to *The Bell Telephone Hour, Camel Caravan, The Ford Sunday Evening Hour, General Motors Concerts, The Magic Key, The NBC Symphony Orchestra, Palmolive Beauty Box Theater, The Prudential Family Hour, The Railroad Hour*; branded radio "most demanding and most frightening" venue (including films, opera): "one mistake over the air goes into the ears of millions ... and can never be taken back"; retired from public life 1954, moved to Italy; d. July 7, 1969.

Deaths

Norman Barry, Dec. 25, 1997, Chicago, Ill.; b. Jan. 19, 1909. Frederick B. Bate, Dec. 25, 1970, Waterford, Va.; b. Nov. 13, 1886. Betty Garde, Dec. 25, 1989, Hollywood, Calif.; b. Sept. 19, 1905.

December 26

Debuting

The American Forum of the Air, Dec. 26, 1937, MBS (debuted as *The Mutual Forum Hour* through Jan. 18, 1949); public affairs panel discussion; hosted by Theodore Granik, law student employed by Gimbel's Department Store as roots planted on emporium's WGBS Radio 1928; turned debates into accepted format on ether; won Peabody Award; NBC-TV 1950–57 with Granik moderating to 1953, succeeded by Stephen McCormick; final radiocast March 11, 1956.

Canceled

Big Sister, Dec. 26, 1952, CBS; debut Sept. 14, 1936. *Fun for All*, Dec. 26, 1953, CBS; debut Sept. 27, 1952. *Give and Take*, Dec. 26, 1953, CBS; debut Aug. 25, 1945. *I Love a Mystery*, Dec. 26, 1952, MBS; debut Jan. 16, 1939. *Maisie* (*The Adventures of Maisie*), Dec. 26, 1952, MBS; debut July 5, 1945 (unconfirmed syndicated run persisted to 1953). *The Shadow*, Dec. 26, 1954, MBS; debut July 31, 1930.

Births

Steve Allen (Stephen V. Allen), Dec. 26, 1921, New York City, N.Y.; actor (film, TV), announcer, author, composer, disc jockey, emcee, lyricist, panelist, pianist, recording artist bka *Tonight Show* variety series original host NBC-TV 1953–57, similarly on like-minded *The Steve Allen Show* NBC-TV 1956–60 with syndication later; launched on Phoenix, Los Angeles radio; hired as DJ by KNX 1947 in L.A., started interviewing some of 1,000 spectators visiting broadcast studio Saturday nights, turning show into crowd-pleaser; CBS gave him radio slot 1950–53, TV time 1950–52; penned more than 5,000 songs, some hits: "This Could Be the Start of Something Big," "Impossible," "Gravy Waltz," "Let's Go to Church Next Sunday Morning," lyrics for movie ballads in *Picnic, Houseboat, On the Beach*, author of 50-plus tomes; played title role in big screen's *The Benny Goodman Story* 1955, acted in other films, hosted more TV shows, panelist on CBS-TV's *What's My Line?, I've Got a Secret*; "never stopped performing" obit scribe noted; many years spent condemning smut on TV; d. Oct. 30, 2000.

James Ralph (Jimmy) Blaine (James William Bunn), Dec. 26, 1924, Greenville, Texas; actor, announcer, emcee, producer, vocalist, writer bka early TV personality (*Cavalcade of Stars, The Howdy Doody Show, Stop the Music!*); after winning local talent contest moved to New York, hired by WNEW as singer; introduced *Get Rich Quick, The Lanny Ross Show, Superstition* late 1940s while acting in *Criminal Casebook*, presiding over *Ladies Be Seated*; presented TV viewers *The Dunninger Show* 1955, 1956 plus animated cartoon series *Ruff and Reddy* 1957–60; formed Jimbo Productions 1960s, penned special features for ABC Radio; d. March 18, 1967.

Richard Widmark, Dec. 26, 1914, Sunrise, Minn.; actor (stage, film, radio, TV), educator (Lake Forest College), emcee bka flick thespian turning up 91 times in cinematic, TV movies 1947–2001; debuted on air 1938 with part in daytime anthology *Aunt Jenny's Real Life Stories*; on Broadway in *Kiss and Tell* 1943; one of five luminaries hosting *The Sears/Mutual Radio Theater* 1979–81, played in *The CBS Radio Mystery Theater* 1974–82; performed multi radio shows in golden age: *Front Page Farrell, Gangbusters, Inner Sanctum Mysteries, Joyce Jordan, Mollé Mystery Theater, Suspense, The Private Lives of Ethel and Albert*, et al., d. March 24, 2008.

Death

Jack Benny, Dec. 26, 1974, Los Angeles, Calif.; b. Feb. 14, 1894.

December 27

Canceled

The Breakfast Club, Dec. 27, 1968, ABC; debut June 23, 1933.*Dear Abby*, Dec. 27, 1974, CBS; debut Dec. 31, 1963. *Strike It Rich*, Dec. 27, 1957, NBC; debut June 29, 1947.

Births

John Jackson (Jack) Latham, Dec. 27, 1914, Davenport, Wash.; announcer, newscaster; while introducing 1940s *The Man Called X, Wake Up America* also dispatched news at Los Angeles KFI; d. Jan. 1, 1987.

Oscar Levant, Dec. 27, 1906, Pittsburgh, Pa.; actor, composer, pianist bka *Information Please* permanent panelist 1938–47; sparred with show's owner, Dan Golenpaul, who eventually made it easy for him to withdraw; played in more than dozen movies; regular appearances on *The Al Jolson Show, Ben Bernie—the Old Maestro*, infrequently on *The Bell Telephone Hour, Kraft Music Hall, Hildegarde's Radio Room*; *A Talent for Genius* released two decades after death chronicled his life's major achievements; d. Aug. 14, 1972.

Cathy Lewis, Dec. 27, 1916, Spokane, Wash.; actress (stage, film, radio, TV), vocalist (Kay Kyser band) bka *My Friend Irma* sitcom cohort-roommate-narrator Jane Stacy 1947–53, *Cathy and Elliott Lewis Onstage* dramatic anthology costar with then-spouse 1953–54; d. Nov. 20, 1968.

Death

Jess Oppenheimer, Dec. 27, 1988, Los Angeles, Calif.; b. Nov. 11, 1913.

December 28

Canceled

Duffy's Tavern, Dec. 28, 1951, NBC; debut March 1, 1941. *Grand Ole Opry*, Dec. 28, 1957, NBC; net debut Oct. 14, 1939, NBC. *Invitation to Learning*, Dec. 28, 1964, CBS; debut May 26, 1940. *Renfro Valley Country Store*, Dec. 28, 1951, CBS; net debut Feb. 19, 1938.

Birth

Dick Joy, Dec. 28, 1915, Putnam, Conn.; announcer, newscaster, sound effects tech, station owner (Palm Springs KCMJ, KTTV television); manifold southern California radio stops: Long Beach KFOX, Hollywood/Los Angeles KNX 1937, KEHE, KHJ, KFAC; presented 1940s-50s features *The Adventures of Bill Lance, The Adventures of Sam Spade, Baby Snooks, Blue Ribbon Town, The Danny Kaye Show, Dr. Kildare, The Nelson Eddy Show, The Saint, Silver Theater, The Spike Jones Show, The Bell Telephone Hour, Those We Love, Vox Pop*; d. Oct. 31, 1991.

Deaths

Arthur Hughes, Dec. 28, 1982, New York City, N.Y.; b. June 24, 1893. Bill Shirer, Dec. 28, 1993, Boston, Mass.; b. Feb. 23, 1904. Bob Warren, Dec. 28, 1984, Santa Clara, Calif.; b. Jan. 22, 1917.

December 29

Births

Robert Latting, Dec. 29, 1921, Michigan; actor, announcer; thespianic talents on 1940s *The Casebook of Gregory Hood, Cavalcade of America, The Story of Sandra Martin, Woman in White* while presenting *Constance Bennett Calls on You*; d. Sept. 29, 1983.

Wendell Edward Niles, Sr., Dec. 29, 1904, Twin Valley, Minn.; announcer, emcee, impresario; after being Montana lightweight boxing champion, coached aeronautical students at Seattle's Boeing Field, formed an orchestra, played vaudeville circuits, master of ceremonies at Seattle hotel floorshow when thrust onto local airwaves 1923 as announcer; moved to Los Angeles 1936 soon introducing *The George Burns and Gracie Allen Show* (applied alias Ronnie Drake to quash uncertainty with sibling Kenneth Niles, their previous interlocutor); linked to score of 1930s-50s aural features like *The Bob Hope Show, The Charlotte Greenwood Show, The Edgar Bergen and Charlie McCarthy Show, The Fitch Bandwagon, Hedda Hopper's Hollywood, Al Pearce and His Gang, Lum and Abner, My Friend Irma, When a Girl Marries*; narrated film shorts, "coming attractions" movie trailers, in 35 Hollywood B-flicks 1932–57, opened NBC-TV game shows *It Could Be You* 1956–61, *Truth or Consequences* 1957–58, *Let's Make a Deal* 1963–64, *Chain Letter* 1966; d. March 28, 1994.

Deaths

Edward John Noble, Dec. 29, 1958, Greenwich, Conn.; b. Aug. 8, 1882. Edward Tomlinson, Dec. 29, 1973, Fairfax, Va.; b. Sept. 27, 1892. Paul Whiteman, Dec. 29, 1967, Doylestown, Pa.; b. March 28, 1890.

December 30

Debuting

Mr. and Mrs. North, Dec. 30, 1942, CBS; amateur sleuth drama; publisher Jerry North (Joseph Curtin, Richard Denning), spouse Pamela (Alice Frost, Barbara Britton) mired in mayhem, murder, stepping over bodies in dark stairwells, accosted by thugs who might offer bodily harm; with support of homicide Lt. Bill Weigand (Frank Lovejoy, Staats Cotsworth, Francis DeSales), Pam usually "stumbled" into plausible solutions by episode end; TV series with Denning, Hale in leads ran CBS 1952–53, NBC 1954; final radiocast April 18, 1955.

Canceled

Perry Mason, Dec. 30, 1955, CBS; debut Oct. 18, 1943. *Stella Dallas*, Dec. 30, 1955, NBC; net debut June 6, 1938.

Births

Edwin Jerome, Dec. 30, 1885, New York City, N.Y.; actor (film, radio, TV); on radio's *Aunt Jenny's Real Life Stories, Blackstone—the Magic Detective* (title), *Call the Police, Mr. Keen—Tracer of Lost Persons, Mystery in the Air, When a Girl Marries*; 16 theatrical films 1929–60—most uncredited, 18 solo roles on TV dramas 1954–59, *Love of Life* daytime serial CBS-TV 1951–53; d. Sept. 10, 1959.

Vincent Lopez, Dec. 30, 1894, Brooklyn, N.Y.; pianist with well-established musical aggregate before network radio's inception; performed NBC (and radio's) inaugural Nov. 15,

1926; fixture of Hotel Taft Grill Room 25 years; headlined 22 chain radio features 1928–56 ("Hello everybody, Lopez speaking"), prominently MBS' *Luncheon with Lopez* 1943–46, 1950–56; d. Sept. 20, 1975.

Jeanette Nolan (McIntire), Dec. 30, 1911, Los Angeles, Calif.; actress (stage, radio, film, TV) bka *Psycho* suspense thriller movie "mother" figure screamer 1960; onstage launch at Pasadena Community Playouse, initially on air on hometown KHJ 1932; support roles on virtually all West Coast-originated crimefighting series, others e.g. *The Adventures of Sam Spade, The Cases of Mr. Ace, Crime Doctor, Dragnet, Gunsmoke, Have Gun—Will Travel, I Love a Mystery, The Lineup, Pursuit, One Man's Family, The Shadow, Sherlock Holmes, The Six Shooter, Tarzan, The Whistler*, more; 41 theatrical films 1948–98, two TV miniseries 1989/1989, 21 made-for-TV flicks 1956–82, *Hotel de Paree* drama figure Annette Deveraux CBS-TV 1959–60 (31 episodes), 193 added performances in scattered solo TV drama outings 1953–90; d. June 5, 1998.

Bert Parks (Bertram Jacobson), Dec. 30, 1914, Atlanta, Ga.; announcer, emcee, showman, stage actor, vocalist bka *Miss America* host 1954–79; game show master of ceremonies on *Break the Bank* 1945–50, *How'm I Doin'?* 1942, *Second Honeymoon* 1948–50, *Stop the Music!* 1948–52—some also on TV, three airing concurrently; interlocutor of more than two dozen audio series; played lead in *The Music Man* on Broadway; *The Bert Parks Show* video host daily 1950–52 while his two-hour radio series *NBC Bandstand* simulcast by NBC-TV 1956; game show emcee in TV with *Double or Nothing* 1952–54, *County Fair* 1958–59, *The Big Payoff* 1959, *Yours for a Song* 1961–63; d. Feb. 2, 1992.

Michael Raffetto, Dec. 30, 1899, Placerville, Calif.; actor (stage, film, radio, TV), director, educator, writer bka *One Man's Family* domestic narrative eldest son Paul Barbour 1932–55, scripted many episodes, replaced acting with directing 1955–59; leading roles on two more Carlton E. Morse-produced series—*I Love a Mystery, I Love Adventure*—plus lead on *Attorney for the Defense*; played in college theatricals, silent films, taught diction; broke into radio penning *Arm of the Law*, hired to play lead 1930; soon NBC West Coast program director; bit parts in 1948, 1956 theatrical films; d. May 31, 1990.

Deaths

Jack Meakin, Dec. 30, 1982, Rancho Mirage, Calif.; b. Sept. 28, 1906. Don Quinn, Dec. 30, 1967, West Hollywood, Calif.; b. Nov. 18, 1900. Artie Shaw, Dec. 30, 2004, Thousand Oaks, Calif.; b. May 26, 1910.

December 31

Sound Bite

In defining moment, on Dec. 31, 1982 NBC ends news-and-features tactic pursued since late 1950s; chain scrubs virtually all daily features, weekend public affairs programming including *Ask Dr. Brothers* (Joyce Brothers), *Here and Now* (Roger Mudd), *The Jensen Report* (Mike Jensen), *Man About Anything* (Gene Shalit), *Willard's Weather* (Willard Scott), *Second Sunday* documentary; all that remains of NBC Radio now: hourly news reports, two-minute weekday *Comment on the News*, Sunday audio repeat of *Meet the Press* from TV.

Debuting

Dear Abby, Dec. 31, 1963, CBS; counsel show; advice columnist Abigail Van Buren meddled in people's personal lives with abandon as one of many mini features CBS offered daytime listeners in epoch; final broadcast Dec. 27, 1974.

Canceled

The CBS Radio Mystery Theater, Dec. 31, 1982, CBS; debut Jan. 6, 1974. *Easy Aces* (*Mr. Ace and Jane*), Dec. 31, 1948, CBS; debut Oct. 5, 1931.

Births

Richard Kollmar, Dec. 31, 1910, Ridgewood, N.J.; actor (film, radio, stage), announcer, emcee, panelist, producer, vocalist bka *Boston Blackie* crime detective drama namesake 1945–50; paired with wife Dorothy Kilgallen on morning chatfest *Breakfast with Dorothy and Dick* New York WOR 1945–63; thespian on 15 or more 1930s-50s audio series e.g. *Armstrong Theater of Today, Big Sister, Bright Horizon, Gangbusters, Grand Central Station, John's Other Wife, Life Can Be Beautiful, The Life of Mary Sothern, Pretty Kitty Kelly, The March of Time,*

When a Girl Marries while singing on *Heartthrobs of the Hills,* narrating *The Adventures of Topper, The Palmolive Beauty Box Theater, Radio Reader's Digest*; linked with several fleeting early TV series, produced handful of stage plays, appeared in solo movie — *Close-Up* 1948; d. Jan. 7, 1971.

Edward Theodore Meyers (some sources incorrectly use Myers), Dec. 31, 1913, Los Angeles County, Calif.; announcer; ushered fans to early 1930s-early 1950s *Calling All Cars, The Lady Esther Screen Guild Theater, People Are Funny, Stop or Go, Tarzan,* others; d. Nov. 25, 1996.

Deaths

Don Douglas, Dec. 31, 1945, Los Angeles, Calif.; b. Aug. 24, 1905. Dirk Fredericks, Dec. 31, 1976, New York City, N.Y.; b. Jan. 19, 1919. Ricky Nelson, Dec. 31, 1985, De Kalb, Texas; b. May 8, 1940.

Bibliography

Anderson, Arthur. *"Let's Pretend": A History of Radio's Best Loved Children's Show by a Longtime Cast Member.* Jefferson, N.C.: McFarland, 1994.

Baber, David. *Television Game Show Hosts: Biographies of 32 Stars.* Jefferson, N.C.: McFarland, 2008.

Balk, Alfred. *The Rise of Radio, from Marconi through the Golden Age.* Jefferson, N.C.: McFarland, 2006.

Barnouw, Erik. *A Tower in Babel: A History of Broadcasting in the United States, Vol. I—to 1933.* New York: Oxford, 1966.

_____. *The Golden Web: A History of Broadcasting in the United States, Vol. II—1933 to 1953.* New York: Oxford, 1968.

_____. *The Image Empire: A History of Broadcasting in the United States, Vol. III—from 1953.* New York: Oxford, 1968.

Bresee, Frank, and Bobb Lynes. *Radio's Golden Years: A Visual Guide to the Shows and the Stars.* Hollywood, Calif.: Frank Bresee Productions, 1998.

Brooks, Tim, and Earle Marsh. *The Complete Directory to Prime Time Network TV Shows, 1946–Present.* 4th ed. New York: Ballantine, 1988.

Buxton, Frank, and Bill Owen. *The Big Broadcast, 1920–1950.* 2nd ed. Lanham, Md.: Scarecrow, 1997.

Campbell, Robert. *The Golden Years of Broadcasting: A Celebration of the First 50 Years of Radio and TV on NBC.* New York: Scribner, 1976.

Castleman, Harry, and Walter J. Podrazik. *505 Radio Questions Your Friends Can't Answer.* New York: Walker, 1983.

Chase, Francis, Jr. *Sound and Fury: An Informal History of Broadcasting.* New York: Harper, 1942.

Cloud, Stanley, and Lynne Olson. *The Murrow Boys: Pioneers on the Front Lines of Broadcast Journalism.* Boston: Houghton Mifflin, 1996.

Columbia Broadcasting System, Inc. *The Sound of Your Life.* New York: CBS, 1950.

Cox, Jim. *The Daytime Serials of Television, 1946–1960.* Jefferson, N.C.: McFarland, 2006.

_____. *Frank and Anne Hummert's Radio Factory: The Programs and Personalities of Broadcasting's Most Prolific Producers.* Jefferson, N.C.: McFarland, 2003.

_____. *The Great Radio Audience Participation Shows: Seventeen Programs from the 1940s and 1950s.* Jefferson, N.C.: McFarland, 2001.

_____. *The Great Radio Sitcoms.* Jefferson, N.C.: McFarland, 2007.

_____. *The Great Radio Soap Operas.* Jefferson, N.C.: McFarland, 1999.

_____. *Historical Dictionary of American Radio Soap Operas.* Lanham, Md.: Scarecrow, 2005.

_____. *Mr. Keen, Tracer of Lost Persons: A Complete History and Episode Log of Radio's Most Durable Detective.* Jefferson, N.C.: McFarland, 2004.

_____. *Music Radio: The Great Performers and Programs of the 1920s through Early 1960s.* Jefferson, N.C.: McFarland, 2005.

_____. *Radio Crime Fighters: Over 300 Programs from the Golden Age.* Jefferson, N.C.: McFarland, 2002.

_____. *Radio Speakers: Narrators, News Junkies, Sports Jockeys, Tattletales, Tipsters, Toastmasters and Coffee Klatch Couples Who Verbalized the Jargon of the Aural Ether from the 1920s to the 1980s—A Biographical Dictionary.* Jefferson, N.C.: McFarland, 2007.

_____. *Say Goodnight, Gracie: The Last Years of Network Radio.* Jefferson, N.C.: McFarland, 2002.

_____. *Sold on Radio: Advertisers in the Golden Age of Broadcasting.* Jefferson, N.C.: McFarland, 2008.

DeLong, Thomas A. *Radio Stars: An Illustrated Biographical Dictionary of 953 Performers, 1920 through 1960.* Jefferson, N.C.: McFarland, 1996.

Duncan, Jacci, ed. *Making Waves: The 50 Greatest*

Women in Radio and Television. Kansas City: Andrews McMeel, 2001.
Dunning, John. *On the Air: The Encyclopedia of Old-Time Radio*. New York: Oxford University Press, 1998.
_____. *Tune in Yesterday: The Ultimate Encyclopedia of Old-Time Radio, 1925–1976*. Englewood Cliffs, N.J.; Prentice-Hall, 1976.
Editors of *The New York Times*. *The New York Times Directory of the Theater*. New York: Arno Press, 1973.
Editors of *TV Guide*. *TV Guide: Guide to TV*. New York: Barnes & Noble, 2004.
Editors of *TV Guide Online's* CineBooks Database. *TV Guide Film & Video Companion, 2004*. New York: Barnes & Noble, 2003.
Fang, Irving E. *Those Radio Commentators!* Ames: Iowa State University Press, 1977.
Gates, Gary Paul. *Air Time: The Inside Story of CBS News*. New York: Harper & Row, 1978.
Godfrey, Donald G., and Frederic A. Leigh, eds. *Historical Dictionary of American Radio*. Westport, Conn.: Greenwood Press, 1998.
Goldin, J. David. *The Golden Age of Radio: The Standard Reference Work of Radio Programs and Radio Performers of the Past*. Sandy Hook, Conn.: Radio Yesteryear, 2000.
Hart, Dennis. *Monitor: The Last Great Radio Show*. San Jose, Calif.: Writers Club Press, 2002.
Harvey, Rita Morley. *Those Wonderful, Terrible Years: George Heller and the American Federation of Television and Radio Artists*. Carbondale.: Southern Illinois University Press, 1996.
Havig, Alan. *Fred Allen's Radio Comedy*. Philadelphia: Temple University Press, 1990.
Hickerson, Jay. *The Third Ultimate History of Network Radio Programming and Guide to All Circulating Shows*. Hamden, Conn.: Presto Print II, 2005.
Hyatt, Wesley. *The Encyclopedia of Daytime Television: Everything You Ever Wanted to Know About Daytime TV but Didn't Know Where to Look! From American Bandstand, As the World Turns, and Bugs Bunny, to Meet the Press, The Price Is Right, and Wide World of Sports, the Rich History of Daytime Television in All Its Glory!* New York: Billboard, 1997.
Inman, David M. *Television Variety Shows: Histories and Episode Guides to 57 Programs*. Jefferson, N.C.: McFarland, 2006.
Julian, Joseph. *This Was Radio: A Personal Memoir*. New York: Viking, 1975.
Lackmann, Ron. *Same Time ... Same Station: An A-Z Guide to Radio from Jack Benny to Howard Stern*. New York: Facts on File, 1996.
Lyons, Eugene. *David Sarnoff: A Biography*. New York: Harper & Row, 1966.
MacDonald, J. Fred. *Don't Touch That Dial!: Radio Programming in American Life from 1920 to 1960*. Chicago: Nelson-Hall, 1991.
Maltin, Leonard. *The Great American Broadcast: A Celebration of Radio's Golden Age*. New York: Penguin Putnam, 1997.
McNeil, Alex. *Total Television: The Comprehensive Guide to Programming from 1948 to the Present*. 4th ed. New York: Penguin Books, 1996.
Nachman, Gerald. *Raised on Radio: In Quest of The Lone Ranger, Jack Benny, Amos 'n' Andy, The Shadow, Mary Noble, The Great Gildersleeve, Fibber McGee and Molly, Bill Stern, Our Miss Brooks, Henry Aldrich, The Quiz Kids, Jack Armstrong, Arthur Godfrey, Bob and Ray, The Barbour Family, Henry Morgan, Joe Friday, and Other Lost Heroes from Radio's Heyday*. New York: Pantheon, 1998.
Passman, Arnold. *The Deejays: How the Tribal Chieftains of Radio Got to Where They're At*. New York: Macmillan, 1971.
Paulson, Roger C. *Archives of the Airwaves*. Vol. 1. Boalsburg, Pa.: BearManor Media, 2005.
_____. *Archives of the Airwaves*. Vol. 2. Boalsburg, Pa.: BearManor Media, 2005.
Poindexter, Ray. *Golden Throats and Silver Tongues: The Radio Announcers*. Conway, Ark.: River Road Press, 1978.
Rayburn, John. *Cat Whiskers and Talking Furniture: A Memoir of Radio and Television Broadcasting*. Jefferson, N.C.: McFarland, 2008.
Robinson, Marc. *Brought to You in Living Color: 75 Years of Great Moments in Television & Radio from NBC*. New York: Wiley, 2002.
Salomonson, Terry. *The Lone Ranger Log: A Radio Broadcast Log of the Western Drama Program The Lone Ranger*. Howell, Mich.: Terry G. Salomonson, 2004.
Schaden, Chuck. *Speaking of Radio: Chuck Schaden's Conversations with the Stars of the Golden Age of Radio*. Morton Grove, Ill.: Nostalgia Digest, 2003.
Settel, Irving. *A Pictorial History of Radio*. 2nd ed. New York: Grosset & Dunlap, 1967.
Sies, Luther F. *Encyclopedia of American Radio, 1920–1960*. Jefferson, N.C.: McFarland, 2000.
Slide, Anthony. *Great Radio Personalities in Historic Photographs*. Vestal, N.Y.: Vestal Press, 1982.
Smith, Sally Bedell. *In All His Glory: The Life of William S. Paley, the Legendary Tycoon and His Brilliant Circle*. New York: Simon and Schuster, 1990.
Sterling, Christopher H., ed. *Telecommunications: Special Reports on American Broadcasting, 1932–1947*. New York: Arno Press, 1974.
Sterling, Christopher H., and John M. Kittross. *Stay Tuned: A Concise History of American Broadcasting*. 2nd ed. Belmont, Calif.: Wadsworth Publishing, 1990.
Summers, Harrison B., ed. *A Thirty-Year History of Programs Carried on National Radio Networks in the United States, 1926–1956*. New York: Arno Press and *The New York Times*, 1971.

Swartz, Jon D., and Robert C. Reinehr. *Handbook of Old-Time Radio: A Comprehensive Guide to Golden Age Radio Listening and Collecting.* Metuchen, N.J.: Scarecrow, 1993.

Terrace, Vincent. *Radio Programs, 1924–1984: A Catalog of Over 1800 Shows.* Jefferson, N.C.: McFarland, 1999.

Tucker, David C. *The Women Who Made Television Funny: Ten Stars of 1950s Sitcoms.* Jefferson, N.C.: McFarland, 2007.

In addition to the texts above, thousands of websites contributed a wealth of data to the factual composition of this volume. It's impossible to cite all of them. Nevertheless, a handful of sources was instrumental literally hundreds of times in corroborating the veracity of information herein and are unconditionally acknowledged.

http://www.ancestry.com (Genealogy); *http://www.easyace.blogspot.com* (Easy Ace — Journal/Classic Radio); *http://www.findagrave.com* (Gravesites of Famous People); *http://www.google.com* (General Search Engine); http://www.ibdb.com (Internet Broadway Database); *http://www.imdb.com* (Internet Movie Database); *http://www.jjonz.us/RadioLogs/index.htm* (Newspaper Radio Logs); *http://www.nytimes.com/pages/obituaries/* (*The New York Times* Obituaries); *http://www.rootsweb.com/* (Social Security Death Index); *http://www.time.com/time/magazine/archives Time* (Archives 1923-Present); http://www.wikipedia.org (Encyclopedia).

Index